THIRD EDITION

ETHICAL ISSUES IN BUSINESS

A Philosophical Approach

Edited by

Thomas Donaldson

Patricia H. Werhane

Loyola University of Chicago

PRENTICE HALL, Englewood Cliffs, New Jersey 07632

Library of Congress Cataloging-in-Publication Data

Ethical issues in business.

Includes bibliographies.
1. Business ethics. 2. Industry — Social aspects.
I. Donaldson, Thomas. II. Werhane, Patricia Hogue.
HF5387.E8 1988   174'.4   87-25847
ISBN 0-13-290172-2

Editorial/production supervision and
  interior design: *Patricia V. Amoroso*
Cover design: *Ben Santora*
Manufacturing buyer: *Margaret Rizzi*

 © 1988 by Prentice-Hall, Inc.
A Division of Simon & Schuster
Englewood Cliffs, New Jersey 07632

Printed in the United States of America

10 9 8 7 6 5 4 3

ISBN 0-13-290172-2 01

PRENTICE-HALL INTERNATIONAL (UK) LIMITED, *London*
PRENTICE-HALL OF AUSTRALIA PTY. LIMITED, *Sydney*
PRENTICE-HALL CANADA INC., *Toronto*
PRENTICE-HALL HISPANOAMERICANA, S.A., *Mexico*
PRENTICE-HALL OF INDIA PRIVATE LIMITED, *New Delhi*
PRENTICE-HALL OF JAPAN, INC., *Tokyo*
SIMON & SCHUSTER ASIA PTE. LTD., *Singapore*
EDITORA PRENTICE-HALL DO BRASIL, LTDA., *Rio de Janeiro*

Contents

Preface *ix*

PART I **GENERAL ISSUES IN ETHICS** *5*

Ethical Relativism *11*

Case Study — The Lockheed Aircraft Corporation *11*
A. CARL KOTCHIAN

A Defense of Cultural Relativism *20*
WILLIAM GRAHAM SUMNER

Ethical Relativity and Ethical Absolutism *27*
WALTER T. STACE

Multinational Decision-Making: Reconciling International Norms *35*
THOMAS DONALDSON

Ethics and the Foreign Corrupt Practices Act *48*
MARK PASTIN AND MICHAEL HOOKER

Moral Dimensions of the Foreign Corrupt Practices Act: Comments on Pastin and Hooker *54*
KENNETH D. ALPERN

Truth Telling *60*

Case Study — Italian Tax Mores *60*
ARTHUR L. KELLY

Ethical Duties Towards Others: "Truthfulness" *63*
IMMANUEL KANT

Is Business Bluffing Ethical?   *69*
ALBERT CARR

The Ethics and Profitability of Bluffing in Business   *77*
RICHARD E. WOKUTCH AND THOMAS L. CARSON

PART II   MORALITY AND CORPORATIONS   *84*

The Moral Status of Corporations   *89*

Case Study—Manville: The Ethics of Economic Efficiency?   *89*
A. R. GINI

When Did Johns-Manville Know?   *98*
JEFF COPLON

The Corporation as a Moral Person   *100*
PETER A. FRENCH

Morality and the Ideal of Rationality in Formal Organizations   *110*
JOHN LADD

The Moral Responsibility of Corporations   *123*

Case Study—"When E. F. Hutton Speaks . . ."   *123*
JOANNE B. CIULLA

Can a Corporation Have a Conscience?   *139*
KENNETH E. GOODPASTER AND JOHN B. MATTHEWS, JR.

Catch 20.5: Corporate Morality as an Organizational Phenomenon   *149*
JAMES A. WATERS

PART III   PROPERTY, PROFIT, AND JUSTICE   *164*

Traditional Theories of Property and Profit   *174*

Case Study—Plasma International   *174*
T. W. ZIMMERER AND P. L. PRESTON

Benefits of the Profit Motive   *176*
ADAM SMITH

The Justification of Private Property   *181*
JOHN LOCKE

Alienated Labour   *187*
KARL MARX

The Communist Manifesto   *192*
KARL MARX AND FRIEDRICH ENGELS

Wealth   *200*
ANDREW CARNEGIE

Property and Profit: Modern Discussions   *206*

Case Study—"Going After the Crooks"   *206*
TIME MAGAZINE

The Social Responsibility of Business Is to Increase Its Profits   *217*
MILTON FRIEDMAN

The New Property   *223*
GEORGE CABOT LODGE

Regulation That Works   *232*
STEVEN KELMAN

Resolving Income and Wealth Differences in a Market Economy: A Dialogue   *237*
JAMES M. GUSTAFSON AND ELMER W. JOHNSON

Justice   *250*

Case Study—International Computer Sales   *250*
LAURA NADEL AND HESH WIENER

Case Study—Who Has First Claim on Health Care Resources?   *256*
ROBERT M. VEATCH

Case Study—Cat Scan   *257*
WALL STREET JOURNAL

Distributive Justice   *258*
JOHN RAWLS

The Principles of a Liberal Social Order   *269*
FRIEDRICH A. HAYEK

Morality and the Liberal Ideal 279
MICHAEL J. SANDEL

PART IV   EMPLOYER-EMPLOYEE RELATIONSHIPS 285

Employee Rights 290

Case Study—The Aircraft Brake Scandal 290
KERMIT VANDIVIER

Case Study—The Copper "O" Company 304
THOMAS F. McMAHON, C. S. V.

A Proposed Bill of Rights 305
DAVID W. EWING

The Myth of the "Oppressive Corporation" 310
MAX WAYS

Employment at Will and Due Process: Contrary Employment
Practices 313
PATRICIA H. WERHANE

The Case for the Polygraph in Employment Screening 319
GORDON H. BARLAND

The Case Against the Polygraph in Employment Screening 323
DAVID T. LYKKEN

Affirmative Action 328

Case Study—Freida Mae Jones 328
MARTIN R. MOSER

Is Turn About Fair Play? 332
BARRY R. GROSS

A Defense of Programs of Preferential Treatment 339
RICHARD WASSERSTROM

Classification by Race in Compensatory Programs 345
JAMES W. NICKEL

How Can Comparable Worth Be Achieved? 350
SEAN DeFORREST

PART V   CONTEMPORARY BUSINESS ISSUES   *356*

The Environment *362*

Case Study—Three Mile Island 362
NEWSWEEK

The Case for Economic Growth 369
WILFRED BECKERMAN

The Scarcity Society 375
WILLIAM OPHULS

Ethics and Ecology 382
WILLIAM T. BLACKSTONE

Advertising *390*

Case Study—Toy Wars 390
MANUEL G. VELASQUEZ

The Dependence Effect 395
JOHN KENNETH GALBRAITH

Advertising and Behavior Control *401*
ROBERT L. ARRINGTON

Corporate Governance *414*

Case Study—A. H. Robins: The Dalkon Shield *414*
A. R. GINI AND T. SULLIVAN

Who Rules the Corporation? *424*
RALPH NADER, MARK GREEN, AND JOEL SELIGMAN

Power and Accountability: The Changing Role of the Corporate
Board of Directors *437*
IRVING S. SHAPIRO

Biographical Information *448*

Preface

The appearance of a third edition always brings a certain pleasure to its originators—for surely no one can smugly predict continued success for one's efforts—but in this instance the pleasure is tied not only to past success, but to present needs. The needs arise from the field of business ethics itself, a field which, more than most others, is tied to the changing, empirical problem context that serves as its subject matter. It is a context that unequivocally demands that published discussions remain relevant.

Some theoretical perspectives do maintain relevance throughout the historical flux (the insights of Adam Smith or the challenges of Karl Marx are no less relevant today than in the eighteenth or nineteenth centuries), yet others are clearly time-bound. When the first edition of this book appeared, Three Mile Island and Chernobol had not darkened our knowledge of the atom, computers were clever gadgets with few ethical implications, and Ivan Boesky had not yet discovered a new route to riches. The reader, consequently, will find that the present edition contains many new case studies, including ones dealing with insider trading, Johns Manville and asbestos, E. F. Hutton and check kiting, the advertising of children's toys, corporate governance, and the Dalkon Shield controversy.

Happily also, changing problems in business have been accompanied by a rapidly growing business ethics literature. At the appearance of the first edition in 1979, *Ethical Issues in Business* was only one of three contenders for college business ethics classrooms; by 1983, at the appearance of the second edition, the selection had grown to ten or fifteen; and today there are at least forty textbooks competing for attention, many of which are of high quality. Alongside the growth of college teaching materials has been an explosion in the production of articles and commentaries. The present edition takes good advantage of this abundance, and contains many new articles, including ones on international business, advertising, employee rights, and corporate governance. Indeed, readers will note that the book contains two entirely new sections: one dealing with the ethics of advertising and the other with corporate governance.

The present edition, as the earlier ones, has not been the simple product of its editors, but owes greatly to those whose suggestions, criticisms, editorial assistance, and moral support made it a better book. These include John Bannan, Raymond Baumhart, S. J., Tom Bennett, John F. Brennen, Thomas Carson, Kendall D'Andrade, A. R. Gini, William Harder, Thomas McMahon, C. S. V., Michael Pritchard, Mark Schneider, Roger J. Sullivan, and Stephen Taylor. We also want to thank F. Marcia Garcia, Jean Jackson, and especially Cindy Rudolph for supurb secretarial help. Finally, we are indebted to the patience and the ingenuity of our production editor at Prentice-Hall, Pattie Amoroso.

THOMAS DONALDSON

PATRICIA H. WERHANE

General Introduction

There is one and only one social responsibility of business . . . to increase its profits. . . .

Milton Friedman

Business executives and the companies they serve have a personal and vested interest in the resolution of ethical and social responsibility dilemmas.

Steven Brenner and Earl Molander

It has often been suggested—though perhaps in jest—that the idea of business ethics constitutes a contradiction in terms. "Business is business," it has been said, "and ethics is not business." Yet each day we hear of the controversies about discrimination in hiring, consumer rights, deceptive advertising, bribery and payoffs, and pollution problems of such magnitude that we cannot remain unaffected.

Ethical problems in business are as old as business itself. Just as we are acutely aware of the problems surrounding the Ivan Boesky case or the Bhopal tragedy, earlier generations were aware of other ethical problems in business. Names such as the "Teapot Dome scandal" or the "Mississippi bubble" are not familiar today, but they were once as well known as "Boesky" and "Bhopal" are now. The issues about which there has been public concern include trusts and monopolies, child labor, working hours and conditions, meat packing standards, the distribution of salaries, and the liability of producers for dangerous products. Not only complaints but attempts at reform have a long and interesting history. The Code of Hammurabi, written nearly two thousand years before Christ, records the fact that Mesopotamian rulers attempted to legislate honest prices from local merchants by instituting wage and price controls.

To explain the special relationship between business and ethics, it is necessary to see how focusing merely on problems of business efficiency and profit making may overlook important moral issues. For example, when the manufacture of a certain product can eventually be linked to human disease or a decrease in the quality of human life, then the issues surrounding it are no longer simply traditional "business" issues. No amount of expertise in marketing, accounting, or management can deal adequately with such problems, and yet they are clearly connected to the activities of the business world. Nor can situations like these be reduced simply to legal problems, understandable only to the lawyer. When Ralph Nader claimed in the late 1960s that General Motors was producing automobiles which, despite their many consumer advantages, were contributing to thousands of highway deaths each year, he was not arguing that GM's practices were against the law—because at that time they were not illegal at all. Rather, Nader was arguing that General Motors had special obligations to its consumers, which were not simply of a traditional business nature, and that the company was not living up to them. Those obligations were *ethical* or *moral* ones.

It appears, then, that confronting questions like those implied by the Nader case—such as, Does business have an obligation to its consumers (or to others) which extends beyond its obligation to make a profit and satisfy its investors?—means confronting ethical and moral issues. The words *ethical* and *moral* in this book are not simply used as they might be by a modern newspaper, for example, "That movie is thoroughly immoral" (meaning, "That movie is pornographic"). Instead, they are used as philosophers have traditionally used them, as words that arise from the study of what is good or right. Although there is dispute even among philosophers over how to define the subject matter of ethics, most would agree that it includes the study of what people ought to pursue, that is, what the *good* is for people, or alternatively, the determination of which actions are the *right* actions for people to perform. Such general definitions may leave one with the feeling that studying ethics must be a hopelessly vague task; yet interestingly, ethical philosophers have succeeded in presenting a great many detailed ethical theses and in conducting a number of successful investigations into specific ethical topics.

The word *ethics*, then, refers generally to the study of whatever is right and good for humans. The study of *business* ethics seeks to understand business practices, institutions, and actions in light of some concept of human value. Traditional business ends—e.g., profit making, growth, or technical advance—are certainly relevant to the subject of business ethics insofar as they can be related to the achievement of some more human good. In other words, business ethics looks at corporate profits not for their own sake but with respect to the achievement of some basic human good, perhaps increased investor satisfaction, higher levels of employment, or increased capacity to improve working conditions.

Because business ethics involves relating business activities to some concept of human good, it is a study which has as one of its aspects the *evaluation* of business practices. Indeed, most of the fundamental criticisms and commendations of contemporary business practices are cast in terms of how modern business either contributes or fails to contribute to the general human good. For example, when modern corporations are criticized for their failure to respond to environmental needs by limiting the amount of pollutants they discharge, they are being evaluated on ethical grounds; the charge is that they are neglecting the public good. Alternatively, when businesses are praised for achieving high levels of efficiency and satisfying consumer needs, it is implied that efficiency and consumer satisfaction contribute directly to the sum total of human good. Even traditional conservative economic theory justifies economic practices in the light of their contribution to human good: The classical economist Adam Smith, for example, justifies the pursuit of self-interest in business by referring to the public benefits that such action secures.

Another aspect of the evaluative dimension in business ethics — or any ethical study — is seen in the contrast between evaluation and simple description. There is a special difference between answering a moral question and answering a question in the areas of, say, marketing and economics. In the latter, it is often sufficient to establish the immediate facts which pertain to the subject. For example, if one hopes to determine the best advertising strategy for the introduction of a new product, one would only need to determine that a certain advertising strategy will have, as a matter of fact, the desired effect, i.e., that it *will* sell the product. It is usually possible in such cases to utilize indicators which more or less establish whether or not a given strategy will be effective: consumer polls, trends in sales, etc. These indicators are then used as factual information upon which one's strategy is based.

However, answering an ethical question may demand very different methods. Determining the immediate and specific facts may only be the first step in a long process which, in the end, may take one far beyond immediate facts. For example, if one wants to determine whether discriminatory hiring practices by corporations *ought* to be corrected by instituting affirmative action programs that favor women and minorities, there may be no question at all about the immediate facts. Two people could thoroughly agree that discrimination of a certain type has taken place and that blacks and women need equal job opportunities to reach relevant levels of social equality. Yet, after agreeing on all these facts the two people may still disagree — and disagree vehemently — over whether affirmative action programs *ought* to be imposed in the wake of past discriminatory practices. Thus, solving an ethical problem may require making *evaluative* judgments about issues which seem far removed from the facts at hand.

Even though business ethics focuses primarily on evaluative issues, its scope is surprisingly large. Insofar as it is concerned with relating business practices to some concept of human good, almost any business issue that relates to human values may become part of its subject matter. Thus the scope of business ethics includes such issues as

1. advertising practices, for example, false or misleading advertising;
2. product safety;
3. monopolistic price schemes and their effects on the consumer;
4. the pursuit of profits;
5. the treatment of workers, including salaries, working conditions, worker participation, and access to pension plans and benefits;
6. the effects of pollution, both economic and environmental;
7. payments of "sensitive" sums of money to foreign governments, foreign agents, or local politicians;
8. the proper roles of shareholders, management, government, and the public in determining corporate policy;
9. discriminatory hiring policies, conditions, and policies of advancement;
10. the limits of private ownership; and
11. insider trading.

The analysis of such issues requires a systematic investigation of both general ethical theory and specific business practices. To accomplish this goal the editors of this anthology have selected a series of writings which includes not only theoretical and philosophical material relevant to business practices but actual case descriptions of ethical problems found in the business world. Much of the philosophical material has gained wide support in traditional ethical philosophy, and the cases include ones that have had a dramatic impact upon our society.

This book has not attempted to provide a list of ethical codes of conduct. Such codes have often proven unsuccessful in achieving their presumed purpose; and more important, their existence can imply something false about the field of business ethics: that the work needed to understand ethical issues can be made unnecessary, and that serious issues can be resolved by simply writing and studying lists of ethical rules.

The advantage of investigating ethical problems from a philosophical point of view should be apparent. One cannot successfully examine a case involving payments made by U.S. corporations to foreign governments until one has considered the more general issue of whether different ethical attitudes (as might exist in the United States and in foreign countries) affect the morality of such actions. This question has traditionally been treated by philosophers under the heading of "ethical relativism," and studying the contributions of philosophers can be of great help.

Part I

GENERAL ISSUES IN ETHICS

At a time when the reputation of business in general is low . . . . at such a time one would expect corporate executives to be especially sensitive even to appearances of conflict of interest. . . . Yet this seems not, on the whole, to be the case. . . .

Irving Kristol

If you were operating a branch of a U.S. company in a foreign country, would you follow the necessary foreign procedures for filing taxes even if (1) these conflicted with procedures in the United States or (2) they clearly involved what you considered unethical practices?

If you were an employee of a large corporation producing equipment for the aircraft industry, would you protest the manufacture of defective products even if it meant the loss of your job?

Suppose you, as an employee of an advertising agency, felt that one of the advertisements for which you were responsible presented false or misleading information about a product. Would you request a change in the advertisement?

Each of these questions is drawn from an actual business situation, and such incidents occur more frequently than one might expect. Understanding their ethical implications requires not only an awareness of the concrete situation but also the ability to subsume business problems under categories of more general ethical concern. The philosophical material in

Part I involves two traditional ethical issues: ethical relativism and truth telling. Stated as questions, these issues are as follows:

1. Ethical relativism: Are values simply relative to the people who espouse them, or is it possible to identify universal values which apply to all? How does one resolve conflicts of values between cultures, social practices, individuals and organizations, or merely between individuals?

2. Truth telling: What obligations exist, if any, for individuals and organizations to communicate honestly? When, if ever, is not telling the truth justified?

ETHICAL RELATIVISM

The issue of honesty is difficult in practice because it must be faced every day. The issue of the relativity of value judgments is less obviously commonplace. It asks whether some moral principles apply universally to all persons or whether, instead, all values and ethical judgments are relative to particular contexts. This question is particularly acute in contemporary business because most major corporations today are "transnational" or "multinational" corporations that conduct business in many countries. How should businesses operate in foreign countries? Should they adopt the practices of the host country even when those practices conflict with an American way of doing business or are morally questionable? Should they lie, bribe, or submit to extortion in a foreign country if that activity is common practice in that culture? According to some views of ethical relativism, one cannot say that bribery is wrong if it is an acceptable practice in that value system; for according to the ethical relativist, there are no universal standards or objective values by which one can judge the moral principles of different cultures.

The relativity of value judgments is also an issue for ordinary business situations. One can argue that values are not merely relative to particular cultures but also relative to different institutions, organizations, or social practices. According to this line of argument, the values of the medical community might differ from, say, those of certain religious groups, or the values espoused by business might differ from, and sometimes even conflict with, ideals espoused by individuals. Because values affect expectations, what is expected of a person as an employee might be different from the values she espouses away from the workplace. The Lockheed case illustrates this well. The president, Carl Kotchian, alleged that he did not want to pay the Japanese in order to get a contract because it was wrong from his personal moral point of view. But he felt he had to make these "sensitive payments" for the well-being of his company.

Ethical relativism frequently uses evidence provided by another, but closely related, point of view known as *cultural* relativism. As William Sumner explains, cultural relativism emphasizes how the ways in which people reason about morality vary in different cultures because of different customs, religious traditions, and methods of education. From the obvious empirical evidence of differences between cultures, a relativist may go further to argue that there are no ultimate, universal ethical principles and that all value judgments are relative to particular cultural contexts. Therefore, the truth of an ethical statement such as "Bribery is wrong" is determined solely by the beliefs of the culture espousing that claim. Although Americans typically think bribery is wrong, in other cultures this is an acceptable part of business and political practice; and according to a relativist, this value conflict cannot be resolved. Value conflicts within a particular society, too, may for the same reason not be resolvable. Cultural relativism is closely linked to the more general theory of ethical relativism, which holds that no ethical assertion or set of assertions has any greater claim to objectivity or universality than any other. For at least some ethical disagreements, because there are no objective or universal standards, there is no single correct view to which even an ideal rational observer can appeal in solving conflicts of values, particularly those of a more serious nature.

An obvious way to challenge either cultural or ethical relativism is to argue that there are some values that are universal, that is, which apply without exception. For example, one might argue that skinning live babies for sport is not acceptable anywhere, despite anyone's belief. W. T. Stace, in his article "Ethical Relativity and Ethical Absolutism," defends just such a point of view. He recognizes that there are practical difficulties in specifying particular ethical principles that apply universally, but these difficulties do not imply that ethical relativism is correct. Although it may in fact be the case that certain value conflicts are never resolved, this does not imply that they are not in principle resolvable. In an intricate set of arguments Stace tries to show that a thoroughgoing position of ethical relativism results in the conclusion that one cannot justify any value judgments whatsoever.

The case study "The Lockheed Aircraft Corporation" raises the specific question of which set of ethical principles or which value system, if any, a multinational corporation should adopt when doing business in a foreign country. Lockheed, trying to gain business favors, made "sensitive payments" to Japanese government officials; but the former president of Lockheed defended these payments, even though they would have been considered both illegal and unethical if made in the United States. He defended them as consistent with (1) practices of other multinational corporations and (2) accepted cultural practices in other countries. Hence, if Lockheed refused to bribe, he concluded, it would lose in the race with its competitors. Arguments such as 1 and 2 involve cultural relativism insofar as right and wrong are assumed to depend on the particular corporate or cultural context being considered. Other U.S. companies involved in foreign bribes have offered a third justification: that (3) American corporations provide needed technology and economic services to foreign countries, thus raising the standards for citizens in these countries. The means through which one makes these goods and services available—for example, sensitive payments—are thus justified by long-range economic results.

If Stace's arguments are correct, they might be used to show that justifications such as 1 and 2 for sensitive payments abroad are questionable and that other justifications, such as 3, are inconsistent with 1 and 2. For when some corporations defend their activities by referring to the economic advantages for the foreign countries in which they operate, are they not assuming that economic growth is a universal value and should be espoused by every country?

In his article "Multinational Decision-Making," Thomas Donaldson considers the vexing problems that arise when moral and legal standards vary between countries, especially between a multinational corporation's home and host countries. How, he asks, should highly placed multinational managers, typically schooled in home-country moral traditions, reconcile conflicts between their values and the practices of the host country? If host-country standards appear lower than home-country ones, should the multinational manager always take the "high road" and implement home-country standards? Or does the "high road" sometimes signal a failure to respect cultural diversity and national integrity? The answer may be fairly obvious in the instance of South Africa (where acquiescing to racism and discrimination would surely be immoral), but how about other instances—ones involving differences in wage rates, pollution standards, or "sensitive payments"? Donaldson constructs and defends what he calls an "ethical algorithm" for multinational managers to use in reconciling such conflicts.

The conduct of multinational corporations has been under severe scrutiny in recent years. As a result of bribery incidents such as Lockheed's, in 1977 the U.S. Congress passed the Foreign Corrupt Practices Act (FCPA). The FCPA is an attempt to legislate standards of conduct for multinational corporations by making it a crime to offer or to acquiesce to sensitive payments to officials of foreign governments. The act implies that what we in this country think is morally right should apply to our dealings with other countries. This position would be criticized by ethical relativists, since according to them, value differences between cultures preclude the justification of such exportation.

The FCPA raises the issue of whether one can justify sensitive payments—that is, bribery and extortion—in any context, and also that of whether one can legislate moral behavior. Michael Hooker and Mark Pastin consider this question in their article "Ethics and the Foreign Corrupt Practices Act." They argue that the moral rule prohibiting bribery is a prima facie rule that can be overridden to prevent a greater harm—the greater harm in this instance being the loss of American business and the accompanying loss of jobs by American multinational corporations which cannot compete in the international market. In response, Kenneth Alpern suggests that one cannot justify overriding a moral rule such as that prohibiting bribery except in dire circumstances, a situation which hardly describes the state of American business. Abolishing the FCPA, according to Alpern, is tantamount to endorsing a general policy of bribery.

TRUTH TELLING

The concept of truth telling can be used to investigate a wide variety of issues, including honesty in advertising, the accuracy of consumer information, and the responsibilities a business has to communicate honestly with its employees and stockholders. A philosopher well known for his vigorous defense of truth telling is the eighteenth-century German philosopher Immanuel Kant. In this section selections from his *Lectures on Ethics* are presented in which Kant claims that truth telling is an essential feature of right communication. He equates honesty both with frankness and reserve, and he supports the principle of never telling a lie on three grounds: First, the principle of truth telling is one which each of us would like everyone else to follow. In other words, it is a principle that philosophers call "universalizable," meaning that each of us would like to see it universally followed by all human beings. Second, truth telling is a necessary element for society because all societies depend upon mutual bonds of honesty and truthfulness to enforce their unity and orderly continuation. Finally, lying destroys the major source of human development—that is, knowledge—since it thwarts the discovery of new truths.

In contrast with Kant, Albert Carr, in a lively article, "Is Business Bluffing Ethical?" suggests that truth telling depends on the context in which the activity takes place. For example, in advertising, although few advertisers actually lie about their products, many advertisements "puff" their products or make unfair comparisons between their product and the competition. This is all right, according to Carr, because everyone understands the "game" of advertising and no one is really fooled by the puffery. As Richard Wokutch and Thomas Carson point out, because perfect market information, and thus in Kant's terms, the "whole truth," is never obtainable, it is usually impossible to determine whether an advertiser or person is bluffing or lying. Wokutch and Carson point out that it is surely not always to the economic advantage of business to reveal the "whole truth" about a product or service, nor is it profitable not to engage in competitive bluffing when other businesses are doing so. Despite Carr's persuasive arguments, many advertisers as well as other business persons and philosophers are worried about the impact of the "game" of advertising on the public. Is bluffing or puffery justified when some persons affected by them do not understand the game and are deceived or misled?

If Carr's game analogy is questionable in advertising, the reader might want to consider its application to other aspects of business. Does the analogy ever justify making an exception to Kant's dictum that one should never lie? Wokutch and Carson argue that bluffing that involves lying about one's bargaining position can be justified if it is necessary to avoid being harmed by the lies of others. The case study "Italian Tax Mores" presents a situation in which truth telling, as well as relativism, is a major issue. The case concerns an American executive working at a branch of a U.S. company in Italy who finds that typical Italian practices encourage actions that he believes constitute both bribery and lying. Is it morally acceptable to misrepresent the company's income tax figures if it appears that most other companies in Italy do the same thing, and if truth telling will do harm to the bank? As a matter of self-defense, should the executive "play the game" and adopt the practices of the Italian tax system when the practices involve outright lying? Or can the manager justify providing the truth to the Italian tax authorities even when this might threaten the well-being of his bank?

Ethical Relativism

Case Study—The Lockheed Aircraft Corporation

A. CARL KOTCHIAN

My initiation into the chill realities of extortion, Japanese style, began in 1972. In August of that year I flew to Tokyo to work for the sale to a Japanese airline of Lockheed's wide-bodied TriStar passenger plane.

Soon after landing I found myself deep in conversation with Toshiharu Okubo, an official of Marubeni, the trading company that was serving as Lockheed's representative and go-between in the already ongoing TriStar negotiations.

Beaming, Okubo reviewed Marubeni's efforts on behalf of TriStar, then gave me the good news that "tomorrow at seven-thirty A.M., we are seeing Prime Minister Tanaka" about the matter. I was quite impressed with an encouraged by the "power of Marubeni"—power that made it possible to make an appointment with the prime minister only 24 hours after I had asked Marubeni to set up such a meeting. Then came an unexpected development: when we began to discuss in detail how to bring about the sale of TriStar, Okubo suddenly suggested that I make a "pledge" to pay money for a major favor like this. Though the proposal did not appall and outrage me, I was nonetheless quite astonished that the question of money had been brought up so abruptly—especially since in broaching the idea Okubo mentioned the name of the prime minister's secretary, Toshio Enomoto.

"How much money do we have to pledge?" I asked.

A. Carl Kotchian, "The Payoff: Lockheed's 70-Day Mission to Tokyo," *Saturday Review*, July 9, 1977, pp. 7–12. © 1977 *Saturday Review* magazine. Reprinted by permission.

"The going rate when asking for a major favor is usually five hundred million yen [roughly $1.7 million]. It can be smaller. . . ."

I was now faced with the problem of whether to make a payment to Japan's highest government office. If I refused, declining Marubeni's advice, and should our sale fail, I was certain that the full responsibility would be placed squarely upon me by Marubeni's officials, who could say to me, "We told you so. You did not listen to us."

Sensing my hesitation, Okubo reiterated, "If you wish to be successful in selling the aircraft, you would do well to pledge five hundred million yen."

During this exchange, Okubo never mentioned for whom the money was intended. But we both knew that our whole conversation had been about the meeting between Prime Minister Tanaka and Chairman Hiyama of Marubeni, scheduled for early in the morning of the next day. Stalling for time and hoping to discover for whom the money was intended, I asked, "How do you deliver that money?"

"We do not have to worry about it," Okubo assured me, "because Mr. Ito [Hiroshi Ito, another executive of Marubeni] is very close to Mr. Enomoto, the prime minister's secretary."

This exchange left me with no doubt that the money was going to the office of Japan's prime minister. Then, in response to my further questions, Okubo concretely spelled out the details of the arrangement—the amount, 500 million yen; the way it had to be put together, in Japanese yen, cash; the fact that it had to be ready when we were given the signal; and the way the delivery of the money was to be accomplished, through the prime minister's secretary. This, then, was how I got involved in the now much publicized secret payments to Japanese government officials.

And "involved" is the word, for later that day I had a meeting near Tokyo's Sony Building with Yoshio Kodama, Lockheed's confidential consultant in Japan. So Byzantine were the TriStar maneuverings that Marubeni, our "above ground" agents and consultants, had no idea that Kodama was on Lockheed's payroll! In keeping with the air of mystery surrounding these dealings, Kodama always insisted on meeting me in the evening, because, I gather, he did not want employees in the other offices to see a highly conspicuous, six-foot-tall *gaijin*—a Japanese word for "foreigner"—going in and out of his office.

During the meeting, I asked about the chances of Lockheed's enlisting the support of Kenji Osano, an intimate of Prime Minister Tanaka whom some people had urged on me as an adviser, since he was "the most influential person in Japan." On this point, Kodama told me without hesitation, "In order to include Mr. Osano, we need an extra five hundred million yen." Frankly, I was quite surprised that he had come up with this figure so readily, as though it had already been decided on well in advance.

So my education in Japanese business practices was proceeding apace: it was the second time that day that I had been asked for "five hundred million yen." I felt that this particular figure must be used quite often in Japan!

In fact, as I thought about it back in my room at the Hotel Okura, I had now had *three* requests for around 500 million yen — 520 million yen for Kodama on our contract with him, a second 500 million yen requested by Okubo to make a "payment pledge," and finally the third 500 million yen requested by Kodama for the inclusion of Osano in our campaign. I could not help thinking about these payments while I was having a room service dinner with my wife, Lucy. I was in fact thinking of calling Okubo to stop the 500 million yen that I had promised to pledge; but if I did that, I thought, I would have to tell him about the 500 million yen requested by Kodama. I decided at the last minute not to do that.

But why, you may wonder, did Lockheed put up at all with these under-the-counter demands? Why not just throw up our hands and try to sell our planes in some other country?

The truth is that — for the moment, at least — Lockheed had nowhere else to go *but* Japan. Although our planes were, and still are, first-rank products, fully competitive with if not superior to any other planes in the world, we had just come off a run of bad luck in the European market. To our chagrin and dismay, we had lost out on contract after airline contract — especially with Italy's Alitalia, Germany's Lufthansa, and Belgium's Sabena airlines.

Further, we were having difficulties with U.S. Defense Department contracts for the "Cheyenne" helicopter and the giant C5A Galaxie transport plane.

This bleak situation all but dictated a strong push for sales in the biggest untapped market left — Japan. This push, if successful, might well bring in revenues upwards of $400 million. Such a cash inflow would go a long way toward helping to restore Lockheed's fiscal health, and it would, of course, save the jobs of thousands of the firm's employees.

Against this background, I could hardly afford simply to fly away in disgust at the mere mention of these payments — payments which were in any case not forbidden under U.S. law. Realistically, the best I could hope for was to bend a bit in the face of these demands, while keeping our payments to a minimum percentage of any sale that went through.

While I was working in the Lockheed office at about 10:00 A.M. the next day, August 23, I received a telephone call from Okubo. He asked me to come to his office.

When I got there an hour or so later, I found him in a very jovial mood. He told me, "I accompanied Mr. Hiyama, Marubeni's chairman, to Prime Minister Tanaka's residence this morning."

According to Okubo, the two men had seen Prime Minister Tanaka briefly, and then Okubo left while Hiyama stayed to talk with the prime minister. He did not tell me what the three of them talked about or what Hiyama talked about with the prime minister. But then Okubo confided:

"That pledge has been made, too."

I do not know specifically how the pledge was made to the office of the prime minister, since these transactions seemed to be such a uniquely Japanese method. All I know is that I was given no paper saying, for instance, "If Lockheed is successful, we will pay 500 million yen," and the like. First of all, it was not clear whether the pledge was made to the prime minister himself or to his secretary. But I did not ask Okubo about this point, nor did I have any intention of doing so. I knew from the beginning that this money was going to the office of the prime minister and there was no need for me to have to pin down exactly to whom it was going or how the money was going to be delivered.

For the next few months, as summer passed over into fall, I stayed on in Tokyo, trying with little success to force-feed the situation, while delays, diversions, and frustrations piled up.

Then, to make things worse, late in October I was knocked flat by the pain and fever of a severe "bug" infection. Doctors, antibiotics, and bed rest seemed to do me no good: all I could do was lie there in my hotel suite, aching and perspiring and thinking darkly about jumping out the window. I suspect that it was only my wife's comforting presence that kept me from doing something drastic.

On October 29, when I was at my lowest ebb physically and mentally, our telephone started ringing. I picked up the receiver thinking, Who can it be at this time on a Sunday night? It was Okubo. Judging from the way his voice sounded, he seemed to be telephoning from a faraway place. After we exchanged pleasantries, he pointed out that the final decision by All Nippon Airlines (ANA)—the largest Japanese domestic carrier—would be made very shortly and said:

"If you do three things, Mr. Kotchian, you will definitely succeed in selling the TriStar."

I was struck with the importance of what Okubo was trying to say to me, and I straightened out the receiver in my hand and asked him, like a pupil asking questions of a teacher, "What are these three things that I have to do?" There was a tension in Okubo's voice, and for my part I listened to him with the phone pressed hard against my ear.

His first few stipulations were relatively minor, having to do with the maintenance of any planes Lockheed might sell to All Nippon Airlines. I readily agreed to them. And then came the "hook." According to Okubo, I had to get together as soon as possible $400,000—that is, 120 million Japanese yen—cash. "If possible, the first thing tomorrow morning, it has to be ready," Okubo urged me. As I'm sure he knew, it would have been impossible to have such a large sum of money ready on such short notice. I began asking questions; above all, What is the money for?

"To give three hundred thousand dollars [90 million yen] to Mr. Wakasa, president of All Nippon Airlines," Okubo blandly explained, "and also to make payments to six politicians."

As Okubo mentioned the six politicians by name, I wrote the names down on a hotel memo pad.

"If we give three hundred thousand dollars to Mr. Wakasa and to each of the six politicians, won't that make two million one hundred thousand dollars—six hundred thirty million yen?" I asked.

Suffering from a high fever and pain, I really became sick at the thought of such a preposterous sum. Okubo had, I reflected, already asked me for 500 million yen in August and I had agreed to make the pledge. Now he's asking more money for payments to politicians. What is he trying to do to me? Okubo hurriedly objected to my 630-million-yen figure: "No, not such a large sum."

"Is it, then, three hundred thousand dollars altogether, including the payments to the politicians?"

"No, that is not correct either. What I am trying to say is . . ."

In the end, it came down to this: the amount of money that had to be delivered to Mr. Wakasa, the president of ANA, was $300,000 altogether. This amount was calculated on the basis of $50,000 for each of the six airplanes ANA planned to purchase initially. In addition to this $300,000 for ANA, Okubo mentioned that an additional $100,000 should be prepared in Japanese yen—cash—and that this money should go to the following six politicians:

Tomisaburo Hashimoto, secretary-general of the Liberal Democratic party.

Susumu Nikaido, chief cabinet secretary.

Hideyo Sasaki, minister of transportation.

Kazuomi Fukunaga, chairman of the Liberal Democratic party's special committee on aviation.

Takayuki Sato, former parliamentary vice-minister of transportation.

Mutsuki Kato, present parliamentary vice-minister of transportation.

Of the six politicians, I had not heard of Kazuomi Fukunaga and Mutsuki Kato. Of the remaining four, I had never met or talked with even one (and have never met them since, either); but I had heard of them and had seen their names in the newspapers. The hotel's telephone memo paper, on which I jotted down their names in romanized Japanese, was the so-called "memo" that had the names of the high Japanese government officials; it is this memo that became a great subject of curiosity when the Lockheed incident was disclosed in the United States.

As for the breakdown of this money for the politicians, Okubo expressed the intention of distributing the money as follows: 7 million yen each to Hashimoto and Nikaido, and 4 million yen each to Sasaki, Fukunaga, Sato, and Kato.

"If you do this first thing tomorrow morning," said Okubo, full of confidence, "we can formally get ANA's order tomorrow without fail." I had a feeling that these figures and the names must have been carefully thought about by someone. The problem, however, was that it was already past midnight and it was going to be very difficult to prepare such a large sum of money so quickly.

"By what time do we have to prepare this amount?" I asked.

"I would like you to have the whole sum of money ready by ten A.M. tomorrow," responded Okubo.

"That is impossible. I could not have it ready so quickly."

"The thirty million yen [for the politicians] is highly important. Couldn't you have that much ready at least?"

"Well, I'll try to do my best," I responded, adding, "and I will have the remaining ninety million yen ready at the earliest possible date. I will let you know on this remaining amount tomorrow morning."

If some third party had heard this conversation, he could ask why I responded to this request for secret payments. However, I must admit that it was extremely persuasive and attractive at that time to have someone come up to me and confidently tell me, "If you do this, you will surely get ANA's order in twenty-four hours." What businessman who is dealing with commercial and trade matters could decline a request for certain amounts of money when that money would enable him to get the contract? For someone like myself, who had been struggling against plots and severe competition for over two months, it was almost impossible to dismiss this opportunity.

At about 10:00 A.M. the next day, a Lockheed representative in Tokyo called to tell me that—persuant to my instructions—he had delivered the 30 million yen to Okubo. (As for the remaining 90 million yen, I believe it was delivered on November 6, after I left Japan.)

Later that day, a group of us who had been working on the TriStar sale met in the lobby of the Kasumigaseki Building; Mr. Matsui of Marubeni got into the elevator with us, and together we went up to the head office of All Nippon Airlines. When we were ushered into one of the conference rooms in the main office, the top management of ANA had already assembled. I was told, "Congratulations, Mr. Kotchian, you have won the contract."

Feverish and light-headed though I was from my illness, I nonetheless felt very happy when I heard this and had a warm feeling inside me. I came back to the hotel at seven o'clock and waited a little bit longer until it was Monday morning, California time. Then I called up our main office in Burbank and informed Mr. Haughton, our chairman, of the good news. He was delighted and told me that on my return they were going to have a big celebration party for all of us who had worked on the sale.

Now, finally, I began to feel a sense of victory after the most intense sales campaign of my life. It was a victory of pain after 70 straight days of battle in which I had literally run around the great city of Tokyo without getting a chance to know it at all. At about seven o'clock on the evening of October 31, our suite was filled with happy Lockheed men and women who had worked many weeks for this occasion. Everybody's face looked so happy and bright; champagne was opened, one bottle after another. I even poured champagne over the head of Peter Mingrone, a Lockheed executive who had helped enormously in the sales campaign.

After returning to the States, I began to take care of the areas of my responsibility other than Japan. Having completed the official signing of the contract document, I thought that the sales campaign of the TriStar in Japan had been completed.

I believe it was around June 25, 1973, although I do not specifically remember the date, that I received an unexpected telephone communication from Okubo, who said, "Now is the time for you to honor that pledge."

For one second, I wondered what he was talking about, but then I realized that by the word *pledge*, he was talking about the pledge of 500 million yen that we made to the office of Prime Minister Tanaka the previous August. The word *pledge* had been used frequently at that time in Okubo's office when we were talking about the subject. Nevertheless, there had been a ten-month lapse since August. It had been almost half a year since Lockheed and ANA officially signed the formal contract in January. I wondered why he was bringing this up now, when the sales campaign of the Tri Star to ANA had long ago been completed.

"I am very surprised, Mr. Okubo, because it all happened six or eight months ago; and we haven't heard anything about it. Frankly, as our campaign has been completed, I don't have that kind of budget now," I told him.

"Yes, but that is the pledge that you agreed upon and accepted," Okubo insisted.

"But you have not communicated with us for such a long time on this matter. The whole deal was completed six months ago," I repeated.

I expressed strong opposition to doing this kind of thing this late. Therefore I asked him: "Are you sure it's necessary, Mr. Okubo?"

Okubo said, "Let me check into it. If it's really necessary, I'll get back to you."

This is how our telephone conversation ended on that day. Three days later, Okubo called me again and said: "This is very serious, Mr. Kotchian, and you must carry out that pledge."

Okubo *sounded* very serious and worried. He said that he had talked to Mr. Hiyama, the chairman of the board of Marubeni, on this matter, and that Mr. Hiyama asked him to tell me that if Lockheed did not stand by its pledge, we would never be able to sell anything in Japan again. Worse still, Okubo said, if the pledge was not honored, "Mr. Hiyama will have to leave Japan."

It was quite shocking for me to hear that the chairman of Marubeni would have to leave Japan. I interpreted this as meaning that Hiyama would be forced into exile.

"You have convinced me, Mr. Okubo, that the matter is indeed serious," I told him, promising that I would get in touch with him early the next week.

After hanging up the phone, I went home and thought about the matter overnight. I decided on the basis of what Okubo had told me that we could not possibly risk any retaliation against Lockheed or against Marubeni. If we did not make the payment on this matter, Hiyama would be forced into exile, Lockheed might not be able to sell anything in Japan again, and our relations with Marubeni might be completely disrupted. Consequently, the more I thought about it, the more I was convinced that there was no alternative but to make the payment. In the end, after talking it over with other Lockheed officials, I called Okubo and told him we would honor the pledge.

Throughout these three international telephone calls on this matter, Okubo never once mentioned the name of the person for whom the money was intended, or the amount; and neither did I. Perhaps we were both mindful of the fact that the conversation was going through the telephone exchange and we did not want to be overheard by anybody; but more than anything else, we were both aware that this 500 million yen was going to the office of the prime minister. I never asked why the payment was necessary at this particular stage, after so many months had passed. All I know is that the designated amount was paid—spread over the remainder of 1973 to early 1974. I did not know then that it was made in four shipments or when it was paid specifically.

When I visited Japan in October 1973, on my way back from Iran, to arrange the date for the delivery of the first plane, All Nippon Airlines had already decided to make a firm order for the additional eight TriStars on which they had an option. After this second contract was concluded, Okubo again demanded $400,000 from us, calculated on the basis of $50,000 per plane for eight planes, to be delivered to Mr. Wakasa, the president of ANA, as a secret payment.

When Okubo called me by international telephone from Tokyo and demanded this amount, I responded rather harshly, saying, "Wasn't it a one-time expenditure at that time only?"

"No," Okubo said emphatically. "I'm sure I told you these payments were necessary for all of the planes—all of the twenty-one planes."

I had no intention of paying this kind of money until the actual order was made and the initial down payment for the next eight planes was made to Lockheed, and I told this to Okubo. Here again, I could have declined. However, if I had declined and they had said, "Well, we will not order any more planes from Lockheed," what would we do?

The most I could say to this additional demand for money was: "When the initial down payment is received, we will pay what we have to."

The down payment started coming in, and by August of the next year, 1974, down payment for the first four of the eight planes had been received by Lockheed. I thought that if I paid the $400,000 requested by Okubo at that stage I would expedite the down payment for the remaining four planes. So it was around this time that I finally approved the payment of $400,000 to ANA and instructed our representative to arrange such a delivery per instructions from Okubo. I don't know how this money was paid, where, and in what manner—or what kind of receipts were used.

As for the purpose of the $700,000 (calculated on the basis of $50,000 per plane for the 14 planes), Okubo never explained to me, nor did I ask any questions about it. It could be inferred, however, from the way that Okubo spoke that the money was to be used at the discretion of the top management of ANA, although none of the ANA people ever talked about this in our meetings.

Such were some of the payments for the sale of the TriStar in Japan, viewed from my perspective. Above all, there are three things I would like to stress about the whole sequence I have described.

The *first* is that the Lockheed payments in Japan, totaling about $12 million, were worthwhile from Lockheed's standpoint, since they amounted to less than 3 percent of the expected sum of about $430 million that we would receive from ANA for 21 TriStars. Further, as I've noted, such disbursements *did not violate American laws.* I should also like to stress that my decision to make such payments stemmed from my judgment that the TriStar payments to ANA would provide Lockheed workers with jobs and thus redound to the benefit of their dependents, their communities, and stockholders of the corporation.

Secondly, I should like to emphasize that the payments to the so-called "high Japanese government officials" were all requested by Okubo and were *not brought up from my side.* When he told me "five hundred million yen is necessary for such sales," from a purely ethical and moral standpoint I would have declined such a request. However, in that case, I would *most certainly* have sacrificed commercial success.

Finally, I want to make it clear that I never discussed money matters with Japanese politicians, government officials, or airline officials.

It would be simple if selling were merely a matter of presenting a product on its merits. Lockheed conducted its business in Japan much as other aircraft companies, its competitors, had done over the years. All have found it helpful to have nationals advise them, in Japan as in many other countries. Much has been made in press accounts in both Japan and the United States of secret agents and secret channels for sales efforts. Of course these consultations with advisers were secret: competitors do not tell each other their strategy or even their sales targets.

And if Lockheed had not remained competitive by the rules of the game as then played, we would not have sold the TriStar and would not have provided work for tens of thousands of our employees or contributed to the future of the corporation. Nor would ANA have had the services of this excellent airplane.

From my experience in international sales, I knew that if we wanted our product to have a chance to win on its own merits, we had to follow the functioning system. If we wanted our product to have a chance, we understood that we would have to pay, or pledge to pay, substantial sums of money in addition to the contractual sales commissions. We never *sought* to make these extra payments. We would have preferred not to have the additional expenses for the sale. But, always, they were recommended by those whose experience and judgment we trusted and whose recommendations we therefore followed.

Every investigation campaign requires an "example," a "scapegoat," and Lockheed is that today in the current international climate of reform. The requirement to assess responsibility in Japan has brought the embarrassment of public accusation to some persons associated with the company. To others it has brought the humiliation of arrest and imprisonment. We, too, have suffered. We are anguished that some of our friends and their families have had to bear this agony. We hope it will not have been without benefit.

A Defense of Cultural Relativism

WILLIAM GRAHAM SUMNER

THE FOLKWAYS ARE "RIGHT." RIGHTS. MORALS

The folkways . . . extend over the whole of life. There is a right way to catch game, to win a wife, to make one's self appear, to cure disease, to honor ghosts, to treat comrades or strangers, to behave when a child is born, on the warpath, in council, and so on in all cases which can arise. The ways are defined on the negative side, that is, by taboos. The "right" way is the way which the ancestors used and which has been handed down. The tradition is its own warrant. It is not held subject to verification by experience. The notion of right is in the folkways. It is not outside of them, of independent origin, and brought to them to test them. In the folkways, whatever is, is right. This is because they are traditional, and therefore contain in themselves the authority of the ancestral ghosts. When we come to the folkways we are at the end of our analysis. The notion of right and ought is the same in regard to all the folkways, but the degree of it varies

William Graham Sumner, *Folkways* (Lexington, Mass.: Ginn and Company, 1907), selections. Reprinted by permission.

with the importance of the interest at stake. The obligation of comformable and cooperative action is far greater under ghost fear and war than in other matters, and the social sanctions are severer, because group interests are supposed to be at stake. Some usages contain only a slight element of right and ought. It may well be believed that notions of right and duty, and of social welfare, were first developed in connection with ghost fear and other-worldliness, and therefore that, in that field also, folkways were first raised to mores. "Rights" are the rules of mutual give and take in the competition of life which are imposed on comrades in the in-group, in order that the peace may prevail there which is essential to the group strength. Therefore rights can never be "natural" or "God-given," or absolute in any sense. The morality of a group at a time is the sum of the taboos and prescriptions in the folkways by which right conduct is defined. Therefore morals can never be intuitive. They are historical, institutional, and empirical.

World philosophy, life policy, right, rights, and morality are all products of the folkways. They are reflections on, and generalizations from, the experience of pleasure and pain which is won in efforts to carry on the struggle for existence under actual life conditions. The generalizations are very crude and vague in their germinal forms. They are all embodied in folklore, and all our philosophy and science have been developed out of them.

INTEGRATION OF THE MORES OF A GROUP OR AGE

In further development of the same interpretation of the phenomena we find that changes in history are primarily due to changes in life conditions. Then the folkways change. The new philosophies and ethical rules are invented to try to justify the new ways. The whole vast body of modern mores has thus been developed out of the philosophy and ethics of the Middle Ages. So the mores which have been developed to suit the system of great secular states, world commerce, credit institutions, contract wages and rent, emigration to outlying continents, etc., have become the norm for the whole body of usages, manners, ideas, faiths, customs, and institutions which embrace the whole life of a society and characterize an historical epoch. Thus India, Chaldea, Assyria, Egypt, Greece, Rome, the Middle Ages, Modern Times, are cases in which the integration of the mores upon different life conditions produced societal states of complete and distinct individuality (ethos). Within any such societal status the great reason for any phenomenon is that it conforms to the mores of the time and place. Historians have always recognized incidentally the operation of such a determining force. What is now maintained is that it is not incidental or subordinate. It is supreme and controlling. Therefore the scientific discussion of a usage, custom, or institution consists in tracing its relation to the mores, and the discussion of societal crises and changes consists in showing their connection with changes in the life conditions, or with the readjustment of the mores to changes in those conditions.

PURPOSE OF THE PRESENT WORK

"Ethology" would be a convenient term for the study of manners, customs, usages, and mores, including the study of the way in which they are formed, how they grow or decay, and how they affect the interests which it is their purpose to serve. The Greeks applied the term "ethos" to the sum of the characteristic usages, ideas, standards, and codes by which a group was differentiated and individualized in character from other groups. "Ethics" were things which pertained to the ethos and therefore the things which were the standard of right. The Romans used "mores" for customs in the broadest and richest sense of the word, including the notion that customs served welfare, and had traditional and mystic sanction, so that they were properly authoritative and sacred. It is a very surprising fact that modern nations should have lost these words and the significant suggestions which inhere in them. The English language has no derivative noun from "mores," and no equivalent for it. The French *moeurs* is trivial compared with "mores." The German *Sitte* renders "mores" but very imperfectly. The modern peoples have made morals and morality a separate domain, by the side of religion, philosophy, and politics. In that sense, morals is an impossible and unreal category. It has no existence, and can have none. The word "moral" means what belongs to or appertains to the mores. Therefore the category of morals can never be defined without reference to something outside of itself. Ethics, having lost connection with the ethos of a people, is an attempt to systematize the current notions of right and wrong upon some basic principle, generally with the purpose of establishing morals on an absolute doctrine, so that it shall be universal, absolute, and everlasting. In a general way also, whenever a thing can be called moral, or connected with some ethical generality, it is thought to be "raised," and disputants whose method is to employ ethical generalities assume especial authority for themselves and their views. These methods of discussion are most employed in treating of social topics, and they are disastrous to sound study of facts. They help to hold the social sciences under the dominion of metaphysics. The abuse has been most developed in connection with political economy, which has been almost robbed of the character of a serious discipline by converting its discussions into ethical disquisitions.

WHY USE THE WORD MORES?

"Ethica," in the Greek sense, or "ethology," as above defined, would be good names for our present work. We aim to study the ethos of groups, in order to see how it arises, its power and influence, the modes of its operation on members of the group, and the various attributes of it (ethica). "Ethology" is a very unfamiliar word. It has been used for the mode of setting forth manners, customs, and mores in satirical comedy. The Latin word "mores" seems to be, on the whole, more practically convenient and available than any other for our purpose, as a name for the folkways with the connotations of right and truth in respect to welfare, embodied in them. The analysis and definition given above show that in the mores we must recognize a dominating force in history, constituting a condition as to what can be done, and as to the methods which can be employed.

MORES ARE A DIRECTIVE FORCE

Of course the view which has been stated is antagonistic to the view that philosophy and ethics furnish creative and determining forces in society and history. That view comes down to us from the Greek philosophy and it has now prevailed so long that all current discussion conforms to it. Philosophy and ethics are pursued as independent disciplines, and the results are brought to the science of society and to statesmanship and legislation as authoritative dicta. We also have *Völkerpsychologie*, *Sozialpolitik*, and other intermediate forms which show the struggle of metaphysics to retain control of the science of society. The "historic sense," the *Zeitgeist*, and other terms of similar import are partial recognitions of the mores and their importance in the science of society. We shall see below that philosophy and ethics are products of the folkways. They are taken out of the mores, but are never original and creative; they are secondary and derived. They often interfere in the second stage of the sequence—act, thought, act. Then they produce harm, but some ground is furnished for the claim that they are creative or at least regulative. In fact, the real process in great bodies of men is not one of deduction from any great principle of philosophy or ethics. It is one of minute efforts to live well under existing conditions, which efforts are repeated indefinitely by great numbers, getting strength from habit and from the fellowship of united action. The resultant folkways become coercive. All are forced to conform, and the folkways dominate the societal life. Then they seem true and right, and arise into mores as the norm of welfare. Thence are produced faiths, ideas, doctrines, religions, and philosophies, according to the stage of civilization and the fashions of reflection and generalization.

WHAT IS GOODNESS OR BADNESS OF THE MORES?

It is most important to notice that, for the people of a time and place, their own mores are always good, or rather that for them there can be no question of the goodness or badness of their mores. The reason is because the standards of good and right are in the mores. If the life conditions change, the traditional folkways may produce pain and loss, or fail to produce the same good as formerly. Then the loss of comfort and ease brings doubt into the judgment of welfare (causing doubt of the pleasure of the gods, or of war power, or of health), and thus disturbs the unconscious philosophy of the mores. Then a later time will pass judgment on the mores. Another society may also pass judgment on the mores. In our literary and historical study of the mores we want to get from them their educational value, which consists in the stimulus or warning as to what is, in its effects, societally good or bad. This may lead us to reject or neglect a phenomenon like infanticide, slavery, or witchcraft, as an old "abuse" and "evil," or to pass by the crusades as a folly which cannot recur. Such a course would be a great error. Everything in the mores of a time and place must be regarded as justified with regard to that time and place. "Good" mores are those which are well adapted to the situation. "Bad" mores are those which are not so adapted. The mores are not so stereotyped and changeless as might appear, because they are forever moving towards more complete adaption to conditions and interests, and also towards more complete adjustment to each other. People in mass have never made or kept up a custom in order to hurt their own interests. They have made innumerable errors as to what their interests were and how to satisfy them, but they have always aimed to serve their interests as well as they could. This gives the standpoint for the student of the mores. All things in them come before him on the same plane. They all bring instruction and warning. They all have the same relation to power and welfare. The mistakes in them are component parts of them. We do not study them in order to approve some of them and condemn others. They are all equally worthy of attention from the fact that they existed and were used. The chief object of study in them is their adjustment to interests, their relation to welfare, and their coordination in a harmonious system of life policy. For the men of the time there are no "bad" mores. What is traditional and current is the standard of what ought to be. The masses never raise any question about such things. If a few raise doubts and questions, this proves that the folkways have already begun to lose firmness and the regulative element in the mores has begun to lose authority. This indicates that the folkways are on their way to a new adjustment. The extreme of folly, wickedness, and absurdity in the mores is witch persecutions, but the best men in the seventeenth century had no doubt that witches existed, and that they ought to be burned. The religion, statecraft, jurisprudence, philosophy, and social system of that age all contributed to maintain that belief. It was rather a culmination than a contradiction of the current faiths and convictions, just as the dogma that all men are equal and that one ought to have as much political power in the state as another was the culmination of the political dogmatism and social philosophy of the nineteenth century. Hence our judgments of the good or evil consequences of folkways are to be kept separate from our study of the historical phenomena of them, and of their strength and the reasons for it. The judgments have their place in plans and doctrines for the future, not in a retrospect.

THE MORES HAVE THE AUTHORITY OF FACTS

The mores come down to us from the past. Each individual is born into them as he is born into the atmosphere, and he does not reflect on them, or criticize them any more than a baby analyzes the atmosphere before he begins to breathe it. Each one is subjected to the influence of the mores, and formed by them, before he is capable of reasoning about them. It may be objected that nowadays, at least, we criticize all traditions, and accept none just because they are handed down to us. If we take up cases of things which are still entirely or almost entirely in the mores, we shall see that this is not so. There are sects of free-lovers amongst us who want to discuss pair marriage. They are not simply people of evil life. They invite us to discuss rationally our inherited customs and ideas as to marriage, which, they say, are by no means so excellent and elevated as we believe. They have never won any serious attention. Some others want to argue in favor of polygamy on grounds of expediency. They fail to obtain a hearing. Others want to discuss property. In spite of some literary activity on their part, no discussion of property, bequest, and inheritance has ever been opened. Property and marriage are in the mores. Nothing can ever change them but the unconscious and imperceptible movement of the mores. Religion was originally a matter of the mores. It became a societal institution and a function of the state. It has now to a great extent been put back into the mores. Since laws with penalties to enforce religious creeds or practices have gone out of use any one may think and act as he pleases about religion. Therefore, it is not now "good form" to attack religion. Infidel publications are now tabooed by the mores, and are more effectually repressed than ever before. They produce no controversy. Democracy is in our American mores. It is a product of our physical and economic conditions. It is impossible to discuss or criticize it. It is glorified for popularity, and is a subject of dithyrambic rhetoric. No one treats it with complete candor and sincerity. No one dares to analyze it as he would aristocracy or autocracy. He would get no hearing and would only incur abuse. The thing to be noticed in all these cases is that the masses oppose a deaf ear to every argument against the mores. It is only insofar as things have been transferred from the mores into laws and positive institutions that there is discussion about them or rationalizing upon them. The mores contain the norm by which, if we should discuss the mores, we should have to judge the mores. We learn the mores as unconsciously as we learn to walk and eat and breathe. The masses never learn how we walk, and eat, and breathe, and they never know any reason why the mores are what they are. The justification of them is that when we wake to consciousness of life we find them facts which already hold us in the bonds of tradition, custom, and habit. The mores contain embodied in them notions, doctrines, and maxims, but they are facts. They are in the present tense. They have nothing to do with what ought to be, will be, may be, or once was, if it is not now.

MORES AND MORALS; SOCIAL CODE

For everyone the mores give the notion of what ought to be. This includes the notion of what ought to be done, for all should cooperate to bring to pass, in the order of life, what ought to be. All notions of propriety, decency, chastity, politeness, order, duty, right, rights, discipline, respect, reverence, cooperation, and fellowship, especially all things in regard to which good and ill depend entirely on the point at which the line is drawn, are in the mores. The mores can make things seem right and good to one group or one age which to another seem antagonistic to every instinct of human nature. The thirteenth century bred in every heart such a sentiment in regard to heretics that inquisitors had no more misgivings in their proceedings than men would have now if they should attempt to exterminate rattlesnakes. The sixteenth century gave to all such notions about witches that witch persecutors thought they were waging war on enemies of God and man. Of course the inquisitors and witch persecutors constantly developed the notions of heretics and witches. They exaggerated the notions and then gave them back again to the mores, in their expanded form, to inflame the hearts of men with terror and hate and to become, in the next stage, so much more fantastic and ferocious motives. Such is the reaction between the mores and the acts of the living generation. The world philosophy of the age is never anything but the reflection on the mental horizon, which is formed out of the mores, of the ruling ideas which are in the mores themselves. It is from a failure to recognize the to and fro in this reaction that the current notion arises that mores are produced by doctrines. The "morals" of an age are never anything but the consonance between what is done and what the mores of the age require. The whole revolves on itself, in the relation of the specific to the general, within the horizon formed by the mores. Every attempt to win an outside standpoint from which to reduce the whole to an absolute philosophy of truth and right, based on an unalterable principle, is a delusion. New elements are brought in only by new conquests of nature through science and art. The new conquests change the conditions of life and the interests of the members of the society. Then the mores change by adaptation to new conditions and interests. The philosophy and ethics then follow to account for and justify the changes in the mores; often, also, to claim that they have caused the changes. They never do anything but draw new lines of bearing between the parts of the mores and the horizon of thought within which they are inclosed, and which is a deduction from the mores. The horizon is widened by more knowledge, but for one age it is just as much a generalization from the mores as for another. It is always unreal. It is only a product of thought. The ethical philosophers select points on this horizon from which to take their bearings, and they think that they have won some authority for their systems when they travel back again from the generalization to the specific custom out of which it was deduced. The cases of the inquisitors and witch persecutors who toiled arduously and continually for their chosen ends, for little or no reward, show us the relation between mores on the one side and philosophy, ethics, and religion on the other.

Ethical Relativity and Ethical Absolutism

WALTER T. STACE

Any ethical position which denies that there is a single moral standard which is equally applicable to all men at all times may fairly be called a species of ethical relativity. There is not, the relativist asserts, merely one moral law, one code, one standard. There are many moral laws, codes, standards. What morality ordains in one place or age may be quite different from what morality ordains in another place or age. The moral code of Chinamen is quite different from that of Europeans, that of African savages quite different from both. Any morality, therefore, is relative to the age, the place, and the circumstances in which it is found. It is in no sense absolute.

This does not mean merely — as one might at first sight be inclined to suppose — that the very same kind of action which is *thought* right in one country and period may be *thought* wrong in another. This would be a mere platitude, the truth of which everyone would have to admit. Even the absolutist would admit this — would even wish to emphasize it — since he is well aware that different peoples have different sets of moral ideas, and his whole

Reprinted with permission of Macmillan Publishing Company from *The Concept of Morals* by Walter T. Stace. Copyright 1937 by Macmillan Publishing Company, renewed 1965 by Walter T. Stace.

point is that some of these sets of ideas are false. What the relativist means to assert is, not this platitude, but that the very same kind of action which is right in one country and period may *be* wrong in another. And this, far from being a platitude, is a very startling assertion.

It is very important to grasp thoroughly the difference between the two ideas. . . . We fail to see that the word "standard" is used in two different senses. It is perfectly true that, in once sense, there are many variable moral standards. We speak of judging a man by the standard of his time. And this implies that different times have different standards. And this, of course, is quite true. But when the word "standard" is used in this sense it means simply the set of moral ideas current during the period in question. It means what people *think* right, whether as a matter of fact it is right or not. On the other hand when the absolutist asserts that there exists a single universal moral "standard," he is not using the word in this sense at all. He means by "standard" what *is* right as distinct from what people merely think right. His point is that although what people think right varies in different countries and periods, yet what actually is right is everywhere and always the same. And it follows that when the ethical relativist disputes the position of the absolutist and denies that any universal moral standard exists he too means by "standard" what actually is right. . . .

To sum up, the ethical relativist consistently denies, it would seem, whatever the ethical absolutist asserts. For the absolutist there is a single universal moral standard. For the relativist there is no such standard. There are only local, ephemeral, and variable standards. For the absolutist there are two senses of the word "standard." Standards in the sense of sets of current moral ideas are relative and changeable. But the standard in the sense of what is actually morally right is absolute and unchanging. For the relativist no such distinction can be made. There is only one meaning of the word standard, namely, that which refers to local and variable sets of moral ideas.

Finally—though this is merely saying the same thing in another way—the absolutist makes a distinction between what actually is right and what is thought right. The relativist rejects this distinction and identifies what is moral with what is thought moral by certain human beings or groups of human beings. . . .

I shall now proceed to consider, first, the main arguments which can be urged in favour of ethical relativity; and secondly, the arguments which can be urged against it. . . .

There are, I think, [two] main arguments in favour of ethical relativity. The first is that which relies upon the actual varieties of moral "standards" found in the world. . . .

The investigations of anthropologists have shown that there exist side by side in the world a bewildering variety of moral codes. On this topic endless volumes have been written, masses of evidence piled up. Anthropologists have ransacked the Melanesian Islands, the jungles of New Guinea, the steppes of Siberia, the deserts of Australia, the forests of central Africa, and have brought back with them countless examples of weird, extravagant, and fantastic "moral" customs with which to confound us. We learn that all kinds of horrible practices are, in this, that, or the other place, regarded as essential to virtue. We find that there is nothing, or next to nothing, which has always and everywhere been regarded as morally good by all men. Where then is our universal morality? Can we, in face of all this evidence, deny that it is nothing but an empty dream?

This argument, taken by itself, is a very weak one. It relies upon a single set of facts—the variable moral customs of the world. But this variability of moral ideas is admitted by both parties to the dispute, and is capable of ready explanation upon the hypothesis of either party. The relativist says that the facts are to be explained by the non-existence of any absolute moral standard. The absolutist says that they are to be explained by human ignorance of what the absolute moral standard is. And he can truly point out that men have differed widely in their opinions about all manner of topics including the subject-matters of the physical sciences—just as much as they differ about morals. And if the various different opinions which men have held about the shape of the earth do not prove that it has no one real shape, neither do the various opinions which they have held about morality prove that there is no one true morality.

Thus the facts can be explained equally plausibly on either hypothesis. There is nothing in the facts themselves which compels us to prefer the relativistic hypothesis to that of the absolutist. And therefore the argument fails to prove the relativist conclusion. If that conclusion is to be established, it must be by means of other considerations. . . .

The [second] argument in favour of ethical relativity is a very strong one. . . . It consists in alleging that no one has ever been able to discover upon what foundation an absolute morality could rest, or from what source a universally binding moral code could derive its authority.

If, for example, it is an absolute and unalterable moral rule that all men ought to be unselfish, from whence does this *command* issue? For a command it certainly is, phrase it how you please. There is no difference in meaning between the sentence "You ought to be unselfish" and the sentence "Be unselfish." Now a command implies a commander. An obligation implies some authority which obliges. Who is this commander, what this authority? Thus the vastly difficult question is raised of *the basis of moral obligation*. Now the argument of the relativist would be that it is impossible to find any basis for a universally binding moral law; but that it is quite easy to discover a basis for morality if moral codes are admitted to be variable, ephemeral, and relative to time, place, and circumstance.

No such easy solution of the problem of the basis of moral obligation is open to the absolutist. He believes in moral commands, obedience to which is obligatory on all men, whether they know it or not, whatever they feel, and whatever their customs may be. Such uniform obligation cannot be founded upon feelings, because feelings are—or are said to be—variable. And there is no set of customs which is more than local in its operation. The will of God as the source of universal law is no longer a feasible suggestion. . . . Where then is the absolutist to turn for an answer to the question? And if he cannot find one, he will have to admit the claims of the ethical relativist; or at least he will have to give up his own claims. . . .

This argument is undoubtedly very strong. It is absolutely essential to solve the problem of the basis of moral obligation if we are to believe in any kind of moral standards other than those provided by mere custom or by irrational emotions. It is idle to talk about a universal morality unless we can point to the source of its authority—or at least to do so is to indulge in a faith which is without rational ground. To cherish a blind faith in morality may be, for the average man whose business is primarily to live aright and not to theorize, sufficient. Perhaps it is his wisest course. But it will not do for the philosopher. His function, or at least one of his functions, is precisely to discover the rational grounds of our everyday beliefs—if they have any. Philosophically and intellectually, then, we cannot accept belief in a universally binding morality unless we can discover upon what foundation its obligatory character rests.

But in spite of the strength of the argument thus posed in favour of ethical relativity, it is not impregnable. For it leaves open one loop-hole. It is always possible that some theory, not yet examined, may provide a basis for a universal moral obligation. The argument rests upon the negative proposition that *there is no theory which can provide a basis for a universal morality*. But it is notoriously difficult to prove a negative. How can you prove that there are no green swans? All you can show is that none have been found so far. And then it is always possible that one will be found tomorrow. So it is here. The relativist shows that no theory of the basis of moral obligation has yet been discovered which could validate a universal morality. Perhaps. But it is just conceivable that one might be discovered in the course of this book.

It is time that we turn our attention from the case in favour of ethical relativity to the case against it. Now the case against it consists, to a very large extent, in urging that, if taken seriously and pressed to its logical conclusion, ethical relativity can only end in destroying the conception of morality altogether, in undermining its practical efficacy, in rendering meaningless many almost universally accepted truths about human affairs, in robbing human beings of any incentive to strive for a better world, in taking the life-blood out of every ideal and every aspiration which has ever ennobled the life of man. . . .

First of all, then, ethical relativity, in asserting that the moral standards of particular social groups are the only standards which exist, renders meaningless all propositions which attempt to compare these standards with one another in respect of their moral worth. And this is a very serious matter indeed. We are accustomed to think that the moral ideas of one nation or social group may be "higher" or "lower" than those of another. We believe, for example, that Christian ethical ideals are nobler than those for the savage races of central Africa. Probably most of us would think that the Chinese moral standards are higher than those of the inhabitants of New Guinea. In short we habitually compare one civilization with another and judge the sets of ethical ideas to be found in them to be some better, some worse. The fact that such judgments are very difficult to make with any justice, and that they are frequently made on very superficial and prejudiced grounds, has no bearing on the question now at issue. The question is whether such judgments have any *meaning*. We habitually assume that they have.

But on the basis of ethical relativity they can have none whatever. For the relativist must hold that there is no *common* standard which can be applied to the various civilizations judged. Any such comparison of moral standards implies the existence of some superior standard which is applicable to both. And the existence of any such standard is precisely what the relativist denies. According to him the Christian standard is applicable only to Christians, the Chinese standard only to Chinese, the New Guinea standard only to the inhabitants of New Guinea.

What is true of comparisons between the moral standards of different races will also be true of comparisons between those of different ages. It is not unusual to ask such questions as whether the standard of our own day is superior to that which existed among our ancestors five hundred years ago. And when we remember that our ancestors employed slaves, practiced barbaric physical tortures, and burnt people alive, we may be inclined to think that it is. At any rate we assume that the question is one which has meaning and is capable of rational discussion. But if the ethical relativist is right, whatever we assert on this subject must be totally meaningless. For here again there is no common standard which could form the basis of any such judgments.

There is indeed one way in which the ethical relativist can give some sort of meaning to judgments of higher or lower as applied to the moral ideas of different races or ages. What he will have to say is that we assume *our* standards to be the best simply because they are ours. And we judge other standards by our own. If we say that Chinese moral codes are better than those of African cannibals, what we *mean* by this is that they are better *according to our standards*. We mean, that is to say, that Chinese standards are *more like our own* than African standards are. "Better" accordingly *means* "more like us." "Worse" means "less like us." It thus becomes clear that judgments of better and worse in such cases do not express anything that is really true at all. They merely give expression to our perfectly groundless satisfaction with our own ideas. In short, they give expression to nothing but our egotism and self-conceit. Our moral ideas are not really better than those of the savage. We are simply deluded by our egotism into thinking they are. The African savage has just as good a right to think his morality the best as we have to think ours the best. His opinion is just as well grounded as ours, or rather both opinions are equally groundless. . . .

Thus the ethical relativist must treat all judgments comparing different moralities as either entirely meaningless; or, if this course appears too drastic, he has the alternative of declaring that they have for their meaning-content nothing except the vanity and egotism of those who pass them. . . .

I come now to a second point. Up to the present I have allowed it to be taken tacitly for granted that, though judgments comparing different races and ages in respect of the worth of their moral codes are impossible for the ethical relativist, yet judgments of comparison between individuals living within the same social group would be quite possible. For individuals living within the same social group would presumably be subject to the same moral code, that of their group, and this would therefore constitute, as between these individuals, a common standard by which they could both be measured. We have not here, as we had in the other case, the difficulty of the absence of any common standard of comparison. It should therefore be possible for the ethical relativist to say quite meaningfully that President Lincoln was a better man than some criminal or moral imbecile of his own time and country, or that Jesus was a better man than Judas Iscariot.

But is even this minimum of moral judgment really possible on relativist grounds? It seems to me that it is not. For when once the whole of humanity is abandoned as the area covered by a single moral standard, what smaller areas are to be adopted as the loci of different standards? Where are we to draw the lines of demarcation? We can split up humanity, perhaps— though the procedure will be very arbitrary—into races, races into nations, nations into tribes, tribes into families, families into individuals. Where are we going to draw the *moral* boundaries? Does the *locus* of a particular moral standard reside in a race, a nation, a tribe, a family, or an individual? Perhaps the blessed phrase "social group" will be dragged in to save the situation. Each such group, we shall be told, has its own moral code which is, for it, right. But what *is* a "group"? Can anyone define it or give its boundaries? . . .

. . . Does the American nation constitute a "group" having a single moral standard? Or does the standard of what I ought to do change continuously as I cross the continent in a railway train? Do different States of the Union have different moral codes? Perhaps every town and village has its own peculiar standard. This may at first sight seem reasonable enough. "In Rome do as Rome does" may seem as good a rule in morals as it is in etiquette. But can we stop there? Within the village are numerous cliques each having its own set of ideas. Why should not each of these claim to be bound only by its own special and peculiar standards? And if it comes to that, why should not the gangsters in Chicago claim to constitute a group having its own morality, so that its murders and debaucheries must be viewed as "right" by the only standard which can legitimately be applied to it? And if it be answered that the nation will not tolerate this, that may be so. But this is to put the foundation of right simply in the superior force of the majority. In that case whoever is stronger will be right, however monstrous his ideas and actions. And if we cannot deny to any set of people the right to have its own morality, is it not clear that, in the end, we cannot even deny this right to the individual? Every individual man and woman can put up, on this view, an irrefutable claim to be judged by no standard except his or her own.

If these arguments are valid, the ethical relativist cannot really maintain that there is anywhere to be found a moral standard binding upon anybody against his will. And he cannot maintain that, even within the social group, there is a common standard as between individuals. And if that is so, then even judgments to the effect that one man is morally better than another become meaningless. All moral valuation thus vanishes. There is nothing to prevent each man from being a rule unto himself. The result will be moral chaos and the collapse of all effective standards.

Perhaps, in regard to the difficulty of defining the social group, the relativist may make the following suggestion. If we admit, he may say, that it is impossible or very difficult to define a group territorially or nationally or geographically, it is still possible to define it logically. We will simply define an ethical group as any set of persons (whether they live together in one place or are scattered about in many places over the earth) who recognizes one and the same moral standard. As a matter of fact such groups will as a rule be found occupying each something like a single locality. The people in one country, or at least in one village, tend to think much alike. But theoretically at least the members of an ethical group so defined might be scattered all over the face of the globe. However that may be, it will now be possible to make meaningful statements to the effect that one individual is morally better or worse than another, so long as we keep within the ethical group so defined. For the individuals of the ethical group will have as their common standard the ethical belief or beliefs the acknowledgment of which constitutes the defining characteristic of the group. By this common standard they can be judged and compared with one another. Therefore it is not true that ethical relativity necessarily makes all such judgments of moral comparison between individuals meaningless.

I admit the logic of this. Theoretically judgments of comparison can be given meaning in this way. Nevertheless there are fatal objections to the suggestion. . . .

. . . Even if we assume that the difficulty about defining moral groups has been surmounted, a further difficulty presents itself. Suppose that we have now definitely decided what are the exact boundaries of the social group within which a moral standard is to be operative. And we will assume—as is invariably done by relativists themselves—that this group is to be some actually existing social community such as a tribe or nation. How are we to know, even then, what actually *is* the moral standard within that group? How is anyone to know? How is even a member of the group to know? For there are certain to be within the group—at least this will be true among advanced peoples—wide differences of opinion as to what is right, what wrong. Whose opinion, then, is to be taken as representing *the* moral standard of the group? Either we must take the opinion of the majority within the group, or the opinion of some minority. If we rely upon the ideas of the majority, the results will be disastrous. Wherever there is found among a people a small band of select spirits, or perhaps one man, working for the establishment of higher and nobler ideals than those commonly accepted by the group, we shall be compelled to hold that, for that people at that time, the majority are right, and that the reformers are wrong and are preaching what is immoral. . . .

The ethical relativists are great empiricists. *What* is the actual moral standard of any group can only be discovered, they tell us, by an examination on the ground of the moral opinions and customs of that group. But will they tell us how they propose to decide, when they get to the ground, which of the many moral opinions they are sure to find there is *the* right one in that group? To some extent they will be able to do this for the Melanesian Islanders—from whom apparently all lessons in the nature of morality are in future to be taken. But it is certain that they cannot do it for advanced peoples whose members have learnt to think for themselves and to entertain among themselves a wide variety of opinions. They cannot do it unless they accept the calamitous view that the ethical opinion of the majority is always right. We are left therefore once more with the conclusion that, even within a particular social group, anybody's moral opinion is as good as anybody else's, and that every man is entitled to be judged by his own standards.

Finally, not only is ethical relativity disastrous in its consequences for moral theory. It cannot be doubted that it must tend to be equally disastrous in its impact upon practical conduct. If men come really to believe that one moral standard is as good as another, they will conclude that their own moral standard has nothing special to recommend it. They might as well then slip down to some lower and easier standard. It is true that, for a time, it may be possible to hold one view in theory and to act practically upon another. But ideas, even philosophical ideas, are not so ineffectual that they can remain for ever idle in the upper chambers of the intellect. In the end they seep down to the level of practice. They get themselves acted on.

These, then, are the main arguments which the anti-relativist will urge against ethical relativity. And perhaps finally he will attempt a diagnosis of the social, intellectual, and psychological conditions of our time to which the emergence of ethical relativism is to be attributed.

Multinational Decision-Making: Reconciling International Norms

THOMAS DONALDSON

Jurisprudence theorists are often puzzled when, having thoroughly analyzed an issue within the boundaries of a legal system, they must confront it again outside those boundaries. For international issues, trusted axioms often fail as the secure grounds of legal tradition and national consensus erode. Much the same happens when one moves from viewing a problem of corporate ethics against a backdrop of national moral consensus to the morally inconsistent backdrop of international opinion. Is the worker who appeals to extra-national opinion while complaining about a corporate practice accepted within his or her country, the same as an ordinary whistle-blower? Is a factory worker in Mexico justified in complaining about being paid three dollars an hour for the same work a U.S. factory worker, employed by the same company, is paid eight dollars?[1] Is he justified when in Mexico the practice of paying workers three dollars an hour—and even much less—is widely accepted? Is an asbestos worker in India justified in drawing world attention to the lower standards of in-plant asbestos pollution maintained by an English multinational relative to standards in England, when the standards in question fall within Indian government guidelines and, indeed, are stricter than the standards maintained by other Indian asbestos manufacturers?

What distinguishes these issues from standard ones about corporate practices is that they involve reference to a conflict of norms, either moral or legal, between home and host country. This paper examines the subclass of conflicts in which host country norms appear substandard from the perspective of home country, and evaluates the claim often made by multinational executives that the prevalence of seemingly lower standards in a host country warrants the adoption by multinationals of the lower standards. It is concerned with cases of the following form: A multinational company (C) adopts a corporate practice (P) which is morally and/or legally permitted in C's host country (B), but not in C's home country (A). The paper argues that the presence of lower standards in B justifies C's adopting the lower standards only in certain, well-defined contexts. It proposes a conceptual test, or ethical algorithm, for multinationals to use in distinguishing justified from unjustified applications of standards. This algorithm ensures that multinational practice will remain faithful at least to the enlightened standards of home country morality.

Journal of Business Ethics 4 (1985): 357–66. © 1985 by Thomas Donaldson.

If *C* is a non-national, that is to say a multinational, corporation, then one may wonder why home country opinion should be a factor in *C*'s decision-making. One reason is that although global companies are multinational in doing business in more than one country, they are uninational in composition and character. They are chartered in a single country, typically have over ninety-five percent of their stock owned by citizens of their home country, and have managements dominated by citizens of their home country. Thus, in an important sense the term "multinational" is a misnomer. For our purposes it is crucial to acknowledge that the moral foundation of a multinational, i.e., the underlying assumptions of its managers infusing corporate policies with a basic sense of right and wrong, is inextricably linked to the laws and mores of the home country.

Modern textbooks dealing with international business consider cultural relativity to be a powerful factor in executive decision-making. Indeed, they often use it to justify practices abroad which, although enhancing corporate profits, would be questionable in the multinational's home country. One prominent text, for example, remarks that "in situations where patterns of dominance-subordination are socially determined, and not a function of demonstrated ability, management should be cautioned about promoting those of inferior social status to positions in which they are expected to supervise those of higher social status."[2] Later, referring to multiracial societies such as South Africa, the same text offers managers some practical advice: ". . . the problem of the multiracial society manifests itself particularly in reference to promotion and pay. An equal pay for equal work policy may not be acceptable to the politically dominant but racial minority group. . . ."[3]

Consider two actual instances of the problem at issue:

Charles Pettis. In 1966 Charles Pettis, employee of Brown and Root Overseas, Inc., an American multinational, became resident engineer for one of his company's projects in Peru: a 146 mile, $46 million project to build a highway across the Andes. Pettis soon discovered that Peruvian safety standards were far below those in the United States. The highway design called for cutting channels through mountains in areas where rock formations were unstable. Unless special precautions were taken, slides could occur. Pettis blew the whistle, complaining first to Peruvian government officials and later to U.S. officials. No special precautions were taken, with the result that thirty-one men were killed by slides during the construction of the road. Pettis was fired for his trouble by Brown and Root and had difficulty finding a job with another company.[4]

American bank in Italy. A new American bank in Italy was advised by its Italian attorneys to file a tax return that misstated income and expenses and consequently grossly underestimated actual taxes due. The bank learned, however, that most other Italian companies regarded the practice as standard operating procedure and merely the first move in a complex negotiating process with the Italian Internal Revenue Service. The bank initially refused to file a fallacious return on moral grounds and submitted an "American style" return instead. But because the resulting tax bill was many times higher than what comparable Italian companies were asked to pay, the bank changed policy in later years to agree with "Italian style."[5]

A. THE MORAL POINT OF VIEW

One may well decide that home country standards were mandatory in one of the above cases, but not in the other. One may decide that despite conforming to Peruvian standards, Peruvian safety precautions were unacceptable, while at the same time acknowledging that however inequitable and inefficient Italian tax mores may be, a decision to file "Italian style" is permissible.

Despite claims to the contrary, one must reject the simple dictum that whenever P violates a moral standard of country A, it is impermissible for C. Arnold Berleant has argued that the principle of equal treatment endorsed by most U.S. citizens requires that U.S. corporations pay workers in less developed countries exactly the same wages paid to U.S. workers in comparable jobs (after appropriate adjustments are made for cost of living levels in the relevant areas).[6] But most observers, including those from the less developed countries, believe this stretches the doctrine of equality too far in a way detrimental to host countries. By arbitrarily establishing U.S. wage levels as the benchmark for fairness one eliminates the role of the international market in establishing salary levels, and this in turn eliminates the incentive U.S. corporations have to hire foreign workers. If U.S. companies felt morally bound to pay Korean workers exactly the wages U.S. workers receive for comparable work, they would not locate in Korea. Perhaps U.S. firms should exceed market rate for foreign labor as a matter of moral principle, but to pay strictly equal rates would freeze less developed countries out of the international labor market.[7] Lacking, then, a simple formula of the sort, "P is wrong when P violates A's norms," one seems driven to undertake a more complex analysis of the types and degrees of responsibilities multinationals possess.

The first task is to distinguish between responsibilities that hold as minimum conditions, and ones that exceed the minimum. We are reminded of the distinction, eloquently articulated by Kant, between perfect and imperfect duties. Perfect duties are owed to a specific class of persons under specified conditions, such as the duty to honor promises. They differ from imperfect duties, such as the duty of charity, which although mandatory, allow considerable discretion as to when, how, and to whom they are fulfilled. The perfect-imperfect distinction, however, is not appropriate for corporations since it is doubtful whether economic entities such as corporations must assume the same imperfect burdens, e.g., of charity, as individual persons.

For purposes of discussing multinationals, then, it is best to recast the distinction into one between 'minimal' and 'enlightened' duties, where a minimal duty is one the persistent failure of which to observe would deprive the corporation of its moral right to exist, i.e., a strictly mandatory duty, and an enlightened duty is one whose fulfillment would be praiseworthy but not mandatory in any sense. In the present context, it is the determination of minimal duties that has priority since in attempting to answer whether P is permissible for C in B, the notion of permissibility must eventually be cashed in terms of minimal standards. Thus, P is not impermissible for C simply because C fails to achieve an ideal vision of corporate conduct; and C's failure to contribute generously to the United Nations is a permissible, if regrettable, act.

Because minimal duties are our target, it is appropriate next to invoke the language of rights, for rights are entitlements that impose minimum demands on the behavior of others.

B. THE APPEAL TO RIGHTS

Theorists commonly analyze the obligations of developed to less developed countries in terms of rights. James Sterba argues that "distant peoples" (e.g., persons in Third World countries) enjoy welfare rights that members of the developed countries are obliged to respect.[8] Welfare rights are defined as rights to whatever is necessary to satisfy "basic needs," and "basic needs," in turn, as needs "which must be satisfied in order not to seriously endanger a person's health and sanity."[9] It follows that multinationals are obliged to avoid workplace hazards that seriously endanger workers' health.

A similar notion is advanced by Henry Shue in his book *Basic Rights*. The substance of a basic right for Shue is "something the deprivation of which is one standard threat to rights generally."[10] He considers it a "minimal demand" that "no individuals or institutions, including corporations, may ignore the universal duty to avoid depriving persons of their basic rights."[11] Since one's physical security, including safety from exposure to harmful chemicals or pollution, is a condition for one's enjoyment of rights generally, it follows that the right to physical security is a basic right that imposes specific obligations on corporations.

Equally important for our purposes is Shue's application elsewhere of the "no harm" principle to the actions of U.S. multinationals abroad.[12] Associated with Mill and traditional liberalism, the "no harm" principle reflects a rights-based approach emphasizing the individual's right to liberty, allowing maximal liberty to each so long as each inflicts no avoidable harm on others. Shue criticizes as a violation of the no-harm principle a plan by a Colorado-based company to export millions of tons of hazardous chemical waste from the United States for processing and disposal in the West African nation of Sierra Leone.[13] Using the same principle, he is able to criticize any U.S. asbestos manufacturing corporation which, in order to escape expensive regulations at home, moves its plant to a foreign country with lower standards.[14]

Thus the Shue-Sterba rights-based approach recommends itself as a candidate for evaluating multinational conduct. It is irrelevant whether the standards of B comply or fail to comply with home country standards; what is relevant is whether they meet a universal, objective minimum. In the present context, the principal advantage of a rights-based approach is to establish a firm limit to appeals made in the name of host country laws and morals—at least when the issue is a clear threat to workers' safety. Clear threats such as in-plant asbestos pollution exceeding levels recommended by independent scientific bodies, are incompatible with employees' rights, especially their right not to be harmed. It is no excuse to cite lenient host country regulations or ill-informed host country public opinion.

But even as a rights-oriented approach clarifies a moral bottom line for extreme threats to workers' safety, it leaves obscure not only the issue of less extreme threats, but of harms other than physical injury. The language of rights and harm is sufficiently vague so as to leave shrouded in uncertainty a formidable list of issues crucial to multinationals.

When refined by the traditions of a national legal system, the language of rights achieves great precision. But left to wander among the concepts of general moral theory, the language proves less exact. Granted, the celebrated dangers of asbestos call for recognizing the right to workers' safety no matter how broadly the language of rights is framed. But what are we to say of a less toxic pollutant? Is the level of sulfur dioxide air pollution we should demand in a struggling nation, say, one with only a few fertilizer plants working overtime to help feed its malnourished population, the same we should demand in Portland, Oregon? Or taking a more obvious case, should the maximal level of thermal pollution generated by a poor nation's electric power plants be the same as West Germany's? Since thermal pollution raises the temperature of a given body of water, it lowers the capacity of the water to hold oxygen and in turn the number of "higher" fish species, e.g., salmon and trout. But whereas the trade-off between more trout and higher output is rationally made by the West German in favor of the trout, the situation is reversed for the citizen of Chad, Africa. This should not surprise us. It has long been recognized that many rights, e.g., the right to medical care, are dependent for their specification on the level of economic development of the country in question.[15]

Nor is it clear how a general appeal to rights will resolve issues that turn on the interpretation of broad social practices. For example, in the Italian tax case mentioned earlier, the propriety of submitting an "Italian" versus "American" style tax return hinges more on the appraisal of the value of honesty in a complex economic and social system, than on appeal to inalienable rights.

C. AN ETHICAL ALGORITHM

What is needed, then, is a test for evaluating P that is more comprehensive than a simple appeal to rights. In the end nothing short of a general moral theory working in tandem with an analysis of the foundations of corporate existence is needed. That is, ultimately there is no escape for the multinational executive from merging the ordinary canons of economic decision-making, of profit maximization and market share, with the principles of basic moral theory.[16] But this formidable task, essential as it is, does not preclude the possibility of discovering lower-order moral concepts to clarify the moral intuitions already in use by multinational decision-makers. Apart from the need for general theories of multinational conduct, there is need for pragmatic aids to multinational decision-making that bring into relief the ethical implications of views already held. This suggests, then, the possibility of generating an interpretive mechanism, or algorithm, that managers of multinationals could use in determining the implications of their own moral views about cases of the form, "Is P permissible for C when P is acceptable in B but not in A?"

The first step in generating such an ethical algorithm is to isolate distinct senses in which B's norms may conflict with the norms of A. Now, if P is morally and/or legally permitted in B, but not in A, then either:

1. The moral reasons underlying B's view that P is permissible refer to B's relative level of economic development; or
2. The moral reasons underlying B's view that P is permissible are independent of B's relative level of economic development.

Let us call the conflict of norms described in (1) a 'type #1' conflict. In such a conflict, an African country that permits slightly higher levels of thermal pollution from electric power generating plants, or a lower minimum wage, than those prescribed in European countries would do so not because higher standards would be undesirable *per se*, but because its level of economic development requires an ordering of priorities. In the future when it succeeds in matching European economic achievements, it may well implement the higher standards.

Let us call the conflict of norms described in (2) a 'type #2' conflict. In such cases levels of economic development play no role. For example, low level institutional nepotism, common in many underdeveloped countries, is justified not on economic grounds, but on the basis of clan and family loyalty. Presumably the same loyalties should be operative even after the country has risen to economic success—as the nepotism prevalent in Saudia Arabia would indicate. The Italian tax case also reflects an Italian cultural style with a penchant for personal negotiation and an unwillingness to formalize transactions, more than a strategy based on level of economic development.

When the conflict of norms occurs for reasons other than relative economic development (type #2), then the possibility is increased that there exists what Richard Brandt has called an "ultimate ethical disagreement." An ultimate disagreement occurs when two cultures are able to consider the same set of facts surrounding a moral issue while disagreeing on the moral issue itself. An ultimate disagreement is less likely in a type #1 case, since after suitable reflection about priorities imposed by differing economic circumstance, the members of A may come to agree that *given* the facts of B's level of economic development, P is permissible. On the other hand, a type #2 dispute about what Westerners call "nepotism" will continue even after economic variables are discounted.[17]

The status of the conflict of norms between A and B, i.e., whether it is of type #1 or #2, does not fix the truth value of B's claim that P is permissible. P may or may not be permissible whether the conflict is of type #1 or #2. This, however, is not to say that the truth value of B's claim is independent of the conflict's type status, for a different test will be required to determine whether P is permissible when the conflict is of type #1 rather than type #2. In a type #1 dispute, the following formula is appropriate:

> P is permissible if and only if the members of A would, under conditions of economic development relevantly similar to those of B, regard P as permissible.

Under this test, excessive levels of asbestos pollution would almost certainly not be tolerated by the members of A under relevantly similar economic conditions, whereas higher levels of thermal pollution would be. The test, happily, explains and confirms our initial moral intuitions.

Yet, when as in type #2 conflicts the dispute between A and B depends upon a fundamental difference of perspective, the step to equalize hypothetically the levels of economic development is useless. A different test is needed. In type #2 conflicts the opposing evils of ethnocentrism and ethical relativism must be avoided. A multinational must forgo the temptation to remake all societies in the image of its home society, while at the same time rejecting a relativism that conveniently forgets ethics when the payoff is sufficient. Thus, the task is to tolerate cultural diversity while drawing the line at moral recklessness.

Since in type #2 cases P is in conflict with an embedded norm of A, one should first ask whether P is necessary to do business in B, for if not, the solution clearly is to adopt some other practice that is permissible from the standpoint of A. If petty bribery of public officials is unnecessary for the business of the Cummins Engine Company in India, then the company is obliged to abandon such bribery. If, on the other hand, P proves necessary for business, one must next ask whether P constitutes a direct violation of a basic human right. Here the notion of a right, specifying a minimum below which corporate conduct should not fall, has special application. If Polaroid, an American company, confronts South African laws that mandate systematic discrimination against non-whites, then Polaroid must refuse to comply with the laws. Thus, in type #2 cases, P would be permissible if and only if the answer to both of the following questions is "no."

> a. Is it possible to conduct business successfully in B without undertaking P?
> b. Is P a clear violation of a basic human right?

What sorts of practice might pass both conditions a and b? Consider the practice of low-level bribery of public officials in some underdeveloped nations. In some South American countries, for example, it is impossible for any company, foreign or national, to move goods through customs without paying low-level officials a few dollars. Indeed, the salaries of such officials are sufficiently low that one suspects they are set with the prevalence of the practice in mind. The payments are relatively small, uniformly assessed, and accepted as standard practice by the surrounding culture. Here, the practice of petty bribery would pass the type #2 test and, barring other moral factors, would be permissible.

A further condition, however, should be placed on multinationals undertaking P in type #2 contexts. The companies should be willing to speak out against, and be willing to work for change of, P. Even if petty bribery or low-level nepotism passes the preceding tests, it may conflict with an embedded norm of country A, and as a representative of A's culture, the company is obliged to take a stand. This would be true even for issues related exclusively to financial practice, such as the Italian tax case. If the practice of underestimating taxes due is (1) accepted in B, (2) necessary for successful business, and (3) does not violate any basic human rights, then it satisfies the necessary conditions of permissibility. Yet insofar as it violates a norm accepted by A, C should make its disapproval of the practice known.

To sum up, then, two complementary tests have been proposed for determining the ultimate permissibility of P. If P occurs in a type #1 context, then P is not permissible if:

> The members of A would not, under conditions of economic development relevantly similar to those of B, regard P as permissible.

If *P* occurs in a type #2 context, then *P* is not permissible if either:

1. It is possible to conduct business successfully in *B* without undertaking *P*, or
2. *P* is a direct violation of a basic human right.

Notice that the type #1 criterion is not reducible to the type #2 criterion. In order for the two criteria to have equivalent outcomes, four propositions would need to be true: (1) If *P* passes #1, it passes #2; (2) if *P* fails #1, it fails #2; (3) if *P* passes #2, it passes #1; and (4) if *P* fails #2, it fails #1. But none of these propositions is true. The possibility matrix below lists in rows *A* and *B* the only combinations of outcomes that are possible on the assumption that the two criteria are equivalent. But they are not equivalent because the combinations of outcomes in *C* and *D* are also possible.

	Criterion #1	*Criterion #2*	
A	Fail	Fail	
			equivalent outcomes
B	Pass	Pass	

C	Fail	Pass	
			nonequivalent outcomes
D	Pass	Fail	

To illustrate, *P* may fail #1 and pass #2; for example, the practice of petty bribery may be necessary for business, may not violate basic human rights, but may nonetheless be unacceptable in *A* under hypothetically lowered levels of economic development; similarly, the practice of allowing a significant amount of sulfur-dioxide pollution (sufficient, say, to erode historical artifacts) may be necessary for business, may not violate basic rights, yet may be hypothetically unacceptable in *A*. Or, *P* may fail #2 and pass #1; for example, the practice of serving alcohol at executive dinners in a strongly Moslem country may not be necessary for business in *B*, and thus impermissible by criterion #2, while being thoroughly acceptable to the members of *A* under hypothetically lowered economic conditions.

It follows, then, that the two tests are not mutually reducible. This underscores the importance of the preliminary step of classifying a given case under either type #1 or type #2. The prior act of classification explains, moreover, why not all cases in row *C* or in row *D* will have the same moral outcome. Consider, for example, the two Fail-Pass cases from row *C* mentioned above, i.e., the cases of artifact-damaging, sulfur-dioxide pollution and petty bribery. The former might be classified properly (depending upon circumstances) as a type #1 practice, and hence would be impermissible, while the latter might be classified as a type #2 practice, and would be permissible.

D. SOME PRACTICAL CONSIDERATIONS AND OBJECTIONS

The algorithm does not obviate the need for multinational managers to appeal to moral concepts both more general and specific than the algorithm itself. It is not intended as a substitute for a general theory of morality or even an interpretation of the basic responsibilities of multinationals. Its power lies in its ability to tease out implications of the moral presuppositions of a manager's acceptance of "home" morality and in this sense to serve as a clarificatory device for multinational decision-making. But insofar as the context of a given conflict of norms categorizes it as a type #1 rather than type #2 conflict, the algorithm makes no appeal to a universal concept of morality (as the appeal to basic human rights does in type #2 cases) save for the purported universality of the ethics endorsed by culture A. This means that the force of the algorithm is relativized slightly in the direction of a single society. When A's morality is wrong or confused, the algorithm can reflect this ethnocentricity, leading either to a mild paternalism or to the imposition of parochial standards. For example, A's oversensitivity to aesthetic features of the environment may lead it to reject a given level of thermal pollution even under hypothetically lowered economic circumstances, thus yielding a paternalistic refusal to allow such levels in B, despite B's acceptance of the higher levels and B's belief that tolerating such levels is necessary for stimulating economic development. Or, A's mistaken belief that the practice of hiring twelve year olds for full-time, permanent work, although happily unnecessary at its relatively high level of economic development, would be acceptable and economically necessary at a level of economic development relevantly similar to B's, might lead it both to tolerate and undertake the practice in B. It would be a mistake, however, to exaggerate this weakness of the algorithm; coming up with cases in which the force of the algorithm would be relativized is extremely difficult. Indeed, I have been unable to discover a single non-hypothetical set of facts fitting such a description.

The algorithm is not intended as a substitute for more specific guides to conduct such as the numerous codes of ethics now appearing on the international scene. A need exists for topic-specific and industry-specific codes that embody detailed safeguards against self-serving interpretations. Consider the Sullivan Standards, designed by the black American minister Leon Sullivan, drafted for the purpose of ensuring non-racist practices by

U.S. multinationals operating in South Africa. As a result of a lengthy lobbying campaign by U.S. activists, the Sullivan principles are now endorsed and followed by almost one third of all American multinationals with South African subsidiaries. Among other things, companies complying with the Sullivan principles must:

> Remove all race designation signs.
>
> Support the elimination of discrimination against the rights of Blacks to form or belong to government registered unions.
>
> Determine whether upgrading of personnel and/or jobs in the lower echelons is needed (and take appropriate steps).[18]

A variety of similar codes are either operative or in the process of development, e.g., the European Economic Community's Vredeling Proposal on labor-management consultations; the United Nation's Code of Conduct for Transnational Corporations and its International Standards of Accounting and Reporting; the World Health Organizations' Code on Pharmaceuticals and Tobacco; the World Intellectual Property Organization's Revision of the Paris Convention for the Protection of Industrial Patents and Trademarks; the International Chamber of Commerce's Rules of Conduct to Combat Extortion and Bribery; and the World Health Organization's Infant Formula code against advertising of breast-milk substitutes.[19]

Despite these limitations, the algorithm has important application in countering the well-documented tendency of multinationals to mask immoral practices in the rhetoric of "tolerance" and "cultural relativity." Utilizing it, no multinational manager can naively suggest that asbestos standards in Chile are permissible because they are accepted there. Nor can he infer that the standards are acceptable on the grounds that the Chilean economy is, relative to his home country, underdeveloped. A surprising amount of moral blindness occurs not because people's fundamental moral views are confused, but because their cognitive application of those views to novel situations is misguided.

What guarantees that either multinationals or prospective whistle-blowers possesses the knowledge or objectivity to apply the algorithm fairly? As Richard Barnet quips, "On the 56th floor of a Manhatten skyscraper, the level of self-protective ignorance about what the company may be doing in Colombia or Mexico is high."[20] Can Exxon or Johns-Manville be trusted to have a sufficiently sophisticated sense of "human rights," or to weigh dispassionately the hypothetical attitudes of their fellow countrymen under conditions of "relevantly similar economic development"? My answer to this is "probably not," at least given the present character of the decision-making procedures in most global corporations. I would add, however, that this problem is a contingent and practical one. It is no more a theoretical flaw of the proposed algorithm that it may be conveniently misunderstood by a given multinational, than it is of Rawl's theory that it may be conveniently misunderstood by a trickle-down capitalist.

What would need to change in order for multinationals to make use of the algorithm? At a minimum they would need to enhance the sophistication of their decision-making mechanisms. They would need to alter established patterns of information flow and collection in order to accommodate moral information. The already complex parameters of corporate decision-making would become more so. They would need to introduce alongside analyses of the bottom line analyses of historical tendencies, nutrition, rights, and demography. And they would need to introduce a new class of employee to provide expertise in these areas. However unlikely such changes are, I believe they are within the realm of possibility. Multinationals, the organizations capable of colonizing our international future, are also capable of looking beyond their national borders and applying—at a minimum—the same moral principles they accept at home.

NOTES

1. An example of disparity in wages between Mexican and U.S. workers is documented in the case study "Twin-Plants and Corporate Responsibilities," by John H. Haddox, in *Profits and Responsibility*, ed. Patricia Werhane and Kendall D'Andrade (New York: Random House, 1985).
2. Richard D. Robinson, *International Business Management: A Guide to Decision Making*, Second Edition (Hinsdale, Ill.: The Dryden Press, 1978), p. 241.
3. Robinson, *International Business Management*, p. 241.
4. Charles Peters and Taylor Branch, *Blowing the Whistle: Dissent in the Public Interest* (New York: Praeger Publishers, 1972), pp. 182–85.
5. Arthur Kelly, "Italian Tax Mores," in *Case Studies in Business Ethics*, ed. T. Donaldson (Englewood Cliffs, N.J.: Prentice-Hall, Inc., 1984). The same case appears in this book, on p. 60.
6. Arnold Berleant, "Multinationals and the Problem of Ethical Consistency," *Journal of Business Ethics* 3 (August 1982), 185–95.
7. One can construct an argument attempting to show that insulating the economies of the less developed countries would be advantageous to the less developed countries in the long run. But whether correct or not, such an argument is independent of the present issue, for it is independent of the claim that if *P* violates the norms of *A*, then *P* is impermissible.
8. James Sterba, "The Welfare Rights of Distant Peoples and Future Generations: Moral Side Constraints on Social Policy," in *Social Theory and Practice* 7 (Spring 1981), p. 110.
9. Sterba, "Distant Peoples," p. 111.
10. Henry Shue, *Basic Rights, Subsistence, Affluence, and U.S. Foreign Policy* (Princeton, N.J.: Princeton University Press, 1981), p. 34.
11. Shue, *Basic Rights*, p. 170.
12. Henry Shue, "Exporting Hazards," *Ethics* 91 (July 1981), 579–606.
13. Shue, "Hazards," pp. 579–80.
14. Considering a possible escape from the principle, Shue considers whether inflicting harm is acceptable in the event overall benefits outweigh the costs.

Hence, increased safety risks under reduced asbestos standards might be acceptable insofar as the economic benefits to the country outweighed the costs. The problem, as Shue correctly notes, is that this approach fails to distinguish between the no-harm principle and a naive greatest happiness principle. Even classical defenders of the no-harm principle were unwilling to accept a simple-minded utilitarianism that sacrificed individual justice on the alter of maximal happiness. Even classical utilitarians did not construe their greatest happiness principle to be a "hunting license." (Shue, "Hazards," pp. 592–93.)

Still another escape might be by way of appealing to the rigors of international economic competition. That is, is it not unreasonable to expect firms to place themselves at a competitive disadvantage by installing expensive safety equipment in a market where other firms are brutally cost conscious? Such policies, argue critics, could trigger economic suicide. The obligation not to harm, in turn, properly belongs to the government of the host country. Here, too, Shue's rejoinder is on-target. He notes first that the existence of an obligation by one party does not cancel its burden on another party; hence, even if the host country's government does have an obligation to protect their citizens from dangerous workplace conditions, its duty does not cancel that of the corporation. (Shue, "Hazards," p. 600.) Second, governments of poor countries are themselves forced to compete for scarce foreign capital by weakening their laws and regulations, with the result that any "competitive disadvantage" excuse offered on behalf of the corporation would also apply to the government. (Shue, "Hazards," p. 601.)

15. Sterba himself reflects this consensus when he remarks that for rights ". . . an acceptable minimum should vary over time and between societies at least to some degree." (Sterba, "Distant Peoples," p. 112.)

16. For the purpose of analyzing the moral foundations of corporate behavior, I prefer a social contract theory, one that interprets a hypothetical contract between society and productive organizations, and which I have argued for in my book *Corporations and Morality*. Thomas Donaldson, *Corporations and Morality* (Englewood Cliffs, N.J.: Prentice-Hall, Inc., 1982); see especially Chapter 3. There I argue that corporations are artifacts; that they are in part the products of our moral and legal imagination. As such, they are to be molded in the image of our collective rights and societal ambitions. Corporations, as all productive organizations, require from society both recognition as single agents, and the authority to own or use land and natural resources, and to hire employees. In return for this, society may expect that productive organizations will, all other things being equal, enhance the general interests of consumers and employees. Society may reasonably expect that in doing so corporations honor existing rights and limit their activities to accord with the bounds of justice. This is as true for multinationals as it is for national corporations.

17. Richard Brandt, "Cultural Relativism," in *Ethical Issues in Business*, Second Edition, ed. T. Donaldson and P. Werhane (Englewood Cliffs, N.J.: Prentice-Hall, Inc., 1983).

18. See "Dresser Industries and South Africa," by Patricia Mintz and Kirk O. Hanson, in *Case Studies in Business Ethics*, ed. Thomas Donaldson (Englewood Cliffs, N.J.: Prentice-Hall, Inc., 1984).

19. For a concise and comprehensive account of the various codes of conduct for international business under consideration, see "Codes of Conduct: Worry over New Restraints on Multinationals," *Chemical Week* (July 15, 1981), pp. 48–52.

20. Richard J. Barnet and Ronald Muller, *Global Reach: The Power of Multinational Corporations* (New York: Simon and Schuster, 1974), p. 185.

Ethics and the Foreign Corrupt Practices Act

MARK PASTIN AND MICHAEL HOOKER

Not long ago it was feared that as a fallout of Watergate, government officials would be hamstrung by artificially inflated moral standards. Recent events, however, suggest that the scapegoat of post-Watergate morality may have become American business rather than government officials.

One aspect of the recent attention paid to corporate morality is the controversy surrounding payments made by American corporations to foreign officials for the purpose of securing business abroad. Like any law or system of laws, the Foreign Corrupt Practices Act (FCPA), designed to control or eliminate such payments, should be grounded in morality, and should therefore be judged from an ethical perspective. Unfortunately, neither the law nor the question of its repeal has been adequately addressed from that perspective.

On December 20, 1977, President Carter signed into law S.305, the Foreign Corrupt Practices Act (FCPA), which makes it a crime for American corporations to offer or provide payments to officials of foreign governments for the purpose of obtaining or retaining business. The FCPA also establishes record keeping requirements for publicly held corporations to make it difficult to conceal political payments proscribed by the Act. Violators of the FCPA, both corporations and managers, face severe penalties. A company may be fined up to $1 million, while its officers who directly participated in violations of the Act or had reason to know of such violations face up to five years in prison and/or $10,000 in fines. The Act also prohibits corporations from indemnifying fines imposed on their directors, officers, employees, or agents. The Act does not prohibit "grease" payments to foreign government employees whose duties are primarily ministerial or clerical, since such payments are sometimes required to persuade the recipients to perform their normal duties.

At the time of this writing, the precise consequences of the FCPA for American business are unclear, mainly because of confusion surrounding the government's enforcement intentions. Vigorous objections have been raised against the Act by corporate attorneys and recently by a few government officials. Among the latter is Frank A. Weil, former Assistant Secretary of Commerce, who has stated, "The questionable payments problem may

Mark Pastin and Michael Hooker, "Ethics and the Foreign Corrupt Practices Act," *Business Horizons*, December 1980, pp. 43–47. Copyright, 1980 by the Foundation for the School of Business at Indiana University. Reprinted by permission.

turn out to be one of the most serious impediments to doing business in the rest of the world."[1]

The potentially severe economic impact of the FCPA was highlighted by the fall 1978 report of the Export Disincentives Task Force, which was created by the White House to recommend ways of improving our balance of trade. The Task Force identified the FCPA as contributing significantly to economic and political losses in the United States. Economic losses come from constricting the ability of American corporations to do business abroad, and political losses come from the creation of a holier-than-thou image.

The Task Force made three recommendations in regard to the FCPA:

- The Justice Department should issue guidelines on its enforcement policies and establish procedures by which corporations could get advance government reaction to anticipated payments to foreign officials.
- The FCPA should be amended to remove enforcement from the SEC, which now shares enforcement responsibility with the Department of Justice.
- The administration should periodically report to Congress and the public on export losses caused by the FCPA.

In response to the Task Force's report, the Justice Department, over SEC objections, drew up guidelines to enable corporations to check any proposed action possibly in violation of the FCPA. In response to such an inquiry, the Justice Department would inform the corporation of its enforcement intentions. The purpose of such an arrangement is in part to circumvent the intent of the law. As of this writing, the SEC appears to have been successful in blocking publication of the guidelines, although Justice recently reaffirmed its intention to publish guidelines. Being more responsive to political winds, Justice may be less inclined than the SEC to rigidly enforce the Act.

Particular concern has been expressed about the way in which bookkeeping requirements of the Act will be enforced by the SEC. The act requires that company records will "acurately and fairly reflect the transactions and dispositions of the assets of the issuer." What is at question is the interpretation of the SEC will give to the requirement and the degree of accuracy and detail it will demand. The SEC's post-Watergate behavior suggests that it will be rigid in requiring the disclosure of all information that bears on financial relationships between the company and any foreign or domestic public official. This level of accountability in record keeping, to which auditors and corporate attorneys have strongly objected, goes far beyond previous SEC requirements that records display only facts material to the financial position of the company.

Since the potential consequences of the FCPA for American businesses and business managers are very serious, it is important that the Act have a rationale capable of bearing close scrutiny. In looking at the foundation of the FCPA, it should be noted that its passage followed in the wake of intense newspaper coverage of the financial dealings of corporations. Such media attention was engendered by the dramatic disclosure of corporate slush funds during the Watergate hearings and by a voluntary disclosure program established shortly thereafter by the SEC. As a result of the SEC program, more than 400 corporations, including 117 of the Fortune 500, admitted to making more than $300 million in foreign political payments in less than ten years.

Throughout the period of media coverage leading up to passage of the FCPA, and especially during the hearings on the Act, there was in all public discussions of the issue a tone of righteous moral indignation at the idea of American companies making foreign political payments. Such payments were ubiquitously termed "bribes," although many of these could more accurately be called extortions, while others were more akin to brokers' fees or sales commissions.

American business can be faulted for its reluctance during this period to bring to public attention the fact that in a very large number of countries, payments to foreign officials are virtually required for doing business. Part of that reluctance, no doubt, comes from the awkwardly difficult position of attempting to excuse bribery or something closely resembling it. There is a popular abhorrence in this country of bribery directed at domestic government officials, and that abhorrence transfers itself to payments directed toward foreign officials as well.

Since its passage, the FCPA has been subjected to considerable critical analysis, and many practical arguments have been advanced in favor of its repeal.[2] However, there is always lurking in back of such analyses the uneasy feeling that no matter how strongly considerations of practicality and economics may count against this law, the fact remains that the law protects morality in forbidding bribery. For example, Gerald McLaughlin, professor of law at Fordham, has shown persuasively that where the legal system of a foreign country affords inadequate protection against the arbitrary exercise of power to the disadvantage of American corporations, payments to foreign officials may be required to provide a compensating mechanism against the use of such arbitrary power. McLaughlin observes, however, that "this does not mean that taking advantage of the compensating mechanism would necessarily make the payment moral."[3]

The FCPA, and questions regarding its enforcement or repeal, will not be addressed adequately until an effort has been made to come to terms with the Act's foundation on morality. While it may be very difficult, or even impossible, to legislate morality (that is, to change the moral character and sentiments of people by passing laws that regulate their behavior), the existing laws undoubtedly still reflect the moral beliefs we hold. Passage of the FCPA in Congress was eased by the simple connection most Congressmen made between bribery, seen as morally repugnant, and the Act, which is designed to prevent bribery.

Given the importance of the FCPA to American business and labor, it is imperative that attention be given to the question of whether there is adequate moral justification for the law. The question we will address is not whether each payment prohibited by the FCPA is moral or immoral, but rather whether the FCPA, given all its consequences and ramifications, is itself moral. It is well known that morally sound laws and institutions may tolerate some immoral acts. The First Amendment's guarantee of freedom of speech allows individuals to utter racial slurs. And immoral laws and institutions may have some beneficial consequences, for example, segregationist legislation bringing deep-seated racism into the national limelight. But our concern is with the overall morality of the FCPA.

The ethical tradition has two distinct ways of assessing social institutions, including laws: *End-Point Assessment* and *Rule Assessment*. Since there is no consensus as to which approach is correct, we will apply both types of assessment to the FCPA.

The End-Point approach assesses a law in terms of its contribution to general social well-being. The ethical theory underlying End-Point Assessment is utilitarianism. According to utilitarianism, a law is morally sound if and only if the law promotes the well-being of those affected by the law to the greatest extent practically achievable. To satisfy the utilitarian principle, a law must promote the well-being of those affected by it at least as well as any alternative law that we might propose, and better than no law at all. A conclusive End-Point Assessment of a law requires specification of what constitutes the welfare of those affected by the law, which the liberal tradition generally sidesteps by identifying an individual's welfare with what he takes to be in his interests.

Considerations raised earlier in the paper suggest that the FCPA does not pass the End-Point test. The argument is not the too facile one that we could propose a better law. (Amendments to the FCPA are now being considered.[4]) The argument is that it may be better to have *no* such law than to have the FCPA. The main domestic consequences of the FCPA seem to include an adverse effect on the balance of payments, a loss of business and jobs, and another opportunity for the SEC and the Justice Department to compete. These negative effects must be weighed against possible gains in the conduct of American business within the United States. From the perspective of foreign countries in which American firms do business, the main consequence of the FCPA seems to be that certain officials now accept bribes and influence from non-American businesses. It is hard to see that who pays the bribes makes much difference to these nations.

Rule Assessment of the morality of laws is often favored by those who find that End-Point Assessment is too lax in supporting their moral codes. According to the Rule Assessment approach: A law is morally sound if and only if the law accords with a code embodying correct ethical rules. This approach has no content until the rules are stated, and different rules will lead to different ethical assessments. Fortunately, what we have to say about Rule Assessment of the FCPA does not depend on the details of a particular ethical code.

Those who regard the FCPA as a worthwhile expression of morality, despite the adverse effects on American business and labor, clearly subscribe to a rule stating that it is unethical to bribe. Even if it is conceded that the payments proscribed by the FCPA warrant classifications as bribes, citing a rule prohibiting bribery does not suffice to justify the FCPA.

Most of the rules in an ethical code are not *categorical* rules; they are *prima facie* rules. A categorical rule does not allow exceptions, whereas a prima facie rule does. The ethical rule that a person ought to keep promises is an example of a prima facie rule. If I promise to loan you a book on nuclear energy and later find out that you are a terrorist building a private atomic bomb, I am ethically obligated not to keep my promise. The rule that one ought to keep promises is "overridden" by the rule that one ought to prevent harm to others.

A rule prohibiting bribery is a prima facie rule. There are cases in which morality requires that a bribe be paid. If the only way to get essential medical care for a dying child is to bribe a doctor, morality requires one to bribe the doctor. So adopting an ethical code which includes a rule prohibiting the payment of bribes does not guarantee that a Rule Assessment of the FCPA will be favorable to it.

The fact that the FCPA imposes a cost on American business and labor weighs against the prima facie obligation not to bribe. If we suppose that American corporations have obligations, tantamount to promises, to promote the job security of their employees and the investments of shareholders, these obligations will also weigh against the obligation not to bribe. Again, if government legislative and enforcement bodies have an obligation to secure the welfare of American business and workers, the FCPA may force them to violate their public obligations.

The FCPA's moral status appears even more dubious if we note that many of the payments prohibited by the Act are neither bribes nor share features that make bribes morally reprehensible. Bribes are generally held to be malefic if they persuade one to act against his good judgment, and consequently purchase an inferior product. But the payments at issue in the FCPA are usually extorted *from the seller*. Further it is arguable that not paying the bribe is more likely to lead to purchase of an inferior product than paying the bribe. Finally, bribes paid to foreign officials may not involve deception when they accord with recognized local practices.

In conclusion, neither End-Point nor Rule Assessment uncovers a sound moral basis for the FCPA. It is shocking to find that a law prohibiting bribery has no clear moral basis, and may even be an immoral law. However, this is precisely what examination of the FCPA from a moral perspective reveals. This is symptomatic of the fact that moral conceptions which were appropriate to a simpler world are not adequate to the complex world in which contemporary business functions. Failure to appreciate this point often leads to righteous condemnation of business, when it should lead to careful reflection on one's own moral preconceptions.

ADDENDUM TO "ETHICS AND THE FOREIGN CORRUPT PRACTICES ACT," AUGUST 1981

There has been an increasing outcry against the FCPA since this article originally appeared. The Reagan administration has called for weakening of the law, especially the burdensome accounting provisions. While we view such weakening of the law as commendable, on the ground that it decreases the cost of the law to business and the American public, the key issue has not been joined. That issue is whether the payments proscribed by the law, heavy-handedly or otherwise, are in fact unethical. There is no doubt that many executives and government officials hold the view that these payments are not unethical. But it is unacceptable to publicly argue that bribes to foreign officials are ethical. Thus it will take considerable audacity to argue for total repeal of the FCPA. Only an increasing appreciation of the barriers to international trade attributable to the law, and of the ethical pointlessness of the law, can be effective.

MARK PASTIN

NOTES

1. *National Journal*, June 3, 1978: 880.
2. David C. Gustman, "The Foreign Corrupt Practices Act of 1977," *The Journal of International Law and Economics*, Vol. 13, 1979: 367–401; and Walter S. Surrey, "The Foreign Corrupt Practices Act: Let the Punishment Fit the Crime," *Harvard International Law Journal*, Spring 1979: 203–303.
3. Gerald T. McLaughlin, "The Criminalization of Questionable Foreign Payments by Corporations," *Fordham Law Review*, Vol. 46: 1095.
4. "Foreign Bribery Law Amendments Drafted," *American Bar Association Journal*, February 1980: 135.

Moral Dimensions of the Foreign Corrupt Practices Act: Comments on Pastin and Hooker

KENNETH D. ALPERN

Michael Hooker and Mark Pastin[1] claim that the Foreign Corrupt Practices Act (FCPA) is not supported by either utilitarian or deontological ("rule-based") moral considerations. I will argue that deontological moral considerations do in fact support the FCPA and that much utilitarian criticism of it is not conceptually well-founded.[2]

Hooker and Pastin offer two argument sketches intended to show that the Act does not receive support from deontological considerations. Spelling out the first gives roughly this:

1. The FCPA is essentially a prohibition of bribery. (Allowed for the sake of argument.)
2. Bribery is morally wrong in the sense that there is a *prima facie* moral obligation not to engage in bribery.
3. Corporations have (*prima facie*) moral obligations to protect the investments of their shareholders and the jobs of their employees. The federal government may also have a *prima facie* moral obligation to secure the welfare of American business and workers.
4. There are situations governed by the FCPA in which the *prima facie* moral obligations of corporations and government override the *prima facie* moral obligation not to bribe.[3]
5. Situations in which the FCPA requires actions that are thus contrary to morality are numerous or of great moral moment.
6. Therefore, the FCPA does not have the support of morality from a deontological perspective.

There is much to agree with in this argument. Its pattern of reasoning is good—the premises do license the conclusion. It is certainly the case that any moral rule prohibiting bribery cannot be absolute. And it is surely true that corporations have some sort of obligation to pursue profit. It could even be allowed that situations are conceivable in which the prohibition of bribery is overridden by other moral obligations of corporations. Nonetheless, the conclusion of the argument is still false.

Much of the argument's appeal derives from its apparent discovery of a second moral principle, the principle that promises should be kept. In situa-

---

Kenneth D. Alpern, "Moral Dimensions of the Foreign Corrupt Practices Act: Comments on Hooker and Pastin." Reprinted with permission of the author.

tions covered by the FCPA, the principle of promise-keeping is supposed to weigh against and outweigh the moral principle prohibiting bribery, though Hooker and Pastin do not go far enough into the argument to indicate which sorts of considerations are supposed to tip the scales in favor of promise-keeping.

Against this position I will argue that the supposed conflict is only apparent and that the introduction of the rule of promise-keeping at this place in the argument is misleading and largely irrelevant. Furthermore, I will argue that the moral considerations which do properly stand in the place thought to be held by the obligation to keep promises are insufficient on conceptual grounds to justify bribery. In order to make my case, it is necessary to look more closely at the way obligations to keep promises enter the picture.

Hooker and Pastin mention three specific obligations deriving from the principle of promise-keeping: (1) an obligation of corporations to promote the investments of their shareholders; (2) an obligation of corporations to protect the security of their employees' jobs; and (3) an obligation which the federal government may possibly be under to protect the welfare of American business and workers. I will focus on the first obligation, which I take to be most important, and comment only briefly on the other two obligations.

The obligation of corporations to their investors seems to come about in this way: corporations are *agents* for their investors. In effect a corporation says: "If you allow us the use of your capital, we promise to return to work to increase the value of your investment."[4] Having made the promise to act as agents, corporations are morally obligated, by virtue of the moral rule that promises be kept, to promote the financial interests of their principals.

What difference does this promise make to the morality of international corporate bribery? The answer is: none. The promise merely *transfers* the responsibility for looking after the investors' interests. It does nothing to affect the type or weight of claim that can be made in behalf of those interests against other moral considerations. In the situations with which we are concerned, who the guardian is and how that guardianship comes about makes no difference outside the relationship between the agent and the principal. If this were not the case, then one could indefinitely increase the moral righteousness of one's causes merely by enlisting a series of agents each promising the other to pursue one's ends.[5]

Talk of the solemn promises or sacred trusts of corporations, while it may refer to actual obligations, is irrelevant to the issue of the weight of investor interests against moral rules. There is no conflict here between a moral principle requiring that promises be kept and a moral principle prohibiting bribery. What stands in opposition to the moral rule prohibiting bribery is not a moral principle at all, but is, at best, merely the *self-interest* of the investors.

Now it must be recognized that unadorned self-interest may carry moral weight. However, it is quite unlikely that this weight will often be great enough to render international corporate bribery moral. For, first of all, within the deontological perspective (which we are being asked to take), moral rules are just the sort of things that override claims of self-interest. As long as we view morality from this perspective, there is strong *a priori* reason to hold that the rule prohibiting bribery controls. Second, though the rule prohibiting bribery may have exceptions — e.g., Hooker and Pastin's case of bribing a doctor as the only means by which to secure essential medical treatment for a dying child — the relevant exceptions appear to exhibit two characteristic features: (1) the personal interest at issue is not a mere desire, but a dire need, and (2) the rule is broken on a special occasion, not as a continuing general policy.[6] In contrast, when we are asked to reject the FCPA, we are asked to endorse a *policy* of bribery, and this for the promotion of interests that are not literally matters of life and death. Finally, to the objection that the moral claim of corporate investors' interests is considerable and thus outweighs the bribery rule, it should be pointed out that not all interests are of equal moral weight. Classical utilitarianism is mistaken in holding that equal additions to the sum total happiness or well-being are morally indifferent. For example, an increase in happiness which satisfies a need is of greater moral moment than the same increment added to the total happiness by way of providing someone with adventitious pleasure. It is morally better to raise a person from poverty to security than to add an equal amount to the total happiness in effecting a person's rise from ease to opulence. So, when it comes to comparing personal interests against moral rules, interests based on mere desires, and not needs, have comparatively little moral weight. This point applies to the FCPA in two ways. First, although American investors include pension plans, philanthropic organizations, and people of modest income, "the average American investor" is nonetheless quite comfortable by world standards and return on investment is not a matter of survival. Secondly, even if return on investment were a matter of survival, corporations can and in fact do derive substantial profits from activities not calling for bribery; most American corporations have dealt successfully in international trade without resorting to payments made unlawful by the FCPA.

One misunderstanding of the preceding argument must be forestalled. At issue is not the comparative need of American investors and the need of citizens of the country in which the bribery takes place. Rather, the point is that because American investors are, on the whole, not in dire need, the moral weight of their financial interests is small compared to the moral weight of moral *principles*.

It remains to say something, necessarily very brief, about the obligation of corporations to their employees and the obligation of the federal government to American business and workers. First, corporations are not morally obligated to secure profits "by whatever means it takes" in order to fulfill their responsibilities to their employees. There are restrictions, such as those imposed by law. If a corporation fails to meet its obligations due to the costs and effects of adhering to the law, then, other things being equal, the employees can have no *moral* complaint against the corporation.

In addition to restrictions imposed on profit-seeking activities through the law, I submit that there are also moral restrictions. For example, corporations are not morally culpable for reduced profits incurred by a failure to be ruthless, even when ruthlessness is within the limits set by the law. Employees (and other interested parties) cannot complain on *moral* grounds that they have suffered because the corporation failed to cheat, lie, deceive, bribe, or pay extortion.

The situation with respect to the moral obligations of the federal government is similar to that of corporations. Roughly, a government can have no *moral* (contrasted with legal or political) obligation to promote the welfare of its citizens by means which are themselves immoral. Bribery, we have been allowing, is immoral. So the government cannot be morally obligated to promote the welfare of American businesses or workers by allowing bribery.

In their second argument against the FCPA, Hooker and Pastin marshal three distinct considerations behind the idea that "many of the payments prohibited by the Act are neither bribes nor share features that make bribes morally reprehensible": (1) payments often are not bribes, but rather are *extorted* from corporations;[7] (2) failure to make payments may lead to the purchase of what are in fact *inferior* products; and (3) such payments may be in accordance with local practices and so lack the deceptiveness of bribery.

Against these considerations it may be pointed out that a payment needn't be bribery to be morally objectionable. Caving in to extortion demands contributes to corruption and fosters its expansion in the country in which payments are made; it leads to unfair competition if the payments are concealed, and even more immediately to the disintegration of free bargaining and a return to a Hobbesian state of nature—in which anything goes— if they are not. These morally objectionable results will generally outweigh harm resulting from the purchase of inferior products. Engaging in such practices *openly* hardly does much to excuse them.

Some business people may feel that international corporate competition *is* in fact a Hobbesian state of nature. However, this is surely hyperbole: murder is still fairly rare in negotiating contracts; not everyone in the business community behaves like the Mafia. But even if they did, that would not make it *moral* to do so. It is also worth pointing out that the state of nature is not a condition that we *want* to be in—few of us *want* to deal with a government like Amin's Uganda or live in a world in which that was the norm.

Hooker and Pastin's third point, that it would be wrong for us to try to impose our standards in countries in which bribery and extortion are commonly practiced, raises important conceptual issues about intercultural social, legal, and moral standards which are too complex to be treated adequately here. However, I can offer a few comments which I think considerably reduce the problems about how one ought to act. First, it is absolutely essential to distinguish between practices that are engaged in, recognized, even tolerated, and those that are condoned and held to be moral. To say simply that in many countries bribery is the norm disguises the fact that what is regularly done may not be what is held to be proper or moral even in the countries where that is the practice. A rough indicator of international moral judgment is the illegality of bribery in every part of the world.[8] Second, requiring American corporations to adhere to "our" moral standards with respect to bribery and extortion is hardly to *impose* our standards on the rest of the world: for a Muslim to refrain from eating pork in England is not for him to impose Muslim standards on the British. Finally, there is some reason for us to refrain from a practice that *we* judge to be wrong and harmful to others even if we do not receive agreement: that settlers in the upper Amazon hunt native Indians for sport does not give us good reason to conform to that practice when in their company. Obviously, more needs to be said on these issues, but I hope that it has been made clear that a passing reference to moral relativism establishes nothing and that there are a number of lines of defense which can be taken against more serious relativistic criticism.

In closing, I want to add a few short remarks. First, in asserting that the FCPA is supported by moral considerations, I am not claiming that the Act defines the morally best behavior in every single case. All laws can be improved; an imperfect law can still be moral and just. Second, it should be noted that if Hooker and Pastin were correct, their arguments would go a long way toward justifying bribery and extortion *within* the United States by both foreign and domestic companies—unless we are to believe that a return to the state of nature is morally acceptable in one place (someone else's country) but not in another. Finally, I think that I have shown that the FCPA is supported by considerations of morality. This should count heavily in favor of retaining the law. However, I do not claim to have necessarily provided *motivation* for supporting this law or adhering to its stipulations. Morality may require sacrifice, in this case at least sacrifice of financial gain. For those who care more for financial gain and for the ruthlessness through which it can be obtained than for the moral values of justice and integrity, I cannot claim to have provided motivation.

NOTES

1. See this volume, pages 48–53.
2. The arguments sketched in this paper are more fully defended in my forthcoming "International Corporate Bribery." The present paper is a considerably shortened

version of a paper read at the Conference on Business and Professional Ethics, in Chicago, May 1981.
3. That is, in some cases, considered individually and other things being equal, corporations *morally ought to bribe* and the government *morally ought not to punish* corporations for bribing. Thus, as the law now stands, some actions are legally required that are contrary to morality.
4. This promise must be understood as a promise to endeavor to a reasonable extent to increase investment value, not to maximize it at all costs.
5. The general moral principle here is, very roughly, that a promise to pursue the interests of another cannot increase the moral weight of those interests against moral considerations external to the relationship of promiser and promisee.
6. For continuing treatment of the child or in situations in which there is continuing and widespread corruption among doctors, it would be necessary to endorse bribery as a policy. However, then one's obligation would not be merely to engage in bribery, but rather to engage in bribery while doing what one can to rectify the situation. Regardless of the precise way this is to be worked out, a simple endorsement of bribery is not what is justified in such cases.
7. In practice it may be difficult to distinguish between bribery and extortion on the one hand, and goodwill gestures (e.g., gifts) and facilitating payments (so-called "grease") on the other. However, the conceptual issue of the wrongness of extortion does not turn on how the practical problem is solved.
8. Judson J. Wambold, "Prohibiting Foreign Bribes: Criminal Sanctions for Corporate Payments Abroad," *Cornell International Law Journal* 10 (1977), pp. 235–237. Wambold also found that though bribery is generally illegal, corporate contributions to political parties are acceptable in many countries. This complicates the moral evaluation of the FCPA. The next two points in my text suggest directions in which to go to defend the Act in this connection.

Truth Telling

Case Study—Italian Tax Mores

ARTHUR L. KELLY

The Italian federal corporate tax system has an official, legal tax structure and tax rates just as the U.S. system does. However, all similarity between the two systems ends there.

The Italian tax authorities assume that no Italian corporation would ever submit a tax return which shows its true profits but rather would submit a return which understates actual profits by anywhere between 30 percent and 70 percent; their assumption is essentially correct. Therefore, about six months after the annual deadline for filing corporate tax returns, the tax authorities issue to each corporation an "invitation to discuss" its tax return. The purpose of this notice is to arrange a personal meeting between them and representatives of the corporation. At this meeting, the Italian revenue service states the amount of corporate income tax which it believes is due. Its position is developed from both prior years' taxes actually paid and the current year's return; the amount which the tax authorities claim is due is generally several times that shown on the corporation's return for the current year. In short, the corporation's tax return and the revenue service's stated position are the opening offers for the several rounds of bargaining which will follow.

The Italian corporation is typically represented in such negotiations by its *commercialista*, a function which exists in Italian society for the primary

---

This case—prepared by Arthur L. Kelly (Managing Partner, KEL Enterprises Ltd.; formerly vice-president—International of A. T. Kearney, Inc.)—was presented at Loyola University of Chicago at a Mellon Foundation symposium entitled "Foundations of Corporate Responsibility to Society," April 1977. Printed with the permission of Arthur L. Kelly.

purpose of negotiating corporate (and individual) tax payments with the Italian tax authorities; thus, the management of an Italian corporation seldom, if ever, has to meet directly with the Italian revenue service and probably has a minimum awareness of the details of the negotiation other than the final settlement.

Both the final settlement and the negotiation are extremely important to the corporation, the tax authorities, and the *commercialista*. Since the tax authorities assume that a corporation *always* earned more money this year than last year and *never* has a loss, the amount of the final settlement, i.e., corporate taxes which will actually be paid, becomes, for all practical purposes, the floor for the start of next year's negotiations. The final settlement also represents the amount of revenue the Italian government will collect in taxes to help finance the cost of running the country. However, since large amounts of money are involved and two individuals having vested personal interests are conducting the negotiations, the amount of *bustarella*—typically a substantial cash payment "requested" by the Italian revenue agent from the *commercialista*—usually determines whether the final settlement is closer to the corporation's original tax return or to the fiscal authority's original negotiating position.

Whatever *bustarella* is paid during the negotiation is usually included by the *commercialista* in his lump-sum fee "for services rendered" to his corporate client. If the final settlement is favorable to the corporation, and it is the *commercialista's* job to see that it is, then the corporation is not likely to complain about the amount of its *commercialista's* fee, nor will it ever know how much of that fee was represented by *bustarella* and how much remained for the *commercialista* as payment for his negotiating services. In any case, the tax authorities will recognize the full amount of the fee as a tax deductible expense on the corporation's tax return for the following year.

About ten years ago, a leading American bank opened a banking subsidiary in a major Italian city. At the end of its first year of operation, the bank was advised by its local lawyers and tax accountants, both from branches of U.S. companies, to file its tax return "Italian-style," i.e., to understate its actual profits by a significant amount. The American general manager of the bank, who was on his first overseas assignment, refused to do so both because he considered it dishonest and because it was inconsistent with the practices of his parent company in the United States.

About six months after filing its "American-style" tax return, the bank received an "invitation to discuss" notice from the Italian tax authorities. The bank's general manager consulted with his lawyers and tax accountants who suggested he hire a *commercialista*. He rejected this advice and instead wrote a letter to the Italian revenue service not only stating that his firm's corporate return was correct as filed but also requesting that they inform him of any specific items about which they had questions. His letter was never answered.

About sixty days after receiving the initial "invitation to discuss" notice, the bank received a formal tax assessment notice calling for a tax of approximately three times that shown on the bank's corporate tax return; the tax authorities simply assumed the bank's original return had been based on generally accepted Italian practices, and they reacted accordingly. The bank's general manager again consulted with his lawyers and tax accountants who again suggested he hire a *commercialista* who knew how to handle these matters. Upon learning that the *commercialista* would probably have to pay *bustarella* to his revenue service counterpart in order to reach a settlement, the general manager again chose to ignore his advisors. Instead, he responded by sending the Italian revenue service a check for the full amount of taxes due according to the bank's American-style tax return even though the due date for the payment was almost six months hence; he made no reference to the amount of corporate taxes shown on the formal tax assessment notice.

Ninety days after paying its taxes, the bank received a third notice from the fiscal authorities. This one contained the statement, "We have reviewed your corporate tax return for 19____ and have determined that [the lira equivalent of] $6,000,000 of interest paid on deposits is not an allowable expense for federal tax purposes. Accordingly, the total tax due for 19____ is lira ____." Since interest paid on deposits is any bank's largest single expense item, the new tax assessment was for an amount many times larger than that shown in the initial tax assessment notice and almost fifteen times larger than the taxes which the bank had actually paid.

The bank's general manager was understandably very upset. He immediately arranged an appointment to meet personally with the manager of the Italian revenue service's local office. Shortly after the start of their meeting, the conversation went something like this:

| General Manager: | "You can't really be serious about disallowing interest paid on deposits as a tax deductible expense." |
| Italian Revenue Service: | "Perhaps. However, we thought it would get your attention. Now that you're here, shall we begin our negotiations?"[1] |

Questions

1. Would you, as the general manager of the Italian subsidiary of an American corporation, "when in Rome" do as other Italian corporations do or adhere strictly to U.S. tax reporting practices?

2. Would you, as chief executive officer of a publicly traded corporation (subject to Securities Exchange Commission rules, regulations, and scrutiny), advise the general manager of your Italian subsidiary to follow common Italian tax reporting practices or to adhere to U.S. standards?

NOTE

1. For readers interested in what happened subsequently, the bank was forced to pay the taxes shown on the initial tax assessment, and the American manager was recalled to the United States and replaced.

Ethical Duties Towards Others: "Truthfulness"

IMMANUEL KANT

The exchange of our sentiments is the principal factor in social intercourse, and truth must be the guiding principle herein. Without truth social intercourse and conversation become valueless. We can only know what a man thinks if he tells us his thoughts, and when he undertakes to express them he must really do so, or else there can be no society of men. Fellowship is only the second condition of society, and a liar destroys fellowship. Lying makes it impossible to derive any benefit from conversation. Liars are, therefore, held in general contempt. Man is inclined to be reserved and to pretend. . . . Man is reserved in order to conceal faults and shortcomings which he has; he pretends in order to make others attribute to him merits and virtues which he has not. Our proclivity to reserve and concealment is due to the will of Providence that the defects of which we are full should not be too obvious. Many of our propensities and peculiarities are objectionable to others, and if they became patent we should be foolish and hateful in their eyes. Moreover, the parading of these objectionable characteristics would so familiarize men with them that they would themselves acquire them. Therefore we arrange our conduct either to conceal our faults or to appear other than we are. We possess the art of simulation. In consequence, our inner weakness and error is revealed to the eyes of men only as an appearance of well-being, while we ourselves develop the habit of dispositions which are conducive to good conduct. No man in his true senses, therefore, is candid. Were man candid, were the request of Momus[1] to be complied with that Jupiter should place a mirror in each man's heart so that his disposition might be visible to all, man would have to be better constituted

From *Lectures on Ethics*, trans. Louis Infield (London: Methuen, 1930; rpt. New York: Harper & Row, 1963), pp. 224–35. Reprinted by permission of the publishers.

and possess good principles. If all men were good there would be no need for any of us to be reserved; but since they are not, we have to keep the shutters closed. Every house keeps its dustbin in a place of its own. We do not press our friends to come into our water-closet, although they know that we have one just like themselves. Familiarity in such things is the ruin of good taste. In the same way we make no exhibition of our defects, but try to conceal them. We try to conceal our mistrust by affecting a courteous demeanour and so accustom ourselves to courtesy that at last it becomes a reality and we set a good example by it. If that were not so, if there were none who were better than we, we should become neglectful. Accordingly, the endeavour to appear good ultimately makes us really good. If all men were good, they could be candid, but as things are they cannot be. To be reserved is to be restrained in expressing one's mind. We can, of course, keep absolute silence. This is the readiest and most absolute method of reserve, but it is unsociable, and a silent man is not only unwanted in social circles but is also suspected; every one thinks him deep and disparaging, for if when asked for his opinion he remains silent people think that he must be taking the worst view or he would not be averse from expressing it. Silence, in fact, is always a treacherous ally, and therefore it is not even prudent to be completely reserved. Yet there is such a thing as prudent reserve, which requires not silence but careful deliberation; a man who is wisely reserved weighs his words carefully and speaks his mind about everything excepting only those things in regard to which he deems it wise to be reserved.

We must distinguish between reserve and secretiveness, which is something entirely different. There are matters about which one has no desire to speak and in regard to which reserve is easy. We are, for instance, not naturally tempted to speak about and to betray our own misdemeanours. Everyone finds it easy to keep a reserve about some of his private affairs, but there are things about which it requires an effort to be silent. Secrets have a way of coming out, and strength is required to prevent ourselves betraying them. Secrets are always matters deposited with us by other people and they ought not to be placed at the disposal of third parties. But man has a great liking for conversation, and the telling of secrets adds much to the interest of conversation; a secret told is like a present given; how then are we to keep secrets? Men who are not very talkative as a rule keep secrets well, but good conversationalists, who are at the same time clever, keep them better. The former might be induced to betray something, but the latter's gift of repartee invariably enables them to invent on the spur of the moment something non-committal.

The person who is as silent as a mute goes to one extreme; the person who is loquacious goes to the opposite. Both tendencies are weaknesses. Men are liable to the first, women to the second. Someone has said that women are talkative because the training of infants is their special charge, and their talkativeness soon teaches a child to speak, because they can chatter to it all day long. If men had the care of the child, they would take much longer to learn to talk. However that may be, we dislike anyone who will not speak: he annoys us; his silence betrays his pride. On the other hand, loquaciousness in men is contemptible and contrary to the strength of the male. All this by the way; we shall now pass to more weighty matters.

If I announce my intention to tell what is in my mind, ought I knowingly to tell everything, or can I keep anything back? If I indicate that I mean to speak my mind, and instead of doing so make a false declaration, what I say is an untruth, a *falsiloquium*. But there can be *falsiloquium* even when people have no right to assume that we are expressing our thoughts. It is possible to deceive without making any statement whatever. I can make believe, make a demonstration from which others will draw the conclusion I want, though they have no right to expect that my action will express my real mind. In that case I have not lied to them, because I had not undertaken to express my mind. I may, for instance, wish people to think that I am off on a journey, and so I pack my luggage; people draw the conclusion I want them to draw; but others have no right to demand a declaration of my will from me.

. . . Again, I may make a false statement (*falsiloquium*), when my purpose is to hide from another what is in my mind and when the latter can assume that such is my purpose, his own purpose being to make a wrong use of the truth. Thus, for instance, if my enemy takes me by the throat and asks where I keep my money, I need not tell him the truth, because he will abuse it; and my untruth is not a lie (*mendacium*) because the thief knows full well that I will not, if I can help it, tell him the truth and that he has no right to demand it of me. But let us assume that I really say to the fellow, who is fully aware that he has no right to demand it, because he is a swindler, that I will tell him the truth, and I do not, am I then a liar? He has deceived me and I deceive him in return; to him, as an individual, I have done no injustice and he cannot complain; but I am none the less a liar in that my conduct is an infringement of the rights of humanity. It follows that a *falsiloquium* can be a *mendacium*—a lie—especially when it contravenes the right of an individual. Although I do a man no injustice by lying to him when he has lied to me, yet I act against the right of mankind, since I set myself in opposition to the condition and means through which any human society is possible. If one country breaks the peace this does not justify the other in doing likewise in revenge, for if it did no peace would ever be secure. Even though a statement does not contravene any particular human right it is nevertheless a lie if it is contrary to the general right of mankind. If a man spreads false news, though he does no wrong to anyone in particular, he offends against mankind, because if such a practice were universal man's desire for knowledge would be frustrated. For, apart from speculation, there are only two ways in which I can increase my fund of knowledge, by experience or by what others tell me. My own experience must necessarily be limited, and if what others told me was false, I could not satisfy my craving for knowledge.

. . . Not every untruth is a lie; it is a lie only if I have expressly given the other to understand that I am willing to acquaint him with my thought. Every lie is objectionable and contemptible in that we purposely let people think that we are telling them our thoughts and do not do so. We have broken our pact and violated the right of mankind. But if we were to be at all times punctiliously truthful we might often become victims of the wickedness of others who were ready to abuse our truthfulness. If all men were well-intentioned it would not only be a duty not to lie, but no one would do so because there would be no point in it. But as men are malicious, it cannot be denied that to be punctiliously truthful is often dangerous. This has given rise to the conception of a white lie, the lie enforced upon us by necessity— a difficult point for moral philosophers. For if necessity is urged as an excuse it might be urged to justify stealing, cheating and killing, and the whole basis of morality goes by the board. Then, again, what is a case of necessity? Everyone will interpret it in his own way. And, as there is then no definite standard to judge by, the application of moral rules becomes uncertain. Consider, for example, the following case. A man who knows that I have money asks me: "Have you any money on you?" If I fail to reply, he will conclude that I have; if I reply in the affirmative he will take it from me; if I reply in the negative, I tell a lie. What am I to do? If force is used to extort a confession from me, if any confession is improperly used against me, and if I cannot save myself by maintaining silence, then my lie is a weapon of defence. The misuse of a declaration extorted by force justifies me in defending myself. For whether it is my money or a confession that is extorted makes no difference. The forcing of a statement from me under conditions which convince me that improper use would be made of it is the only case in which I can be justified in telling a white lie. But if a lie does no harm to anyone and no one's interests are affected by it, is it a lie? Certainly. I undertake to express my mind, and if I do not really do so, though my statement may not be to the prejudice of the particular individual to whom it is made, it is none the less *in praejudicium humanitatis*. Then, again, there are lies which cheat. To cheat is to make a lying promise, while a breach of faith is a true promise which is not kept. A lying promise is an insult to the person to whom it is made, and even if this is not always so, yet there is always something mean about it. If, for instance, I promise to send some one a bottle of wine, and afterwards make a joke of it, I really swindle him. It is true that he has no right to demand the present of me, but in Idea it is already a part of his own property.

    . . . If a man tries to extort the truth from us and we cannot tell it [to] him and at the same time do not wish to lie, we are justified in resorting to equivocation in order to reduce him to silence and put a stop to his questionings. If he is wise, he will leave it at that. But if we let it be understood that we are expressing our sentiments and we proceed to equivocate we are in a different case; for our listeners might then draw wrong conclusions from our statements and we should have deceived them. . . . But a lie is a lie, and is in itself intrinsically base whether it be told with good or bad intent. For formally a lie is always evil; though if it is evil materially as well, it is a much meaner thing. There are no lies which may not be the source of evil. A liar is a coward; he is a man who has recourse to lying because he is unable to help himself and gain his ends by any other means. But a stout-hearted man will love truth and will not recognize a *casus necessitatis*. All expedients which take us off our guard are thoroughly mean. Such are lying, assassination, and poisoning. To attack a man on the highway is less vile than to attempt to poison him. In the former case he can at least defend himself, but, as he must eat, he is defenceless against the poisoner. A flatterer is not always a liar; he is merely lacking in self-esteem; he has no scruple in reducing his own worth and raising that of another in order to gain something by it. But there exists a form of flattery which springs from kindness of heart. Some kind souls flatter people whom they hold in high esteem. There are thus two kinds of flattery, kindly and treacherous; the first is weak, while the second is mean. People who are not given to flattery are apt to be fault-finders.

If a man is often the subject of conversation, he becomes a subject of criticism. If he is our friend, we ought not invariably to speak well of him or else we arouse jealousy and grudge against him; for people, knowing that he is only human, will not believe that he has only good qualities. We must, therefore, concede a little to the adverse criticism of our listeners and point out some of our friend's faults; if we allow him faults which are common and unessential, while extolling his merits, our friend cannot take it in ill part. Toadies are people who praise others in company in hope of gain. Men are meant to form opinions regarding their fellows and to judge them. Nature has made us judges of our neighbors so that things which are false but are outside the scope of the established legal authority should be arraigned before the court of social opinion. Thus, if a man dishonours some one, the authorities do not punish him, but his fellows judge and punish him, though only so far as it is within their right to punish him and without doing violence to him. People shun him, and that is punishment enough. If that were not so, conduct not punished by the authorities would go altogether unpunished. What then is meant by the enjoinder that we ought not to judge others? As we are ignorant of their dispositions we cannot tell whether they are punishable before God or not, and we cannot, therefore, pass an adequate moral judgment upon them. The moral dispositions of others are for God to judge, but we are competent judges of our own. We cannot judge the inner core of morality: no man can do that; but we are competent to judge its outer manifestations. In matters of morality we are not judges of our fellows, but nature has given us the right to form judgments about others and she also has ordained that we should judge ourselves in accordance with judgments that others form about us. The man who turns a deaf ear to other people's opinion of him is base and reprehensible. There is nothing that happens in this world about which we ought not to form an opinion, and we show considerable subtlety in judging conduct. Those who judge our conduct with exactness are our best friends. Only friends can be quite candid and open with each other. But in judging a man a further question arises. In what terms are we to judge him? Must we pronounce him either good or evil? We must proceed from the assumption that humanity is lovable, and, particularly in regard to wickedness, we ought never to pronounce a verdict either of condemnation or of acquittal. We pronounce such a verdict whenever we judge from his conduct that a man deserves to be condemned or acquitted. But though we are entitled to form opinions about our fellows, we have no right to spy upon them. Everyone has a right to prevent others from watching and scrutinizing his actions. The spy arrogates to himself the right to watch the doings of strangers; no one ought to presume to do such a thing. If I see two people whispering to each other so as not to be heard, my inclination ought to be to get farther away so that no sound may reach my ears. Or if I am left alone in a room and I see a letter lying open on the table, it would be contemptible to try to read it; a right-thinking man would not do so; in fact, in order to avoid suspicion and distrust he will endeavour not to be left alone in a room where money is left lying about, and he will be averse from learning other people's secrets in order to avoid the risk of the suspicion that he has betrayed them; other people's secrets trouble him, for even between the most intimate of friends suspicion might arise. A man who will let his inclination or appetite drive him to deprive his friend of anything, of his fiancée, for instance, is contemptible beyond a doubt. If he can cherish a passion for my sweetheart, he can equally well cherish a passion for my purse. It is very mean to lie in wait and spy upon a friend, or on anyone else, and to elicit information about him from menials by lowering ourselves to the level of our inferiors, who will thereafter not forget to regard themselves as our equals. Whatever militates against frankness lowers the dignity of man. Insidious, underhand conduct uses means which strike at the roots of society because they make frankness impossible; it is far viler than violence; for against violence we can defend ourselves, and a violent man who spurns meanness can be tamed to goodness, but the mean rogue, who has not the courage to come out into the open with his roguery, is devoid of every vestige of nobility of character. For that reason a wife who attempts to poison her husband in England is burnt at the stake, for if such conduct spread, no man would be safe from his wife.

As I am not entitled to spy upon my neighbour, I am equally not entitled to point out his faults to him; and even if he should ask me to do so he would feel hurt if I complied. He knows his faults better than I, he knows that he has them, but he likes to believe that I have not noticed them, and if I tell him of them he realizes that I have. To say, therefore, that friends ought to point out each other's faults, is not sound advice. My friend may know better than I whether my gait or deportment is proper or not, but if I will only examine myself, who can know me better than I can know myself? To point out his faults to a friend is sheer impertinence; and once fault finding begins between friends their friendship will not last long. We must turn a blind eye to the faults of others, lest they conclude that they have lost our respect and we lose theirs. Only if placed in positions of authority over others should we point out to them their defects. Thus a husband is entitled to teach and correct his wife, but his corrections must be well-intentioned and kindly and must be dominated by respect, for if they be prompted only by displeasure they result in mere blame and bitterness. If we must blame, we must temper the blame with a sweetening of love, good-will, and respect. Nothing else will avail to bring about improvement.

NOTE

1. CF. *Babrii fabulae Aesopeae*, ed. O. Cousins, 1897, Fable 59, p. 54.

Is Business Bluffing Ethical?

Albert Carr

A respected businessman with whom I discussed the theme of this article remarked with some heat, "You mean to say you're going to encourage men to bluff? Why, bluffing is nothing more than a form of lying! You're advising them to lie!"

I agreed that the basis of private morality is a respect for truth and that the closer a businessman comes to the truth, the more he deserves respect. At the same time, I suggested that most bluffing in business might be regarded simply as game strategy—much like bluffing in poker, which does not reflect on the morality of the bluffer.

I quoted Henry Taylor, the British statesman who pointed out that "falsehood ceases to be falsehood when it is understood on all sides that the truth is not expected to be spoken"—an exact description of bluffing in poker, diplomacy, and business. I cited the analogy of the criminal court, where the criminal is not expected to tell the truth when he pleads "not guilty." Everyone from the judge down takes it for granted that the job of the defendant's attorney is to get his client off, not to reveal the truth; and this is considered ethical practice. I mentioned Representative Omar Burleson, the Democrat from Texas, who was quoted as saying, in regard to the ethics of Congress, "Ethics is a barrel of worms"[1]—a pungent summing up of the problem of deciding who is ethical in politics.

I reminded my friend that millions of businessmen feel constrained every day to say *yes* to their bosses when they secretly believe *no* and that this is generally accepted as permissible strategy when the alternative might be the loss of a job. The essential point, I said, is that the ethics of business are game ethics, different from the ethics of religion.

He remained unconvinced. Referring to the company of which he is president, he declared: "Maybe that's good enough for some businessmen, but I can tell you that we pride ourselves on our ethics. In 30 years not one customer has ever questioned my word or asked to check our figures. We're loyal to our customers and fair to our suppliers. I regard my handshake on a deal as a contract. I've never entered into price-fixing schemes with my competitors. I've never allowed my salesmen to spread injurious rumors about other companies. Our union contract is the best in our industry. And, if I do say so myself, our ethical standards are of the highest!"

He really was saying, without realizing it, that he was living up to the ethical standards of the business game—which are a far cry from those of private life. Like a gentlemanly poker player, he did not play in cahoots with others at the table, try to smear their reputations, or hold back chips he owed them.

But this same fine man, at that very time, was allowing one of his products to be advertised in a way that made it sound a great deal better than it actually was. Another item in his product line was notorious among dealers for its "built-in-obsolescence." He was holding back from the market a much-improved product because he did not want to interfere with sales of the inferior item it would have replaced. He had joined with certain of his competitors in hiring a lobbyist to push a state legislature, by methods that he preferred not to know too much about, into amending a bill then being enacted.

In his view these things had nothing to do with ethics; they were merely normal business practice. He himself undoubtedly avoided outright falsehoods—never lied in so many words. But the entire organization that he ruled was deeply involved in numerous strategies of deception.

PRESSURE TO DECEIVE

Most executives from time to time are almost compelled, in the interests of their companies or themselves, to practice some form of deception when negotiating with customers, dealers, labor unions, government officials, or even other departments of their companies. By conscious misstatements, concealment of pertinent facts, or exaggeration—in short, by bluffing— they seek to persuade others to agree with them. I think it is fair to say that if the individual executive refuses to bluff from time to time—if he feels obligated to tell the truth, the whole truth, and nothing but the truth—he is ignoring opportunities permitted under the rules and is at a heavy disadvantage in his business dealings.

But here and there a businessman is unable to reconcile himself to the bluff in which he plays a part. His conscience, perhaps spurred by religious idealism, troubles him. He feels guilty; he may develop an ulcer or a nervous tic. Before any executive can make profitable use of the strategy of the bluff, he needs to make sure that in bluffing he will not lose self-respect or become emotionally disturbed. If he is to reconcile personal integrity and high standards of honesty with the practical requirements of business, he must feel that his bluffs are ethically justified. The justification rests on the fact that business, as practiced by individuals as well as by corporations, has the impersonal character of a game—a game that demands both special strategy and an understanding of its special ethics.

The game is played at all levels of corporate life, from the highest to the lowest. At the very instant that a man decides to enter business, he may be forced into a game situation, as is shown by the recent experience of a Cornell honor graduate who applied for a job with a large company:

• This applicant was given a psychological test which included the statement, "Of the following magazines, check any that you have read either regularly or from time to time, and double-check those which interest you most. *Reader's Digest, Time, Fortune, Saturday Evening Post, The New Republic, Life, Look, Ramparts, Newsweek, Business Week, U.S. News & World Report, The Nation, Playboy, Esquire, Harper's, Sports Illustrated.*

His tastes in reading were broad, and at one time or another he had read almost all of these magazines. He was a subscriber to *The New Republic*, an enthusiast for *Ramparts*, and an avid student of the pictures in *Playboy*. He was not sure whether his interest in *Playboy* would be held against him, but he had a shrewd suspicion that if he confessed to an interest in *Ramparts* and *The New Republic*, he would be thought a liberal, a radical, or at least an intellectual, and his chances of getting the job, which he needed, would greatly diminish. He therefore checked five of the more conservative magazines. Apparently it was a sound decision, for he got the job.

He had made a game player's decision, consistent with business ethics.

A similar case is that of a magazine space salesman who, owing to a merger, suddenly found himself out of a job:

• This man was 58, and, in spite of a good record, his chances of getting a job elsewhere in a business where youth is favored in hiring practice was not good. He was a vigorous, healthy man, and only a considerable amount of gray in his hair suggested his age. Before beginning his job search he touched up his hair with a black dye to confine the gray to his temples. He knew that the truth about his age might well come out in time, but he calculated that he could deal with that situation when it arose. He and his wife decided that he could easily pass for 45, and he so stated his age on his résumé.

This was a lie; yet within the accepted rules of the business game, no moral culpability attaches to it.

THE POKER ANALOGY

We can learn a good deal about the nature of business by comparing it with poker. While both have a large element of chance, in the long run the winner is the man who plays with steady skill. In both games ultimate victory requires intimate knowledge of the rules, insight into the psychology of the other players, a bold front, a considerable amount of self-discipline, and the ability to respond swiftly and effectively to opportunities provided by chance.

No one expects poker to be played on the ethical principles preached in churches. In poker it is right and proper to bluff a friend out of the rewards of being dealt a good hand. A player feels no more than a slight twinge of sympathy, if that, when—with nothing better than a single ace in his hand—he strips a heavy loser, who holds a pair, of the rest of his chips. It was up to the other fellow to protect himself. In the words of an excellent poker player, former President Harry Truman, "If you can't stand the heat, stay out of the kitchen." If one shows mercy to a loser in poker, it is a personal gesture, divorced from the rules of the game.

Poker has its special ethics, and here I am not referring to rules against cheating. The man who keeps an ace up his sleeve or who marks the cards is more than unethical; he is a crook, and can be punished as such—kicked out of the game or, in the Old West, shot.

In contrast to the cheat, the unethical poker player is one who, while abiding by the letter of the rules, finds ways to put the other players at an unfair disadvantage. Perhaps he unnerves them with loud talk. Or he tries to get them drunk. Or he plays in cahoots with someone else at the table. Ethical poker players frown on such tactics.

Poker's own brand of ethics is different from the ethical ideals of civilized human relationships. The game calls for distrust of the other fellow. It ignores the claim of friendship. Cunning deception and concealment of one's strength and intentions, not kindness and openheartedness, are vital in poker. No one thinks any the worse of poker on that account. And no one should think any the worse of the game of business because its standards of right and wrong differ from the prevailing traditions of morality in our society. . . .

WE DON'T MAKE THE LAWS

Wherever we turn in business, we can perceive the sharp distinction between its ethical standards and those of the churches. Newspapers abound with sensational stories growing out of this distinction:

- We read one day that Senator Philip A. Hart of Michigan has attacked food processors for deceptive packaging of numerous products.[2]
- The next day there is a Congressional to-do over Ralph Nader's book, *Unsafe At Any Speed*, which demonstrates that automobile companies for years have neglected the safety of car-owning families.[3]
- Then another Senator, Lee Metcalf of Montana, and journalist Vic Reinemer show in their book, *Overcharge*, the methods by which utility companies elude regulating government bodies to extract unduly large payments from users of electricity.[4]

These are merely dramatic instances of a prevailing condition; there is hardly a major industry at which a similar attack could not be aimed. Critics of business regard such behavior as unethical, but the companies concerned know that they are merely playing the business game.

Among the most respected of our business institutions are the insurance companies. A group of insurance executives meeting recently in New England was startled when their guest speaker, social critic Daniel Patrick Moynihan, roundly berated them for "unethical" practices. They had been guilty, Moynihan alleged, of using outdated actuarial tables to obtain unfairly high premiums. They habitually delayed the hearings of lawsuits against them in order to tire out the plaintiffs and win cheap settlements. In their employment policies they used ingenious devices to discriminate against certain minority groups.[5]

It was difficult for the audience to deny the validity of these charges. But these men were business game players. Their reaction to Moynihan's attack was much the same as that of the automobile manufacturers to Nader, of the utilities to Senator Metcalf, and of the food processors to Senator Hart. If the laws governing their business change, or if public opinion becomes clamorous, they will make the necessary adjustments. But morally they have in their view done nothing wrong. As long as they comply with the letter of the law, they are within their rights to operate their businesses as they see fit.

The small business is in the same position as the great corporation in this respect. For example:

• In 1967 a key manufacturer was accused of providing master keys for automobiles to mail-order customers, although it was obvious that some of the purchasers might be automobile thieves. His defense was plain and straightforward. If there was nothing in the law to prevent him from selling his keys to anyone who ordered them, it was not up to him to inquire as to his customers' motives. Why was it any worse, he insisted, for him to sell car keys by mail, than for mail-order houses to sell guns that might be used for murder? Until the law was changed, the key manufacturer could regard himself as being just as ethical as any other businessman by the rules of the business game.[6]

Violations of the ethical ideals of society are common in business, but they are not necessarily violations of business practices. Each year the Federal Trade Commission orders hundreds of companies, many of them of the first magnitude, to "cease and desist" from practices which, judged by ordinary standards, are of questionable morality but which are stoutly defended by the companies concerned.

In one case, a firm manufacturing a well-known mouthwash was accused of using a cheap form of alcohol possibly deleterious to health. The company's chief executive, after testifying in Washington, made this comment privately:

> We broke no law. We're in a highly competitive industry. If we're going to stay in business, we have to look for profit wherever the law permits. We don't make up the laws. We obey them. Then why do we have to put up with this 'holier than thou' talk about ethics? It's sheer hypocrisy. We're not in business to promote ethics. Look at the cigarette companies, for God's sake! If the ethics aren't embodied in the laws by the men who made them, you can't expect businessmen to fill the lack. Why, a sudden submission to Christian ethics by businessmen would bring about the greatest economic upheaval in history!

It may be noted that the government failed to prove its case against him.

CAST ILLUSIONS ASIDE

Talk about ethics by businessmen is often a thin decorative coating over the hard realities of the game:

• Once I listened to a speech by a young executive who pointed to a new industry code as proof that his company and its competitors were deeply aware of their responsibilities to society. It was a code of ethics, he said. The industry was going to police itself, to dissuade constituent companies from wrongdoing. His eyes shone with conviction and enthusiasm.

The same day there was a meeting in a hotel room where the industry's top executives met with the "czar" who was to administer the new code, a man of high repute. No one who was present could doubt their common attitude. In their eyes the code was designed primarily to forestall a move by the federal government to impose stern restrictions on the industry. They felt that the code would hamper them a good deal less than new federal laws would. It was, in other words, conceived as a protection for the industry, not for the public.

The young executive accepted the surface explanation of the code; these leaders, all experienced game players, did not deceive themselves for a moment about its purpose.

The illusion that business can afford to be guided by ethics as conceived in private life is often fostered by speeches and articles containing such phrases as, "It pays to be ethical," or, "Sound ethics is good business." Actually this is not an ethical position at all; it is a self-serving calculation in disguise. The speaker is really saying that in the long run a company can make more money if it does not antagonize competitors, suppliers, employees, and customers by squeezing them too hard. He is saying that oversharp policies reduce ultimate gains. That is true, but it has nothing to do with ethics. The underlying attitude is much like that in the familiar story of the shopkeeper who finds an extra $20 bill in the cash register, debates with himself the ethical problem—should he tell his partner?—and finally decides to share the money because the gesture will give him an edge over the s.o.b. the next time they quarrel.

I think it is fair to sum up the prevailing attitude of businessmen on ethics as follows:

We live in what is probably the most competitive of the world's civilized societies. Our customs encourage a high degree of aggression in the individual's striving for success. Business is our main area of competition, and it has been ritualized into a game of strategy. The basic rules of the game have been set by the government, which attempts to detect and punish business frauds. But as long as a company does not transgress the rules of the game set by law, it has the legal right to shape its strategy without reference to anything but its profits. If it takes a long-term view of its profits, it will preserve amicable relations, so far as possible, with those with whom it deals. A wise businessman will not seek advantage to the point where he generates dangerous hostility among employees, competitors, customers, government, or the public at large. But decisions in this area are, in the final test, decisions of strategy, not of ethics.

PLAYING TO WIN

. . . If a man plans to make a seat in the business game, he owes it to himself to master the principles by which the game is played, including its special ethical outlook. He can then hardly fail to recognize that an occasional bluff may well be justified in terms of the game's ethics and warranted in terms of economic necessity. Once he clears his mind on this point, he is in a good position to match his strategy against that of the other players. He can then determine objectively whether a bluff in a given situation has a good chance of succeeding and can decide when and how to bluff, without a feeling of ethical transgression.

To be a winner, a man must play to win. This does not mean that he must be ruthless, cruel, harsh, or treacherous. On the contrary, the better his reputation for integrity, honesty, and decency, the better his chances of victory will be in the long run. But from time to time every businessman, like every poker player, is offered a choice between certain loss or bluffing within the legal rules of the game. If he is not resigned to losing, if he wants to rise in his company and industry, then in such a crisis he will bluff—and bluff hard.

Every now and then one meets a successful businessman who has conveniently forgotten the small or large deceptions that he practiced on his way to fortune. "God gave me my money," old John D. Rockefeller once piously told a Sunday school class. It would be a rare tycoon in our time who would risk the horse laugh with which such a remark would be greeted.

In the last third of the twentieth century even children are aware that if a man has become prosperous in business, he has sometimes departed from the strict truth in order to overcome obstacles or has practiced the more subtle deceptions of the half-truth or the misleading omission. Whatever the form of the bluff, it is an integral part of the game, and the executive who does not master its techniques is not likely to accumulate much money or power.

NOTES

1. *The New York Times*, March 9, 1967.
2. *The New York Times*, November 21, 1966.
3. New York, Grossman Publishers, Inc., 1965.
4. New York, David McKay Company, Inc., 1967.
5. *The New York Times*, January 17, 1967.
6. Cited by Ralph Nader in "Business Crime," *The New Republic*, July 1, 1967, p. 7.

The Ethics and Profitability of Bluffing in Business

RICHARD E. WOKUTCH AND THOMAS L. CARSON

Consider a standard case of bluffing in an economic transaction. I am selling a used car and say that $1,500 is my final offer, even though I know that I would accept considerably less. Or, suppose that I am a union representative in a labor negotiation. Although I have been instructed to accept $10 an hour if that is the highest offer I receive, I say that we will not accept a wage of $10 an hour under any circumstances. This sort of bluffing is widely practiced and almost universally condoned. It is thought to be morally acceptable. It is our contention, however, that bluffing raises serious ethical questions. For bluffing is clearly an act of deception; the bluffer's intent is to deceive the other parties about the nature of his bargaining position. Furthermore, bluffing often involves lying. The two examples of bluffing presented here both fit the standard definition of lying; they are deliberate false statements made with the intent of deceiving others.[1]

Common sense holds that lying and deception are prima facie wrong. One could also put this by saying that there is a presumption against lying and deception; that they require some special justification in order to be permissible.[2] Almost no one would agree with Kant's view that it is wrong to lie even if doing so is necessary to protect the lives of innocent people. According to Kant it would be wrong to lie to a potential murderer concerning the whereabouts of his intended victim.[3]

Assuming the correctness of the view that there is a moral presumption against lying and deception, and assuming that we are correct in saying that bluffing often involves lying, it follows that bluffing and other deceptive business practices require some sort of special justification in order to be considered permissible. Business people frequently defend bluffing and other deceptive practices on the grounds that they are profitable or economically necessary. Such acts are also defended on the grounds that they are standard practice in economic transactions. We will argue that these standard justifications of bluffing are unacceptable. Then we will propose an alternative justification for lying and deception about one's bargaining position.

There are those who hold that lying and deception are never profitable or economically necessary. In their view, honesty is always the best policy.

Richard E. Wokutch and Thomas L. Carson, "The Ethics and Profitability of Bluffing in Business," *Westminster Institute Review* vol. 1, no. 2, May 1981. Revised 1986. Reprinted by permission of the publisher and the authors.

One incentive for telling the truth is the law, but here we are referring to lying or bluffing which is not illegal, or for which the penalty or risk of being caught is not great enough to discourage the action.

Those who hold that honesty is always in one's economic self-interest argue that economic transactions are built on trust and that a violation of that trust discourages an individual or organization from entering into further transactions with the lying party for fear of being lied to again. Thus, some mutually beneficial transactions may be foregone for lack of trust. Moreover, word of deceitful practices spreads through the marketplace and others also avoid doing business with the liar. Thus, while some short run profit might accrue from lying, in the long run it is unprofitable. If this argument were sound, we would have a non-issue. Lying, like inefficiency, would be a question of bad management that would be in one's own best interest to eliminate.

Unfortunately, there are some anomalies in the marketplace which prevent the system from operating in a perfectly smooth manner. The very existence of bluffing and lying in the first place suggests that the economists' assumption of perfect (or near perfect) market information is incorrect. Some transactions, such as buying or selling a house, are one-shot deals with little or no chance of repeat business. Thus, there is no experience on which to base an assessment of the seller's honesty, and no incentive to build trust for future transactions. Even when a business is involved in an ongoing operation, information flows are such that a large number of people can be duped before others hear about it (e.g., selling Florida swampland or Arizona desertland sight unseen). Other bluffs and lies are difficult or even impossible to prove. If a union negotiator wins a concession from management on the grounds that the union would not ratify the contract without it—even though he has reason to believe that this is untrue—it would be extremely difficult for management to prove later that ratification could have been achieved without the provision. By the same token, some product claims, such as the salesman's contention that "this is the best X on the market," are inherently subjective. When the competing products are of similar quality, it is difficult to prove such statements untrue, even if the person making the statement believes them to be untrue. Another exception to the assumption of perfect information flows is the confusion brought on by the increasing technological complexity of goods and services. In fact, a product information industry in the form of publications like *Consumer Reports, Canadian Consumer, Consumer Union Reports, Money,* and *Changing Times* has arisen to provide, for a price, the kind of product information that economic theory assumes consumers have to begin with.

These arguments suggest not only that the commonly cited disincentives to bluffing and lying are often ineffective, but that there are some distinct financial incentives for these activities. If you can convince consumers that your product is better than it really is, you will have a better chance of selling them that product and you may be able to charge them a higher price than they would otherwise be willing to pay. It is also obvious that in a negotiating setting there are financial rewards for successful lies and bluffs. If you can conceal your actual minimal acceptable position, you may be able to achieve a more desirable settlement. By the same token, learning your negotiating opponent's true position will enable you to press towards his minimal acceptable position. This is, of course, why such intrigues as hiding microphones in the opposing negotiating team's private quarters or hiring informants are undertaken in negotiations—they produce valuable information.

An individual cannot, however, justify lying simply on the grounds that it is in his own self-interest to lie, for it is not always morally permissible to do what is in one's own self-interest. I would not be justified in killing you or falsely accusing you of a crime in order to get your job, even if doing so would be to my advantage. Similarly, a businessman cannot justify lying and deception simply on the grounds that they are advantageous, i.e., profitable, to his company. This point can be strengthened if we remember that any advantages that one gains as a result of bluffing are usually counter-balanced by corresponding disadvantages on the part of others. If I succeed in getting a higher price by bluffing when I sell my house, there must be someone else who is paying more than he would have otherwise.

Economic necessity is a stronger justification for lying than mere profitability. Suppose that it is necessary for a businessman to engage in lying or deception in order to insure the survival of his firm. Many would not object to a person stealing food to prevent himself or his children from starving to death. Perhaps lying in an extreme situation to get money to buy food or to continue employing workers so that *they* can buy food would be equally justifiable. This case would best be described as a conflict of duties—a conflict between the duty to be honest and the duty to promote the welfare of those for/to whom one is responsible (one's children, one's employees, or the stockholders whose money one manages). However, it is extremely unlikely that bankruptcy would result in the death or starvation of anyone in a society which has unemployment compensation, welfare payments, food stamps, charitable organizations, and even opportunities for begging. The consequences of refraining from lying in transactions might still be very unfavorable indeed, involving, for example, the bankruptcy of a firm, loss of investment, unemployment, and the personal suffering associated with this. But a firm which needs to practice lying or deception in order to continue in existence is of doubtful value to society. Perhaps the labor, capital and raw materials which it uses could be put to better use elsewhere. At least in a free market situation, the interests of economic efficiency would be best served if such firms were to go out of business. An apparent exception to this argument about economic efficiency would be a situation in which a firm was pushed to the edge of bankruptcy by the lies of competitors or others. It seems probable that the long term consequences of the bankruptcy of a firm which needs to lie in order to continue in existence would be better, or no worse, than those of its continuing to exist.

Suppose, however, that the immediate bad consequences of bankruptcy would not be offset by any long term benefits. In that case it is not clear that it would be wrong for a company to resort to lying and deception out of economic necessity. One can, after all, be justified in lying or deceiving to save individuals from harms far less serious than death. I can be justified in lying about the gender of my friend's roommate to a nosy relative or boss in order to protect him from embarrassment or from being fired. If the degree of harm prevented by lying or deception were the only relevant factor, and if bankruptcy would not have any significant long term benefits, then it would seem that a businessman could easily justify lying and deceiving in order to protect those associated with his business from the harm which would result from the bankruptcy of the firm. There is, however, another relevant factor which clouds the issue. In the case of lying about the private affairs of one's friends, one is lying to others about matters about which they have no right to know. Our present analogy warrants lying and deception for the sake of economic survival only in cases in which the persons being lied to or deceived have no right to the information in question. Among other things, this rules out deceiving customers about dangerous defects in one's products, because customers have a right to this information; but it does not rule out lying to someone or deceiving them about one's minimal bargaining position.

We have argued that personal or corporate profit is no justification for lying in business transactions, and that lying for reasons of economic necessity is also morally objectionable in many cases. But what about lying in order to benefit the party being lied to? There are certainly many self-serving claims to this effect. Some have argued that individuals derive greater satisfaction from a product or service if they can be convinced that it is better than is actually the case. On the other hand, an advertising executive made the argument in the recent Federal Trade Commission hearings on children's advertising that the disappointment children experience when a product fails to meet their commercial-inflated expectations is beneficial because it helps them develop a healthy skepticism. These arguments are not convincing. In fact, they appear to be smoke screens for actions taken out of self-interest. It is conceivable that consumers might benefit from it. For example, deceptive advertising claims may cause one to purchase a product which is of genuine benefit. While lying and deception can sometimes be justified by reference to the interests of those being lied to or deceived, such cases are very atypical in business situations. As was argued earlier, successful bluffing almost always harms the other party in business negotiations. The net effect of a successful bluff is paying more or receiving less than would otherwise have been the case. . . .

A further ground on which lying or deception in bargaining situations is sometimes held to be justifiable is the claim that the other parties do not have a right to know one's true bargaining position. It is true that the other parties do not have a right to know one's position, i.e., it would not be wrong to refuse to reveal it to them. But this is not to say that it is permissible to lie or deceive them. You have no right to know where I was born, but it would be prima facie wrong for me to lie to you about the place of my birth. So, lying and deception in bargaining situations cannot be justified simply on the grounds that the other parties have no right to know one's true position. However, other things being equal, it is much worse to lie or deceive about a matter concerning which the other parties have a right to know than one about which they have no right to know.

But what of the justification that lying and deception are standard practice in economic transations? Certainly, lying and deception are very common, if not generally accepted or condoned. Bluffing and other deceptive practices are especially common in economic negotiations, and bluffing, at least, is generally thought to be an acceptable practice.[4] Does this fact in any way justify bluffing? We think not. The mere fact that something is standard practice or generally accepted is not enough to justify it. Standard practice and popular opinion can be in error. Such things as slavery were once standard practice and generally accepted. But they are and *were* morally wrong. Bluffing cannot be justified simply *because* it is a common and generally accepted practice. However, we shall now use the prevalence of bluffing involving lying and deception as a premise of an argument to show that there is a presumption for thinking that bluffing of this sort is morally permissible. If one is involved in a negotiation, it is very probable that the other parties with whom one is dealing are themselves bluffing. The presumption against lying and deception does not hold when the other parties with whom one is dealing are themselves lying to or otherwise attempting to deceive one. Given this, there is no presumption against lying or deceiving others about one's bargaining position in the course of an ordinary business negotiation, since the parties with whom one is dealing may be presumed to be doing the same themselves.

It is prima facie wrong to use violence against another person, but when one is a victim of violence oneself, it is permissible to use violence if doing so is necessary in order to prevent or limit harm to oneself. One is not morally required to refrain from self-defense. Similarly, other things being equal, if X is being harmed by the lies or deception of Y and if X can avoid or mitigate that harm only by lying to or deceiving Y, then it is permissible for X to lie to or deceive Y. These intuitions are captured by the following principle:

> (P) Other things being equal, it is permissible for X to do a to Y, even if a is a prima facie wrong, provided that X's doing a to Y is necessary in order to prevent or mitigate harm to X caused by Y's doing a to X.[5]

In business negotiations an individual can typically gain some benefit (balanced by corresponding harm to the other party) if he is willing to lie or deceive the other person about his own negotiating position. The other party can avoid or mitigate this harm only by being willing to do the same. In our society most people routinely practice this sort of lying and/or deception in business negotiations. Given this, (P) implies that one may presume that one is justified in bluffing (by means of lying and deception about one's negotiating position) in ordinary circumstances, unless either: (i) one has special reasons to suppose that the other party will not do the same (e.g., one might know that the individual with whom one is dealing is unusually scrupulous or naive), or (ii) one has special reasons for thinking that one will not be harmed by the bluffing of the other party, even if one does not bluff oneself.

Space does not permit an extended discussion or defense of (P). We would, however, like to forestall two possible objections. (i) (P) does not constitute a blanket endorsement of retaliation or the policy of "an eye for an eye and a tooth for a tooth." (P) would not justify my killing your child in retaliation for your having killed mine. (P) would justify my killing another person X only if my killing X is necessary in order to prevent X from killing me. (ii) It is standard practice for people involved in negotiations to misrepresent the terms they are willing to accept. In ordinary circumstances (P) will justify such actions. However, there are types of lying and deception which are not generally practiced in negotiations. For example, while meeting with a prospective buyer a person selling a house might have a friend pretend to make an offer to buy the house in order to pressure the prospective buyer. (P) does not imply that there is any presumption for thinking that such a ruse would be morally permissible.

NOTES

We are indebted to Thomas Beauchamp for comments on a previous version of this paper. Earlier versions of this paper were presented to a conference on Business and Professional Ethics at Kalamazoo College and Western Michigan University, November 1979, and to the Philosophy Department at Denison University.

1. For a much more thorough defense of the claim that bluffing involves lying, with an appeal to a somewhat different definition of lying, see our paper "The Moral Status of Bluffing and Deception in Business" in *Business and Professional Ethics*, ed. Wade L. Robison and Michael S. Pritchard (New York: Humana Press). Also see our paper "Bluffing in Labor Negotiations: Legal and Ethical Issues," with Kent F. Mursmann, *Journal of Business Ethics*, vol. 1, no. 1, January 1982.
2. The classic statement of this view is included in Chapter II of Sir David Ross' *The Right and the Good* (Oxford: Oxford University Press, 1930).
3. Immanual Kant, "On the Supposed Right to Tell Lies from Benevolent Motives,"

(1797), in *Moral Rules and Particular Circumstances*, ed. Baruch Brody (Englewood Cliffs, New Jersey: Prentice-Hall, 1970), pp. 32 and 33.

4. In a well-known defense of bluffing, Albert Carr claims that it is permissible to make false statements in the course of business negotiations because doing so is "normal business practice," and part of what is involved in "playing the business game." See "Is Business Bluffing Ethical?," *Harvard Business Review*, Jan.–Feb. 1968.

5. It seems plausible to say that it would be permissible to do an act that is prima facie wrong to another person (X) if doing so were necessary in order to prevent X from harming a third party by doing the same act. For example, one would be justified in killing another person if doing so were necessary in order to prevent him from killing a third party. We accept the following stronger version of P:

> P′ Other things being equal, it is permissible for X to do *a* to Y, even if *a* is prima facie wrong, provided that X's doing *a* to Y is necessary in order to prevent or mitigate harm to *someone* caused by Y's doing *a* to that person.

The weaker principle (P) is sufficient for the purposes of our argument.

Part II

MORALITY
AND CORPORATIONS

People eat, sleep, vote, love, hate, and suffer guilt. Corporations do none of these. Yet corporations are considered "persons" under the law and have many of the same rights as humans: to sue, to own property, to conduct business and conclude contracts, and to enjoy freedom of speech, of the press, and freedom from unreasonable searches and seizures. Corporations are legal citizens of the state in which they are chartered. They even possess two rights not held by humans: unlimited longevity and limited liability. This means that corporations have unlimited charters—they never "die"— and that their shareholders are liable for corporate debts *only* up to the extent of their personal investment.

One of the most stubborn ethical issues surrounding the corporation is, not what it should *do*, but how it should be *considered*. What is a corporation? Is it a distinct individual in its own right, or merely an aggregate of individuals, for example, stockholders, managers, and employees? The answer to this question is crucial for understanding corporations and their activities. We must know, morally speaking, whether a corporation has responsibilities and rights *in addition to* the rights and responsibilities of the aggregate of individuals that make it up. We already know that individual members of a corporation can be held morally responsible. For example, if a chemical engineer intentionally puts a dangerous chemical in a new cosmetic product, he is morally blameworthy. But can we hold the corporation, considered as something distinct from its individual members, morally blameworthy too?

On the one hand, the very concept of a corporation seems to involve more than the individual actions of specific persons. The corporation is understood to exist even after all its original members are deceased; it is said to "hire" employees or fire them when only a handful of the corporate members are involved in the decision, and it is said to have obligations through its charter that override the desires of its individual members. But even granting that the corporation is a distinct entity such that its actions are not reducible—at least in a straightforward way—to the actions of individuals, does it follow that the corporation has moral characteristics that are not reducible to the moral characteristics of its members? Philosophers have addressed this issue by asking whether the corporation is a "moral agent." Rocks, trees, and machines clearly are not moral agents. People clearly are. What are we to say about corporations?

Whatever the answer to this question, a second immediately follows, namely, What should society expect from corporations? The two questions are closely connected. For if we answer the first by concluding that the corporation is a moral agent, then we will formulate the second by asking, What is the nature of a corporation's rights and obligations? If, on the other hand, we answer the first question by denying that the corporation is a moral agent, and hence refuse to ascribe to it any rights or obligations, we will formulate the second question by asking, What behavior should society expect from the individual persons that make up the corporation, that is, those who hold its offices, perform its tasks, and construct its rules? By phrasing the second question this way, we do not attribute moral agency to the corporation but treat it as a powerful nonmoral entity.

Both the first and second questions have enormous practical and philosophical significance, for if corporations are true moral agents, we should expect them to develop and manifest a sense of right and wrong, and to possess certain rights, privileges, and responsibilities. But if they are not moral agents, we must proceed to determine what sorts of entities they really are, in order to discover how best to treat them and what to expect from them. For example, if it is determined that corporations are similar to large machines, they must be externally controlled like any large machine with the capacity to harm society. According to this view, we must abandon hope of a corporation exercising genuine moral responsibility. But then we are forced to regulate those corporate activities which are societally unacceptable, a move which may not be altogether palatable to the business community.

THE MORAL STATUS OF CORPORATIONS

When discussing whether corporations are moral agents, a good place to begin is with corporate legal history, that is, with the series of legislative acts and court decisions that have defined the corporation's existence. From its beginning in the Middle Ages, the corporation has been subject to differing legal interpretations. In the Middle Ages the law did not recognize any profit-making organizations as corporations; instead, it granted corporate status only to guilds, boroughs, and the church. In some instances the law decreed that corporations follow strict guidelines; for example, in 1279 the French Statute of Mortmain declared that a corporation's property could not exceed a specified amount. Even hundreds of years after its beginning, the corporation remained subject to strict legal sanctions on the conditions of its charter. As late as the nineteenth century, some U.S. corporations were granted charters only on the condition that they restrict land purchases to a certain geographic location and to a maximum number of acres. Thus corporations were viewed merely as artificial beings, created by the state and owing their very existence to a decree by the government.

But in the latter part of the nineteenth century and in the twentieth century, especially in the United States, this view suffered a dramatic change. Instead of treating corporations as mere creations of the state, the courts began to see them as natural outcomes of the habits of business persons. It saw them as the predictable results of the actions of business persons who, exercising their inalienable right to associate freely with others, gathered together to conduct business and pursue a profit. As such, incorporation came to be seen less as a privilege granted by the state and more as a right to be protected by the state. Chartering a corporation became easier, and government restrictions less severe. Even so, the traditional view of a corporation continues to influence the law. The most accepted legal definition of a corporation remains the one offered by Chief Justice Marshall in 1819: "A corporation," he wrote, "is an artificial being, invisible, intangible, and existing only in the contemplation of law. Being the mere creation of law, it possesses only those properties which the charter of its creation confers upon it. . . ."

Throughout the evolution of corporate law the problem of whether and how to ascribe responsibility to the corporation persisted. In the sixteenth century the large trading corporations were not themselves held responsible when one ship collided with another; instead, the individual boat owners, who participated in the corporation only to secure special trading rights, were held individually responsible. By the seventeenth century, the notion of "corporate" responsibility was thoroughly established in the law, but some sticky issues remained. Could a corporation be *criminally* liable? What rights, if any, did corporations share with ordinary persons? In the early twentieth century and again in recent years, U.S. corporations have been charged with homicide—one such case involved the Ford Pinto's exploding gas tank—but in every instance so far, although the court has been willing to impose stiff fines, it has stopped short of entering a verdict of guilty of homicide.

In 1978 the U.S. Supreme Court delivered a landmark verdict in the case of *First National Bank of Boston v. Bellotti*. The fundamental issue raised was whether a corporation should be allowed the right to free speech even when exercising that right means spending corporate money to promote political causes not directly related to corporate profits. Should corporations have full-fledged first amendment rights to free speech even when that means that they can use their vast financial reserves to support partisan political ends? In a split decision the Supreme Court decided in favor of recognizing such a right, although the decision itself remains controversial.

Whatever the courts eventually decide about the legal status of a corporation, questions about its moral status will remain. Two distinct and dramatically opposed moral views on this topic are presented in this section. The first, represented in the article by the contemporary philosopher Peter French, holds that corporations are moral agents in the sense that they can have moral responsibility attributed to them more or less on a par with persons. The second, represented by John Ladd, takes a reverse stand. Ladd argues that corporations are not "persons" at all—even of the fictional kind—and hence cannot truly be said to possess rights and responsibilities.

Professor French, in his article "The Corporation as a Moral Person," constructs an argument for corporate moral agency by relying on the nature of a corporation's "internal decision-making structure." Corporations have policies, rules, and decision-making procedures, all of which when considered together qualify them for the status of a moral agent. They can be praised or blamed for such decisions, and their decision-making capacity entails that they are "intentional beings" and have essentially the same responsibilities and rights as ordinary persons.

John Ladd, in his well-known article "Morality and the Ideal of Rationality in Formal Organizations," argues that a corporation is structured to achieve certain goals. In contrast with French, Ladd challenges the claim that corporation is an autonomous, independent formal organization which has its own self-determined goals. Because of its very structure, it can try to achieve only its formal ends, which cannot, by definition, be moral ones. Consequently a corporation is not a moral agent at all but more like a complicated machine; and like a machine, a corporation cannot be said to have genuine moral and social responsibilities.

The debate between French and Ladd is of more than abstract philosophical interest, as the Manville case illustrates. The Manville Corporation has been accused of causing injuries and deaths to thousands of workers who were exposed to asbestos dust over long periods of time. The managers originally in charge of developing and manufacturing asbestos when the majority of those workers were exposed are no longer at Manville. Yet Manville, the corporation, still exists. Can we hold it morally responsible? Or, if Ladd is correct, must we simply regulate undesirable corporate activities to prevent further incidents such as asbestos poisoning?

In a compromise between French and Ladd, Kenneth Goodpaster and John Matthews, in an article that appears in the next section of this part, argue that because corporations act as individuals and perform actions that are similar to human actions, corporations are analogous to, but not identical with, moral persons. Therefore it is not preposterous to project moral responsibility onto corporations, indeed, the same kind of moral responsibility we expect from persons. If Goodpaster and Matthews are correct, corporations can and should be expected to exercise moral awareness and to recognize ethical limitations on their actions.

THE MORAL RESPONSIBILITIES OF CORPORATIONS

The second section deals with a more difficult issue: What should we hope for in terms of corporate behavior? Whether a corporation is a moral agent or not, it must adhere to certain norms of behavior. For example, at a minimum a corporation must not deliberately murder or systematically harm others. But beyond specifying bare minimum conditions, what can one say? How can one evaluate acceptable and unacceptable behavior in corporations?

Goodpaster and Matthews, as we noted, find corporate and individual behavior analogous. Corporations are responsible bodies, so that we can expect as much of them in terms of moral accountability as we do of individuals. The question is, If corporations can be morally responsible, why is it that sometimes corporations, run by morally decent individuals, go astray? The E. F. Hutton case illustrates just such a problem. E. F. Hutton had been an outstanding brokerage house with a fine national reputation, but its well-paid employees became involved in a complex bank overdraft scheme that was illegal and unfair both to the banks and to their customers. Why did this happen?

James Waters, in his article "Catch 20.5: Corporate Morality as an Organizational Phenomenon," tackles this problem. Waters acknowledges that corporations can and should be morally responsible, but he shows that morally responsible activities are in fact sometimes hard to achieve within an organization. Morally acceptable corporate behavior must originate in morally acceptable individual behavior. Sometimes the organizational structures and goal expectations of a corporation interfere with ethical behavior by individuals who are ordinarily upstanding people. Waters's analysis raises the question, How can corporations be structured so that incidents like E. F. Hutton can be prevented? Waters offers a number of fruitful suggestions for the thoughtful reader.

The Moral Status
of Corporations

Case Study—Manville: The Ethics of Economic Efficiency?

A. R. GINI

On Friday, July 30, 1982, a short article appeared on page four of the *Wall Street Journal* announcing that yet another company, UNR Industries Inc. of Chicago, had filed for Chapter 11 of the Federal Bankruptcy Code of 1978. Given the present state of the economy the public notification of a bankruptcy proceeding is hardly a novel occurrence. However, the circumstances leading to the UNR petition were certainly far from usual.

At the time of filing UNR assets exceeded $200 million with debts totaling only about $100 million. While sales had marginally declined, 4.2% in the second quarter of 1982, yearly sales figures were expected to remain relatively strong. UNR chairman, David S. Leavitt, said that the company was forced to file for bankruptcy because of the nearly 17,000 suits filed against it in regard to their asbestos pipe insulation product line. Although the company had stopped manufacturing asbestos insulation in 1970, the suits seek damages for alleged injuries and wrongful deaths supposedly attributable to exposure to the insulation. Mr. Leavitt claimed that the company simply could not survive the burden of the costs of all the present and possible future litigation.[1] While the general business community probably paid little or no attention to UNR's plight, their predicament did not go unnoticed by the Denver based Manville Corporation, the nation's, if not the world's, single largest producer of asbestos and asbestos products.

On Thursday, August 26, 1982, the Manville Corporation (formerly Johns-Manville) and its principal American and Canadian affiliates filed for reorganization under Chapter 11 in the United States District Court for the Southern District of New York. Manville's unexpected bankruptcy petition stunned the financial community, surprised Congress, shocked their creditors, suppliers, and customers, totally outraged those who had filed damage suits against them, and raised a complex tangle of legal, political, and ethical issues that will have far-reaching implications for millions of Americans. The drama of the Manville announcement stems from the fact that this is the same Manville Corporation that last year earned $60.3 million on sales exceeding $2 billion with an unencumbered net worth of $1.1 billion. This is the same Manville that ranks 181 on the "Fortune 500" list of American corporations. And this is the same Manville that has been traditionally included in the 30 companies used to calculate the prestigious Dow Jones industrial average, the most watched indicator of prices on the New York Stock Exchange. While there are many factors in the equation that resulted in Manville's final decision, like UNR's unprecedented decision less than a month earlier, Manville Chairman John A. McKinney angrily announced that this company could no longer sustain or survive the blitz of "toxic torts" that it was now facing.

Many of Manville's critics have claimed that Manville, and by implication UNR, is acting in an immoral and illegal manner. They are held to be immoral insofar as their critics feel that they are using the "bankruptcy boom" as a means of avoiding just compensation for those who have truly been injured or killed due to excessive or abusive exposure to asbestos. Manville is accused of acting illegally in that the spirit and purpose of the 1978 Bankruptcy Act is being violated because no company has ever filed for Chapter 11 given the size of their assets, their net worth, and their yearly sales figures. Other observers suggest that this is much too simplistic a response to the situation and that whatever the final merits of Manville's petition the factors involved in their decision warrant a careful and detailed analysis.

Asbestos is a naturally occurring mineral found in various concentrations across the earth's surface. Asbestos is the best known member of a family of fibrous silicate minerals, which share the common attribute of being able to be separated into relatively soft, silky strands. Because of its high tensile strength, superior flexibility, and durability and because of its resistance to fire, heat, and corrosion, asbestos finds broad use in many essential applications. In all, asbestos is a component in more than 3,000 industrial and consumer products. It is an essential ingredient in plastics, textiles, roofing tiles, brake linings, insulation and fire wall materials, cement water and sewerage pipes, and vinyl floor coverings. Because it is plentiful in nature and relatively inexpensive in cost, asbestos continues to be widely used. According to the Bureau of Mines, 349,000 metric tons of asbestos was used to make various products in this country in 1981.

Industry spokesmen are quick to point out that its unique combination of properties makes asbestos superior to any other natural or man-made fiber. After more than a decade of intense well-financed research for an asbestos substitute, none has been found that works as well or makes as much economic sense. Robert Clifton, asbestos commodities specialist for the National Bureau of Mines, stated that while there are substitutes for practically every application in which asbestos is used, they are either inferior, more costly, or contain serious health hazards.[2]

Like many of the naturally occurring materials, asbestos may also pose a health hazard unless properly handled. Today there is little doubt that excessive exposure to airborne asbestos fiber can cause disease, principally of the respiratory tract. Some forms of asbestos consist of fibers so small that 1,600 particles can occupy the space of a single human hair. Because of their minute size and needle-like shape asbestos fibers can be inhaled into the lungs; and because they are relatively indestructible they may be substantially resistant to the body's normal defense mechanisms.[3]

The insidious aspect of asbestos-related illnesses is that they have an incubation period of 10 to 40 years. Diseases of this type are usually referred to as "delayed emergence diseases." Asbestos has been primarily associated with three forms of respiratory illness: asbestosis, mesothelioma, lung cancer. Asbestosis is a chronic and sometimes fatal lung disease characterized by extensive scarring of the lung tissue and progressive shortness of breath much like emphysema. This disease has a latency period of 10 to 20 years. Mesothelioma is a fatal if rare cancer of the chest or abdomen lining. Its average latency is 25 to 40 years. Asbestos-related lung cancer is a highly virulent and always fatal form of the disease which has a latency period of 20 to 40 years. Moreover, modern research has also suggested a link between asbestos fibers and cancer of the gastrointestinal tract, larynx, and kidney.

In a recent statement in *Newsweek* magazine Dr. William Blot of the National Cancer Institute claims that excessive exposure to asbestos fibers "appears to be the greatest single source of occupational cancer."[4] Medical specialists estimate that over the past 40 years 9 to 20 million Americans have been exposed to large amounts of asbestos in the workplace and that *at least* 5,000 cancer related deaths directly linked to asbestos will occur annually until the end of the century. According to Manville, the major occupational groups that may have been exposed to excessive amounts of asbestos in the past are divided into three categories: (1) Workers in mines, mills, and factories where raw asbestos was used; (2) Insulation workers who worked with non-bonded or non-encapsulated asbestos-containing products; (3) Workers exposed to asbestos while in government controlled naval shipyards.[5]

For all intents and purposes the origins of Manville's present predicament begins with this country's preparation for World War II. Because of its
fire resistant qualities, asbestos was extensively used in government owned
or controlled shipyards in the production of 6,000 new warships and freight-
ers and the refitting of 65,000 other vessels. Over 4 million workers were
directly exposed to clouds of asbestos dust in their race to build and repair
America's naval arsenal.[6] While it is the case that after the war asbestos
came to be looked upon as the "miracle mineral" and was extensively used
throughout the construction industry, the shipyard workers remain the largest single group exposed to the possible effects of asbestos poisoning. It is
from this group that Manville is experiencing the largest number of lawsuits
and claims.

By the summer of 1982 Manville was being sued at the rate of 500 new
cases a month. Having already settled 3,500 suits at a cost of over $50
million[7] and with 16,500 suits still pending, Manville commissioned a study
by Epidemiology Resources, Inc., a small, Boston based, health data research company, to determine how many new lawsuits would probably be
filed against them. The report was filed on August 4, 1982, and it forecast
that by the year 2009 Manville could conservatively expect another 32,000
suits. Together these pending and probable suits could cost the company
anywhere between $2 to $5 billion, budgeting $40,000 per settlement based
on the assumption of a modest rate of inflation and an average win/loss
ratio.

While many critics contend that Manville's figures are an excessive
extrapolation, a number of independent authorities maintain that Manville's figures are not only conservative but very low estimates indeed. Dr.
Irving J. Selikoff, chief of Environmental Health at Mt. Sinai Hospital in
New York and a leading authority on asbestos-related disease, claims that
Manville is vastly underestimating their future rate of litigation and probable liabilities. According to Dr. Selikoff's figures, from 1940 to 1980 about 27
million workers were exposed to asbestos. He claims that while only a fraction of those exposed developed cancer, the number of cancer deaths
among asbestos workers exceeds the average in the population by 8,000 to
10,000 a year. This means, said Dr. Selikoff, that the total liabilities to
Manville and other asbestos companies could reach $40 to $80 billion![8]

Based on the "Epidemiology Resources Report" and after an intensive
review by a "blue-ribbon committee," Manville's board of directors announced their decision to file for reoiganization under Chapter 11 of the
Bankruptcy Act. In filing for reorganization Manville has won at least a
temporary respite from its legal woes. Although the company will continue
operating during the reorganization, all suits now pending are frozen and no
new suits can be filed. While the company develops a plan to handle its
liabilities, it is up to the bankruptcy courts to deal with all present claims as
well as establishing guidelines for the handling of any future claims.

In a full-page interview that appeared as an ad in 21 major newspapers one day after the bankruptcy filing, Manville Chairman John A. McKinney contended that while the decision to apply for Chapter 11 was a dramatic one, he stressed that the company was not acting in a desperate manner. "This is not a financial failure," McKinney emphasized.

> Nothing is wrong with our business. Filing under Chapter 11 does not mean that the company is going out of business and that its assets will be liquidated. Lawsuits are the problem. We will continue to manufacture and ship high quality products and provide the same services, as always.[9]

McKinney went on to say that he was personally angered by and opposed to the decision to file for bankruptcy, but he agreed with the board of directors that there was no other logical recourse legally left to the company.

Mr. G. Earl Parker, Manville Senior Vice-President, in testimony before a "House Subcommittee on Labor Standards" on September 9, 1982, itemized the four chief reasons that forced Manville to the bankruptcy courts:

1. to avoid the largest tort litigation ever witnessed;
2. federal standards in regard to accounting principles and requirements;
3. legal disputes with insurance companies;
4. the federal government's unwillingness to establish a compensation fund for asbestos victims.[10]

The first two points are interconnected. With Manville being faced with the possibility of a minimum of $2 billion in litigation costs and liabilities, the company found itself, at least on paper, in a difficult financial position. As John McKinney pointed out, the company's net worth is only $1.1 billion. Therefore, if Manville did not file for bankruptcy

> we would have to strangle the company slowly, by deferring maintenance and postponing capital expenditures. We would also have to cannibalize our good businesses to just keep going. . . . We would have to mortgage our plants and properties and new credit would be most difficult and expensive to obtain.[11]

Because Manville is a publicly-held company it is required to comply with certain accounting requirements. Federal law states that a company is supposed to estimate the costs of all current and probable litigation whenever possible and create a reserve fund for the liability in an amount equal to the estimated costs. Given the volume of present and projected litigation facing Manville, it is clearly impossible for them to establish such a fund even on a liquidation basis. "Without court protection," McKinney insisted, "the lawsuits, one way or another, would cripple us."[12]

Perhaps the least appreciated factor in the equation that led Manville to Chapter 11 is the long disputes it has been having with its major insurance carriers. According to Manville spokesman John Lonnquist, "Except for one company, all are essentially withholding payments."[13] The insurance industry has been split into two warring camps by the flood of asbestos-related lawsuits that led Manville to declare bankruptcy. Some insurance experts suggest that it is the insurance industry's war, more than any other factor, that has prompted the bankruptcy filing. At the heart of the insurance battle is the question of whether an insurer's liability begins when the workers were exposed to asbestos or when the asbestos-related disease manifests itself, typically many years after exposre. As one might expect, insurance firms who covered the asbestos manufacturers in the early years favor the manifestation theory. And the insurers who have written coverage for the asbestos industry more recently are fighting for the exposure theory. Manville's problem is that as long as the insurance companies are fighting among themselves about whose policies cover what, Manville must use its corporate assets to pay both the fees and damages involved in all suits. For its part, Manville is presently suing all of its insurers (27 companies); they are asking that all outstanding claims be paid as well as $5 billion in punitive damages.[14]

No matter what the other reasons that have led Manville to apply for Chapter 11, in so doing it clearly hopes to encourage the support and active participation of the federal government in establishing a compensation program for all asbestos victims. Up until now the government has steadfastly denied responsibility and refused to participate in any further compensation fund beyond the presently mandated compensation programs.[15] John McKinney vigorously rejects the allegation that Manville is simply seeking a federal "bailout" vis-á-vis Chrysler or the railroads. Manville maintains that the government should pay a large portion of the astestos claims for three reasons:

1. The government was the chief contractor for the shipyards and the major employer of the asbestos-exposed workers.
2. The government established the specifications for all aspects of the sale and use of asbestos in wartime shipbuilding.
3. Since the war the government has been responsible for the establishment and policing of all safety standards regarding asbestos.[16]

Manville insists that it has always conformed to government standards and that it always tried to establish company regulations that reflected the latest word in scientific achievement. Tragically for many workers, however, it has taken decades for the medical/scientific community, industry, and the government to obtain the broad knowledge we have today. The public literature has reported since the 1930s that factory workers exposed to 100 percent raw asbestos fiber experienced an increased risk of contracting a pulmonary fibrosis that has come to be called asbestosis. But there was no reason to believe that any worker faced a health risk from using finished asbestos products, and there was no reason to believe that workers faced any health risks other than asbestosis.[17] In 1964 Dr. Irving Selikoff of Mt. Sinai School of Medicine in New York reported the results of a study of insulation workers and changed everyone's understanding of the extent of potential health problems from excessive exposure to asbestos. Dr. Selikoff's findings showed that exposure to asbestos from products such as asbestos insulation, even though below the accepted standard, heightened the risk of disease among insulation workers. In addition, he showed that there was a markedly increased risk of lung cancer in asbestos insulation workers who smoked cigarettes. Studies since then have supported Dr. Selikoff's findings.[18]

Given this information and the new standards that have evolved, Manville is convinced that asbestos can and is being used safely. Today's disease problems, Manville contends, are a legacy of the past when the state of medical knowledge concerning asbestos was inadequate. Therefore, while Manville recognizes that it has participated in the mistakes of the past, the company feels that the government has been a full partner in these errors. As a partner Manville is willing to share costs with the government in the establishment of a statutory compensation program to aid all those who have contracted an asbestos disease. According to John McKinney, without such a program there will be no help for present and future victims of asbestos, and there will be no way to save the Manville Corporation from going defunct!

The issues raised by the Manville bankruptcy proceedings are many and highly complex.

1. Is Manville telling the truth about their knowledge of the health factors involved in excessive exposure to asbestos? Is it true that they had no awareness of the connection between asbestos and certain respiratory distress diseases, including cancer? Or is it the case, as many of their critics contend, that they conspired for over 40 years to both deny and cover up any knowledge of the long-term ill effects of working with and around asbestos and asbestos products?

2. If it is true that Manville did conspire to cover up any knowledge of ill effects of asbestos, are they justified in petitioning the government for their support in establishing a compensation program for asbestos victims?

3. Can the 1978 Federal Bankruptcy Act be used as a means of seeking relief from possible future claims and liabilities?

4. In regard to general product liability, how far back can claims be made against a company? More importantly, is it just to sue a company when, at the time, it acted legally, cautiously, and in good faith?

5. Given the fact that Manville was simply the producer/supplier of a product and not the contractor, designer, or an agent in charge, is the federal government justified in denying further responsibility?

6. Manville's effort to protect itself from financial claims by asbestos victims is a dramatic reminder that the nation has not come to grips with the problems created by environmentally caused diseases. The company's petition underscores the financial impact on both industry and the victims of health problems arising from hazardous substances.[19]

7. A major by-product of Manville's actions may be the restructuring of the legal responsibilities of industrial insurance carriers. Specifically, how does an insurance company determine a valid claim and when may a company decide to deny or withhold a claim?

8. Because of the new laws regarding product liability as well as the legal requirements and public expectations regarding corporate responsibility, the question arises: "Is any company totally safe from being put out of business?"[20]

After all is said and done, the central issue in this case for most people is not that Manville is filing for Chapter 11 to avoid immediate and future liability, but that Manville is alive, doing well, highly solvent, and not even close to closing up shop and yet it is filing for bankruptcy! Manville claims that just because their actions are unprecedented (save for UNR) and highly unorthodox, it does not follow that they are acting in an immoral or illegal fashion. Manville officials insist that filing for bankruptcy was unavoidable and in the best interest of its stockholders, employees, and creditors. Moreover, they feel that in the long run their decision will better benefit the victims of asbestos-related diseases. Earl Parker testified that only by filing now could Manville ensure that the asbestos disease claimants will receive the money owed them in the coming decades.[21] Manville Chairman John McKinney insists that Chapter 11 is the only orderly way possible for the company to treat everyone fairly. He emphasized that Manville's failure is really our court and legislative systems' failure to provide a reasonable way to compensate victims of an unexpected occupational health catastrophe. McKinney is firmly convinced that Manville's problems are America's problems and the government should and must help![22]

In all candor it must be remembered that Manville's actions are not without danger. To the extent that Manville is using Chapter 11 as a shelter against the rush of asbestos litigation, the company is nevertheless taking a risky gamble. Manville must now operate under the eye of a federal bankruptcy judge, and, said Lawrence King, Professor of Law at New York University, "once you file, there is always a risk of liquidation." "It is not yet clear," said King, "that the bankruptcy proceeding will succeed in mooting the claims against Manville."[23] No one really knows how Manville's decision to apply for Chapter 11 will ultimately affect the status of the litigation and claims now in the courts. The only thing that is clear is that each decision in the Manville controversy will be breaking new legal ground each step of the way, whether it be in regard to Manville itself, the asbestos industry in general, government regulations and responsibilities, and/or the future status of public health and environmental policy.[24]

NOTES

1. *Wall Street Journal,* July 30, 1982, p. 4.
2. *New York Times,* September 2, 1982, Sec. D, p. 2.
3. *Compensating Workers for Asbestos-Related Disease,* Asbestos Compensation Coalition, 1981, p. 1.
4. *Newsweek,* September 6, 1982, pp. 54, 55.
5. *Asbestos, Health and John-Manville,* Johns-Manville Corporate Relations Department, September 1981, p. 5.
6. "Kirkland & Ellis Report: The Government's Legal Responsibilities," Manville Corporate Relations Department, September 8, 1982.
7. *Time,* September 6, 1982, p. 17.
8. *New York Times,* August 31, 1982, Sec. A, p. 13.
9. *New York Times,* August 27, 1982, Sec. D, p. 3.
10. "The Testimony of G. Earl Parker, U.S. House of Representatives," Manville Corporate Relations Department, September 9, 1982.
11. *New York Times,* August 27, 1982, Sec. D, p. 3.
12. Ditto.
13. *Science News,* September 18, 1982, Vol. 122, p. 183.
14. *New York Times,* September 7, 1982, Sec. D, p. 2.
15. *Sci Now,* September 18, 1982, Vol. 122, p. 182. *New York Times,* September 10, 1982, Sec. D, p. 1.
16. "Kirkland & Ellis Report: The Government's Legal Responsibilities," Manville Corporate Relations Department, September 8, 1982.
17. "The Testimony of G. Earl Parker, The Senate Subcommittee on Courts," Manville Corporate Relations Department, November 19, 1982.
18. *Asbestos, health and John-Manville,* Johns-Manville Corporate Relations Department, September 1981, p. 6.
19. *New York Times,* August 31, 1982, Sec. A, p. 13.
20. *Chemical and Engineering News,* September 6, 1982, p. 6.
21. "The Testimony of G. Earl Parker, U.S. House of Representatives," Manville Corporate Relations Department, September 9, 1982.
22. *New York Times,* August 27, 1982, Sec. D, p. 3.
23. *Newsweek,* September 6, 1982, p. 55.
24. Whatever the final legal outcome of Manville's actions the company has so far been able to survive and accrue some capital in preparation for claims still pending. On October 29, 1982, Curtis G. Linke, a Manville spokesman, reported that the earnings for the third quarter in 1982 were higher than the corresponding quarter in 1981, $24.3 million as compared with $12.6 million. Linke suggested that the increase in net earnings in the third quarter was due to cost control measures, higher productivity, a national advertisement campaign, relief from litigations costs, and the deferral of interest payments as a result of filing for Chapter 11. *New York Times,* December 10, 1982, Sec. D, p. 1, p. 23.

When Did Johns-Manville Know?

JEFF COPLON

Even if the Manville Corp. is thrown out of bankruptcy court, Ted Kowalski and his fellow plaintiffs will be fighting uphill to collect on their damage suits. To date, New Jersey workers have been shunted to workers' compensation in cases of job-related illness or injury; no one has ever successfully sued an employer in civil court.

But in California, the state Supreme Court ruled in 1980 that the family of a dead J-M employee could sue the company for "fraud and conspiracy" in concealing the dangers of long-term exposure to asbestos.

By 1981, under the same principle, several judges throughout the country had ordered six-figure punitive awards to people outside the company who had taken sick after handling J-M products. In one case, a widow of a Cleveland insulation worker won $350,000 in punitive damages, in addition to $500,000 in compensatory damages.

For the victims in Manville, then, the legal issue is this: what did J-M know, and when did the company know it?

In its defense, J-M says it protected its own workers from asbestosis as best it could since the 1930s, that it followed the U.S. Public Health Service standard set in 1938, and that it was aware of no cancer threat until 1964.

But a growing body of evidence suggests otherwise—that J-M knew more than it admits, and that it deliberately suppressed medical information from its workers in Manville.

The first case of asbestosis was reported in 1907 in England, followed by conclusive medical research in 1930 and documentation of a link with lung cancer in 1934. In this country, the Journal of the American Medical Association reported on asbestosis in 1928—the same year Prudential Insurance suspended all policies on the lives of asbestos workers.

In the 1930s, J-M responded by taking annual chest X rays at the Manville plant and partially funding a study of asbestosis at Saranac Lake. But at the same time, recently disclosed correspondence between officers at J-M and other asbestos firms shows they sought to keep the bad news from spreading.

In December 1934, after reviewing galley proofs of the Saranac Lake study, J-M attorney Vandiver Brown requested revisions: "All we ask is that . . . none of the unfavorable [aspects] be unintentionally pictured in darker tones than the circumstances justify." The study was duly revised.

Jeff Coplon, "When Did J-M Know?" *Village Voice*, XXVIII, March 1, 1983, p. 16. Reprinted with permission.

In 1942 an outside attorney named Charles Roemer met with Brown. After his cousin, a doctor at a Paterson asbestos plant, found "lung changes" among many workers, Roemer approached J-M "to see how they were handling the asbestos health problem."

The answer, included in a sworn affidavit taken from the 83-year-old Roemer last September, pulled no punches: "Vandiver Brown stated that Johns-Manville's physical examination program had, indeed, also produced findings of X-ray evidence of asbestos disease among workers exposed to asbestos and that it was Johns-Manville's policy not to do anything, nor to tell the employees of the X-ray findings. Vandiver Brown went on to say that . . . if Johns-Manville's workers were told, they would stop working and file claims against Johns-Manville, and that it was Johns-Manville's policy to let them work until they quit work because of asbestosis or died as a result of asbestos-related diseases."

In 1952, Dr. Kenneth Smith, J-M's medical director, asked company executives to place a warning label on some asbestos products, which he felt could be dangerous to insulation workers. Their reply, he attested in a 1975 deposition, was that the corporation "is in business . . . to provide jobs for people and make money for stockholders, and they had to take into consideration the effects of everything they did and if the application of caution label would cut out sales, there would be serious financial implications." The warning labels were deferred until 1964.

In 1950 Dr. Nicholas Demy, a Somerset radiologist, found asbestos fibers imbedded within the lung cancer of a deceased J-M worker—demonstrating a link the industry would deny for 14 more years. Subsequently, J-M refused to supply Demy with occupational histories he needed to pursue the lead.

When it was clear the controversy over asbestos would not blow over, J-M was selective as to what research it backed. When Dr. Maxwell Borow, a surgeon at Somerset Medical Center, asked for $3500 in 1966 to mount an exhibit on the worst Manville cancer of all, the company declined: "They said they were not prepared to admit a causal relationship between asbestos and mesothelioma."

Even as the conflagration raged full blast, some say the company shrank from sounding an alarm. According to Wilber Ruff, a former J-M manager at its Pittsburgh, California, plant, company doctors were barred until 1971 from telling workers about their X rays or referring them to outside specialists.

"The company did not want to talk about these things and get employees upset," Ruff testified before Congress, "until such time as we knew our ground."

Few people will question a doctor who tells them they're healthy. It's what they want to hear, after all, that all will be well in the morning. And in a company town like Manville, filled with immigrants who spoke little English, the doctor was a man of learning, a high authority. If he said the X ray showed nothing, they must be fine. They weren't much for complaining.

"They're good people, strong people, with strong beliefs," said Ted Kowalski. "Someone took advantage of their goodness."

That remains true today. For all the hoopla and network specials about the lethal white fiber, there is no research to determine why certain workers are susceptible to asbestosis and related cancers, or how they might get sick under current workplace conditions.

"Neither the companies nor the insurance companies nor the government have shown the slightest interest in finding out how these diseases occur," said Dr. Irving Selikoff, the Mt. Sinai researcher whose 1964 paper was the first accepted by J-M. "One side says the other should pay for it. There's been no interest. So people will continue to die."

The Corporation as a Moral Person

Peter A. French

In one of his *New York Times* columns of not too long ago Tom Wicker's ire was aroused by a Gulf Oil Corporation advertisement that "pointed the finger of blame" for the energy crisis at all elements of our society (and supposedly away from the oil company). Wicker attacked Gulf Oil as the major, if not the sole, perpetrator of that crisis and virtually every other social ill, with the possible exception of venereal disease. It does not matter whether Wicker was serious or sarcastic in making his charges (I suspect he was in deadly earnest). I am interested in the sense ascriptions of moral responsibility make when their subjects are corporations. I hope to provide the foundation of a theory that allows treatment of corporations as members of the moral community, of equal standing with the traditionally acknowledged residents: biological human beings, and hence treats Wicker-type responsibility ascriptions as unexceptionable instances of a perfectly proper sort without having to paraphrase them. In short, corporations can be full-fledged moral persons and have whatever privileges, rights and duties as are, in the normal course of affairs, accorded to moral persons.

It is important to distinguish three quite different notions of what constitutes personhood that are entangled in our tradition: the metaphysi-

Peter A. French, "The Corporation as a Moral Person," *American Philosophical Quarterly*, 3 (1979), pp. 207–15. Reprinted with permission.

cal, moral and legal concepts. The entanglement is clearly evident in Locke's account of personal identity. He writes that the term "person" is "a *forensic* term, appropriating actions and their merit; and so belongs only to *intelligent agents*, capable of law, and happiness, and misery."[1] He goes on to say that by consciousness and memory persons are capable of extending themselves into the past and thereby become "concerned and *accountable*."[2] Locke is historically correct in citing the law as a primary origin of the term "person." But he is incorrect in maintaining that its legal usage somehow entails its metaphysical sense, agency; and whether or not either sense, but especially the metaphysical, is interdependent on the moral sense, accountability, is surely controversial. Regarding the relationship between metaphysical and moral persons there are two distinct schools of thought. According to one, to be a metaphysical person is to be a moral one; to understand what it is to be accountable one must understand what it is to be an intelligent or a rational agent and vice versa; while according to the other, being an agent is a necessary but not sufficient condition of being a moral person. Locke holds the interdependence view with which I agree, but he roots both moral and metaphysical persons in the juristic person, which is, I think, wrongheaded. The preponderance of current thinking tends to some version of the necessary pre-condition view, but it does have the virtue of treating the legal person as something apart.

It is of note that many contemporary moral philosophers and economists both take a pre-condition view of the relationship between the metaphysical and moral person and also adopt a particular view of the legal personhood of corporations that effectually excludes corporations *per se* from the class of moral persons. Such philosophers and economists champion the least defensible of a number of possible interpretations of the juristic personhood of corporations, but their doing so allows them to systematically sidestep the question of whether corporations can meet the conditions of metaphysical personhood.[3]

*   *   *

Many philosophers, including, I think, Rawls, have rather uncritically relied upon what they incorrectly perceive to be the most defensible juristic treatment of collectivities such as corporations as a paradigm for the treatment of corporations in their moral theories. The concept of corporate legal personhood under any of its popular interpretations is, I want to argue, virtually useless for moral purposes.

Following many writers on jurisprudence, a juristic person may be defined as any entity that is a subject of a right. There are good etymological grounds for such an inclusive neutral definition. The Latin *"persona"* originally referred to *dramatis personae*, and in Roman law the term was adopted to refer to anything that could act on either side of a legal dispute. [It was not until Boethius' definition of a person: *"Persona est naturae rationabilis individua substantia* (a person is the individual subsistence of a rational nature)" that metaphysical traits were ascribed to persons.] In effect, in Roman legal tradition persons are creations, artifacts, of the law itself, i.e., of the legislature that enacts the law, and are not considered to have, or only have incidentally, existence of any kind outside of the legal sphere. The law, on the Roman interpretation, is systematically ingorant of the biological status of its subjects.

The Roman notion applied to corporations is popularly known as the Fiction Theory. . . .

∗   ∗   ∗

The Fiction Theory's major rival in American jurisprudence and the view that does seem to inform Rawls' account is what I shall call "the Legal Aggregate theory of the Corporation." It holds that the names of corporate bodies are only umbrellas that cover (but do not shield) certain biological persons. The Aggregate Theory treats biological status as having legal priority and corporate existence as a contrivance for purposes of summary reference. (Generally, it may be worth mention, Aggregate Theorists tend to ignore employees and identify corporations with directors, executives and stockholders. The model on which they stake their claim is no doubt that of the primitive partnership.) I have shown elsewhere[4] that to treat a corporation as an aggregate for any purposes is to fail to recognize the key logical differences between corporations and mobs. The Aggregate Theory, then, despite the fact that it has been quite popular in legislatures, courtrooms, and on street corners, simply ignores key logical, socio-economic and historical facts of corporate existence. It might prove of some value in clarifying the dispute between Fiction and Aggregate theorists to mention a rather famous case in the English law. (The case is cited by Hallis.) It is that of *Continental Tyre and Rubber Co., Ltd.* vs. *Daimler Co., Ltd.* Very sketchily, the Continental Tyre company was incorporated in England and carried on its business there. Its business was the selling of tires made in Germany, and all of its directors were German subjects in residence in Germany, and all but one of its shares were held by German subjects. The case arose during the First World War, and it turned on the issue of whether the company was an English subject by virtue of its being incorporated under the English law and independent of its directors and stockholders, and could hence bring suit in an English court against an English subject while a state of war existed. The majority opinion of The Court of Appeals (5–1) was that the corporation was an entity created by statute and hence was "a different person altogether from the subscribers to the memorandum or the shareholders on the register."[5]

∗   ∗   ∗

Underlying all of these interpretations of corporate legal personhood is a distinction, embedded in the law itself, that renders them unhelpful for our purposes. Being a subject of rights is often contrasted in the law with being an "administrator of rights." Any number of entities and associations can and have been the subjects of legal rights. Legislatures have given rights to unborn human beings, they have reserved rights for human beings long after their death, and in some recent cases they have invested rights in generations of the future.[6] Of course such subjects of rights, though they are legal persons, cannot dispose of their rights, cannot administer them, because to administer a right one must be an agent, i.e., able to act in certain ways. It may be only an historical accident that most legal cases are cases in which "the subject of right X" and "the administrator of right X" are co-referential. It is nowhere required by law, under any of the three above theories or elsewhere, that it be so. Yet, it is possession of the attributes of an administrator of rights and not those of a subject of rights that are among the generally regarded conditions of moral personhood. It is a fundamental mistake to regard the fact of juristic corporate personhood as having settled the question of the moral personhood of a corporation one way or the other.

Two helpful lessons however, are learned from an investigation of the legal personhood of corporations: (1) biological existence is not essentially associated with the concept of a person (only the fallacious Aggregate Theory depends upon reduction to biological referents) and (2) a paradigm for the form of an inclusive neutral definition of a moral person is provided: "a subject of a right." I shall define a moral person as the referent of any proper name or description that can be a non-eliminatable subject of what I shall call (and presently discuss) a responsibility ascription of the second type. The non-eliminatable nature of the subject should be stressed because responsibility and other moral predicates are neutral as regards person and *personum* prediction.[7] Though we might say that the Ox-Bow mob should be held responsible for the death of three men, a mob is an example of what I have elsewhere called an aggregate collectivity with no identity over and above that of the sum of the identities of its component membership, and hence to use "the Ox-Bow mob" as the subject of such ascriptions is to make summary reference to each member of the mob. For that reason mobs do not qualify as metaphysical or moral persons.

There are at least two significantly different types of responsibility ascriptions that should be distinguished in ordinary usage (not counting the laudatory recommendation, "He is a responsible lad.") The first type pins responsibility on someone or something, the who-dun-it or what-dun-it sense. Austin has pointed out that it is usually used when an event or action is thought by the speaker to be untoward. (Perhaps we are most interested in the failures rather than the successes that punctuate our lives.)

The second type of responsibility ascription, parasitic upon the first, involves the notion of accountability. "Having a responsibility" is interwoven with the notion "Having a liability to answer," and having such a liability or obligation seems to imply (as Anscombe has noted[8]) the existence of some sort of authority relationship either between people or between people and a deity or in some weaker versions between people and social norms. The kernel of insight that I find intuitively compelling, is that for someone to legitimately hold someone else responsible for some event there must exist or have existed a responsibility relationship between them such that in regard to the event in question the latter was answerable to the former. In other words, "X is responsible for y," as a second-type ascription, is properly uttered by someone Z if X in respect to y is or was accountable to Z. Responsibility relationships are created in a multitude of ways, e.g., through promises, contracts, compacts, hirings, assignments, appointments, by agreeing to enter a Rawlsian original position, etc. The right to hold responsible is often delegatable to third parties; though in the case of moral responsibility no delegation occurs because no person is excluded from the relationship: moral responsibility relationships hold reciprocally and without prior agreements among all moral persons. No special arrangement needs to be established between parties for anyone to hold someone morally responsible for his acts or, what amounts to the same thing, every person is a party to a responsibility relationship with all other persons as regards the doing or refraining from doing of certain acts: those that take descriptions that use moral notions.

Because our interest is in the criteria of moral personhood and not the content of morality we need not pursue this idea further. What I have maintained is that moral responsibility, although it is neither contractual nor optional, is not a class apart but an extension of ordinary, garden-variety, responsibility. What is needed in regard to the present subject then is an account of the requirements for entry into any responsibility relationship, and we have already seen that the notion of the juristic person does not provide a sufficient account. For example, the deceased in a probate case cannot be held responsible in the relevant way by anyone, even though the deceased is a juristic person, a subject of rights.

A responsibility ascription of the second type amounts to the assertion of a conjunctive proposition, the first conjunct of which identifies the subject's actions with or as the cause of an event (usually an untoward one) and the second conjunct asserts that the action in question was intended by the subject or that the event was the direct result of an intentional act of the subject. In addition to what it asserts it implies that the subject is accountable to the speaker (in the case at hand) because of the subject's relationship to the speaker (who the speaker is or what the speaker is, a member of the "moral community," a surrogate for that aggregate). The primary focus of responsibility ascriptions of the second type is on the subject's intentions rather than, though not to the exclusion of, occasions. Austin wrote: "In considering responsibility, few things are considered more important than to establish whether a man *intended* to do A, or whether he did A intentionally."[9] To be the subject of a responsibility ascription of the second type, to be a party in responsibility relationships, hence to be a moral person, the subject must be at minimum, what I shall call a Davidsonian agent.[10] If corporations are moral persons, they will be non-eliminatable Davidsonian agents.

For a corporation to be treated as a Davidsonian agent it must be the case that some things that happen, some events, are describable in a way that makes certain sentences true, sentences that say that some of the things a corporation does were intended by the corporation itself. That is not accomplished if attributing intentions to a corporation is only a shorthand way of attributing intentions to the biological persons who comprise e.g. its board of directors. If that were to turn out to be the case then on metaphysical if not logical grounds there would be no way to distinguish between corporations and mobs. I shall argue, however, that a Corporation's Internal Decision Structure (its CID Structure) is the requisite redescription device that licenses the predication of corporate intentionality.

* * *

Certain events, that is, actions, are describable as simply the bodily movements of human beings and sometimes those same events are redescribable in terms of their upshots, as bringing about something, e.g., (from Austin[11]) feeding penguins *by* throwing them peanuts ("by" is the most common way we connect different descriptions of the same event[12]), and sometimes those events can be redescribed as the effects of some prior cause; then they are described as done for reasons, done in order to bring about something, e.g., feeding the penguins peanuts in order to kill them. Usually what we single out as that prior cause is some desire or felt need combined with the belief that the object of the desire will be achieved by the action undertaken. (This, I think, is what Aristotle meant when he maintained that acting requires desire.) Saying "someone (X) did y intentionally" is to describe an event (y) as the upshot of X's having had a reason for doing it which was the cause of his doing it.

It is obvious that a corporation's doing something involves or includes human beings doing things and that the human beings who occupy various positions in a corporation usually can be described as having reasons for *their* behavior. In virtue of those descriptions they may be properly held responsible for their behavior, *ceteris paribus*. What needs to be shown is that there is sense in saying that corporations and not just people who work in them, have reasons for doing what they do. Typically, we will be told that it is the directors, or the managers, etc., that really have the corporate reasons and desires, etc., and that although corporate actions may not be reducible without remainder, corporate intentions are always reducible to human intentions.

Every corporation has an internal decision structure. CID Structures have two elements of interest to us here: (1) an organizational or responsibility flow chart that delineates stations and levels within the corporate power structure and (2) corporate decision recognition rule(s) (usually embedded in something called "corporation policy"). The CID Structure is the personnel organization for the exercise of the corporation's power with respect to its ventures, and as such its primary function is to draw experience from various levels of the corporation into a decision-making and ratification process. When operative and properly activated, the CID Structure accomplishes a subordination and synthesis of the intentions and acts of various biological persons into a corporate decision. When viewed in another way, as already suggested, the CID Structure licenses the descriptive transformation of events, seen under another aspect as the acts of biological persons (those who occupy various stations on the organizational chart), to corporate acts by exposing the corporate character of those events. A functioning CID Structure *incorporates* acts of biological persons. For illustrative purposes, suppose we imagine that an event E has at least two aspects, that is, can be described in two non-identical ways. One of those aspects is "Executive X's doing y" and one is "Corporation C's doing z." The corporate act and the individual act may have different properties; indeed they have different causal ancestors though they are causally inseparable. (The causal inseparability of these acts I hope to show is a product of the CID Structure, X's doing y is not the cause of C's doing z nor is C's doing z the cause of X's doing y although if X's doing y causes event F then C's doing z causes F and vice versa.

✻　✻　✻

Supose, for illustrative purposes, we activate a CID Structure in a corporation, Wicker's favorite, the Gulf Oil Corporation. Imagine that three executives X, Y and Z have the task of deciding whether or not Gulf Oil will join a world uranium cartel. X, Y, and Z have before them an Everest of papers that have been prepared by lower echelon executives. Some of the papers will be purely factual reports, some will be contingency plans, some will be formulations of positions developed by various departments, some will outline financial considerations, some will be legal opinions and so on. Insofar as these will all have been processed through Gulf's CID Structure system, the personal reasons, if any, individual executives may have had when writing their reports and recommendations in a specific way will have been diluted by the subordination of individual inputs to peer group input even before X, Y and Z review the matter. X, Y and Z take a vote. Their taking of a vote is authorized procedure in the Gulf CID Structure, which is to say that under these circumstances the vote of X, Y and Z can be redescribed as the corporation's making a decision: that is, the event "XYZ voting" may be redescribed to expose an aspect otherwise unrevealed, that is quite different from its other aspects, e.g., from X's voting in the affirmative. Redescriptive exposure of a procedurally corporate aspect of an event, however, is not to be confused with a description of an event that makes true a sentence that says that the corporation did something intentionally. But the

CID Structure, as already suggested, also provides the grounds in its other type of recognitor for such an attribution of corporate intentionality. Simply, when the corporate act is consistent with an instantiation or an implementation of established corporate policy, then it is proper to describe it as having been done for corporate reasons, as having been caused by a corporate desire coupled with a corporate belief and so, in other words, as corporate-intentional.

An event may, under one of its aspects, be described as the conjunctive act "X did a (or as X intentionally did a) & Y did a (or as Y intentionally did a) & Z did a (or as Z intentionally did a)" (where a = voted in the affirmative on the question of Gulf Oil joining the cartel). Given the Gulf CID Structure, formulated in this instance as the conjunction of rules: when the occupants of positions A, B and C on the organizational chart unanimously vote to do something and if doing that something is consistent with an instantiation or an implementation of general corporate policy and *ceteris paribus*, then the corporation has decided to do it for corporate reasons, the event is redescribable as "the Gulf Oil Corporation did j for corporate reasons f" (where j is "decided to join the cartel" and f is any reason (desire + belief) consistent with basic policy of Gulf Oil, e.g., increasing profits) or simply as "Gulf Oil Corporation intentionally did j." This is a rather technical way of saying that in these circumstances the executives' voting is, given its CID Structure, also the corporation deciding to do something, and that regardless of the personal reasons the executives have for voting as they do and even if their reasons are inconsistent with established corporate policy or even if one of them has no reason at all for voting as he does, the corporation still has reasons for joining the cartel; that is, joining is consistent with the inviolate corporate general policies as encrusted in the precedent of previous corporate actions and its statements of purpose as recorded in its certificate of incorporation, annual reports, etc. The corporation's only method of achieving its desires or goals is the activation of the personnel who occupy its various positions. However, if X voted affirmatively purely for reasons of personal monetary gain (suppose he had been bribed to do so) that does not alter the fact that the corporate reason for joining the cartel was to minimize competition and hence pay higher dividends to its shareholders. Corporations have reasons because they have interest in doing those things that are likely to result in realization of their established corporate goals regardless of the transient self-interest of directors, managers, etc. If there is a difference between corporate goals and desires and those of human beings it is probably that the corporate ones are relatively stable and not very wide ranging, but that is only because corporations can do relatively fewer things than human beings, being confined in action predominately to a limited socio-economic sphere. The attribution of corporate intentionality is opaque with respect to other possible descriptions of the event in question. It is, of course, in a corporation's interest that its component membership view the corporate purposes as instrumental in the achievement of their own goals. (Financial reward is the most common way this is achieved.)

It will be objected that a corporation's policies reflect only the current goals of its directors. But that is certainly not logically necessary nor is it in practice true for most large corporations. Usually, of course, the original incorporators will have organized to further their individual interests and/or to meet goals which they shared. But even in infancy the melding of disparate interests and purposes gives rise to a corporate long-range point of view that is distinct from the intents and purposes of the collection of incorporators viewed individually. Also, corporate basic purposes and policies, as already mentioned, tend to be relatively stable when compared to those of individuals and not couched in the kind of language that would be appropriate to individual purposes. Furthermore, as histories of corporations will show, when policies are amended or altered it is usually only peripheral issues that are involved. Radical policy alteration constitutes a new corporation, a point that is captured in the incorporation laws of such states as Delaware. ("Any power which is not enumerated in the charter and the general law or which cannot be inferred from those two sources is *ultra vires* of the corporation.") Obviously underlying the objection is an uneasiness about the fact that corporate intent is dependent upon policy and purpose that is but an artifact of the socio-psychology of a group of biological persons. Corporate intent seems somehow to be a tarnished illegitimate offspring of human intent. But this objection is another form of the anthropocentric bias. By concentrating on possible descriptions of events and by acknowledging only that the possibility of describing something as an agent depends upon whether or not it can be properly described as having done something (the description of some aspect of an event) for a reason, we avoid the temptation to look for extensional criteria that would necessitate reduction to human referents.

The CID Structure licenses redescriptions of events as corporate and attributions of corporate intentionality while it does not obscure the private acts of executives, directors, etc. Although X voted to support the joining of the cartel because he was bribed to do so, X did not join the cartel, Gulf Oil Corporation joined the cartel. Consequently, we may say that X did something for which he should be held morally responsible, yet whether or not Gulf Oil Corporation should be held morally responsible for joining the cartel is a question that turns on issues that may be unrelated to X's having accepted a bribe.

Of course Gulf Oil Corporation cannot join the cartel unless X or somebody who occupies position A on the organizational chart votes in the affirmative. What that shows, however, is that corporations are collectivities. That should not, however, rule out the possibility of their having metaphysical status, as being Davidsonian agents, and being thereby full-fledged moral persons.

This much seems to me clear: we can describe many events in terms of certain physical movements of human beings and we also can sometimes describe those events as done for reasons by those human beings, but further we can sometimes describe those events as corporate and still further as done for corporate reasons that are qualitatively different from whatever personal reasons, if any, component members may have for doing what they do.

Corporate agency resides in the possibility of CID Structure licensed redescription of events as corporate-intentional. That may still appear to be downright mysterious, although I do not think it is, for human agency as I have suggested, resides in the possibility of description as well.

Although further elaboration is needed, I hope I have said enough to make plausible the view that we have good reasons to acknowledge the non-eliminatable agency of corporations. I have maintained that Davidsonian agency is a necessary and sufficient condition of moral personhood. I cannot further argue that position here (I have done so elsewhere). On the basis of the foregoing analysis, however, I think that grounds have been provided for holding corporations *per se* to account for what they do, for treating them as metaphysical persons *qua* moral persons.

NOTES

1. John Locke, *An Essay Concerning Human Understanding* (1960), Bk. II, Ch. XXVII.
2. Ibid.
3. For a particularly flagrant example see Michael Jensen and William Meckling, "Theory of the Firm: Managerial Behavior, Agency Costs and Ownership Structure," *Journal of Financial Economics*, vol. 3 (1976), pp. 305–60. On p. 311 they write, "The private corporation or firm is simply one form of legal fiction which serves as a nexus for contracting relationships. . . ."
4. "Types of Collectivities and Blame," *The Personalist*, vol. 56 (1975), pp. 160–69, and in the first chapter of my *Corporate and Collective Responsibility*, Columbia University Press, 1984.
5. "Continental Tyre and Rubber Co., Ltd. vs. Daimler Co., Ltd." (1915) K.B., p. 893.
6. And, of course, in earlier times animals have been given legal rights.
7. See Gerald Massey, "Tom, Dick, and Harry, and All The King's Men," *American Philosophical Quarterly*, vol. 13 (1976), pp. 89–108.
8. G. E. M. Anscombe, "Modern Moral Philosophy," *Philosophy*, vol. 33 (1958), pp. 1–19.
9. J. L. Austin, "Three Ways of Spilling Ink," in *Philosophical Papers* (Oxford, 1970), p. 273.
10. See, for example, Donald Davidson, "Agency," in *Agent, Action, and Reason*, ed. by Binkley, Bronaugh, and Marras (Toronto, 1971).
11. Austin, p. 275.
12. See Joel Feinberg, *Doing and Deserving* (Princeton, 1970), p. 134f.

Morality and the Ideal of Rationality in Formal Organizations

JOHN LADD

I. INTRODUCTORY

The purpose of this paper is to explore some of the moral problems that arise out of the interrelationships between individuals and formal organizations (or bureaucracies) in our society. In particular, I shall be concerned with the moral implications of the so-called ideal of rationality of formal organizations with regard to, on the one hand, the obligations of individuals both inside and outside an organization to that organization and, on the other hand, the moral responsibilities of organizations to individuals and to the public at large. I shall argue that certain facets of the organizational ideal are incompatible with the ordinary principles of morality and that the dilemma created by this incompatibility is one source of alienation in our contemporary, industrial society. The very conception of a formal organization or bureaucracy presents us with an ideological challenge that desperately needs to be met in some way or other.

The term "formal organization" will be used in a more or less technical sense to cover all sorts of bureaucracies, private and public. A distinctive mark of such organizations is that they make a clear-cut distinction between the acts and relationships of individuals in their official capacity within the organization and in their private capacity. Decisions of individual decision-makers in an organization are attributed to the organization and not to the individual. In that sense, they are impersonal. Individual office-holders are in principle replaceable by other individuals without affecting the continuity or identity of the organization. In this sense, it has sometimes been said that an organization is "immortal."

This kind of impersonality, in particular, the substitutability of individuals, is one way in which formal organizations differ from other kinds of social systems, e.g. the family, the community or the nation, which are collectivities that are dependent for their existence on specific individuals or groups of specific individuals and that change when they change. . . .

Social critics, e.g., W. H. Whyte, use phrases like the "smothering of the individual" to describe the contemporary situation created by organizations. It is not my purpose here to decry once more the unhappy condition of man occasioned by his submergence as an individual in the vast social, economic and political processes created by formal organizations. Instead, I shall try to show that the kind of alienation that we all feel and complain about is, at least in part, a logical necessity flowing from the concept of formal organizations itself, that is, it is a logical consequence of the particular language-game one is playing in organizational decision-making. My analysis is intended to be a logical analysis, but one that also has important ethical implications. . . .

Here we may find the concept of a language-game, as advanced by Wittgenstein and others, a useful tool of analysis. The point about a language-game is that it emphasizes the way language and action are interwoven: "I shall call the whole, consisting of language and the actions into which it is woven, the language-game."[1] A language-game is thus more than simply an abstract set of propositions constituting, say, a formal system. The game not only determines what should and what should not be done, but also sets forth the goals and the moves by which they are to be attained. More important even than these, a particular language-game determines how the activities within it are to be conceptualized, prescribed, justified and evaluated. Take as an example what is meant by a "good" move in chess: we have to refer to the rules of chess to determine what a "move" is, how to make one, what its consequences will be, what its objective is and whether or not it is a good move in the light of this objective.[2] Finally, this system of rules performs the logical function of defining the game itself. . . .

If we pursue the game-analogy one step further, we find that there may be even more striking similarities between the language-game of formal organizations and the language-game of other types of games. For instance, the rules and rationale obtaining in most typical games like chess and baseball tend to make the activity logically autonomous, i.e. the moves, defenses and evaluations are made independently of external considerations. In this sense they are self-contained. Furthermore, while playing a game it is thought to be "unfair" to challenge the rules. Sometimes it is even maintained that any questioning of the rules is unintelligible. In any case, there is a kind of sanctity attached to the rules of a game that renders them immune to criticism on the part of those engaged in playing. The resemblance of the autonomy of the activity and the immunity of the rules governing the game to the operations of bureaucracies can hardly be coincidental![3]

II. THE CONCEPTS OF SOCIAL DECISION AND SOCIAL ACTION

Let us take as our point of departure Herbert Simon's definition of a formal organization as a "decision-making structure."[4] The central concept with which we must deal is that of a decision (or action) that is attributable to the organization rather than to the individuals who are actually involved in the decisional process. The decision is regarded as the organization's decision even though it is made by certain individuals acting as its representatives. The latter make the decision only for and on behalf of the organization. Their role is, i.e. is supposed to be, impersonal. Such nonindividual decisions will be called *social decisions*, choices or actions. (I borrow the term "social choice" from Arrow, who uses it to refer to a choice made on behalf of a group as distinct from the aggregate of individual choices.)[5]

The officials of an organization are "envisaged as more or less ethically neutral . . . (and) the values to be taken as data are not those which would guide the individual if he were a private citizen. . . ."[6] When the official decides for the organization, his aim is (or should be) to implement the objectives of the organization *impersonally*, as it were. The decisions are made for the organization, with a view to its objectives and not on the basis of the personal interests or convictions of the individual official who makes the decision. This is the theory of organizational decision-making.

One might be tempted to call such organizational decisions "collective decisions," but that would be a misnomer if we take a collective decision to be a decision made by a collection of individuals. Social decisions are precisely decisions (or actions) that are to be *attributed* to the organizations themselves and not to collections of individuals. In practice, of course, the organizational decisions made by officials may actually be collective decisions. But in theory the two must be kept separate; for the "logic" of decisions attributed to organizations is critically different from the "logic" of collective decisions, i.e. those attributed to a collection of individuals.

Underlying the concept of social decisions (choices, actions) as outlined here is the notion that a person (or group of persons) can make decisions that are not his, i.e. are not attributable to him. He makes the decisions on behalf of someone else and with a view to the latter's interest, not his own. In such cases, we ordinarily consider the person (or group) that acts to be a representative or agent of the person or thing he is acting for. . . .

Accordingly, a social decision, as intended here, would be an action performed by an official as actor but owned by the organization as author. For all the consequences of the decision so made are imputed to the organization and not to the individual decision-maker. The individual decision-making official is not personally bound by the agreements he makes for the organization, nor is he personally responsible for the results of these decisions.

The theory of social decision-making that we are considering becomes even clearer if we examine the theory of organizational authority with which it is conjoined. Formal organizations are hierarchical in structure, that is, they are organized along the principle that superiors issue commands to those below them. The superior exercises authority over the subordinates. . . .

In summary, then, the organizational order requires that its social decisions be attributed to the organization rather than to the individual decision-maker, the "decision is to be made nonpersonally from the point of view of its organization effect and its relation to the organizational purpose."[7] and the officials, as its agents, are required to abdicate their choice in obedience to the impersonal organizational order.

We now turn to another essential facet of the organizational language-game, namely, that every formal organization must have a goal, or a set of goals. In fact, organizations are differentiated and defined by reference to their aims or goals, e.g. the aim of the Internal Revenue Service is to collect taxes. The goal of most business ventures is to maximize profits, etc. We may find it useful to distinguish between the real and stated goals of an organization. Thus, as Galbraith has pointed out, although the stated goal of large industrial organizations is the maximization of profits, that is a pure myth; their actual, operative goals are the securing of their own survival, autonomy and economic growth.[8] There may, indeed, be a struggle over the goals of an organization, e.g. a power play between officials.[9]

For our present purposes, we may consider the real goal of an organization to be that objective (or set of objectives) that is used as a basis for decision-making, i.e. for prescribing and justifying the actions and decisions of the organization itself, as distinct from the actions and decisions of individual persons within the organization. As such, then, the goal is an essential element in the language-game of a formal organization's activities in somewhat the way as the goal of checkmating the king is an essential element in the game of chess. Indeed, formal organizations are often differentiated from other kinds of social organizations in that they are "deliberately constructed and reconstructed to seek specific goals."[10]

The logical function of the goal in the organizational language-game is to supply the value premises to be used in making decisions, justifying and evaluating them. "Decisions in private management, like decisions in public management, must take as their ethical premises the objectives that have been set for the organization."[11]

It follows that any considerations that are not related to the aims or goals of the organization are automatically excluded as irrelevant to the organizational decision-making process. This principle of the exclusion of the irrelevant is part of the language-game. It is a logical requirement of the process of prescribing, justifying and evaluating social decisions. Consequently, apart from purely legal considerations, decisions and actions of individual officers that are unrelated to the organization's aims or goals are construed, instead, as actions of those individuals rather than of the organization. If an individual official makes a mistake or does something that fails to satisfy this criterion of social decision, he will be said to have "exceeded his authority," and will probably be sacked or made a vice-president! Again, the point is a logical one, namely, the only those actions that are related to the goal of the organization are to be attributed to the organization; those actions that are inconsistent with it are attributed to the individual officers as individuals. The individual, rather than the organization, is then forced to take the blame for whatever evil results.

Thus, for example, a naval officer who runs his ship aground is court-martialed because what he did was inconsistent with the aims of the naval organization; the action is attributed to him rather than to the Navy. On the other hand, an officer who successfully bombards a village, killing all of its inhabitants, in accordance with the objectives of his organization, is performing a social action, an action that is attributable to the organization and not to him as an individual. Whether or not the organization should take responsibility in a particular case for the mistakes of its officials is a policy decision to be made in the light of the objectives of the organization.

In other words, the concept of a social decision or action is bound up logically with the notion of an organization aim. The consequence of this co-implication of action and aim is that the notion of an action or decision taken by an organization that is not related to one of its aims makes no sense. It is an unintelligible notion within the language-game of formal organizations. Within that language-game such an action would be as difficult to understand as it would be to understand how a man's knocking over the pieces in a chess game can be part of playing chess.

We finally come to the concept of "rationality," the so-called "ideal of pure rationality."[12] From the preceding observations concerning the organizational language-game, it should be clear that the sole standard for the evaluation of an organization, its activities and its decisions, is its effectiveness in achieving its objectives—within the framework of existing conditions and available means. This kind of effectiveness is called "rationality." Thus rationality is defined in terms of the category of means and ends. . . .

"Rationality," so construed, is relative, that is, to be rational means to be efficient in pursuing a desired goal, whatever it might be. In the case of organizations, "a decision is 'organizationally' rational if it is oriented to the organization's goals."[13] Rationality is consequently neutral as to "what goals are to be attained."[14] Or to be more accurate, "rationality" is an incomplete term that requires reference to a goal before it is completely intelligible. . . .

Let us return to the organizational language-game. It was observed that within that game the sole standard of evaluation of, e.g. a decision, is the "rational" one, namely, that it be effective in achieving the organization's goal. Hence, any considerations that are taken into account in deliberation about these social decisions and in the evaluation of them are relevant only if they are related to the attainment of the organization's objectives. Let us suppose that there are certain factual conditions that must be considered in arriving at a decision, e.g. the available means, costs, and conditions of feasibility. The determination of such conditions is presumably a matter of empirical knowledge and a subject for empirical investigation. Among these empirical conditions there is a special class that I shall call *limiting operating conditions*. These are conditions that set the upper limits to an organization's operations, e.g. the scarcity of resources, of equipment, of trained personnel, legal restrictions, factors involving employee morale. Such conditions must be taken into account as *data*, so to speak, in organizational decision-making and planning. In this respect information about them is on a par logically with other information utilized in decision-making, e.g. cost-benefit computations.

Now the only way that moral considerations could be relevant to the operations of a formal organization in the language-game that I have been describing is by becoming limiting operating conditions. Strictly speaking, they could not even be introduced as such, because morality is itself not a matter of empirical knowledge. Insofar as morality in the strict sense enters into practical reasoning it must do so as an "ethical" premise, not as an empirical one. Hence morality as such must be excluded as irrelevant in organizational decision-making—by the rules of the language-game. The situation is somewhat parellel to the language-game used in playing chess: moral considerations are not relevant to the decisions about what move to make there either.

Morality enters in only indirectly, namely, as moral opinion, what John Austin calls "positive morality."[15] Obviously the positive morality, laws and customs of the society in which the organization operates, must be taken into account in decision-making and planning. The same thing goes for the religious beliefs and practices of the community. A decision-maker cannot ignore them, and it makes no difference whether he shares them or accepts them himself personally. But the determination of whether or not there are such limiting conditions set by positive morality, customs, law, and religion is an empirical matter. Whether there are such limitations is simply a matter of fact and their relevance to the decision-making is entirely dependent upon how they affect the efficiency of the organization's operations.

Social decisions, then, are not and cannot be governed by the principles of morality, or, if one wishes, they are governed by a different set of moral principles from those governing the conduct of individuals as individuals. For, as Simon says: "Decisions in private management, like decisions in public management, must take as their ethical premises the objectives that have been set for the organization."[16] By implication, they cannot take their ethical premises from the principles of morality.

Thus, for logical reasons it is improper to expect organizational conduct to conform to the ordinary principles of morality. We cannot and must not expect formal organizations, or their representatives acting in their official capacities, to be honest, courageous, considerate, sympathetic, or to have any kind of moral integrity. Such concepts are not in the vocabulary, so to speak, of the organizational language-game. (We do not find them in the vocabulary of chess either!) Actions that are wrong by ordinary moral standards are not so for organizations; indeed, they may often be required. Secrecy, espionage and deception do not make organizational action wrong; rather they are right, proper and, indeed, *rational*, if they serve the objectives of the organization. They are no more or no less wrong than, say, bluffing is in poker. From the point of view of organizational decision-making they are "ethically neutral."

Of course, I do not want to deny that it may be in the best interests of a formal organization to pay lip service to popular morality (and religion). That is a matter of public relations. But public relations operations themselves are evaluated and justified on the same basis as the other operations of the organization. The official function of the public relations officer is to facilitate the operations of the organization, not to promote morality. . . .

The upshot of our discussion so far is that actions are subject to two entirely different and, at times, incompatible standards: social decisions are subject to the standard of rational efficiency (utility) whereas the actions of individuals as such are subject to the ordinary standards of morality. An action that is right from the point of view of one of these standards may be wrong from the point of view of the other. Indeed, it is safe to say that our own experience attests to the fact that our actual expectations and social approvals are to a large extent based on a tacit acceptance of a double-standard—one for the individual when he is in his office working for the company and another for him when he is at home among friends and neighbors. Take as an example the matter of lying: nobody would think of condemning Joe X, a movie star, for lying on a TV commercial about what brand of cigarettes he smokes, for it is part of his job. On the other hand, if he were to do the same thing when he is at home among friends, we should consider his action to be improper and immoral. Or again, an individual who, acting in his official capacity, refuses help to a needy suppliant, would be roundly condemned if he were to adopt the same course of action in his private life.

III. THE MORAL RELATIONSHIP OF INDIVIDUALS TO ORGANIZATIONS

It follows from what has already been said that the standard governing an individual's relationship to an organization is likely to be different from the one governing the converse relationship, i.e. of an organization to individuals. The individual, for his part, is supposed to conduct himself in his relationship to an organization according to the same standards that he would employ in his personal relationships, i.e. the standards of ordinary morality. Thus, he is expected to be honest, open, respectful, conscientious, and loyal towards the organization of which he is a member or with which he has dealings. The organization, reprsented by its officials, can, however, be none of these in return. "Officials are expected to assume an impersonal orientation. . . . Clients are to be treated as cases . . . and subordinates are to be treated in a similar fashion."[17]

The question I now want to explore is whether or not the individual is justified in applying the standard of individual morality to his relations with formal organizations. It will, of course, generally be in the interest of the formal organizations themselves to encourage him to do so, e.g. to be honest, although the organization as such cannot "reciprocate." But we must ask this question from the point of view of the individual or, if you wish, from the moral point of view: what good moral reasons can be given for an individual to assume a moral stance in his conduct and relations with formal organizations, in contradistinction, say, to his conduct and relations with individuals who happen to be employees of such an organization?

The problem, which may be regarded as a question of loyalty and fidelity, puts the age-old problem of authority and obedience in a new light. Authority has become diffused, as I have already pointed out, and the problem of obedience can no longer be treated in terms of the personal relationship of an individual to his sovereign lord. The problem today is not so easily focused on one relationship; for the demands of authority, as represented in modern organizations, are at once more extensive, more pervasive and less personal. The question we face today is, for example, why should I, as an individual, comply with the mass of regulations laid down by an impersonal order, a bureaucratic organization? Why, for example, should I comply with draft-registration procedures? with passport regulations? with income-tax requirements? with mortage, credit, licensing, fair-trade regulations or with anti-trust laws? Or, indeed, has the individual any moral obligation at all to comply with them?[18]

It might be thought that, before trying to answer such questions, we must be careful to distinguish between individuals within an organization, e.g. officials and employees, and those outside it who have dealings with it, e.g. clients and the general public: what each of these classes ought to do is different. Granting that the specific demands placed on individuals in these various categories may be quite different, they all involve the question of authority in one way or another. Hence, for our purposes, the distinction is unimportant. For example, the authority, or the claims to it, of governmental bureaucracies extends far beyond those who are actually in their employ, e.g. the Internal Revenue Service. For convenience, I shall call those who come under the authority of an organization in some capacity or other, directly or indirectly, the *subjects* of the organization. Thus, we are all subjects of the IRS.

Can any moral reasons be given why individual subjects should comply with the decisions of organizations? Or, what amounts to the same thing, what is the basis of the authority of organizations by virtue of which we have an obligation to accept and obey their directives? And why, if at all, do we owe them loyalty and fidelity?

The most obvious answer, although perhaps not the most satisfactory one ethically, is that it is generally expedient for the individual to go along with what is required by formal organizations. If I want a new automobile, I have to comply with the financing requirements. If I want to avoid being harassed by an internal revenue agent, I make out my income tax form properly. If I want to be legally married, I comply with the regulations of the Department of Public Health. In other words, I comply from practical necessity, that is, I act under a hypothetical imperative.

Still, this sort of answer is just as unsatisfactory from the point of view of moral philosophy as the same kind of answer always has been with regard to political obligation, namely, it fails to meet the challenge of the conscientious objector.

Furthermore, there are many occasions and even whole areas where self-interest is not immediately or obviously involved in which, nevertheless, it makes good sense to ask: why comply? The traditional Lockean argument that our acceptance of the benefits of part of the social and political order commits us morally to the acceptance and conformity with the rest of it rests on the dubious assumption that the social and political order is all of one piece, a seamless web. But when we apply the argument to formal organizations it becomes especially implausible, because there are so many competing claims and conflicting regulations, not to mention loyalties. Not only logically, but as a matter of practicality, it seems obvious that accepting the benefits of one bureaucratic procedure, e.g., mailing letters, does not, from the moral point of view, *eo ipso* bind us to accept and comply with all the other regulations and procedures laid down by the formal organization and, much less, those laid down by formal organizations in general. . . .

In sum, we cannot make compacts with organizations because the standard of conduct which requires that promises be honored is that of individual conduct.[19] It does not and cannot apply to formal organizations. This follows from the fact of a double standard. . . .

I have been able to touch only on some very limited aspects of the relationship of individuals to organizations. I hope, however, that it is now abundantly clear that some sort of crisis is taking place in our moral relationships, and in particular in our conceptions of authority, and that this crisis is due not only to complex historical, psychological and sociological factors, but also to an inherent *logical* paradox in the foundations of our social relations.

IV. THE MORAL RELATIONSHIP OF ORGANIZATIONS TO INDIVIDUALS

For logical reasons that have already been mentioned, formal organizations cannot assume a genuine moral posture towards individuals. Although the language-game of social decision permits actions to be attributed to organizations as such, rather than to the officials that actually make them, it does not contain concepts like "moral obligation," "moral responsibility," or "moral integrity." For the only relevant principles in rational decision-making are those relating to the objectives of the organization. Hence individual officers who make the decisions for and in the name of the organization, as its representatives, must decide solely by reference to the objectives of the organization.

According to the theory, then, the individuals who are officers of an organization, i.e. those who run it, operate simply as vehicles or instruments of the organization. The organizational language-game requires that they be treated as such. That is why, in principle at least, any individual is dispensable and replaceable by another. An individual is selected for a position, retained in it, or fired from it solely on the grounds of efficiency, i.e. of what will best serve the interests of the organization. The interests and needs of the individuals concerned, as individuals, must be considered only insofar as they establish limiting operating conditions. Organizational rationality dictates that these interests and needs must not be considered in their own right or on their own merits. If we think of an organization as a machine, it is easy to see why we cannot reasonably expect it to have any moral obligations to people or for them to have any to it.

For precisely the same reason, the rights and interests of persons outside the organization and of the general public are *eo ipso* ruled out as logically irrelevant to rational organizational decision, except insofar as these rights and interests set limiting conditions to the effectiveness of the organization's operations or insofar as the promoting of such rights and interests constitutes part of the goal of the organization. Hence it is fatuous to expect an industrial organization to go out of its way to avoid polluting the atmosphere or to refrain from making napalm bombs or to desist from wire-tapping on purely moral grounds. Such actions would be irrational.

It follows that the only way to make the rights and interests of individuals or of the people logically relevant to organizational decision-making is to convert them into pressures of one sort or another, e.g. to bring the pressure of the law or of public opinion to bear on the organizations. Such pressures would then be introduced into the rational decision-making as limiting operating conditions. . . .

Since, as I have argued in some detail, formal organizations are not moral persons, and have no moral responsibilities, they have no moral rights. In particular, they have no *moral* right to freedom or autonomy. There can be nothing morally wrong in exercising coercion against a formal organization as there would be in exercising it against an individual. Hence, the other side of the coin is that it would be irrational for us, as moral persons, to feel any moral scruples about what we do to organizations. (We should constantly bear in mind that the officials themselves, as individuals, must still be treated as moral persons with rights and responsibilities attached to them as individuals.) . . .

V. UTILITARIANISM AND ALIENATION

It is abundantly evident that the use of a double standard for the evaluation of actions is not confined to the operations of formal organizations, as I have described them. The double standard for social morality is pervasive in our society. For almost all our social decisions, administrative, political and economic, are made and justified by reference to the "rational" standard, which amounts to the principle that the end justifies the means; and yet as individuals, in our personal relations with one another, we are bound by the ordinary principles of morality, i.e. the principles of obligation, responsibility and integrity. . . .

A great deal more needs to be said about the effects of working from a double standard of morality. In our highly organized (and utilitarian) society, most of us, as individuals, are forced to live double lives, and in order to accommodate ourselves to two different and incompatible standards, we tend to compartmentalize our lives, as I have already pointed out. For the most part, however, the organizational (or utilitarian) standard tends to take over.

Accordingly, our actions as individuals are increasingly submerged into social actions, that is, we tend more and more to use the social standard as a basis for our decisions and to evaluate our actions. As a result, the individual's own decisions and actions become separated from himself as a person and become the decisions and actions of another, e.g. of an organization. They become social decisions, not decisions of the individual. And in becoming social decisions, they are, in Hobbes's terms, no longer "his," they are "owned" by another, e.g. an organization or society.

This is one way of rendering the Marxian concept of alienation. As his actions are turned into social decisions, the individual is alienated from them and is *eo ipso* alienated from other men and from morality. In adopting the administrator's point of view (or that of a utilitarian) and so losing his actions, the individual becomes dehumanized and demoralized. For morality is essentially a relation between men, as individuals, and in losing this relation, one loses morality itself.

VI. CLOSING REMARKS ON THE SOURCE OF THE PARADOX

It is unnecessary to dwell on the intolerable character of the moral schizophrenia in which we find ourselves as the result of the double standard of conduct that has been pointed out. The question is: what can be done about it? The simplest and most obvious solution is to jettison one of the conflicting standards. But which one? The choice is difficult, if not impossible. If we give up the standard of "rationality," e.g. of organizational operations, then we surrender one of the chief conditions of civilized life and progress as well as the hope of ever solving mankind's perennial practical problems, e.g. the problems of hunger, disease, ignorance and overpopulation. On the other hand, if we give up the standard of ordinary moral conduct, then in effect we destroy ourselves as moral beings and reduce our relationships to each other to purely mechanical and materialistic ones. To find a third way out of the dilemma is not only a practical, political and sociological necessity, but a moral one as well. . . .

NOTES

1. Ludwig Wittgenstein, *Philosophical Investigations* (New York: Macmillan Company, 1953), p. 7.
2. These rules are called "constitutive rules" by John Searle. See his *Speech Acts* (Cambridge: The University Press, 1969), Ch. 2, Sec. 5.
3. For further discussion of the game-model and this aspect of rules see my "Moral and Legal Obligation," in J. Roland Pennock and John W. Chapman, editors, *Political and Legal Obligations*, Nomos, 12 (New York: Atherton Press, 1970).
4. Herbert A. Simon, *Administrative Behavior*, 2nd ed. (New York: Free Press, 1965), p. 9. Hereinafter cited as Simon, AB. For a useful survey of the subject of formal organizations see Peter M. Blau and W. Richard Scott, *Formal Organizations* (San Francisco: Chandler Publishing Company, 1962), p. 36. Hereinafter cited as Blau and Scott, FO.
5. See Kenneth Arrow, *Social Choice and Individual Values* (New York: John Wiley, 1951), *passim*.
6. Quoted from A. Bergson by Kenneth Arrow in "Public and Private Values," in *Human Values and Economic Policy*, ed. S. Hook (New York: New York University Press, 1967), p. 14.
7. Quoted from Chester I. Barnard in Simon, AB, p. 203.
8. See John Kenneth Galbraith, *The New Industrial State* (Boston: Houghton Mifflin, 1967), pp. 171–78. Hereinafter cited in NIS.
9. Amitai Etzioni, *Modern Organizations* (Englewood Cliffs, N.J.: Prentice-Hall, 1964), p. 4. Hereinafter cited as MO.
10. Etzioni, MO, p. 3. See also Blau and Scott, FO, p. 5. In a forthcoming article on "Community," I try to show that communities, as distinct from formal organizations, do not have specific goals. Indeed, the having of a specific goal may be what differentiates a *Gesellschaft* from a *Gemeinschaft* in Tönnies's sense. See Ferdinand Tönnies, *Community and Society*, trans. Charles P. Loomis (New York: Harper and Row, 1957), *passim*.

11. Simon, AB, p. 52.
12. "The ideal of pure rationality is basic to operations research and the modern management sciences." Yehezkel Dror, *Public Policymaking Reexamined* (San Francisco: Chandler Publishing Company, 1968), p. 336. Dror gives a useful bibliography of this subject on pp. 336–40.
13. Simon, AB, p. 77.
14. Simon, AB, p. 14.
15. "The name *morality*, when standing unqualified or alone, may signify the human laws which I style positive morality, without regard to their goodness or badness. For example, such laws of the class as are peculiar to a given age, or such laws of the class as are peculiar to a given nation, we style the morality of that given age or nation, whether we think them good or bad, etc." John Austin, *Province of Jurisprudence Determined*, ed. H. L. A. Hart (New York: Noonday Press, 1954), p. 125. The study of positive moralities belongs to what I call "descriptive ethics." See my *Structure of a Moral Code* (Cambridge, Mass: Harvard University Press, 1957).
16. Simon, AB, p. 52.
17. Blau and Scott, FO, p. 34.
18. See my "Moral and Legal Obligation," referred to in note 3.
19. The fact that promising involves an extremely personal relation between individuals is almost universally overlooked by philosophers who discuss promises.

The Moral Responsibility of Corporations

Case Study—When E. F. Hutton Speaks . . .

JOANNE B. CIULLA

On May 2, 1985, E. F. Hutton pleaded guilty to mail and wire fraud. The brokerage house had been charged with fradulently obtaining the use of more than $1 billion in interest-free funds by systematically overdrawing checking accounts at some 400 banks. Hutton's attorneys bargained with the Justice Department and agreed on a $2 million fine plus $750,000 to cover the cost of the investigation. Since the fine for mail fraud was $1000 per case, Hutton's attorneys pleaded guilty to 2000 counts of fraud. (Ironically, around the time of Hutton's settlement the fine for mail fraud was raised to $500,000 per count.)

Robert Fomon, CEO of E. F. Hutton, hoped that the guilty plea would minimize public scrutiny and put an end to the scandal—but it didn't. Investigations of the firm continued and were closely monitored by the press. E. F. Hutton, one of the most respected brokerage houses on Wall Street, became "the company that pleaded guilty to 2000 counts of fraud."

COMPANY BACKGROUND

E. F. Hutton was founded by Edward F. Hutton and George Ellis, Jr., in 1904. The Hutton partnership aimed at maintaining a strong financial base

Joanne B. Ciulla, "E. F. Hutton." Reprinted by permission of the author.

and providing complete service to elite investors. It was the first New York Stock Exchange firm to open an office on the West Coast. Since Western Union had no wires over the Rockies, Hutton advanced it $50,000 to complete its first coast-to-coast wire. The system was completed in 1905, establishing Hutton as a firm dedicated to speedy service.

Because of the importance of the wire to their business, brokerage firms were called "wire houses." This ability to move funds and to buy and sell quickly benefitted Hutton's West Coast clients. For example, during the 1906 San Francisco earthquake Hutton office managers retrieved their records from the destroyed office, and knowing that clients would need cash but could not be reached, liquidated their positions before news of the quake hit the East Coast.

While sharing in the prosperity of the 1920s, Hutton pursued a conservative course in keeping within margin requirements. So when the market crashed in 1929, it lost less than $50,000 on its unsecured accounts. Even during the depression, Hutton continued to expand and improve its communications networks. By 1962 the firm had grown so much that it dissolved the partnership and became a corporation.[1]

ROBERT FOMON AND THE HUTTON ORGANIZATION

After graduating from the University of Southern California with a degree in English, Fomon was hired by Hutton as a sales trainee in 1951. He told one interviewer that his first impression of the securities industry was an unrealistic one which came from reading F. Scott Fitzgerald novels.[2] Nonetheless, Fomon learned the business and worked his way up to the head of the company's West Coast corporate finance, syndicate, and institutional sales. He then became CEO in 1970. The choice of Fomon was controversial. Some people in the firm had wanted John Shad, who was then head of corporate finance, to be CEO (Shad later left Hutton in 1981 to become chairman of the SEC).

When Fomon became CEO, Hutton was losing money because the market was depressed and the firm's staff had grown too large—commissions accounted for almost 68 percent of Hutton's revenues (by 1979 commissions would shrink to 38 percent). Fomon began his term of office by firing 600 employees and trimming losses that had reached $1 million a month. This aggressive move, combined with the healthy market of 1972, got Hutton out of the red.

In 1972 Hutton became a publicly owned company, but Fomon continued to run the firm in the loose style of a partnership. The managing partners all sat on the board of directors. There were no outsiders on the board until 1974 when Harvard Business School Professor Warren Law became a member. Ten years later Edward F. Hutton's daughter, actress

Dina Merrill, and California attorney Edward Cazier, Jr., joined the board. Baseball commissioner Peter Ueberroth became a member in 1984.

Disliking tight organizational systems, Fomon believed that "charts and boxes do not solve your problems." He said, "It's much more important to select the right people and I think that I'm pretty good at that."[3] But Fomon, who was described as moody and aloof, took little interest in the details of management. He did, however, pay close attention to business deals and was known to veto certain projects for ethical reasons or because of his personal tastes. For example, he refused to let Hutton underwrite a casino project and once vetoed a deal because it included a fast food business.[4] Under Foman's leadership, Hutton went from 95 branch offices and 1250 account executives in 1972 to 400 offices worldwide and 6600 account executives in 1985.

Hutton's strength was its retail sales force and distribution system. Hutton's rewards system plus its decentralized management system engendered a strong independent entrepreneurial spirit among employees in its branch offices. While the large and bureaucratic Merrill Lynch was symbolized by the herd, Hutton was best symbolized by the lone cowboy. At Hutton it was said that the client belonged to the account executive, whereas at other places like Merrill Lynch, the client belonged to the company.

INTEREST INCOME IN THE SECURITIES INDUSTRY

Interest income is very important to a brokerage firm. Basically, said one industry specialist, "Wire houses are giant factories designed to collect money from customers and lend it out." In order to do business with a brokerage house, both retail and institutional customers must either have money on hand to buy shares, or they can buy shares on credit (or margin). To buy on margin, they must borrow from the broker and deposit the shares as collateral. If clients want to sell short (sell stocks that they do not own so as to profit from a falling market), they must deposit the cash value of those shares in their brokerage account. This system boosts profits whenever interests rates rise—especially since customers often hold their profits in their brokerage account until another investment opportunity comes along.

Brokerage firms are allowed by the SEC to use the credit balances left by customers to lend out to other clients. For example, in 1981 the Bache Group described its policy this way:

> A portion of the funds loaned to customers by the company is derived from sources which are largely interest free to the company. [As a result of this] the company earns income in some cases equal to the entire interest rate charged to its customers. A primary source of such funds are the excess funds left with the company by its customers.[5]

With interest rates at 17 percent in 1981, Shearson Loeb Rhoades was able to cover all of its overhead with "Saturday and Sunday money," which is interest income derived from waiting until Monday to move customers' money into their private accounts.

	(1) PRE-TAX EARNINGS $m	(2) NET INTEREST REVENUES $m	(2) AS % OF (1)
Merrill Lynch	366.1	251.8	69
E. F. Hutton	155.8	95.8	61
Shearson Loeb Rhoades	105.0	71.5	68
Dean Witter Reynolds	62.3	61.2	98
Bache	47.5	52.6	110
Donaldson Lufkin & Jenrette	15.9	21.8	137
Paine Webber	−16.2	20.3	—

Source: The Economist, June 20, 1981, p. 9.

Motivation in the brokerage business was mostly based on monetary rewards. The main source of account executives' income was the 1/2 to 2 percent commission they made on each trade—the more they traded, the higher the commission. High producers were treated like prima donnas. Firms regularly tried to steal good sales people from each other by offering them bonuses—which were sometimes as much as $300,000—to defect. The top producers at Hutton tended to gravitate to managerial positions. Branch managers received 10 percent of the net profit of their office; however, some successful sales people preferred to stay in sales, where they could earn more money.

GEORGE BALL

In 1977 Fomon named 38-year-old George Ball as President and head of retail operations. Ball was an aggressive salesman who had quickly worked his way up through the branch system. He began as an account executive trainee in 1962, became the Newark branch manager in 1967, and then regional sales manager in 1969. A charismatic public person, Ball was always out talking to employees—making sure that new sales ideas were in the pipeline. As one ex-Hutton employee said: "It wasn't a surprise to see him [Ball] anywhere. But when Fomon went anyplace other than the twelfth floor [the site of the executive offices], people would say, 'what the hell is he up to?' "[6] Ball's managerial abilities complemented those of the moody and sometimes reclusive Fomon, who was described as a "backroom deal maker" and talented investment banker.

All of the regional offices reported to Ball. The chain of command was short and loose—account executives reported to branch managers, who reported to their regional VPs, who reported to Ball. Ball and the executive VPs reported directly to Fomon. But in actual practice Ball was the dominant figure in the company and other senior officers reported to him ex-officio (see Exhibit 1). Hutton was described as a "comfortable" organization without a fixed hierarchy. The benefit of this arrangement, according to Ball, was that without a formal organizational chart, management could make fast decisions.[7]

CASH MANAGEMENT AT HUTTON

In 1980, with interest rates hovering around 18 percent, Hutton began to explore ways to maximize its interest earnings. Hutton managers recognized that if they could receive one-day credit on checks deposited with local banks, while checks written by Hutton required two days to clear, they could capture some of the "float" inherent in the banking system. By drawing checks on Monday, e.g., based on anticipated deposits on Tuesday, sufficient funds would be available in the bank to cover Hutton's checks when presented for payment on Wednesday. This required an estimate of the next day's deposits. A formula was derived which used past experience to produce a reasonable estimate. Since checks were written when funds were not on deposit, Hutton was technically overdrafting its account. If next day deposits were overestimated, the account would be overdrawn and in reality have a negative balance. This could cause the bank either to demand immediate reimbursement by wire transfer of funds or refuse payment of Hutton's checks—although sometimes, for various reasons, the banks did nothing.

William Sullivan, designated as Hutton's "money mobilizer," had designed Hutton's cash management system in the late seventies. The system moved money from branch office accounts to regional office bank accounts and then to national concentration accounts where the funds could be used by the company. Often delays in the processing of Hutton's checks between banks denied the company same-day availability of funds. To remedy this delay, funds were transferred as soon as possible. The objective of this system was to leave enough money in the bank account to compensate the bank for its services and withdraw the rest. From Hutton's point of view, it was compensating itself by overdrafting for the day in which the bank was holding its money.

When these alterations had been made in the cash management system, Sullivan and other Hutton officials met with its auditors, Arthur Anderson & Co. (AA&Co), to discuss the legality of the new procedures. A memorandum dated March 7, 1980, described that meeting:

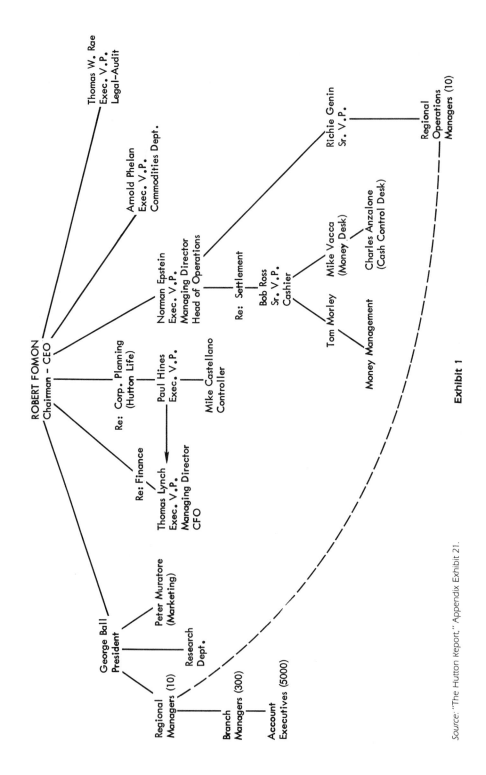

ROBERT FOMON
Chairman – CEO

Thomas W. Rae
Exec. V.P.
Legal–Audit

Arnold Phelan
Exec. V.P.
Commodities Dept.

Norman Epstein
Exec. V.P.
Managing Director
Head of Operations

Richie Genin
Sr. V.P.

Re: Settlement

Bob Ross
Sr. V.P.
Cashier

Mike Vacca
(Money Desk)

Charles Anzalone
(Cash Control Desk)

Regional
Operations
Managers (10)

Tom Morley

Money Management

Re: Corp. Planning
(Hutton Life)

Paul Hines
Exec. V.P.

Mike Castellano
Controller

Re: Finance

Thomas Lynch
Exec. V.P.
Managing Director
CFO

George Ball
President

Peter Muratore
(Marketing)

Research
Dept.

Regional
Managers (10)

Branch
Managers (300)

Account
Executives (5000)

Exhibit 1

Source: "The Hutton Report," Appendix Exhibit 21.

After the discussion of the procedure employed and its legality, Joel Miller, AA&Co engagement partner, requested that Tom Rae (Hutton's general council and former SEC lawyer) render a written legal opinion stating that Hutton's activities in this area don't present any legal problems. Mr. Rae declined to render such an opinion, stating that the banks are fully cognizant of Hutton's procedures, that this is an accepted banking practice, and that there is no question as to the propriety of such a transaction, again making reference to the "means of payment" principles. [The legal concept of check writing requires that you have the intent and the ability to cover the check on time.] After Tom Rae declined to issue an opinion on this matter, Bill Sullivan offered to call one of the banks that Hutton uses, Morgan Guaranty, and ask them what the banks would do if a company were to issue checks with no book balances. Joel Miller then stated that he would discuss the matter with other partners at AA&Co, whose clients include major money center banks, to ascertain what the banks' "point of view" is regarding these transactions.[8]

THE BANKS

Banks are compensated for their services to corporate customers by either requiring a minimum balance in the account or by charging set fees, or a combination of both. Most of the banks Hutton used required the firm to leave an average amount of money in the account so that the bank could produce a yield that would compensate it for its services. The bank and the customer agreed on the sum of the average balance and the time period over which the adequacy of compensation would be measured. If this arrangement did not yield enough compensation for a particular bank, it would inform the customer. Bank of America charged Hutton set fees for its services and only required Hutton to have sufficient funds in its account to cover a check when it was presented for payment—the rest of the time the account could have a zero balance.

Commercial banks, however, normally required corporate customers to maintain average account balances at negotiated target levels, and did not expect corporate customers to overdraft their accounts without prior consent. Nevertheless, bank managers expected occasional overdrafts to occur because of errors or inadvertence, such as the failure of an incoming wire to arrive on time. Most bank managers tolerated overdrafting by creditworthy customers as long as the amounts of money were relatively small and the overdrafts were infrequent.

The time that it takes for a check to clear, called "collection float," is based on the inefficiency of the payments system in this country. A check that is not cashed in person must be physically taken from the bank to a clearing house before its funds can become available. Electronic banking systems would eliminate this time lag by moving funds instantly. However, according to one Federal Reserve Board representative, an electronic payments system is not likely to displace checks during the remainder of this century.[9]

THE CAMPAIGN FOR INTEREST PROFITS BEGINS

On October 21, 1980, a memo written by Tom Morley (who had replaced William Sullivan as the money mobilizer) was sent to all branch managers. The memo emphasized the importance of interest income and suggested ways to increase interest profits. The memo pointed out that "net interest income accounted for approximately 50 percent of the average branch's profits. And by paying insufficient attention to net interest profits, a branch may be ignoring potential revenue." Four major areas generated interest profits: margin accounts, short positions, free credit balances, and interest on general ledger balances. Morley pointed out that the last category had the greatest potential for profit. The memo said:

> The branch earns interest on all credit balances in its general ledger and is charged for all debit balances, both at the call rate. The lion's share of the interest profit generated in this category is due to the float earned on Bank of America checks and overdrafting the branch's account.[10]

At the time, interest from overdrafting was reported as part of a single line item on profit and loss statements. This item included interest generated by the overdrafting of branch bank accounts as well as interest generated by other bank transactions. Morley's memo broke down the components of interest in the Southeast Region. He noted that the first three categories accounted for approximately 55 percent of the interest earned, while the general ledger interest accounted for 45 percent of the net interest profits.

In November 1980 Morley gave a speech to the regional operations managers and noted that it was a good idea for branch managers to inform local banks of Hutton's cash management system. However, one of Morley's staff members later sent a memo in June 1981 to Regional Operations managers, advising: "If an office is overdrafting its ledger balance consistently, it is probably best not to request an account analysis."[11]

EXPLAINING THE CASH MANAGEMENT POLICY

Tom Morley told branch managers how to use Hutton's money management system in a memo dated March 10, 1981:

> In collecting our branch receipts, we usually assign one-day availability to our local deposit. In doing this we anticipate our drawdown check clearing the bank the next business day, which will be when our local deposit becomes available. If the drawdown check fails to clear the bank the next business day, we attempt to capture the excess balances by increasing subsequent drawdowns. In handling our collections in this manner, we give the same clearing value to our drawdown check as we expect to receive on our branch deposit.

This system is the standard cash management collection process used in the industry. What the system fails to address and cultivate is the situation where we can receive one day availability on our drawdown check, but it actually takes two days for the check to clear our bank.[12]

With the emphasis on interest income, the branch office cashier's job became more important because the cashier was the one who moved the money in and out of a branch office's account. In a memo to Tom Morley dated May 12, 1981, Tom Lillis, the vice president of accounting services, emphasized the importance of a good branch cashier, giving the following example:

> One branch had earned a consistent $30,000 per month in interest "just from overdrafting of the bank account." When the branch manager changed cashiers, the office only earned $10,000 from overdrafting.[13]

The overdrafting principle was implemented through a formula that incorporated a multiplier, which took weekends into account. Many cashiers found the formula difficult to understand and use. In July 1980 and May 1981 Morley's assistant, Kevin Mahoney, suggested automating the procedure at the branch office level. Using a computer software program, offices could only overdraft as much as would allow Hutton to maintain a zero balance.[14] Hutton did not, at either time, purchase this software.

The Mountain Region offices received instructions on how to use the formula in a memorandum. The Pacific region was given instructions by telephone. Some branch offices did not get any instructions on how to use the formula. Traditionally, branch office practices were determined by the instructions that the branch manager gave to the office cashier.

Branch operations personnel in the Atlantic Region learned how to use the formula in a seminar. A memo from that seminar titled "Reminders from Seminar," dated June 2, 1981, contains this tip: "Drawdown as discussed. You may drawdown more than formula but not less! This will depend on individual branch/bank circumstances."[15]

Interest profits became a frequent topic of conversation at meetings of branch and regional personnel. Branch managers were concerned with interest profits because their compensation and job evaluation was based on their office's net profit. However, because of the sharp division in the Hutton organization between sales and operations, branch managers were mainly responsible for sales and reported to the regional vice president of sales, while their cashiers were answerable to the regional operations managers. Under this arrangement it was possible for a branch manager to assume that if the drawdown worksheets were being used incorrectly, he or she would be notified by operations.

GEORGE BALL'S ENCOURAGEMENT

Throughout 1981 Ball wrote memos encouraging greater interest profits. A memo dated April 27, 1981, named New England as "The Region of the Month." In it, Ball recommended that managers get in touch with Tom Morley to find out how to maximize interest income and said, "Interest is an excellent way to legitimately optimize a branch's or region's results."[16] On June 25, 1981, Tom Lillis wrote in a memo

> I noticed that George Ball suggested to a number of RVPs [regional vice presidents] that they get in touch with Tom Morley to see if they can improve their interest profits. Tom Morley is only concerned with overdrafting at the branch level and I believe that there is far more to be done to improve interest profits.

Lillis went on to say

> I would like to spearhead a retail system campaign to make branch managers aware of interest profit opportunities, but without a means of monitoring branch performance the program would be at best hit or miss. I need a priority for the proposed interest program so that we can improve the profitability of this $100,000,000 product.[17]

Ball continued to encourage interest earnings. In his memo dated August 5, 1981, he wrote: "High fences make good neighbors and high interest profits create good margins."[18] His December 18, 1981, memo states, "We have certainly had the luxury of high interest profits, profits which may be importantly lower in the year ahead. Our corporate goal is to earn in excess of $100,000,000 [in interest]. Together we can do it, but it will take a mighty push."[19]

THE BRANCHES PUSH

Branch managers became very conscious of their interest income stacked up against other branch offices. Baltimore branch manager, Anthony Read, worried about his branch's poor interest earnings. His cashier informed him that the way in which managers increased interest was to arbitrarily increase drawdowns. Read began to do so periodically, adding $500,000 to $3 million to his account. The bank complained to Morley and Hutton deposited a large sum of money and left it there for several days. Read was charged with the interest on that money and stopped overdrafting his account.

Alexandria branch manager, Perry Bacon, was known as a bright young manager. After someone in the Alexandria branch inadvertently added an extra zero to an overdraft, making the figure 9 million instead of

900 thousand, Bacon noticed that the bank did nothing. So he began to aggressively overdraft his account. Letters from Bacon's local bank indicated that he maintained excellent relations with it.

In November 1981 Bacon's office was ranked as the number one profit center in the central region. George Ball sent a memo to the Central Regional vice president asking why the Alexandria office's interest earnings were so high. Ball queried, "Were these accounting adjustments?" The response was, "No, but the office does a superb job of money management."[20] Ball, Morley, and others later suggested that branch managers get advice from Bacon on how to increase their interest income.

Earnest Dipple, a VP for the Central Region, told Louisville branch manager, William Wilcox, to contact Bacon about how to improve his branch's interest earnings. Wilcox increased the multiplier used in connection with the drawdown formula and arbitrarily increased the amount of the branch drawdown. However, unlike Bacon and Read, Wilcox had negotiated a minimum service fee with his bank, The First National Bank of Louisville, in the fall of 1981. In order to assess the fees owed to it, the bank closely analyzed Wilcox's account and was fully aware of its status from day to day.

THE BIG OVERDRAFT

In December 1981 the Genesee County Bank in Batavia, New York, was presented with a large check that had been deposited in a New York bank. Genesee had received Hutton checks drawn on the United Penn bank in Wilkes-Barre, Pennsylvania. The Genesee branch manager called United Penn to see if Hutton had $8 million available in its account. United Penn said Hutton only had uncollected money in the form of checks that were deposited the day before. Genesee and United Penn then refused to honor Hutton checks and closed the firm's account. Hutton immediately wired $18.8 million to United Penn and $20 million to Genesee.

This movement of money between the Genesee Bank and United Penn was called "chaining" (see Exhibit 2). The system had been developed by the Atlantic Region's operations manager, Arthur Jensen, and similar systems were used in other regions. These chains served the purpose of generating clearing delays in order to ease the region's task of concentrating funds from branches within the region. Clearing delays increased interest profits by giving Hutton one-day availability of checks written to Hutton and two-day clearance of checks written by Hutton. It was generally considered convenient and it improved the availability of funds. Unlike overdrafting, which was used to compensate Hutton for the float that was built into the banking system, chaining created additional float.

Exhibit 2

THE GENESEE CHAIN AS IDENTIFIED BY THE DEPARTMENT OF JUSTICE

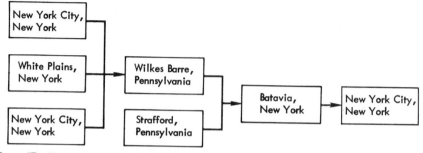

Source: "The Hutton Report," Appendix Exhibit 14.

HUTTON'S AUDITORS ASK QUESTIONS

Hutton's AA&Co auditors called a meeting in early 1982 with CFO Tom Lynch, General Council Tom Rae and his assistants, and an attorney from Hutton's outside law firm, Cahill, Gordon & Reindel. They discussed Hutton's overdraft policy, the $8 million overdraft at the Genesee County Bank, and inquiries by banking regulators into excessive overdrafting of accounts at Manufacturers' Hanover Bank and Chemical Bank. A memo describing the meeting said the Federal Reserve Board had expressed concern that Hutton might be "creating float" as opposed to taking advantage of the float inherent in the banking system. The memo reported that "We were assured of the fact that no action has been brought against Hutton and that Hutton officials believed that banking regulators had no jurisdiction over their firm." The memo further stated that "the major concern of management was the potential negative publicity if the media were informed."[21]

Many other questions began to surface at Hutton. George Ball, in a March 19, 1982, memo again questioned the interest profits of the Alexandria office. Commenting on the contents of a memorandum on interest earnings, Ball said: "Note — commentary seems very aggressive. Who is calling the shots, and were the shots well called?"[22]

Four months later, in July 1982, to the surprise of some and the disappointment of many, Ball left Hutton to become the president and chief executive of Prudential-Bache Securities. His departure was based on the desire for professional advancement and did not, according to Ball, have anything to do with problems at Hutton.[23] Ball's departure left a huge managerial gap in the Hutton organization. Fomon was without his public "hands on manager."

HUTTON ATTRACTS ATTENTION

The Genesee incident attracted the attention of a young Assistant U.S. Attorney from the Middle District of Pennsylvania named Albert Murray. Murray doggedly traced the movement of Hutton's checks between banks and initiated a Justice Department investigation of Hutton's activities. On May 10, 1982, the Justice Department subpoenaed CEO Robert Fomon and Controller Michael Castellano, asking for virtually every document in E. F. Hutton's files.

At that time Attorney General Edwin Meese III had just taken office. Meese's appointment had been opposed by congressmen and senators who questioned the propriety of some low interest loans that Meese obtained while working in the White House. The Democrats in particular not only questioned Meese's moral character, but worried that he would be soft on white collar crime.

The Justice Department's investigation covered the firm's overdrafting from mid-1980 to February 1982. Hutton was charged with overdrafting its accounts and intentionally delaying check collection. Altogether, the Justice Department estimated that by shuffling $10 billion in uncollected funds from one account to another, Hutton obtained the interest free use of $1 billion in uncollected funds from July 1980 through February 1982 (which was when the short-term interest rates were 18 percent to 20 percent).[24]

HUTTON'S RESPONSE

The investigation dragged on from February 1982 until May 1985. When it was completed in the spring of 1985, the audit committee of the board of directors met. The committee, which consisted of the outside members of the board of directors, did not think that the case against Hutton was very strong (a representative of the Justice Department later testified that, in the department's opinion, chances of convicting Hutton were fifty-fifty).[25] However, a guilty plea would avoid a long jury trial with the attendant publicity, and the risk that Hutton employees would be found guilty of fraud (in which case they could be barred from the securities industry). It was tentatively agreed to enter a guilty plea, if a satisfactory settlement could be worked out with the Justice Department.

One factor contributing to this decision was a memo that surfaced in February 1985. It was written on April 23, 1982, by Perry Bacon in response to a memo by Washington branch manager, Steve Bralove. Bralove had complained to Bacon about causing problems with the bank by overdrafting excessively. Bacon replied in reference to overdrafting:

Exhibit 3

E. F. HUTTON (A)

TO: Steve Bralove

FROM: Perry H. Bacon

DATE: April 23, 1982

SUBJECT: Your Memo—Banking Activities

EFHutton

INTER-OFFICE MEMORANDUM

Our banking activities during the last six months have been no different than our banking activities off and on for the last five years. Additionally, I believe those activities are encouraged by the firm and are in fact identical to what the firm practices on a national basis. Specifically, we will from time to time draw down not only deposits plus anticipated deposits, but also bogus deposits. One day prior to that incremental drawdown arriving at our bank, we may need to cover with a New York (Chemical, U.S. Trust) check. As long as the local bank honors that check with same day availability, the firm profits at both the branch and the national level. We profit at the branch level by creating a surplus in general ledger revenues which are credited at the broker call rate. We profit at the national level for two reasons: (1) Because New York is doing the same thing with the U.S. Trust check by reacting to our bank wire and floating checks based on those deposits which deposits may not really exist. (2) Because those bogus deposits create a reduction in our net capital ratio requirement which allows the firm to deploy capital elsewhere. Furthermore, we (as a firm) learned to use the float because it is exactly what the banks do to us (see enclosed article). I know of at least a dozen managers at E. F. Hutton—managers who along with Bill Sullivan and Tom Morley taught me the system—who do precisely the same thing. Presumably, any manager who was willing to take the time to learn the system would want to use the system.

The obvious drawback to the system is that it can cost the bank money. If the bank honors a New York deposit check with same day availability and subsequently have those funds withdrawn by a New York drawdown check before they get FED usage of the funds, they have a net debit. On the other hand, the bank is not quite the defenseless amoeba that your memo suggests. FIRST, the system only exists because, peculiarly, our mammoth federal banking system is more hand processed than automated—NB—a system which the banks well know how to use as the enclosed article discusses. SECOND, the system we use does not happen the day we open an account. We spend months working up to larger drawdowns leaving the bank surplus deposits, and I do not recall any bank offering to send us their earnings on those deposits.

NB—There is not much difference between what we do and when a bank tells you not to write checks on your out of state deposit for 10 days, clears that check through the FED in 2 days, and enjoys the float for 8 days. Essentially, the bank has created a net debit against you in the form of 8 day nonusable funds. By the way, Tom Morley believes that within 2–3 years the entire system will be automated and all domestic checks will clear in one day. Therefore, as Tom stated in our New York BOM meeting, the time to take advantage of the system is now. (See second enclosed article.)

Exhibit 3 (*continued*)

THIRD, all banks either know or eventually figure out our system. When they do, they simply cease giving same day availability, and often will not count regular checks as collected funds. In fact, contrary to your implication that all banks are *now* holding your checks, NBW (a bank with whom we have never dealt) had been doing that to you months *before* this issue arose. FOURTH, if a bank is slow to move on #3 above, documents a net loss and asks us for same, we will probably give it to them. Our objective is not to steal money from the banks. Whatever the bank may have lost, we have enjoyed a greater profit due to the spread float.* I am aware of four branches that have had to write checks within the last six months for just the reasons listed above. On the other hand, many banks accept their losses as a cost of doing business and never ask for the money.

This last point leads to some of the specific remarks in your memo. FIRST, when you called a few months ago and asked if I was aware that due to our over-drafts, 1st American was giving you trouble with your secondary account there, you will recall that I replied that I was not aware, and I replied that I would not do any more overdrafting at that bank. If I sounded unconcerned, it was because your terse interrogatory was limited to your secondary bank account. The first time I heard about an institutional problem was from Ernie some weeks ago. Your conclusion that my attitude to Hutton's reputation in the city is "indifferent" is ridiculous. I confess to an emotion somewhere between indifference and astonishment at your suggestion that the solution to your secondary account problem was to call and offer money to a bank that had not, and to this date has not called me to complain, ask for money or request to discuss the issue — in fact has never called me at all. SECOND, your remark that since 1st American has contacted all of the area banks and now all banks are holding checks is not only contradicted by your knowledge that NBW had already been doing that, but would further suggest violation of any number of federal and banking stat-utes regarding collusion and anti-trust. THIRD, and what really troubles me, is that your constant use of terminology such as "excessive," "blatant disregard," "casually damaged" and "indifferent" is way out of line — and I think you know it. I plead guilty to simply never having considered that an institutional relation-ship could be jeopardized. Importantly, if our zeal with the bank has in any way impaired your ability to do business with that bank, I am genuinely sorry and would like to apologize to you and anyone else adversely effected. However, your sweeping implication that such an isolated incident immeasurably damages our reputation and ability to transact . . .

* Ex. — The average balance that we earned on during the months to which you refer was significantly greater than the 2 million figure that the bank stated.

Source: "The Hutton Report," Appendix Exhibit 17.

I believe those activities are encouraged by the firm and are in fact identical to what the firm practices on a national basis. Specifically we will from time to time draw down not only deposits plus anticipated deposits, but also bogus deposits. (See Exhibit 3.)

Some Hutton insiders said that this memo was "the nail in the coffin" that forced Hutton to plead guilty.[26] But the most compelling reason why Fomon chose to plead guilty was the hope that it would end the affair quickly.[27]

Hutton's board of directors later approved the settlement and the firm pleaded guilty to the agreed-upon 2000 counts of fraud. Attorney General Meese said that the government had foregone prosecution of Hutton employees in order to avoid lengthy litigation. Meese believed that the overdrafting was a "corporate scheme" and "no one personally benefited from defrauding the banks."[28] The Justice Department had also agreed to send a letter to the SEC saying, "the interests of the U.S. government have been served."

But many constituencies were not satisfied with the Justice Department's investigation. The Chairman of the House Judiciary Crime subcommittee, N. J. Democrat William J. Hughes, believed that individuals in the corporate hierarchy should be charged. Stephen Trott, Justice Department Criminal Division chief, was unhappy with the way that Hutton delivered subpoenaed documents and thought the case should be reopened.[29] And the SEC wanted its own investigation. On top of all this, some banks considered filing a class action suit under the Racketeer Influenced & Corrupt Organizations Act.

So it did not look like the guilty plea was going to put the scandal to rest. The press was keeping a watchful eye on Hutton and its publicity-shy CEO. After two years of investigations, even Fomon was not sure what had gone wrong. One thing that the 34-year Hutton veteran did know was that he would have to do something to keep his prized employees from defecting, and regain Hutton's credibility as a financial institution.[28]

NOTES

1. "The Story of E. F. Hutton's Founding and Growth," published by E. F. Hutton.
2. "The Undoing of Robert Fomon," by James Steingold, *The New York Times*, Sept. 29, 1985, sec. 3, p. 10.
3. Ibid., p. 11.
4. "Bob Fomon: Is Being Tough Still Enough?" by Gregory Miller, *Institutional Investor*, April 1985, p. 62.
5. Ibid., p. 60.
6. "The Productivity Game at E. F. Hutton," by Nigel Adam, *Euromoney*, Dec. 1981, p. 79.

7. Appendix to "The Hutton Report," by Griffin B. Bell, Sept. 4, 1985, Exhibit 45.
8. "The Hutton Report," by Griffin Bell, Sept. 4, 1985, p. 21.
9. Appendix to "The Hutton Report," Exhibit 35.
10. Ibid., Exhibit 6.
11. Ibid., Exhibit 31.
12. Ibid., Exhibit 13.
13. Ibid., Exhibits 26, 27, & 28.
14. Ibid., Exhibit 20.
15. Ibid., Exhibit 40.
16. Ibid., Exhibit 39.
17. Ibid., Exhibit 13.
18. Ibid., Exhibit 13.
19. Ibid., Exhibit 19.
20. "Hutton Auditor Defends Role," by Nathaniel Nash, *The New York Times*, October 4, 1985, sec. D, p. 3.
21. Appendix Exhibit 40.
22. "E. F. Hutton Appears Headed for a Long Siege," by Scott McMurray, *The Wall Street Journal* May 4, 1985, p. 1.
23. "What Did Hutton's Managers Know—And When Did They Know It?" by Anthony Bianco, David Wallace, and Daniel Moskowitz, *Business Week*, May 20, 1985, p. 110.
24. "Why the E. F. Hutton Scandal May Be Far from Over," by Chris Wells, *Business Week*, Feb. 24, 1986, p. 98.
25. "The Undoing of Robert Fomon," sec. 3, p. 1.
26. "What Did Hutton's Managers Know—And When Did They Know It?" p. 111.
27. "Why the Hutton Scandal May Be Far from Over," p. 101.
28. Special thanks to Professor E. Raymond Corey for his helpful advice on this case.

Can a Corporation Have a Conscience?

KENNETH E. GOODPASTER AND JOHN B. MATTHEWS, JR.

During the severe racial tensions of the 1960s, Southern Steel Company (actual case, disguised name) faced considerable pressure from government and the press to explain and modify its policies regarding discrimination both within its plants and in the major city where it was located. SSC was the largest employer in the area (it had nearly 15,000 workers, one-third of whom were black) and had made great strides toward removing barriers to equal job opportunity in its several plants. In addition, its top executives (especially its chief executive officer, James Weston) had distinguished themselves as private citizens for years in community programs for black housing, education, and small business as well as in attempts at desegregating all-white police and local government organizations.

SSC drew the line, however, at using its substantial economic influence in the local area to advance the cause of the civil rights movement by pressuring banks, suppliers, and the local government:

> "As individuals we can exercise what influence we may have as citizens," James Weston said, "but for a corporation to attempt to exert any kind of economic compulsion to achieve a particular end in a social area seems to me to be quite beyond what a corporation should do and quite beyond what a corporation can do. I believe that while government may seek to compel social reforms, any attempt by a private organization like SSC to impose its views, its beliefs, and its will upon the community would be repugnant to our American constitutional concepts and that appropriate steps to correct this abuse of corporate power would be universally demanded by public opinion."

Weston could have been speaking in the early 1980s on any issue that corporations around the United States now face. Instead of social justice, his theme might be environmental protection, product safety, marketing practice, or international bribery. His statement for SSC raises the important issue of corporate responsibility. Can a corporation have a conscience?

Weston apparently felt comfortable saying it need not. The responsibilities of ordinary persons and of "artificial persons" like corporations are, in his view, separate. Persons' responsibilities go beyond those of corporations. Persons, he seems to have believed, ought to care not only about themselves but also about the dignity and well-being of those around them—ought not only to care but also to act. Organizations, he evidently thought, are creatures of, and to a degree prisoners of, the systems of economic incentive and political sanction that give them reality and therefore should not be expected to display the same moral attributes that we expect of persons.

Others inside business as well as outside share Weston's perception. One influential philosopher, John Ladd, carries Weston's view a step further:

> "It is improper to expect organizational conduct to conform to the ordinary principles of morality," he says. "We cannot and must not expect formal organizations, or their representatives acting in their official capacities, to be honest, courageous, considerate, sympathetic, or to have any kind of moral integrity. Such concepts are not in the vocabulary, so to speak, of the organizational language game."[1]

In our opinion, this line of thought represents a tremendous barrier to the development of business ethics both as a field of inquiry and as a practical force in managerial decision making. This is a matter about which executives must be philosophical and philosophers must be practical. A corporation can and should have a conscience. The language of ethics does have a place in the vocabulary of an organization. There need not be and there should not be a disjunction of the sort attributed to SSC's James Weston. Organizational agents such as corporations should be no more and no less morally responsible (rational, self-interested, altruistic) than ordinary persons.

We take this position because we think an analogy holds between the individual and the corporation. If we analyze the concept of moral responsibility as it applies to persons, we find that projecting it to corporations as agents in society is possible.

DEFINING THE RESPONSIBILITY OF PERSONS

When we speak of the responsibility of individuals, philosophers say that we mean three things: someone is to blame, something has to be done, or some kind of trustworthiness can be expected.

We apply the first meaning, what we shall call the *causal* sense, primarily to legal and moral contexts where what is at issue is praise or blame for a past action. We say of a person that he or she was responsible for what happened, is to blame for it, should be held accountable. In this sense of the word, *responsibility* has to do with tracing the causes of actions and events, of finding out who is answerable in a given situation. Our aim is to determine someone's intention, free will, degree of participation, and appropriate reward or punishment.

We apply the second meaning of *responsibility* to rule following, to contexts where individuals are subject to externally imposed norms often associated with some social role that people play. We speak of the responsibilities of parents to children, of doctors to patients, of lawyers to clients, of citizens to the law. What is socially expected and what the party involved is to answer for are at issue here.

We use the third meaning of *responsibility* for decision making. With this meaning of the term, we say that individuals are responsible if they are trustworthy and reliable, if they allow appropriate factors to affect their judgment; we refer primarily to a person's independent thought processes and decision making, processes that justify an attitude of trust from those who interact with him or her as a responsible individual.

The distinguishing characteristic of moral responsibility, it seems to us, lies in this third sense of the term. Here the focus is on the intellectual and emotional processes in the individual's moral reasoning. Philosophers call this "taking a moral point of view" and contrast it with such other processes as being financially prudent and attending to legal obligations. . . .

We maintain that the processes underlying moral responsibility can be defined and are not themselves vague, even though gaining consensus on specific moral norms and decisions is not always easy.

What, then, characterizes the processes underlying the judgment of a person we call morally responsible? Philosopher William K. Frankena offers the following answer

> "A morality is a normative system in which judgments are made, more or less consciously, [out of a] consideration of the effects of actions . . . on the lives of persons . . . including the lives of others besides the person acting. . . . David Hume took a similar position when he argued that what speaks in a moral judgment is a kind of sympathy. . . . A little later, . . . Kant put the matter somewhat better by characterizing morality as the business of respecting persons as ends and not means or as things. . . ."[2]

Frankena is pointing to two traits, both rooted in a long and diverse philosophical tradition:

1. *Rationality.* Taking a moral point of view includes the features we usually attribute to rational decision-making, that is, lack of impulsiveness, care in mapping out alternatives and consequences, clarity about goals and purposes, attention to details of implementation.
2. *Respect.* The moral point of view also includes a special awareness of and concern for the effects of one's decisions and policies on others, special in the sense that it goes beyond the kind of awareness and concern that would ordinarily be part of rationality, that is, beyond seeing others merely as instrumental to accomplishing one's own purposes. This is respect for the lives of others and involves taking their needs and interests seriously, not simply as resources in one's own decision making but as limiting conditions which change the very definition of one's habitat from a self-centered to a shared environment. It is what philosopher Immanuel Kant meant by the "categorical imperative" to treat others as valuable in and for themselves.

It is this feature that permits us to trust the morally responsible person. We know that such a person takes our point of view into account not merely as a useful precaution (as in "honesty is the best policy") but as important in its own right. . . .

PROJECTING RESPONSIBILITY TO CORPORATIONS

Now that we have removed some of the vagueness from the notion of moral responsibility as it applies to persons, we can search for a frame of reference in which we can meaningfully and appropriately say that corporations are morally responsible. This is the issue reflected in the SSC case.

To deal with it, we must ask two questions: Is it meaningful to apply moral concepts to actors who are not persons but who are instead made up of persons? And even if meaningful, is it advisable to do so?

If a group can act like a person in some ways, then we can expect it to behave like a person in other ways. For one thing, we know that people organized into a group can act as a unit. As business people well know, legally a corporation is considered a unit. To approach unity, a group usually has some sort of internal decision structure, a system of rules that spell out authority relationships and specify the conditions under which certain individuals' actions become official actions of the group.[3]

If we can say that persons act responsibly only if they gather information about the impact of their actions on others and use it in making decisions, we can reasonably do the same for organizations. Our proposed frame of reference for thinking about and implementing corporate responsibility aims at spelling out the processes associated with the moral responsibility of individuals and projecting them to the level of organizations. This is similar to, though an inversion of, Plato's famous method in the *Republic*, in which justice in the community is used as a model for justice in the individual.

Hence, corporations that monitor their employment practices and the effects of their production processes and products on the environment and human health show the same kind of rationality and respect that morally responsible individuals do. Thus, attributing actions, strategies, decisions, and moral responsibilities to corporations as entities distinguishable from those who hold offices in them poses no problem.

And when we look about us, we can readily see differences in moral responsibility among corporations in much the same way that we see differences among persons. Some corporations have built features into their management incentive systems, board structures, internal control systems, and research agendas that in a person we would call self-control, integrity, and conscientiousness. Some have institutionalized awareness and concern for consumers, employees, and the rest of the public in ways that others clearly have not.

As a matter of course, some corporations attend to the human impact of their operations and policies and reject operations and policies that are questionable. Whether the issue be the health effects of sugared cereal or cigarettes, the safety of tires or tampons, civil liberties in the corporation or the community, an organization reveals its character as surely as a person does.

Indeed, the parallel may be even more dramatic. For just as the moral responsibility displayed by an individual develops over time from infancy to adulthood,[4] so too we may expect to find stages of development in organizational character that show significant patterns.

EVALUATING THE IDEA OF MORAL PROJECTION

Concepts like moral responsibility not only make sense when applied to organizations but also provide touchstones for designing more effective models than we have for guiding corporate policy.

Now we can understand what it means to invite SSC as a corporation to be morally responsible both in-house and in its community, but *should* we issue the invitation? Here we turn to the question of advisability. Should we require the organizational agents in our society to have the same moral attributes we require of ourselves?

Our proposal to spell out the processes associated with moral responsibility for individuals and then to project them to their organizational counterparts takes on added meaning when we examine alternative frames of reference for corporate responsibility.

Two frames of reference that compete for the allegiance of people who ponder the question of corporate responsibility are emphatically opposed to this principle of moral projection—what we might refer to as the "invisible hand" view and the "hand of government" view.

The Invisible Hand

The most eloquent spokesman of the first view is Milton Friedman (echoing many philosophers and economists since Adam Smith). According to this pattern of thought, the true and only social responsibilities of business organizations are to make profits and obey the laws. The workings of the free and competitive marketplace will "moralize" corporate behavior quite independently of any attempts to expand or transform decision making via moral projection.

A deliberate amorality in the executive suite is encouraged in the name of systemic morality: the common good is best served when each of us and our economic institutions pursue not the common good or moral purpose, advocates say, but competitive advantage. Morality, responsibility, and conscience reside in the invisible hand of the free market system, not in the hands of the organizations within the system, much less the managers within the organizations.

To be sure, people of this opinion admit, there is a sense in which social or ethical issues can and should enter the corporate mind, but the filtering of such issues is thorough: they go through the screens of custom, public opinion, public relations, and the law. And, in any case, self-interest maintains primacy as an objective and a guiding star.

The reaction from this frame of reference to the suggestion that moral judgment be integrated with corporate strategy is clearly negative. Such an integration is seen as inefficient and arrogant, and in the end both an illegitimate use of corporate power and an abuse of the manager's fiduciary role. With respect to our SSC case, advocates of the invisible hand model would vigorously resist efforts, beyond legal requirements, to make SSC right the wrongs of racial injustice. SSC's responsibility would be to make steel of high quality at least cost, to deliver it on time, and to satisfy its customers and stockholders. Justice would not be part of SSC's corporate mandate.

The Hand of Government

Advocates of the second dissenting frame of reference abound, but John Kenneth Galbraith's work has counterpointed Milton Friedman's with insight and style. Under this view of corporate responsibility, corporations are to pursue objectives that are rational and purely economic. The regulatory hands of the law and the political process rather than the invisible hand of the marketplace turns these objectives to the common good.

Again, in this view, it is a system that provides the moral direction for corporate decision making—a system, though, that is guided by political managers, the custodians of the public purpose. In the case of SSC, proponents of this view would look to the state for moral direction and responsible management, both within SSC and in the community. The corporation would have no moral responsibility beyond political and legal obedience.

What is striking is not so much the radical difference between the economic and social philosophies that underlie these two views of the source of corporate responsibility but the conceptual similarities. Both views locate morality, ethics, responsibility, and conscience in the systems of rules and incentives in which the modern corporation finds itself embedded. Both views reject the exercise of independent moral judgment by corporations as actors in society.

Neither view trusts corporate leaders with stewardship over what are often called noneconomic values. Both require corporate responsibility to march to the beat of drums outside. In the jargon of moral philosophy, both views press for a rule-centered or a system-centered ethics instead of an agent-centered ethics. These frames of reference countenance corporate rule-following responsibility for corporations but not corporate decision-making responsibility.

The Hand of Management

To be sure, the two views under discussion differ in that one looks to an invisible moral force in the market while the other looks to a visible moral force in government. But both would advise against a principle of moral projection that permits or encourages corporations to exercise independent, noneconomic judgment over matters that face them in their short- and long-term plans and operations.

Accordingly, both would reject a third view of corporate responsibility that seeks to affect the thought processes of the organization itself—a sort of "hand of management" view—since neither seems willing or able to see the engines of profit regulate themselves to the degree that would be implied by taking the principle of moral projection seriously. Cries of inefficiency and moral imperialism from the right would be matched by cries of insensitivity and illegitimacy from the left, all in the name of preserving us from corporations and managers run morally amok.

Better, critics would say, that moral philosophy be left to philosophers, philanthropists, and politicians than to business leaders. Better that corporate morality be kept to glossy annual reports, where it is safely insulated from policy and performance.

The two conventional frames of reference locate moral restraint in forces external to the person and the corporation. They deny moral reasoning and intent to the corporation in the name of either market competition or society's system of explicit legal constraints and presume that these have a better moral effect than that of rationality and respect.

Although the principle of moral projection, which underwrites the idea of a corporate conscience and patterns it on the thought and feeling processes of the person, is in our view compelling, we must acknowledge that it is neither part of the received wisdom, nor is its advisability beyond question or objection. Indeed, attributing the role of conscience to the corporation seems to carry with it new and disturbing implications for our usual ways of thinking about ethics and business.

Perhaps the best way to clarify and defend this frame of reference is to address the objections to the principle found in the last pages of this article. There we see a summary of the criticisms and counterarguments we have heard during hours of discussion with business executives and business school students. We believe that the replies to the objections about a corporation having a conscience are convincing. . . .

IS A CORPORATION A MORALLY RESPONSIBLE "PERSON"?

Objection 1 to the Analogy

Corporations are not persons. They are artificial legal constructions, machines for mobilizing economic investments toward the efficient production of goods and services. We cannot hold a corporation responsible. We can only hold individuals responsible.

Reply

Our frame of reference does not imply that corporations are persons in a literal sense. It simply means that in certain respects concepts and functions normally attributed to persons can also be attributed to organizations made up of persons. Goals, economic values, strategies, and other such personal attributes are often usefully projected to the corporate level by managers and researchers. Why should we not project the functions of conscience in the same way? As for holding corporations responsible, recent criminal prosecutions such as the case of Ford Motor Company and its Pinto gas tanks suggest that society finds the idea both intelligible and useful.

Objection 2

A corporation cannot be held responsible at the sacrifice of profit. Profitability and financial health have always been and should continue to be the "categorical imperatives" of a business operation.

Reply

We must of course acknowledge the imperatives of survival, stability, and growth when we discuss corporations, as indeed we must acknowledge them when we discuss the life of an individual. Self-sacrifice has been identified with moral responsibility in only the most extreme cases. The pursuit of profit and self-interest need not be pitted against the demands of moral responsibility. Moral demands are best viewed as containments—not replacements—for self-interest.

This is not to say that profit maximization never conflicts with morality. But profit maximization conflicts with other managerial values as well. The point is to coordinate imperatives, not deny their validity. . . .

Objection 3

The idea of moral projection is a useful device for structuring corporate responsibility only if our understanding of moral responsibility at the level of the person is in some sense richer than our understanding of moral responsibility on the level of the organization as a whole. If we are not clear about individual responsibility, the projection is fruitless.

Reply

The objection is well taken. The challenge offered by the idea of moral projection lies in our capacity to articulate criteria or frameworks of reasoning for the morally responsible person. And though such a challenge is formidable, it is not clear that it cannot be met, at least with sufficient consensus to be useful.

For centuries, the study and criticism of frameworks have gone on, carried forward by many disciplines, including psychology, the social sciences, and philosophy. And though it would be a mistake to suggest that any single framework (much less a decision mechanism) has emerged as the right one, it is true that recurrent patterns are discernible and well enough defined to structure moral discussion.

In the body of the article, we spoke of rationality and respect as components of individual responsibility. Further analysis of these components would translate them into social costs and benefits, justice in the distribution of goods and services, basic rights and duties, and fidelity to contracts. The view that pluralism in our society has undercut all possibility of moral agreement is anything but self-evident. Sincere moral disagreement is, of course, inevitable and not clearly lamentable. But a process and a vocabulary for articulating such values as we share is no small step forward when compared with the alternatives. Perhaps in our exploration of the moral projection we might make some surprising and even reassuring discoveries about ourselves. . . .

Objection 4

Why is it necessary to project moral responsibility to the level of the organization? Isn't the task of defining corporate responsibility and business ethics sufficiently discharged if we clarify the responsibilities of men and women in business as individuals? Doesn't ethics finally rest on the honesty and integrity of the individual in the business world?

Reply

Yes and no. Yes, in the sense that the control of large organizations does finally rest in the hands of managers, of men and women. No, in the sense that what is being controlled is a cooperative system for a cooperative purpose. The projection of responsibility to the organization is simply an acknowledgment of the fact that the whole is more than the sum of its parts. Many intelligent people do not an intelligent organization make. Intelligence needs to be structured, organized, divided, and recombined in complex processes for complex purposes.

Studies of management have long shown that the attributes, successes, and failures of organizations are phenomena that emerge from the coordination of persons' attributes and that explanations of such phenomena require categories of analysis and description beyond the level of the individual. Moral responsibility is an attribute that can manifest itself in organizations as surely as competence or efficiency. . . .

Objection 5

Is the frame of reference here proposed intended to replace or undercut the relevance of the "invisible hand" and the "government hand" views, which depend on external controls?

Reply

No. Just as regulation and economic competition are not substitutes for corporate responsibility, so corporate responsibility is not a substitute for law and the market. The imperatives of ethics cannot be relied on—nor have they ever been relied on—without a context of external sanctions. And this is true as much for individuals as for organizations.

This frame of reference takes us beneath, but not beyond, the realm of external systems of rules and incentives and into the thought processes that interpret and respond to the corporation's environment. Morality is more than merely part of that environment. It aims at the projection of conscience, not the enthronement of it in either the state or the competitive process.

The rise of the modern large corporation and the concomitant rise of the professional manager demand a conceptual framework in which these phenomena can be accommodated to moral thought. The principle of moral projection furthers such accommodation by recognizing a new level of agency in society and thus a new level of responsibility. . . .

NOTES

1. See John Ladd, "Morality and the Ideal of Rationality in Formal Organizations," *The Monist*, October 1970, p. 499.
2. See William K. Frankena, *Thinking About Morality* (Ann Arbor: University of Michigan Press, 1980), p. 26.
3. See Peter French, "The Corporation as a Moral Person," *American Philosophical Quarterly*, July 1979, p. 207.
4. A process that psychological researchers from Jean Piaget to Lawrence Kohlberg have examined carefully; see Jean Piaget, *The Moral Judgement of the Child* (New York: Free Press, 1965) and Lawrence Kohlberg, *The Philosophy of Moral Development* (New York: Harper & Row, 1981).

Catch 20.5: Corporate Morality as an Organizational Phenomenon

JAMES A. WATERS

On a snowy February day in 1960 in Philadelphia, seven electrical equipment manufacturing company executives received jail sentences for their part in a widespread price-fixing and bid rigging conspiracy in the industry. In reference to one of the defendants, a *Fortune* magazine writer noted: "Gray-haired Westinghouse Vice-President, J. H. Chiles, Jr., vestryman of

Excerpted, by permission of the publisher, from "Catch 20.5: Corporate Morality as an Organizational Phenomenon," by James A. Waters, *Organizational Dynamics*, Spring, 1978. © 1978, American Management Association, New York. All rights reserved.

St. John's Episcopal Church in Sharon, Pennsylvania, got thirty days in prison, a $2000 fine."

The description is instructive. It is one thing to be caught with your hand in the till, but in our culture you're likely to receive a great deal more tongue clucking and scorn if you conspicuously represent a contrary set of values through some other activities; if, for example, you are a church elder, a political leader, a den mother, or a teacher. One suspects that the message of the clucking tongues was something like this: There goes Mr. Chiles. He was pretending to be an ethical, moral man, but he was really a crook. He was a hypocrite.

However, there might have been another response, reversed but equally valid, given the importance of situational determinants of behavior. People might have said: There goes Mr. Chiles. Really an ethical, moral man, he was pretending to be a crook. He was a pawn in the system.

INDIVIDUAL VERSUS ORGANIZATIONAL FOCUS

Over the past decade or so, corporate morality has been a subject of continual interest to managers, academics, social critics, and others. Much of this interest has focused on the ethical orientation or morality of corporate managers. However, there are hidden consequences to entering the topic from this perspective.

First, the approach leads to an individual level of analysis as distinguished from an organizational level of analysis. Both kinds of analysis are valid, but they lead to different ideas about action. Once started on an individual-level analysis, one is likely to end up with a kind of "moral exhortation" response to the issue—"What business needs is good people." The exhortation is appropriate, but it may divert attention from other substantive issues.

Second, a person-centered approach flies in the face of what is a subtle but altogether reasonable assumption that the people employed in the business world *are* good people. That is, taken as a whole, they are probably not any different from people in general. There are some crooks and some saints, but most people fall somewhere in between. Moreover, excluding a few businesses in which questionable practices are common, it is not unreasonable to say that the employees of most companies are typically good people within the limits and distribution of people in business, which is the same as people anywhere else.

But if the employees of any given organization are "typically good," why do various unsavory practices (graft, use of call girls, price fixing, and so on) keep reoccurring?

One answer is that sometimes the chief executive of an organization is directly involved. Most lower-level employees may not know what is going on or, if they do, they don't have anywhere within the organization to go with their concerns. . . .

However, another class of problem is probably more common and leaves us with more questions. That is when illegal or unethical activities take place in the organization *without* the knowledge and *against* the wishes of top management. What happens to the "typically good" employees then? . . .

ORGANIZATIONAL BLOCKS

As noted by K. D. Walters, the political right of employees to blow the whistle on employer practices that offend their consciences has been fairly well established, especially when they have exhausted internal grievance procedures. However, the question of *why they don't always do so*, that is, why they don't take steps internally to respond to their own disapproval of and discomfort with certain practices, even when they have no reason to believe that top management supports those practices, may be a more important consideration in understanding why those practices continue.

In the discussion that follows, the term "organizational blocks" will be used to describe those aspects of organizations that may get in the way of the natural tendency of people to react against illegal and unethical practices. The approach puts a positive value on internal whistle blowing. Note also that this way of getting into the topic leads to a different question about the disclosure of such practices. Rather than ask "What was going on with those *people* to make them act that way?" we ask "What was going on in that *organization* that made people act that way?". . .

The first two blocks deal with aspects of supervisor-subordinate relations that can be found in many organizations. The next four relate to more broadly based organizational phenomena: cohesiveness of work groups, ambiguity regarding organizational priorities, separation of strategic and operating decisions, and division of labor. The last block has to do with the relation of the organization to its environment. After a brief review of the nature and functioning of these seven blocks, we will turn to how the concerned manager might respond to the issues raised.

Block 1: Strong Role Models

One of the recurring tasks in organizations is teaching job incumbents the behavior that is required in their jobs. Written job descriptions and performance standards do part of the job, but a lot of teaching and training is accomplished less formally through the efforts of the jobholder's superior and more experienced peers.

Moving into a new job is a time of unusually high dependence on one's superior. To the extent that pressure, both internal and external, is exerted to "get on board and up to speed" quickly, the new jobholder must look to his or her superior for guidance and will attempt to imitate the superior's behavior.

When such socialization includes indoctrination into illegal and un-ethical practices, this same organizational dynamic makes it difficult for the executive to redefine the reality of his or her job so as to exclude such practices. He or she is led to conclude that nothing different can be done, that there is no way to disengage from such practices and still fulfill the requirements of the job.

Examples abound in the electrical equipment case. In describing how, as a proposition engineer-in-training for General Electric, he first became involved in meetings with competitors for purposes of price-fixing, one man recalled that "I got into it in the beginning when I was young. I probably was impressed by the manager of marketing asking me to go to a meeting with him (where price-fixing discussions took place). I probably was naive" (16652). (In what follows, three- to five-digit references are to page numbers in testimony transcripts described in the selected bibliography). Another felt that when he became a sales manager for Wagner Electric, he was simply "filling a spot in carrying out a pattern that had been in existence for some time" (17823). . . .

Block 2: Strict Line of Command

One of the popular principles of formal organization is establishment of a chain of command. Each person has one boss, and authority is vested in the office of that superior. It is a widespread belief that efficiency is best achieved through strict adherence to this approach, labeled the "one-over-one" in the General Electric vernacular of the 1950s.

Time and again, throughout the testimony, deeply ingrained respect for the line-of-command concept is evident. When asked directly why he did not report illegal activities to higher management, one witness simply replied: "I had no power to go higher. I do not report to anyone else except my superior" (16584).

Another consequence of the strict line of command is that assumptions are generated about where orders really come from:

> I had to assume that whatever he told me came from his superior, just as my subordinate would have to assume that what I told him came from my superior. *That is the way business is run.* (16864)

The power of the line of command is not simply a social norm: Unethical executives often have the raw power at their disposal to enforce compliance without tipping off higher-ups. Threats of transfer to lesser positions, subtle character assassination on appraisal forms, manipulation of rewards, and the like are used to keep the more conscience-troubled employee in line.

Whether or not such coercive power and control are necessary tools in the modern management tool bag can be argued. However, their existence may be a natural outgrowth of other dimensions of organizational life, such as task specialization, delegation of authority, and supervisor responsibility for performance appraisal and implementation of reward systems. A major effort would probably be necessary to eliminate them.

In any event, in terms of speed and efficiency, the existence of a strict line of command in the hierarchy has obvious pay-offs. Similarly, the prevalence of a strong loyalty ethic allows an executive to deal more efficiently with the relations between his unit and the larger organization. Loyalty from the troops is a source of sustenance and power.

This same organizational dynamic becomes a block to the executive who wants to eliminate his involvements in illegal or unethical activities. Even if he gets past the on-going socialization by his boss (Block 1) he is still in a bind. If he defies orders, he is subject to manipulation by his boss. If he exposes the practice, he is defying the organizational chain-of-command ethos and is likely to be stigmatized as disloyal. Also, since there is a logical presumption that his boss is simply passing along orders, to whom does he report the illegal goings-on?

Block 3: Task Group Cohesiveness

A ubiquitous phenomenon of organizational life is the presence of groups. People work in groups, draw their social support from groups, and look to groups as referents to define reality in vague and ambiguous situations.

When people work interdependently on common tasks it is in the organization's best interest for them to be a cohesive group in order to facilitate communication and work. Investments are frequently made both formally (team-building programs) and informally (luncheons, travel together) to build group cohesion.

However, a possible consequence of increased intragroup cohesion is reduced intergroup cohesion. Communication and cooperation among groups in the same organization can become restricted and reduce the impact or influence of some organizational directives. At the time, conspirators at General Electric referred to themselves as "members of the club" (17040). There is repeated testimony about how the group functioned to exclude outsiders. For example:

> We were continually reminded that whenever we got instructions that we were going to start this contacting up again, be sure not to let the lawyers know anything about it, and do not keep any records so they can find out anything about it. (16737)

> You were never to let the manufacturing people, the engineers, and especially the lawyers, know anything about it. (17040)

While there are organizational gains to be made from tightly cohesive work groups, these groups can also function as organizational blocks. The group provides social support for continued involvements in the illegal activity. More importantly, efforts to disengage from such practices will conflict with the executive's loyalty to the group, especially if there is no way to get out without exposing the other members. Last, external pressure to expose illegal goings-on is a threat to the group, which in turn may cause it to draw even tighter and inhibit the executive still more from withdrawing from those activities.

Block 4: Ambiguity about Priorities

Richard Cyert and J. G. March have noted that organizations can often maintain mutually inconsistent or even conflicting objectives (for example, to increase market share *and* increase margin on sales) by devoting attention to them sequentially rather than simultaneously. When the directive to obey the law creates a tug-of-war with the general pressure for profits, *how* the organization presents these messages may be as important as *what* the messages contain. Subtle cues may determine the manner in which employees resolve perceived conflict among objectives and they may also determine the degree of uncertainty employees experience about how much social support they will recieve if they expose some illegal practice. If I expose shady selling practices, will I be a hero or an outcast?

For example, General Electric had a very clearly written antitrust directive called "policy 20.5." But the directive received a curious treatment in the organization; it was often dominated by line-of-command directions to the contrary.

One executive was adamant about the ambiguity of the message in 20.5:

> I feel that if the company really meant that all the employees should follow this 20.5, that the company and all the officers of the company should take the same interest in that, and talk just as much about the 20.5 at every meeting as they talk about engineering, marketing, finance, profits, labor relations, and everything else. They never did that. (16829)

Another executive suggested there was some question in his mind as to whether the top line-of-command people were behind the policy:

> At no time during this period did they use what we call the one-over-one system in the General Electric Company (concerning policy 20.5). That is the man over the other man, to sit down with that policy and say "You are to observe this policy and here, sign this." All they did was to issue that policy,

and send [it] to us through the mail from the legal side of it, which was an advisory side, not a line-of-command side, and ask us to sign it. (16788)

Two factors interact to create and maintain this ambiguity. First, hard measurable performance criteria (for example, profitability, sales volume, costs) tend to drive out softer, less measurable criteria (for example, social responsiveness, ethical practices). Because the former are easier to discuss, agree on, and control for, they attract more executive time and energy than the latter. As Robert Ackerman points out, this is especially true for divisionalized structures, where the autonomy of operating divisions rests on their willingness to perform against hard, measurable financial targets, and communication with corporate management tends to be limited to those targets. It becomes easy to create the impression that the softer criteria are less important.

The general pressure within organizations to enhance profitability reinforces that impression. In GE at the time, there was considerable evidence that if a manager wanted to continue to have a profit-center responsibility, he would be well advised to keep achieving his profit budget.

Simply announcing that compliance with the law was a paramount value in the array of corporate objectives would have eliminated any ambiguity in the minds of employees about how they would be received if they blew the whistle. However, such a stance would have depressurized the forces exerted on employees for profits. The profit manager would have had an "out" about realized price levels. Thus the policy may have been perceived as being presented with an implicit message of "Do this, but make sure that doing it doesn't keep you from meeting your profit objectives." It would be a "Catch 20.5."

Block 5: Separation of Decisions

Ideally, the experiences of operating-level people in attempting to implement organization strategy are used as data input for the constant revision of basic strategy. Sometimes strategic decisions are made by middle managers. However, in large, hierarchically structured organizations, lower-level people are usually expected to accept strategy as a given and to work to achieve the stated objectives. An executive might feel free to ask about objectives one or two levels up, but no avenues are available for routine questioning of more basic starting points in what amounts to a hierarchy of ends and means.

This organizational reality can function as a block when strategy constrains an executive to operate in a business or in a locale in which practices he perceives to be of questionable legality or ethicality are accepted as commonplace. The dilemmas faced by employees of multinational corporations with respect to payments that would be considered bribes (and illegal) in this country but are a way of life in others have been well publicized.

Analogies closer to home are available. One knowledgeable observer points out

> that in New York City it is well known that graft and bribes are an integral part of "doing business" in the construction industry. At the opposite end of the scale, no graft is paid in Atlanta, Georgia, where it is considered inappropriate.

The point to be emphasized is that the lower-level executive who finds himself in a "New York City type of business" is in a peculiar bind. Suppose, for example, that as part of a diversification program, your company has acquired a subsidiary with completely new marketing channels. As part of your plan to integrate that acquisition into the corporate fold, you transfer some mid-level managers from the main business area to the new acquisition.

One executive who made just such a move discovered that selling practices in the new business routinely involved kickbacks, graft, elaborate promotional considerations (for example, giving buyers automobiles), and other, similar practices. The old-timers in the company had become desensitized to the ethical issues implicit in these practices. Moreover, they believed (quite correctly) that avoiding these practices would cause a drastic reduction in marketshare.

What could this man do? It would be extremely costly for a single company to avoid such practices in this industry. The only realistic choices would be to stay in the business, to abandon it, or to sell the company to an unsuspecting buyer. This man's organization simply had no channels through which he could raise questions about the ethics of staying in this business.

Also, as James March and Herbert Simon point out, closely related to the idea of available channels is the issue of communication efficiency. Shared organizational vocabularies tend to develop such that large amounts of information can be communicated with relatively few words. For example, such short phrases as "ROI," "payback period," "he's a producer," "she's on the fast track," often convey a constellation of facts and judgments far beyond the literal meaning of the words. In contrast, anything that doesn't fit the system is communicated only with great difficulty.

In the organizations being discussed, as in most organizations, a widely shared organizational vocabulary concerning issues of morality and ethics does not exist. Just as the presence of a shared vocabulary facilitates identification and discussion of topics like marketshare, inventory levels, capital budgets, competitors' actions, and the like, the absence of a richly elaborated common language for issues of morality acts to block discussion.

Conversations about moral and ethical issues are almost doomed to be awkward, halting, and time-consuming to the point of painfulness. If an organizational environment normally demands snappy and efficient presentations and discussions, such conversations are unlikely to take place.

Block 6: Division of Work

The total work to be done in any organization must be subdivided. The most familiar division of work is horizontal in nature; this is the basis of task specialization. A consequence of rigid division is that things often get "left to channels." Employees in one part of an organization can be aware of illegal activities in another part, yet believe that they are in no position to do anything about it or that it just isn't done. As one witness put it: "I happen to have a great distaste for tale-bearing and I simply did not do that kind of thing". (17228)

Channels can also be changed to isolate and neutralize an executive who might be critical of a corporate practice.

. . . Somewhat like the effect of a strict chain of command, exaggerated respect for channels could convince employees that they must *not* do what they're *not* told. A person who knows of or is associated with illegal or unethical practices may be blocked from reacting by the difficulty of working across channels and by the disfavor with which any such activity is viewed in a tight organization.

Vertical fractionation of work also occurs. Different levels in the hierarchy may make qualitatively different contributions to the organization. For example, the same information may mean different things to people at succeeding levels in the hierarchy. People at each level may filter or use selectively the data provided by the previous level because, by virtue of their position, they have a more accurate sense of the purpose for which the information was collected and/or have different factual input that supports revisions.

A possible consequence is that lower-level employees may have uncomfortable suspicions that what they are doing is illegal or unethical, yet not have enough command of the facts to report their suspicions without fear of finding that they have completely misread the situation. In short, the absence of sufficient knowledge of the "big picture" acts to immobilize the employee at the same time that the knowledge he does have about certain practices is spurring him to take action. In large organizations very few people have the "big picture." Each level tends to reserve a portion of the facts, perhaps in order to maintain differentiation of levels. Hence, the employee is afraid to act on what he knows. . . .

Block 7: Protection from Outside Intervention

Any investigation into illegal and unethical practices by an organization only increases its risk of exposure to prosecution, damage claims, and soiled public image. Every pressure exists, even for the organization that wants to eliminate such practices, to avoid looking at what has happened in the past.

Thus the affidavit accompanying 20.5 in GE read in part as follows:

I have received a copy of directive policy general no. 20.5 dated October 23, 1953. I have read and understood this policy. I am observing it and will observe it in the future. (16737)

The focus of the affidavit is on the present and the future. It is certainly understandable that a sincere desire to obey the law would take its first form in a desire to clean things up from then on. It would take a qualitatively different type of motivation to engage in public confessions of past misdeeds, and that is probably what an organization would have to do if a full-scale investigation of past practices were launched. . . .

The way the organization is encouraged to exercise a tight control over its interface with the social system becomes an organizational block for the executive who wishes to stop illegal and unethical activities. To cease and desist, one must first clean house. Cleaning house could mean public exposure, which conflicts with reasonable organizational loyalty.

The tight control organizations are forced to maintain also limits research into instances of unethical behavior in organizational settings. The resulting lack of published cases and analyses limits public discussion and appreciation of the conflicting pressures on an employee with respect to illegal or unethical practices.

In something of a vicious cycle, this lack of open discussion in schools and among managers makes employees more susceptible to the organizational blocks. Conversely, to the extent that business school graduates and young managers have been able to read about and discuss cases in which people like themselves got mired in some unsavory practice, they are more capable of resisting pressures from inappropriate role models and simplistic norms about the chain of command.

The lack of open discussion also deprives the organizational policy formulation process of important input. If there can be no data-based analyses of the roots and flowering of past illegal and unethical practices, managerial attempts to eliminate such practices are forced to rely on vague and anecdotal feedback. The development of policies and change strategies that could reduce or eliminate organizational blocks is thus impeded.

RESPONSE: TIGHTENING DOWN OR LOOSENING UP?

As noted earlier, all these factors are natural concomitants of a complex organization. The extent to which they also act to block people from blowing the whistle on practices they find ethically objectionable might be described as an unintended consequence. In a few cases it might also be said that the same methods of control instituted by the leaders of an organization to achieve organizational objectives can be used by the occasional "bad apple" to block effective reaction by those who are offended by specific practices. How should the concerned manager react? Should he or she make the controls even more stringent?

Such an approach, however instinctive, can be seen to focus on the "bad guys" (assumed to be few in number) and to ignore the "good guys" (assumed to be most of the employees in the company). Based on a consideration of the notion of organizational blocks, I suggest that "battening down the hatches" can have exactly the opposite effect from the one intended. Increasing the clarity of control procedures may enable the few bad guys to navigate their way around the system easily.

For example, establishing a "watchdog" position, perhaps in the legal department, with great fanfare may enable those who are so inclined to rope that person off from crucial information more easily. Focusing guardianship in this way may also diminish the felt responsibilities in others to detect and report unethical practices. A mechanistic approach—such as having everybody sign a standard affidavit like GE's "20.5"—can impersonalize and desensitize the issue. Such an approach can create the illusion that all is taken care of while the main effect may be to allow a few conspirators to lay low for a while or develop persuasive stories as to why this "routine staff request" should be treated lightly.

More importantly, such an approach doesn't tap into the tremendous reservoir of energy that exists among employees to root out such practices. By reversing the focus and thinking more about the "good guys," it may be possible to unblock some of the natural forces that exist in the organization to raise questions about practices of uncertain ethicality.

In other words, instead of asking how to block people from engaging in unsavory practices, it might be better to ask how to unblock the natural ethical instincts of most of your employees.

ACTION PLANNING

How can the concerned manager proactively approach the job of ensuring ethical business operations? A spirit of inquiry must be brought to a *preventive maintenance program*: just as you can do maintenance on a machine while it is running rather than wait for a possibly calamitous breakdown, you can work to reduce or eliminate the effects of organizational blocks before unethical practices take root or there is a costly scandal. . . .

The challenge in all this for the concerned management is to integrate a healthy pressure for performance and profitability with a healthy respect for individual consciences and differences of opinion. If top management has been relatively more articulate about the former than about the latter, there may be no more potent way of signaling a more balanced interest than to invest time and energy in a collaborative program aimed at minimizing the impact of organizational blocks.

What might such a program look like? As suggested earlier, it would have to be shaped to fit the organization, and it would be best if both its design and execution were carried out by the key people in that organization. Nevertheless, most programs contain some common basic elements.

1. Removing ambituity concerning organizational priorities. If top management really wants to obey the law and operate according to the general ethical standards of society, it must say so unambiguously. It should state clearly that such constraints come *before,* and in that sense have a *higher priority than,* such traditional objectives as sales volume, marketshare, and profits.

[In] A. B. Carroll's survey, 78 percent of all the managers responding agreed to some extent with the following statement: "I can conceive of a situation where you have sound ethics running from top to bottom but, because of pressures from top to achieve results, the person down the line compromises." To facilitate internal whistle blowing, everyone must be made acutely aware that organizational priorities will be maintained even when the pressure is on for profits and performance. This has to be a starting point.

2. Moving from abstract generality to concrete example. A presidential letter that stays at the "do good and avoid evil" level of abstraction can be a pretty ambiguous signal to people who are afraid to respond to their own distaste for certain practices. "I wonder if he means this" will be the most common reaction. Avoiding specific examples that would be obvious to anyone in the industry will create doubt about the seriousness of the message.

For instance, if your firm is involved in real estate transactions such as buying retail sites and working with zoning commissions, it is dysfunctional to pretend that bribery is not a frequent occurrence in this area and to avoid saying that you do not want your people to pay bribes of any sort, even if it hurts your business. If your firm is selling a relatively undifferentiated product to retail channels dominated by a few chains and their powerful buyers and buying/selling practices are notoriously corrupt, your field salespeople will feel uncertain about a message that does not acknowledge the existence of such practices and does not clearly state your views on how you want them to deal with the pressures they face.

Some brainstorming sessions with employees who have long and diverse experience in your industry can probably generate a lengthy list of examples. It can be done in a nonthreatening way by asking people what *could* be going on that shouldn't rather than what *is* going on. A corollary to Murphy's Law would be that illegal or unethical practices that could exist probably do.

3. Providing concrete steps for internal whistle blowers. If people are convinced of your position and want to take action on a questionable practice, what steps should they take? If you don't provide direction for them, they may still feel blocked. Leaving communications to the regular chain of command is obviously inadequate.

Should they ask for a meeting with you? Write you a memo? Call you at home? Perhaps you will want to establish an ombudsman in the organization. Although ombudsmen traditionally respond to employee complaints about such matters as compensation inequities, job performance appraisals, and benefit programs, it is not difficult to imagine the position also serving as a receiving point for internal whistle blowing.

Perhaps those who want to report wrongdoing could be encouraged by assurances that *initial* explorations would take place under the security of guaranteed anonymity. Subsequent serious action and change, if any, would necessarily and appropriately involve open discussion between the whistle blower and those engaged in the practice in question.

A system of secret informers is unthinkable, since it would destroy the spirit of openness and questioning that is being sought. However, an initial ice-breaking confidential discussion with a manager tuned in to these kinds of questions may help the would-be whistle blower to think through whether the issue in question warrants open investigation and, if so, may help him to gather his courage to proceed.

The exact channel used here may be less important than the clarity with which the proper procedure is spelled out. The person who wants to take action probably feels anxious and uncertain. Providing a reasonable procedure for reporting problems and a picture of what will happen to those reports will help make the anxiety manageable and will facilitate action.

4. Developing an appropriate organizational vocabulary. As suggested earlier, one of the blocks to internal whistle blowing is the difficulty of discussing issues of morality and ethics in the absence of an appropriate organizational vocabulary. Training programs can be devised that focus directly on this problem. Peopled by employees from diagonal slices of the organization, so that different departments and hierarchical levels are involved, workshops can allow those attending to wrestle with cases that are directly pertinent to their company and to see the issues from different perspectives.

Note that such programs would be organization-level interventions rather than attempts to change individuals. First, they would serve to legitimize the topic—ethical concerns or pangs of conscience would become proper subjects to bring up with one's boss or at a staff meeting.

Second, by being exposed to a common framework of cases and anecdotes, organization members would begin to develop a shared appreciation of ethical questions and dilemmas. Analogies could be drawn. "The situation we're in here seems just like that of the sales manager in that XYZ Pump Company case we discussed." A crisper vocabulary could be used. "There appears to be a vast discrepancy between our intended values and our operational values in the case of this ad copy." In short, the purpose of these programs would be to create a rich and differentiated vocabulary within the organization so that when the time came to discuss ethical questions, everyone would be speaking the same language. They would *not* be set up to make people more ethical.

There are specific reasons for the diagonal-slice approach to selecting people for such workshops. If someone feels blocked because of strong pressure from a group of conspirators, working intensively with people from other parts of the organization can give that person a chance to build the social support necessary to break away from the old group.

Furthermore, the workshops, instead of being based on a one-way communication model, could be designed as deep-sensing sessions. Additonal insights could be gathered about what might be going on in the way of illegal and unethical practices. Since people from different departments would be joining together on this work, norms that exist against commenting on business areas other than one's own would be challenged and revised. The cross-level nature of the participation would signal the seriousness of the commitment at all levels of the organization.

By having all *new* management employees participate in such training programs, you could bring about an evolutionary change. If appropriate norms about dealing with questionable practices could be instilled early in people's organizational careers, they would be less blocked from acting on their own ethical concerns.

In a longer-range effort to build appropriate vocabularies and prepare new employees for the pressures they will face on the job, top management can also influence the training they receive *before* they reach the organization. They can demand that business schools explicitly devote research and teaching time to questions of ethics and morality. They can offer to work with serious researchers and to give guest lectures on the topic. It is hard to picture a contemporary management school faculty that would not be responsive to such influence.

5. Launching sensitive investigative efforts. Several firms (Seagram, Northrop, Gulf, and so on) have employed audit committees to search out and report illegal campaign contributions or overseas bribery payments. These have generally had a financial accounting orientation, but it seems reasonable to think that the mission of such audit committees could be expanded so that moral and ethical questions outside the existing financial control procedures are also explored.

In some ways, this would convert the ombudsman role mentioned earlier to a more proactive posture. Rather than being simply a receiving post for whistle blowers, such a person could go out into the organization and actively seek to uncover unintended organizational blocks. However, it would be important for this searching activity to be perceived as facilitating the general opening up of communication in the organization. If it is not part of an overall change program, it might be seen as detective work, and skillful operators will devise ways to circumvent it and rope it off from pertinent information. . . .

. . . To greater or lesser degrees, we all have boundaries on our courage. From an institutional leadership perspective, the individual as citizen is a natural integrating link between the organization and the laws and ethical customs of the larger society. Practices that are badly out of synchronization with the prevailing moral sense of society won't take place if they are exposed to the light of reasonable debate among "good people." The concerned manager might ask whether his or her organization makes it easy for employees to act on their consciences or whether it tests the boundaries of their courage.

SELECTED BIBLIOGRAPHY

For some after-the-fact accounts by actual whistle blowers, Ralph Nadar, Peter Petkas, and Kate Blackwell's *Whistle Blowing* (Grossman Publishers, 1972) and Robert L. Heilbroner's *In the Name of Profit* (Doubleday, 1972) are interesting. The actual transcripts from congressional investigating committees provide perhaps the most engaging insight into organizational life with respect to illegal and unethical activities. The primary sources for this article were "Price Fixing and Bid Rigging in the Electrical Manufacturing Industry," Hearings Before the Subcommittee on Antitrust and Monopoly of the Committee on the Judiciary, U.S. Senate, Parts 27–28, 1961; "Competitive Problems in the Drug Industry," Hearings Before the Monopoly Subcommittee of the Select Committee on Small Business, U.S. Senate, 1969; and "Air Force A-7D Brake Problem," Hearing Before the Subcommittee on Economy in Government of the Joint Economic Committee, U.S. Congress, 1969.

Additional examples of whistle blowing can be found in K. D. Walters's "Your Employee's Right to Blow the Whistle" (*Harvard Business Review*, July–August 1975), which discusses the political and legal rights of sincere whistle blowers. H. Gordon Fitch and Charles B. Saunders's "Blowing the Whistle: The Limits of Obedience to the Organization" (*Business and Society*, Fall 1976, Vol. 17, No. 1) provides an interesting counterperspective to the one presented here, since they take the same cases and describe an individual level problem, that is, excessive obedience. In contrast, and more in parallel with the line of thinking presented here, Chapter 4 of Robert Ackerman's *The Social Challenge to Business* (Harvard University Press, 1975) discusses the impact of divisionalized organization structures on social criteria of performance.

For some insight into attitudes of managers toward ethical questions and into differing views by upper- and lower-level managers, see Archie B. Carroll's "Managerial Ethics: A Post Watergate View" (*Business Horizons*, April 1975) and Rama Krishnan's "Business Philosophy and Executive Responsibility" (*Academy of Management Journal*, December 1973).

Part III

PROPERTY, PROFIT, AND JUSTICE

Issues about money and economics are often connected to those of ethics and values. If a friend borrows five dollars and later refuses to repay it, then the issue quickly becomes an ethical one: we say the friend really *should* repay the money. At all levels of economics, ethics plays an important role. For example, to decide how society should distribute wealth, one must know what ethical standards distinguish fair from unfair distributions. Thus it is not surprising that two well-known economists, Adam Smith and Karl Marx (both of whom are discussed in this section), began their careers as philosophers.

Two of the most volatile issues in economics have ethical implications: the importance of the profit motive, and the restrictions to be placed, if any, on private property. The pursuit of profit and the existence of private property are said by some economists to be the foundation of a free society. The seventeenth-century philosopher John Locke argued that each person has a natural *right* to own property. However, others argue that the profit motive and private property are corrupting and result in labor abuses, unfair income distribution, monopolistic practices, and misuse of the environment.

A third issue involving both ethics and economics is the nature of justice. For example, is there such a thing as a just distribution of wealth, resources, and opportunities in society, and if so, what does that distribution look like? Is it fair that one person buys yachts and racehorses while another cannot even buy food? Or is it true, instead, that any time government attempts to insure "fairness" by interfering with the free accumulation of wealth, its attempt to redistribute wealth, resources, or opportunities commits a fundamental injustice by violating the liberty of those who have freely earned power, position, or property?

TRADITIONAL THEORIES OF PROFIT AND PROPERTY

The Profit Motive

It is not uncommon today to hear a person or corporation condemned for being greedy. Such an attitude, which questions the morality of emphasizing profit, is not new. If anything, people today are more accepting of the profit motive than at any other time in history. Especially prior to the nineteenth century, pursuing wealth, and sometimes even lending money, were targets of intense criticism.

The greatest defender of the profit motive was the eighteenth-century philosopher-economist Adam Smith. Today, nearly two hundred years after Smith presented his ideas in *The Wealth of Nations* (excerpts of which are presented in this section), his name is almost synonymous with the defense of the free market or "laissez-faire" economic system. However, Smith did not believe that economic gain was our most noble goal; rather, he agreed with his professor of moral philosophy, Francis Hutcheson, who claimed that benevolence, not self-interest, was humanity's crowning virtue. But in contrast with his teacher, Smith asserted that the pursuit of profit, at least in the context of a free market, was not always bad. In a famous quotation from *The Wealth of Nations* he writes

> It is not from the benevolence of the butcher, the brewer, or the baker that we expect our dinner, but from their regard of their own interest. We address ourselves not to their humanity, but to their self-love and never talk to them of our own necessities, but of their advantage.

Thus Smith emphasized the way in which pursuing one's own economic self-interest in the free marketplace could enhance public welfare. Smith believed that the world was designed so that people's pursuing their own selfish economic ends would tend to generate, in the absence of governmental intervention, great public good. He calls this special tendency the "invisible hand," a tendency that guides each person's pursuit of self-interest into a pattern of healthy competition, which, in turn, yields high quality products at the lowest possible prices. It has been said that Smith showed how a "private vice," that is, the self-interested pursuit of profit, can be transformed into a "public virtue."

Criticisms of the Invisible Hand

By the time the Industrial Revolution was under way in the early nineteenth century, Smith's ideas dominated economic theory, and interestingly, many of the emerging social patterns of that era were justified by appealing to his philosophy. The increased specialization, the reduction of quotas and tariffs, and the decreased role of government in business were all justified by appealing to Smith's *Wealth of Nations*. Smith himself, however, did not live to see the changes, nor the human misery rampant during the Industrial Revolution. Labor was poorly paid, working conditions deplorable, and working hours long. One of the most depressing sights of all was children working in factories for sixteen hours a day, six days a week. For many children, such work was necessary to supplement their family's meager income.

Many witnesses to the Industrial Revolution were persuaded that the real villain was the economic system. The German philosopher and economist Karl Marx argued that the "free market" Smith championed was little more than a convenient fiction for capitalist property owners. Whereas Smith had praised the competitive market because of its ability to generate better products at lower prices, Marx argued that in the marketplace workers were mere commodities, available to the factory owners at the lowest possible wages. Indeed, he thought the pressures of the marketplace would force workers, who could not refuse to work without starving, to accept wages barely above a subsistence level. Meanwhile the owners of the means of production, the capitalists, could exploit workers by using their labor and then selling the resulting product at a profit. Marx identified the difference between the costs of production, including wages, and the selling price of the product as "surplus value." For Marx, then, profits always meant exploitation of the worker by the capitalist. And he added that whenever technology develops, the economic gap between the capitalist and the worker must widen further, since technology allows products to be manufactured with less human labor and thus creates unemployment and lower wages.

In the selections taken from *Economic and Philosophic Manuscripts of 1844*, Marx outlines his influential theory of alienation, in which he asserts that workers in capitalistic society are separated from, and deprived of, their own labor. When forced to work for the capitalist, workers are also forced to give the capitalist what most belongs to them: their own work. Factory employees toil away producing products that the factory owner will eventually sell, and they feel no connection to those products; rather, they have been *alienated* from the effects of their labor. Thus, through the concept of alienation Marx offers a fundamental condemnation of modern capitalism.

At the same time that Marx was developing his criticisms of capitalism, there was another equally dramatic development occurring. In 1859 the English naturalist Charles Darwin published his monumental work on evolution, *The Origin of the Species*. Darwin argued, in short, that (1) organisms in the biological kingdom had evolved from simple to more complex species; and (2) during this process organisms less adaptable to the environment failed to survive, while the more adaptable ones flourished. Darwin himself expressly stated that his ideas applied only to the biological kingdom, but many thinkers extended them to social and economic issues. The resulting theory of society, popularized by Herbert Spencer and industrialists such as Andrew Carnegie (whose article "Wealth" is reproduced in this section), was known as Social Darwinism.

Social Darwinism was to have its effect on issues dealt with by Adam Smith and Karl Marx, but in point of fact it agreed with neither. The Darwinists argued that the Industrial Revolution exemplified social evolution from simple to complex societies. In the evolution of a capitalistic industrial system, then, some individuals may suffer; but the system itself enhances human welfare, since it weeds out the unsuccessful, weak competitors while allowing the tougher ones to flourish. Thus, both marketplace and nature operate according to the same "natural" laws. Those who can, survive; those who cannot, perish. In this way the thesis of Social Darwinism came to view the profit motive in business as the essential motivating force in the struggle for economic survival. Unfortunately, Social Darwinism was also touted by a few wealthy tycoons in the nineteenth century as a justification for deplorable working conditions and massive economic inequalities.

The key issues of Part III—human motivation, human nature, and which economic system is preferable—are interrelated. For example, the ethical question of when, if at all, it is best for people to be motivated by profit is directly connected to the question of whether there is a common human nature. If, as some have argued, people must and will pursue their own self-interest because of their *very nature*, it can be claimed, as Smith does, that the pursuit of self-interest in the form of economic gain is often morally justified. In a similar fashion both issues are tied to that of discovering the best economic system. If people are naturally self-interested and will inevitably act on the basis of self-interest in the marketplace, perhaps society needs an economic system that acknowledges and reflects this fact. On the other hand, if while being naturally self-interested people can regularly subordinate their self-interest to higher motives such as benevolence, then perhaps society needs a somewhat different economic system, one that encourages such higher motives.

Private Ownership

Another issue closely connected to that of profit is public versus private ownership. A common argument used by those who criticize private property asserts that the elimination of private property makes it impossible for people to strive to accumulate wealth, and thus discourages them from acting from a bad motive, that is, the profit motive. Defenders of the institution of private property disagree, citing the incentive for hard work and creativity that private property provides. But by far the most ingenious argument in favor of private property is the classical one offered by the seventeenth-century English philosopher John Locke.

Locke believed that human beings have a fundamental right to own private property, and the basic premises that establish this right can be found in the selection from his *Second Treatise on Government*. Even today his "social contract" argument is commonly used in defending the right to own property. Locke asserts what he claims is a truism: in the absence of any formally structured society—that is, in the "state of nature"—all people may be said to *own their own bodies*. Moreover, all people living in such a state may be said also to possess the *right* to own their own bodies. It was upon this seemingly obvious premise that Locke rested his defense. If one admits that one has the right to own one's body, it follows that one owns the actions of that body, or in other words, one's own labor. Finally, one may also be said to own, and to have a right to own, the things with which one mixes one's labor. For example, if in the state of nature a person picks fruit from wild bushes, that person may be said to own the fruit. And if we grant that property may be freely traded, given, and accumulated, we have the beginning of the basis for justification of vast ownership of capital and land.

In sharp contrast with Locke's seemingly benign defense of private property, Karl Marx argues that it is actually an institution that perpetuates the class struggle. He believes that it is likely that no such state of nature as Locke described ever existed, and he tries to give an accurate historical account of the evolution of the institution of private property. In the selections from *The Communist Manifesto*, Marx tries to show how at every stage in the struggle for private property one class succeeds in exploiting another. He argues that the institution of private property in a capitalistic economic system is nothing other than the means by which the privileged class—the capitalists or bourgeoisie—exploits the class of the less privileged, the workers.

We should remind ourselves that the immediate question confronting most people in the Western world is probably not whether to adopt a purely communistic or a purely free-market form of economy. Of more immediate practical significance is the question of *how much* of society's goods and services should be placed in public ownership. How important is it, for example, that certain of society's economic institutions remain in the hands of private ownership? Can businesses that are privately owned contribute as much to the public welfare as those that are publicly owned? Is it possible for the latter, such as the post office or public utilities, to violate basic human rights and freedoms? In this context the case study "Plasma International" raises the question of the good or bad effects of allowing the market to distribute goods and services—especially when the good is a human necessity such as blood.

PROFIT AND PROPERTY: MODERN DISCUSSIONS

One of the most outspoken critics of public ownership in the twentieth century is the economist Milton Friedman. Strongly opposing Marx, Friedman argues that the maintenance of the economic institution of private property is necessary to ensure basic political rights and freedoms. In his article "The Social Responsibility of Business Is to Increase Its Profits," Friedman denies the claim that businesses have obligations to society over and above their obligation to make a profit. In the spirit of Adam Smith, Friedman believes that the free market works best, and makes its greatest contribution, when companies compete for consumers' business and for the maximization of profits. Consequently, says Friedman, if a company were to make ethics or social responsibility a primary goal, it would be failing in its duty and hence, ironically, would not be fulfilling its real "social responsibility." Rather, the social responsibility of a corporate manager is simply to maximize profits on behalf of the corporation's owners, the shareholders.

Friedman strongly objects to placing society's major economic institutions in public ownership. Not only would the competitive marketplace be undermined, resulting in poorer products and services for the consumer, but a basic freedom would be denied insofar as the government would be interfering with the right to own property. In other of his writings Friedman even argues that certain institutions that are now public, such as the post office and national parks, should be turned over to private investors.

How seriously one takes either Friedman's arguments or arguments asserting the opposite—that the railroads or oil industry, for example, should become publicly owned—will hinge on how seriously one takes the arguments of Locke and Marx. Is Locke correct in arguing that there is a natural right to private property? And how does his argument relate to Marx's claim that private property makes it possible for one class to exploit another?

Friedman's proposal for a free market has received widespread attention in the 1980s as a potential solution to our economic problems. But the proposal has also been sharply criticized. In a reading included in this section, George Cabot Lodge contends that the Lockean notion of private property, a notion fundamental to Friedman's views, is no longer faithful to contemporary property relationships. Lodge notes the disintegration of the absolute right to private property and suggests that this disintegration has occurred both because the courts have systematically weakened property rights for the sake of public interest and because corporations have "dispersed" ownership by selling shares of stock. Locke's notion of private property has given way to a broader sense of community where basic human claims to survival, a decent standard of living, and a clean environment override traditional property claims. The result, in brief, is a reevaluation not only of private property but of labor rights and the traditional ideas of freedom and responsibility.

Friedman's thesis raises another issue. Should the government police the activities of private corporations and business persons? Or should it intervene only when a clear and present danger exists for persons (as in the instance of poisoned pain killers), or any time it believes that doing so will enhance general welfare? Two articles dealing with this issue are Steven Kelman's "Regulation that Works" and James Gustafson and Elmer Johnson's "Resolving Income and Wealth Differences in a Market Economy." In the former, Kelman argues against those who would attempt to dismantle or significantly reduce existing regulatory apparatus. Government regulation of pollution, safety, consumer products, and even business competition, he asserts, is good for the country. It is good on moral as well as economic grounds. In the latter article, Gustafson and Johnson highlight the issue of the rich and the poor: To what extent should the government intervene to improve the lot of the poor, the uneducated, and the handicapped? Gustafson, a prominent theologian, argues for a crucial government role in insuring economic fairness. Johnson, a leading business executive, finds a role for government, but he argues that unless it is sharply limited, there is a risk of denying personal freedom and stifling economic efficiency.

In the case study "Going After the Crooks," issues of government regulation and market freedom come to a head. The case describes the activities—many of them illegal—through which stock speculators using "inside" information have been able to reap enormous profits. By using information unavailable to other investors—say, about the impending takeover of a company—speculators such as Ivan Boesky can purchase stock destined to rise quickly in value. The Securities and Exchange Commission in the United States regulates such activities and forbids the use of inside information on the grounds that it rigs the game against other investors. In other words, because other investors lack the information relevant, say, to a corporate takeover, the person who, like Ivan Boesky, buys the stock of the company to be acquired and makes a killing has essentially robbed the persons from whom he purchased the stock of the increased value their stock was bound to accrue. A few voices, however, have criticized the laws that have trapped Boesky and others because they feel such laws violate the spirit of market freedom and property rights. Are not the very transactions for which Boesky was made to pay a whopping fine ($100 million) *voluntary* ones, and is it not wrong on principle for the government to interfere in voluntary market transactions? Is it not true, moreover, that many, if not most, business transactions are ones in which one party to the transaction has information that the other does not? Why penalize a person, they ask, for being smart enough to acquire information others lack? Such defenders of a more laissez-faire, unregulated approach to stock market transactions call attention to the fact that other industrialized countries, notably in Western Europe, either do not prohibit insider trading or do not enforce such prohibitions if they have them.

JUSTICE

The subject of social justice, both for traditional and modern philosophers, is directly connected to economics and ethical theory. One important subcategory of justice dealt with in this section—namely, distributive justice—concerns the issue of how, and according to what principle, society's goods should be distributed. When thinking about justice it is important to remember that the concept of "justice" cannot include all ethical and political values. Thus, no matter how desirable it may be to have justice established in society, we must acknowledge other ideals such as benevolence and charity. Justice refers to a minimal condition that should exist in a good society, a condition that traditionally has been interpreted as "giving each individual his or her due."

The notion of distributive justice, or of what constitutes justice in distributing goods to persons, is an evasive concept, as is illustrated by the following story: Once a group of soldiers found themselves defending a fort against an enemy. The soldiers were in desperate need of water, and the only source was 200 yards from the fort in enemy territory. Courageously, a small group sneaked outside the fort, filled their canteens with water, and returned safely. After showing the water to their fellow soldiers, the successful adventurers proposed that it should be distributed in accordance with the principles of justice. Since justice requires distribution on the basis of *merit*, they said, they themselves should get the water because they risked their lives in obtaining it. There was considerable disagreement. Although agreeing that justice requires distribution on the basis of deserving characteristics, a different group of soldiers, which had been longest without water, claimed they deserved it more because they *needed* it more than the others. After all, they were the thirstiest. And still a different group, agreeing with the same general principle of justice, argued that *everyone* deserved *equal* amounts of water because all human beings, considered generally, have equal worth. The moral, obviously, is that intepretations of justice have difficulty specifying a particular characteristic or set of characteristics which, when possessed by human beings, will serve as the basis for "giving each person his or her due."

Although the subject of distributive justice is a popular topic among modern philosophers, some claim that the mere idea is prejudicial and controversial. If a society's goods are to be distributed, doesn't this imply the existence of a distributing agency (such as the government) to enforce certain principles of distribution, thus taking away from those who have more than they deserve and giving to those who have and deserve less? It can be argued that the very existence of such a process violates basic principles of individual liberty because it denies individuals the opportunity to engage freely in exchanges of goods and property. In this way it is maintained that distributive and redistributive practices necessitate the violation of basic liberties and freedoms, and therefore that no willful distribution can itself be just.

The fundamental issue of individual liberty, along with questions about the right of government to interfere with such liberty, are found in F. A. Hayek's essay "The Principles of a Liberal Social Order." As one of the best-known defenders in the twentieth century of a free and unregulated social order, Hayek is anxious to distinguish the kind of society in which the free actions of individuals combine to yield a "spontaneous" social order from the closed, regulated society in which the social order is a consequence of design. It is only in a spontaneous social order, Hayek believes, that individual liberty can be meaningful. As soon as one begins to demand that a certain order be imposed (for example, that people should receive goods and services in proportion to their needs), it becomes necessary to abolish the spontaneous social order and to institute strong government control, both of which open the door to totalitarian practices. Hayek admits that a free society does not always yield a direct correspondence between personal merit or need and the distribution of goods and services; yet he emphatically denies that such a correspondence can be brought about without sacrificing an even more important political value, namely, an open society which protects individual liberty. Thus Hayek is one of the foremost advocates of spontaneous social order as the foundation for a just society, and, incidentally, his views have had a significant impact upon other well-known modern theorists, such as John Hospers and Robert Nozick.

Another modern writer presented in this section, John Rawls, also considers questions of justice and the social order. In contrast to Hayek, Rawls believes that the idea of distributive justice can be coordinated with principles of individual rights and liberties. He argues that a just society is one in which agreements are freely made, in which no one is left out, and in which deserving people are not shortchanged. Rawls argues that a just society is based on two principles: (1) ". . . each person engaged in an institution or affected by it has an equal right to the most extensive liberty compatible with a like liberty for all . . ." and (2) ". . . inequalities as defined by the institutional structure . . . are arbitrary unless it is reasonable to expect that they will work out to everyone's advantage and provided that the positions and offices to which they attach or from which they may be gained are open to all." Thus, Rawls is not arguing that in a just society things would be structured so as to give all people an equal number of goods—for example, money, education, or status; and he allows that some people may have a great deal more than others. However, for a society to be just, such inequalities are only acceptable if their existence is to the advantage of the least fortunate as well as to everyone else. Rawls further specifies that no form of distribution in any society is just unless it satisfies the first condition of justice: freedom. Rawls's article "Distributive Justice," excerpts of which are presented in this section, first appeared in 1967 and is a precursor of his influential book A *Theory of Justice*,[1] in which he more fully develops the views presented here.

The contemporary debate over the interpretation of justice begun by persons such as Rawls, Nozick, and Hayek in the 1970s was joined in the 1980s by a variety of voices, many of them critical of the very assumptions underlying the debate. One philosopher in particular, Michael Sandel, has criticized key assumptions held about justice. In the article included in this section, "Morality and the Liberal Ideal," he argues that the modern political mind-set is preoccupied with individual liberty and fair procedures at the expense of a fuller and more positive concept of social-personal good.

NOTES

1. John Rawls, A *Theory of Justice* (Cambridge, Mass.: Harvard University Press, 1971).

Traditional Theories of Property and Profit

Case Study—Plasma International

T. W. ZIMMERER AND P. L. PRESTON

The Sunday headline in the Tampa, Florida, newspaper read:

Blood Sales Result in Exorbitant Profits for Local Firm

The story went on to relate how the Plasma International Company, head-quartered in Tampa, Florida, purchased blood in underdeveloped countries for as little as 45[1] cents a pint and resold the blood to hospitals in the United States and South America. A recent disaster in Nicaragua produced scores of injured persons and the need for fresh blood. Plasma International had 10,000 pints of blood flown to Nicaragua from West Africa and charged the hospitals $75 per pint, netting the firm nearly three quarters of a million dollars.

    As a result of the newspaper story, a group of irate citizens, led by prominent civic leaders, demanded that the City of Tampa, and the State of Florida, revoke Plasma International's licenses to practice business. Others protested to their congressmen to seek enactment of legislation designed to halt the sale of blood for profit. The spokesperson was reported as saying, "What kind of people are these—selling life and death? These men prey on the needs of dying people, buying blood from poor, ignorant Africans for 45 cents worth of beads and junk, and selling it to injured people for $75 a pint.

Well, this company will soon find out that the people of our community won't stand for their kind around here."

"I just don't understand it. We run a business just like any other business; we pay taxes and we try to make an honest profit," said Sol Levin as he responded to reporters at the Tampa International Airport. He had just returned home from testifying before the House Subcommittee on Medical Standards. The recent publicity surrounding his firm's activities during the recent earthquakes had once again fanned the flames of public opinion. An election year was an unfortunate time for the publicity to occur. The politicians and the media were having a field day.

Levin was a successful stockbroker when he founded Plasma International Company three years ago. Recognizing the world's need for safe, uncontaminated, and reasonably priced whole blood and blood plasma, Levin and several of his colleagues pooled their resources and went into business. Initially, most of the blood and plasma they sold was purchased through store-front operations in the southeast United States. Most of the donors were, unfortunately, men and women who used the money obtained from the sale of their blood to purchase wine. While sales increased dramatically on the base of an innovative marketing approach, several cases of hepatitis were reported in recipients. The company wisely began a search for new sources.

Recognizing their own limitations in the medical-biological side of the business they recruited a highly qualified team of medical consultants. The consulting team, after extensive testing, and a worldwide search, recommended that the blood profiles and donor characteristics of several rural West African tribes made them ideal prospective donors. After extensive negotiations with the State Department and the government of the nation of Burami, the company was able to sign an agreement with several of the tribal chieftains.

As Levin reviewed these facts, and the many costs involved in the sale of a commodity as fragile as blood, he concluded that the publicity was grossly unfair. His thoughts were interrupted by the reporter's question: "Mr. Levin, is it necessary to sell a vitally needed medical supply, like blood, at such high prices especially to poor people in such a critical situation?" "Our prices are determined on the basis of a lot of costs that we incur that the public isn't even aware of," Levin responded. However, when reporters pressed him for details of these "relevant" costs, Levin refused any further comment. He noted that such information was proprietary in nature and not for public consumption.

NOTE

1. Prices have been adjusted in this article to allow for inflation occurring since the article was written (ed.).

Benefits of the Profit Motive

ADAM SMITH

BOOK I

OF THE CAUSES OF IMPROVEMENT IN THE PRODUCTIVE POWERS OF LABOR AND OF THE ORDER ACCORDING TO WHICH ITS PRODUCE IS NATURALLY DISTRIBUTED AMONG THE DIFFERENT RANKS OF THE PEOPLE

Chapter I
Of the Division of Labor

The greatest improvement in the productive powers of labor, and the greater part of the skill, dexterity, and judgment with which it is anywhere directed, or applied, seem to have been the effects of the division of labor. . . .

To take an example, therefore, from a very trifling manufacture; but one in which the division of labor has been very often taken notice of, the trade of the pin-maker; a workman not educated to this business (which the division of labor has rendered a distinct trade), nor acquainted with the use of the machinery employed in it (to the invention of which the same division of labor has probably given occasion), could scarce, perhaps, with his utmost industry, make one pin in a day, and certainly could not make twenty. But in the way in which this business is now carried on, not only the whole work is a peculiar trade, but it is divided into a number of branches, of which the greater part are likewise peculiar trades. One man draws out the wire, another straights it, a third cuts it, a fourth points it, a fifth grinds it at the top for receiving the head; to make the head requires two or three distinct operations; to put it on is a peculiar business, to whiten the pins is another; it is even a trade by itself to put them into the paper; and the important business of making a pin is, in this manner, divided into about eighteen distinct operations, which is some manufactories, are all performed by distinct hands, though in others the same man will sometimes perform two or three of them. I have seen a small manufactory of this kind where ten men only were employed, and where some of them consequently performed two or three distinct operations. But though they were very poor, and therefore but indifferently accommodated with the necessary machinery, they could, when they exerted themselves, make among them about

From Adam Smith, *The Wealth of Nations*, Books I and IV (1776; rpt. Chicago: University of Chicago Press, 1976).

twelve pounds of pins a day. There are in a pound upwards of four thousand pins of a middling size. Those ten persons, therefore, could make among them upwards of forty-eight thousand pins in a day. Each person, therefore, making a tenth part of forty-eight thousand pins, might be considered as making four thousand eight hundred pins in a day. But if they had all wrought separately and independently, and without any of them having been educated to this peculiar business, they certainly could not each of them have made twenty, perhaps not one pin in a day; that is, certainly, not the two hundred and fortieth, perhaps not the four thousand eight hundredth part, of what they are at present capable of performing in consequence of a proper division and combination of their different operations.

In every other art and manufacture, the effects of the division of labor are similar to what they are in this very trifling one; though in many of them, the labor can neither be so much subdivided, nor reduced to so great a simplicity of operation. The division of labor, however, so far as it can be introduced, occasions, in every art, a proportionate increase of the productive powers of labor. . . .

This great increase of the quantity of work, which in consequence of the division of labor, the same number of people are capable of performing, is owing to three different circumstances: first, to the increase of dexterity in every particular workman; secondly, to the saving of the time which is commonly lost in passing from one species of work to another; and lastly, to the invention of a great number of machines which facilitate and abridge labor, and enable one man to do the work of many.

First, the improvement of the dexterity of the workman necessarily increases the quantity of the work he can perform; and the division of labor, by reducing every man's business to some one simple operation and by making this operation the sole employment of his life, necessarily increases very much the dexterity of the workman. A common smith, who, though accustomed to handle the hammer, has never been used to make nails, if upon some particular occasion he is obliged to attempt it, will scarce, I am assured, be able to make about two or three hundred nails in a day, and those too very bad ones. A smith who has been accustomed to make nails, but whose sole or principal business has not been that of a nailer, can seldom with his utmost diligence make more than eight hundred or a thousand nails in a day. I have seen several boys under twenty years of age who had never exercised any other trade but that of making nails, and who, when they exerted themselves, could make, each of them, upwards of two thousand three hundred nails in a day. The making of a nail, however, is by no means one of the simplest operations. The same person blows the bellows, stirs or mends the fire as there is occasion, heats the iron, and forges every part of the nail: In forging the head too he is obliged to change his tools. The different operations into which the making of a pin or of a metal button is subdivided, are all of them much more simple; and the dexterity of the person, of whose life it has been the sole business to perform them, is usually much greater. The rapidity with which some of the operations of those manufacturers are performed exceeds what the human hand could, by those who had never seen them, be supposed capable of acquiring.

Secondly, the advantage which is gained by saving the time commonly lost in passing from one sort of work to another is much greater than we should at first view be apt to imagine it. It is impossible to pass very quickly from one kind of work to another, that is carried on in a different place, and with quite different tools. A country weaver who cultivates a small farm must lose a good deal of time in passing from his loom to the field, and from the field to his loom. When the two trades can be carried on in the same workhouse, the loss of time is no doubt much less. It is even in this case, however, very considerable. . . .

Thirdly, and lastly, every body must be sensible how much labor is facilitated and abridged by the application of proper machinery. . . .

. . . A great part of the machines made use of in those manufactures in which labor is most subdivided were originally the inventions of common workmen, who, being each of them employed in some very simple operation, naturally turned their thoughts toward finding out easier and readier methods of performing it. Whoever has been much accustomed to visit such manufacturers must frequently have been shown very pretty machines which were inventions of such workmen in order to facilitate and quicken their own particular part of the work. In the first fire-engines, a boy was constantly employed to open and shut alternately the communication between the boiler and the cylinder, according as the piston either ascended or descended. One of those boys, who loved to play with his companions, observed that, by tying a string from the handle of the valve which opened this communication to another part of the machine, the valve would open and shut without his assistance, and leave him at liberty to divert himself with his play-fellows. One of the greatest improvements that has been made upon this machine, since it was first invented, was in this manner the discovery of a boy who wanted to save his own labor. . . .

It is the great multiplication of the productions of all the different arts, in consequence of the division of labor, which occasions, in a well-governed society, that universal opulence which extends itself to the lowest ranks of the people. Every workman has a great quantity of his own work to dispose of beyond what he himself has occasion for; and every other workman being exactly in the same situation, he is enabled to exchange a great quantity of his own goods for a great quantity, or, what comes to the same thing, for the price of a great quantity of theirs. He supplies them abundantly with what they have occasion for, and they accommodate him as amply with what he has occasion for, and a general plenty diffuses itself through all the different ranks of the society. . . .

Chapter II
Of the Principle Which Gives Occasion
to the Division of Labor

This division of labor, from which so many advantages are derived, is not originally the effect of any human wisdom which foresees and intends that general opulence to which it gives occasion. It is the necessary, though very slow and gradual, consequence of a certain propensity in human nature which has in view no such extensive utility: the propensity to truck, barter, and exchange one thing for another.

. . . In almost every other race of animals each individual, when it is grown up to maturity, is entirely independent, and in its natural state has occasion for the assistance of no other living creature. But man has almost constant occasion for the help of his brethren, and it is in vain for him to expect it from their benevolence only. He will be more likely to prevail if he can interest their self-love in his favor, and show them that it is for their own advantage to do for him what he requires of them. Whoever offers to another a bargain of any kind, proposes to do this. Give me that which I want, and you shall have this which you want, is the meaning of every such offer; and it is in the manner that we obtain from one another the far greater part of those good offices which we stand in need of. It is not from the benevolence of the butcher, the brewer, or the baker, that we expect our dinner, but from their regard to their own interest. We address ourselves, not to their humanity but to their self-love, and never talk to them of our own necessities but of their advantages. Nobody but a beggar chooses to depend chiefly upon the benevolence of his fellow-citizens. Even a beggar does not depend upon it entirely. The charity of well-disposed people, indeed, supplies him with the whole fund of his subsistence. But though this principle ultimately provides him with all the necessaries of life which he has occasion for, it neither does nor can provide him with them as he has occasion for them. The greater part of his occasional wants are supplied in the same manner as those of other people, by treaty, by barter, and by purchase. With the money which one man gives him he purchases food. The old clothes which another bestows upon him he exchanges for other old clothes which suit him better, or for lodging, or for food, or for money, with which he can buy either food, clothes, or lodging, as he has occasion.

As it is by treaty, by barter, and by purchase that we obtain from one another the greater part of those mutual good offices which we stand in need of, so it is this same trucking disposition which originally gives occasion to the division of labor. In a tribe of hunters or shepherds a particular person makes bows and arrows, for example, with more readiness and dexterity than any other. He frequently exchanges them for cattle or for venison with his companions; and he finds at last that he can in this manner get more cattle and venison than if he himself went to the field to catch them.

From a regard to his own interest, therefore, the making of bows and arrows grows to be his chief business, and he becomes a sort of armorer. Another excels in making the frames and covers of their little huts or movable houses. He is accustomed to be of use in this way to his neighbors, who reward him in the same manner with cattle and with venison till at last he finds it his interest to dedicate himself entirely to this employment, and to become a sort of house carpenter. In the same manner a third becomes a smith or a brazier; a fourth a tanner or dresser of hides or skins, the principal part of the clothing of savages. And thus the certainty of being able to exchange all that surplus part of the produce of his own labor, which is over and above his own consumption, for such parts of the produce of other men's labor as he may have occasion for, encourages every man to apply himself to a particular occupation, and to cultivate and bring to perfection whatever talent or genius he may possess for that particular species of business.

The difference of natural talents in different men is, in reality, much less than we are aware of; and the very different genius which appears to distinguish men of different professions, when grown up to maturity, is not upon many occasions so much the cause as the effect of the division of labor. The difference between the most dissimilar characters, between a philosopher and a common street porter, for example, seems to arise not so much from nature as from habit, custom, and education. When they came into the world, and for the first six or eight years of their existence, they were, perhaps, very much alike, and neither their parents nor play-fellows could perceive any remarkable difference. About that age, or soon after, they come to be employed in very different occupations. The difference of talents comes then to be taken notice of, and widens by degrees, till at last the vanity of the philosopher is willing to acknowledge scarce any resemblance. But without the disposition to truck, barter, and exchange, every man must have procured to himself every necessary and conveniency of life which he wanted. All must have had the same duties to perform, and the same work to do, and there could have been no such difference of employment as could alone give occasion to any great difference of talents. . . . .

BOOK IV

Chapter II

Every individual is continually exerting himself to find out the most advantageous employment for whatever capital he can command. It is his own advantage, indeed, and not that of the society, which he has in view. But the study of his own advantage, naturally, or rather necessarily, leads him to prefer that employment which is most advantageous to the society. . . .

As every individual, therefore, endeavours as much as he can both to employ his capital in the support of domestic industry, and so to direct that industry that its produce may be of the greatest value, every individual necessarily labors to render the annual revenue of the society as great as he can. He generally, indeed, neither intends to promote the public interest, nor knows how much he is promoting it. By preferring the support of domestic to that of foreign industry, he intends only his own security: and by directing that industry in such a manner as its produce may be of the greatest value, he intends only his own gain, and he is in this, as in many other cases, led by an invisible hand to promote an end which was no part of his intention. Nor is it always the worse for society that it was no part of it. By pursuing his own interest he frequently promotes that of the society more effectually than when he really intends to promote it. I have never known much good done by those who affected to trade for the public good. It is an affectation, indeed, not very common among merchants, and very few words need be employed in dissuading them from it.

The Justification of Private Property

JOHN LOCKE

. . . God, who hath given the world to men in common, hath also given them reason to make use of it to the best advantage of life and convenience. The earth and all that is therein is given to men for the support and comfort of their being. And though all the fruits it naturally produces, and beasts it feeds, belong to mankind in common, as they are produced by the spontaneous hand of nature; and nobody has originally a private dominion exclusive of the rest of mankind in any of them as they are thus in their natural state; yet being given for the use of men, there must of necessity be a means to appropriate them some way or other before they can be of any use or at all beneficial to any particular man. The fruit or venison which nourishes the wild Indian, who knows no enclosure, and is still a tenant in common, must be his, and so his, i.e., a part of him, that another can no longer have any right to it, before it can do any good for the support of his life.

Though the earth and all inferior creatures be common to all men, yet every man has a property in his own person; this nobody has any right to but

From John Locke, *Second Treatise on Government* (1764; rpt. New York: MacMillan, 1956).

himself. The labor of his body and the work of his hands we may say are properly his. Whatsoever, then, he removes out of the state that nature hath provided and left it in, he hath mixed his labor with, and joined to it something that is his own, and thereby makes it his property. It being by him removed from the common state nature placed it in, it hath by this labor something annexed to it that excludes the common right of other men. For this labor being the unquestionable property of the laborer, no man but he can have a right to what that is once joined to, at least where there is enough, and as good left in common for others.

He that is nourished by the acorns he picked up under an oak, or the apples he gathered from the trees in the wood, has certainly appropriated them to himself. Nobody can deny but the nourishment is his. I ask, then, When did they begin to be his—when he digested, or when he ate, or when he boiled, or when he brought them home, or when he picked them up? And 'tis plain if the first gathering made them not his, nothing else could. That labor put a distinction between them and common; that added something to them more than nature, the common mother of all, had done, and so they became his private right. And will anyone say he had no right to those acorns or apples he thus appropriated, because he had not the consent of all mankind to make them his? Was it robbery thus to assume to himself what belonged to all in common? If such a consent as that was necessary, man had starved, notwithstanding the plenty God had given him. We see in commons which remains so by compact that 'tis the taking any part of what is common and removing it out of the state nature leaves it in, which begins the property; without which the common is of no use. And the taking of this or that does not depend on the express consent of all the commoners. Thus the grass my horse has bit, the turfs my servant has cut, and the ore I have dug in any place where I have a right to them in common with others, become my property without the assignation or consent of anybody. The labor that was mine removing them out of that common state they were in, hath fixed my property in them. . . .

It will perhaps be objected to this, that if gathering the acorns, or other fruits of the earth, etc., makes a right to them, then anyone may engross as much as he will. To which I answer, Not so. The same law of nature that does by this means give us property, does also bound that property too. "God has given us all things richly" (I Tim. vi. 17), is the voice of reason confirmed by inspiration. But how far has He given it us? To enjoy. As much as anyone can make use of any advantage of life before it spoils, so much he may by his labor fix a property in; whatever is beyond this, is more than his share, and belongs to others. Nothing was made by God for man to spoil or destroy. And thus considering the plenty of natural provisions there was a long time in the world, and the few spenders, and to how small a part of that provision the industry of one man could extend itself, and engross it to the prejudice of others—especially keeping within the bounds, set by reason, of what might serve for his use—there could be then little room for quarrels or contentions about property so established.

But the chief matter of property being now not the fruits of the earth, and the beasts that subsist on it, but the earth itself, as that which takes in and carries with it all the rest, I think it is plain that property in that, too, is acquired as the former. As much land as a man tills, plants, improves, cultivates, and can use the product of, so much is his property. He by his labor does as it were enclose it from the common. Nor will it invalidate his right to say, everybody else has an equal title to it; and therefore he cannot appropriate, he cannot enclose, without the consent of all his fellow-commoners, all mankind. God, when He gave the world in common to all mankind, commanded man also to labor, and the penuary of his condition required it of him. God and his reason commanded him to subdue the earth, i.e., improve it for the benefit of life, and therein lay out something upon it that was his own, his labor. He that, in obedience to this command of God, subdued, tilled, and sowed any part of it, thereby annexed to it something that was his property, which another had no title to, nor could without injury take from him.

Nor was this appropriation of any parcel of land, by improving it, any prejudice to any other man, since there was still enough and as good left; and more than the yet unprovided could use. So that in effect, there was never the less left for others because of his enclosure for himself. For he that leaves as much as another can make use of, does as good as take nothing at all. Nobody could think himself injured by the drinking of another man, though he took a good draught, who had a whole river of the same water left him to quench his thirst; and the case of land and water, where there is enough of both, is perfectly the same.

God gave the world to men in common; but since He gave it them for their benefit, and the greatest conveniences of life they were capable to draw from it, it cannot be supposed He meant it should always remain common and uncultivated. He gave it to the use of the industrious and rational (and labor was to be his title to it), not to the fancy or coveteousness of the quarrelsome and contentious. He that had as good left for his improvement as was already taken up, needed not complain, ought not to meddle with what was already improved by another's labor; if he did, it is plain he desired the benefit of another's pains, which he had no right to, and not the ground which God had given him in common with others to labor on, and whereof there was as good left as that already possessed, and more than he knew what to do with, or his industry could reach to.

It is true, in land that is common in England, or any other country where there is plenty of people under Government, who have money and commerce, no one can enclose or appropriate any part without the consent of all his fellow-commoners: because this is left common by compact, i.e., by the law of the land, which is not to be violated. And though it be common in respect of some men, it is not so to all mankind; but is the joint property of this country, or this parish. Besides, the remainder, after such enclosure, would not be as good to the rest of the commoners as the whole was, when they could all make use of the whole, whereas in the beginning and first peopling of the great common of the world it was quite otherwise. The law man was under was rather for appropriating. God commanded, and his wants forced him, to labor. That was his property, which could not be taken from him wherever he had fixed it. And hence subduing or cultivating the earth, and having dominion, we see are joined together. The one gave title to the other. So that God, by commanding to subdue, gave authority so far to appropriate. And the condition of human life, which requires labor and materials to work on, necessarily introduces private possessions.

The measure of property nature has well set by the extent of men's labor and the conveniency of life. No man's labor could subdue or appropriate all, nor could his enjoyment consume more than a small part; so that it was impossible for any man, this way, to entrench upon the right of another or acquire to himself a property to the prejudice of his neighbor, who would still have room for as good and as large a possession (after the other had taken out his) as before it was appropriated. Which measure did confine every man's possession to a very moderate proportion, and such as he might appropriate to himself without injury to anybody in the first ages of the world, when men were more in danger to be lost, by wandering from their company, in the then vast wilderness of the earth than to be straitened for want of room to plant in. . . .

And thus, without supposing any private dominion and property in Adam over all the world, exclusive of all other men, which can no way be proved, nor any one's property be made out from it, but supposing the world, given as it was to the children of men in common, we see how labor could make men distinct titles to several parcels of it for their private uses, wherein there could be no doubt of right, no room for quarrel.

Nor is it so strange, as perhaps before consideration it may appear, that the property of labor should be able to overbalance the community of land. For it is labor indeed that puts the difference of value on everything; and let anyone consider what the difference is between an acre of land planted with tobacco or sugar, sown with wheat or barley, and an acre of the same land lying in common without any husbandry upon it, and he will find that the improvement of labor makes the far greater part of the value. I think it will be but a very modest computation to say that of the products of the earth useful to the life of man nine-tenths are the effects of labor; nay, if we will rightly estimate things as they come to our use, and cast up the several expenses about them—what in them is purely owing to nature, and what to labor—we shall find that in most of them ninety-nine hundredths are wholly to be put on the account of labor. . . .

From all which it is evident that, though the things of nature are given in common, yet man, by being master of himself and proprietor of his own person and the actions or labor of it, had still in himself the great foundation of property; and that which made up the great part of what he applied to the support or comfort of his being, when invention and arts had improved the conveniences of life, was perfectly his own, and did not belong in common to others.

Thus labor, in the beginning, gave a right of property, wherever anyone was pleased to employ it upon what was common, which remained a long while the far greater part, and is yet more than mankind makes use of. Men at first, for the most part, contented themselves with what unassisted nature offered to their necessities; and though afterwards, in some parts of the world (where the increase of people and stock, with the use of money, had made land scarce, and so of some value), the several communities settled the bounds of their distinct territories, and by laws within themselves, regulated the properties of the private men of their society, and so, by compact and agreement, settled the property which labor and industry began — and the leagues that have been made between several states and kingdoms, either expressly or tacitly disowning all claim and right to the land in the other's possession, have, by common consent, given up their pretenses to their natural common right, which originally they had to those countries; and so have, by positive agreement, settled a property amongst themselves in distant parts of the world — yet there are still great tracts of ground to be found which, the inhabitants thereof not having joined with the rest of mankind in the consent of the use of their common money, lie waste, and more than the people who dwell on it do or can make use of, and so still lie in common; though this can scarce happen amongst that part of mankind that have consented to the use of money.

The greatest part of things really useful to the life of man, and such as the necessity of subsisting made the first commoners of the world look after, as it doth the Americans now, are generally things of short duration, such as, if they are not consumed by use, will decay and perish of themselves: gold, silver, and diamonds are things that fancy or agreement have put the value on more than real use and the necessary support of life. Now of those good things which nature hath provided in common, everyone hath a right, as hath been said, to as much as he could use, and had a property in all he could effect with his labor — all that his industry could extend to, to alter from the state nature had put it in, was his. He that gathered a hundred bushels of acorns or apples had thereby a property in them; they were his goods as soon as gathered. He was only to look that he used them before they spoiled, else he took more than his share, and robbed others; and, indeed, it was a foolish thing, as well as dishonest, to hoard up more than he could make use of. If he gave away a part to anybody else, so that it perished not uselessly in his possession, these he also made use of; and if he also bartered away plums that would have rotted in a week, for nuts that would last good for his eating a whole year, he did no injury; he wasted not the common stock, destroyed no part of the portion of goods that belonged to others, so long as nothing perished uselessly in his hands. Again, if he would give his nuts for a piece of metal, pleased with its color, or exchange his sheep for shells, or wool for a sparkling pebble or a diamond, and keep those by him all his life, he invaded not the right of others; he might heap up as much as these durable things as he pleased, the exceeding of the bounds of his just property not lying in the largeness of his possessions, but the perishing of anything uselessly in it.

And thus came in the use of money—some lasting thing that men might keep without spoiling, and that, by mutual consent, men would take in exchange for the truly useful but perishable supports of life.

And as different degrees of industry were apt to give men possessions in different proportions, so this invention of money gave them the opportunity to continue and enlarge them; for supposing an island, separate from all possible commerce with the rest of the world, wherein there were but a hundred families—but there were sheep, horses, and cows, with other useful animals, wholesome fruits, and land enough for corn for a hundred thousand times as many, but nothing in the island, either because of its commonness or perishableness, fit to supply the place of money—what reason could anyone have there to enlarge his possessions beyond the use of his family and a plentiful supply to its consumption, either in what their own industry produced, or they could barter for like perishable useful commodities with others? Where there is not something both lasting and scarce, and so valuable to be hoarded up, there men will not be apt to enlarge their possessions of land, were it never so rich, never so free for them to take; for I ask, what would a man value ten thousand or a hundred thousand acres of excellent land, ready cultivated, and well stocked too with cattle, in the middle of the inland parts of America, where he had no hopes of commerce with other parts of the world, to draw money to him by the sale of the product? It would not be worth the enclosing, and we should see him give up again to the wild common of nature whatever was more than would supply the conveniences of life to be had there for him and his family.

Thus in the beginning all the world was America, and more so than that is now, for no such thing as money was anywhere known. Find out something that hath the use and value of money amongst his neighbors, you shall see the same man will begin presently to enlarge his possessions.

But since gold and silver, being little useful to the life of man in proportion to food, raiment, and carriage, has its value only from the consent of men, whereof labor yet makes, in great part, the measure, it is plain that the consent of men have agreed to a disproportionate and unequal possession of the earth—I mean out of the bounds of society and compact; for in governments the laws regulate it; they having, by consent, found out and agreed in a way how a man may rightfully and without injury possess more than he himself can make use of by receiving gold and silver, which may continue long in a man's possession, without decaying for the overplus, and agreeing those metals should have a value.

And thus, I think, it is very easy to conceive without any difficulty how labor could at first begin a title of property in the common things of nature, and how the spending it upon our uses bounded it; so that there could then be no reason of quarrelling about title, nor any doubt about the largeness of possession it gave. Right and conveniency went together; for as a man had a right to all he could employ his labor upon, so he had no temptation to labor for more than he could make use of. This left no room for controversy about the title, nor for encroachment on the right of others; what portion a man carved to himself was easily seen, and it was useless, as well as dishonest, to carve himself too much, or take more than he needed.

Alienated Labour

KARL MARX

We shall begin from a *contemporary* economic fact. The worker becomes poorer the more wealth he produces and the more his production increases in power and extent. The worker becomes an ever cheaper commodity the more goods he creates. The *devaluation* of the human world increases in direct relation with the *increase in value* of the world of things. Labour does not only create goods; it also produces itself and the worker as a *commodity*, and indeed in the same proportion as it produces goods. . . .

All these consequences follow from the fact that the worker is related to the *product of his labour* as to an *alien* object. For it is clear on this presupposition that the more the worker expends himself in work the more powerful becomes the world of objects which he creates in face of himself, the poorer he becomes in his inner life, and the less he belongs to himself. It is just the same as in religion. The more of himself man attibutes to God the less he has left in himself. The worker puts his life into the object, and his life then belongs no longer to himself but to the object. The greater his activity, therefore, the less he possesses. What is embodied in the product of his labour is no longer his own. The greater this product is, therefore, the

From *Karl Marx: Early Writings, The Economic and Philosophic manuscripts of 1844*, trans. T. B. Bottomore. Copyright © 1963 by McGraw-Hill Book Company. Used with permission of McGraw-Hill Book Co., New York, and Pitman Publishing, London.

more he is diminished. The *alienation* of the worker in his product means not only that his labour becomes an object, assumes an *external* existence, but that it exists independently, *outside himself*, and alien to him, and that it stands opposed to him as an autonomous power. The life which he has given to the object sets itself against him as an alien and hostile force.

. . . The worker becomes a slave of the object; first, in that he receives an *object of work*, i.e. receives *work*, and secondly, in that he receives *means of subsistence*. Thus the object enables him to exist, first as a *worker* and secondly, as a *physical subject*. The culmination of this enslavement is that he can only maintain himself as a *physical subject* so far as he is a *worker*, and that it is only as a *physical subject* that he is a worker. . . .

What constitutes the alienation of labour? First, that the work is *external* to the worker, and that it is not part of his nature; and that, consequently, he does not fulfill himself in his work but denies himself, has a feeling of misery rather than well-being, does not develop freely his mental and physical energies but is physically exhausted and mentally debased. The worker, therefore, feels himself at home only during his leisure time, whereas at work he feels homeless. His work is not voluntary but imposed, *forced labour*. It is not the satisfaction of a need, but only a *means* for satisfying other needs. Its alien character is clearly shown by the fact that as soon as there is no physical or other compulsion it is avoided like the plague. External labour, labour in which man alienates himself, is a labour of self-sacrifice, of mortification. Finally, the external character of work for the worker is shown by the fact that it is not his own work but work for someone else, that in work he does not belong to himself but to another person. . . .

We arrive at the result that man (the worker) feels himself to be freely active only in his animal functions — eating, drinking and procreating, or at most also in his dwelling and in personal adornment — while in his human functions he is reduced to an animal. The animal becomes human and the human becomes animal.

Eating, drinking and procreating are of course also genuine human functions. But abstractly considered, apart from the environment of human activities, and turned into final and sole ends, they are animal functions.

We have now considered the act of alienation of practical human activity, labour, from two aspects: (1) the relationship of the worker to the *product of labour* as an alien object which dominates him. This relationship is at the same time the relationship to the sensuous external world, to natural objects, as an alien and hostile world; (2) the relationship of labour to the *act of production* within *labour*. This is the relationship of the worker to his own activity as something alien and not belonging to him, activity as suffering (passivity), strength as powerlessness, creation as emasculation, the *personal* physical and mental energy of the worker, his personal life (for what is life but activity?), as an activity which is directed against himself, independent of him and not belonging to him. This is *self-alienation* as against the above-mentioned alienation of the *thing*.

We have now to infer a third characteristic of *alienated labour* from the two we have considered.

Man is a species-being not only in the sense that he makes the community (his own as well as those of other things) his object both practically and theoretically, but also (and this is simply another expression for the same thing) in the sense that he treats himself as the present, living species, as a *universal* and consequently free being.[1]

Species-life, for man as for animals, has its physical basis in the fact that man (like animals) lives from inorganic nature, and since man is more universal than an animal so the range of inorganic nature from which he lives is more universal. . . . The universality of man appears in practice in the universality which makes the whole of nature into his inorganic body: (1) as a direct means of life; and equally (2) as the material object and instrument of his life activity. Nature is the inorganic body of man; that is to say nature, excluding the human body itself. To say that man *lives* from nature means that nature is his *body* with which he must remain in a continuous interchange in order not to die. The statement that the physical and mental life of man, and nature, are interdependent means simply that nature is interdependent with itself, for man is a part of nature.

Since alienated labour: (1) alienates nature from man; and (2) alienates man from himself, from his own active function, his life activity; so it alienates him from the species. It makes *species-life* into a means of individual life. In the first place it alienates species-life and individual life, and secondly, it turns the latter, as an abstraction, into the purpose of the former, also in its abstract and alienated form.

For labour, *life activity, productive life*, now appear to man only as *means* for the satisfaction of a need, the need to maintain his physical existence. Productive life is, however, species-life. It is life creating life. In the type of life activity resides the whole character of a species, its species-character; and free, conscious activity is the species-character of human beings. Life itself appears only as a *means of life*.

The animal is one with its life activity. It does not distinguish the activity from itself. It is *its activity*. But man makes his life activity itself an object of his will and consciousness. He has a conscious life activity. It is not a determination with which he is completely identified. Conscious life activity distinguishes man from the life activity of animals. Only for this reason is he a species-being. Or rather, he is only a self-conscious being, i.e. for his own life is an object for him, because he is a species-being. Only for this reason is his activity free activity. Alienated labour reverses the relationship, in that man because he is a self-conscious being makes his life activity, his *being*, only a means for his *existence*.

The practical construction of an *objective world*, the *manipulation* of inorganic nature, is the confirmation of man as a conscious species-being, i.e., a being who treats the species as his own being or himself as a species-being. . . .

It is just in his work upon the objective world that man really proves himself as a *species-being*. This production is his active species-life. By means of it nature appears as *his* work and his reality. The object of labour is, therefore, the *objectification of man's species-life:* for he no longer reproduces himself merely intellectually, as in consciousness, but actively and in a real sense, and he sees his own reflection in a world which he has constructed. While, therefore, alienated labour takes away the object of production from man, it also takes away his *species-life*, his real objectivity as a species-being, and changes his advantage over animals into a disadvantage in so far as his inorganic body, nature, is taken from him.

Just as alienated labour transforms free and self-directed activity into a means, so it transforms the species-life of man into a means of physical existence.

Consciousness, which man has from his species, is transformed through alienation so that species-life becomes only a means for him. (3) Thus alienated labour turns the *species-life of man*, and also nature as his mental species-property, into an *alien* being and into a *means* for his *individual existence*. It alienates from man his own body, external nature, his mental life and his *human* life. (4) A direct consequence of the alienation of man from the product of his labour, from his life activity and from his species-life, is that *man is alienated* from other *men*. When man confronts himself he also confronts *other* men. What is true of man's relationship to his work, to the product of his work and to himself, is also true of his relationship to other men, to their labour and to the objects of their labour.

In general, the statement that man is alienated from his species-life means that each man is alienated from others, and that each of the others is likewise alienated from human life.

Human alienation, and above all the relation of man to himself, is first realized and expressed in the relationship between each man and other men. Thus in the relationship of alienated labour every man regards other men according to the standards and relationships in which he finds himself placed as a worker.

We began with an economic fact, the alienation of the worker and his production. We have expressed this fact in conceptual terms as *alienated labour*, and in analysing the concept we have merely analysed an economic fact. . . .

The *alien* being to whom labour and the product of labour belong, to whose service labour is devoted, and to whose enjoyment the product of labour goes, can only be *man* himself. If the product of labour does not belong to the worker, but confronts him as an alien power, this can only be because it belongs to *a man other than the worker*. . . .

Thus, through alienated labour the worker creates the relation of another man, who does not work and is outside the work process, to this labour. The relation of the worker to work also produces the relation of the capitalist (or whatever one likes to call the lord of labour) to work. *Private property* is, therefore, the product, the necessary result, of *alienated labour*, of the external relation of the worker to nature and to himself.

Private property is thus derived from the analysis of the concept of *alienated labor*; that is, alienated man, alienated labour, alienated life, and estranged man.

We have, of course, derived the concept of *alienated labour (alienated life)* from political economy, from the analysis of the *movement of private property*. But the analysis of this concept shows that although private property appears to be the basis and cause of alienated labour, it is rather a consequence of the latter, just as the gods are *fundamentally* not the cause but the product of confusion of human reason. At a later stage, however, there is a reciprocal influence.

Only in the final state of the development of private property is its secret revealed, namely, that it is on one hand the *product* of alienated labour, and on the other hand the *means* by which labour is alienated, *the realization of this alienation. . . .*

Just as *private property* is only the sensuous expression of the fact that man is at the same time an *objective* fact for himself and becomes an alien and non-human object for himself; just as his manifestation of life is also his alienation of life and his self-realization a loss of reality, the emergence of an *alien* reality; so the positive supersession of private property, i.e. the *sensuous* appropriation of the human essence and of human life, of objective man and of human *creations*, by and for man, should not be taken only in the sense of *immediate*, exclusive *enjoyment*, or only in the sense of *possession* or *having*. Man appropriates his manifold being in an all-inclusive way, and thus as a whole man. All his *human* relations to the world—seeing, hearing, smelling, tasting, touching, thinking, observing, feeling, desiring, acting, loving—in short, all the organs of his individuality, like the organs which are directly communal in form, are in their objective action (their *action in relation to the object*) the appropriation of this object, the appropriation of human reality. The way in which they react to the object is the confirmation of *human reality*. It is human effectiveness and human *suffering*, for suffering humanly considered is an enjoyment of the self for man.

Private property has made us so stupid and partial that an object is only *ours* when we have it, when it exists for us as capital or when it is directly eaten, drunk, worn, inhabited, etc., in short, *utilized* in some way. But private property itself only conceives these various forms of possession as *means of life*, and the life for which they serve as means is the life of *private property*—labour and creation of capital.

The supersession of private property is, therefore, the complete *emancipation* of all the human qualities and senses. It is such an emancipation because these qualities and senses have become *human*, from the subjective as well as the objective point of view. The eye has become a *human* eye when its *object* has become a *human*, social object, created by man and destined for him. The senses have, therefore, become directly theoreticians in practice. They relate themselves to the thing for the sake of the thing, but the thing itself is an *objective human* relation to itself and to man, and vice versa. Need and enjoyment have thus lost their *egoistic* character and nature has lost its mere *utility* by the fact that its utilization has become *human* utilization. . . .

NOTE

1. In this passage Marx reproduces Feuerbach's argument in *Das Wesen des Christentums.*

The Communist Manifesto

KARL MARX AND FRIEDRICH ENGELS

I. BOURGEOIS AND PROLETARIANS

The history of all hitherto existing society is the history of class struggles.

Freeman and slave, patrician and plebeian, lord and serf, guildmaster and journeyman, in a word, oppressor and oppressed, stood in constant opposition to one another, caried on an uninterrupted, now hidden, now open fight, a fight that each time ended, either in a revolutionary reconstitution of society at large, or in the common ruin of the struggling classes.

In the earlier epochs of history, we find almost everywhere a complicated arrangement of society into various orders, a manifold gradation of social rank. In ancient Rome we have patricians, knights, plebians, slaves; in the Middle Ages, feudal lords, vassals, guildmasters, journeymen, apprentices, serfs; and in almost all of these particular classes, again, other subordinate gradations.

The modern bourgeois society that has sprouted from the ruins of feudal society has not done away with class antagonisms. It has only estab-

From Karl Marx and Friedrich Engels, *The Communist Manifesto*, trans. Samuel Moore (New York: Washington Square Press, 1934); © 1964 by Washington Square Press. Reprinted by permission of the publisher.

lished new classes, new conditions of oppression, new forms of struggle in place of the old ones.

Our epoch, the epoch of the bourgeoisie, shows, however, this distinctive feature: it has simplified the class antagonisms. Society as a whole is more and more splitting up into two great hostile camps, into two great classes directly facing each other: *bourgeoisie* and *proletariat*.

From the serfs of the Middle Ages sprang the chartered burghers of the earliest towns. From these burghers the first elements of the bourgeoisie were developed.

The discovery of America, the rounding of the Cape, opened the fresh ground for the rising bourgeoisie. The East-Indian and Chinese markets, the colonization of America, trade with the colonies, the increase in the means of exchange and in commodities generally, gave to commerce, to navigation, to industry, an impulse never before known, and thereby, to the revolutionary element in the tottering feudal society, a rapid development.

The feudal system of industry, under which industrial production was monopolized by closed guilds, now no longer sufficed for the growing wants of the new markets. The manufacturing system took its place. The guild-masters were pushed on one side by the manufacturing middle class; division of labor between the different corporate guilds vanished in the face of division of labor in each single workshop.

Meanwhile the markets kept on growing; demand went on rising. Manufacturing no longer was able to keep up with this growth. Then, steam and machinery revolutionized industrial production. The place of manufacture was taken by the giant, *modern industry*; the place of the industrial middle class, by industrial millionaires, the leaders of whole industrial armies, the modern bourgeois.

Modern industry has established the world market, for which the discovery of America paved the way. This market has given an immense development to commerce, to navigation, to communication by land. This development has, in its turn, reacted on the extension of industry; and in proportion as industry, commerce, navigation, railways extended, in the same proportion the bourgeoisie developed, increased its capital, and pushed into the background every class handed down from the Middle Ages.

We see, therefore, how the modern bourgeoisie is itself the product of a long course of development, of a series of revolutions in the modes of production and of exchange. . . .

The need of a constantly expanding market for its products chases the bourgeoisie over the whole surface of the globe. It must nestle everywhere, settle everywhere, establish connections everywhere.

The bourgeoisie has through its exploitation of the world market given a cosmopolitan character to production and consumption in every country. To the great chagrin of reactionaires, it has drawn from under the feet of industry the national ground on which it stood. All old-established national industries have been destroyed or are daily being destroyed. They are dislodged by new industries, whose introduction becomes a life and death question for all civilized nations, by industries that no longer work up indigenous raw material, but raw material drawn from the remotest zones; industries whose products are consumed, not only at home, but in every quarter of the globe. In place of the old wants, satisfied by the productions of the country, we find new wants, requiring for their satisfaction the products of distant lands and climates. In place of the old local and national seclusion and self-sufficiency, we have intercourse in every direction, universal interdependence of nations. And as in material, so also in intellectual production. The intellectual creations of individual nations become common property. National one-sidedness and narrow-mindedness become more and more impossible, and from the numerous national and local literatures, there emerges a world literature.

The bourgeoisie, by the rapid improvement of all instruments of production, by the immensely facilitated means of communications, draws all, even the most backward, nations into civilization. The cheap prices of its commodities are the heavy artillery with which it batters down all Chinese walls, with which it forces the underdeveloped nations' intensely obstinate hatred of foreigners to capitulate. It compels all nations, on pain of extinction, to adopt the bourgeois mode of production; it compels them to introduce what it calls civilization into their midst, *i.e.*, to become bourgeois themselves. In one word, it creates a world in its own image.

The bourgeoisie has subjected rural areas to the rule of cities. It has created enormous cities, has greatly increased the urban population as compared with the rural, and has thus rescued a considerable part of the population from the idiocy of rural life. Just as it has made the country dependent on the cities, so has it made barbarian and semi-underdeveloped countries dependent on the civilized ones, nations of peasants on nations of bourgeois, the East on the West.

The bourgeoisie keeps more and more doing away with the scattered state of the population, of the means of production, and of property. It has agglomerated population, centralized means of production, and has concentrated property in a few hands. The necessary consequence of this was political centralization. Independent, or but loosely connected, provinces with separate interests, laws, governments, and systems of taxation became lumped together into one nation, with one government, one code of laws, one national class-interest, one frontier, and one customs-tariff.

The bourgeoisie, during its rule of scarcely one hundred years, has created more massive and more colossal productive forces than have all preceding generations together. Subjection of Nature's forces to man, machinery, application of chemistry to industry and agriculture, steam-navigation, railways, electric telegraphs, clearing of whole continents for cultivation, canalization of rivers, whole populations conjured out of the ground—what earlier century had even a presentiment that such productive forces slumbered in the lap of social labor?

We see then: the means of production and of exchange, on whose foundation the bourgeoisie built itself up, were generated in feudal society. At a certain stage in the development of these means of production and of exchange, the conditions under which feudal society produced and exchanged, the feudal organization of agriculture and manufacturing industry, in one word, the feudal relations of property became no longer compatible with the already developed productive forces; they became so many fetters. They had to be burst asunder; they were burst asunder.

Into their place stepped free competition, accompanied by a social and political constitution adapted to it, and by the economical and political sway of the bourgeois class.

A similar movement is going on before our own eyes. Modern bourgeois society with its relations of production, of exchange and of property, a society that has conjured up such gigantic means of production and of exchange, is like the sorcerer, who is no longer able to control the powers of the subterranean world which he has called up by his spells. For many decades now the history of industry and commerce has been but the history of the revolt of modern productive forces against modern conditions of production, against the property relations that are the conditions for the existence of the bourgeoisie and of its rule. It is enough to mention the commercial crises that by their periodical return put on trial, each time more threateningly, the existence of the entire bourgeois society. In these crises a great part not only of the existing products, but also of the previously created productive forces, are periodically destroyed. In these crises there breaks out an epidemic that, in all earlier epochs, would have seemed an absurdity—the epidemic of overproduction. Society suddenly finds itself put back into a state of momentary barbarism; it appears as if a famine, a universal war of devastation had cut off the supply of every means of subsistence; industry and commerce seem to be destroyed; and why? Because there is too much civilization, too much means of subsistence, too much industry, too much commerce. The productive forces at the disposal of society no longer tend to further the development of the conditions of bourgeois property; on the contrary, they have become too powerful for these conditions, by which they are fettered, and so soon as they overcome these fetters, they bring disorder into the whole of bourgeois society, endanger the existence of bourgeois property. The conditions of bourgeois society are too narrow to comprise the wealth created by them. And how does the bourgeoisie get over these crises? On the one hand by enforced destruction of mass productive forces; on the other, by the conquest of new markets, and by the more thorough exploitation of the old ones. That is to say, by paving the way for more extensive and more destructive crises, and by diminishing the means whereby crises are prevented.

The weapons with which the bourgeoisie felled feudalism to the ground are now turned against the bourgeoisie itself.

But not only has the bourgeoisie forged the weapons that bring death to itself; it has also called into existence the men who are to wield those weapons—the modern working class—the proletarians.

In proportion as the bourgeoisie, *i.e.*, capital, is developed, in the same proportion is the proletariat, the modern working class, developed—a class of laborers, who live only so long as they find work, and who find work only so long as their labor increases capital. These laborers, who must sell themselves piecemeal, are a commodity, like every other article of commerce, and are consequently exposed to all the vicissitudes of competition, to all the fluctuations of the market.

Owing to the extensive use of machinery and to division of labor, the work of the proletarians has lost all individual character, and, consequently, all charm for the workman. He becomes an appendage of the machine, and it is only the most simple, most monotonous, and most easily acquired knack that is required of him. Hence, the cost of production of a workman is restricted, almost entirely, to the means of subsistence that he requires for his maintenance, and for the propagation of his race. But the price of a commodity, and therefore also of labor, is equal to its cost of production. In proportion, therefore, as the repulsiveness of the work increases, the wage decreases. What is more, in proportion as the use of machinery and division of labor increases, in the same proportion the burden of toil also increases, whether by prolongation of the working hours, by increase of the work exacted in a given time or by increased speed of the machinery, etc.

Modern industry has converted the little workshop of the patriarchal master into the great factory of the industrial capitalist. Masses of laborers, crowded into the factory, are organized like soldiers. As privates of the industrial army they are placed under the command of a perfect hierarchy of officers and sergeants. Not only are they slaves of the bourgeois class, and of the burgeois state; they are daily and hourly enslaved by the machine, by the foreman, and, above all, by the individual bourgeois manufacturer himself. The more openly this despotism proclaims gain to be its end and aim, the more petty, the more hateful, and the more embittering it is. . . .

But with the development of industry the proletariat not only increases in number; it becomes concentrated in greater masses, its strength grows, and it feels that strength more. The various interests and conditions of life within the ranks of the proletariat are more and more equalized, in proportion as machinery obliterates all distinctions of labor, and nearly everywhere reduces wages to the same low level. The growing competition among the bourgeoisie, and the resulting commercial crises, make the wages of the workers ever more fluctuating. The unceasing improvement of machinery, ever more rapidly developing, makes their livelihood more and more precarious; the collisions between individual workmen and individual bourgeoisie take more and more the character of collisions between two classes. Thereupon the workers begin to form combinations (trade unions) against the bourgeoisie; they club together in order to keep up the rate of wages; they found permanent associations in order to make provision beforehand for these occasional revolts. Here and there the contest breaks out into riots.

From time to time the workers are victorious, but only for a time. The real fruit of their battles lies not in the immediate result, but in the ever-expanding union of the workers. This union is helped by the improved means of communication that are created by modern industry and that place the workers of different localities in contact with one another. It was just this contact that was needed to centralize the numerous local struggles, all of the same character, into one national struggle between classes. But every class struggle is a political struggle. And that union, to attain which the burghers of the Middle Ages, with their miserable highways, required centuries, the modern proletarians, thanks to railways, achieve in a few years. . . .

Hitherto, every form of society has been based, as we have already seen, on the antagonism of oppressing and oppressed classes. But in order to oppress a class, certain conditions must be assured to it under which it can, at least, continue its slavish existence. The serf, in the period of serfdom, raised himself to membership in the commune, just as the petty bourgeois, under the yoke of feudal absolutism, managed to develop into a bourgeois. The modern laborer, on the contrary, instead of rising with the progress of industry, sinks deeper and deeper below the conditions of existence of his own class. He becomes a pauper, and pauperism develops more rapidly than population and wealth. And here it becomes evident that the bourgeoisie is unfit any longer to be the ruling class in society, and to impose its conditions of existence upon society as an overriding law. It is unfit to rule because it is incompetent to assure an existence to its slave within his slavery, because it cannot help letting him sink into such a state, that it has to feed him, instead of being fed by him. Society can no longer live under this bourgeoisie, in other words, its existence is no longer compatible with society.

The essential condition for the existence, and for the sway of the bourgeois class, is the formation and augmentation of capital; the condition for capital is wage labor. Wage labor rests exclusively on competition between the laborers. The advance of industry, whose involuntary promoter is the bourgeoisie, replaces the isolation of the laborers, due to competition, by their revolutionary combination, due to association. The development of modern industry, therefore, cuts from under its feet the very foundation on which the bourgeoisie produces and appropriates products. What the bourgeoisie, therefore, produces, above all, is its own grave-diggers. Its fall and the victory of the proletariat are equally inevitable.

II. PROLETARIANS AND COMMUNISTS

. . . All property relations in the past have continually been subject to historical change consequent upon the change in historical conditions.

The French Revolution, for example, abolished feudal property in favor of bourgeois property.

The distinguishing feature of communism is not the abolition of property generally, but the abolition of bourgeois property. But modern bourgeois private property is the final and most complete expression of the system of producing and appropriating products that is based on class antagonisms, on the exploitation of the many by the few.

In this sense, the theory of the Communists may be summed up in the single phrase: Abolition of private property.

We Communists have been reproached with the desire of abolishing the right of personally acquiring property as the fruit of man's own labor, which property is alleged to be the groundwork of all personal freedom, activity and independence.

Hard-won, self-acquired, self-earned property! Do you mean the property of the petty artisan and of the small peasant, a form of property that preceded the bourgeois form? There is no need to abolish that; the development of industry has to a great extent already destroyed it, and is still destroying it daily.

Or do you mean modern bourgeois private property?

But does wage labor create any property for the laborer? Not a bit. It creates capital, *i.e.*, the kind of property that exploits wage labor, and that cannot increase except upon condition of begetting a new supply of wage labor for fresh exploitation. Property, in its present form, is based on the antagonism of capital and wage labor. Let us examine both sides of this antagonism.

To be a capitalist, is to have not only a purely personal, but a social *status* in production. Capital is a collective product, and only by the united action of many members, nay, in the last resort, only by the united action of all members of society, can it be set in motion.

Capital is, therefore, not a personal, it is a social power.

When, therefore, capital is converted into common property, into the property of all members of society, personal property is not thereby transformed into social property. It is only the social character of the property that is changed. It loses its class character.

Let us now take wage labor.

The average price of wage labor is the minimum wage, *i.e.*, that quantum of the means of subsistence, which is absolutely requisite to keep the laborer in bare existence as a laborer. What, therefore, the wage laborer appropriates by means of his labor, merely suffices to prolong and reproduce a bare existence. We by no means intend to abolish this personal appropria-

tion of the products of labor, an appropriation that is made for the maintenance and reproduction of human life, and that leaves no surplus where-
with to command the labor of others. All that we want to do away with is the
miserable character of this appropriation, under which the laborer lives
merely to increase capital, and is allowed to live only in so far as the interest
of the ruling class requires it.

In bourgeois society, living labor is but a means to increase accumulated labor. In communist society, accumulated labor is but a means to
widen, to enrich, to promote the existence of the laborer.

In bourgeois society, therefore, the past dominates the present; in
communist society the present dominates the past. In bourgeois society
capital is independent and has individuality, while the living person is dependent and has no individuality.

And the abolition of this state of things is called by the bourgeoisie,
abolition of individuality and freedom! And rightly so. The abolition of
bourgeois individuality, bourgeois independence, and bourgeois freedom is
undoubtedly aimed at.

By freedom is meant, under the present bourgeois conditions of production, free trade, free selling and buying.

But if selling and buying disappears, free selling and buying disappears
also. This talk about free selling and buying, and all the other "brave words"
of our bourgeoisie about freedom in general, have a meaning, if any, only in
contrast with restricted selling and buying, with the fettered traders of the
Middle Ages, but have no meaning when opposed to the communist abolition of buying and selling, of the bourgeois conditions of production, and of
the bourgeoisie itself.

You are horrified at our intending to do away with private property.
But in your existing society, private property is already done away with for
nine-tenths of the population; its existence for the few is solely due to its
non-existence in the hands of those nine-tenths. You reproach us, therefore, with intending to do away with a form of property, the necessary
condition for whose existence is the nonexistence of any property for the
immense majority of society.

In one word, you reproach us with intending to do away with your
property. Precisely so; that is just what we intend.

From the moment when labor can no longer be converted into capital,
money, or rent, into a social power capable of being monopolized, *i.e.*, from
the moment when individual property can no longer be transformed into
bourgeois property, into capital, from that moment, you say, individuality
vanishes.

You must, therefore, confess that by "individual" you mean no other
person than the bourgeois, than the middle-class owner of property. This
person must, indeed, be swept out of the way, and made impossible.

Communism deprives no man of the power to appropriate the products of society; all that it does is to deprive him of the power to subjugate the labor of others by means of such appropriation.

It has been objected that upon the abolition of private property all work will cease, and universal laziness will overtake us.

According to this, bourgeois society ought long ago to have gone to the dogs through sheer idleness; for those of its members who work, acquire nothing, and those who acquire anything, do not work. The whole of this objection is but another expression of the tautology: that there can no longer be any wage labor when there is no longer any capital.

Wealth

Andrew Carnegie

This article is one of the clearest attempts to justify Social Darwinism. Written in 1889, it defends the pursuit of wealth by arguing that society is strengthened and improved through the struggle for survival in the marketplace. Interestingly, it was written by one of the world's wealthiest men, Andrew Carnegie, who came to the United States as a poor immigrant boy and quickly rose to enormous power. He began his career as a minor employee in a telegraph company, but emerged in a few years as superintendent of the Pennsylvania Railroad. After the Civil War he entered the iron and steel business, and by 1889 he controlled eight companies which he eventually consolidated into the Carnegie Steel Corporation. Shortly before he died, he merged the Carnegie Steel Corporation with the United States Steel Company.

Carnegie took seriously the task of managing his vast fortune, and he made use of many of the ideas which are presented in the following article. He gave generously to many causes, including public libraries, public education, and the development of international peace.

The problem of our age is the proper administration of wealth, so that the ties of brotherhood may still bind together the rich and poor in harmonious relationship. The conditions of human life have not only been changed, but

First published in the *North American Review*, June 1889.

revolutionized, within the past few hundred years. In former days there was little difference between the dwelling, dress, food, and environment of the chief and those of his retainers. The Indians are today where civilized man then was. When visiting the Sioux, I was led to the wigwam of the chief. It was just like the others in external appearance, and even within the difference was trifling between it and those of the poorest of his braves. The contrast between the palace of the millionaire and the cottage of the laborer with us today measures the change which has come into civilization.

This change, however, is not to be deplored, but welcomed as highly beneficial. It is well, nay essential, for the progress of the race, that the houses of some should be homes for all that is highest and best in literature and art, and for all the refinements of civilization, rather than that none should be so. Much better this great irregularity than universal squalor. Without wealth there can be no Maecetions. When these apprentices rose to be masters, there was little or no change in their mode of life, and they, in turn, educated in the same routine succeeding apprentices. There was, substantially, social equality, and even political equality, for those engaged in industrial pursuits had then little or no political voice in the State.

But the inevitable result of such a mode of manufacture was crude articles at high prices. Today the world obtains commodities of excellent quality at prices which even the generation preceding this would have deemed incredible. In the commercial world similar causes have produced similar results, and the race is benefited thereby. The poor enjoy what the rich could not before afford. What were the luxuries have become the necessaries of life. The laborer has now more comforts than the farmer had a few generations ago. The farmer has more luxuries than the landlord had, and is more richly clad and better housed. The landlord has books and picturers rarer, and appointments more artistic, than the King could then obtain.

The price we pay for this salutary change is, no doubt, great. We assemble thousands of operatives in the factory, in the mine, and in the counting-house, of whom the employer can know little or nothing, and to whom the employer is little better than a myth. All intercourse between them is at an end. Rigid Castes are formed, and, as usual, mutual ignorance breeds mutual distrust. Each Caste is without sympathy for the other, and ready to credit anything disparaging in regard to it. Under the law of competition, the employer of thousands is forced into the strictest economies, among which the rates paid to labor figure prominently, and often there is friction between the employer and the employed, between capital and labor, between rich and poor. Human society loses homogeneity.

The price which society pays for the law of competition, like the price it pays for cheap comforts and luxuries, is also great; but the advantages of this law are also greater still, for it is to this law that we owe our wonderful material development, which brings improved conditions in its train. But, whether the law be benign or not, we must say of it, as we say of the change in the conditions of men to which we have referred: It is here; we cannot evade it; no substitutes for it have been found; and while the law may be sometimes hard for the individual, it is best for the race, because it insures the survival of the fittest in every department. We accept and welcome, therefore, as conditions to which we must accomodate ourselves, great inequality of environment, the concentration of business, industrial and commercial, in the hands of a few, and the law of competition between these, as being not only beneficial, but essential for the future progress of the race. Having accepted these, it follows that there must be great scope for the exercise of special ability in the merchant and in the manufacturer who has to conduct affairs upon a great scale. That this talent for organization and management is rare among men is proved by the fact that it invariably secures for its possessor enormous rewards, no matter where or under what laws or conditions. The experienced in affairs always rate the MAN whose services can be obtained as a partner as not only the first consideration, but such as to render the question of his capital scarcely worth considering, for such men soon create capital; while, without the special talent required, capital soon takes wings. Such men become interested in firms or corporations using millions; and estimating only simple interest to be made upon the capital invested, it is inevitable that their income must exceed their expenditures, and that they must accumulate wealth. Nor is there any middle ground which such men can occupy, because the great manufacturing or commercial concern which does not earn at least interest upon its capital soon becomes bankrupt. It must either go forward or fall behind: to stand still is impossible. It is a condition essential for its successful operation that it should be thus far profitable, and even that, in addition to interest on capital, it should make a profit. It is a law, as certain as any of the others named, that men possessed of this peculiar talent for affairs, under the free play of economic forces, must, of necessity, soon be in receipt of more revenue than can be judiciously expended upon themselves, and this law is as beneficial for the race as the others.

Objections to the foundations upon which society is based are not in order, because the condition of the race is better with these than it has been with any others which have been tried. Of the effect of any new substitutes proposed we cannot be sure. The Socialist or Anarchist who seeks to overturn present conditions is to be regarded as attacking the foundation upon which civilization itself rests, for civilization took its start from the day that the capable, industrious workman said to his incompetent and lazy fellow, "If thou dost not sow, thou shalt not reap," and thus ended primitive Communism by separating the drones from the bees. One who studies this subject will soon be brought face to face with the conclusion that upon the sacredness of property civilization itself depends—the right of the laborer to his hundred dollars in the savings bank, and equally the legal right of the millionaire to his millions. To those who propose to substitute Communism for this intense Individualism the answer, therefore, is: The race has tried that. All progress from that barbarous day to the present time has resulted from its displacement. Not evil, but good, has come to the race from the accumulation of wealth by those who have the ability and energy that produce it. But even if we admit for a moment that it might be better for the race to discard its present foundation, Individualism—that it is a nobler ideal that man should labor, not for himself alone, but in and for a brotherhood of his fellows, and share with them all in common, realizing Swedenborg's idea of Heaven, where, as he says, the angels derive their happiness, not from laboring for self, but for each other—even admit all this, and a sufficient answer is, This is not evolution, but revolution. It necessitates the changing of human nature itself—a work of aeons, even if it were good to change it, which we cannot know. It is not practicable in our day or in our age. Even if desirable theoretically, it belongs to another and long-succeeding sociological stratum. Our duty is with what is practicable now; with the next step possible in our day and generation. It is criminal to waste our energies in endeavoring to uproot, when all we can profitably or possibly accomplish is to bend the universal tree of humanity a little in the direction most favorable to the production of good fruit under existing circumstances. We might as well urge the destruction of the highest existing type of man because he failed to reach our ideal as to favor the destruction of Individualsim, Private Property, the Law of Accumulation of Wealth, and the Law of Competition; for these are the highest results of human experience, the soil in which society so far has produced the best fruit. Unequally or unjustly, perhaps, as these laws sometimes operate, and imperfect as they appear to the Idealist, they are nevertheless, like the highest type of man, the best and most valuable of all that humanity has yet accomplished.

We start, then, with a condition of affairs under which the best interests of the race are promoted, but which inevitably gives wealth to the few. Thus far, accepting conditions as they exist, the situation can be surveyed and pronounced good. The question then arises—and, if the foregoing be correct, it is the only question with which we have to deal—What is the proper mode of administering wealth after the laws upon which civilization is founded have thrown it into the hands of the few? And it is of this great question that I believe I offer the true solution. It will be understood that *fortunes* are here spoken of, not moderate sums saved by many years of effort, the returns from which are required for the comfortable maintenance and education of families. This is not *wealth*, but only *competence*, which it should be the aim of all to acquire.

. . . Indeed, it is difficult to set bounds to the share of a rich man's estate which should go at his death to the public through the agency of the state, and by all means such taxes should be graduated, beginning at nothing upon moderate sums to dependents, and increasing rapidly as the amounts swell, until of the millionaire's hoard, as of Shylock's at least

> "_____ The other half
> Comes to the privy coffer of the state."

This policy would work powerfully to induce the rich man to attend to the administration of wealth during his life, which is the end that society should always have in view, as being that by far most fruitful for the people. Nor need it be feared that this policy would sap the root of enterprise and render men less anxious to accumulate, for to the class whose ambition it is to leave great fortunes and be talked about after their death, it will attract more attention, and, indeed, be a somewhat nobler ambition to have enormous sums paid over to the state from their fortunes.

There remains, then, only one mode of using great fortunes; but in this we have the true antidote for the temporary unequal distribution of wealth, the reconciliation of the rich and the poor—a reign of harmony—another ideal, differing, indeed, from that of the Communist in requiring only the further evolution of existing conditions, not the total overthrow of our civilization. It is founded upon the present most intense individualism, and the race is prepared to put it in practice by degrees whenever it pleases. Under its sway we shall have an ideal state, in which the surplus wealth of the few will become, in the best sense, the property of the many, because administered for the common good, and this wealth, passing through the hands of the few, can be made a much more potent force for the elevation of our race than if it had been distributed in small sums to the people themselves. Even the poorest can be made to see this, and to agree that great sums gathered by some of their fellow-citizens and spent for public purposes, from which the masses reap the principal benefit, are more valuable to them than if scattered among them through the course of many years in trifling amounts.

The best uses to which surplus wealth can be put have already been indicated. Those who would administer wisely must, indeed, be wise, for one of the serious obstacles to the improvement of our race is indiscriminate charity. It were better for mankind that the millions of the rich were thrown into the sea than so spent as to encourage the slothful, the drunken, the unworthy. Of every thousand dollars spent in so-called charity today, it is probable that $950 is unwisely spent; so spent, indeed, as to produce the very evils which it proposes to mitigate or cure. A well-known writer of philosophic books admitted the other day that he had given a quarter of a dollar to a man who approached him as he was coming to visit the house of his friend. He knew nothing of the habits of this beggar; knew not the use that would be made of this money, although he had every reason to suspect that it would be spent improperly. This man professed to be a disciple of Herbert

Spencer; yet the quarter-dollar given that night will probably work more injury than all the money which its thoughtless donor will ever be able to give in true charity will do good. He only gratified his own feelings, saved himself from annoyance—and this was probably one of the most selfish and very worst actions of his life, for in all respects he is most worthy.

In bestowing charity, the main consideration should be to help those who will help themselves; to provide part of the means by which those who desire to improve may do so; to give those who desire to rise the aids by which they may rise; to assist, but rarely or never to do all. Neither the individual nor the race is improved by alms-giving. Those worthy of assistance, except in rare cases, seldom require assistance. The really valuable men of the race never do, except in cases of accident or sudden change. Every one has, of course, cases of individuals brought to his own knowledge where temporary assistance can do genuine good, and these he will not overlook. But the amount which can be wisely given by the individual for individuals is necessarily limited by his lack of knowledge of the circumstance connected with each. He is the only true reformer who is as careful and as anxious not to aid the unworthy as he is to aid the worthy, and perhaps, even more so, for in alms-giving more injury is probably done by rewarding vice than by relieving virtue.

Thus is the problem of Rich and Poor to be solved. The laws of accumulation will be left free; the laws of distribution free. Individualism will continue, but the millionaire will be but a trustee for the poor; intrusted for a season with a great part of the increased wealth of the community, but administrating it for the community far better than it could or would have done for itself. The best minds will thus have reached a stage in the development of the race in which it is clearly seen that there is no mode of disposing of surplus wealth creditable to thoughtful and earnest men into whose hands it flows save by using it year by year for the general good. This day already dawns. But a little while, and although, without incurring the pity of their fellows, men may die sharers in great business enterprises from which their capital cannot be or has not been withdrawn, and is left chiefly at death for public uses, yet the man who dies leaving behind him millions of available wealth, which was his to administer during life, will pass away "unwept, unhonored, and unsung," no matter to what uses he leaves the dross which he cannot take with him. Of such as these the public verdict will then be: "The man who dies thus rich dies disgraced."

Such, in my opinion, is the true Gospel concerning Wealth, obedience to which is destined some day to solve the problems of the Rich and the Poor, and to bring "Peace on earth, among men Good-Will."

Property and Profit: Modern Discussions

Case Study—"Going After the Crooks"

The affair has quickly become known as Wall Street's Watergate. That hardly seems an exaggerated description for the drama of financial power and corruption that was exploding on both coasts of the U.S. last week. An enormous scandal was spreading at the core of America's investment community, touching some of the biggest moneymen in the country. A civil and criminal investigation was peeling back layer after layer of evidence in a bid to uncover the full pattern of illegalities that had come to light in the $2.5 trillion U.S. stock market. There was even that ultimate Watergate touch: the disclosure that for weeks, perhaps months, conversations had been secretly tape-recorded in an effort to plumb the depths of the worst insider-trading scandal in U.S. history.

In the paneled corridors of Manhattan's brokerage firms and investment houses, the scandal was reverberating in an atmosphere that one eminent Wall Street lawyer described as "hysteria." At blue-chip law firms, telephones rang incessantly as worried players of the multi-billion-dollar business-takeover game sought advice and protection. Said a nervous Manhattan brokerage executive: "Everyone is scared to read the newspaper in case his name might be in it." Similar jitters struck in Los Angeles, where guards carefully screened visitors to the offices of one of the country's hottest investment firms, now the focus of curiosity and controversy.

All across the U.S., investors were raging at the discovery that Wall Street high rollers had been ripping off millions of dollars by trading on knowledge not available to the general public. That sweeping form of sophisticated fraud did not merely touch the pocketbooks of professional stock-market players. The illicit profits came from taking unfair advantage of price movements in a broad range of stocks. That meant, in the end, that the speculators had pilfered from funds that countless thousands of ordinary investors had contributed to the market, in the form of their own stock purchases or investments in pension and mutual funds that in turn had bought securities.

At the center of last week's maelstrom was a shadowy figure whom few people had heard of until last week: Ivan Boesky. On November 14 the Securities and Exchange Commission electrified the financial world with news that Boesky, 49, one of America's richest and savviest stock market speculators, had been caught in an ongoing insider-trading probe. Boesky had agreed to pay $100 million in penalties, return profits and accept eventual banishment from professional stock trading for life for his alleged wrongdoings. He also faces a single, as yet unspecified, criminal charge, which could lead to a five-year prison term.

News of Boesky's misdoings echoed as far away as London, where he resigned his chairmanship of an investment trust known as Cambrian and General Securities. London brokers were reportedly told they could still trade with Boesky, but must inform the surveillance division of the London Stock Exchange of any such dealings.

In the process of striking his settlement with U.S. authorities, the relentless wheeler-dealer who earned the nickname "Ivan the Terrible" talked long and hard to investigators about the stock trades he had made using insider knowledge. He also reportedly allowed regulators to eavesdrop on and tape his telephone conversations as he conducted his business dealings. Last week Boesky's singing began to discomfit some of the biggest names in the corporate-takeover business. Said Pierre Rinfret, head of a Wall Street investment and consulting firm: "This may be the end of an era."

If so, the age of Boesky threatened to close with a bang rather than a whimper. Process servers working for both the SEC and the U.S. Attorney's office in Manhattan had delivered subpoenas to at least a dozen important figures in the stock-trading pantheon. The subpoenas did not imply guilt on the part of those who got them, but requested information about any dealings and relationships with Boesky. Among those said to have received the documents:

- TWA Chairman Carl Icahn, 50, the Manhattan-based corporate raider currently involved in an $8 billion takeover bid for Pittsburgh-based USX. The Washington *Post* last week quoted unnamed sources to the effect that Icahn and Boesky, who in 1985 owned more than 5% of Gulf & Western's stock, had collaborated to run up the price of those shares by fueling rumors that the company would be a takeover target. The two then sold their shares back to Gulf & Western for a profit. That ploy would have amounted to illegal stock manipulation. In a memorandum to his TWA staff, Icahn denounced the accusation: "I have never traded on insider information."

- Victor Posner, 67, another well-known corporate raider who lives in Miami Beach. Between 1984 and 1985, Posner paid about $80 million to acquire control of New York City–based Fischbach, the largest electrical contractor in the U.S. Boesky had also bought 13.4% of the shares of that company. In September, Posner was granted a new trial by a federal judge who overturned his July conviction on charges of evading $1.2 million in income taxes. Posner will neither confirm nor deny that he was subpoenaed.

- Boyd Jefferies, 56, chairman of the Los Angeles–based Jefferies & Co. investment firm, which specializes in assembling large blocks of stock in takeover targets. Jefferies recently supplied Canadian raider Robert Campeau with $1.8 billion worth of stock in Allied Stores, a move that eased a $3.6 billion takeover of the retail chain. Jefferies has acknowledged receiving a subpoena, and told the *New York Times* that he was innocent of wrongdoing. Also served was Michael Singer, 37, a former Jefferies senior vice president who switched in October to the Manhattan-based Salomon Brothers investment firm. Singer resigned his new post last week, but said, "I have done nothing wrong."

- Michael Milken, 40, senior executive vice president of New York City's Drexel Burnham Lambert investment firm. Milken, who works out of branch offices at the tony corner of Beverly Hills' Wilshire Boulevard and Rodeo Drive, is the guru of the so-called junk bond, the high-interest but risky investment vehicle that has provided much of the financing for the stock market's takeover frenzy. At least five other Drexel Burnham employees, including Milken's younger brother Lowell, have also been subpoenaed.

In addition to the individuals, Drexel Burnham as a corporation was subpoenaed by the SEC and by a federal grand jury. For the past two years Drexel Burnham has been Wall Street's most profitable investment firm; its 1985 gross earnings were an estimated $1.1 billion. In a bid to head off a run on accounts held with the company, Drexel Burnham declared it was "providing information" to investigators and emphasized that it "will not condone or tolerate any activities which violate the integrity of the markets."

Meanwhile, the stock market suffered some profound jitters of its own. On the day after disclosure of the SEC subpoenas, the Dow Jones index of 30 blue-chip industrial stocks plummeted 43.31 points, to 1,817.21, the fourth largest drop on record. If anything, the Dow understated the market's nervous collapse. On the New York Stock Exchange, 1,390 issues fell that Tuesday, and only 283 gained. Many of the hardest hit were stocks that had been heavily traded by speculators in the anticipation of takeover action. Later in the week, as opportunistic traders saw many stocks as bargains, the Dow stormed back 76.35 points, to finish at 1,893.56.

Even amid that recovery, however, many Wall Streeters were livid to discover that Boesky and the SEC had apparently collaborated in what many considered another stock-trading outrage. Prior to the November 14 announcement of his penalties, Boesky had been allowed by the federal regulators to unload quietly some $440 million in stocks from the estimated

$2 billion worth of portfolios he controlled. In effect, Boesky avoided the market slump caused by the news of his own spectacular downfall. Steamed one senior Wall Street trading executive: "This was the ultimate insider deal." Raged another investor: "It's incredible! This guy was allowed to protect himself while the rest of us had to take a hit for being honest."

At the week's end the SEC offered a defense of the $440 million sell-off. Boesky's action was legal, the commission declared, and the regulators had been fully aware of it. The SEC realized that there was a danger of a stock-market slide after the announcement of the action against Boesky. If that happened, Boesky would have been forced because of margin debts on his stock accounts to liquidate huge amounts of securities quickly. That could have sent the market into a steeper downward spiral. The SEC apparently decided it would be better for Boesky to dispose of some of his portfolio in advance.

Little investor rancor but presumably considerable discomfort was in evidence at a meeting Boesky held on Thursday at the office of his lawyers in downtown Manhattan. In attendance were some of the 43 limited partners who had anted up $221 million in capital for his major arbitrage fund, Ivan F. Boesky & Co. L. P. Boesky's tribulations had cast an unwelcome spotlight on a heterogeneous group of investors who suddenly found themselves unwitting participants in the scandal. The list of partners included several high-profile companies, such as Rapid-American (investment in Boesky: $5 million) and National Can ($6.5 million). Prominent individuals ranged from Manhattan investor Jeffry Picower ($28 million) to Martin Peretz, editor in chief of the liberal weekly *New Republic* ($250,000). Even the British Water Authority Superannuation Fund had chipped in $10 million.

At the meeting Boesky read a brief statement essentially apologizing for his actions, then handed the three- to four-hour session over to his legal advisors. They explained that the fund would be liquidated as part of Boesky's agreement with the SEC to remove himself from stock-trading activities over the next 16½ months. Said Lewis Lehrman, a former Republican gubernatorial candidate in New York State, who had plunked down $1 million on Boesky's speculative endeavors but who skipped the session: "I would say that Mr. Boesky disappointed a lot of people, me included."

In Washington, Congressmen raised questions about the need for new regulation of the securities industry and promised lengthy hearings on the insider-trading issue. A more aggressive response came from Angelo Oriolo, 66, a retired businessman from Pennsville, N.J., who last week filed a class-action lawsuit in U.S. district court against Boesky and others implicated in the scandal. Oriolo alleged that he had been injured financially in September 1985 when he sold 100 shares of General Foods stock. According to the SEC's complaint against Boesky, he made illegal profits from insider trading on General Foods. The Oriolo lawsuit is only the start of an expected avalanche of civil litigation that is expected to descend in the aftermath of the Boesky affair.

For many Americans, the Boesky case seemed to symbolize boundless avarice on Wall Street. Boesky's declared specialty was the high-return game known as risk arbitrage, which involves buying and selling stocks in companies that appear on the verge of being taken over by others. In little more than a decade, Boesky parlayed that arcane activity into an estimated net worth of at least $200 million.

Arbitrage based on public knowledge of acquisition bids has long been recognized as a legitimate exercise in which professional traders assume much of the risk inherent in trading stocks involved in takeover battles. But Boesky's illegal use of secret tips on takeovers has tarnished the reputations of all arbitragers and ordinary stock traders. Says Jack Steele, recently retired dean of the University of Southern California business school: "Where we're at today is really no different from the age of the robber barons." Agrees Robert Hanisee, president of Seidler Amdec Securities, a Los Angeles brokerage [firm]: "The popular perception among investors is that this kind of Boesky crap goes on all the time. The real tragedy is that we keep living up to people's worst expectations." Says John Baker, a broker with Shearson Lehman/American Express: "In the eyes of the public, we are all bad guys now."

Behind that admission of public cynicism was a growing crisis of confidence in the functions of Wall Street itself. Over the past decade, the place where American business raises money for its operations and expansion has been transformed into a high-tech, high-volume supermarket in which institutional investors move billions of dollars in the blink of an electronic eye. In all, some $130 billion in stocks, bonds and other securities now change hands daily simply on the basis of telephone calls alone.

At the same time, the number of small individual investors who own stock has been steadily shrinking, and the Boesky scandal may well accelerate that trend. Says Bill Kasten, an account executive in the Chicago offices of the E. F. Hutton investment firm: "Smaller investors now think that they're just crumbs in the pie, that they have no control." Agrees Robert Nichols, president of Los Angeles-based RNC Capital Management: "If we don't restore the public's confidence the public is going to exit and not come back."

Ironically, the offense that Boesky was charged with committing is anything but clear-cut. Insider trading is a crime that goes virtually undescribed in U.S. securities statutes, although it is roughly defined in court cases as the illicit profiting from information about private corporate behavior before that knowledge has reached the public domain. It has been compared to playing poker with marked cards. But deciding when the cards have been improperly marked—and, above all, proving it—is no mean feat, since rumor, innuendo and split-second inference are the stuff of ordinary stock trading.

Walter Wriston, former chairman of Citicorp, the largest U.S. bank, observes, "I have great trouble in knowing the difference between insider information and a very fine research report." On Wall Street, says an SEC official, "knowledge is power is money. It's worth a fortune." Deciding whether that fortune is ill-gotten is one of the regulators' most forbidding tasks.

Beneath all the wrongdoing, panic and disaffection with Wall Street lies a deeper issue. The lanky, impeccably tailored Boesky rode to staggering success and then to disaster on the wave of takeovers that have swamped the stock market in the '80s, dramatically reshaping the way that corporate America does business. Some 2,806 mergers and buyouts worth nearly $130 billion have occurred so far this year, up from 2,755 deals worth about $100 billion during a comparable period of 1985. The feverish activity has created a climate in which corporate raiders can reap quick, huge profits simply by buying a block of stock in a company, driving up the share price and then selling the securities back to the firm or to a higher bidder.

In 1984, for example, Fort Worth's Sid Bass and his brothers bought and sold 9.9% of Texaco's shares for a swift profit of $300 million. Manhattan financier Saul Steinberg earned $60 million that year by buying 11.1% of Walt Disney Productions and then reselling it to the company at a premium, a practice known as greenmail. Boesky made much of his fortune by guessing—and sometimes knowing—where the corporate raiders would strike next. Says an eminent Washington securities lawyer: "The millions and millions that are made out of nonproductive deal making represent the collapse of real morality in our markets."

The Boesky case had an instant sobering effect on the takeover game. As the thunder of the insider-trading disclosures rose in volume, a number of big plays suddenly came to a halt. Wickes, a Santa Monica, Calif., retailing and manufacturing conglomerate headed by Sanford Sigoloff, 56, announced that it might not be able to carry out the estimated $1.7 billion acquisition of California's Lear Siegler, the aerospace and automotive-products concern. Sigoloff's bankers, spooked by the Boesky scandal, apparently balked at financing the deal.

Sir James Goldsmith, 53, the Anglo-French raider, abruptly ended his 2½-week siege of Goodyear Tire & Rubber, the Akron manufacturer, after being grilled before the House Subcommittee on Monopolies and Commercial Law in Washington. "My question is: Who the hell are you?" said Ohio Democrat John Seiberling, whose family founded Goodyear. Goldsmith's sharp retort was that he represented the "rough, tough world of competition . . . a world in which you run a business as a business and not as an institution." But the aggressive tycoon, who owned 11.5% of Goodyear's stock and had offered $4.7 billion for the whole company, was in the end bought off by the management, which promised to repurchase his holdings for $618.8 million plus expenses. The profit to Goldsmith and partners: $93 million. He said that his change of plans resulted in part from what he called, with lordly British disdain, "this ghastly Boesky affair."

Boesky's name popped up again in the ongoing takeover battle between Gillette, of shaving-blade renown, and Revlon Group, the cosmetics conglomerate. Revlon, headed by raider Ronald Perelman, offered $4.12 billion for Gillette two weeks ago, just hours before the Boesky case broke. Gillette counterattacked last week with a claim in Boston's Federal District Court that charged Perelman with violating insider-trading laws. Gillette's lawyers issued a blizzard of demands for records from Boesky and a host of other Wall Street investment firms. Perelman called the Gillette accusations "totally without merit and self-serving." He denied that he had ever had any dealings with Boesky and vowed that he would press on with his takeover suit.

Other merger bids were seemingly not affected. Undeterred by its frustrated advances toward Lear Siegler, Wickes announced it would proceed with a $1.16 billion bid for New York–based Collins & Aikman, a textile concern. In California, First Interstate Bancorp is continuing its more-than-$3-billion bid to win giant BankAmerica.

The acquisition trend, however, is still vulnerable to further Boesky-related disclosures, and the odds are good that there will be plenty. Most of the furor that the Boesky case has caused so far comes from the SEC's November 14 judgment against the arbitrage superstar. That, in turn, was based on the relationship investigators uncovered between Boesky and Dennis Levine, the former managing director of Drexel Burnham who first blew open the scandal when he was charged last May with illegal trading in 54 stocks.

In its case against Boesky, the SEC charged that he had in effect contracted for insider information with Levine, who as a merger-and-acquisition specialist with Drexel Burnham had advance knowledge of takeover bids. Levine has been ordered to pay back $11.6 million in illegal profits and awaits sentencing on four criminal counts. In the spring of 1985 Boesky allegedly promised to pay Levine a percentage of profits for his tips, and subsequently the two agreed on a $2.4 million lump-sum payment. The SEC's complaint detailed a number of stock-trading situations in which Boesky had profited illegally to the tune of "more than $50 million." Among the stocks cited: Nabisco Brands, Houston Natural Gas, General Foods, Union Carbide and Boise Cascade.

Last week Irving Einhorn, the SEC's West Coast regional director, observed that "nobody has said that Boesky's trading was limited to tips only from Dennis Levine." In addition to the cases mentioned by the SEC in its complaint, regulators were believed to be studying as many as a dozen others for evidence of illegal trading activity.

Among them were January 1985 merger talks between Diamond Shamrock, a Dallas energy firm, and Occidental Petroleum—discussions that subsequently broke off. Another case is said to involve T. Boone Pickens' February 1985 takeover bid for Unocal. Pickens eventually backed away after Unocal bought up his holdings in the company. Analysts estimate that he broke even on the takeover bid. Yet another situation reportedly involves a successful June 1985 offer by the voracious Wickes for Gulf & Western's consumer- and industrial-products group, which manufactures such products as Simmons mattresses and Burlington hosiery.

Among more recent takeovers, the SEC is said to be looking at the action of traders amid the turbulence surrounding Broadcaster Ted Turner's acquisition of MGM/UA, for which the Atlanta buccaneer paid $1.6 billion last March. In October 1985 the New York–based Maxxam Group, an investment and real estate–holdings firm, made an $800 million tender offer for San Francisco's Pacific Lumber, leading to the companies' merger early this year. Boesky is said to have bought 10,000 shares of Pacific Lumber stock three days before the tender was made public, and he may eventually have owned 5.1% of the company's shares. Another case reportedly receiving scrutiny is the $400 million merger in February of Lorimar, producer and syndicator of *Dallas* and *Falcon Crest*, with Telepictures.

One thing that seemed to tie many of those deals together was the financing role played by Drexel Burnham. In one sense that was unsurprising, since the company completely dominates the market for the high-interest junk bonds that have been issued to finance so many corporate mergers and buyouts. For other Wall Street firms even remotely connected with suspect deals, a major source of concern was the sheer sweep of Boesky's operations over the years. Said a member of the Goldman, Sachs investment house: "Most major brokerage firms executed trading orders for Boesky." Agreed another Wall Street analyst: "We are all scared that it will work its way back here."

New deals continue to leak out about the way the insider-trading ring was discovered, starting with the exposure of Levine. The investment banker's covert role began to surface as far back as May 1985, when an anomymous letter from Caracas to the giant Merrill Lynch investment house alleged trading irregularities on the part of two of the company's employees in Venezuela, both of whom have since left the firm. In tracking down the accusation, Merrill Lynch authorities discovered that their employees' actions mirrored trades ordered through an account at the Bahamas branch of Switzerland's Bank Leu International. The brokerage did not know it, but the account was the main conduit used by Levine for making his own insider moves. Merrill Lynch passed on the information about Bank Leu to U.S. authorities in June 1985; it took almost a year before Swiss authorities agreed to divulge the name behind the account number.

Levine soon led federal officials to smaller fish in his insider-trading network, but Boesky's role may also have been uncovered as early as the end of last August. If that is true, the ten-week hiatus between then and the November 14 revelations would mark a truly substantial period of clandestine cooperation between the speculator, the SEC enforcement unit commanded by Gary Lynch, and the Manhattan branch of the U.S. Attorney's office headed by Rudolph Giuliani. The aggressive Giuliani, who has over-seen the criminal side of the investigation since Levine was snared, may eventually become almost as renowned for chasing insider traders as for bringing Mafia bosses to justice.

The help that Boesky has given to authorities may explain what many Wall Streeters feel has been extraordinary leniency shown toward the specu-lator, given the extent of his alleged misdoings. In 1984 U.S. securities laws were amended to allow confiscation of as much as three times the illegal profits earned from insider trading. But Boesky's $100 million penalty in-cludes only $50 million in returned illegal profits, or about the same amount of ill-gotten gains cited in the SEC's November 14 complaint. What many Wall Streeters found even more surprising, in view of the sweep of his illegal activities, was the mildness of a single unspecified criminal charge against Boesky. Says a securities lawyer in Washington: "He must have made a very attractive offer to them."

Boesky's appeal to investigators lies in the central role he has played in so many takeover deals. As practiced in the go-go stock market of the '80s, the corporate-takeover game often resembles a feeding frenzy; even in per-fectly legal situations it brings together, in a swift sequence of events, raid-ers, arbitrage specialists like Boesky, financiers and brokers.

In a typical takeover, a corporate raider might begin by buying a few million shares of a target stock, acquiring them on the open market through a major Wall Street broker. Under SEC rules, however, a raider is obliged to announce his holdings and his intentions once 5% or more of a company's shares are in his grasp. The first result of such an announcement is usually a boost in the stock's price. After the offer is made public, arbitragers, betting that a takeover bid will succeed, jump in and buy as much of the target stock as they can. Shareholders who are willing to sell then have the opportunity to win profits without staying the full course of the takeover, which may not succeed. Of course, the activities of the arbitragers boost the share price again.

Meantime, the raider would make plans with an investment banker to raise the cash or credit needed for the takeover, often by launching a junk-bond issue. With such financial backing lined up, the raider could then announce a bid for the controlling interest in the target company's stock. By then, the necessary holdings might be in the hands of arbitragers, who would be waiting to sell at a still higher price than their own efforts had created.

If the intended takeover victim fights back, outside brokers who are unregistered with the major stock exchanges might enter the game, usually as stalking horses for the raider. The job of the so-called third-market bro-kers is to "sweep the Street" quickly and quietly for any available blocks of stock in the target company, usually after regular market hours or when normal trading in a stock has been suspended under exchange rules. Then they turn the shares over to the raider.

All those operations are completely legal. But the close proximity of a small core of professional takeover specialists, and their towering importance in the market of the '80s, makes the prospects for collusion virtually endless. Since brokers and junk-bond dealers often know about the raider's plans well in advance of the general public, those professionals have the opportunity to tip off other investors or to make their own profits by trading in the target stock.

Lawyer Daniel Bergstein, a senior partner in the New York firm of Finley Kumble Wagner, which has many Wall Street clients, notes that raiders and arbitragers can form what he calls an "unholy alliance." In a typical maneuver, they might have a mutual commitment to buy up stock in a company, limiting their blocks to less than 5% to avoid the SEC's required disclosure rule. Then one member of the ring can leak the rumor of an impending takeover. When legitimate arbitragers leap into the fray, the group can unload at the inflated stock price and make off with enormous profits. Says Bergstein: "Both the raider and the arbitrager have an incentive to tell the other side what they are doing."

As reports of abuses in the takeover game proliferate, the political pressure to put new curbs on corporate raiders is sure to rise. At last week's hearing before the House Monopolies Subcommittee, A. A. Sommer, a Washington securities lawyer and former SEC commissioner, delivered a strong denunciation of takeover mania. Said he: "American enterprise, at a time when all its energies are needed for the worldwide economic struggle, is being driven by a handful of opportunists into a massive restructuring with consequences that may be disastrous." Sommer's argument struck a responsive chord among the legislators. Said Democratic Representative Mary Rose Oakar of Ohio: "Corporate America is being held hostage by the corporate raider. Profitable companies are being driven into debt, American jobs lost, and American businesses are being taken overseas, all so that a few enormously wealthy individuals can add to their personal fortunes."

But the issue is not that simple. In many cases a raider's acquisition bid may be one of the few defenses that shareholders have against inept, self-serving and complacent management. Many economists, along with key figures in the Reagan Administration, believe executives should be subjected to the full discipline of the marketplace, including the threat of takeover.

In recent criticisms of American companies, some Administration officials have sounded as harsh as the corporate raiders. Only three weeks ago Deputy Treasury Secretary Richard Darman launched a slashing attack on what he called "corpocracy." By that, Darman said, he meant the tendency of U.S. corporations to become similar to the Government bureaucracies that company executives frequently deplore: "bloated, risk averse, inefficient and unimaginative." Corporate raiders, Darman added, "are gaining attention as a new kind of populist folk hero, taking on not only big corporations but the phenomenon of corpocracy itself."

The Administration's reluctance to offer companies protection against takeovers may be tested in the new Democrat-controlled Congress. A number of suggestions for legislative reform are already beginning to percolate. Felix Rohatyn, a partner in the New York City investment-banking firm of Lazard Frères and a longtime critic of the stock market's speculative excesses, has proposed a sharp limit on the right of Government-insured pension funds, thrift institutions and trusts to invest in junk bonds. He suggests that takeover bids that are conditional on anticipated junk-bond financing be forbidden as an unfair manipulation of public markets. Rohatyn also thinks that offers to acquire a large number of shares in a firm should be voted on by all stockholders on both sides of the transaction. That would help to prevent managements from paying inflated prices to buy back stock from raiders in greenmail deals.

One of the most controversial suggestions on how to limit takeovers comes up for SEC hearings next month. It involves a New York Stock Exchange proposal to remove its 60-year-old "one share, one vote" rule, which prohibits the trading of shares in companies that issue both voting and nonvoting common stock. The revision would allow corporate managers and other insiders to keep the voting stock for themselves and to raise money by selling the nonvoting shares to other investors. Critics of the proposal see it merely as a way for managements to make themselves impregnable.

Whether or not anything should be done to restrict takeovers, specific steps can be taken to slow down insider trading. One would be to cut back steeply on the time speculators have to maneuver before a takeover bid is publicly announced. Under current SEC rules, corporate raiders have ten days between the time they acquire 5% of a target stock and the date when a public announcement of their intentions is necessary. It is precisely at such times, when insiders know that something is happening and outsiders are in the dark, that the potential for abuse—and for profit—is greatest.

Says Samuel Winer, a former SEC enforcement lawyer now in private practice in Washington: "You can get away with all kinds of discussions and not tell anyone." Winer would require companies to announce publicly whenever preliminary takeover negotiations begin. He would also mandate companies to release much more quickly such important data as earnings projections and year-end financial results.

Almost everyone agrees that one of the best defenses against illicit insider trading is to increase the likelihood that offenders will be caught—and that getting caught will hurt. So far the SEC has been reluctant to use the powers of treble confiscation of illegal profits granted to the agency in 1984. That should change. At the same time, the SEC under Chairman John Shad has shown greater eagerness than it had under his predecessors to pursue insider cases. Says Shad: "If the public believes that a few have privileged information and take advantage of it, it is going to shake confidence in the fairness and integrity of the securities market." Shad's crackdown on insider trading would be greatly helped by an increase in the SEC's budget, which is currently $106 million, or only a little more than Boesky's total penalty.

A highly regarded Washington securities lawyer who is familiar with the Boesky case probably speaks truly when he observes that "we may well get a whole string of new laws or regulations. Whether they're fundamental changes, however, depends on whether the public will care enough to push for them." In that regard, the widening stain surrounding Ivan Boesky may be serving a perverse kind of service to the integrity of the marketplace. If the stock and dismay engendered by his case are bolstered by further disclosures, popular indignation could guarantee a regulatory shake-up. It may be that further fallout resulting from Boesky's cooperation with the authorities will also help to clean up the marketplace the old-fashioned way: by deterring insiders from succumbing to Wall Street's temptations.

The Social Responsibility of Business Is to Increase Its Profits

MILTON FRIEDMAN

When I hear businessmen speak eloquently about the "social responsibilities of business in a free-enterprise system," I am reminded of the wonderful line about the Frenchman who discovered at the age of 70 that he had been speaking prose all his life. The businessmen believe that they are defending free enterprise when they declaim that business is not concerned "merely" with profit but also with promoting desirable "social" ends; that business has a "social conscience" and takes seriously its responsibilities for providing employment, eliminating discrimination, avoiding pollution and whatever else may be the catchwords of the contemporary crop of reformers. In fact they are—or would be if they or anyone else took them seriously—preaching pure and unadulterated socialism. Businessmen who talk this way are unwitting puppets of the intellectual forces that have been undermining the basis of a free society these past decades.

The discussions of the "social responsibilities of business" are notable for their analytical looseness and lack of rigor. What does it mean to say that "business" has responsibilities? Only people can have responsibilities. A corporation is an artificial person and in this sense may have artificial responsibilities, but "business" as a whole cannot be said to have responsibilities, even in this vague sense. The first step toward clarity to examining the doctrine of the social responsibility of business is to ask precisely what it implies for whom.

Presumably, the individuals who are to be responsible are businessmen, which means individual proprietors or corporate executives. Most of the discussion of social responsibility is directed at corporations, so in what follows I shall mostly neglect the individual proprietors and speak of corporate executives.

In a free-enterprise, private-property system, a corporate executive is an employee of the owners of the business. He has direct responsibility to his employers. That responsibility is to conduct the business in accordance with their desires, which generally will be to make as much money as possible while conforming to the basic rules of the society, both those embodied in law and those embodied in ethical custom. Of course, in some cases his employers may have a different objective. A group of persons might establish a corporation for an eleemosynary purpose—for example, a hospital or a school. The manager of such a corporation will not have money profit as his objectives but the rendering of certain services.

In either case, the key point is that, in his capacity as a corporate executive, the manager is the agent of the individuals who own the corporation or establish the eleemosynary institution, and his primary responsibility is to them.

Needless to say, this does not mean that it is easy to judge how well he is performing his task. But at least the criterion of performance is straightforward, and the persons among whom a voluntary contractual arrangement exists are clearly defined.

Of course, the corporate executive is also a person in his own right. As a person, he may have many other responsibilities that he recognizes or assumes voluntary—to his family, his conscience, his feelings of charity, his church, his clubs, his city, his country. He may feel impelled by these responsibilities to devote part of his income to causes he regards as worthy, to refuse to work for particular corporations, even to leave his job, for example, to join his country's armed forces. If we wish, we may refer to some of these responsibilities as "social responsibilities." But in these respects he is acting as a principal, not an agent; he is spending his own money or time or energy, not the money of his employers or the time or energy he has contracted to devote to their purposes. If these are "social responsibilities," they are the social responsibilities of individuals, not of business.

What does it mean to say that the corporate executive has a "social responsibility" in his capacity as businessman? If this statement is not pure rhetoric, it must mean that he is to act in some way that is not in the interest of his employers. For example, that he is to refrain from increasing the price of the product in order to contribute to the social objective of preventing inflation, even though a price increase would be in the best interests of the corporation. Or that he is to make expenditures on reducing pollution beyond the amount that is in the best interests of the corporation or that is required by law in order to contribute to the social objective of improving the environment. Or that, at the expense of corporate profits, he is to hire "hardcore" unemployed instead of better qualified available workmen to contribute to the social objective of reducing poverty.

In each of these cases, the corporate executive would be spending someone else's money for a general social interest. Insofar as his actions in accord with his "social responsibility" reduce returns to stockholders, he is spending their money. Insofar as his his actions raise the price to customers, he is spending customers' money. Insofar as his actions lower the wages of some employees, he is spending their money.

The stockholders or the customers or the employees could separately spend their own money on the particular action if they wished to do so. The executive is exercising a distinct "social responsibility," rather than serving as an agent of the stockholders or the customers or the employees, only if he spends the money in a different way than they would have spent it.

But if he does this, he is in effect imposing taxes, on the one hand, and deciding how the tax proceeds shall be spent, on the other.

This process raises political questions on two levels: principle and consequences. On the level of political principle, the imposition of taxes and the expenditure of tax proceeds are governmental functions. We have established elaborate constitutional, parliamentary and judicial provisions to control these functions, to assure that taxes are imposed so far as possible in accordance with the preferences and desires of the public—after all, "taxation without representation" was one of the battle cries of the American Revolution. We have a system of checks and balances to separate the legislative function of imposing taxes and enacting expenditures from the executive function of collecting taxes and administering expenditure programs and from the judicial function of mediating disputes and interpreting the law.

Here the businessman—self-selected or appointed directly or indirectly by stockholders—is to be simultaneously legislator, executive and jurist. He is to decide whom to tax by how much and for what purpose, and he is to spend the proceeds—all this guided only by general exhortations from on high to restrain inflation, improve the environment, fight poverty and so on and on.

The whole justification for permitting the corporate executive to be selected by the stockholders is that the executive is an agent serving the interests of his principal. This justification disappears when the corporate executive imposes taxes and spends the proceeds for "social" purposes. He becomes in effect a public employee, a civil servant, even though he remains in name an employee of a private enterprise. On grounds of political principle, it is intolerable that such civil servants—insofar as their actions in the name of social responsibility are real and not just window dressing—should be selected as they are now. If they are to be civil servants, then they must be elected through a political process. If they are to impose taxes and make expenditures to foster "social" objectives, then political machinery must be set up to make the assessment of taxes and to determine through a political process the objectives to be served.

This is the basic reason why the doctrine of "social responsibility" involves the acceptance of the socialist view that political mechanisms, not market mechanisms, are the appropriate way to determine the allocation of scarce resources to alternative uses.

On the grounds of consequences, can the corporate executive in fact discharge his alleged "social responsibilities"? On the one hand, suppose he could get away with spending the stockholders' or customers' or employees' money. How is he to know how to spend it? He is told that he must contribute to fighting inflation. How is he to know what action of his will contribute to that end? He is presumably an expert in running his company—in producing a product or selling it or financing it. But nothing about his selection makes him an expert on inflation. Will his holding down the price of his product reduce inflationary pressure? Or, by leaving more spending power in the hands of his customers, simply divert it elsewhere? Or, by forcing him to produce less because of the lower price, will it simply contribute to shortages? Even if he could answer these questions, how much cost is he justified in imposing on his stockholders, customers, and employees for this social purpose? What is his appropriate share and what is the appropriate share of others?

And, whether he wants to or not, can he get away with spending his stockholders', customers' or employees' money? Will not the stockholders fire him? (Either the present ones or those who take over when his actions in the name of social responsibility have reduced the corporation's profits and the price of its stock.) His customers and his employees can desert him for other producers and employers less scrupulous in exercising their social responsibilities.

This facet of "social responsibility" doctrine is brought into sharp relief when the doctrine is used to justify wage restraint by trade unions. The conflict of interest is naked and clear when union officials are asked to subordinate the interest of their members to some more general purpose. If union officials try to enforce wage restraint, the consequence is likely to be wildcat strikes, rank-and-file revolts and the emergence of strong competitors for their jobs. We thus have the ironic phenomenon that union leaders—at least in the U.S.—have objected to Government interference with the market far more consistently and courageously than have business leaders.

The difficulty of exercising "social responsibility" illustrates, of course, the great virtue of private competitive enterprise—it forces people to be responsible for their own actions and makes it difficult for them to "exploit" other people for either selfish or unselfish purposes. They can do good—but only at their own expense.

Many a reader who has followed the argument this far may be tempted to remonstrate that it is all well and good to speak of Government's having the responsibility to impose taxes and determine expenditures for such "social" purposes as controlling pollution or training the hard-core unemployed, but that the problems are too urgent to wait on the slow course of political processes, that the exercise of social responsibility by businessmen is a quicker and surer way to solve pressing current problems.

Aside from the question of fact—I share Adam Smith's skepticism about the benefits that can be expected from "those who affect to trade for the public good"—this argument must be rejected on grounds of principle. What it amounts to is an assertion that those who favor the taxes and expenditures in question have failed to persuade a majority of their fellow citizens to be of like mind and that they are seeking to attain by undemocratic procedures what they cannot attain by democratic procedures. In a free society, it is hard for "evil" people to do "evil," especially since one man's good is another's evil.

I have, for simplicity, concentrated on the special case of the corporate executive, except only for the brief digression on trade unions. But precisely the same argument applies to the newer phenomenon of calling upon stockholders to require corporations to exercise social responsibility (the recent G.M. crusade for example). In most of these cases, what is in effect involved is some stockholders trying to get other stockholders (or customers or employees) to contribute against their will to "social" causes favored by the activists. Insofar as they succeed, they are again imposing taxes and spending the proceeds.

The situation of the individual proprietor is somewhat different. If he acts to reduce the returns of his enterprise in order to exercise his "social responsibility," he is spending his own money, not someone else's. If he wishes to spend his money on such purposes, that is his right, and I cannot see that there is any objection to his doing so. In the process, he, too, may impose costs on employees and customers. However, because he is far less likely than a large corporation or union to have monopolistic power, any such side effects will tend to be minor.

Of course, in practice the doctrine of social responsibility is frequently a cloak for actions that are justified on other grounds rather than a reason for those actions.

To illustrate, it may well be in the long-run interest of a corporation that is a major employer in a small community to devote resources to providing amenities to that community or to improving its government. That may make it easier to attract desirable employees, it may reduce the wage bill or lessen losses from pilferage and sabotage or have other worthwhile effects. Or it may be that, given the laws about the deductibility of corporate charitable contributions, the stockholders can contribute more to charities they favor by having the corporation make the gift than by doing it themselves, since they can in that way contribute an amount that would otherwise have been paid as corporate taxes.

In each of these—and many similar—cases, there is a strong temptation to rationalize these actions as an exercise of "social responsibility." In the present climate of opinion, with its widespread aversion to "capitalism," "profits," and "soulless corporation" and so on, this is one way for a corporation to generate goodwill as a by-product of expenditures that are entirely justified in its own self-interest.

It would be inconsistent of me to call on corporate executives to refrain from this hypocritical window-dressing because it harms the foundations of a free society. That would be to call on them to exercise a "social responsibility"! If our institutions, and the attitudes of the public make it in their self-interest to cloak their actions in this way, I cannot summon much indignation to denounce them. At the same time, I can express admiration for those individual proprietors or owners of closely held corporations or stockholders of more broadly held corporations who disdain such tactics as approaching fraud.

Whether blameworthy or not, the use of the cloak of social responsibility, and the nonsense spoken in its name by influential and prestigious businessmen, does clearly harm the foundations of a free society. I have been impressed time and again by the schizophrenic character of many businessmen. They are capable of being extremely far-sighted and clear-headed in matters that are internal to their businesses. They are incredibly short-sighted and muddle-headed in matters that are outside their businesses but affect the possible survival of business in general. This short-sightedness is strikingly exemplified in the calls from many businessmen for wage and price guidelines or controls or income policies. There is nothing that could do more in a brief period to destroy a market system and replace it by a centrally controlled system than effective governmental control of prices and wages.

The short-sightedness is also exemplified in speeches by businessmen on social responsibility. This may gain them kudos in the short run. But it helps to strengthen the already too prevalent view that the pursuit of profits is wicked and immoral and must be curbed and controlled by external forces. Once this view is adopted, the external forces that curb the market will not be the social consciences, however highly developed, of the pontificating executives; it will be the iron fist of Government bureaucrats. Here, as with price and wage controls, businessmen seem to me to reveal a suicidal impulse.

The political principle that underlies the market mechanism is unanimity. In an ideal free market resting on private property, no individual can coerce any other, all cooperation is voluntary, all parties to such cooperation benefit or they need not participate. There are no values, no "social" responsibilities in any sense other than the shared values and responsibilities of individuals. Society is a collection of individuals and of the various groups they voluntarily form.

The political principle that underlies the political mechanism is conformity. The individual must serve a more general social interest—whether that be determined by a church or a dictator or a majority. The individual may have a vote and say in what is to be done, but if he is overruled, he must conform. It is appropriate for some to require others to contribute to a general social purpose whether they wish to or not.

Unfortunately, unanimity is not always feasible. There are some respects in which conformity appears unavoidable, so I do not see how one can avoid the use of the political mechanism altogether.

But the doctrine of "social responsibility" taken seriously would extend the scope of the political mechanism to every human activity. It does not differ in philosophy from the most explicitly collectivist doctrine. It differs only by professing to believe that collectivist ends can be attained without collectivist means. That is why, in my book *Capitalism and Freedom*, I have called it a "fundamentally subversive doctrine" in a free society, and have said that in such a society, "there is one and only one social responsibility of business—to use its resources and engage in activities designed to increase its profits so long as it stays within the rules of the game, which is to say, engages in open and free competition without deception or fraud."

The New Property

GEORGE CABOT LODGE

The Lockean ideology attached supreme importance to property rights as a means to fulfilling the values of survival, justice, and self-respect. We have seen that by the term "property," Locke meant both body and estate, and that by "estate" he meant essentially land or clearly owned artifacts; and that

From *The New American Ideology* by George Cabot Lodge. Copyright © 1975 by George Cabot Lodge. Reprinted by permission of Alfred A. Knopf, Inc.

he regarded the sole role of the state as being the protection of property, a man's body and estate. He was speaking for a clientele who owned property and were anxious to keep it from the king. For them, property was the means to political and economic independence, the guarantor of freedom. Those who did not own property, those who had sold even their bodies through wage labor, were so deprived of independence as to be incapable of voting freely and, therefore, were made ineligible to vote. In early America, property was widely diffused—nearly everyone had a reasonable chance to own some. (Slaves were, of course, excepted, being property themselves. In fact, slavery was justified in part because of the enormous power of property rights as an idea in America.)

After a period in which the corporation was seen as the creation of a legislature for the fulfillment of a specific community need, the idea of individual property rights came to make the corporation legitimate. Time and again this right was used to protect the corporation as an individual against the intervention of the state. And although the ownership of the corporation became more and more diffused until it was nothing but a myth, the idea of property was maintained, its unreality ignored in the name of efficiency and growth.[1] Today, the concept of private property when applied to the large public corporation is so obscure as to be nearly useless for legitimization. At the same time, uncertainty about the definition of efficiency and the acceptability of growth deprive these two notions of their old force.

The beginning of the disintegration of the idea of property rights in America can be set in the year 1877, when Chief Justice Morrison R. Waite found in *Munn* v. *Illinois*[2] that property "affected with a public interest" ceases to be purely private. Waite employed this concept to justify state regulation of rates charged by a private warehouse. The doctrine was taken further in 1934 in *Nebbia* v. *New York*,[3] when the Supreme Court found that the state could intervene whenever the public needed protection in the name of community need. It is hard to improve on the much earlier statement of the problem of private property rights versus the public interest made by Chief Justice Shaw in Massachusetts in 1839:

> It is difficult, perhaps impossible, to lay down any general rule, that would precisely define the power of the government in the acknowledged right of eminent domain. It must be large and liberal, so as to meet the public exigencies, and it must be so limited and constrained, as to secure effectually the rights of citizens; and it must depend, in some instances, upon the nature of the exigencies as they arise, and the circumstances of individual cases.[4]

The continuing disintegration of property rights as a legitimizing idea today is rooted in two factors: the changes that have come about in the nature of the American community (Shaw's "public exigencies"), and the continued dispersion of "ownership" of some 2,000 large publicly held corporations which account for something like 70–80 percent of the nation's corporate assets.[5] As the right to property gives way, a new idea is taking its place—the communitarian right of all members to survival, to income, to health, education, green space, natural beauty, and so on. It is not that the right to property needs to be abolished or that it is evil. It can continue to be appropriate in some settings, including most of the nation's several million small and clearly proprietary enterprises. But it has lost its dominant place as the prime guarantor and arbiter of human rights. In particular, it has lost its utility with respect to the large nonproprietary corporation.

The transformation is observable in several key areas. In the first place, technology has opened access to new sectors of our universe in which the traditional notions of property rights and ownership are simply irrelevant. Outer space and the seabed, for example, are defined by international law as "the common province of mankind" and "the common heritage of mankind," respectively.[6] No person, no corporation, no state may own these areas. They belong to all; they are of "the commons."

In the second place, scarce resources are coming to be placed in the public domain. We are increasingly aware of the scarcity of vital commodities: clean air to breathe, pure water to drink, fertile soil, natural beauty, fuel for energy, and perhaps food to eat. In the name of survival, these resources are moving inexorably beyond property to a new cradle of legitimacy composed of two related ideas: community need, and harmony between man and nature.

Examples of this transformation in new law are abundant, none more dramatic than the National Environmental Protection Act and the Clean Air Act. In 1972, for example, a land developer began construction of a high-rise apartment building on a small plot of land near Mammoth Lake in the High Sierras of California. Residents sued to halt the construction even though it was on private land. It offended the environment, they said. The case worked its way to the California Supreme Court, and in a 6–1 decision the court ruled in favor of the residents. In consequence, state and local governments now must make environmental-impact studies and expose them to public scrutiny before they can approve private construction projects which may have a significant impact on the environment. The California decision meant that citizens can sue to halt any such project that is not accompanied by such a study. According to the attorney who represented the Mammoth Lake residents, the California court decision was "the first time that any U.S. law has given citizens the right to participate directly in private land-use decisions before they are made." A number of land development and housing companies are in a quandary about what to do. "I think they want to put the builders out of business," said Gene Meyers, executive vice president of Levitt United.[7]

In much the same vein a federal task force on land use, headed by Laurance S. Rockefeller, advised President Nixon in 1973 that henceforth "development rights" on private property must be regarded as resting with the community rather than with property owners:

> There is a new mood in America. Increasingly, citizens are asking what urban growth will add to the quality of their lives. They are questioning the way relatively unconstrained piecemeal urbanization is changing their communities, and are rebelling against the traditional processes of government and the market place which they believe have inadequately guided development in the past. . . . They are measuring new development proposals by the extent to which environmental criteria are satisfied.[8]

Even with declining fertility rates, the report said, the nation's population will keep growing until well into the twenty-first century. It put present growth at the rate of 27,000 new households a week. The Constitution guarantees these families the right to move about freely, a fact that caused the task force to raise some long-range questions. May not the "new mood" force this attribute of individualism to change, in the face of community need? May it not be necessary for every level of government, covering every locality, to plan its growth, to provide for open space, proper housing, and the rest? And may this not require that communities establish population ceilings? Specifically, the report urged that all levels of government engage in buying up land for public uses and adopt strict regulations governing the use of privately held land. It observed that the states have the power to do this, "but must overcome a tradition of inactivity."

The strength of this tradition cannot be underestimated. Colorado Springs, for example, is a heavenly place nestled beneath the majesty of the Rocky Mountains on the edge of the Great Plains. Recently, its population has been growing by leaps and bounds, with industrial sprawl marring its perimeters. Youths abound, and there is insufficient work for them to do; vandalism is high. The community is running out of water and inversion makes the air foul on certain days. It is turning from heaven to hell before the stricken eyes of its business and civic leaders. I spoke to those leaders in 1972 about their ideology, which is as near to pure Lockeanism as one is likely to find in America today. They heard me out and shuffled silently from the hall. Later, in the hotel bar, I met the city manager who had heard the speech. He told me, "You're right. We have to plan as a community, but every time I suggest it, they call me a socialist or something worse." Others from the hall joined us in the bar. Relaxed, they lamented their plight, the waywardness of their children, the decline of what they had held dear. I made my speech again; this time the ideological barriers were more permeable. Since then, even Colorado Springs has begun to plan—its Lockeanism eroded by crisis.

In April 1974 the Environmental Protection Agency, acting under the National Environmental Protection Act, moved indirectly to limit the population size of Ocean County, New Jersey. An official of the EPA said, "We intend to do this all over the country." The EPA ruled that the national pollution standards set by the act required a total population of no more than 250,000 in sixteen municipalities of the county. It sought to enforce this ruling by refusing to grant the Ocean County Sewage Authority either the required discharge permit or federal funds to build a system which would serve a larger population.[9]

In the third place, mass urbanization has undermined the traditional theory of private domain. The old ideas simply fade, slowly but surely, as increasing numbers of people pay rent in vast complexes where ownership guarantees none of the political, social, and economic independence described by Locke and formerly provided by the family farm or business. The old idea of property is powerless to prevent the deterioration of low-cost housing blocs; already the federal government owns large tracts of faltering or abandoned inner-city housing. In 1972, for example, the Department of Housing and Urban Development found itself the reluctant owner of 5,000 single-family homes in Detroit's wasteland; the situation is as bad in other cities.[10] Cities and neighborhoods within cities are communities, and can only function if they are treated as such. But this requires entirely different ideological foundations, an entirely new collective consciousness.

In the fourth place, there has been a shift in the nature and function of work and in the means that workers have to fulfillment and self-respect. Of primary importance here is the fact that virtually all members of the American community now have at least a theoretical right that would have been unthinkable as recently as fifty years ago: the right, in effect, to survive. Along with this go other rights of community membership—to a minimum income, to health services, even to entertainment as in public television. (And further rights derive from membership in certain communities, such as IBM or AT&T, Oregon or Los Angeles.) The definition of survival has now become disconnected from work, being guaranteed by the community.

This has several important implications for the idea of property rights. The right to survive as a right of membership is obviously more important than property rights. And the idea of one's body being one's property, which was so central to Lockean individualistic thought, loses force.

Other factors have eroded the old notion of labor as a man's use of his own body. Today, labor increasingly means skill, knowledge, education, and organization. These are not owned by anybody; they are the product of the community. Further, as Robert L. Heilbroner has put it: "In the advanced capitalist nations, new elites based on science and technology are gradually displacing the older elites based on wealth."[11] At the same time, other wealth-producing factors such as resources and capital are becoming less clearly "owned" and of decreasing importance compared with the intangibles of knowledge and organization.

The ascendancy of community-created labor resources, coupled with the communitarian guarantee of survival and the decline in the legitimacy of property rights — and thus in the old basis of managerial authority–is having profound organizational effects. There need be no top or bottom in the managerial hierarchy; there must merely be a gradient of different skills and roles. Authority can derive from a variety of sources, which may have nothing to do with property. . . . And because the number, size, and importance of organizations (particularly the corporation) are growing, the terms of membership in those organizations are of increasing concern. Once, private ownership of his labor conferred a degree of individual independence upon a worker, even if it was only his body that he owned. But the worker today is increasingly compelled to function in a large organization in which any rights he may have depend upon his locus there and upon his dedication to the organization's goals.

Charles Reich has stated the dilemma well:

> When status and relationships to organizations replace private property, the result is a change in the degree of independent sovereignty enjoyed by the individual. Private property gave each person a domain in which he could be independent, and it enabled him to tell the rest of the world to go fly a kite. But a person whose "property" consists of a position in an organization is tied to the fate of the organization; if the organization goes down he goes with it.[12]

This redefinition of property plays havoc with some profoundly traditional notions of individual incentive and responsibility. As Aristotle wrote:

> that which is common to the greatest number has the least care bestowed upon it. Every one thinks chiefly of his own, hardly at all of the common interest, and only when he is himself concerned as an individual. For besides other considerations, everybody is more inclined to neglect the duty which he expects another to fulfill; as in families many attendants are often less useful than a few.[13]

Western man has seemed to husband best that which is his. Furthermore, we derive important psychological satisfaction from owning something, even though it be but a knick-knack. Surely this trait in our culture will not wither soon; nonetheless; we must adjust to the new concept of place in the communitarian order.

Other cultures have succeeded in reaching a solution here. In Japan, for example, the common interest has always been placed above that of the individual. Indeed, the individual achieves fulfillment only insofar as he contributes to his family, to his village, to the greater Japan. Centuries of cultural development and environmental adaptation have created this ideology — if a break in the dike around your rice paddy causes a flood in mine, our individual interests become inseparable from our common interest and the latter must prevail. Tightly delimited in resources, the Japanese have consequently produced a radically different ideology and radically different institutions from the United States or the West in general. As we move into an era of communitarianism, we can see that these institutions are functioning in many ways more effectively than ours. The role of the state and its relationship to business, for example, have given Japan a substantial edge in its strategic planning in the world economy. But the difficulty of moving away from our Western bias is as great as the seeming inevitability of such a movement.

Finally, the 2,000 or so largest corporations in America, which control most of the nation's corporate assets, have over the years detached themselves from the old idea of property. Even when managers cling to it for legitimacy, what authority they have derives from their place in a hierarchy of uncertain legitimacy. Since large corporations have obvious potential power and influence, this uncertainty renders them vulnerable to charges of abuse and conspiracy. Whether or not their power and influence are in fact abusive or conspiratorial, their estrangement from the old bases of legitimacy makes them suspect. The problem is heightened when the community is unclear or inexplicit about what it expects of corporations.

Myth has it that a share of General Motors, for example, is philosophically as important as a share in the ownership of the corporation. The myth, however, is empty of reality. A share of GM is nothing more than a claim on income and is generally disposed of if a share of IBM pays more. The claim that the shareholders elect the board of directors which in turn controls the "hired hands" of management is vapid. Myles Mace, in his study of corporate boards of directors, quotes one typical executive vice president:

> Management creates policies. We decide what course we are going to paddle our canoe in. We tell our directors the direction of the company and the reasons for it. Theoretically, the board has a right of veto, but they never exercise it. . . . We communicate with them. But they are in no position to challenge what we propose to do.[14]

So management appoints the board and the board endorses management in a mystical, self-perpetuating process, which albeit efficient, is plainly illegitimate.[15] We were willing to live with the illegitimacy as long as efficiency and growth were of overriding importance, but now that other factors have called into question the previously uncounted costs of growth, our willingness is evaporating. The individual components of corporate America— what Galbraith calls the planning system—are too large and powerful to be left to themselves; and collectively, in the complexes these organizations have formed with each other and in the economic sectors they dominate, they have become political forces to be reckoned with on the very largest scale. No one can doubt that the intentions of the utility industry, the oil industry, the automobile industry, and the communications industry have become matters of national concern politically and socially, as well as economically. Yet although in fact these are vast industrial complexes, the terms in which they regard themselves are frequently individualistic and proprietary.

Even in the equity markets that serve these industries, the trend from the individual to the collective is apparent and sweeping. Investors in the equity markets, theoretically the owners of the corporations, are increasingly unidentifiable as individuals to whom the ownership of corporations could conceivably be attached. "Like the curator of the National Zoo," said G. Bradford Cook, when he retired as chairman of the Securities and Exchange Commission, "I feel constrained to warn: The individual investor has acquired the status of an endangered species."[16] The place of the individual investor has been taken by huge organizations whose ownership is also extremely obscure: mutual funds, insurance companies, pension funds, and bank trust departments. Whereas such groups accounted for only 35 percent of the dollar value of New York Stock Exchange trading volume in 1963, the percentage is well over 70 today. This development has changed and perhaps profoundly threatened capital market structures; John C. Whitehead, a Goldman, Sachs partner, asserts that institutional dominance has endangered the market's valuation capability and demolished its liquidity: "We can look forward in another decade to complete dominance of our markets and of our corporations by a relatively small handful of institutions—the kind of industrial society that currently exists in Europe and Japan."[17]

This phenomenon of gigantism is having an interesting side effect on the innovation and enterprise which historically have been the handmaidens of the traditional ideology. Because the big institutions show market interest in relatively few stocks, newer and smaller companies are finding it increasingly difficult to go public at all. The vulnerability of our system to the acquisitiveness of the giants can be sensed in the example of Morgan Guaranty, which in 1972 owned more common stock than any other institution on earth—$2 billion worth of IBM, $1.1 billion of Kodak, and $500 million or more of Avon, Sears, and Xerox.[18] Taken together, all these factors have thoroughly confused our original notions of the role of the publicly held corporation and eroded its legitimacy. Ideologically, it has become a mere collection of persons and matter with considerable potential power—political and social as well as economic—floating dangerously in a philosophic limbo. If it survives, as it probably will, it has to be made legitimate. The only questions are how and by whom. The issues surrounding these questions fall into two categories:

1. Those having to do with the external relationships between the corporate collective and the communities that it affects.
2. Those having to do with the internal structure of the organization and thus with managerial authority and collective discipline.

NOTES

1. James Willard Hurst, *The Legitimacy of the Business Corporation in the Law of the United States, 1780–1970* (Charlottesville: The University Press of Virginia, 1970), pp. 234–53.
2. *Munn* v. *Illinois*, 94 U.S. 113 (1877).
3. *Nebbia* v. *New York*, 291 U.S. 502 (1934).
4. J. Shaw, *per curiam*, *Boston Water Power Co.* v. *Boston and Worcester Railroad*, 3 Pick, 360 (1839). Quoted in Harry N. Scheiber, "The Road to *Munn*: Eminent Domain and the Concept of Public Purpose in the State Courts," *Perspectives in American History*, vol. v, (1971): 399.
5. In 1968 the United States contained about 1.6 million profit-seeking corporations. Forty-three percent of those possessed assets of less than $50,000 and 94 percent had assets of less than $1 million. On the other hand, 1,900 companies, constituting 0.13 percent of the corporate population, had assets of $100 million or more and held about 60 percent of total corporate assets. This concentration of assets in large publicly-owned firms whose shares are traded on the stock exchanges has been increasing steadily since World War II. Neil Jacoby has estimated that 10,000 of the 1.6 million corporations have stock which is publicly traded — Neil H. Jacoby, *Corporate Power and Social Responsibility* (New York: The Macmillan Co., 1973), pp. 28, 49, and 179. Jacoby used data from *Statistics of Income: Corporation Returns 1965* (Washington, D.C.: U.S. Government Printing Office, 1965), pp. 4–5; Betty Bock, *Concentration, Oligopoly and Profit: Concept and Data* (New York: The Conference Board, 1972).
6. Elisabeth Mann Borgese, "The Promise of Self Management," *The Center Magazine*, June 1972.
7. Earl C. Gottschalk, Jr., "Guarding the Land," *Wall Street Journal*, Oct. 9, 1972.
8. Quoted in Gladwin Hill, "Authority to Develop Land Is Termed a Public Right," *The New York Times*, May 30, 1973.
9. U.S. Environmental Protection Agency, Region II, "Conclusions and Recommendations on the Central Service Area Sewage Project of Ocean County, New Jersey," April 1974.
10. John Herbers, "U.S. Now Big Landlord in Decaying Inner City," *The New York Times*, Jan. 2, 1972.
11. Robert L. Heilbroner in *The New York Times Magazine*, as quoted in John K. Galbraith, *Economics and the Public Purpose* (Boston: Houghton Mifflin Co., 1973), p. 81.
12. Charles Reich, *The Greening of America* (New York: Random House, Inc., 1970), p. 111.
13. Aristotle, *Politics*, Book II, 1261b, in Benjamin Jowett, *The Politics of Aristotle* (Oxford, England: The Clarendon Press, 1885), p. 30.
14. Myles L. Mace, "The President and the Board of Directors," *Harvard Business Review*, March–April 1972, p. 41.
15. The fact that the courts are holding directors increasingly liable for the sins of managers does not really help the legitimacy problem, even though it has probably increased the wariness of directors. The amount of liability insurance sold to directors and officers has increased from practically nothing to more than $1 billion — "The Law: Trouble for the Top," *Forbes*, Sept. 1, 1968, p. 23.
16. *Business Week*, June 2, 1973, pp. 58 and 59.
17. In Japan equity capital is rarely more than 25 percent of the corporation's total capitalization. Management controls companies with virtually no interference from stockholders. Ultimate control lies with the company's bank. The bank has

no vote, but the company's dependence on the bank gives it what a Japanese manager once described as the "power of irresistible persuasion." Banks in turn are heavily influenced by government. See Peter F. Drucker, "Global Management," *Challenge to Leadership* (New York: The Free Press, 1973), p. 240.
18. *Business Week,* June 2, 1973, p. 59.

Regulation That Works

STEVEN KELMAN

The last decade has seen dramatic restrictions in the freedom of action society chooses to allow to business firms. A series of laws in areas like environmental protection, occupational safety and health, consumer product safety and equal opportunity has restricted the prerogatives of business firms to pursue production, hiring and marketing practices that would have continued without these laws. Business and conservatives have now launched a counterattack against these changes. Cleverly exploiting various popular resentments, the counterattacking forces seek to lump "excessive government regulation" together with themes as diverse as high taxes and school busing to generate an all-embracing demand to "get the government out of our hair." To hear the critics of the new government regulatory programs tell it, nothing less fundamental than our very freedom is at stake in the battle against meddlesome bureaucrats. And now, with national concern over inflation growing, we are being told that the new regulatory programs are an important cause of the increased cost of living, and must be reduced for that reason as well.

One fact it is important to get clear from the beginning is that the alleged popular ground swell against government regulation of business does not exist. A recent Louis Harris survey asked Americans, "In the future, do you think there should be more government regulation of business, less government regulation, or the same amount there is now?" By 53 percent to 30 percent, those polled favored either more regulation or the same amount as now, over less regulation. In fact, almost as many respondents (24 percent) favored more regulation as favored less regulation (30 percent). Repeated polls have shown wide popular support for measures to make workplaces safe, and to clean up the environment.

This absence of any ground swell against the new regulatory thrust of the last decade is reassuring, because the conservative and business counterattack is, I believe, largely wrong. New regulatory programs neither threaten freedom nor contribute significantly to inflation. On the whole, the new regulation is a good thing. Certainly there have been excesses by bureaucrats, but what is more impressive than these excesses is the unfinished work the new agencies still have before them to deal with the injustices that prompted their creation in the first place.

There are two kinds of activities often lumped together as "government regulation." When denouncing the "costs of government regulation," opponents of the new regulatory agencies tend to forget this distinction. An older generation of liberals, fond of asserting that regulatory agencies always get captured by those they regulate, also ignore this distinction.

Most of the regulatory agencies established before the last decade were set up to regulate prices and conditions of entry in various industries. The grandfather of such agencies was the Interstate Commerce Commission, established in 1887 to regulate railroads. There is a lively dispute among historians about whether the ICC, when it was established, was an attempt to tame a powerful and oppressive industry, or a government-sanctioned effort by the railroads themselves to set up a cartel to avoid price competition. It is much clearer, however, that other agencies regulating market conditions in various industries, such as the Civil Aeronautics Board and the Federal Communications Commission, *were* originally established at the behest of industries seeking to avoid "excessive" competition. These agencies, by maintaining artificially high prices in various industries, have been very costly to consumers and to the economy as a whole. But you do not hear the voices of business complaining about them. Indeed, when proposals are made to deregulate surface transportation, airlines, or television, the main opponents of such proposals have been the industries being "regulated."

The situation is very different, both politically and conceptually, for the regulatory agencies—which have blossomed especially during the last decade—intended to regulate non-market behavior by business firms. Usually they regulate acts that injure third parties. These "social" regulatory agencies include the Environmental Protection Agency, the Occupational Safety and Health Administration, the National Highway Transportation Safety Board, the Consumer Product Safety Commission, and the Equal Employment Opportunity Commission. These agencies generally came into being despite genuine business resistance. Business representatives certainly have ample opportunity to participate in developing the regulations these agencies promulgate, but there are other organized constituencies interested in their work as well (environmentalists at EPA, trade unions at OSHA, civil rights and women's groups at EEOC, for instance). Few reasonable people believe the social regulatory agencies have been "captured" by business—least of all, as the current attacks demonstrate, business itself.

The conceptual basis for the social regulatory agencies also is different from that of agencies intended to limit or replace the free market. In any society, one of the basic tasks of government and the legal system is to decide which acts of individuals are so harmful to others that they cannot be freely permitted (and which harmful acts may rightfully be performed, even though others are indeed harmed). The social regulatory agencies are engaged in this age-old task. There is nothing conceptually new about their activities. What *is* new is that they have redefined certain acts by business firms previously regarded as acceptable, and determined that they are henceforth unacceptable.

Government has never left businessmen "unregulated," as business spokesmen now wistfully, but erroneously, imagine. The voluminous case and statute law of property, contracts and torts along with large chunks of the criminal law, comprise an elaborate system—far more complex and intricate than any OSHA standard—regulating acts that injure property holders, as well as acts by property holders that injure others. A starving person does not have the freedom to injure a rich man by appropriating the rich man's money in order to buy food. People do not have the freedom to injure a landowner by trespassing on his land. Furthermore, the process by which these older rules were elucidated and enforced through litigation was much more cumbersome and arbitrary than the rule making of today's regulatory agencies.

The plethora of regulations regarding property that has grown up over the centuries is not some sort of natural order, onto which new regulations of business behavior in areas like safety, health, environmental protection, consumer fraud, and discrimination represent an unnatural intrusion. As long as the regulations were restricting the freedom of non–property-holders to injure *them*, businessmen raised no chorus of complaints about an oppressive government stifling freedom. The chorus of complaints from business has begun only as regulations have begun increasingly to restrict the freedom of business firms to injure others.

The harms that social regulations of the last decade were intended to curb were not insignificant. Urban air had become unhealthy as well as unpleasant to breathe. Rivers were catching on fire. Many working people were dying from exposure to chemicals on their jobs. Firms were selling products of whose hazards consumers were ignorant. And the nation faced a legacy of racial and sexual discrimination. Frequently the harm was borne disproportionately by the more disadvantaged members of society, while the more advantaged produced the harm. The social regulation of the past decade grew largely, then, out of a sense of fairness—a view that people, frequently disadvantaged people, were being victimized by others in unacceptable ways.

The impact of the new agencies in alleviating these injuries has begun to be felt. Racial and sexual discrimination have decreased, partly thanks to broader social trends, but partly thanks to government efforts. There has

been a vast increase in the amount of information manufacturers are required to tell consumers about their products, and surveys indicate that
many consumers use this information in making purchasing decisions.

Since the much-maligned OSHA and its sister agency regulating coal
mining safety have come into existence, the number of accidental workplace deaths has been cut almost in half. Worker exposures to harmful
amounts of coal dust and chemicals like vinyl chloride, asbestos and lead
have been reduced, and this will reduce the toll of occupational sickness and
death in the years to come. Improvements in emergency medical care and
some changes in workforce composition since 1970 may be partially responsible for the dramatic reduction in workplace deaths. But today's figures
don't even reflect the reduction in deaths due to occupational disease,
which will be felt mainly in future years because of the frequently lengthy
period separating exposure to harmful levels of chemicals and death or
illness due to that exposure.

Environmental regulation has produced significant improvements in
the quality of air in the United States. Without regulation the situation
would have gotten worse because economic growth tends to increase the
level of pollution. Carbon monoxide levels in eight representative cities
declined 46 percent between 1972 and 1976. Carbon monoxide levels that
had been found in urban air were enough to increase the incidence of heart
attacks and of painful angina attacks among people with heart disease.
There has been a major decline in heart attack deaths in the United States
during the 1970s. No one yet knows why, but I predict that studies will show
that improvement in air quality has played a role in this decline. Another
common air pollutant, sulfur dioxide, which definitely causes respiratory
illness and death and is suspected of causing cancer, has now declined to a
point where almost every place in the country is in compliance with EPA
standards.

The critics ask: have the benefits outweighed the costs? Are they feeding inflation, for example? Allegations that health, safety, environmental
and antidiscrimination regulations are a major cause of inflation are little
short of grotesque. Much of the business thunder about regulation begins
by citing some overall figure for the "cost of regulation," and then goes on to
zero in on agencies like OSHA and EPA. These agencies are chosen, however, only because business dislikes them especially, not because they are
major contributors to the "cost of regulation." Most of the cost of regulation
is imposed by the market-fixing agencies, like the ICC, that the business
world likes. Murray Weidenbaum, director of the Center for the Study of
American Business and an adjunct scholar at the American Enterprise Institute, estimated that in 1976 federal regulation in the areas he examined cost
$62.3 billion to comply with. But of this sum, approximately $26 billion—or
42 percent—was the estimated impact on consumer prices of tariff protection against imports and of price and entry regulations by the ICC, CAB and
FCC. (The largest figure in this category was the cost of ICC regulation of

transportation). Another $18 billion—29 percent of the estimated total cost—represented the alleged cost of federal paperwork. Certainly there are plenty of pointless federal paperwork requirements. But few of these relate to what would normally be thought of as "government regulation." Much federal paperwork takes the form of reports for statistical purposes and of requirements for federal contractors or other citizens receiving federal benefits.

Only five percent of Weidenbaum's estimated total—$3.2 billion in 1976—was spent on complying with OSHA regulations. Another $7.8 billion allegedly was spent to comply with EPA regulations—less than 13 percent of the total. (Weidenbaum also estimated a $3.7 billion retail cost for auto safety and emissions requirements.)

Even these modest figures do not reflect the direct savings that result from some of these regulations. The actual monetary cost of pollution abatement measures, for example, is the cost to firms of capital equipment, energy and maintenance, *minus* the savings in medical bills, damaged crops, premature corrosion of property, laundering expenses and so forth, that would otherwise be borne by victims of pollution. Most accounts of the "inflationary impact" of government regulation do not calculate such savings.

More fundamentally, these estimates of the "cost" of regulation ignore widespread benefits that do not have a direct monetary value, but are real nonetheless. In the case of pollution control, for example, the air smells a bit better for five million people; 100,000 people get to see mountains in the distance which they would not have seen had the air not been as clean; and 50 lives are saved. There is no way of objectively determining whether these non-priced benefits justify the net monetary costs.

The costs and benefits of the business behavior now coming under regulation have not been distributed randomly. Much of the new social regulation benefits more disadvantaged groups in society. To put it somewhat simply—but not, in my view, unfairly—those who argue, say, that OSHA should "go soft" on its health regulations in order to spare the country the burden of additional costs, are saying that some workers should die so that consumers can pay a few bucks less for the products they purchase, and stockholders can make a somewhat higher return on their investments. It is hard to see why workers exposed to health hazards should be at the front line of the battle against inflation, however the overall costs and benefits tally up.

There are, to be sure, those sudden friends of the poor who allege that environmental regulation has significantly added to unemployment, or who point out that regulation-induced price increases weigh most heavily on the poor. But studies have concluded that, on balance, environmental legislation has probably created many more jobs than it has cost. And one must wonder whether there aren't more direct ways to help the poor than to eliminate the health, safety, and environmental regulations that slightly increase the costs of goods they buy.

None of this means that every regulation promulgated by social regulatory agencies in the last few years is justified. In some instances, as with some affirmative action requirements, regulations may have gone beyond their conceptual justifications. In other instances the administrative burden, the paperwork requirements or the monetary costs of regulating may be too great to justify the benefits, however real, received by those whom the regulations are intended to protect. Offhand, for example, it appears to me that the costs of retrofitting older urban subway systems to accommodate the handicapped, only a small number of whom could be expected to use those systems anyway, appear unjustified, even though failure to retrofit does indeed injure some disadvantaged people. Questions like this should be considered case-by-case, but with sympathy for those people injured by the failure to regulate.

The thrust of the current movement against social regulation in the United States is a wish by the strong to regain prerogatives whose disappearance, for the most part, is one of the most welcome events of the past decade. Individual regulations can and should be criticized. But the assault on the concept of regulation must be resisted if we are to continue to be a decent people living in a decent society.

Resolving Income and Wealth Differences in a Market Economy: A Dialogue

JAMES M. GUSTAFSON AND ELMER W. JOHNSON*

JMG:

Let me begin this discussion by recounting a few facts concerning the distribution of wealth and income in the United States. According to Arthur Okun, the top 1 percent of American families have about as much after-tax

* James M. Gustafson is University Professor of Theological Ethics at the University of Chicago. Elmer W. Johnson is Vice President, Group Executive, and General Counsel of General Motors.

James M. Gustafson and Elmer W. Johnson, "Income and Wealth Differences in a Market Economy," presented at Loyola University of Chicago, November 18, 1980, under the auspices of the Mellon Foundation. Reprinted by permission of the authors.

income as nearly all families in the bottom 20 percent and the top fifth of families have about as much after-tax income as the bottom three-fifths. The distribution of wealth is even more skewed. The richest 1 percent of American families have about one-third of all wealth, and the bottom half of all families hold only 5 percent of total wealth. Even worse, I understand, is the concentration of investment assets, since homes account for most of the wealth of the bulk of the population. It has been estimated that the top half percent of the adult population owns 49 percent of all privately owned corporate stock.[1]

According to Lester Thurow, the distribution of family income has remained essentially the same over the last thirty years, but only by reason of the rapid rise in income transfer payments ($224 billion in 1978) and labor force participation rates for women. Without these two factors the income differences might have been substantially greater. In short, welfare-state capitalism under our present tax system has made almost no dent in the distribution patterns of thirty years ago.[2]

Given these circumstances can capitalism be defended as a just system? Does it facilitate or impede the realization and develop a just distribution of the economic benefits that it produces?

There are two dominant ways of stating the formal principle of justice in the Western tradition: "To each his or her due," and "equals shall be treated equally." To apply these principles three questions must be kept in mind. *To whom* is X due? (Who are the equals to be treated equally?) *What* kind of things are due to whom? (What is to be duly distributed?) And, on *what principle* is the distribution to be made? The third is obviously the most critical question.

There is a spectrum of possible principles of distribution. (1) To each the same things. This is the most radical egalitarian principle. (2) To each according to needs. (3) To each according to ascribed social status, that is to "rank" determined by, for example, social tradition. (4) To each according to merit. Merit, like needs, begs for refinement. Merit can refer to contributions to social well-being, to culture, to productivity, etc.; what holds merit criteria together is the assumption that a person is causally accountable for achievements, and thus deserves reward.

In one sense a capitalist social order is radically egalitarian, at least in principle, namely that respect is due to all persons as free agents. The liberty of each is to be respected; the capacities that each has to be self-determining are to be respected. Respect is due each person; respect for persons ought to be evenly distributed to all.

The humane forms of capitalism today attempt to see that the fundamental human needs of persons in the society are met; at least this tends to be the case for "the deserving poor," for those who desire to work and who accept a considerable measure of accountability for the conduct of their lives. On what basis should the "undeserving poor" be treated? The "free-riders"? Those who do not seek work, or in other ways conduct their lives "irresponsibly"?

We do not have a social structure based on the ascription of status such as the designation of various "estates," but the powers that accrue to families of large inherited wealth are not totally dissimilar. Many of the benefits of power and authority, income and education, that families have in our society are certainly not attributable to the merits and achievements of their individual members. Present inheritance tax policies would seem to sustain a kind of "ascribed" social status.

Merit, it would seem, is the dominant, operative principle in the "justice" of present income distribution. And the most determinative kind of merit or achievement in the corporate and professional worlds is that of contributions to the economic well-being of particular organizations. The merit principle is clearly an incentive to achievement; it maximizes the degree to which persons are accountable for what they receive, and it motivates the acceptance of high performance standards. It appeals to self-interest, and sustains aggressive and competitive drives. In principle it operates not only within organizations, but among them. Units that deserve to flourish presumably do, and their flourishing is the result of the collective merits of the leadership and policies that make them successful.

EWJ:

I cannot begin to consider the justice questions you have raised without making some preliminary observations about the case for capitalism. The more thoughtful advocates of capitalism, to my knowledge, have never rested their case on whether it results in a just distribution of the economic output among the members of the society.

Rather they argue on grounds of efficiency and freedom and contend that excessive efforts to approximate economic equality will ultimately undermine liberty and severely contract output. The idea that the material welfare of the masses should depend on society's toleration of substantial wealth and income differences is not easily grasped, but this is the key to achieving adequate long-term capital formation, rewarding managerial training and responsibility, and providing the entrepreneurial incentives for innovation and risk-taking. Our current problems of declining productivity and inadequate capital formation, these advocates argue, are attributable not to capitalism but rather to such factors as (1) a tax system that has favored consumption over saving and investing and (2) a program of social legislation and over-regulation that has sapped the vigor of our market system.

Hayek, Lindblom, and others have all paid tribute to the marvelous coordinating function performed by market systems, a function that must otherwise be carried out by government planners. To date, no government has demonstrated the competence to perform this function very well.

We should also remind ourselves that capitalism has raised the material well-being of the masses of citizens in the advanced societies of the world to levels that were never dreamed possible, and this despite the population growth of the last two hundred years. The deliverance of the masses of people in democratic capitalist societies from grinding poverty, they argue, has been accomplished not by pursuing economic justice but by harnessing the energy of private, self-interest. In addition, the capitalist would remind us that our strivings for justice are subject to important constraints. Among these constraints is the need for a strong military defense capability, which in a democratic society requires a great deal of efficiency and dynamism in the economy.

The advocates of market capitalism would point out another important limiting condition: the corrupting nature of power. Capitalism works as well as it does in part because it decentralizes power and responsibility. All utopian forms of economic organization, dedicated to achieving greater economic equality, require an even greater centralization of power than obtains in the case of managerial capitalism. In the process, the managers of the centrally ordered economy tend to be corrupted by the exercise of power, and the system tends to break down. This danger might be less where there has been a long tradition of high ethical standards of conduct in the central government, continually maintained by institutions for the moral nurture and education of central managers, as obtained periodically in ancient China when Confucian ethicists played an important role. But it is doubtful whether the forces for moral nurture in our society today are sufficiently strong that we can be optimistic along these lines. We have enough trouble trying to cope with the corruptibility of corporate managers under capitalism.

Another limiting condition is the obligation to maintain and pass on from generation to generation the torch of high civilization. Surely, the capitalist argues, the preservation and enhancement of our cultural and intellectual heritage require a substantial degree of economic inequality. Tocqueville is good authority on this point.

Having summarized the very powerful utilitarian case for capitalism, I am ready to address your justice concerns. But I think it is important that these concerns be addressed in light of the possible downside risks: the subordination of national defense and international peace-keeping concerns; the spread of mediocrity and the loss of intellectual and cultural richness; declining productivity as self-interest incentives are removed and as government bureaucracy is augmented to handle redistributive schemes; the resulting increase in free-riders throughout the society; the erosion of the capital formation system as incentives to save are removed; the disappearance of what Schumpeter calls the "gales of creative destruction" that make for innovation and progress over the long term; the threat to civil liberties as government comes to pervade every area of our lives; and so forth. With this understanding, the question remains: Can the distributional principles operative in capitalism be defended as Just?

I would generally agree with your very brief summary of the mix of distributive principles that are presently operative in our particular system. Does this mix satisfy my normative concerns? By no means. First, it seems unfair that persons should be rewarded so heavily on the basis of their genetic endowments. Second, I am bothered that so many persons are rewarded on the basis of how well they pander to the basest of consumer desires, desires intensified by a powerful advertising engine. Third, it is not fair that some people inherit vast non-human capital assets for whose employment they are richly rewarded without having to develop and apply their own human skills. Fourth, it is unfair that the child who is born into a home where the educational and moral nurture is of the highest order, should therefore be able to earn many times more than the unlucky child born into a home at the opposite end of the spectrum.

The trick, I suppose, is to address these normative concerns without losing sight of the various downside risks that I mentioned earlier. Is it possible to articulate a workable concept of justice, one that takes these kinds of considerations into account? I remember John Rawls qualifying his theory of justice by saying that there are other institutional values besides justice that need to be taken into account, such as stability and efficiency, but that justice is primary. Yet, by the time he has worked out his difference principle (which in effect justifies the unequal distribution of wealth, income and the powers and prerogatives of authority to the extent that such inequality maximizes the well-being of the least advantaged), it seems to me he has incorporated into his concept of justice a great deal of what I would call efficiency values. I just wonder if justice doesn't include efficiency as a component value. Also, Rawls specifically makes the preservation of equal liberty prior to the fair distribution of the other social primary goods, thus taking into account my concerns about freedom and world peace.

JMG:

Let me remark on some of the points of your response.

First you raise an issue that probably gets us into an eddy. The question is, what are the causes of the increase in material well-being of persons in many societies over the past two centuries? You attribute the cause to capitalism. I would attribute it more to the rise of modern technology, which can be supported by various systems of economic organization. The point to be raised is whether modern technology arose only under the incentives of capitalism. But that gets us into a historical argument.

Second, you gradually move toward normative concerns by stating some things that bother you about present arrangements. Three of the four things you list I would put under the heading of luck in the lottery of birth. You do not think people should be especially rewarded for being lucky in their genetic endowments, in being born into wealthy families, and being born into families that provide commendable moral and educational advantages. Underlying this seems to me to be a principle that can be stated in this way: Persons should be rewarded according to their desserts, and their desserts are to be judged according to their individual efforts. Persons should not be rewarded for their luck in the lottery of birth. I take it that one can also say that persons should not be penalized for their unluck in the lottery of birth. We could persue this point. Should persons be compensated for their unluck in the lottery? How should this be done? What compensation at the expense of the lucky would be fair to the unlucky because they are unlucky? Maybe the lucky, and the lucky who achieve, should be taxed so that the unlucky, and especially the unlucky who achieve to the best of their circumstances, can be compensated. I do not think this line of inquiry gets us into an eddy; it is one route into how different benefits of the economy might, or should be distributed. My impression is that if this route is taken, we are not distributing according to need, or certainly not need alone. We are distributing according to desserts for achievements, with non-penalization (or compensation) of those who have less advantages due to no responsibility of their own.

Next, you indicate the "downside" risks for the health of the economy of a generally more egalitarian distribution system. What might be risks for the economy might also make possible benefits for persons in the relevant community—they would not need to be anxious about the things Jesus had confidence that God would provide, but if God does not, the state should—like adequate nutrition, and so forth. So the downside risks for the economy might be upside benefits for persons and families. And we are coming to the trade-off problem. To the risks for the economy you add the threat to civil liberties. On that I have an empirical query. Are civil liberties put at risk in economies more "mixed" than ours, such as the British and the Scandinavian ones? What civil liberties are put at risk?

Finally, you ask whether justice includes efficiency as a component value. Efficiency is a relational term that needs to be specified according to the ends of activity. Something that is economically efficient—producing a marketable product at very low cost—might be an inefficient procedure for some other human ends.

I think we need now to turn to further specification of what sorts of distribution of benefits from the economy we would deem to be more or less just, and defend them on some moral or religious grounds. Second, we need to ask what we would be willing to "trade off " either of the benefits and their distribution, or of the economic costs that are involved in the downside risk.

Let me propose. I would argue on religious and moral grounds that distribution according to needs is proper. Then I should have to differenti-

ate between real needs and superficial desires, and formulate some gradation of needs so that those deemed basic were sure to be met, and that
distribution with reference to others would be graded according to resources
available and willingness to make certain trade-offs in the process of meeting
them. Meeting "health" needs would be a case in point; while certain forms
of medical care ought to be available regardless of capacity to pay for them
by the patient, high cost, high technology interventions under certain conditions cannot be provided to all. But to put my point as an assertion, I
believe that our society and its government have an obligation of justice to
meet a range of human needs that could be defended as basic to all persons.
We do not respect persons without providing the necessary conditions for
them to survive, and to develop some of their capacities.

My second proposal is that a merit principle of distribution should
operate on the second floor of this social structure. This is not simply a
concession to "sin," in terms of the observation that persons will not work
hard, achieve many things, etc., without some recognition and reward. It is
also that having persons accept accountability (within the range of their
capacities, obviously) for their own actions is itself a matter of moral worth,
and that some reward system (it might be honor and respect as well as
money) is fitting recognition. If you agree, we can begin to work these things
out in more detail.

There will be no perfect system. Those who are ahead by the lottery of
birth might always be ahead (though many of them will squander their
gifts), but we cannot penalize persons simply for being lucky. I believe
compensatory measures ought to be made available to the unlucky so that
they can make the most of their unluck. I believe that we will always have
free-riders, and the number that can be tolerated, and the extent to which
their costs can be tolerated, has to be looked at in particular classes of cases.

EWJ:

Your suggestion, that a just organization of economic life would meet the
basic needs of every member of society without reference to notions of merit
and would permit the excess output of the society to be distributed in accordance with some principle of merit, is really what our country has been
groping after for several decades, particularly with the social legislation of
the last ten or fifteen years. Even Milton Friedman has proposed a negative
income tax as a means of further ensuring that each family will be able to
satisfy its basic needs, regardless of merit.

Your two-tier concept has an immediate appeal to me. I start with the
view that this world is an arena for our moral and rational development, in
community. Our economic arrangements provide a limited but indispensable portion of the conditions for this development.

Having agreed with the substance of your two very general proposals, let me now raise some problems that call for clearer definition. As to the first principle, you have already mentioned one of the serious definitional problems: i.e., that of distinguishing between basic needs and all other needs and desires for goods and services. A second, related problem is how should the needs principle be carried out: by means of a negative income tax or through an extensive array of governmental programs for the distribution of basic goods and services in kind, or by some combination of both mechanisms? In other words, how paternalistic should we be if our aim is to produce free and responsible human beings? A third problem is whether the society is obliged by considerations of justice to meet even the basic needs of the able-bodied poor who refuse to work when work is available? If it is not, then perhaps the government should have comprehensive work programs available for the reserve army of the unemployed.

As to your second proposal for some kind of merit principle, what do you think of our present free market idea as a principle of distribution, subject to the heavy qualification it receives in our society by virtue of government regulation and taxation? Or did you have some quite different principle in mind? As I stated earlier, the market principle is basically an efficiency criterion, and it appeals to me for this reason. I mentioned some aspects of this principle that I don't like. Your proposal for a floor eliminates some of my concerns. Appropriate tax reforms would eliminate other concerns of mine. I would then still be left with one more, perhaps insoluble, defect of the market: that it leaves people free, and many people almost certain, to make a mess of their lives, as Schumpeter puts it.

JMG:

I am happy that you consent to the view that respect for persons requires more than respect for their liberty. That, I take it, is a critical difference between us and the radical libertarians. Second, I am pleased that you note the intergenerational responsibilities. I suspect you would not argue against the view that maintenance and improvement of the capital base of our civilization comprehends natural and cultural conservation and preservation as well.

First, the distinction between basic and other needs and desires. There are efforts to draw the distinction more precisely than I have thus far. Basic needs would include food, clothing, and shelter; protection from crime and from rash invasions of privacy, and so forth. But I think no sharp lines, valid through time and across cultures, can be drawn with precision. The minimal conditions for well-being vary. Some opportunities to nurture the human spirit are necessary; that which nurtures differs between cultures. In American cities it can be argued that a telephone is a necessary instrument to meet many needs; in Calcutta it is not. In certain conditions modern transportation is not needed (though it is convenient), and in others it is. One thing I think we can agree upon; a percentage figure of those at the bottom of the income scale ought not to determine "the needy" in a more basic sense. Swedish social services, for example, are so broadly distributed that to call a fixed percentage of the lower-income levels "needy" does not make sense.

Across cultures and national economies the issue of meeting basic needs must be kept in mind, though we cannot get into international economic arrangements here. Not only the luck of the birth lottery, but the fact that some human populations must survive in adverse climatic and geographical circumstances is important to remember.

So, on the point of basic needs, I cannot "define" them in a satisfactory way to meet all circumstances. Historical, technological, and cultural conditions will always make the distinction a moving, rather than fixed, one.

To sum up, I believe that "voluntary consent" and exercise of capacities of self-determination provide a basic line of concern, but I do not believe the community needs to provide the resources that will be used wantonly for the sake of maximizing liberty. The basic point on which I think we agree is that (to polarize) any maximally libertarian way of meeting the needs principle, or any maximally paternalistic way, will have its deleterious as well as approvable consequences. Policy must be based on which risks seem to be worth taking.

There is one term we have not developed much that I think needs some reflection, and that is "power." Just distribution pertains to the distribution of power as well as economic benefits. How the actual distribution of power occurs in the society will be affected by other choices along the way. I take it that distribution according to the need "floor" requires concentration of power in government, for that is the institution that has responsibility for attending to the welfare of all of the citizenry (and by welfare I do not mean doles, but even the preservation of liberties). One of the functions of government is to attend to the interests of those whose interests are not met by other institutional arrangements. The state has an interest in the neglected child not only because the child does not have capacities and power to defend his or her own interests, but also because the common good is threatened in some way. There are legitimate interests of persons that are overlooked without the power of the state attending to them. The civil rights movement in recent history has made that point. Part of what has occurred is the development of new power groups with legitimation by law and court decisions, and with new power groups come different distributions of aspects of the capitalistic social organization's benefits. It is not only power that tends to corrupt, but also the absence of power.

Another term is common good. What is the relation between distributive justice and the common good of the society? That asks the question abstractly. But it can be asked with reference to particular policies for just distribution. And when we get down to particular policies we have to ask about various elements in the common good. Your argument might be that a free system of economic life serves the common good by providing capital accumulation, by setting conditions for the emergence of good leaders in competitive situations, and by providing conditions that serve the common good by maximizing individual responsibility. From another side, one can ask whether the common good in other respects is not served by more egalitarian distribution of more things under the auspices of the state, which is the institution that in principle is concerned for the common good of the nation. I only raise the question here.

EWJ:

Let me summarize our ethical concerns and considerations and then propose to you some very general policy guidelines that I believe are responsive to these concerns.

Much oversimplified, here are the fundamental principles and assumptions on which our policies will be based:

1. Our society is not merely an aggregation of individuals, as the nineteenth-century liberals and their philosophic successors suppose. That is, our ideal of the person is not comprehended by such phrases as "free to choose" or "free and responsible." Because the individual can flourish only in community, government is much more than a night watchman and a market referee. Government exists not only to ensure individual freedom, a negative value, but also to provide positively for the common good. Gewirth, Maritain, and Rawls have spoken eloquently to this point.

2. All members of our society are entitled to equal respect simply because they are human beings. Through our government institutions we accord this respect not only by guaranteeing individual freedom but also (at our advanced stage of cultural and economic development) by (a) meeting the minimum needs for food, clothing, shelter, education, and health of those who are unable to work and thereby meet these needs on their own and (b) by providing work opportunities for the unemployed who are able to work. We cannot be at all precise in defining "minimum needs" in kind or amount for all times and places. We cannot even be very precise in respect to our particular time and our particular community.

3. Above the "needs" floor, this equal respect can be roughly accorded by means of a market principle of economic organization, which (despite its many imperfections) tends to operate as a merit principle and hold us accountable to each other and to ourselves for successfully developing our talents and making the most productive use of those talents. The effectiveness of the market depends heavily on broad government guarantees to all members of society of positive rights to equality of opportunity and to open access to positions of power and responsibility, based on merit. This is especially important in a highly hierarchical society such as ours in which most persons earn their livings as employees of large organizations. These

considerations would seem to call for a tax system designed to prevent undue concentrations of economic wealth from being passed on from generation to generation.

4. In providing for basic needs, questions as to whether and to what extent goods and services should be delivered in kind will be resolved not by reference to abstract principles of freedom versus paternalism but by considering how these needs can be met in ways that are least costly to the community, least demeaning to the recipient, and most likely to encourage self-help and self-respect.

I think this fairly summarizes our joint conclusions thus far in our discussion. What are the implications of these ethical notions for the organization of our economic life? First, we are not calling for any basic alteration from capitalism to socialism. That is, we are not only content with, but our merit notion calls for, a market principle of economic organization, one of the two chief defining terms of capitalism.

The other defining term, private ownership of the means of production, is also an aspect of capitalism that is entirely consistent with our ethical notions. I really believe the critics of capitalism who think that this second principle is a great evil are quite misguided. That is, there are two basic ways by which the government can see to it that productive resources are deployed so as to promote the common good. One way is to permit individuals and non-governmental associations to "own" and deploy these assets subject to the regulatory and taxing powers of the state. This way reflects a policy that says in effect: "We want as much of the best of both worlds as possible: the much superior efficiency and adaptability afforded by the market accountability of competitive capitalism; and the governmental tools of regulation and taxation for seeing to the common good and eliminating excessive differences in wealth and income. The second way is for government directly to own these capital assets and for everyone in society to work for government. In theory our merit principle could work just as well if the salary and bonus schemes were artfully designed and fairly implied, but with government being the dominant employer and having to rely on the command system of the legislature or agencies to establish appropriate incentive systems, the prospects for our merit principle would be quite dim. Certainly my observations of other societies as well as of our post office confirm this conclusion.

Second, we *are* calling for the kinds of reforms that will (a) help carry out our generation's obligations to maintain and improve the capital base for succeeding generations, and (b) moderate income and wealth differences in light of our "needs" and "merit" principles. Edmund Burke is my authority for the proposition that government is among other things a partnership among generations. A chief function of the state is to ensure that we who are living fulfill our intergenerational responsibilities, particularly in a time such as ours when the institution of the family cannot be relied upon to play the major role in inculcating this aspect of stewardship.

Specifically, I would tend to favor tax reforms (i) replacing the present income tax system with a consumption tax on the lines proposed by Professor William Andrews at Harvard Law School,[3] (ii) removing the tax discrimination against equity capital of corporations, and (iii) imposing a more severe inheritance tax system that is yet consistent with the need for entrepreneurial incentives. Professor Cooper has spoken eloquently to this last point.[4] I would favor such tax reforms because (a) we need to encourage saving for investment and discourage consumption, (b) we must prevent long-term, undue concentrations of wealth if we are to have a vigorous merit system, (c) we need to create more fluid markets for the allocation of capital resources, and (d) we should afford to the children of all economic levels, even the wealthy, the opportunity to blossom forth to their full potential under a meritocracy.

My conclusion is that our two principles of "needs" and "merit," far from being mutually incompatible or requiring tragic trade-offs, are mutually supportive. Persons with freedom, but whose basic needs are unmet, never reach the stage of being able to develop under a merit system. Persons with excess wealth likewise often inherit positions of economic power for which they are not fit. Finally, I believe that the downside risks that I referred to much earlier in this dialogue have been adequately taken into account.

JMG:

I am not sufficiently informed about the more technical matters implied in your proposals to say that I am either in firm agreement with all of them, or in firm disagreement with any of them. I think they are very important ways to bring greater justice into the system, and are really quite strong without being revolutionary.

I will make one comment, and then state vigorously one dissent.

I believe that the *most general* principles we agree on can probably be worked out in a democratic quasi-socialist system as well as in the democratic quasi-capitalist system your proposals lead to. The policy proposals you make protect the interests of developing capitalism, and serve the common good in that way. Someone who might favor quasi socialism would be dissatisfied with your proposals. The difference is that your proposals are readier to limit some justice considerations, and the efficiency considerations require a larger range of freedom of economic choice and a wider spread in income and wealth. Your proposals do, however, lay the groundwork for the need tier of this justice principle. The debate between you and someone to your left would be primarily about what—economically, legally and socially—conditions are necessary, and how to establish them, so as to bring about a more equitable distribution. You probably worry more than such a person would about maximizing accountability for one's self as a moral value to be preserved. I, a "liberal" but not a socialist, can live with these proposals comfortably, and support them heartily.

My leaning toward the center continues to be from the left side; yours is from the right side. That is a good thing; if it were not so we would have a monologue.

NOTES

1. George Cooper, "Taking Wealth Taxation Seriously," *Record of the Association of the Bar of the City of New York* 34 (1979).
2. Lester Thurow, *The Zero Sum Society* (New York: Basic Books, 1980).
3. William D. Andrews, "A Consumption-Type or Cash Flow Personal Income Tax," *Harvard Law Review* 87, p. 1113. A consumption or expenditures tax is one which taxes only that portion of income or wealth that is devoted to spending for consumption purposes as opposed to savings and investment.
4. Cooper, p. 34.

Justice

Case Study—International Computer Sales

LAURA NADEL AND HESH WIENER

Would you sell a computer to Hitler?

You remember Hitler. He maimed, tortured, and killed millions of people. They were, as far as he was concerned, enemies of the state. That, he felt, was enough.

Some people escaped. But imagine if Hitler had had a computer to keep track of his victims and intended victims. Log in. Type GIVE ME THE NAMES OF 20 JEWS AND 30 CATHOLICS IN BERLIN. And . . . but why go on? Hitler died a long time ago. These things don't happen anymore. Or do they?

There are countries on this earth with governments so cruel that you can't find words to condemn their actions. And these governments carry out their missions, it seems, with the aid of computers. American computers.

In Chile, Uruguay, Argentina, or Brazil, and agent of the secret police can come to your door and ask you detailed questions about one of your friends—or even about someone you hardly know. If you do not answer satisfactorily, you may be threatened or taken away.

If you are taken away by the secret police, you may be tortured. According to the United Nations report, you could be hung upside down in a vat of urine or forced to eat vomit until your memory improves. If it doesn't

Laura Nadel and Hesh Wiener, "Would You Sell a Computer to Hitler?" Reprinted from *Computer Decisions*, February 1977, pp. 22–26, © 1977, Hayden Publishing Company.

what follows will make you wish you had drowned in the tank in which you were hanging. You may be told that your loved ones will be treated even more harshly, although you probably can't imagine what more harshly means.

Like all modern police forces, secret police agencies have the latest in crime information systems, as sophisticated as their governments can afford. For example, according to a knowledgeable refugee, the Chilean government's computer systems store complete information about "the opposition, those considered leftists or suspects. The computer has all the facts." In South America, such systems are running on American computers—the United States is the technological supplier of choice in this hemisphere.

The American computer manufacturers that supply Latin American governments with computers say they are not aware that their machines are used by the secret police. But they do concede that it is not possible for them to control how their machines are used by their customers. Most vendors say that they cannot take responsibility for the ultimate use to which their products are put.

"We are in a position similar to a car manufacturer," says IBM's director of information, Dan Burnham. "If General Motors sells you a car, and you use it to kill someone, that doesn't make General Motors responsible.

"Once the manufacturer sells the automobile, there's no guarantee it won't be used to commit a crime."

Control Data Corp.'s vice president Roger G. Wheeler, speaking for that company, concedes the responsibility of a manufacturer, especially a manufacturer of computers of awesome capacity. CDC, alone among American mainframe vendors, has a corporate policy governing the sale of its machines.

"Our own sense of responsibility," says Wheeler, "would not permit us to provide a computer system for any purpose that abridges human rights and dignity.

Asked whether IBM has a similar policy, Dan Udell, and IBM public relations officer, said that "IBM's official policy is to act in accordance with U.S. national policy in dealing with all countries."

IBM has substantial interests in Latin America. In Brazil, for example, IBM's factory in São Paulo makes System 370s. In Argentina, IBM builds high-speed line printers. In Uruguay, IBM has an enormous service bureau and data center. In Chile, IBM has no plants but does have a data center in Santiago.

It is in Santiago that the DINA, Chile's secret police is headquartered. In the old offices of the Pan American Bank, an eight-story building, the DINA directors oversee their work. Sources say that there are computers in this building, computers of American manufacture, which may well be linked to other DINA offices and police organizations by Chile's sophisticated telecommunications complex.

Communications links in Chile include a modern ITT telephone system said to be as good as any in the United States, an extensive microwave network for long distance communications, satellite links, and government radio channels. These facilities enable the DINA to keep in touch with its more specialized offices.

On Jose Arietta street, on the outskirts of the Chilean capital, is a building officially known as Villa Grimaldi, commonly called the Palace of Laughter. It is here that victims of the secret police may be taken for torture. Ultimately, victims are sent to concentration camps or prisons, of which there are many in Chile. Villa Grimalde, according to United Nations sources, has extensive communications equipment.

The use of computers by the secret police in Chile was first brought to public attention by the National Council of Churches. Reports received by the council indicated that an American computer was destined to become a tool of the DINA.

NCC representatives went to an IBM shareholder's meeting on April 28, 1975, with the hope that they could halt IBM's planned installation of a 370/145 at the University of Chile in Santiago. They claimed that the system would be used by the police agencies of that country, not the university.

"The Chileans did purchase a 145," IBM's Burnham explains, "and they told us they weren't doing it for intelligence purposes." IBM decided to trust the Chileans.

"If I was the Chilean military junta, I wouldn't put my computer in the University of Chile," reasons Burnham. However, he says, he does "understand the generals have taken over the university."

The National Council of Churches is more definite on this issue than any IBM spokesman. William Wipfler, the Latin-American director of NCC feels that IBM does indeed have a responsibility in this matter.

"We called the attention of IBM to the repeated violations of human rights in Chile and asked them to reconsider their plans to install the 145."

The National Council of Churches backed their pleas with proxies totaling 200,000 shares of IBM stock.

"The question is not whether they would sell computers to Hitler," says Wipfler, "but whether they would sell gas chambers to Hitler. Either way you're giving him weapons. When you know who Hitler is, you can't pretend you don't know what he's doing with your equipment."

Frank Cary, IBM chairman, spoke at the 1975 meeting in response to the church group's protest.

"We don't think the installation of a computer on the campus of the University of Chile has any sinister implications at all."

Sinister, according to Washington journalist Tom Mechling, is hardly the word. "The University of Chile would be a real Machiavellian place to put the things. On the basis of what I've learned from extremely reliable sources, I'm very much convinced that that computer is being used for name, rank, and serial number. These people who say they can't know what it's being used for suffer from the Eichmann syndrome. They claim they're only carrying out orders."

But IBM did send Dan Udell down to Santiago.

"We checked it out in detail. It's used for payroll, for processing student aptitude tests, for enrollment statistics and applications to college. To the best of our knowledge there are no other applications."

Perhaps the 145 at the University of Chile is not used by the secret police. But there is another, more direct link between the university and the Chilean secret police, a link typical of those that connect various Chilean institutions.

The leading computer service bureau in Chile is ECOM (Empressa Nacional de Computacion), an organization that provides extensive computer support to the government. This relationship is a long-standing one, according to the Chilean refugee now living in England. But, our source indicates, that relationship now includes computer support for DINA operation.

The president of ECOM is Rene Peralta, a former official of the Chilean Navy. He is also the former head of computation at the University of Chile, the very organization now training people in the use of a 370/145. The chairman of ECOM is an active general in the Chilean Army.

Our source claims that the systems at ECOM include modern powerful American computers. The services provided by ECOM include teleprocessing—the software there is capable of running database applications.

On May 20, 1975, General Pinochet, head of Chile's military junta, dedicated a 370/145 at the Technical University. This computer has been linked to other campuses by telex lines, according to Chilean sources.

The Technical University system is one of several shared by the Chilean Association of University Computing Centers. Among the members of this association are the University of Chile, Catholic University, University of Concepción, and ECOM.

Today, the Technical University is headed by Army Colonel Reyes. Commenting on this, an informed exile said "interrelationships between the universities and the military are natural" in Chile.

In addition to Peralta, there is another figure whose name comes up whenever computers and repression in Chile is discussed. He is Patricio Leniz, a former civil engineer who, according to informed sources, was a key software man on the computer projects of the DINA.

Patricio Leniz is the brother of Fernando Leniz, former minister of the military junta ruling Chile. Fernando Leniz is also the former chairman of *El Mercurio*, Chile's right-wing newspaper.

Further substantiation of the DINA's use of computers comes from refugees' accounts of mass arrests in Chile. Those rounded up surrender their identification cards which are quickly processed. Suspects are separated from the detainees and ID cards are soon returned to those free. The rapid checking of names against police files requires an on-line computer facility. Other stories from individuals detained by police corroborate the rapid checking of dossiers.

IBM is not the only American manufacturer that sells computers to Chile. Burroughs also sells machines there. Neil Jackson, Burroughs director of communications, said that the Chileans have one older machine which Burroughs sold them in 1970. This, he points out, was three governments ago.

Jackson's statement conflicts with a report that there are Burroughs maniframes at the Technical University, the Catholic University, and at the government's service bureau, ECOM.

Jackson stated that "Burroughs's official policy is that we never comment on the political affairs of any of the 120 countries with which we do business, including our own."

Suppose a B3500 is now used for police purposes? "Obviously we hope it's not," said Jackson. "We're not aware of any use by any of our customers for any purposes that violate human rights."

Refugees from other Latin American police states also tell of the use of computer printouts during interrogations to cross-check data provided by detainees. According to these exiles, dossiers are shared among the police forces of Argentina, Chile, Uruguay, and Brazil.

The most detailed report of the use of computer-generated information during a police interrogation comes from a clergyman. He entered Uruguay and was picked up by the police there for questioning. During the ordeal the police tried to get him to talk about a Catholic priest they were investigating.

When detained for questioning, the clergymay was presented with a computer printout describing the details of the career of his colleague. On the printout were all the addresses at which the sought-after priest had lived, his salary at each point in his career, his telephone numbers and his relations with other Catholics in Uruguay.

The interrogated clergyman said that the most incredible thing about the questioning was that, as far as he could tell, the man the police sought had never been in Uruguay.

This printout, a church spokesman claims, could not have been stolen from the personnel files of the Catholic church; it must have come from some police computer system. Police in Latin America, he said, keep close tabs on many priests.

The idea of using computing equipment to support police activities in Latin America has been promoted by the United States government. During the early years of this decade the Agency for International Development (AID) provided South American police forces with weapons, training, and data processing equipment under its "public safety" programs.

In the AID document describing U.S. assistence to the government of Venezuela, contract 529-11-710-022, U.S. officials report that "the technical groundwork has been laid for the country's public safety agencies, through electronic data processing and related processes, to pool their identification and intelligence data in a central location for more efficient coordination and rapid distribution of relevant facts and leads."

AID's Office of Public Safety, in a report on its assistance to Brazilian authorities, specifically lists IBM systems among police equipment shipped to that country.

Is this practice continuing? An AID official said that that agency no longer provides police equipment to Latin states. But AID does "provide computers to Chile."

The computers are included with moneys earmarked for activities other than "public safety." An AID official said that a recent grant for agriculture included a "computer component." He added that there is no practical way for AID personnel in Washington to check on the ultimate use to which such a computer is put. Informed sources state that the Chilean Institute of Agriculture building in Calle Belgrado, Santiago, is a center of communications for the DINA.

Evidence that Latin American authorities use computers for repression is abundant. Yet there seems to be no way for either computer manufacturers or humane government to halt this activity.

What little hope there is for a change in these practices may lie with the United Nations, a body limited to persuasive power.

The United Nations has been concerned about the possible use of computers as an aid to police in dictatorships. The proposed United Nations code of ethics states:

"It would seem imperative for computer experts to have some training in human rights concepts and in certain aspects of the law.

"In computer based decision-making, the computer user should bear in mind the need to protect and promote the rights of the individual."

Can the United Nations actually halt the use of computers by police states? Can it prevent automation of the "the final solution"?

"The U.N. has no methods of enforcing its principles," says Leonore Hooley, a United Nations human rights officer.

"We operate on the principle of nonintervention in the internal affairs of countries."

Case Study—Who Has First Claim on Health Care Resources?

ROBERT M. VEATCH

State Bill 529 calls for the establishment of community-based homes for the care and education of the mentally retarded. The bill provides one home for every fifteen persons presently institutionalized in four state institutions for the mentally retarded at a cost of $55.8 million. The estimated costs for the new care for the present population of 7,600 will be $70 million a year.

The bill was introduced by Representative John Sheehan who spoke in favor of it. He painted a dismal picture of antiquated institutions bereft of basic human necessities or amenities. Thousands of human beings, many unclothed, spend their lives huddled in dark, drab rooms, where they are supervised by an overworked staff, many of whom have no professional training. Sheehan, who has the support of the parents' organization, the State Department of Mental Health, the local ACLU, and the religious leadership, concluded his case by pleading, "Justice requires that we extend this token contribution to these citizens, burdened by physical and psychological suffering, and by the degradation of our society's past inhumanity to its fellow humans."

Representative James Hudson and Dr. Robert Simmons, while emphasizing their concern for care of the retarded, spoke in opposition to the bill. Representative Hudson, noting that he was elected representative of all the citizens in his district, argued that he had an obligation to examine the alternative uses for the $14 million in additional funds called for by the bill. But first, he pointed out that the new total sum of $70 million equalled 1.5 percent of the state's budget, a budget raised by all its citizens, while the institutionalized population equalled only one-tenth of one percent of the state's population. The proposed increase of $14 million could buy hot lunches for all the state's school children; it could also provide job training for productive members of society. Hudson argued that the fairest thing to do would be to spread the money evenly among those who would be productive. "Our task as legislators," he concluded, "must be to serve the greatest good of the greatest number."

Dr. Simmons, as a physician, argued that the money could be used more efficiently in providing health care for three groups: normal or more nearly normal children (thousands of whom could be reached for every

Robert M. Veatch, "Who Has First Claim on Health Care Resources?" *Hastings Center Report*, August 1975, reprinted by permission of the author and The Hastings Center: Institute of Society, Ethics, and the Life Sciences.

mentally retarded child), those potentially engaged in productive labor, and pregnant women. He showed that much mental retardation can be eliminated through prenatal diagnosis which he estimated to cost $200 per case for Down's syndrome compared to $60,000 for each institutionalized child. Even allowing that some of the institutionalized retarded might be gainfully employed if they were in high-quality, community-based homes, the savings from spending the funds on detection rather than on more expensive forms of institutionalized care are enormous.

The legislative committee must now make its decision on the bill.

Case Study—Cat Scan

In a typical governmental response to a problem of its own making, Congress in 1974 entered into the business of health planning to try to reduce medical costs that were being inflated by badly designed Medicare and Medicaid programs. One feature of the scheme required hospitals to obtain "certificates of need" from a "Health Systems Agency" in order to make any sizable capital investment.

While the HSAs were theoretically controlled by local citizens, many in practice became tools of state and federal health bureaucrats. One of the outcomes was a limitation on use of some of the more expensive forms of medical technology, even where there were clearly demonstrated cost, and life, saving benefits. One such device was the complex machine commonly known as the CT or "CAT" scanner, which uses a computer and X-rays to formulate "pictures" of the internal organs of the body.

Doctors find this machine invaluable, particularly for diagnosing diseases and injuries affecting the brain. When health planners denied them to some hospitals, doctors in some cases raised the $500,000 on their own, installing what the bureaucrats chose to call "fugitive scanners" near hospitals for lifesaving diagnostic work.

One hospital that was, until this year, denied a CAT scanner was Harlem Hospital Center, a big New York municipal facility. Health planners ruled that doctors there could use scanners in nearby hospitals, but for various reasons, either because patients were too ill or the equipment was not free when needed, the use of CAT scans by Harlem Hospital doctors was sharply limited.

Three doctors at the hospital have just published an article in the New England Journal of Medicine detailing the effects of this, based on a retrospective analysis of hospital records for 1979.

Their conclusion:

> "Lack of a CT scanner at Harlem Hospital led to prolonged hospitalization, discharge without adequate diagnosis and probably in some cases morbidity and mortality. We do not claim that all or even most of the 163 medical and surgical patients who were thought to need CT, but who died without it, would have survived had it been available. Autopsies were infrequent. Individual analysis of these cases, however, raises the possibility of treatable lesions detectable only with CT—a possibility that was regarded with considerable anxiety during each patient's hospitalization."

The Harlem case is but one more example of the risks of bureaucrat-controlled medicine. The Reagan administration has proposed to phase out federal funding of Health Systems Agencies, leaving it up to state and local groups to decide whether they are worthwhile. Federal administration of Professional Standards Review Organizations, set up to monitor whether doctors are wasting hospital resources, also is slated for phase-out.

Both efforts are being resisted in Congress, naturally. But the Harlem experience tells us that in this one area, the loss of decision-making power by local professionals and boards can be a matter of life and death.

Distributive Justice

JOHN RAWLS

We may think of a human society as a more or less self-sufficient association regulated by a common conception of justice and aimed at advancing the good of its members.[1] As a co-operative venture for mutual advantage, it is characterized by a conflict as well as an identity of interests. There is an identity of interests since social co-operation makes possible a better life for all than any would have if everyone were to try to live by his own efforts; yet at the same time men are not indifferent as to how the greater benefits produced by their joint labours are distributed, for in order to further their own aims each prefers a larger to a lesser share. A conception of justice is a

From John Rawls, "Distributive Justice," *Philosophy, Politics, and Society*, 3rd series, ed. by Peter Laslett and W. G. Runciman (Basil Blackwell, Oxford; Barnes & Noble Books, Div. Harper & Row, Publishers, New York, 1967). Reprinted by permission of the author and publisher.

set of principles for choosing between the social arrangements which determine this division and for underwriting a consensus as to the proper distributive shares.

Now at first sight the most rational conception of justice would seem to be utilitarian. For consider: each man in realizing his own good can certainly balance his own losses against his own gains. We can impose a sacrifice on ourselves now for the sake of a greater advantage later. A man quite properly acts, as long as others are not affected, to achieve his own greatest good, to advance his ends as far as possible. Now, why should not a society act on precisely the same principle? Why is not that which is rational in the case of one man right in the case of a group of men? Surely the simplest and most direct conception of the right, and so of justice, is that of maximizing the good. This assumes a prior understanding of what is good, but we can think of the good as already given by the interests of rational individuals. Thus just as the principle of individual choice is to achieve one's greatest good, to advance so far as possible one's own system of rational desires, so the principle of social choice is to realize the greatest good (similarly defined) summed over all the members of society. We arrive at the principle of utility in a natural way: by this principle a society is rightly ordered, and hence just, when its institutions are arranged so as to realize the greatest sum of satisfactions.

The striking feature of the principle of utility is that it does not matter, execpt indirectly, how this sum of satisfactions is distributed among individuals, any more than it matters, except indirectly, how one man distributes his satisfactions over time. Since certain ways of distributing things affect the total sum of satisfactions, this fact must be taken into account in arranging social institutions; but according to this principle the explanation of common-sense precepts of justice and their seemingly stringent character is that they are those rules which experience shows must be strictly respected and departed from only under exceptional circumstances if the sum of advantages is to be maximized. The precepts of justice are derivative from the one end of attaining the greatest net balance of satisfactions. There is no reason in principle why the greater gains of some should not compensate for the lesser losses of others; or why the violation of the liberty of a few might not be made right by a greater good shared by many. It simply happens, at least under most conditions, that the greatest sum of advantages is not generally achieved in this way. From the standpoint of utility the strictness of common-sense notions of justice has a certain usefulness, but as a philosophical doctrine it is irrational.

If, then, we believe that as a matter of principle each member of society has an inviolability founded on justice which even the welfare of everyone else cannot override, and that a loss of freedom for some is not made right by a greater sum of satisfactions enjoyed by many, we shall have to look for another account of the principles of justice. The principle of utility is incapable of explaining the fact that in a just society the liberties of equal citizenship are taken for granted, and the rights secured by justice are not subject to political bargaining nor to the calculus of social interests. Now, the most natural alternative to the principle of utility is its traditional rival, the theory of the social contract. The aim of the contract doctrine is precisely to account for the strictness of justice by supposing that its principles arise from an agreement among free and independent persons in an original position of equality and hence reflect the integrity and equal sovereignty of the rational persons who are the contractees. Instead of supposing that a conception of right, and so a conception of justice, is simply an extension of the principle of choice for one man to society as a whole, the contract doctrine assumes that the rational individuals who belong to society must choose together, in one joint act, what is to count among them as just and unjust. They are to decide among themselves once and for all what is to be their conception of justice. This decision is thought of as being made in a suitably defined initial situation one of the significant features of which is that no one knows his position in society, nor even his place in the distribution of natural talents and abilities. The principles of justice to which all are forever bound are chosen in the absence of this sort of specific information. A veil of ignorance prevents anyone from being advantaged or disadvantaged by the contingencies of social class and fortune; and hence the bargaining problems which arise in everyday life from the possession of this knowledge do not affect the choice of principles. On the contract doctrine, then, the theory of justice, and indeed ethics itself, is part of the general theory of rational choice, a fact perfectly clear in its Kantian formulation.

Once justice is thought of as arising from an original agreement of this kind, it is evident that the principle of utility is problematical. For why should rational individuals who have a system of ends they wish to advance agree to a violation of their liberty for the sake of a greater balance of satisfactions enjoyed by others? It seems more plausible to suppose that, when situated in an original position of equal right, they would insist upon institutions which returned compensating advantages for any sacrifices required. A rational man would not accept an institution merely because it maximized the sum of advantages irrespective of its effect on his own interests. It appears, then, that the principle of utility would be rejected as a principle of justice, although we shall not try to argue this important question here. Rather, our aim is to give a brief sketch of the conception of distributive shares implicit in the principles of justice which, it seems, would be chosen in the original position. The philosophical appeal of utilitarianism is that it seems to offer a single principle on the basis of which a consistent and complete conception of right can be developed. The problem is to work out a contractarian alternative in such a way that it has comparable if not all the same virtues.

In our discussion we shall make no attempt to derive the two principles of justice which we shall examine; that is, we shall not try to show that they would be chosen in the original position.[2] It must suffice that it is plausible that they would be, at least in preference to the standard forms of traditional theories. Instead we shall be mainly concerned with three questions: first, how to interpret these principles so that they define a consistent and complete conception of justice; second, whether it is possible to arrange the institutions of a constitutional democracy so that these principles are satisfied, at least approximately; and third, whether the conception of distributive shares which they define is compatible with common-sense notions of justice. The significance of these principles is that they allow for the strictness of the claims of justice; and if they can be understood so as to yield a consistent and complete conception, the contractarian alternative would seem all the more attractive.

The two principles of justice which we shall discuss may be formulated as follows: first, each person engaged in an institution or affected by it has an equal right to the most extensive liberty compatible with a like liberty for all; and second, inequalities as defined by the institutional structure or fostered by it are arbitrary unless it is reasonable to expect that they will work out to everyone's advantage and provided that the positions and offices to which they attach or from which they may be gained are open to all. These principles regulate the distributive aspects of institutions by controlling the assignment of rights and duties throughout the whole social structure, beginning with the adoption of a political constitution in accordance with which they are then to be applied to legislation. It is upon a correct choice of a basic structure of society, its fundamental system of rights and duties, that the justice of distributive shares depends.

The two principles of justice apply in the first instance to this basic structure, that is, to the main institutions of the social system and their arrangement, how they are combined together. Thus, this structure includes the political constitution and the principal economic and social institutions which together define a person's liberties and rights and affect his life-prospects, what he may expect to be and how well he may expect to fare. The intuitive idea here is that those born into the social system at different positions, say in different social classes, have varying life-prospects determined, in part, by the system of political liberties and personal rights, and by the economic and social opportunities which are made available to these positions. In this way the basic structure of society favours certain men over others, and these are the basic inequalities, the ones which affect their whole life-prospects. It is inequalities of this kind, presumably inevitable in any society, with which the two principles of justice are primarily designed to deal.

Now the second principle holds that an inequality is allowed only if there is reason to believe that the institution with the inequality, or permitting it, will work out for the advantage of every person engaged in it. In the case of the basic structure this means that all inequalities which affect life-prospects, say the inequalities of income and wealth which exist between social classes, must be to the advantage of everyone. Since the principle applies to institutions, we interpret this to mean that inequalities must be to the advantage of the representative man for each relevant social position; they should improve each such man's expectation. Here we assume that it is possible to attach to each position an expectation, and that this expectation is a function of the whole institutional structure: it can be raised and lowered by reassigning rights and duties throughout the system. Thus the expectation of any position depends upon the expectations of the others, and these in turn depend upon the pattern of rights and duties established by the basic structure. But it is not clear what is meant by saying that inequalities must be to the advantage of every representative man. . . . [One] . . . interpretation [of what is meant by saying that inequalities must be to the advantage of every representative man] . . . is to choose some social position by reference to which the pattern of expectations as a whole is to be judged, and then to maximize with respect to the expectations of this representative man consistent with the demands of equal liberty and equality of opportunity. Now, the one obvious candidate is the representative man of those who are least favoured by the system of institutional inequalities. Thus we arrive at the following idea: the basic structure of the social system affects the life-prospects of typical individuals according to their initial places in society, say the various income classes into which they are born, or depending upon certain natural attributes, as when institutions make discriminations between men and women or allow certain advantages to be gained by those with greater natural abilities. The fundamental problem of distributive justice concerns the differences in life-prospects which come about in this way. We interpret the second principle to hold that these differences are just if and only if the greater expectations of the more advantaged, when playing a part in the working of the whole social system, improve the expectations of the least advantaged. The basic structure is just throughout when the advantages of the more fortunate promote the well-being of the least fortunate, that is, when a decrease in their advantages would make the least fortunate even worse off than they are. The basic structure is perfectly just when the prospects of the least fortunate are as great as they can be.

In interpreting the second principle (or rather the first part of it which we may, for obvious reasons, refer to as the difference principle), we assume that the first principle requires a basic equal liberty for all, and that the resulting political system, when circumstances permit, is that of a constitutional democracy in some form. There must be liberty of the person and political equality as well as liberty of conscience and freedom of thought. There is one class of equal citizens which defines a common status for all.

We also assume that there is equality of opportunity and a fair competition for the available positions on the basis of reasonable qualifications. Now, given this background, the differences to be justified are the various economic and social inequalities in the basic structure which must inevitably arise in such a scheme. These are the inequalities in the distribution of income and wealth and the distinctions in social prestige and status which attach to the various positions and classes. The difference principle says that these inequalities are just if and only if they are part of a larger system in which they work out to the advantage of the most unfortunate representative man. The just distributive shares determined by the basic structure are those specified by this constrained maximum principle.

Thus, consider the chief problem of distributive justice, that concerning the distribution of wealth as it affects the life-prospects of those starting out in the various income groups. These income classes define the relevant representative men from which the social system is to be judged. Now, a son of a member of the entrepreneurial class (in a capitalist society) has a better prospect than that of the son of an unskilled labourer. This will be true, it seems, even when the social injustices which presently exist are removed and the two men are of equal talent and ability; the inequality cannot be done away with as long as something like the family is maintained. What, then, can justify this inequality in life-prospects? According to the second principle it is justified only if it is to the advantage of the representative man who is worst off, in this case the representative unskilled labourer. The inequality is permissible because lowering it would, let's suppose, make the working man even worse off than he is. Presumably, given the principle of open offices (the second part of the second principle), the greater expectations allowed to entrepreneurs has the effect in the longer run of raising the life-prospects of the labouring class. The inequality in expectation provides an incentive so that the economy is more efficient, industrial advance proceeds at a quicker pace, and so on, the end result of which is that greater material and other benefits are distributed throughout the system. Of course, all of this is familiar, and whether true or not in particular cases, it is the sort of thing which must be argued if the inequality in income and wealth is to be acceptable by the difference principle.

We should now verify that this interpretation of the second principle gives a natural sense in which everyone may be said to be made better off. Let us suppose that inequalities are chain-connected: that is, if an inequality raises the expectations of the lowest position, it raises the expectations of all positions in between. For example, if the greater expectations of the representative entrepreneur raises that of the unskilled labourer, it also raises that of the semi-skilled. Let us further assume that inequalities are close-knit: that is, it is impossible to raise (or lower) the expectation of any representative man without raising (or lowering) the expectations of every other representative man, and in particular, without affecting one way or the other that of the least fortunate. There is no loose-jointedness, so to speak, in the way in which expectations depend upon one another. Now with these assumptions, everyone does benefit from an inequality which satisfies the difference principle, and the second principle as we have formulated it reads correctly. For the representative man who is better off in any pair-wise comparison gains by being allowed to have his advantage, and the man who is worse off benefits from the contribution which all inequalities make to each position below. Of course, chain-connection and close-knitness may not obtain; but in this case those who are better off should not have a veto over the advantages available for the least advantaged. The stricter interpretation of the difference principle should be followed, and all inequalities should be arranged for the advantage of the most unfortunate even if some inequalities are not to the advantage of those in middle positions. Should these conditions fail, then, the second principle would have to be stated in another way.

It may be observed that the difference principle represents, in effect, an original agreement to share in the benefits of the distribution of natural talents and abilities, whatever this distribution turns out to be, in order to alleviate as far as possible the arbitrary handicaps resulting from our initial starting places in society. Those who have been favoured by nature, whoever they are, may gain from their good fortune only on terms that improve the well-being of those who have lost out. The naturally advantaged are not to gain simply because they are more gifted, but only to cover the costs of training and cultivating their endowments and for putting them to use in a way which improves the position of the less fortunate. We are led to the difference principle if we wish to arrange the basic social structure so that no one gains (or loses) from his luck in the natural lottery of talent and ability, or from his initial place in society, without giving (or receiving) compensating advantages in return. (The parties in the original position are not said to be attracted by this idea and so agree to it; rather, given the symmetries of their situation, and particularly their lack of knowledge, and so on, they will find it to their interest to agree to a principle which can be understood in this way.) And we should note also that when the difference principle is perfectly satisfied, the basic structure is optimal by the efficiency principle. There is no way to make anyone better off without making someone worse off, namely, the least fortunate representative man. Thus the two principles of justice define distributive shares in a way compatible with efficiency, at least as long as we move on this highly abstract level. If we want to say (as we do, although it cannot be argued here) that the demands of justice have an absolute weight with respect to efficiency, this claim may seem less paradoxical when it is kept in mind that perfectly just institutions are also efficient.

Our second question is whether it is possible to arrange the institutions of a constitutional democracy so that the two principles of justice are satisfied, at least approximately. We shall try to show that this can be done provided the government regulates a free economy in a certain way. More fully, if law and government act effectively to keep markets competitive, resources fully employed, property and wealth widely distributed over time, and to maintain the appropriate social minimum, then if there is equality of opportunity underwritten by education for all, the resulting distribution will be just. Of course, all of these arrangements and policies are familiar. The only novelty in the following remarks, if there is any novelty at all, is that this framework of institutions can be made to satisfy the difference principle. To argue this, we must sketch the relations of these institutions and how they work together.

First of all, we assume that the basic social structure is controlled by a just constitution which secures the various liberties of equal citizenship. Thus the legal order is administered in accordance with the principle of legality, and liberty of conscience and freedom of thought are taken for granted. The political process is conducted, so far as possible, as a just procedure for choosing between governments and for enacting just legislation. From the standpoint of distributive justice, it is also essential that there be equality of opportunity in several senses. Thus, we suppose that, in addition to maintaining the usual social overhead capital, government provides for equal educational opportunities for all either by subsidizing private schools or by operating a public school system. It also enforces and underwrites equality of opportunity in commercial ventures and in the free choice of occupation. This result is achieved by policing business behaviour and by preventing the establishment of barriers and restriction to the desirable positions and markets. Lastly, there is a guarantee of a social minimum which the government meets by family allowances and special payments in times of unemployment, or by a negative income tax.

In maintaining this sytem of institutions the government may be thought of as divided into four branches. Each branch is represented by various agencies (or activities thereof) charged with preserving certain social and economic conditions. These branches do not necessarily overlap with the usual organization of government, but should be understood as purely conceptual. Thus the allocation branch is to keep the economy feasibly competitive, that is, to prevent the formation of unreasonable market power. Markets are competitive in this sense when they cannot be made more so consistent with the requirements of efficiency and the acceptance of the facts of consumer preferences and geography. The allocation branch is also charged with identifying and correcting, say by suitable taxes and subsidies wherever possible, the more obvious departures from efficiency caused by the failure of prices to measure accurately social benefits and costs. The stabilization branch strives to maintain reasonably full employment so that there is no waste through failure to use resources and the free choice of occupation and the deployment of finance is supported by strong effective demand. These two branches together are to preserve the efficiency of the market economy generally.

The social minimum is established through the operations of the transfer branch. Later on we shall consider at what level this minimum should be set, since this is a crucial matter; but for the moment, a few general remarks will suffice. The main idea is that the workings of the transfer branch take into account the precept of need and assign it an appropriate weight with respect to the other common-sense precepts of justice. A market economy ignores the claims of need altogether. Hence there is a division of labour between the parts of the social system as different institutions answer to different common-sense precepts. Competitive markets (properly supplemented by government operations) handle the problem of the efficient allocation of labour and resources and set a weight to the conventional precepts associated with wages and earnings (the precepts of each according to his work and experience, or responsibility and the hazards of the job, and so on), whereas the transfer branch guarantees a certain level of well-being and meets the claims of need. Thus it is obvious that the justice of distributive shares depends upon the whole social system and how it distributes total income, wages plus transfers. There is with reason strong objection to the competitive determination of total income, since this would leave out of account the claims of need and of a decent standard of life. From the standpoint of the original position it is clearly rational to insure oneself against these contingencies. But now, if the appropriate minimum is provided by transfers, it may be perfectly fair that the other part of total income is competitively determined. Moreover, this way of dealing with the claims of need is doubtless more efficient, at least from a theoretical point of view, than trying to regulate prices by minimum wage standards and so on. It is preferable to handle these claims by a separate branch which supports a social minimum. Henceforth, in considering whether the second principle of justice is satisfied, the answer turns on whether the total income of the least advtantaged, that is, wages plus transfers, is such as to maximize their long-term expectations consistent with the demands of liberty.

Finally, the distribution branch is to preserve an approximately just distribution of income and wealth over time by affecting the background conditions of the market from period to period. Two aspects of this branch may be distinguished. First of all, it operates a system of inheritance and gift taxes. The aim of these levies is not to raise revenue, but gradually and continually to correct the distribution of wealth and to prevent the concentrations of power to the detriment of liberty and equality of opportunity. It is perfectly true, as some have said,[3] that unequal inheritance of wealth is no more inherently unjust than unequal inheritance of intelligence; as far as possible the inequalities founded on either should satisfy the difference principle. Thus, the inheritance of greater wealth is just as long as it is to the advantage of the worst off and consistent with liberty, including equality of opportunity. Now by the latter we do not mean, of course, the equality of expectations between classes, since differences in life-prospects arising from the basic structure are inevitable, and it is precisely the aim of the second principle to say when these differences are just. Indeed, equality of opportunity is a certain set of institutions which assures equally good education and chances of culture for all and which keeps open the competition for positions on the basis of qualities reasonably related to performance, and so on. It is these institutions which are put in jeopardy when inequalities and concentrations of wealth reach a certain limit; and the taxes imposed by the distribution branch are to prevent this limit from being exceeded. Naturally enough where this limit lies is a matter for political judgment guided by theory, practical experience, and plain hunch; on this question the theory of justice has nothing to say.

The second part of the distribution branch is a scheme of taxation for raising revenue to cover the costs of public goods, to make transfer payments, and the like. This scheme belongs to the distribution branch since the burden of taxation must be justly shared. Although we cannot examine the legal and economic complications involved, there are several points in favour of proportional expenditure taxes as part of an ideally just arrangement. For one thing, they are preferable to income taxes at the level of common-sense precepts of justice, since they impose a levy according to how much a man takes out of the common store of goods and not according to how much he contributes (assuming that income is fairly earned in return for productive efforts). On the other hand, proportional taxes treat everyone in a clearly defined uniform way (again assuming that income is fairly earned) and hence it is preferable to use progressive rates only when they are necessary to preserve the justice of the system as a whole, that is, to prevent large fortunes hazardous to liberty and equality of opportunity, and the like. If proportional expenditure taxes should also prove more efficient, say because they interfere less with incentives, or whatever, this would make the case for them decisive provided a feasible scheme could be worked out.[4] Yet these are questions of political judgment which are not our concern; and, in any case, a proportional expenditure tax is part of an idealized scheme which we are describing. It does not follow that even steeply progressive income taxes, given the injustice of existing systems, do not improve justice and efficiency all things considered. In practice we must usually choose between unjust arrangements and then it is a matter of finding the lesser injustice.

Whatever form the distribution branch assumes, the argument for it is to be based on justice: we must hold that once it is accepted the social system as a whole—the competitive economy surrounded by a just constitutional legal framework—can be made to satisfy the principles of justice with the smallest loss in efficiency. The long-term expectations of the least advantaged are raised to the highest level consistent with the demands of equal liberty. In discussing the choice of a distribution scheme we have made no reference to the traditional criteria of taxation according to ability to pay or benefits received; nor have we mentioned any of the variants of the sacrifice principle. These standards are subordinate to the two principles of justice; once the problem is seen as that of designing a whole social system, they assume the status of secondary precepts with no more independent force than the precepts of common sense in regard to wages. To suppose otherwise is not to take a sufficiently comprehensive point of view. In setting up a just distribution branch these precepts may or may not have a place depending upon the demands of the two principles of justice when applied to the entire system. . . .

The sketch of the system of institutions satisfying the two principles of justice is now complete. . . .

In order . . . to establish just distributive shares a just total system of institutions must be set up and impartially administered. Given a just constitution and the smooth working of the four branches of government, and so on, there exists a procedure such that the actual distribution of wealth, whatever it turns out to be, is just. It will have come about as a consequence of a just system of institutions satisfying the principles to which everyone would agree and against which no one can complain. The situation is one of pure procedural justice, since there is no independent criterion by which the outcome can be judged. Nor can we say that a particular distribution of wealth is just because it is one which could have resulted from just institutions although it has not, as this would be to allow too much. Clearly there are many distributions which may be reached by just institutions, and this is true whether we count patterns of distributions among social classes or whether we count distributions of particular goods and services among particular individuals. There are indefinitely many outcomes and what makes one of these just is that it has been achieved by actually carrying out a just scheme of co-operation as it is publicly understood. It is the result which has arisen when everyone receives that to which he is entitled given his and others' actions guided by their legitimate expectations and their obligations to one another. We can no more arrive at a just distribution of wealth except by working together within the framework of a just system of institutions than we can win or lose fairly without actually betting.

This account of distributive shares is simply an elaboration of the familiar idea that economic rewards will be just once a perfectly competitive price system is organized as a fair game. But in order to do this we have to begin with the choice of a social system as a whole, for the basic structure of the entire arrangement must be just. The economy must be surrounded with the appropriate framework of institutions, since even a perfectly efficient price system has no tendency to determine just distributive shares when left to itself. Not only must economic activity be regulated by a just constitution and controlled by the four branches of government, but a just saving-function must be adopted to estimate the provision to be made for future generations. . . .

NOTES

1. In this essay I try to work out some of the implications of the two principles of justice discussed in "Justice as Fairness," which first appeared in the *Philosophical Review*, 1958, and which is reprinted in *Philosophy, Politics and Society*, Series II, pp. 132–57.
2. This question is discussed very briefly in "Justice as Fairness," see pp. 138–41. The intuitive idea is as follows. Given the circumstances of the original position, it is rational for a man to choose as if he were designing a society in which his enemy is to assign him his place. Thus, in particular, given the complete lack of knowledge (which makes the choice one uncertainty), the fact that the decision involves one's life-prospects as a whole and is constrained by obligations to third parties (e.g., one's descendants) and duties to certain values (e.g., to religious truth), it is rational to be conservative and so to choose in accordance with an analogue of the maximum principle. Viewing the situation in this way, the interpretation given to the principles of justice earlier is perhaps natural enough. Moreover, it seems clear how the principle of utility can be interpreted; it is the analogue of the Laplacean principle for choice uncertainty. (For a discussion of these choice criteria, see R. D. Luce and H. Raiffa, *Games and Decisions* [1957], pp. 275–98.)
3. Example F. von Hayek, *The Constitution of Liberty* (1960), p. 90.
4. See N. Kaldor, *An Expenditure Tax* (1955).

The Principles of a Liberal Social Order

FRIEDRICH A. HAYEK

1. By 'liberalism' I shall understand here the conception of a desirable political order which in the first instance was developed in England from the time of the Old Whigs in the later part of the seventeenth century to that of Gladstone at the end of the nineteenth. David Hume, Adam Smith, Edmund Burke, T. B. Macaulay and Lord Acton may be regarded as its typical representatives in England. It was this conception of individual liberty under the law which in the first instance inspired the liberal movements on the Continent and which became the basis of the American political tradition. A few of the leading political thinkers in those countries like B. Constant and A. de Tocqueville in France, Immanuel Kant, Friedrich von Schiller and Wilhelm von Humboldt in Germany, and James Madison, John Marshall, and Daniel Webster in the United States belong wholly to it.

Published in *Il Politico*, 1966. Reprinted in *Studies in Philosophy, Politics and Economics*, ed. Friedrich A. Hayek, by permission of the University of Chicago Press. © 1967 by F. A. Hayek. All rights reserved. Reprinted by permission of the editors of *Il Politico*.

2. This liberalism must be clearly distinguished from another, originally Continental European tradition, also called 'liberalism' of which what now claims this name in the United States is a direct descendant. This latter view, though beginning with an attempt to imitate the first tradition, interpreted it in the spirit of a constructivist rationalism prevalent in France and thereby made of it something very different, and in the end, instead of advocating limitations on the powers of government, ended up with the ideal of the unlimited powers of the majority. This is the tradition of Voltaire, Rousseau, Condorcet and the French Revolution which became the ancestor of modern socialism. English utilitarianism has taken over much of this Continental tradition and the late-nineteenth-century British liberal party, resulting from a fusion of the liberal Whigs and the utilitarian Radicals, was also a product of this mixture.

3. Liberalism and democracy, although compatible, are not the same. The first is concerned with the extent of governmental power, the second with who holds this power. The difference is best seen if we consider their opposites: the opposite of liberalism is totalitarianism, while the opposite of democracy is authoritarianism. In consequence, it is at least possible in principle that a democratic government may be totalitarian and that an authoritarian government may act on liberal principles. The second kind of 'liberalism' mentioned before has in effect become democratism rather than liberalism and, demanding *unlimited* power of the majority, has become essentially anti-liberal. . . .

6. Liberalism . . . derives from the discovery of a self-generating or spontaneous order in social affairs (the same discovery which led to the recognition that there existed an object for theoretical social sciences), an order which made it possible to utilize the knowledge and skill of all members of society to a much greater extent than would be possible in any order created by central direction, and the consequent desire to make as full use of these powerful spontaneous ordering forces as possible.

7. It was thus in their efforts to make explicit the principles of an order already existing but only in an imperfect form that Adam Smith and his followers developed the basic principles of liberalism in order to demonstrate the desirability of their general application. In doing this they were able to presuppose familiarity with the common law conception of justice and with the ideals of the rule of law and of government under the law which were little understood outside the Anglo-Saxon world; with the result that not only were their ideas not fully understood outside the English-speaking countries, but that they ceased to be fully understood even in England when Bentham and his followers replaced the English legal tradition by a constructivist utilitarianism derived more from Continental rationalism than from the evolutionary conception of the English tradition.

8. The central concept of liberalism is that under the enforcement of universal rules of just conduct, protecting a recognizable private domain of

individuals, a spontaneous order of human activities of much greater complexity will form itself than could ever be produced by deliberate arrangement, and that in consequence the coercive activities of government should be limited to the enforcement of such rules, whatever other services government may at the same time render by administering those particular resources which have been placed at its disposal for those purposes.

9. The distinction between a *spontaneous order* based on abstract rules which leave individuals free to use their own knowledge for their own purposes, and an *organization or arrangement* based on commands, is of central importance for the understanding of the principles of a free society and must in the following paragraphs be explained in some detail, especially as the spontaneous order of a free society will contain many organizations (including the biggest organization, government), but the two principles of order cannot be mixed in any manner we may wish.

10. The first peculiarity of a spontaneous order is that by using its ordering forces (the regularity of the conduct of its members) we can achieve an order of a much more complex set of facts than we could ever achieve by deliberate arrangement, but that, while availing ourselves of this possibility of inducing an order of much greater extent than we otherwise could, we at the same time limit our power over the details of that order. We shall say that when using the former principle we shall have power only over the abstract character but not over the concrete detail of that order.

11. No less important is the fact that, in contrast to an organization, neither has a spontaneous order a purpose nor need there be agreement on the concrete results it will produce in order to agree on the desirability of such an order, because, being independent of any particular purpose, it can be used for, and will assist in the pursuit of, a great many different, divergent and even conflicting individual purposes. Thus the order of the market, in particular, rests not on common purposes but on reciprocity, that is on the reconciliation of different purposes for the mutual benefit of the participants. . . .

16. The spontaneous order of the market resulting from the interaction of many . . . economies is something so fundamentally different from an economy proper that it must be regarded as a great misfortune that it has ever been called by the same name. I have become convinced that this practice so constantly misleads people that it is necessary to invent a new technical term for it. I propose that we call this spontaneous order of the market a *catallaxy* in analogy to the term 'catallactics', which has often been proposed as a substitute for the term 'economics'. (Both 'catallaxy' and 'catallactics' derive from the ancient Greek verb *katallattein* which, significantly, means not only 'to barter' and 'to exchange' but also 'to admit into the community' and 'to turn from enemy into friend'.)

17. The chief point about the catallaxy is that, as a spontaneous order, its orderliness does *not* rest on its orientation on a single hierarchy of ends,

and that, therefore, it will *not* secure that for it as a whole the more important comes before the less important. This is the chief cause of its condemnation by its opponents, and it could be said that most of the socialist demands amount to nothing less than that the catallaxy should be turned into an economy proper (i.e., the purposeless spontaneous order into a purpose-oriented organization) in order to assure that the more important be never sacrificed to the less important. The defence of a free society must therefore show that it is due to the fact that we do not enforce a unitary scale of concrete ends, nor attempt to secure that some particular view about what is more and what is less important governs the whole of society, that the members of such a free society have as good a chance successfully to use their individual knowledge for the achievement of their individual purposes as they in fact have.

18. The extension of an order of peace beyond the small purpose-oriented organization became thus possible by the extension of purpose-independent ("formal") rules of just conduct to the relations with other men who did not pursue the same concrete ends or hold the same values except those abstract rules—which did not impose obligations for particular actions (which always presuppose a concrete end) but consisted solely in prohibitions from infringing the protected domain of each which these rules enable us to determine. Liberalism is therefore inseparable from the institution of private property which is the name we usually give to the material part of this protected individual domain. . . .

20. Liberalism recognizes that there are certain other services which for various reasons the spontaneous forces of the market may not produce or may not produce adequately, and that for this reason it is desirable to put at the disposal of government a clearly circumscribed body of resources with which it can render such services to the citizens in general. This requires a sharp distinction between the coercive powers of government, in which its actions are strictly limited to the enforcement of rules of just conduct and in the exercise of which all discretion is excluded, and the provision of services by government, for which it can use only the resources put at its disposal for this purpose, has no coercive power or monopoly, but in the use of which resources it enjoys wide discretion. . . .

22. Liberalism has indeed inherited from the theories of the common law and from the older (pre-rationalist) theories of the law of nature, and also presupposes, a conception of justice which allows us to distinguish between such rules of just individual conduct as are implied in the conception of the 'rule of law' and are required for the formation of a spontaneous order on the one hand, and all the particular commands issued by authority for the purpose of organization on the other. This essential distinction has been made explicit in the legal theories of two of the greater philosophers of modern times, David Hume and Immanuel Kant, but has not been adequately restated since and is wholly uncongenial to the governing legal theories of our day.

23. The essential points of this conception of justice are (a) that justice can be meaningfully attributed only to human action and not to any state of affairs as such without reference to the question whether it has been, or could have been, deliberately brought about by somebody; (b) that the rules of justice have essentially the nature of prohibitions, or, in other words, that injustice is really the primary concept and the aim of rules of just conduct is to prevent unjust action; (c) that the injustice to be prevented is the infringement of the protected domain of one's fellow men, a domain which is to be ascertained by means of these rules of justice; and (d) that these rules of just conduct which are in themselves negative can be developed by consistently applying to whatever such rules a society has inherited the equally negative test of universal applicability — a test which, in the last resort, is nothing else than the self-consistency of the actions which these rules allow if applied to the circumstances of the real world. These four crucial points must be developed further in the following paragraphs.

24. *Ad (a):* Rules of just conduct can require the individual to take into account in his decisions only such consequences of his actions as he himself can foresee. The concrete results of the catallaxy for particular people are, however, essentially unpredictable; and since they are not the effect of anyone's design or intentions, it is meaningless to describe the manner in which the market distributed the good things of this world among particular people as just or unjust. This, however, is what the so-called 'social' or 'distributive' justice aims at in the name of which the liberal order of law is progressively destroyed. We shall later see that no test or criteria have been found or can be found by which such rules of 'social justice' can be assessed, and that, in consequence, and in contrast to the rules of just conduct, they would have to be determined by the arbitrary will of the holders of power.

25. *Ad (b):* No particular human action is fully determined without a concrete purpose it is meant to achieve. Free men who are to be allowed to use their own means and their own knowledge for their own purposes must therefore not be subject to rules which tell them what they must positively do, but only to rules which tell them what they must not do; except for the discharge of obligations an individual has voluntarily incurred, the rules of just conduct thus merely delimit the range of permissible actions but do not determine the particular actions a man must take at a particular moment. (There are certain rare exceptions to this, like actions to save or protect life, prevent catastrophes, and the like, whether either rules of justice actually do require, or would at least generally be accepted as just rules if they required, some positive action. It would lead far to discuss here the position of such rules in the system.) The generally negative character of the rules of just conduct, and the corresponding primacy of the injustice which is prohibited, has often been noticed but scarcely ever been thought through to its logical consequences.

26. *Ad (c):* The injustice which is prohibited by rules of just conduct is any encroachment on the protected domain of other individuals, and they

must therefore enable us to ascertain what is the protected sphere of others. Since the time of John Locke it is customary to describe this protected domain as property (which Locke himself had defined as 'the life, liberty, and possessions of a man'). This term suggests, however, a much too narrow and purely material conception of the protected domain which includes not only material goods but also various claims on others and certain expectations. If the concept of property is, however, (with Locke) interpreted in this wide sense, it is true that law, in the sense of rules of justice, and the institution of property are inseparable.

27. *Ad (d)*: It is impossible to decide about the justice of any one particular rule of just conduct except within the framework of a whole system of such rules, most of which must for this purpose be regarded as unquestioned: values can always be tested only in terms of other values. The test of the justice of a rule is usually (since Kant) described as that of its 'universalizability', i.e., of the possibility of willing that the rules should be applied to all instances that correspond to the conditions stated in it (the 'categorical imperative'). What this amounts to is that in applying it to any concrete circumstances it will not conflict with any other accepted rules. The test is thus in the last resort one of the compatibility or non-contradictoriness of the whole system of rules, not merely in a logical sense but in the sense that the system of actions which the rules permit will not lead to conflict.

28. It will be noticed that only purpose-independent ('formal') rules pass this test because, as rules which have originally been developed in small, purpose-connected groups ('organizations') are progressively extended to larger and larger groups and finally universalized to apply to the relations between any members of an Open Society who have no concrete purposes in common and merely submit to the same abstract rules, they will in this process have to shed all references to particular purposes.

29. The growth from the tribal organization, all of whose members served common purposes, to the spontaneous order of the Open Society in which people are allowed to pursue their own purposes in peace, may thus be said to have commenced when for the first time a savage placed some goods at the boundary of his tribe in the hope that some member of another tribe would find them and leave in turn behind some other goods to secure the repetition of the offer. From the first establishment of such a practice which served reciprocal but not common purposes, a process has been going on for millennia which, by making rules of conduct independent of the particular purposes of those concerned, made it possible to extend these rules to ever wider circles of undetermined persons and eventually might make possible a universal peaceful order of the world. . . .

32. The progressive displacement of the rules of conduct of private and criminal law by a conception derived from public law is the process by which existing liberal societies are progressively transformed into totalitar-

ian societies. This tendency has been most explicitly seen and supported by Adolf Hitler's 'crown jurist' Carl Schmitt who consistently advocated the replacement of the 'normative' thinking of liberal law by a conception of law which regards as its purpose the 'concrete order formation' (*konkretes Ordnungsdenken*). . . .

34. If it was the nature of the constitutional arrangements prevailing in all Western democracies which made this development possible, the driving force which guided it in the particular direction was the growing recognition that the application of uniform or equal rules to the conduct of individuals who were in fact very different in many respects, inevitably produced very different results for the different individuals; and that in order to bring about by government action a reduction in these unintended but inevitable differences in the material position of different people, it would be necessary to treat them not according to the same but according to different rules. This gave rise to a new and altogether different conception of justice, namely that usually described as 'social' or 'distributive' justice, a conception of justice which did not confine itself to rules of conduct for the individual but aimed at particular results for particular people, and which therefore could be achieved only in a purpose-governed organization but not in a purpose-independent spontaneous order.

35. The concepts of a 'just price', a 'just remuneration' or a 'just distribution of incomes' are of course very old; it deserves notice, however, that in the course of the efforts of two thousand years in which philosophers have speculated about the meaning of these concepts, not a single rule has been discovered which would allow us to determine what is in this sense just in a market order. Indeed the one group of scholars which have most persistently pursued the question, the schoolmen of the latter middle ages and early modern times, were finally driven to define the just price or wage as that price or wage which would form itself on a market in the absence of fraud, violence or privilege—thus referring back to the rules of just conduct and accepting as a just result whatever was brought about by the just conduct of all individuals concerned. This negative conclusion of all the speculations about 'social' or 'distributive' justice was, as we shall see, inevitable, because a just remuneration or distribution has meaning only within an organization whose members act under command in the service of a common system of ends, but can have no meaning whatever in the catallaxy or spontaneous order which can have no such common system of ends.

36. A state of affairs as such, as we have seen, cannot be just or unjust as a mere fact. Only in so far as it has been brought about designedly or could be so brought about does it make sense to call just or unjust the actions of those who have created it or permitted it to arise. In the catallaxy, the spontaneous order of the market, nobody can foresee, however, what each participant will get, and the results for particular people are not determined by anyone's intentions; nor is anyone responsible for particular peo-

ple getting particular things. We might therefore question whether a deliberate choice of the market order as the method for guiding economic activities, with the unpredictable and in a great measure chance incidence of its benefits, is a just decision, but certainly not whether, once we have decided to avail ourselves of the catallaxy for that purpose, the particular results it produces for particular people are just or unjust.

37. That the concept of justice is nevertheless so commonly and readily applied to the distribution of incomes is entirely the effect of an erroneous anthropomorphic interpretation of society as an organization rather than as a spontaneous order. The term 'distribution' is in this sense quite as misleading as the term 'economy', since it also suggests that something is the result of deliberate action which in fact is the result of spontaneous ordering forces. Nobody distributes income in a market order (as would have to be done in an organization) and to speak, with respect to the former, of a just or unjust distribution is therefore simple nonsense. It would be less misleading to speak in this respect of a 'dispersion' rather than a 'distribution' of incomes.

38. All endeavors to secure a 'just' distribution must thus be directed towards turning the spontaneous order of the market into an organization or, in other words, into a totalitarian order. It was this striving after a new conception of justice which produced the various steps by which rules of organization ('public law'), which were designed to make people aim at particular results, came to supersede the purpose-independent rules of just individual conduct, and which thereby gradually destroyed the foundation on which a spontaneous order must rest.

39. The ideal of using the coercive powers of government to achieve 'positive' (i.e., social or distributive) justice leads, however, not only necessarily to the destruction of individual freedom, which some might not think too high a price, but it also proves on examination a mirage or an illusion which cannot be achieved in any circumstances, because it presupposes an agreement on the relative importance of the different concrete ends which cannot exist in a great society whose members do not know each other or the same particular facts. It is sometimes believed that the fact that most people today desire social justice demonstrates that this ideal has determinable content. But it is unfortunately only too possible to chase a mirage, and the consequence of this is always that the result of one's striving will be utterly different from what one had intended.

40. There can be no rules which determine how much everybody 'ought' to have unless we make some unitary conception of relative 'merits' or 'needs' of the different individuals, for which there exists no objective measure, the basis of a central allocation of all goods and services—which would make it necessary that each individual, instead of using *his* knowledge for *his* purposes, were made to fulfil a duty imposed upon him by somebody else, and were remunerated according to how well he has, in the opinion of others, performed this duty. This is the method of remuneration appropri-

ate to a closed organization, such as an army, but irreconcilable with the forces which maintain spontaneous order.

41. It ought to be freely admitted that the market order does not bring about any close correspondence between subjective merit or individual needs and rewards. It operates on the principle of a combined game of skill and chance in which the results for each individual may be as much determined by circumstances wholly beyond his control as by his skill or effort. Each is remunerated according to the value his particular services have to the particular people to whom he renders them, and this value of his services stands in no necessary relation to anything which we could appropriately call his merits and still less to his needs.

42. It deserves special emphasis that, strictly speaking, it is meaningless to speak of a value 'to society' when what is in question is the value of some services to certain people, services which may be of no interest to anybody else. A violin virtuoso presumably renders services to entirely different people from those whom a football star entertains, and the maker of pipes altogether different people from the maker of perfumes. The whole conception of a 'value to society' is in a free order as illegitimate an anthropomorphic term as its description as 'one economy' in the strict sense, as an entity which 'treats' people justly or unjustly, or 'distributes' among them. The results of the market process for particular individuals are neither the result of anybody's will that they should have so much, nor even foreseeable by those who have decided upon or support the maintenance of this kind of order. . . .

45. The aim of economic policy of a free society can therefore never be to assure particular results to particular people, and its success cannot be measured by any attempt at adding up the value of such particular results. In this respect the aim of what is called 'welfare economics' is fundamentally mistaken, not only because no meaningful sum can be formed of the satisfactions provided for different people, but because its basic idea of a maximum of need-fulfilment (or a maximum social product) is appropriate only to an economy proper which serves a single hierarchy of ends, but not to the spontaneous order of a catallaxy which has no common concrete ends.

46. Though it is widely believed that the conception of an optimal economic policy (or any judgment whether one economic policy is better than another) presupposes such a conception of maximizing aggregate real social income (which is possible only in value terms and therefore implies an illegitimate comparison of the utility to different persons), this is in fact not so. An optimal policy in a catallaxy may aim, and ought to aim, at increasing the chances of any member of society taken at random of having a high income, or, what amounts to the same thing, the chance that, whatever his share in total income may be, the real equivalent of this share will be as large as we know how to make it.

47. This condition will be approached as closely as we can manage, irrespective of the dispersion of incomes, if everything which is produced is

being produced by persons or organizations who can produce it more cheaply than (or at least as cheaply as) anybody who does not produce it, and is sold at a price lower than that at which it would be possible to offer it for anybody who does not in fact so offer it. (This allows for persons or organizations to whom the costs of producing one commodity or service are lower than they are for those who actually produce it and who still produce something else instead, because their comparative advantage in that other production is still greater; in this case the total costs of their producing the first commodity would have to include the loss of the one which is not produced.)

48. It will be noticed that this optimum does not presuppose what economic theory calls 'perfect competition' but only that there are no obstacles to the entry into each trade and that the market functions adequately in spreading information about opportunities. It should also be specially observed that this modest and achievable goal has never yet been fully achieved because at all times and everywhere governments have both restricted access to some occupations and tolerated persons and organizations deterring others from entering occupations when this would have been to the advantage of the latter.

49. This optimum position means that as much will be produced of whatever combination of products and services is in fact produced as can be produced by any method we know, because we can through such a use of the market mechanism bring more of the dispersed knowledge of the members of society into play than by any other. But it will be achieved only if we leave the share in the total, which each member will get, to be determined by the market mechanism and all its accidents, because it is only through the market determination of incomes that each is led to do what this result requires.

50. We owe, in other words, our chances that our unpredictable share in the total product of society represents as large an aggregate of goods and services as it does to the fact that thousands of others constantly submit to the adjustments which the market forces on them; and it is consequently also our duty to accept the same kind of changes in our income and position, even if it means a decline in our accustomed position and is due to circumstances we would not have foreseen and for which we are not responsible. The conception that we have 'earned' (in the sense of morally deserved) the income we had when we were more fortunate, and that we are therefore entitled to it so long as we strive as honestly as before and had no warning to turn elsewhere, is wholly mistaken. Everybody, rich or poor, owes his income to the outcome of a mixed game of skill and chance, the aggregate results of which and the shares in which are as high as they are only because we have agreed to play that game. And once we have agreed to play the game and profited from its results, it is a moral obligation on us to abide by the results even if they turn against us. . . .

61. In conclusion, the basic principles of a liberal society may be

summed up by saying that in such a society all coercive functions of government must be guided by the overruling importance of what I like to call
THE THREE GREAT NEGATIVES: PEACE, JUSTICE AND LIBERTY. Their
achievement requires that in its coercive functions government shall be
confined to the enforcement of such prohibitions (stated as abstract rules) as
can be equally applied to all, and to exacting under the same uniform rules
from all a share of the costs of the other, noncoercive services it may decide
to render to the citizens with the material and personal means thereby
placed at its disposal.

Morality and the Liberal Ideal

MICHAEL J. SANDEL

Liberals often take pride in defending what they oppose—pornography, for
example, or unpopular views. They say the state should not impose on its
citizens a preferred way of life, but should leave them as free as possible to
choose their own values and ends, consistent with a similar liberty for
others. This commitment to freedom of choice requires liberals constantly
to distinguish between permission and praise, between allowing a practice
and endorsing it. It is one thing to allow pornography, they argue, something else to affirm it.

Conservatives sometimes exploit this distinction by ignoring it. They
charge that those who would allow abortions favor abortion, that opponents
of school prayer oppose prayer, that those who defend the rights of Communists sympathize with their cause. And in a pattern of argument familiar in
our politics, liberals reply by invoking higher principles; it is not that they
dislike pornography less, but rather that they value toleration, or freedom of
choice, or fair procedures more.

But in contemporary debate, the liberal rejoinder seems increasingly
fragile, its moral basis increasingly unclear. Why should toleration and freedom of choice prevail when other important values are also at stake? Too
often the answer implies some version of moral relativism, the idea that it is
wrong to "legislate morality" because all morality is merely subjective. "Who
is to say what is literature and what is filth? That is a value judgment, and
whose values should decide?"

Relativism usually appears less as a claim than as a question: "Who is to

From *The New Republic*, May 7, 1984, pp. 15–17. Copyright *The New Republic*, 1984.
Reprinted by permission of the New Republic, Inc.

judge?" But it is a question that can also be asked of the values that liberals defend. Toleration and freedom and fairness are values too, and they can hardly be defended by the claim that no values can be defended. So it is a mistake to affirm liberal values by arguing that all values are merely subjective. The relativist defense of liberalism is no defense at all.

What, then, can be the moral basis of the higher principles the liberal invokes? Recent political philosophy has offered two main alternatives — one utilitarian, the other Kantian. The utilitarian view, following John Stuart Mill, defends liberal principles in the name of maximizing the general welfare. The state should not impose on its citizens a preferred way of life, even for their own good, because doing so will reduce the sum of human happiness, at least in the long run; better that people choose for themselves, even if, on occasion, they get it wrong. "The only freedom which deserves the name," writes Mill in *On Liberty*, "is that of pursuing our own good in our own way, so long as we do not attempt to deprive others of theirs, or impede their efforts to obtain it." He adds that his argument does not depend on any notion of abstract right, only on the principle of the greatest good for the greatest number. "I regard utility as the ultimate appeal on all ethical questions; but it must be utility in the largest sense, grounded on the permanent interests of man as a progressive being."

Many objections have been raised against utilitarianism as a general doctrine of moral philosophy. Some have questioned the concept of utility, and the assumption that all human goods are in principle commensurable. Others have objected that by reducing all values to preferences and desires, utilitarians are unable to admit qualitative distinctions of worth, unable to distinguish noble desires from base ones. But most recent debate has focused on whether utilitarianism offers a convincing basis for liberal principles, including respect for individual rights.

In one respect, utilitarianism would seem well suited to liberal purposes. Seeking to maximize overall happiness does not require judging people's values, only aggregating them. And the willingness to aggregate preferences without judging them suggests a tolerant spirit, even a democratic one. When people go to the polls we count their votes, whatever they are.

But the utilitarian calculus is not always as liberal as it first appears. If enough cheering Romans pack the Colosseum to watch the lion devour the Christian, the collective pleasure of the Romans will surely outweigh the pain of the Christian, intense though it be. Or if a big majority abhors a small religion and wants it banned, the balance of preferences will favor suppression, not toleration. Utilitarians sometimes defend individual rights on the grounds that respecting them now will serve utility in the long run. But this calculation is precarious and contingent. It hardly secures the liberal promise not to impose on some the values of others. As the majority will is an inadequate instrument of liberal politics — by itself it fails to secure individual rights — so the utilitarian philosophy is an inadequate foundation for liberal principles.

The case against utilitarianism was made most powerfully by Immanuel Kant. He argued that empirical principles, such as utility, were unfit to serve as basis for the moral law. A wholly instrumental defense of freedom and rights not only leaves rights vulnerable, but fails to respect the inherent dignity of persons. The utilitarian calculus treats people as means to the happiness of others, not as ends in themselves, worthy of respect.

Contemporary liberals extend Kant's arguments with the claim that utilitarianism fails to take seriously the distinction between persons. In seeking above all to maximize the general welfare, the utilitarian treats society as a whole as if it were a single person; it conflates our many, diverse desires into a single system of desires. It is indifferent to the distribution of satisfactions among persons, except insofar as this may affect the overall sum. But this fails to respect our plurality and distinctness. It uses some as means to the happiness of all, and so fails to respect each as an end in himself.

In the view of modern-day Kantians, certain rights are so fundamental that even the general welfare cannot override them. As John Rawls writes in his important work, A *Theory of Justice*, "Each person possesses an inviolability founded on justice that even the welfare of society as a whole cannot override. . . . The rights secured by justice are not subject to political bargaining or to the calculus of social interests."

So Kantian liberals need an account of rights that does not depend on utilitarian considerations. More than this, they need an account that does not depend on any particular conception of the good, that does not presuppose the superiority of one way of life over others. Only a justification neutral about ends could preserve the liberal resolve not to favor any particular ends, or to impose on its citizens a preferred way of life. But what sort of justification could this be? How is it possible to affirm certain liberties and rights as fundamental without embracing some vision of the good life, without endorsing some ends over others? It would seem we are back to the relativist predicament—to affirm liberal principles without embracing any particular ends.

The solution proposed by Kantian liberals is to draw a distinction between the "right" and the "good"—between a framework of basic rights and liberties, and the conceptions of the good that people may choose to pursue within the framework. It is one thing for the state to support a fair framework, they argue, something else to affirm some particular ends. For example, it is one thing to defend the right to free speech so that people may be free to form their own opinions and choose their own ends, but something else to support it on the grounds that a life of political discussion is inherently worthier than a life unconcerned with public affairs, or on the grounds that free speech will increase the general welfare. Only the first defense is available in the Kantian view, resting as it does on the ideal of a neutral framework.

Now, the commitment to a framework neutral with respect to ends can be seen as a kind of value—in this sense the Kantian liberal is no relativist—but its value consists precisely in its refusal to affirm a preferred way of life or conception of the good. For Kantian liberals, then, the right is prior to the good, and in two senses. First, individual rights cannot be sacrificed for the sake of the general good; and second, the principles of justice that specify these rights cannot be premised on any particular vision of the good life. What justifies the rights is not that they maximize the general welfare or otherwise promote the good, but rather that they comprise a fair framework within which individuals and groups can choose their own values and ends, consistent with a similar liberty for others.

Of course, proponents of the rights-based ethic notoriously disagree about what rights are fundamental, and about what political arrangements the ideal of the neutral framework requires. Egalitarian liberals support the welfare state, and favor a scheme of civil liberties together with certain social and economic rights—rights to welfare, education, health care, and so on. Libertarian liberals defend the market economy, and claim that redistributive policies violate peoples' rights; they favor a scheme of civil liberties combined with a strict regime of private property rights. But whether egalitarian or libertarian, rights-based liberalism begins with the claim that we are separate, individual persons, each with our own aims, interests, and conceptions of the good; it seeks a framework of rights that will enable us to realize our capacity as free moral agents, consistent with a similar liberty for others.

Within academic philosophy, the last decade or so has seen the ascendance of the rights-based ethic over the utilitarian one, due in large part to the influence of Rawls's A *Theory of Justice*. The legal philosopher H. L. A. Hart recently described the shift from "the old faith that some form of utilitarianism must capture the essence of political morality" to the new faith that "the truth must lie with a doctrine of basic human rights, protecting specific basic liberties and interests of individuals. . . . Whereas not so long ago great energy and much ingenuity of many philosophers were devoted to making some form of utilitarianism work, latterly such energies and ingenuity have been devoted to the articulation of theories of basic rights."

But in philosophy as in life, the new faith becomes the old orthodoxy before long. Even as it has come to prevail over its utilitarian rival, the rights-based ethic has recently faced a growing challenge from a different direction, from a view that gives fuller expression to the claims of citizenship and community than the liberal vision allows. The communitarian critics, unlike modern liberals, make the case for a politics of the common good. Recalling the arguments of Hegel against Kant, they question the liberal claim for the priority of the right over the good, and the picture of the freely choosing individual it embodies. Following Aristotle, they argue that we cannot justify political arrangements without reference to common purposes and ends, and that we cannot conceive of ourselves without reference to our role as citizens, as participants in a common life.

This debate reflects two contrasting pictures of the self. The rights-based ethic, and the conception of the person it embodies were shaped in large part in the encounter with utilitarianism. Where utilitarians conflate our many desires into a single system of desire, Kantians insist on the separateness of persons. Where the utilitarian self is simply defined as the sum of its desires, the Kantian self is choosing self, independent of the desires and ends it may have at any moment. As Rawls writes, "The self is prior to the ends which are affirmed by it; even a dominant end must be chosen from among numerous possibilities."

The priority of the self over its ends means I am never defined by my aims and attachments, but always capable of standing back to survey and assess and possibly to revise them. This is what it means to be a free and independent self, capable of choice. And this is the vision of the self that finds expression in the ideal of a state as a neutral framework. On the rights-based ethic, it is precisely because we are essentially separate, independent selves that we need a neutral framework, a framework of rights that refuses to choose among competing purposes and ends. If the self is prior to its ends, then the right must be prior to the good.

Communitarian critics of rights-based liberalism say we cannot conceive ourselves as independent in this way, as bearers of selves wholly detached from our aims and attachments. They say that certain of our roles are partly constitutive of the persons we are—as citizens of a country, or members of a movement, or partisans of a cause. But if we are partly defined by the communities we inhabit, then we must also be implicated in the purposes and ends characteristic of those communities. As Alasdair MacIntyre writes in his book, *After Virtue*, "What is good for me has to be the good for one who inhabits these roles." Open-ended though it be, the story of my life is always embedded in the story of those communities from which I derive my identity—whether family or city, tribe or nation, party or cause. In the communitarian view, these stories make a moral difference, not only a psychological one. They situate us in the world and give our lives their moral particularity.

What is at stake for a politics in the debate between unencumbered selves and situated ones? What are the practical differences between a politics of rights and a politics of the common good? On some issues, the two theories may produce different arguments for similar policies. For example, the civil rights movement in the 1960s might be justified by liberals in the name of human dignity and respect for persons, and by communitarians in the name of recognizing the full membership of fellow citizens wrongly excluded from the common life of the nation. And where liberals might support public education in hopes of equipping students to become autonomous individuals, capable of choosing their own ends and pursuing them effectively, communitarians might support public education in hopes of equipping students to become good citizens, capable of contributing meaningfully to public deliberations and pursuits.

On other issues, the two ethics might lead to different policies. Communitarians would be more likely than liberals to allow a town to ban pornographic bookstores, on the grounds that pornography offends its way of life and the values that sustain it. But a politics of civic virtue does not always part company with liberalism in favor of conservative policies. For example, communitarians would be more willing than some rights-oriented liberals to see states enact laws regulating plant closings, to protect their communities from the disruptive effects of capital mobility and sudden industrial change. More generally, where the liberal regards the expansion of individual rights and entitlements as unqualified moral and political progress, the communitarian is troubled by the tendency of liberal programs to displace politics from smaller forms of association to more comprehensive ones. Where libertarian liberals defend the private economy and egalitarian liberals defend the welfare state, communitarians worry about the concentration of power in both the corporate economy and the bureaucratic state, and the erosion of those intermediate forms of community that have at times sustained a more vital public life.

Liberals often argue that a politics of the common good, drawing as it must on particular loyalties, obligations, and traditions, opens the way to prejudice and intolerance. The modern nation-state is not the Athenian polis, they point out; the scale and diversity of modern life have rendered the Aristotelian political ethic nostalgic at best and dangerous at worst. Any attempt to govern by a vision of the good is likely to lead to a slippery slope of totalitarian temptations.

Communitarians reply, rightly in my view, that intolerance flourishes most where forms of life are dislocated, roots unsettled, traditions undone. In our day, the totalitarian impulse has sprung less from the convictions of confidently situated selves than from the confusions of atomized, dislocated, frustrated selves, at sea in a world where common meanings have lost their force. As Hannah Arendt has written, "What makes mass society so difficult to bear is not the number of people involved, or at least not primarily, but the fact that the world between them has lost its power to gather them together, to relate and to separate them." Insofar as our public life has withered, our sense of common involvement diminished, we lie vulnerable to the mass politics of totalitarian solutions. So responds the party of the common good to the party of rights. If the party of the common good is right, our most pressing moral and political project is to revitalize those civic republican possibilities implicit in our tradition but fading in our time.

Part IV

EMPLOYER-EMPLOYEE RELATIONSHIPS

EMPLOYEE RIGHTS

A large U.S. corporation, B. F. Goodrich, became involved in serious ethical problems over the testing procedures it used in the fulfillment of a government contract for jet aircraft brakes. The pressures upon corporate employees, including those of job security and advancement in this incident, were strong enough to result in the falsifying of engineering specifications so that Goodrich could market dangerous and defective aircraft brakes. The dilemma of one employee, Vandivier, who finally "blew the whistle" on Goodrich, is a revealing illustration of some of the conflicts that can occur between self-interest, job responsibility, and one's sense of right and wrong.

This case illustrates a pressing contemporary concern: the relationship between employers and employees, especially in the area of employee rights. Do employees have rights in the workplace despite having voluntarily entered into a formal employee-employer relationship? For example, does a worker have the right to blow the whistle on a dangerous product without reprisal from management? Does he or she have a right to refuse a lie detector, or polygraph, test without being fired? Does he or she have the right to participate, directly or indirectly, in the management of the organization for which he or she works? And what are the concomitant rights of employers vis-à-vis their employees? What might an employer justifiably and reasonably expect in terms of loyalty and trust from his or her employees? These questions are among those falling under the heading of "employee rights," and their discussion has become one of the most heated and controversial in the field of business ethics.

When talking about employee rights, a few philosophical distinctions about the concept of a right are in order. We take the term *right* for granted, often forgetting that only a few centuries ago, the term was unknown. The first instance of the word in English appeared during the sixteenth century in the phrase "the rights of Englishmen." But the "rights of Englishmen" referred literally to English*men*, not English*women*, and included only those who owned property. History waited for the English philosopher John Locke to provide the word *right* with its present, far-reaching significance. In Locke's writings the word came to refer to something which, by definition, is possessed unconditionally by *all* rational adult human beings. The talk of rights in our own Declaration of Independence and Constitution owes much to Locke's early doctrine of rights.

Philosophers disagree about the precise definition of a right. Three of the most widely used definitions are (1) a right is a justified claim (for example, the right to freedom); (2) a right is an entitlement *to* something, held *against* someone else (for example, the right to equal protection is an entitlement which requires positive action on the part of others, including the government); and (3) a right is a "trump" over a collective goal. The right to worship as one pleases, for example, overrides or "trumps" the collective goal of ideological unity within our society, and thus overrides any claims by certain groups or a government that certain religions must be suppressed for the sake of the common good.

Rights may be divided into legal rights and moral rights. The former are rights that are either specified formally by law or protected by it. In the United States, the right to sue, to have a jury trial, to own property, and to have a free public education are legal rights. Not all such rights were included in the founding documents of the U.S. government: The right to free publication, the right of women and blacks to vote, and the right of workers to form unions were historical additions made in the nineteenth and twentieth centuries. Moral rights, on the other hand, are rights that are not necessarily protected and specified by the laws. Moral rights are rights everyone has or *should* have—that is, they are normative claims about what people are entitled to—but they may not be universally recognized or incorporated into law. They would include, for example, the right to be treated with equal respect, the right to equal freedom, and the right not to be systematically deceived or harmed. The law might stop short of preventing private clubs, for instance, from excluding Jews and blacks, yet most of us would agree that Jews and blacks have a *moral* right in such situations not to be excluded. Similarly, South African law protects the apartheid system, yet few of us feel that those laws are morally correct.

Turning to employee rights, although the Constitution and the Bill of Rights protect the political rights of citizens, as late as 1946 the Supreme Court argued that the protection of the right to due process under the Fourteenth Amendment does not extend to private industry unless a particular business is performing a public function.[1] It is not that some rights are denied to employees in private industry but rather that they are not always explicitly protected nor are employers always restrained when rights are abrogated.

One of the most controversial issues in the area of employee rights, then, is whether, given that employees have some moral rights, those rights should remain only moral rights or also be protected as legal rights. David Ewing, perhaps the best known modern defender of employee rights, postulates a specific list of rights in his well-known "A Proposed Bill of Rights," reprinted in this section. This list, Ewing believes, specifies rights that should be guaranteed in all modern organizations. His list has sparked a spirited controversy in which his critics attack both the general idea of employee rights and the specific entitlements he endorses. One of his critics, Max Ways, takes Ewing to task in the article "The Myth of the 'Oppressive Corporation.'"

Until recently the lack of protection of employee rights has been rationalized by appealing to the common-law doctrine, the principle of Employment at Will (EAW), a principle that states that in the absence of law or a specific contract an employer may hire, fire, demote, or promote an employee whenever the employer wishes without having to justify that action. In criticizing Employment at Will, Patricia Werhane defends what she considers to be the most important employee right, namely, the right to due process. Werhane argues that due process should be extended and protected in the workplace as part of the employee–employer labor exchange. Professor Werhane's argument is close in spirit to the social practices of Western Europe, where, unlike their U.S. counterparts, corporations are unable to fire or lay off employees for arbitrary reasons, although Werhane does not argue specifically for a legal enforcement of the right to due process in the workplace.

In the past 10 years the principle of EAW has gradually been eroded in the courts, and today some employers argue that *their* rights are not always given equal consideration. The relationship between employee and employer rights is particularly an issue with the prolific use of the polygraph in employment. The polygraph appears to threaten job applicants' right to privacy. On the other hand, employers argue that they also have rights—in particular, the right not to be harmed by employee misbehavior. Can this conflict of rights be adjudicated so that the claims of both parties are respected, or must one party, the employer or the employee, sacrifice his or her rights for another goal? In a heated debate, Gordon Barland and David Lykken argue both sides of the question: Should the polygraph be used in employment?

AFFIRMATIVE ACTION

One important moral right that directly concerns business is the right of everyone to be treated equally in matters of hiring, pay, and promotion. If a person may be said to have such rights, business managers presumably have a corresponding obligation not to pursue discriminatory policies. For example, business organizations should be obliged to hire on the basis of applicant competence without being swayed by irrelevant factors such as sex, race, or ethnic origin. Most business people today recognize this obligation, one which is enforced fully in the law. A more controversial issue is whether business has an obligation to go beyond the point of merely not discriminating, to pursue what is called affirmative action. Affirmative action programs are of at least three sorts:

1. those which pursue a policy of deliberately hiring and promoting equally qualified minorities and women when considering candidates for a position;
2. those which pursue a policy of deliberately favoring qualified, but not necessarily equally qualified, minorities and women when hiring or promoting; and
3. those which establish quota systems to regulate the percentage of minority members hired or promoted in accordance with an ideal distribution of race, sex, creed, or ethnicity.

Perhaps the most common objection to affirmative action programs is that they are inconsistent, that is, that they make the same mistakes they hope to remedy. If discrimination entails using a morally irrelevant characteristic, such as a person's skin color, as a factor in hiring, is affirmative action itself perpetuating unjust discrimination? In giving preference to, say, blacks over whites, are such programs using the same morally irrelevant characteristic previously used in discriminatory practices, thus themselves committing discrimination? This and other criticisms of affirmative action programs are offered by Barry Gross in his article "Is Turn About Fair Play?"

Defenders of affirmative action argue that these programs are, all things considered, fair and consistent. They are not merely necessary to compensate past injustices in employment practices, injustices which clearly damaged the well-being and prospects of many members of society. Rather, they are also necessary to guarantee fairness in hiring and promotion for future generations. How will minority applicants ever seriously compete for positions in, say, medical school unless the educational and economic opportunities for minorities and nonminorities are equalized? And how will educational and economic opportunities be equalized unless minorities are able to attain a fair share of society's highest level of jobs? The case study "Freida Mae Jones" illustrates a special problem relating to discrimination. Ms. Jones, a black female, had little problem finding a good job for which she was qualified, but she met with a peculiar kind of discrimination. Her employer may not have been an evil person, but he placed customer preference above Ms. Jones's rights to equal opportunity. Can such a trade-off ever be justified?

In articles reprinted in this section, both Richard Wasserstrom and James Nickel defend the legitimacy of claims against society by minorities. Nickel defends affirmative action as a form of compensation because what is being compensated in affirmative action programs is not racial (or sexual) discrimination, as Gross alleges, but rather the wrongs suffered by those qualified persons not originally hired because of their race or sex.

Wasserstrom argues that although affirmative action programs may be discriminatory, they are not as discriminatory as the original discrimination which was part of a whole social structure relegating women and minorities to second-class citizenship. Although affirmative action programs in employment *do* take into account race and sex, this is no less fair than other common employment practices which do not always hire or promote the most qualified either. Wasserstrom suggests that since we do not live in a perfect meritocracy, those who are minimally qualified deserve an equal opportunity with those who are the more able. Furthermore, this seems a small price to pay for the resulting improvement in the racial-sexual mix in society.

The issues of discrimination and affirmative action are connected to, but distinct from, another important issue, namely, the question of comparable worth. Comparable worth entails the notion of fair treatment in job classification and compensation. It includes the idea of equal pay for equal work in similar jobs, a notion of particular importance for women in the workplace who, according to recent surveys, are still paid almost 40 percent below males. Most important, the principle of comparable worth tries to establish guidelines for fairness in job measurement for jobs of comparable value—even when those jobs are radically different. Although equal pay for similar jobs is achievable, as Sean DeForrest points out, it is difficult to determine and compare the worth of jobs that are dissimilar. One has to take into account such subjective qualities as skill level, effort, responsibility, and working conditions to ascertain whether job segregation, as well as wage discrimination, has occurred. Comparable worth, then, is a concept which must be carefully defined and clarified.

NOTE

1. *Marsh v. State of Alabama*, 66 S.Ct. 276 (1946).

Employee Rights

Case Study—The Aircraft Brake Scandal

KERMIT VANDIVIER

The B. F. Goodrich Company is what business magazines like to refer to as "a major American corporation." It has operations in a dozen states and as many foreign countries; and of these far-flung facilities, the Goodrich plant at Troy, Ohio, is not the most imposing. It is a small, one-story building, once used to manufacture airplanes. Set in the grassy flatlands of west-central Ohio, it employs only about six hundred people. Nevertheless, it is one of the three largest manufacturers of aircraft wheels and brakes, a leader in a most profitable industry. Goodrich wheels and brakes support such well-known planes as the F111, the C5A, the Boeing 727, the XB70, and many others.

Contracts for aircraft wheels and brakes often run into millions of dollars, and ordinarily a contract with a total value of less than $70,000, though welcome, would not create any special stir of joy in the hearts of Goodrich sales personnel. But purchase order P-237138—issued on June 18, 1967, by the LTV Aerospace Corporation, ordering 202 brake assemblies for a new Air Force plane at a total price of $69,417—was received by Goodrich with considerable glee. And there was good reason. Some ten years previously, Goodrich had built a brake for LTV that was, to say the least, considerably less than a rousing success. The brake had not lived up to

Goodrich's promises, and after experiencing considerable difficulty, LTV had written off Goodrich as a source of brakes. Since that time, Goodrich salesmen had been unable to sell so much as a shot of brake fluid to LTV. So in 1967, when LTV requested bids on wheels and brakes for the new A7D light attack aircraft it proposed to build for the Air Force, Goodrich submitted a bid that was absurdly low, so low that LTV could not, in all prudence, turn it down.

Goodrich had, in industry parlance, "bought into the business." The company did not expect to make a profit on the initial deal; it was prepared, if necessary, to lose money. But aircraft brakes are not something that can be ordered off the shelf. They are designed for a particular aircraft, and once an aircraft manufacturer buys a brake, he is forced to purchase all replacement parts from the brake manufacturer. The $70,000 that Goodrich would get for making the brake would be a drop in the bucket when compared with the cost of the linings and other parts the Air Force would have to buy from Goodrich during the lifetime of the aircraft.

There was another factor, besides the low bid, that had undoubtedly influenced LTV. All aircraft brakes made today are of the disk type, and the bid submitted by Goodrich called for a relatively small brake, one containing four disks and weighing only 106 pounds. The weight of any aircraft is extremely important: the lighter a part is, the heavier the plane's payload can be.

The brake was designed by one of Goodrich's most capable engineers, John Warren. A tall, lanky, blond graduate of Purdue, Warren had come from the Chrysler Corporation seven years before and had become adept at aircraft brake design. The happy-go-lucky manner he usually maintained belied a temper that exploded whenever anyone ventured to offer criticism of his work, no matter how small. On these occasions, Warren would turn red in the face, often throwing or slamming something and then stalking from the scene. As his co-workers learned the consequences of criticizing him, they did so less and less readily, and when he submitted his preliminary design for the A7D brake, it was accepted without question.

Warren was named project engineer for the A7D, and he, in turn, assigned the task of producing the final production design to a newcomer to the Goodrich engineering stable, Searle Lawson. Just turned twenty-six, Lawson had been out of the Northrop Institute of Technology only one year when he came to Goodrich in January 1967. He had been assigned to various "paper projects" to break him in, and after several months spent reviewing statistics and old brake designs, he was beginning to fret at the lack of challenge. When told he was being assigned to his first "real" project, he was elated and immediately plunged into his work.

The major portion of the design had already been completed by Warren, and major subassemblies for the brake had already been ordered from Goodrich suppliers. Naturally, however, before Goodrich could start making the brakes on a production basis, much testing would have to be done. Lawson would have to determine the best materials to use for the linings and discover what minor adjustments in the design would have to be made.

Then, after the preliminary testing and after the brake was judged ready for production, one whole brake assembly would undergo a series of grueling, simulated braking stops and other severe trials called qualification tests. These tests are required by the military, which gives very detailed specifications on how they are to be conducted, the criteria for failure, and so on. They are performed in the Goodrich plant's test laboratory, where huge machines called dynamometers can simulate the weight and speed of almost any aircraft.

Searle Lawson was well aware that much work had to be done before the A7D brake could go into production, and he knew that LTV had set the last two weeks in June 1968 as the starting dates for flight tests. So he decided to begin testing immediately. Goodrich's suppliers had not yet delivered the brake housing and other parts, but the brake disks had arrived, and using the housing from a brake similar in size and weight to the A7D brake, Lawson built a prototype. The prototype was installed in a test wheel and placed on one of the big dynamometers in the plant's test laboratory. Lawson began a series of tests, "landing" the wheel and brake at the A7D's landing speed and braking it to a stop. The main purpose of these preliminary tests was to learn what temperatures would develop within the brake during the simulated stops and to evaluate lining materials tentatively selected for use.

During a normal aircraft landing the temperatures inside the brake may reach 1,000 degrees, and occasionally a bit higher. During Lawson's first simulated landings, the temperature of his prototype brake reached 1,500 degrees. The brake glowed a bright cherry-red and threw off incandescent particles of metal and lining material as the temperature reached its peak. After a few such stops, the brake was dismantled and the linings were found to be almost completely disintegrated. Lawson chalked this first failure up to chance, and ordering new lining materials, tried again.

The second attempt was a repeat of the first. The brake became extremely hot, causing the lining materials to crumble into dust.

After the third such failure, Lawson, inexperienced though he was, knew that the fault lay not in defective parts or unsuitable lining material but in the basic design of the brake itself. Ignoring Warren's original computations, Lawson made his own, and it didn't take him long to discover where the trouble lay—the brake was too small. There simply was not enough surface area on the disks to stop the aircraft without generating the excessive heat that caused the linings to fail.

The answer to the problem was obvious, but far from simple—the four-disk brake would have to be scrapped, and a new design, using five disks, would have to be developed. The implications were not lost on Lawson. Such a step would require junking the four-disk-brake subassemblies, many of which had now begun to arrive from the various suppliers. It would also mean several weeks of preliminary design and testing and many more weeks of waiting while the suppliers made and delivered the new subassemblies.

Yet, several weeks had already gone by since LTV's order had arrived, and the date for delivery of the first production brakes for flight testing was only a few months away.

Although John Warren had more or less turned the A7D over to Lawson, he knew of the difficulties Lawson had been experiencing. He had assured the younger engineer that the problem resolved around getting the right kind of lining material. Once that was found, he said, the difficulties would end.

Despite the evidence of the abortive tests and Lawson's careful computations, Warren rejected the suggestion that the four-disk brake was too light for the job. He knew that his superior had already told LTV, in rather glowing terms, that the preliminary tests on the A7D brake were very successful. Indeed, Warren's superiors weren't aware at this time of the troubles on the brake. It would have been difficult for Warren to admit not only that he had made a serious error in his calculations and original design but that his mistakes had been caught by a green kid, barely out of college.

Warren's reaction to a five-disk brake was not unexpected by Lawson, and seeing that the four-disk brake was not to be abandoned so easily, he took his calculations and dismal test results one step up the corporate ladder.

At Goodrich, the man who supervises the engineers working on projects slated for production is called, predictably, the projects manager. The job was held by a short, chubby, bald man named Robert Sink. Some fifteen years before, Sink had begun working at Goodrich as a lowly draftsman. Slowly, he worked his way up. Despite his geniality, Sink was neither respected nor liked by the majority of the engineers, and his appointment as their supervisor did not improve their feelings toward him. He possessed only a high-school diploma, and it quite naturally rankled those who had gone through years of college to be commanded by a man whom they considered their intellectual inferior. But, though Sink had no college training, he had something even more useful: a fine working knowledge of company politics.

Puffing on a meerschaum pipe, Sink listened gravely as young Lawson confided his fears about the four-disk brake. Then he examined Lawson's calculations and the results of the abortive tests. Despite the fact that he was not a qualified engineer, in the strictest sense of the word, it must certainly have been obvious to Sink that Lawson's calculations were correct and that a four-disk brake would never work on the A7D.

But other things of equal importance were also obvious. First, to concede that Lawson's calculations were correct would also mean conceding that Warren's calculations were incorrect. As projects manager, not only was he responsible for Warren's activities, but in admitting that Warren had erred he would also have to admit that he had erred in trusting Warren's judgment. It also meant that, as projects manager, it would be he who would have to explain the whole messy situation to the Goodrich hierarchy, not only at Troy but possibly on the corporate level at Goodrich's Akron offices. And having taken Warren's judgment of the four-disk brake at face value, he had assured LTV, not once but several times, that about all there was left to do on the brake was pack it in a crate and ship it out the door.

There's really no problem at all, he told Lawson. After all, Warren was an experienced engineer, and if he said the brake would work, it would work. Just keep on testing and probably, maybe even on the very next try, it'll work out just fine.

Lawson was far from convinced, but without the support of his superiors there was little he could do except keep on testing. By now, housings for the four-disk brake had begun to arrive at the plant, and Lawson was able to build a production model of the brake and begin the formal qualification tests demanded by the military.

The first qualification attempts went exactly as the tests on the prototype had. Terrific heat developed within the brakes, and after a few short, simulated stops the linings crumbled. A new type of lining material was ordered and once again an attempt to qualify the brake was made. Again, failure.

Experts were called in from lining manufacturers, and new lining "mixes" were tried, always with the same result. Failure.

It was now the last week in March 1968, and flight tests were scheduled to begin in seventy days. Twelve separate attempts had been made to qualify the brake, and all had failed. It was no longer possible for anyone to ignore the glaring truth that the brake was a dismal failure and that nothing short of a major design change could ever make it work.

On April 4, the thirteenth attempt at qualification was begun. This time no attempt was made to conduct the tests by the methods and techniques spelled out in the military specifications. Regardless of how it had to be done, the brake was to be "nursed" through the required fifty simulated stops.

Fans were set up to provide special cooling. Instead of maintaining pressure on the brake until the test wheel had come to a complete stop, the pressure was reduced when the wheel had decelerated to around 15 mph, allowing it to "coast" to a stop. After each stop, the brake was disassembled and carefully cleaned, and after some of the stops, internal brake parts were machined in order to remove warp and other disfigurations caused by the high heat.

By these and other methods, all clearly contrary to the techniques established by the military specifications, the brake was coaxed through the fifty stops. But even using these methods, the brake could not meet all the requirements. On one stop the wheel rolled for a distance of 16,000 feet, or over three miles, before the brake could bring it to a stop. The normal distance required for such a stop was around 3,500 feet.

On April 11, the day the thirteenth test was completed, I became personally involved in the A7D situation.

I had worked in the Goodrich test laboratory for five years, starting first as an instrumentation engineer, then later becoming a data analyst and technical writer. As part of my duties, I analyzed the reams and reams of instrumentation data that came from the many testing machines in the lab, then transcribed all of it to a more usable form for the engineering department. When a new-type brake had successfully completed the required qualification tests, I would issue a formal qualification report.

Qualification reports are an accumulation of all the data and test logs compiled during the qualification tests and are documentary proof that a brake has met all the requirements established by the military specifications and is therefore presumed safe for flight testing. Before actual flight tests are conducted on a brake, qualification reports have to be delivered to the customer and to various government officials.

On April 11, I was looking over the data from the latest A7D test, and I noticed that many irregularities in testing had been noted on the test logs.

Technically, of course, there was nothing wrong with conducting tests in any manner desired, so long as the test was for research purposes only. But qualification test methods are clearly delineated by the military, and I knew that this test had been a formal qualification attempt. One particular notation on the test logs caught my eye. For some of the stops, the instrument that recorded the brake pressure had been deliberately miscalibrated so that, while the brake pressure used during the stops was recorded as 1,000 psi (pounds per square inch)—the maximum pressure that would be available on the A7D aircraft—the pressure had actually been 1,100 psi.

I showed the test logs to the test lab supervisor, Ralph Gretzinger, who said he had learned from the technician who had miscalibrated the instrument that he had been asked to do so by Lawson. Lawson, said Gretzinger, readily admitted asking for the miscalibration, saying he had been told to do so by Sink.

I asked Gretzinger why anyone would want to miscalibrate the data-recording instruments.

"Why? I'll tell you why," he snorted. "That brake is a failure. It's way too small for the job, and they're not ever going to get it to work. They're getting desperate, and instead of scrapping the damned thing and starting over, they figure they can horse around down here in the lab and qualify it that way."

An expert engineer, Gretzinger had been responsible for several innovations in brake design. It was he who had invented the unique brake system used on the famous XB70. "If you want to find out what's going on," said Gretzinger, "ask Lawson; he'll tell you."

Curious, I did ask Lawson the next time he came into the lab. He seemed eager to discuss the A7D and gave me the history of his months of frustrating efforts to get Warren and Sink to change the brake design. "I just can't believe this is really happening," said Lawson, shaking his head slowly. "This isn't engineering, at least not what I thought it would be. Back in school, I thought that when you were an engineer, you tried to do your best, no matter what it cost. But this is something else."

He sat across the desk from me, his chin propped in his hand. "Just wait," he warned. "You'll get a chance to see what I'm talking about. You're going to get in the act too, because I've already had the word that we're going to make one more attempt to qualify the brake, and that's it. Win or lose, we're going to issue a qualification report!"

I reminded him that a qualification report could be issued only after a brake had successfully met all military requirements, and therefore, unless the next qualification attempt was a success, no report would be issued.

"You'll find out," retorted Lawson. "I was already told that regardless of what the brake does on test, it's going to be qualified." He said he had been told in those exact words at a conference with Sink and Russell Van Horn.

This was the first indication that Sink had brought his boss, Van Horn, into the mess. Although Van Horn, as manager of the design engineering section, was responsible for the entire department, he was not necessarily familiar with all phases of every project, and it was not uncommon for those under him to exercise the what-he-doesn't-know-won't-hurt-him philosophy. If he was aware of the full extent of the A7D situation, it meant that Sink had decided not only to call for help but to look toward that moment when blame must be borne and, if possible, shared.

Also, if Van Horn had said, "Regardless of what the brake does on test, it's going to be qualified," then it could only mean that, if necessary, a false qualification report would be issued. I discussed this possibility with Gretzinger, and he assured me that under no circumstances would such a report ever be issued.

"If they want a qualification report, we'll write them one, but we'll tell it just like it is," he declared emphatically. "No false data or false reports are going to come out of this lab."

On May 2, 1968, the fourteenth and final attempt to qualify the brake was begun. Although the same improper methods used to nurse the brake through the previous tests were employed, it soon became obvious that this too would end in failure.

When the tests were about half completed, Lawson asked if I would start preparing the various engineering curves and graphic displays that were normally incorporated in a qualification report. I flatly refused to have anything to do with the matter and immediately told Gretzinger what I had been asked to do. He was furious and repeated his previous declaration that under no circumstances would any false data or other matter be issued from the lab.

"I'm going to get this settled right now, once and for all," he declared. "I'm going to see Line [Russell Line, manager of the Goodrich Technical Services Section, of which the test lab was a part] and find out just how far this thing is going to go!" He stormed out of the room.

In about an hour, he returned and called me to his desk. He sat silently for a few moments, then muttered, half to himself, "I wonder what the hell they'd do if I just quit?" I didn't answer and I didn't ask him what he meant. I knew. He had been beaten down. He had reached the point when the decision had to be made. Defy them now while there was still time — or knuckle under, sell out.

"You know," he went on uncertainly, looking down at his desk, "I've been an engineer for a long time, and I've always believed that ethics and integrity were every bit as important as theorems and formulas, and never once has anything happened to change my beliefs. Now this . . . Hell, I've got two sons I've got to put through school and I just . . ." His voice trailed off.

He sat for a few more minutes, then, looking over the top of his glasses, said hoarsely, "Well, it looks like we're licked. The way it stands now, we're to go ahead and prepare the data and other things for the graphic presentation in the report, and when we're finished, someone upstairs will actually write the report.

"After all," he continued, "we're just drawing some curves, and what happens to them after they leave here — well, we're not responsible for that."

I wasn't at all satisfied with the situation and decided that I too would discuss the matter with Russell Line, the senior executive in our section.

Tall, powerfully built, his teeth flashing white, his face tanned to a coffee-brown by a daily stint with a sunlamp, Line looked and acted every inch the executive. He had been transferred from the Akron offices some two years previously, and he commanded great respect and had come to be well liked by those of us who worked under him.

He listened sympathetically while I explained how I felt about the A7D situation, and when I had finished, he asked me what I wanted him to do about it. I said that as employees of the Goodrich Company we had a responsibility to protect the company and its reputation if at all possible. I said I was certain that officers on the corporate level would never knowingly allow such tactics as had been employed on the A7D.

"I agree with you," he remarked, "but I still want to know what you want me to do about it."

I suggested that in all probability the chief engineer at the Troy plant,

H. C. "Bud" Sunderman, was unaware of the A7D problem and that he, Line, could tell him what was going on.

Line laughed, good-humoredly. "Sure, I could, but I'm not going to. Bud probably already knows about this thing anyway, and if he doesn't, I'm sure not going to be the one to tell him."

"But why?"

"Because it's none of my business, and it's none of yours. I learned a long time ago not to worry about things over which I had no control. I have no control over this."

I wasn't satisfied with this answer, and I asked him if his conscience wouldn't bother him if, say, during flight tests on the brake, something should happen resulting in death or injury to the test pilot.

"Look," he said, becoming somewhat exasperated, "I just told you I have no control over this. Why should my conscience bother me?"

His voice took on a quiet, soothing tone as he continued. "You're just getting all upset over this thing for nothing. I just do as I'm told, and I'd advise you to do the same."

I made no attempt to rationalize what I had been asked to do. It made no difference who would falsify which part of the report or whether the actual falsification would be by misleading numbers or misleading words. Whether by acts of commission or omission, all of us who contributed to the fraud would be guilty. The only question left for me to decide was whether or not I would become a party to the fraud.

Before coming to Goodrich in 1963, I had held a variety of jobs, each a little more pleasant, a little more rewarding than the last. At forty-two, with seven children, I had decided that the Goodrich Company would probably be my "home" for the rest of my working life. The job paid well, it was pleasant and challenging, and the future looked reasonably bright. My wife and I had bought a home and we were ready to settle down into a comfortable, middle-age, middle-class rut. If I refused to take part in the A7D fraud, I would have either to resign or be fired. The report would be written by someone anyway, but I would have the satisfaction of knowing I had no part in the matter. But bills aren't paid with personal satisfaction, nor house payments with ethical principles. I made my decision. The next morning, I telephoned Lawson and told him I was ready to begin on the qualification report.

I had written dozens of qualification reports, and I knew what a "good" one looked like. Resorting to the actual test data only on occasion, Lawson and I proceeded to prepare page after page of elaborate, detailed engineering curves, charts, and test logs, which purported to show what had happened during the formal qualification tests. Where temperatures were too high, we deliberately chopped them down a few hundred degrees, and where they were too low, we raised them to a value that would appear reasonable to the LTV and military engineers. Brake pressure, torque values, distances, times—everything of consequence was tailored to fit.

Occasionally, we would find that some test either hadn't been performed at all or had been conducted improperly. On those occasions, we "conducted" the test—successfully, of course—on paper.

For nearly a month we worked on the graphic presentation that would be a part of the report. Meanwhile, the final qualification attempt had been completed, and the brake, not unexpectedly, had failed again.

We finished our work on the graphic portion of the report around the first of June. Altogether, we had prepared nearly two hundred pages of data, containing dozens of deliberate falsifications and misrepresentations. I delivered the data to Gretzinger, who said that he had been instructed to deliver it personally to the chief engineer, Bud Sunderman, who in turn would assign someone in the engineering department to complete the written portion of the report. He gathered the bundle of data and left the office. Within minutes, he was back with the data, his face white with anger.

"That damned Sink's beat me to it," he said furiously. "He's already talked to Bud about this, and now Sunderman says no one in the engineering department has time to write the report. He wants us to do it, and I told him we couldn't."

The words had barely left his mouth when Russell Line burst in the door. "What the hell's all the fuss about this damned report?" he demanded.

Patiently, Gretzinger explained. "There's no fuss. Sunderman just told me that we'd have to write the report down here, and I said we couldn't. Russ," he went on, "I've told you before that we weren't going to write the report. I made my position clear on that a long time ago."

Line shut him up with a wave of his hand and, turning to me, bellowed "I'm getting sick and tired of hearing about this damned report. Now, write the goddamn thing and shut up about it!" He slammed out of the office.

Gretzinger and I just sat for a few seconds looking at each other. Then he spoke.

"Well, I guess he's made it pretty clear, hasn't he? We can either write the thing or quit. You know, what we should have done was quit a long time ago. Now, it's too late."

Somehow I wasn't at all surprised at the turn of events, and it didn't really make that much difference. As far as I was concerned, we were all up to our necks in the thing anyway, and writing the narrative portion of the report couldn't make me more guilty than I already felt myself to be.

Within two days, I had completed the narrative, or written portion, of the report. As a final sop to my own self-respect, in the conclusion of the report I wrote, "The B. F. Goodrich P/N 2–1162–3 brake assembly does not meet the intent or the requirements of the applicable specification documents and therefore is not qualified."

This was a meaningless gesture, since I knew that this would certainly be changed when the report went through the final typing process. Sure enough, when the report was published, the negative conclusion had been made positive.

One final and significant incident occurred just before publication.

Qualification reports always bear the signature of the person who has prepared them. I refused to sign the report, as did Lawson. Warren was later asked to sign the report. He replied that he would "when I receive a signed statement from Bob Sink ordering me to sign it."

The engineering secretary who was delegated the responsibility of "dogging" the report through publication told me later that after I, Lawson, and Warren had all refused to sign the report, she had asked Sink if he would sign. He replied, "On something of this nature, I don't think a signature is really needed."

On June 5, 1968, the report was officially published and copies were delivered by hand to the Air Force and LTV. Within a week flight tests were begun at Edwards Air Force Base in California. Searle Lawson was sent to California as Goodrich's representative. Within approximately two weeks, he returned because some rather unusual incidents during the tests had caused them to be canceled.

His face was grim as he related stories of several near crashes during landings—caused by brake troubles. He told me about one incident in which, upon landing, one brake was literally welded together by the intense heat developed during the test stop. The wheel locked, and the plane skidded for nearly 1,500 feet before coming to a halt. The plane was jacked up and the wheel removed. The fused parts within the brake had to be pried apart.

That evening I left work early and went to see my attorney. After I told him the story, he advised that, while I was probably not actually guilty of fraud, I was certainly part of a conspiracy to defraud. He advised me to go to the Federal Bureau of Investigation and offered to arrange an appointment. The following week he took me to the Dayton office of the FBI and after I had been warned that I would not be immune from prosecution, I disclosed the A7D matter to one of the agents. The agent told me to say nothing about the episode to anyone and to report any further incidents to him. He said he would forward the story to his superiors in Washington.

A few days later, Lawson returned from a conference with LTV in Dallas and said that the Air Force, which had previously approved the qualification report, had suddenly rescinded that approval and was demanding to see some of the raw test data. I gathered that the FBI had passed the word.

Omitting any reference to the FBI, I told Lawson I had been to an attorney and that we were probably guilty of conspiracy.

"Can you get me an appointment with your attorney?" he asked. Within a week, he had been to the FBI and told them of his part in the mess. He too was advised to say nothing but to keep on the job reporting any new development.

Naturally, with the rescinding of Air Force approval and the demand to see raw test data, Goodrich officials were in a panic. A conference was

called for July 27, a Saturday morning affair at which Lawson, Sink, Warren, and I were present. We met in a tiny conference room in the deserted
engineering department. Lawson and I, by now openly hostile to Warren
and Sink, ranged ourselves on one side of the conference table while Warren sat on the other side. Sink, chairing the meeting, paced slowly in front
of a blackboard, puffing furiously on a pipe.

The meeting was called, Sink began, "to see where we stand on the
A7D." What we were going to do, he said, was to "level" with LTV and tell
them the "whole truth" about the A7D. "After all," he said, "they're in this
thing with us, and they have the right to know how matters stand."

"In other words," I asked, "we're going to tell them the truth?"

"That's right," he replied. "We're going to level with them and let them
handle the ball from there."

"There's one thing I don't quite understand," I interjected. "Isn't it
going to be pretty hard for us to admit to them that we've lied?"

"Now, wait a minute," he said angrily. "Let's don't go off half-cocked
on this thing. It's not a matter of lying. We've just interpreted the information the way we felt it should be."

"I don't know what you call it," I replied, "but to me it's lying, and it's
going to be damned hard to confess to them that we've been lying all along."

He became very agitated at this and repeated, "We're not lying," adding, "I don't like this sort of talk."

I dropped the matter at this point, and he began discussing the various
discrepancies in the report.

We broke for lunch, and afterward, I came back to the plant to find
Sink sitting alone at his desk, waiting to resume the meeting. He called me
over and said he wanted to apologize for his outburst that morning. "This
thing has kind of gotten me down," he confessed, "and I think you've got the
wrong picture. I don't think you really understand everything about this."

Perhaps so, I conceded, but it seemed to me that if we had already told
LTV one thing and then had to tell them another, changing our story
completely, we would have to admit we were lying.

"No," he explained patiently, "we're not really lying. All we were doing
was interpreting the figures the way we knew they should be. We were just
exercising engineering license."

During the afternoon session, we marked some forty-three discrepant
points in the report; forty-three points that LTV would surely spot as occasions where we had exercised "engineering license."

After Sink listed those points on the blackboard, we discussed each one
individually. As each point came up, Sink would explain that it was probably
"too minor to bother about," or that perhaps it "wouldn't be wise to open
that can of worms," or that maybe this was a point that "LTV just wouldn't
understand." When the meeting was over, it had been decided that only
three points were "worth mentioning."

Similar conferences were held during August and September, and the summer was punctuated with frequent treks between Dallas and Troy and demands by the Air Force to see the raw test data. Tempers were short, and matters seemed to grow worse.

Finally, early in October 1968, Lawson submitted his resignation, to take effect on October 25. On October 18, I submitted my own resignation, to take effect on November 1. In my resignation, addressed to Russell Line, I cited the A7D report and stated: "As you are aware, this report contains numerous deliberate and willfull misrepresentations which, according to legal counsel, constitute fraud and expose both myself and others to criminal charges of conspiracy to defraud . . . The events of the past seven months have created an atmosphere of deceit and distrust in which it is impossible to work. . . ."

On October 25, I received a sharp summons to the office of Bud Sunderman. Tall and graying, impeccably dressed at all times, he was capable of producing a dazzling smile or a hearty chuckle or immobilizing his face into marble hardness, as the occasion required.

I faced the marble hardness when I reached his office. He motioned me to a chair. "I have your resignation here," he snapped, "and I must say you have made some rather shocking, I might even say irresponsible, charges. This is very serious."

Before I could reply, he was demanding an explanation. "I want to know exactly what the fraud is in connection with the A7D and how you can dare accuse this company of such a thing!"

I started to tell some of the things that had happened during the testing, but he shut me off saying, "There's nothing wrong with anything we've done here. You aren't aware of all the things that have been going on behind the scenes. If you had known the true situation, you would never have made these charges." He said that in view of my apparent "disloyalty" he had decided to accept my resignation "right now," and said it would be better for all concerned if I left the plant immediately. As I got up to leave he asked me if I intended to "carry this thing further."

I answered simply, "Yes," to which he replied, "Suit yourself." Within twenty minutes, I had cleaned out my desk and left. Forty-eight hours later, the B. F. Goodrich Company recalled the qualification report and the four-disk brake, announcing that it would replace the brake with a new, improved, five-disk brake at no cost to LTV.

Ten months later, on August 13, 1969, I was the chief government witness at a hearing conducted before Senator William Proxmire's Economy in Government Subcommittee. I related the A7D story to the committee, and my testimony was supported by Searle Lawson, who followed me to the witness stand. Air Force officers also testified, as well as a four-man team from the General Accounting Office, which had conducted an investigation of the A7D brake at the request of Senator Proxmire. Both Air Force and GAO investigators declared that the brake was dangerous and had not been tested properly.

Testifying for Goodrich was R. G. Jeter, vice-president and general counsel of the company, from the Akron headquarters. Representing the Troy plant was Robert Sink. These two denied any wrongdoing on the part of the Goodrich Company, despite expert testimony to the contrary by Air Force and GAO officials. Sink was quick to deny any connection with the writing of the report or directing of any falsifications, claiming to have been on the West Coast at the time. John Warren was the man who had supervised its writing, said Sink.

As for me, I was dismissed as a high-school graduate with no technical training, while Sink testified that Lawson was a young, inexperienced engineer. "We tried to give him guidance," Sink testified, "but he preferred to have his own convictions."

About changing the data to figures in the report, Sink said: "When you take data from several different sources, you have to rationalize among those data what is the true story. This is part of your engineering know-how." He admitted that changes had been made in the data, "but only to make them more consistent with the overall picture of the data that is available."

Jeter pooh-poohed the suggestion that anything improper occurred, saying: "We have thirty-odd engineers at this plant . . . and I say to you that it is incredible that these men would stand idly by and see reports changed or falsified. . . . I mean you just do not have to do that working for anybody . . . Just nobody does that."

The four-hour hearing adjourned with no real conclusion reached by the subcommittee. But the following day the Department of Defense made sweeping changes in its inspection, testing, and reporting procedures. A spokesman for the DOD said the changes were a result of the Goodrich episode.

The A7D is now in service, sporting a Goodrich-made five-disk brake, a brake that works very well, I'm told. Business at the Goodrich plant is good. Lawson is now an engineer for LTV and has been assigned to the A7D project, possibly explaining why the A7D's new brakes work so well. And I am now a newspaper reporter.

At this writing, those remaining at Goodrich—including Warren—are still secure in the same positions, all except Russell Line and Robert Sink.

Line has been rewarded with a promotion to production superintendent, a large step upward on the corporate ladder. As for Sink, he moved up into Line's old job.

Case Study—The Copper "O" Company

THOMAS F. McMAHON, C.S.V.

The XYZ Company is a multinational electronics corporation. It is listed in *Forbes* as one of the top fifty companies in total assets. XYZ has a plant on Chicago's near northwest side, which manufactures printed circuit boards. High concentrations of copper are flushed down the sewer. The Metropolitan Sanitary District allows 3 milligrams per litre; any amount above 3 milligrams per litre is in violation of the city's Pure Air and Water Ordinance. XYZ has been flushing 5 to 6 milligrams per litre of copper—both particulate and solution—into the city sewerage system. Copper is toxic to water creatures but has little effect on humans (unless it becomes copper sulfate). The sanitary district is much more concerned with cadmium and cyanide than with copper contamination. When the engineers of the sanitary district observe excessive chemical discharge, they generally provide a "reasonable" time (six months) to correct the infringement through systems of filters, settling tanks, or other equipment.

On a number of occasions during the past three years, Bill Jones, plant manager, has confronted his immediate superiors about the existing violation. They keep postponing any definite answer about installing antipollution equipment. During Bill's most recent confrontation six months ago, they told Bill (1) that the present plant has been sold to another company; (2) that XYZ is building a new plant installed with the most advanced antipollution equipment in the suburbs within two years; (3) that no city inspector has ever tested this particular discharge since the inception of the printed circuit boards about four years ago.

Bill frequently wonders about his responsibility to the firm, his superiors, his workers, and his own family, as well as his obligation to his profession, local community, and a healthy environmental "quality-of-life." During the last few months, he found out that XYZ hired a public relations firm to promote the "concerned citizen about the environment" stance which XYZ is taking on its new plant. He wondered whether he should "blow the whistle" on the XYZ Company. He also mused over the role of the public relations firm: one black shoe from the sludge in Chicago; one white shoe from the clean environment in the suburbs.

Reprinted by permission of the author.

A Proposed Bill of Rights

DAVID W. EWING

What should a bill of rights for employees look like?

First, it should be presented in the form of clear and practical injunctions, not in the language of desired behavior or ideals.

In 1789, when James Madison and other members of the first U.S. Congress settled down to write the Bill of Rights (the first ten amendments to the Constitution), Madison insisted on using the imperative "shall" instead of the flaccid "ought," which had been used in the declarations of rights by the states, from which the ideas for the federal Bill of Rights were taken. For instance, where Virginia's historic Declaration of Rights of 1776 stated that "excessive bail ought not to be required," and where the amendments proposed in 1788 by Virginia legislators were identically worded, the amendment proposed by Madison (and later accepted) read: "Excessive bail shall not be required. . . ."

The imperative has precisely the same advantage in a bill of rights for members of a corporation, government bureau, university administration, or other organization. An analogy is a traffic light. It does not contain various shades of red but just one shade which means clearly and unequivocally, "Stop." Nor does a stop sign say "Stop If Possible" or "Stop If You Can." It says simply "Stop."

Second, as a general rule, it is wise to phrase a bill of rights in terms of negative injunctions rather than positive ones. A bill of rights does not aim to tell officials what they can do so much as it aims to tell them what they cannot do. It is not like the delegation of powers found in constitutions. Here again it is instructive to recall the writing of the federal Bill of Rights in 1789. Madison insisted that the positive grants of government powers had been well provided for in the main body of the Constitution and did not need to be reiterated in the first ten amendments.

In addition, a "Thou shalt not" type of commandment generally can be more precise than a "Thou shalt" type of commandment; the latter must be worded and interpreted to cover many possibilities of affirmative action. Since it is more precise, a "Thou shalt not" injunction is more predictable — not quite as predictable as a traffic light, but more so than most positive injunctions can be.

Also, since it is more limited, a negative injunction is less of a threat to the future use of executive (and legislative) powers. For instance, the in-

From *Freedom Inside the Organization*, by David W. Ewing. Copyright © 1977 by David W. Ewing. Reprinted by permission of the publisher, E. P. Dutton, a division of NAL Penguin Inc.

junction "Congress shall make no law respecting an establishment of religion" (first item in the U.S. Bill of Rights) inhibits Congress less, simply because it is so precise, than a positive command such as "Congress shall respect various establishments of religion" (rejected by the Founding Fathers when proposed in the 1789 discussions), which is more protean and expansible.

Third, an organization's bill of rights should be succinct. It should read more like a recipe in a cookbook than the regulations of the Internal Revenue Service. It is better to start with a limited number of rights that apply to familiar situations and that may have to be extended and amended in a few years than to try to write a definitive listing for all time. Rights take time to ingest.

Fourth, a bill of rights should be written for understanding by employees and lay people rather than by lawyers and personnel specialists. It should not read like a letter from a credit company or a Massachusetts auto insurance policy. If an organization desires to make everything clear for experts, it could add a supplement or longer explanation that elaborates in technical terms on the provisions and clarifies questions and angles that might occur to lawyers.

Fifth, a bill of rights should be enforceable. Existence as a creed or statement of ideals is not enough. While creeds indeed may influence behavior in the long run, in the short run they leave too much dependent on good will and hope.

The bill of rights that follows is one person's proposal, a "working paper" for discussion, not a platform worked out in committee. . . . The slight variations in style are purposeful—partly to reduce monotony and partly to suggest different ways of defining employee rights and management prerogatives.

1. *No organization or manager shall discharge, demote, or in other ways discriminate against any employee who criticizes, in speech or press, the ethics, legality, or social responsibility of management actions.*

Comment: This right is intended to extend the U.S. Supreme Court's approach in the *Pickering* case‡ to all employees in business, government, education, and public service organizations.

What this right does not say is as important as what it does say. Protection does not extend to employees who make nuisances of themselves or who balk, argue, or contest managerial decisions on normal operating and planning matters, such as the choice of inventory accounting method, whether to diversify the product line or concentrate it, whether to rotate workers on a certain job or specialize them, and so forth. "Committing the truth," as Ernest Fitzgerald called it, is protected only for speaking out on

---

‡ [ed.] In the *Pickering* case the Supreme Court found in favor of a public employee, a school teacher, who had been fired for criticizing school policies in the local newspaper.

issues where we consider an average citizen's judgment to be as valid as an expert's—truth in advertising, public safety standards, questions of fair disclosure, ethical practices, and so forth.

Nor does the protection extend to employees who malign the organization. We don't protect individuals who go around ruining other people's reputations, and neither should we protect those who vindictively impugn their employers.

Note, too, that this proposed right does not authorize an employee to disclose to outsiders information that is confidential.

This right puts publications of nonunionized employees on the same basis as union newspapers and journals, which are free to criticize an organization. Can a free press be justified for one group but not for the other? More to the point still, in a country that practices democratic rites, can the necessity of an "underground press" be justified in any socially important organization?

2. *No employee shall be penalized for engaging in outside activities of his or her choice after working hours, whether political, economic, civic, or cultural, nor for buying products and services of his or her choice for personal use, nor for expressing or encouraging views contrary to top management's on political, economic, and social issues.*

Comment: Many companies encourage employees to participate in outside activities, and some states have committed this right to legislation. Freedom of choice of products and services for personal use is also authorized in various state statutes as well as in arbitrators' decisions. The third part of the statement extends the protection of the First Amendment to the employee whose ideas about government, economic policy, religion, and society do not conform with the boss's. It would also protect the school-teacher who allows the student newspaper to espouse a view on sex education that is rejected by the principal . . . , the staff psychologist who endorses a book on a subject considered taboo in the board room, and other independent spirits.

Note that this provision does not authorize an employee to come to work "beat" in the morning because he or she has been moonlighting. Participation in outside activities should enrich employees' lives, not debilitate them; if on-the-job performance suffers, the usual penalties may have to be paid.

3. *No organization or manager shall penalize an employee for refusing to carry out a directive that violates common norms of morality.*

Comment: The purpose of this right is to . . . afford job security (not just unemployment compensation) to subordinates who cannot perform an action because they consider it unethical or illegal. It is important that the conscientious objector in such a case hold to a view that has some public acceptance. Fad moralities—messages from flying saucers, mores of occult religious sects, and so on—do not justify refusal to carry out an order. Nor in any case is the employee entitled to interfere with the boss's finding another person to do the job requested.

4. *No organization shall allow audio or visual recordings of an employee's conversations or actions to be made without his or her prior knowledge and consent. Nor may an organization require an employee or applicant to take personality tests, polygraph examinations, or other tests that constitute, in his opinion, an invasion of privacy.*

Comment: This right is based on policies that some leading organizations have already put into practice. If an employee doesn't want his working life monitored, that is his privilege so long as he demonstrates (or, if an applicant, is willing to demonstrate) competence to do a job well.

5. *No employee's desk, files, or locker may be examined in his or her absence by anyone but a senior manager who has sound reason to believe that the files contain information needed for a management decision that must be made in the employee's absence.*

Comment: The intent of this right is to grant people a privacy right as employees similar to that which they enjoy as political and social citizens under the "searches and seizures" guarantee of the Bill of Rights (Fourth Amendment to the Constitution). Many leading organizations in business and government have respected the principle of this rule for some time.

6. *No employer organization may collect and keep on file information about an employee that is not relevant and necessary for efficient management. Every employee shall have the right to inspect his or her personnel file and challenge the accuracy, relevance, or necessity of data in it, except for personal evaluations and comments by other employees which could not reasonably be obtained if confidentiality were not promised. Access to an employee's file by outside individuals and organizations shall be limited to inquiries about the essential facts of employment.*

Comment: This right is important if employees are to be masters of their employment track records instead of possible victims of them. It will help to eliminate surprises, secrets, and skeletons in the clerical closet.

7. *No manager may communicate to prospective employers of an employee who is about to be or has been discharged gratuitous opinions that might hamper the individual in obtaining a new position.*

Comment: The intent of this right is to stop blacklisting. The courts have already given some support for it.

8. *An employee who is discharged, demoted, or transferred to a less desirable job is entitled to a written statement from management of its reasons for the penalty.*

Comment: The aim of this provision is to encourage a manager to give the same reasons in a hearing, arbitration, or court trial that he or she gives the employee when the cutdown happens. The written statement need not be given unless requested; often it is so clear to all parties why an action is being taken that no document is necessary.

9. *Every employee who feels that he or she has been penalized for assert-ing any right described in this bill shall be entitled to a fair hearing before an impartial official, board, or arbitrator. The findings and conclusions of the hearing shall be delivered in writing to the employee and manage-ment.*

Comment: This very important right is the organizational equivalent of due process of law as we know it in political and community life. Without due process in a company or agency, the rights in this bill would all have to be enforced by outside courts and tribunals, which is expensive for society as well as time-consuming for the employees who are required to appear as complainants and witnesses. The nature of a "fair hearing" is purposely left undefined here so that different approaches can be tried, expanded, and adapted to changing needs and conditions.

Note that the findings of the investigating official or group are not binding on top management. This would put an unfair burden on an om-budsperson or "expedited arbitrator," if one of them is the investigator. Yet the employee is protected. If management rejects a finding of unfair treat-ment and then the employee goes to court, the investigator's statement will weigh against management in the trial. As a practical matter, therefore, employers will not want to buck the investigator-referee unless they fer-vently disagree with the findings.

In Sweden, perhaps the world's leading practitioner of due process in organizations, a law went into effect in January 1977 that goes a little farther than the right proposed here. The new Swedish law states that except in unusual circumstances a worker who disputes a dismissal notice can keep his or her job until the dispute has been decided by a court.

Every sizable organization, whether in business, government, health, or another field, should have a bill of rights for employees. Only small organizations need not have such a statement—personal contact and oral communications meet the need for them. However, companies and agen-cies need not have identical bills of rights. Industry custom, culture, past history with employee unions and associations, and other considerations can be taken into account in the wording and emphasis given to different provisions.

For instance, Booz, Allen, and Hamilton, the well-known consulting company, revised a bill of rights for its employees in 1976 (the list included several of the rights suggested here). One statement obligated the company to "respect the right of employees to conduct their private lives as they choose, while expecting its employees' public conduct to reflect favorably upon the reputation of the Firm." The latter part of this provision reflects the justifiable concern of a leading consulting firm with outward appear-ances. However, other organizations—a mining company, let us say, or a testing laboratory—might feel no need to qualify the right of privacy be-cause few of their employees see customers.

In what ways can due process be assured? There are certain procedures that the organization itself can establish. . . . In addition, society can undertake to assure due process for employees. . . .

The Myth of the "Oppressive Corporation"

MAX WAYS

If enough voices declare that the pace of change in the workplace is "too slow," and that this should be blamed on concentrated corporate power, then, obviously, somebody is going to limit the power of the corporate Leviathan.

Proposals along this line are set forth in *Freedom Inside the Organization* by David W. Ewing, an editor of the *Harvard Business Review*. Subtitled *Bringing Civil Liberties to the Workplace*, the book falls into a familiar pattern: generalizations about existing conditions are drawn from atrocity stories and selected opinions of employees. In the dark picture of corporate oppression that results, the author sees an urgent need for drastic legal remedies.

"For nearly two centuries," Ewing begins, "Americans have enjoyed freedom of press, speech, and assembly, due process of law, privacy, freedom of conscience, and other important rights—in their homes, churches, political forums, and social and cultural life. But Americans have not enjoyed these civil liberties in most companies, government agencies, and other organizations where they work. Once a U.S. citizen steps through the plant or office door at 9:00 A.M., he or she is nearly rightless until 5:00 P.M., Monday through Friday."

Ewing has in this opening passage disclosed a fundamental misconception about the nature of our cherished rights. A few pages later, this mistake leads him into a shocking distortion.

"For all practical purposes," he writes, "employees are required to be as obedient to their superiors, regardless of ethical and legal considerations, as are workers in totalitarian countries."

A writer so insensitive that he can equate U.S. corporate practices, even at their worst, with the system that produced the Gulag Archipelago is hardly qualified to lecture businessmen on their lack of concern for human rights.

The historic rights enjoyed by Americans protect them against the abuse of government police power, not against all unpleasant consequences that may follow from their speech or action. Free speech, for instance, means that Americans cannot be fined or imprisoned for what they say; the exceptions are a small and shrinking number. It does not mean that they cannot be sued for slander. It does not mean that what they say may not deprive them of the respect of their children, the affection of their parents or spouses, the company of their friends. If an American's speech is rude enough, or malicious enough, or silly enough he may find that people don't listen to him and he may even be ostracized. Cases where such penalties are "unjust" do occur. But these instances are not violations of our right of free speech.

The human damage that can be done by words is so great and so plain that (most) children learn early to watch what they say. These inhibitions can be psychologically or socially hurtful, but civilized life would be impossible without them and the person-to-person sanctions by which they are maintained.

Most corporations today allow employees great latitude in their personal behavior, including speech. But corporations, like individuals, retain the power to employ all private sanctions that are not illegal in themselves (e.g., assault and battery) to express disapproval of an individual's speech. They can argue, remonstrate, and warn. The most extreme penalty at their disposal is to dissolve their association with the speaker by firing him. This can be, indeed, a serious penalty—but not necessarily more serious than divorce, which is frequently provoked by speech.

Reciting a number of instances where corporations have fired employees for what they said, Ewing deems many, though not all, of these to be "unjust." He points out that some companies invoke penalties only after a scrupulously enforced "due process." He cites an IBM policy that guarantees many freedoms to employees and establishes internal procedures to review penalties imposed by managers. More and more companies have moved in this direction.

Ewing's argument is that if some corporations choose to behave in this way then all corporations should be required by law to do likewise. The legal reasoning is reminiscent of that which produced the Eighteenth Amendment. First, the human damage done by alcohol was exaggerated, then "the power of the liquor interest" was blown up out of all proportion to reality, then attention was called to the fact that many Americans—perhaps half the adult population—hardly ever used alcohol. Ergo, let's have a law requiring everyone to conform to the best practice.

Sure enough, Ewing, too, wants an amendment to the Constitution of the United States. His draft starts, "No public or private organization shall discriminate against an employee for criticizing the ethical, moral, or legal policies and practices of the organization. . . ."

In addition to protecting individual employees, Ewing frankly desires to encourage "whistle blowing" in cases of corporate wrongdoing. That might accomplish some desirable changes in corporate behavior. But this hypothesized advantage has to be weighed against some foreseeable disadvantages. Who is to distinguish between whistle blowing and spiteful accusation? Speech now is protected from government penalty, in most cases, even if the utterance is proved untrue. Would Ewing's amendment continue this broad protection? Or would courts have to sift evidence to discover whether the employee's charge against the corporation was true? In the first case an organization might be required to keep on its payroll an employee who continually lied about it. In the second case, courts, which are not winning much public applause for the way they discharge their present responsibilities, would have to take on a huge new burden of deciding not only whether charges were true or false, but whether ethical norms had or had not been violated by the defendant organization.

The incidence of these cases could become such a nuisance to companies that all employees might wind up having, in effect, life tenure in their jobs, like the Civil Service or the tenured faculty of universities. Neither of these examples is necessarily reassuring.

It's true, of course, that a company's right to fire has long been limited by the National Labor Relations Act, which has worked rather well in forbidding firing for union activity. In this narrow class of cases it is relatively easy to determine whether the forbidden practice has occurred. In a much larger group of cases under equal-opportunity acts, corporations are forbidden to discriminate in respect to race or sex. Enforcement here has been less effective and has caused more confusion. Ewing's amendment is so much broader than the equal-opportunity laws, and its criteria so much vaguer, that the imagination boggles at the legal chaos that might ensue.

Such practical objections Ewing brushes aside with a quote from Judge Learned Hand: "To keep our democracy, there must be one commandment: Thou shalt not ration justice." The distinguished jurist said many wise things, but this was not one of them. In any society justice must always be less than perfect. A free society recognizes that its government should not pretend to dispense total justice. In that sense justice in a democracy must always be "rationed."

Much injustice that occurs among citizens is beyond the reach of courts or of any government instrument. The state in which that limitation is not recognized, the state that believes itself empowered to set all norms of conduct and to deal with every incident of ethical transgression, is the absolute state, Leviathan.

Employment at Will and Due Process: Contrary Employment Practices

Patricia H. Werhane

In 1981 the Supreme Court of the State of Illinois made what was purported to be a monumental decision. It said that an employee of International Harvester Corporation, Ray Palmateer, was wrongly fired for supplying information to local police about employee theft at International Harvester. The company had tried to justify its firing of Palmateer on the basis of a doctrine called Employment at Will. Under this common law principle in this country, unless specified by law or by contract, an employer has the right to hire, demote, promote, or fire "at will" whom and when it wishes. The Palmateer decision was said to be a landmark decision, because it reversed the standing tradition that employer wishes take precedence over employee rights in the workplace. The case was said to indicate a changing view toward employee rights in this country—recognition that employees or workers have certain claims even though they are working for someone else.[1] Yet in 1986 the Supreme Court of Oregon, ordinarily "liberal" in honoring implied employment contracts and in reversing "at will" practices, upheld J. C. Penney's dismissal of an employee, Mr. Patton, fired for dating a co-worker.[2]

It would appear that if one has constitutional guarantees to basic human rights, including the right to due process, equal opportunity, and freedom of speech, such guarantees would be enough to assure fair treatment in the workplace. Interestingly, however, until recently rights of the majority of employees in this country have not been enforced in employment. At least 64 percent of all employees in this country are "at will," employees unprotected by collective bargaining agreements or legislation.[3] These employees can be hired or fired at the discretion of the employer without cause, due process, or prior notice. And the principle of Employment at Will is sometimes used as a weapon to "punish" unruly, disobedient, as well as inefficient employees. In these instances it is not literally the case that the Constitution does not protect employee rights in the workplace. Rather it is that the law does not restrain employers who penalize employees for their exercise of rights. So in fact constitutional guarantees are not enforced in private places of business. This position was upheld by the Supreme Court in a 1946 decision that stated that the due process clause of the Fourteenth Amendment does not extend to private industry unless it is in the interest of public policy.[4] When due process procedures, for example, are not instituted in a private organization or when employees are fired or demoted without reason or redress, the courts have little precedent for questioning that employer action. The Palmateer and Patton cases illustrate a much overlooked issue in the workplace, and the subject of employee rights is a very current and controversial issue.

I shall present a theoretical argument that employees have rights in employment. Specifically, employees, all employees in whatever job, have the right to procedural due process. It shall be claimed that the common law doctrine of Employment at Will (hereafter abbreviated EAW) is an unjust principle because it does not recognize equal employer and employee rights. Due process procedures in the workplace, it will be argued, help to alleviate these inequalities created as a result of the practice of EAW. Due process is an important employee *and* employer right, because it provides fairness and consistency in employment, two goals coveted by any organization.

In what follows, the terms "employee" and "worker" will be used interchangeably to refer to any person who is in the employ of another. For the sake of abbreviating the argument the term "employer" or "manager" will represent the person or institution who has the power to hire, demote, promote, or fire another person. Thus in this context "employer" could refer to an individual, an owner, a corporation, a personnel officer, a manager, a supervisor, or a foreman.

One point should be emphasized at the outset. It is not true that most employers are ogres. Many places of employment are decent places to work, jobs are not unpleasant, and a manager or employer normally treats her employees with decency and respect. What is troublesome is not that fair treatment never occurs in the workplace. Fair treatment and respect for employee interests are growing focuses of concern of manager. Nor is it the case that EAW is universally or consistently applied in employment practices. The facts are to the contrary. What is at issue is that EAW is still used as a justification for arbitrary employment procedures so that the *right* to fair treatment has not been firmly established in employment nor supported by the courts. The determination of this right is important in order that one need not depend merely on the kindness of one's superiors for fairness and respect.

Due process, that is, procedural due process, is a means by which one can appeal a decision in order to get a disinterested, objective, or fair judgment as to its rightness or wrongness. In the workplace due process is, or should be, the right of employees and employers to grievance, arbitration, or some other appeals procedure in questioning a decision in hiring, firing, promotion, demotion, transfer, or other employment activity. Due process should not be confused with a claim to a right not to be fired or demoted. Due process is meant to insure fair procedures in firing, but not to rule out that employer action. The right to due process simply reiterates what is standardly accepted, that every accused person, guilty or innocent, has a right to a fair hearing and an objective evaluation of his or her guilt or innocence. To deny due process in the workplace would appear to argue that this right does not extend to every sector of society, or it might be to claim that employer interests may sometimes override an employee's right to due process.

In response, it is argued that because most businesses are not publicly owned, due process need not be instituted in the workplace. Moreover, EAW is defended as a fair principle of employment. The justifications for EAW originated in the rationale for property rights. In brief, it was argued that because the employer or the corporation owns the means of production, and because every person (and thus by analogy every organization) has the right to freedom, the employer has the right to do what he pleases with his business. An employee works for someone else and is paid for his or her work; so the employer has the right, in the absence of any contract, to employ or dismiss whom and when he wishes. Because the business is his, an employer need not explain or defend his treatment of employees in this regard, nor give a hearing to an employee before she is dismissed. In dismissing or demoting employees, one is not denying persons the political right to due process; rather, the employer is simply excluding that person from working or working at a particular job at the employer's place of business.

Changes in ownership relationships in this century have outdated this sort of justification. Today employers are by and large corporations. At least in principle, managers are agents for a changing group of owner-shareholders whose interests are represented by a board of directors, and the latter have little say in the day-to-day employment practices within a corporation. As agents of the corporation, managers are given power as employers over their unit or division. There is, then, a "hangover" effect of the nineteenth-century notion of property rights where those rights are translated into management prerogatives to control employment. Interestingly, managers are themselves employees of other managers or the board of directors, and thus they are subject to restraints similar to those they impose on their employees. However, a manager's dual role as an employer and an employee seldom influences how a manager perceives her role responsibilities and job priorities. Because managers see themselves as agents for the corporation and its shareholders, managers place corporate concerns such as profitability, growth, or company survival as their primary management goals. Whomever or whatever obstructs or interferes with corporate goals should be removed in order to progress, or in an unprofitable setting, in order to survive. Managers are given control of their units just for that purpose, to ensure economic efficiency and a well-run operation.

Employment at Will preserves the right of managers to create, continue, or perpetuate corporate ends. Erosion of that principle with union contracts, equal opportunity and age discrimination legislation, and other restrictions legislate against efficiency, economic growth, and even sometimes corporate financial viability. Ultimately, such restrictions affect the economy in general. The erosion of EAW interferes with the workings of a market economy where competition, both domestic and foreign, requires highly-skilled innovative employees working together to produce quality goods and services for the marketplace. The principle of EAW, then, preserves freedom and competition in the marketplace as well as economic efficiency. Finally, according to defenders of EAW, the principle recognizes equal rights of employees, because any employee, like any employer, is free and may choose or change his or her job at any time. And our Federal court system provides an arena of legal appeal for any employee who feels she has been mistreated. EAW, then, reflects our traditional democratic values of freedom and redress in the courts.

Given this line of reasoning, it would appear that attacking EAW is paramount to an attack on the rights and benefits of a free enterprise system. However, I shall argue that EAW does not respect the freedoms of everyone equally, that economic efficiency is not dependent on EAW, and that fair and consistent management practices require its abolishment.

The first objection to the principle of EAW is that it appears to value economic efficiency more than it values persons. In fact, it values arbitrariness rather than consistency. In allowing managers to fire employees "at will" in the name of efficiency, survival, or other economic goals without having to justify that dismissal, EAW appears to defend itself on the grounds that these goals are more important than the future of some employees. What most managers whant is a well-run organization. Employees who do not work well or in some way impede that functioning hurt the organization. So a good manager sees the need to fire, transfer, or demote those employees. The manager, then, focuses on the contribution (or lack thereof) of the employee to the unit or the business, and it is her responsibility as manager to do so. It is not that managers want to harm employees; it is that they want to achieve corporate economic aims, and these aims take precedence in management decisions.

The difficulty is, however, that in focussing on corporate goals, sometimes a manager treats employees unfairly. One kind of unfair treatment is to dismiss someone without any grievance or appeal procedure. Both Palmateer and Patton met with that fate. When a manager denies an employee due process in the workplace that manager is presuming that he or she has a right to decide what should be done even when that action ignores important rights of other persons. This presumption is questionable. When an employer arbitrarily fires an employee, the employer is not merely rejecting the contributions of an employee; the employer is rejecting that person as well. In treating employees "at will" this treatment is analogous to regarding the employee as if he or she was at the disposal of the employer. Now, an employee's contribution belongs to the employer (if the latter has paid a fair wage). But an employee does not. Because "at will" demotion or dismissal does not allow employees to defend themselves, an employee is assumed guilty without an opportunity to appeal, and thus is denied a very basic right.

Now, most managers have reasons, good reasons, for demoting or dismissing an employee. Economic efficiency, survival, loss of revenue, or poor workmanship are all good reasons. The problem with the principle of EAW is that it permits arbitrary decision-making in employment. So it allows managers to make employment decisions without having to justify them even when they have good reasons. Such decisions appear to be arbitrary, harmful, or unfair even when they are not. EAW, then, serves as a justification for arbitrariness, injustices, and even inconsistencies in management decisions, three qualities antithetical to good management practice. It permitted the "at will" firing of Palmateer and Patton where the *prima facie* public evidence appears to show that they were unjustly dismissed. That may be true, but had the employer in each instance been required to justify those dismissals, other reasons, good reasons, might have been presented for those actions. The "at will" dismissal of Palmateer and Patton presented their employers in an unfavorable light. As a result Palmateer was reinstated, although he might not have been, and will not be, an ideal employee. It might be to an *employer's* as well as an employee's disadvantage not to have a grievance procedure in place in some of these instances.

Secondly, while it is contended that EAW supports equally the freedoms of employees and employers, this is not true. Defenders of EAW claim that EAW balances employee and employer rights because, just as a manager has the right to control her unit or division, so too, an employee has the right to accept or refuse a job, and he also has the absolute freedom to quit "at will." According to this argument, due process creates an imbalance of rights, because it restricts the freedom of an employer or manager without restricting the choices of employees.

What this defense of EAW fails to notice is that when one is demoted or fired the reduction or loss of the job is only part of an employee's disadvantage. In these circumstances it is commonly taken for granted that one deserved that treatment, whether or not this is the case. Without a hearing or an objective appraisal no employee can appeal when he is mistreated, nor has the employee any way to demonstrate that she was fired arbitrarily without good reason. Fired or demoted employees have more difficulty getting new jobs or getting promoted than those who are not fired or demoted, even when employee dismissal was unjustified. So those who are dismissed unfairly are treated equally with those who should have been fired. The absence of due process denies employees the right to equal opportunity since those who do not deserve to be fired are treated equally with those who do. This of course is too simple. Market factors play a role too, for in a full-employment economy even fired persons do not have difficulty in finding new employment. My argument is that given two equally qualified persons, one of whom was dismissed or demoted, the person who was not demoted or dismissed is more likely to be hired or promoted, even if the other person was dismissed or demoted unfairly. While it is true that those who feel they are dismissed unfairly can take their grievances to the courts, most employees have neither the resources nor the time to do so, and the outcome is not always promising, as Patton found out. Moreover, whistle blowers like Palmateer who are not reinstated are often considered poor risks and are seldom hired elsewhere. Again, management is at an advantage because they are more likely to find financial resources to support a legal battle than an individual employee, and because blackballing an employer or an industry is seldom an effective employee weapon.

Moreover, while a dismissed employee is placed at an unfair advantage vis-a-vis other workers, a manager's freedom to hire and promote is not equally disadvantaged when an employee quits. So an employee's freedom to change jobs is affected adversely when she is arbitrarily fired, while the manager's freedom to hire someone else when an employee quits is not. This phenomenon is somewhat affected by market conditions. A uniquely qualified employee is very hard to replace, but the manager's *freedom* to hire someone else is not affected, while an arbitrarily dismissed employee's freedom to find another job is.

Third, although EAW is defended on grounds of economic efficiency, often good employees are lost because of arbitrary dismissals. Lee Iacocca and Reggie Jackson are only two such examples. Fourth, the institution of objective grievance procedures uniformly throughout a corporation both expands managers' responsibilities and improves their overall performance as managers. The management ideal of consistent, reasoned, and well-documented decision-making is extended to employment practices so that the same *kinds* of judgments are made about employees as are made about other corporate activities. This is an extension of management roles and responsibilities, an extension that is both humane and consistent with good management practice.

Finally, even the most fair-minded managers are sometimes afraid of due process, grievance procedures, or arbitration, because of the likelihood of its abuse. The abuses may be of two sorts. Some managers equate arbitration with mandatory employee retention. But due process does not require that employers never dismiss anyone. Due process simply requires that any employee have a hearing and an objective evaluation before being dismissed or demoted. Secondly, some employers fear that making public reasons for dismissals may be used against that employer in libel suits brought by disgruntled employees. But careful documentation of the rationale for demotion or dismissal and carefully constructed procedures fair to both sides allow the dismissal of problematic employees while protecting managers from retaliation in the courts.

The principle of EAW, then, is an inconsistent doctrine because it violates rights and creates disadvantages for one set of persons, employees, while granting prerogatives on the basis of arbitrary decision-making to managers. Due process in the workplace helps to alleviate inconsistencies in employment practices by adjudicating unfair disadvantages created because of arbitrary employment decision-making by those in the position to control employment. Due process reduces injustices in the workplace by extending good management procedures to include employment practices. Therefore its importance for employees and employers cannot be exaggerated.[5]

NOTES

1. *Palmateer v. International Harvester Corporation*, 85 Ill. App. 3rd 50 (1981). See Patricia H. Werhane, "A Theory of Employee Rights," in *Ethical Issues in Business*, second edition, ed. T. Donaldson and P. Werhane (Englewood Cliffs, N.J.: Prentice-Hall, Inc, 1983), p. 315.
2. *Patton v. J. C. Penney*, 105 Ore. S.Ct. 532302 (1986).
3. Mary Ann Glendon and Edward R. Lev, "Changes in the Bonding of the Employment Relationship: An Essay on the New Property," *Boston College Law Review* XX (1979), pp. 457–84.
4. *Marsh v. State of Alabama*, 66 S. Ct. 276 (1946).
5. This paper profited a great deal from comments by Stephen C. Taylor of Delaware State College. Its errors are my own.

The Case for the Polygraph in Employment Screening

Gordon H. Barland

Many arguments have been made against the use of the polygraph to screen job applicants. These have included claims that it is coercive, that it invades privacy, that it is un-American, and that it is wrong as often as it is right. Fortunately, these claims simply are not true when the polygraph is intelligently administered by experienced examiners. If it were but half as bad as its critics claim, it would have died out decades ago. Instead, the use of the polygraph in pre-employment screening is burgeoning. Business people have a reputation for being pragmatic and cost-conscious. In my home state of Utah, the number of polygraph exams given annually increased 40 percent in the five years from 1979 through 1983. Only 10 percent of all polygraph examinations conducted in 1983 were on criminal suspects; an astonishing 90 percent were done for employers, and nearly half of those were to screen job applicants. Perhaps the main reason why the use of the polygraph is increasing so rapidly is that, in my experience, an employer who starts using the polygraph to screen applicants almost never stops. That speaks eloquently for its usefulness to the business community.

There are many reasons why more and more employers are using the polygraph to screen applicants. Traditional methods such as checking with former employers never were fully adequate because applicants often omitted jobs from which they were fired. Such methods are becoming even less effective, for the rise in lawsuits makes employers increasingly reluctant to release derogatory information. The polygraph, on the other hand, provides a quick source of highly pertinent and accurate information about the applicant's whole employment history. The polygraphic interview is surprisingly inexpensive in view of the quantity and quality of information it produces, yet it is eminently fair, for the applicant controls the release of information and is able to provide extenuating and mitigating information of which the former employer may not have been aware.

Although many critics have said that the use of the polygraph with applicants is coercive, none has ever produced any evidence to support that. They also claim that the anger that applicants feel about being coerced into taking the test causes them to look guilty. No critic has ever produced any evidence to support that claim either. However, more than half a dozen surveys of applicants who have undergone polygraph screening have showed that the applicants understand the need for the polygraph, did not feel coerced into taking it, and did not feel that their privacy was invaded. During the six years I operated a polygraph screening service for employers, we screened thousands of job applicants. Although I was always alert for errors, I *never* found a single error attributable to anger or resentment over taking the test. The very few applicants who claimed to be angry about being asked to take the test reacted deceptively on the test, but almost all of them also admitted that they had lied. The claim that questions about the use of drugs on the job invade one's privacy are usually made by those who are guilty of having done so. But society must always balance the individual's right to privacy against the rights of the employer to hire the best, most honest, and most productive employees that are available.

ACCURACY AND UTILITY OF THE POLYGRAPH

Just how accurate is the polygraph in preemployment screening? Nobody knows for sure, yet nobody can deny that it is highly effective in providing the personnel director with a great deal of useful and accurate information about the applicants. While scientists are trying to determine the accuracy of chart interpretation, businesses that use the polygraph know that a polygraph test consists of far more than just an interpretation of the charts. The skilled examiner spends considerable time interviewing the job applicant, asking the same work-related questions that every competent personnel director must ask. Most applicants are a great deal more frank and detailed in their answers to the examiner than in their earlier interview with the personnel director because they know that the completeness and accuracy of their answers are about to be tested. The information they reveal is quite accurate, for no one knows the applicant better than he does himself.

It is precisely this increase in frank and accurate information about the applicant that makes the polygraph so cost-effective. For example, I once examined an accountant applying for the position of bookkeeper with a small business. Following deceptive reactions on the test regarding theft of money from previous employers, the bookkeeper admitted that he had embezzled some money—he refused to say just how much—from his last employer. The embezzlement had been discovered, and to avoid prosecution he had agreed to make restitution in the amount of $25,000. When I reported this information immediately following the exam, the personnel director was astonished. The last thing he had done before scheduling the polygraph exam was to call the previous employer, who had given the applicant an unqualified endorsement!

Unfortunately, this type of situation is all too common, for the threat of being sued has a way of making employers reluctant to say anything bad about a former employee. In this case a second factor may have been involved: The former employer was motivated to foist the ex-bookkeeper off on the new employer, for how else could he pay off what he had embezzled? It is likely that the savings resulting from that one test paid for several years' worth of polygraph tests.

Although the polygraph's critics concede that widespread dishonesty by workers makes the polygraph useful, the polygraphic interview does far more than expose the applicant's history of theft. Most polygraphists also cover which jobs were deliberately omitted from the application and why; any health problems that could interfere with work; how often the applicant is late for work and how many days of work were missed last year for various reasons, including truancy; and the use of drugs on the job or in such a way as to endanger fellow workers.

Perhaps more than any other screening method, information obtained from polygraph screening allows management to make an intelligent hiring decision. Another example illustrates this rather nicely. I once tested an experienced trucker who was applying for a position as a long-haul driver. He had told the personnel manager that he had quit his job as a driver in another state in order to be closer to his family here. During the polygraph test, the driver told me that he had a drinking problem. He had caused a fatal accident when driving under the influence of alcohol on his last job which, for obvious reasons, he had not listed on his application. He had fled that state in hopes of avoiding a lawsuit filed by a survivor of the accident. Surprisingly, the new company hired him despite his alcohol problem — not as a driver, but as a worker on the loading dock! The results of this one test probably saved the hiring company a great deal of money and may even have saved people's lives.

Indeed, a company may be found legally negligent if it does not adequately screen job applicants. In a 1984 case in Texas, the maintenance man at an apartment complex used his passkey to enter a woman's apartment, where he raped her. When the investigation showed that the man had a prior criminal record for rape, the victim sued the management company for failing to investigate the maintenance man's background, *failing to have him take a lie detector test*, and failing to verify his employment application. She was awarded $325,000 in cash and lifetime annual payments ranging from $12,000 to $67,398, guaranteed for 20 years. In addition, she will receive periodic lump sum payments totaling $450,000 [*Allison v. Herman Management & Investment Co.*, Texas, Tarrant County District Court, No. 342-75424, 82, August 1, 1984].

WHEN TO USE PRE-EMPLOYMENT SERVICE

Not all states permit the employer to screen applicants on the polygraph. Alaska, Connecticut, Massachusetts, Michigan, Minnesota, New Jersey, Oregon, Vermont, and West Virginia prohibit an employer from even requesting an applicant to take a polygraph test. An additional 11 states prohibit an employer from *requiring* a polygraph test as a condition of employment, although it is well within an employer's rights to ask an applicant to take a polygraph test. Those states are California, Hawaii, Idaho, Maryland, Montana, Nebraska, Pennsylvania, Rhode Island, Virginia, Washington, and Wisconsin. No other states restrict the employer's use of the polygraph to screen applicants.

A case can certainly be made that everybody should be screened on the polygraph prior to being hired. First, management has a responsibility to its stockholders to take all reasonable and prudent steps to protect the company's property and assets. Second, no one would be able to claim that the company is discriminating against any particular employee group if everyone must be screened. However, many companies only screen employees who handle money or merchandise, including janitors and others who have opportunity to steal.

Either way, the exams should be administered *prior* to hiring the applicant. All too often an employer is surprised by the amount of derogatory information revealed by the polygraph test of a promising applicant; if the individual has already been hired before being given the polygraph test, the company's position is unnecessarily complicated.

Most polygraph services are able to examine an applicant within 24 hours of the time an appointment is requested, and the company is notified of the results by telephone immediately upon completion of the exam. Although some polygraph services do make a recommendation about hiring an applicant, that decision must be made by the personnel director after being provided with a summary of all significant information from the exam.

CONCLUSION

Most employers who have used the polygraph for pre-employment screening have found it to be an extremely useful, cost-effective tool for assessing the backgrounds of job applicants. Although the accuracy of the polygraph in screening is not fully known, the skilled examiner is able to provide the user with a great deal of accurate and relevant information about the applicant which, in many cases, has not been revealed previously. When properly used, the polygraph does not invade the applicant's privacy or create any morale problems for the company. The key to the effective use of the polygraph is the skill of the examiner who conducts the test.

The Case Against the Polygraph in Employment Screening

DAVID T. LYKKEN

The private practice of polygraphy has become a big business in the United States. As many as 10,000 examiners are now practicing, most of them trained in one of the dozens of polygraph schools that have sprung up about the country—schools where the curriculum lasts from six to eight weeks. (To become a licensed *barber* in my state requires attendance at barber

David T. Lykken, "The Case Against the Polygraph in Employment Screening," reprinted from the September 1985 issue of *Personnel Administrator*, copyright 1985, The American Society for Personnel Administration, 606 North Washington Street, Alexandria, Virginia 22314, $40 per year.

college for at least 12 months.) Businesses use the polygraph for pre-employment screening, for periodic testing of current employees, and for in-house
investigations of actual theft or sabotage.

The latter application is perhaps the most offensive. Suspected employees are required to submit to a trial-by-polygraph, a kind of kangaroo
court in which the polygrapher sits as judge and jury. These tests are alleged
to be "voluntary"; indeed, every examinee must sign a waiver of rights
attesting to willingness to submit before the test is administered. All this
really means is that the examinee was not tested under actual physical
restraint—that when the boss asked him to "prove his innocence" on the lie
detector, he did not feel able to refuse.

Consider a letter from a minister in Texas who explains that he supported himself and his church by working as bookkeeper for a small firm in
Dallas; he had been with them more than seven years. Some months ago the
boss's wife stopped by the office with a $5,000 bank deposit in her purse;
when she got to the bank the money was missing. Could an employee have
rifled her purse? All 13 employees were required to take polygraph tests.
Reverend Russell was identified as the thief and he was fired. "I am completely devastated about this. I have a deep feeling about right and wrong
and would never take anything from anyone, even if I was starving. I don't
know how to clear my name. . . ."

A second example: A Piggly Wiggly store in Lake City, South Carolina,
had been reporting losses; the head office hired Truth Associates (!), a local
polygraph firm, to test all 52 employees. Mack Coker, the assistant manager,
was the scapegoat in this case and, within a few days, his children were
being taunted at school that their daddy was a thief. Coker, disgraced in his
community and unemployable, consulted an attorney who brought suit for
defamation. In addition to a substantial cash settlement, Piggly Wiggly published an apology in the Lake City newspaper.

A growing number of victims of polygraph tests are resorting to the
courts. A Michigan jury brought in a verdict of $100,000 against Kresge
Corporation on behalf of a young woman who was fired on the advice of a
polygrapher; the Zayre Corporation settled a similar case in Florida for
$300,000; a Maryland jury awarded $5 million to some employees of a large
east coast drugstore chain. In addition to the stress and humiliation of the
test itself, defendants in these trials-by-polygraph can suffer not just the loss
of their jobs but often the loss of their reputations and perhaps their ability
to obtain future employment. That such sanctions are imposed with no
semblance of due process seems to anger American juries.

The type of polygraph test that is used most commonly is some type of
Control Question Test (CQT), the same technique that is employed in
criminal investigation. There have been three scientifically credible studies
of the accuracy of the CQT in real-life situations; they indicate that the test
is wrong about one-third of the time overall. Each of the three studies

examined the fates of those who were later proved innocent: 37 percent, 49 percent, and 55 percent of these truthful people, respectively, were mistakenly classified as "deceptive" on the basis of their polygraph results. It is now well established that the CQT is strongly biased against the innocent. If the waivers that employees are required to sign before submitting to the polygraph honestly revealed the perils of submitting to the test, we might expect many more refusals, fewer victims and, hence, fewer costly lawsuits.

PRE-EMPLOYMENT SCREENING

The type of polygraph test format used in preemployment screening differs substantially from the CQT. The screening test—I call it the Relevant Control Test (RCT)—is essentially a list of questions about possible misconduct that the employer considers to be job relevant. As the U.S. Congress's Office of Technology Assessment reported in 1983, there has been *no* scientifically acceptable study of the accuracy of the RCT. There is not even any indirect evidence—no properly controlled study to determine whether instituting a polygraph screening program reduces losses or produces a better work force.

The alarming growth of the polygraph industry in the absence of any evidence that their product works is a curious phenomenon. Perhaps employers feel that a technique that is good enough for President Reagan and the Defense Department is good enough for them.

But, then, the faith of the federal government in polygraphy is a curious phenomenon also. Embarrassed by recent spy scandals involving employees with high security clearances—most of whom had passed polygraph tests to get and keep their clearances—the government's response has been to call for *more* use of the polygraph. In 1982 information from a top-secret meeting of the Pentagon's Defense Resources Board was leaked to the *Washington Post.* Secretary Weinberger ordered all 36 persons present at the meeting—including the Service Secretaries and the Chairman of the Joint Chiefs—to submit to polygraph testing. One lower-level civil servant was identified as the culprit but, just before he was fired, his career in shambles, the *Post*'s reporter sent the Pentagon an affidavit stating that the man was not his source.

Why does our government not learn from these experiences? Perhaps some government polygrapher explained that even if they did get the wrong man in this instance and failed to detect the true culprit, only two errors out of 36 tries is still 94 percent accuracy! Or perhaps they agree with former President Nixon's remark on the Oval Office tape of 14 July 1971: "Listen, I don't know anything about polygraphs and I don't know how accurate they are but I know they'll scare the hell out of people!"

DAMAGING ADMISSIONS

Because it is frightening and stressful, polygraph testing frequently elicits damaging admissions from subjects gulled into thinking that they might survive the ordeal if they can only clear their consciences of all guilty secrets. "Think of it as a kind of mental cleansing" is the way one examiner puts it. Literature from the American Polygraph Association states that 75 percent of job applicants make damaging admissions during preemployment testing; some examiners claim that 90 percent of the adverse reports they make to employers are based not upon the actual test results, but on admissions from the applicant's own mouth.

I do not believe that 75 percent of all Americans are thieves in any useful sense of that term. I think most of these damaging admissions concern peccadillos that most readers of this article could also expect to recall when examined before the Divine Bar of Justice, or by some less-than-divine graduate of a six-week course in polygraph school. And what about those 25 percent who do *not* make damaging admissions? They are the interesting minority, the literally "abnormal" ones. This group will include those saintly persons who truly have nothing to confess and also, undoubtedly, most of the real villains—the habitual liars and thieves who expect to cheat and steal at every opportunity—and to whom it would never occur to volunteer an admission of any kind. It is not as if the polygraph or the clever examiner elicits a damaging admission against the will and resistance of the respondent. In most instances, one must assume, the admissions that emerge in a polygraph session reflect impulses of guilt and shame, the normal pangs of conscience, and the urge to be honest and straightforward. For many of those who receive adverse reports, one might argue that their damaging admissions should have been counted *in* their favor rather than *against* them.

The basic question is this: Do employees who "fail" screening tests or offer damaging admissions prove to be less satisfactory or less trustworthy than those who do not? A study published in 1979 indicated that highly socialized persons, the kind of conscientious individuals whom most employers covet, tend to fail polygraph tests—even though they are truthful—while the undersocialized or psychopathic types of individual tend to pass them, even though they are lying. It is possible that the main effect of preemployment screening is to enable those with something to hide—and who also will not admit anything—to be considered seriously for a particular position.

I cannot prove this possibility, but then I am not selling a product. Those who *are* selling polygraphy cannot prove that their product works or even that it is not, as I suspect, counterproductive. The polygraph industry has shrugged off the burden of proof, relying instead on the peculiar mystique that the "lie detector" possesses in American folklore. Every culture has its myths. French employers commonly employ graphologists to assist them in selecting among job applicants — again, needless to say, in the absence of any credible proof that one can determine character from handwriting. But some myths are more objectionable than others. No one will brand someone as a liar or a thief because of the divination of a graphologist, but an American who tends to fail polygraph tests may be in real trouble.

One serious consequence of relying upon polygraph screening is the tendency to slight other, more expensive (but more reliable) security precautions. A recent example is the case of the California engineer who sold to the Soviets the plans of the "stealth" bomber, armloads of documents obtained from his lady friend who worked as secretary to an executive of a defense contractor. This woman had a high-security clearance that was obtained with the aid of a polygraph test, and could simply walk into the vault at night and carry off whatever she wanted. Without the false sense of security provided by the polygraph, it might have occurred to someone that secretaries did not need to have access to topsecret blueprints and specifications.

Polygraph tests are inherently stressful and intrusive. They antagonize employees and instill an atmosphere of suspicion and distrust. Invalid tests victimize untold numbers of honorable and truthful persons. Because of these and other reasons there should be concern about the use of polygraphic screening in the private sector even if evidence existed that the practice yielded savings to businesses that use it. But there is no such evidence. A personnel manager who subjects the company to the danger of expensive litigation by subjecting the employees to polygraph testing is spending the company's money on a wholly unproven (and inherently implausible) technology.

Affirmative Action

Case Study—Freida Mae Jones

MARTIN R. MOSER

Freida Mae Jones was born in her grandmother's Georgia farm house on June 1, 1949. She was the sixth of George and Ella Jones's ten children. Mr. and Mrs. Jones moved to New York City when Freida was four because they felt that the educational and career opportunities for their children would be better in the north. With the help of some cousins, they settled in a five-room apartment in the Bronx. George worked as a janitor at Lincoln Memorial Hospital and Ella was a part-time housekeeper in a nearby neighborhood. The Joneses were conservative and strict parents. They kept a close watch on their children's activities and demanded they be home by a certain hour. The Joneses believed that because they were black, the children would have to perform and behave better than their peers to be successful. They believed that their children's education would be the most important factor in their success as adults.

Freida entered Memorial High School, a racially integrated public school, in September 1963. Seventy percent of the student body was caucasian, twenty percent black, and ten percent Hispanic. About sixty percent of the graduates went on to college. Of this sixty percent, four percent were black and Hispanic and all were male. In the middle of her senior year Freida was academically the top student in her class. Following school regulations, Freida met with her guidance counselor to discuss her plans upon graduation. The counselor advised her to consider training in a "prac-

Prepared by Martin R. Moser, Ph.D., Assistant Professor of Management, The Graduate School of Management, Clark University, © 1980 by Martin R. Moser. Reprinted by permission.

tical" field such as housekeeping, cooking, or sewing, so that she could find a job.

George and Ella Jones were furious when Freida told them what the counselor had advised. Ella said, "Don't they see what they are doing? Freida is the top rated student in her whole class and they are telling her to become a manual worker. She showed that she has a fine mind and can work better than any of her classmates and still she is told not to become anybody in this world. It's really not any different in the north than back home in Georgia, except that they don't try to hide it down south. They want her to throw away her fine mind because she is a black girl and not a white boy. I'm going to go up to her school tomorrow and talk to the principal."

As a result of Mrs. Jones's visit to the principal, Freida was assisted in applying to ten fine eastern colleges, each of which offered her full scholarships. In September 1966 Freida entered Werbley College, an exclusive private women's college in Massachusetts. In 1970 Freida graduated summa cum laude in history. She decided to return to New York to teach grade school in the city's public school system. Freida was unable to obtain a full-time position, so she substituted. She also enrolled as a part-time student in Columbia University's Graduate School of Education. By 1975 she had [attained] her Master of Arts degree in Teaching (MAT) from Columbia, but could not find a permanent teaching job. New York City was laying off teachers and had instituted a hiring freeze due to the city's financial problems.

Feeling frustrated about her future as a teacher, Freida decided to get an MBA. She thought that there was more opportunity in business than in education. Churchill Business School, a small, prestigious school located in upstate New York, accepted Freida into its MBA program.

Freida completed her MBA in 1977 and accepted an entry-level position at the Industrialist World Bank of Boston in a fast-track management development program. The three-year program introduced her to all facets of bank operations, from telling to loan training and operations management. She was rotated to branch offices throughout New England. After completing the program she became an Assistant Manager for Branch Operations in the West Springfield Branch Office.

During her second year in the program, Freida had met James Walker, a black doctoral student in business administration at the University of Massachusetts. Her assignment to West Springfield precipitated their decision to get married. They originally anticipated that they would marry when James finished his doctorate and he could move to Boston. Instead, they decided he would pursue a job in the Springfield-Hartford area.

Freida was not only the first black but also the first woman to hold an executive position in the West Springfield Branch Office. Throughout the training program Freida felt somewhat uneasy, although she did very well.

There were six other blacks in the training program, five men and one woman and she found support and comfort in sharing her feelings with them. The group spent much of their free time together. Freida had hoped that she would be located near one or more of the group when she went out into the "real world." She felt that, although she was able to share her feelings about work with James, he did not have the full appreciation or understanding of her co-workers. However, the nearest group member was located one hundred miles away.

Freida's boss in Springfield was Stan Luboda, a fifty-five-year-old native New Englander. Freida felt that he treated her differently than he did the other trainees. He always tried to help her and took a lot of time (too much according to Freida) explaining things to her. Freida felt that he was treating her like a child and not an intelligent and able professional.

"I'm really getting frustrated and angry about what is happening at the bank," Freida said to her husband. "The people don't even realize it, but their prejudice comes through all the time. I feel as if I have to fight all the time just to start off even. Luboda gives Paul Cohen more responsibility than me, and we both started at the same time with the same amount of training. He's meeting customers alone and Luboda has accompanied me to each meeting I've had with a customer."

"I run into the same thing at school," said James. "The people don't even know that they are doing it. The other day I met with a professor on my dissertation committee. I've known and worked with him for over three years. He said he wanted to talk with me about a memo he had received. I asked him what it was about and he said that the records office wanted to know about my absence during the spring semester. He said that I had to sign some forms. He had me confused with Martin Jordan, another black student. Then he realized that it wasn't me, but Jordan, who he wanted. All I could think was that we all must look alike to him. I was angry. Maybe it was an honest mistake on his part, but whenever something like that happens, and it happens often, it gets me really angry."

"Something like that happened to me," said Freida. "I was using the copy machine, and Luboda's secretary was talking to someone in the hall. She had just gotten a haircut and was saying that her hair was now like Freida's—short and kinky, and that she would have to talk to me about how to take care of it. Luckily, my back was to her. I just bit my lip and went on with my business. Maybe she was trying to be cute, because I know she saw me standing there, but comments like that are not cute, they are racist."

"I don't know what to do," said James. "I try to keep things in perspective. Unless people interfere with my progress, I try to let it slide. I only have so much energy and it doesn't make any sense to waste it on people who don't matter. But that doesn't make it any easier to function in a racist environment. People don't realize that they are being racist. But a lot of times their expectations of black people or women, or whatever, are different because of skin color or gender. They expect you to be different, al-though if you were to ask them they would say that they don't. In fact, they would be highly offended if you implied that they were racist or sexist. They don't see themselves that way."

"Luboda is interfering with my progress," said Freida. "The kinds of experiences I have now will have a direct bearing on my career advancement. If decisions are being made because I am black or a woman, then they are racially and sexually biased. It's the same kind of attitude that the guidance counselor had when I was in high school, although not as blatant.

In September 1980 Freida decided to speak to Luboda about his treatment of her. She met with him in his office. "Mr. Luboda, there is something that I would like to discuss with you, and I feel a little uncomfortable because I'm not sure how you will respond to what I am going to say."

"I want you to feel that you can trust me," said Luboda. "I am anxious to help you in any way I can."

"I feel that you treat me differently than you treat the other people around here," said Freida. "I feel that you are over-cautious with me, and that you always try to help me, and never let me do anything on my own."

"I always try to help the new people around here," answered Luboda. "I'm not treating you any differently than I treat any other person. I think that you are being a little too sensitive. Do you think that I treat you differently because you are black?"

"The thought had occurred to me," said Freida. "Paul Cohen started here the same time that I did and he has much more responsibility than I do." Cohen had started at the bank at the same time as Freida and completed the management training program with Freida. Cohen was already handling accounts on his own, while Freida had not yet been given that responsibility.

"Freida, I know you are not a naive person," said Luboda. "You know the way the world works. There are some things which need to be taken more slowly than others. There are some assignments for which Cohen has been given more responsibility than you, and there are some assignments for which you are given more responsibility than Cohen. I try to put you where you do the most good."

"What you are saying is that Cohen gets the most visible, customer contact assignments and I get the behind-the-scenes running of the operations assignments," said Freida. "I'm not naive, but I'm also not stupid either. Your decisions are unfair. Cohen's career will advance more quickly than mine because of the assignments that he gets."

"Freida, that is not true," said Luboda. "Your career will not be hurt because you are getting different responsibilities than Cohen. You both need the different kinds of experiences you are getting. And you have to face the reality of the banking business. We are in a conservative business. When we speak to customers we need to gain their confidence, and we put the best people for the job in the positions to achieve that end. If we don't get their confidence they can go down the street to our competitors and do business with them. Their services are no different than ours. It's a competitive business in which you need every edge you have. It's going to take time for people to change some of their attitudes about whom they borrow money from or where they put their money. I can't change the way people feel. I am running a business, but believe me I won't make any decisions that are detrimental to you or to the bank. There is an important place for you here at the bank. Remember, you have to use your skills to the best advantage of the bank as well as your career."

"So what you are saying is that all things being equal, except my gender and my race, Cohen will get different treatment than me in terms of assignments," said Freida.

"You're making it sound like I am making a racist and sexist decision," said Luboda. "I'm making a business decision using the resources at my disposal and the market situation in which I must operate. You know exactly what I am talking about. What would you do if you were in my position?"

Is Turn About Fair Play?

BARRY R. GROSS

. . . The balance of argument weighs against reverse discrimination for four interrelated sets of reasons. First, the procedures designed to isolate the discriminated are flawed. Second, the practice has undesirable and dangerous consequences. Third, it fails to fit any of the models of compensation or reparations. Fourth, it falls unjustly upon both those it favors and those it disfavors. I conclude that if to eliminate discrimination against the members of one group we find ourselves discriminating against another, we have gone too far.

Sociologically, groups are simply not represented in various jobs and at various levels in percentages closely approximating their percentage of the population. When universities in general and medical schools in particular discriminated heavily against them, Jews were represented in the medical profession in far greater percentages than their percentage of the population. At the same time, they were represented in far lower percentages in

From *Reverse Discrimination*, ed. Barry R. Gross (Buffalo, N.Y.: Prometheus Books, 1977). Reprinted from the *Journal of Critical Analysis*, Vol. 5 (Jan.–Apr. 1975).

banking, finance, construction, and engineering than their percentage in the population, especially the population of New York City. A similar analysis by crudely drawn group traits—Jew, Roman Catholic, WASP, Irish, and so forth—of almost any trade, business or profession would yield similar results.

But the argument from population percentages may be meant not as an analysis of what is the case, but as an analysis of what ought to be the case. A proponent might put it this way: It is true that groups are not usually represented in the work force by their percentage in the population at large, but minority C has been systematically excluded from the good places. Therefore, in order to make sure that they get some of them, we should systematically include them in the good places, and a clear way of doing it is by their percentage in the population. Or we might conclude instead: therefore, in order to make up for past exclusion, they should be included in the good places as reparation, and an easy way to do it is by their percentage in the population.

If the definition of a minority discriminated against is ipso facto their representation in certain jobs in percentages less than their percentage in the general population, then one has to remark that the reasoning is circular. For we are trying to prove: (1) that minority C is discriminated against. We use a premise (3) that minority C is underrepresented in good jobs. Since (1) does not follow from (3) (mere underrepresentation not being even prima facie evidence of discrimination), it is necessary to insert (2) that their underrepresentation is due to discrimination. But this completes the circle.

A critic might reply that we know perfectly well what is meant. The groups discriminated against are blacks, Puerto Ricans, Mexican-Americans, American Indians, and women. He is correct, though his answer does not tell us *how to find out* who is discriminated against. This critic, for example, left out Jews and Orientals. If he should reply that Jews and Orientals do well enough, we point out that the question was not "Who fails to do well?" but rather, "Who is discriminated against?" This argument shows that the mechanisms for identifying the victims of discrimination and for remedying it are seriously deficient.

Even if we allow that the percentage of the group in the work force versus its percentage in the population is the criterion of discrimination, who is discriminated against will vary depending upon how we divide the groups. We may discover that Republicans are discriminated against by our literary or intellectual journals—*New York Review, Dissent, Commentary.* We may also discover that wealthy Boston residents are discriminated against by the Los Angeles Dodgers, that women are discriminated against by the Army, and that idiots (we hope) are discriminated against by universities.

What employment or profession a person chooses depends upon a number of variables—background, wealth, parents' employment, schooling, intelligence, drive, ambition, skill, and not least, luck. Moreover, the analysis will differ depending upon what group identification or stratification you choose. None seems to have priority over the others. Every person can be typed according to many of these classifications. It seems, therefore, that the relevant analysis cannot even be made, much less justified.

In addition, some proponents of the population-percentage argument seem to hold: (4) From the contingent fact that members of the group C were discriminated against, it follows necessarily that they are underrepresented in the good positions. They then go on to assert (5) if members of group C were not discriminated against they would not be underrepresented, or (6) if they are underrepresented, then they are discriminated against.

But clearly (4) is itself a contingent, not a necessary truth. Clearly also neither (5) nor (6) follows from it, (5) being the fallacy of denying the antecedent and (6) the fallacy of affirming the consequent. Lastly, neither (5) nor (6) is necessarily true. The members of a group might simply lack interest in certain jobs (for example, Italians in the public-school system are in short supply). Could one argue that, even though neither (4), (5), nor (6) is *necessarily* true, the mere fact of underrepresentation in certain occupations does provide evidence of discrimination? The answer is no—no more than the fact of "overrepresentation" in certain occupations is evidence of favoritism.

At most, underrepresentation can be used to support the contention of discrimination when there is *other* evidence as well.

FAIR PLAY: OUGHT WE TO DISCRIMINATE IN REVERSE?

There are at least three difficulties with reverse discrimination: first, it is inconsistent; second, it licenses discrimination; third, it is unfair.

If we believe the principle that equal opportunity is a right of everyone, then if members of group C are excluded from enjoying certain opportunities merely because they are members of group C, their right is being abrogated. They are entitled to this right, but so is everybody else, even those persons who presently deny it to them. If both are made to enjoy equal opportunity, then both are enjoying their right. To give either oppressors or oppressed more than equal opportunity is equally to deny the rights of one or the other in violation of the principle of equal opportunity.

Proponents of reverse discrimination seem to be caught on the horns of a dilemma: either discrimination is illegitimate or it is not. If it is illegitimate, then it ought not to be practiced against anyone. If it is not, then there exists no reason for *now* favoring blacks, Puerto Ricans, Chicanos, Indians, women, and so forth over whites.

Two strategies present themselves. Either we can analyze one disjunct with a view to showing that distinctions can be made which require compensation or reparations in the form of reverse discrimination to be made to wronged individuals or groups; or we can try to soften one of the disjuncts so as to make a case for exceptions in favor of the wronged. The first appeals both to our reason and our sense of justice. The second appeals to our emotions. I shall argue that neither strategy works.[1]

Now reverse discrimination can take several forms, but I think that what many of its proponents have in mind is a strong form of compensation — a form which requires us to discriminate against non-C members and favor C members even if less qualified. One may well wonder whether there is not a little retribution hidden in this form of compensation.

THE "SOFTENED" GENERAL PRINCIPLE

The argument for construing reverse discrimination as compensation or reparation has a great appeal which can be brought out by contrasting it with another approach. One might agree that as a general rule reverse discrimination is illegitimate but that it need not be seen as universally illegitimate. In particular, in the case where people have been so heavily discriminated against as to make it impossible for them now to gain a good life, there is no possibility of their having a fair chance, no possibility of their starting out on anything like equal terms, then and only then is it legitimate to discriminate in their favor and hence against anyone else.

Against this "softened" general principle I shall urge two sorts of objections which I call respectively "practical" and "pragmatic." Against the reparations type of argument, I shall urge first that there is some reason to think the conditions for exacting and accepting them are lacking, and second that, owing to the peculiar nature of their reparations to be exacted (reverse discrimination), the very exaction of them is unreasonable and unfair to both parties — exactors and exactees.

I mention briefly two sorts of practical objections to the "softened" general principle. First, it is simply the case that when discrimination is made in favor of someone regardless of his qualifications, there is the greatest possible danger that the person getting the position will not be competent to fill it. Second, when a person is placed in a position because of discrimination in his favor, he may come to feel himself inferior.[2] This may easily lead to the permanent conferral of inferior status on the group, an inferiority which is all the stronger because self-induced. Its psychological effects should not be underestimated.

The pragmatic objection to the "softened" general principle is much stronger. Discrimination in any form is invidious. Once licensed, its licenses rebound upon its perpetrators as well as others. Principles tend to be generalized without consideration of restrictions or the circumstances to which they were intended to apply. Students of the Nazi movement will have noticed that in licensing the discrimination, isolation, persecution, and "final solution" of the Jews, the Nazis (foreign and German) licensed their own. (Hitler's plans for extermination included political groups, for example, the Rohm faction of the SA, as well as other racial groups, for example, Slavs and Balts who fought on the German side.) It is necessary to be quite careful what principles one adopts. In view of the long and bloody history of discrimination, one ought to be very chary of sanctioning it.

COMPENSATIONS, REPARATIONS, AND RESTITUTION

Because it escapes most of these objections, the reparations argument becomes very attractive. What is more obvious than the principle that people ought to be compensated for monetary loss, pain and suffering inflicted by others acting either as agents of government or as individuals? From the negligence suit to reparations for war damage, the principle is comfortable, familiar, and best of all, legal. For victims of broken sidewalks, open wells, ignored stop signs, the conditions under which damages are awarded are quite clear. (1) There is specific injury, specific victim, specific time and place. (2) A specific individual or set of individuals must be found responsible either (a) by actually having done the injury, or (b) by failing to act in such a way (for example, repairing the sidewalk, sealing the well) so as to remove a particular potential source of injury on their property. (3) A reasonable assessment of the monetary value of the claim can be made. In such cases no moral blame is attached to the person forced to pay compensation.

But reparations are somewhat less clear. How much does Germany owe France for causing (losing?) World War I? Can we say that *Germany* caused the war? Germany did pay, at least in part, based upon rough calculations of the cost of the Allied armies, including pensions, the loss of allied GNP, indemnities for death and for the destruction of property. . . .

INAPPLICABILITY OF THESE PARADIGMS

Can reverse discrimination be construed to fit any of these paradigms? Can favoring blacks, Chicanos, Indians, women, and so forth over whites or males be seen as compensation, reparations, or restitution? The answer is no for two general reasons and for several which are specific to the various paradigms. The general reasons are, first, that responsibility for discrimination past and present and for its deleterious consequences is neither clearly assigned nor accepted. Some seem to think that the mere fact of its existence makes all whites (or males in the case of antifeminism) responsible.[3] But I do not know an analysis of responsibility which bears out this claim.

Second, there is a great difficulty, if not an impossibility, in assigning a monetary value to the damage done and compensation allegedly owed— that is to say, reverse discrimination.

If we turn to the negligence paradigm, all the conditions seem to fail. *Specific* injury is lacking, *specific* individual responsibility is lacking, and there is no way to assess the monetary value of the "loss." Indeed, in the case of reverse discrimination it is not monetary value which is claimed but preferential treatment. Under the large-scale reparations paradigm two conditions beyond responsibility are lacking. There are no governments or government-like agencies between which the transfer could take place, and there is no *modus agendi* for the transfer to take place.

Where the transfer is to be of preferential treatment, it is unclear how it is even to be begun. So we come to the third paradigm: individual restitution. This is much closer, for it deals with compensating individual victims of persecution. Again, however, it fails to provide a model, first, because reverse discrimination cannot be looked at in monetary terms, and second, even if it could, the restitution is designed to bring a person back to where he was before deprivation. In the case of the minorities in question, there can be no question of restoring them to former positions or property. Precisely, the point of the reparation is to pay them for what they, because of immoral social practices, never had in the first place. . . .

JUSTICE

Finally, if we ignore all that has been said and simply go ahead and discriminate in reverse, calling it reparation, it remains to ask whether it would be either reasonable or just? I think the answer is no. It is possible to hold that in some set of cases, other things being equal, compensation is required and yet to argue either that since other things are not equal compensation is not required, or that even if some compensation is required it ought not to take the form of reverse discrimination. Certainly, from the fact that some form of compensation or reparation must be made it does not follow that any *specific* form of compensation is in order. If X is discriminated against in awarding professorships because he is a member of C group, it scarcely follows that if compensation is in order it *must* take the form of his being discriminated in favor of for another professorship, at least not without adopting the principle of "an eye for an eye" (and only an *eye* for an eye?). Consider X being turned down for an apartment because he is a C member. Must compensation consist just in his being offered another ahead of anybody else? Even if he has one already? To go from the relatively innocuous principle that where *possible* we ought to compensate for damages, to sanction reverse discrimination as the proper or preferred form of redress, requires us to go beyond mere compensation to some principle very much like "let the punishment mirror the crime." But here the person "punished," the person from which the compensation is exacted, is often not the "criminal." Nor will it help to say that the person deprived of a job or advancement by reverse discrimination is not really being punished or deprived, since the job did not belong to him in the first place. Of course it didn't; nor did it belong to the successful candidate. What belonged to both is equal consideration, and that is what one of them is being deprived of.[4]

There is an element of injustice or unfairness in all reparations. The money derived from taxes paid by all citizens is used for reparations regardless of whether they were responsible for, did nothing about, opposed, or actually fought the policies or government in question. Yet we say that this is the only way it can be done, that the element of unfairness is not great, and that on the whole it is better that this relatively painless way of appropriating money from Jones, who is innocent, be used than that the victims of persecution or crime go uncompensated. But the consequences of reverse discrimination are quite different, especially when it is based upon group membership rather than individual desert. It is possible and is sometimes the case that though most C members are discriminated against, Y is a C member who had met with no discrimination at all. Under the principle that all C members should be discriminated in favor of, we would offer "compensation" to Y. But what are we compensating him *for?* By hypothesis he was no victim of discrimination. Do we compensate him for what happened to others? Do we pay Jones for what we buy from Smith? We seem to be compensating him for being a C member, but why? Do we secretly hold C members inferior? Some claim that society as a whole must bear the burden of reparation. But then reverse discrimination will hardly do the trick. It does not exact redress from the government, or even from all white (responsible?) citizens equally, but falls solely against those who apply for admissions, or jobs *for which blacks or other minorities are applying at the same time.* By the same token, it does not compensate or "reparate" all minority persons equally but merely those applying for admission, jobs, promotions, and so forth. Those whose positions are secure would not be paid. A white person who fought for civil rights for blacks may be passed over for promotion or displaced, a victim of reverse discrimination, while a Ku Klux Klan man at the top of the job ladder pays nothing. This would be a laughably flawed system if it were not seriously advocated by responsible people, and partly implemented by the government. Surely, it violates the principles of both compensatory and distributive justice.

NOTES

1. For examples of these strategies, see the article by J. W. Nickel . . . herein.
2. *Contra* this objection see Irving Thalberg, "Justifications of Institutional Racism," *The Philosophical Forum*, Winter 1972.

3. See Thalberg. For an interesting catalogue of "irresponsible use of 'responsibility,' " see Robert Stover, "Responsibility for the Cold War—A Case Study in Historical Responsibility," *History and Theory*, 1972. For a clear-cut analysis that more than mere presence on the scene is required to show responsibility, see S. Levinson, "Responsibility for Crimes of War," *Philosophy and Public Affairs*, Spring 1973.
4. See Gertrude Ezorsky, "It's Mine," *Philosophy and Public Affairs*, Spring 1974.

A Defense of Programs
of Preferential Treatment

RICHARD WASSERSTROM

Many justifications of programs of preferential treatment depend upon the claim that in one respect or another such programs have good consequences or that they are effective means by which to bring about some desirable end, e.g., an integrated, equalitarian society. I mean by "programs of preferential treatment" to refer to programs such as those at issue in the *Bakke* case—programs which set aside a certain number of places (for example, in a law school) as to which members of minority groups (for example, persons who are non-white or female) who possess certain minimum qualifications (in terms of grades and test scores) may be preferred for admission to those places over some members of the majority group who possess higher qualifications (in terms of grades and test scores).

Many criticisms of programs of preferential treatment claim that such programs, even if effective, are unjustifiable because they are in some important sense unfair or unjust. In this paper I present a limited defense of such programs by showing that two of the chief arguments offered for the unfairness or injustice of these programs do not work in the way or to the degree supposed by critics of these programs.

The first argument is this. Opponents of preferential treatment programs sometimes assert that proponents of these programs are guilty of intellectual inconsistency, if not racism or sexism. For, as is now readily acknowledged, at times past employers, universities, and many other social institutions did have racial or sexual quotas (when they did not practice overt racial or sexual exclusion), and many of those who were most concerned to bring about the eradication of those racial quotas are now untrou-

Richard Wasserstrom, "A Defense of Programs of Preferential Treatment," *Phi Kappa Phi Journal*, LVIII (Winter 1978).

bled by the new programs which reinstitute them. And this, it is claimed, is inconsistent. If it was wrong to take race or sex into account when blacks and women were the objects of racial and sexual policies and practices of exclusion, then it is wrong to take race or sex into account when the objects of the policies have their race or sex reversed. Simple considerations of intellectual consistency—of what it means to give racism or sexism as a reason for condemning these social policies and practices—require that what was a good reason then is still a good reason now.

The problem with this argument is that despite appearances, there is no inconsistency involved in holding both views. Even if contemporary preferential treatment programs which contain quotas are wrong, they are not wrong for the reasons that made quotas against blacks and women pernicious. The reason why is that the social realities do make an enormous difference. The fundamental evil of programs that discriminated against blacks or women was that these programs were a part of a larger social universe which systematically maintained a network of institutions that un-justifiably concentrated power, authority, and goods in the hands of white male individuals, and which systematically consigned blacks and women to subordinate positions in the society.

Whatever may be wrong with today's affirmative action programs and quota systems, it should be clear that the evil, if any, is just not the same. Racial and sexual minorities do not constitute the dominant social group. Nor is the conception of who is a fully developed member of the moral and social community one of an individual who is either female or black. Quotas that prefer women or blacks do not add to an already relatively overabundant supply of resources and opportunities at the disposal of members of these groups in the way in which the quotas of the past did maintain and argument the overabundant supply of resources and opportunities already available to white males.

The same point can be made in a somewhat different way. Sometimes people say that what was wrong, for example, with the system of racial discrimination in the South was that it took an irrelevant characteristic, namely race, and used it systematically to allocate social benefits and burdens of various sorts. The defect was the irrelevance of the characteristic used—race—for that meant that individuals ended up being treated in a manner that was arbitrary and capricious.

I do not think that was the central flaw at all. Take, for instance, the most hideous of the practices, human slavery. The primary thing that was wrong with the institution was not that the particular individuals who were assigned the place of slaves were assigned there arbitrarily because the assignment was made in virtue of an irrelevant characteristic, their race. Rather, it seems to me that the primary thing that was and is wrong with slavery is the practice itself—the fact of some individuals being able to own other individuals and all that goes with that practice. It would not matter by what criterion individuals were assigned; human slavery would still be wrong. And the same can be said for most if not all of the other discrete practices and institutions which comprised the system of racial discrimination even after human slavery was abolished. The practices were unjustifiable—they were oppressive—and they would have been so no matter how the assignment of victims had been made. What made it worse, still, was that the institutions and the supporting ideology all interlocked to create a system of human oppression whose effects on those living under it were as devastating as they were unjustifiable.

Again, if there is anything wrong with the programs of preferential treatment that have begun to flourish within the past ten years, it should be evident that the social realities in respect to the distribution of resources and opportunities make the difference. Apart from everything else, there is simply no way in which all of these programs taken together could plausibly be viewed as capable of relegating white males to the kind of genuinely oppressive status characteristically bestowed upon women and blacks by the dominant social institutions and ideology.

The second objection is that preferential treatment programs are wrong because they take race or sex into account rather than the only thing that does matter—that is, an individual's qualifications. What all such programs have in common and what makes them all objectionable, so this argument goes, is that they ignore the persons who are more qualified by bestowing a preference on those who are less qualified in virtue of their being either black or female.

There are, I think, a number of things wrong with this objection based on qualifications, and not the least of them is that we do not live in a society in which there is even the serious pretense of a qualification requirement for many jobs of substantial power and authority. Would anyone claim, for example, that the persons who comprise the judiciary are there because they are the most qualified lawyers or the most qualified persons to be judges? Would anyone claim that Henry Ford II is the head of the Ford Motor Company because he is the most qualified person for the job? Part of what is wrong with even talking about qualifications and merit is that the argument derives some of its force from the erroneous notion that we would have a meritocracy were it not for programs of preferential treatment. In fact, the higher one goes in terms of prestige, power and the like, the less qualifications seem ever to be decisive. It is only for certain jobs and certain places that qualifications are used to do more than establish the possession of certain minimum competencies.

But difficulties such as these to one side, there are theoretical difficulties as well which cut much more deeply into the argument about qualifications. To begin with, it is important to see that there is a serious inconsistency present if the person who favors "pure qualifications" does so on the ground that the most qualified ought to be selected because this promotes maximum efficiency. Let us suppose that the argument is that if we have the most qualified performing the relevant tasks we will get those tasks done in the most economical and efficient manner. There is nothing wrong in principle with arguments based upon the good consequences that will flow from maintaining a social practice in a certain way. But it is inconsistent for the opponent of preferential treatment to attach much weight to qualifications on this ground, because it was an analogous appeal to the good consequences that the opponent of preferential treatment thought was wrong in the first place. That is to say, if the chief thing to be said in favor of strict qualifications and preferring the most qualified is that it is the most efficient way of getting things done, then we are right back to an assessment of the different consequences that will flow from different programs, and we are far removed from the considerations of justice or fairness that were thought to weigh so heavily against these programs.

It is important to note, too, that qualifications—at least in the educational context—are often not connected at all closely with any plausible conception of social effectiveness. To admit the most qualified students to law school, for example—given the way qualifications are now determined—is primarily to admit those who have the greatest chance of scoring the highest grades at law school. This says little about efficiency except perhaps that these students are the easiest for the faulty to teach. However, since we know so little about what constitutes being a good, or even successful lawyer, and even less about the correlation between being a very good law student and being a very good lawyer, we can hardly claim very confidently that the legal system will operate most effectively if we admit only the most qualified students to law school.

To be at all decisive, the argument for qualifications must be that those who are the most qualified deserve to receive the benefits (the job, the place in law school, etc.) because they are the most qualified. The introduction of the concept of desert now makes it an objection as to justice or fairness of the sort promised by the original criticism of the programs. But now the problem is that there is no reason to think that there is any strong sense of "desert" in which it is correct that the most qualified deserve anything.

Let us consider more closely one case, that of preferential treatment in respect to admission to college or graduate school. There is a logical gap in the inference from the claim that a person is most qualified to perform a task, e.g., to be a good student, to the conclusion that he or she deserves to be admitted as a student. Of course, those who deserve to be admitted should be admitted. But why do the most qualified deserve anything? There is simply no necessary connection between academic merit (in the sense of being most qualified) and deserving to be a member of a student body. Suppose, for instance, that there is only one tennis court in the community. Is it clear that the two best tennis players ought to be the ones permitted to use it? Why not those who were there first? Or those who will enjoy playing the most? Or those who are the worst and, therefore, need the greatest opportunity to practice? Or those who have the chance to play least frequently?

We might, of course, have a rule that says that the best tennis players get to use the court before the others. Under such a rule the best players would deserve the court more than the poorer ones. But that is just to push the inquiry back on stage. Is there any reason to think that we ought to have a rule giving good tennis players such a preference? Indeed, the arguments that might be given for or against such a rule are many and varied. And few if any of the arguments that might support the rule would depend upon a connection between ability and desert.

Someone might reply, however, that the most able students deserve to be admitted to the university because all of their earlier schooling was a kind of competition, with university admission being the prize awarded to the winners. They deserve to be admitted because that is what the rule of the competition provides. In addition, it might be argued, it would be unfair now to exclude them in favor of others, given the reasonable expectations they developed about the way in which their industry and performance would be rewarded. Minority-admission programs, which inevitably prefer some who are less qualified over some who are more qualified, all possess this flaw.

There are several problems with this argument. The most substantial of them is that it is an empirically implausible picture of our social world. Most of what are regarded as the decisive characteristics for higher education have a great deal to do with things over which the individual has neither control nor responsibility: such things as home environment, socioeconomic class of parents, and, of course, the quality of the primary and secondary schools attended. Since individuals do not deserve having had any of these things vis-à-vis other individuals, they do not, for the most part, deserve their qualifications. And since they do not deserve their abilities they do not in any strong sense deserve to be admitted because of their abilities.

To be sure, if there has been a rule which connects say, performance at high school with admission to college, then there is a weak sense in which those who do well at high school deserve, for that reason alone, to be admitted to college. In addition, if persons have built up or relied upon their reasonable expectations concerning performance and admission, they have a claim to be admitted on this ground as well. But it is certainly not obvious that these claims of desert are any stronger or more compelling than the competing claims based upon the needs of or advantages to women or blacks from programs of preferential treatment. And as I have indicated, all rule-based claims of desert are very weak unless and until the rule which creates the claim is itself shown to be a justified one. Unless one has a strong preference for the status quo, and unless one can defend that preference, the practice within a system of allocating places in a certain way does not go very far at all in showing that that is the right or the just way to allocate those places in the future.

A proponent of programs of preferential treatment is not at all committed to the view that qualifications ought to be wholly irrelevant. He or she can agree that, given the existing structure of any institution, there is probably some minimal set of qualifications without which one cannot participate meaningfully within the institution. In addition, it can be granted that the qualifications of those involved will affect the way the institution works and the way it affects others in the society. And the consequences will vary depending upon the particular institution. But all of this only establishes that qualifications, in this sense, are relevant, not that they are decisive. This is wholly consistent with the claim that race or sex should today also be relevant when it comes to matters such as admission to college or law school. And that is all that any preferential treatment program—even one with the kind of quota used in the *Bakke* case—has ever tried to do.

I have not attempted to establish that programs of preferential treatment are right and desirable. There are empirical issues concerning the consequences of these programs that I have not discussed, and certainly not settled. Nor, for that matter, have I considered the argument that justice may permit, if not require, these programs as a way to provide compensation or reparation for injuries suffered in the recent as well as distant past, or as a way to remove benefits that are undeservedly enjoyed by those of the dominant group. What I have tried to do is show that it is wrong to think that programs of preferential treatment are objectionable in the centrally important sense in which many past and present discriminatory features of our society have been and are racist and sexist. The social realities as to power and opportunity do make a fundamental difference. It is also wrong to think that programs of preferential treatment are in any strong sense either unjust or unprincipled. The case for programs of preferential treatment could, therefore, plausibly rest both on the view that such programs are not unfair to white males (except in the weak, rule-dependent sense described above) and on the view that it is unfair to continue the present set of unjust—often racist and sexist—institutions that comprise the social reality. And the case for these programs could rest as well on the proposition that, given the distribution of power and influence in the United States today, such programs may reasonably be viewed as potentially valuable, effective means by which to achieve admirable and significant social ideals of equality and integration.

Classification by Race in Compensatory Programs

JAMES W. NICKEL

Suppose that a person who favors compensatory programs for American blacks because of America's history of slavery and discrimination is charged with inconsistency in the following way: "When blacks are denied benefits and given heavier burdens because of race you claim that race is irrelevant and hence claim that discimination is being practiced.[1] But when racial classifications are used to give preferential treatment to blacks you claim that race is a relevant consideration and deny that this is reverse discrimination." I want to consider two replies that can be made to this charge of inconsistency. The first reply holds that race, the characteristic which is held to be irrelevant when blacks are mistreated, is not the characteristic which is being held to be relevant when compensatory programs are defended. This reply denies that race is the basis for compensation; it claims that the real basis is the wrongs and losses blacks have suffered and the special needs that they have. Hence the characteristic which is held to be relevant in connection with compensatory programs is not race but a different characteristic, and there is no inconsistency. I will call this the "different-characteristics reply." The second reply allows that race is the characteristic about which differing relevance claims are made, but it denies that there is any inconsistency since claiming that race is irrelevant to whether someone should be mistreated is not incompatible with claiming that race is relevant to whether someone should be helped. Different issues are involved, and what is relevant to one issue can be irrelevant to another. I will call this the "different-issues reply."

This reply claims that there is no inconsistency in condemning racial discrimination while favoring compensatory programs for blacks because race, the characteristic which is held to be irrelevant when blacks are mistreated, is not the characteristic which is the basis for providing compensation to blacks. And since race is not the basis for compensatory programs, it need not be claimed that race is relevant in such contexts. The reason for providing compensatory programs for blacks is not their race but the fact that they have been victimized by slavery and discrimination. Not race, but the wrongs that were done, the losses that were suffered and the special needs

James W. Nickel, "Classification by Race in Compensatory Programs," from *Ethics*, Vol. 84 (1974), pp. 146–50. © 1974 by the University of Chicago. Reprinted by permission of the author and the publisher, The University of Chicago Press.

resulting from these provide the basis for special treatment now. On this view, race is not held to be relevant in defending compensatory programs, and hence there is no inconsistency with the original claim that race is irrelevant to how people should be treated.[2]

I think this reply is helpful in many cases, but in cases where explicit racial classifications are used by compensatory programs, the person who takes this approach must either claim that such explicit racial classifications are unjustifiable or suggest that they are an unavoidable administrative expediency. To suggest the latter is to suggest that this is a case where the administrative basis for a program (i.e., the characteristic which is used by administrators to decide who is to be served by the program) is different from the justifying basis (i.e., the characteristic which is the reason for having the program). It is not uncommon for these two to differ, although they should overlap substantially. If the justifying basis is a characteristic which occurs in more individuals than the characteristic which is the administrative basis, the latter is underinclusive. And if the justifying basis is a characteristic which occurs in fewer individuals than the characteristic which is the administrative basis, the latter is overinclusive. When resources are limited it is not uncommon to use an underinclusive administrative basis (e.g., when a poverty program only serves those with an income of less than $2,000 per year), even though this forces the program to ignore deserving cases. And difficulties in identifying those with the characteristic which is the justifying basis may cause the program, for reasons of efficiency, to serve more people than those who have the characteristic which is the justifying basis (e.g., when everyone in a certain county—the administrative basis—is inoculated in order to eliminate a disease—the justifying basis—which 60 percent of the people have but which is difficult to detect except in advanced stages).[3]

The advocate of the "different-characteristics reply" is committed to denying that race is the justifying basis for compensatory programs. But if the justifying basis for such programs is the losses and needs resulting from slavery and discrimination there will be a high correlation between being black and having suffered these losses and having these needs, and because of this the advocate of this reply can allow, without inconsistency, that race can serve as part of the administrative basis for such a program. Efficiency in administering large-scale programs often requires that detailed investigations of individual cases be kept to a minimum, and this means that many allocative decisions will have to be made on the basis of gross but easily discernible characteristics. This may result in a certain degree of unfairness, but it does help to decrease administrative costs so that more resources can be directed to those in need. Programs designed to help victims of discrimination are probably of this sort. Since it is usually quite difficult to determine the extent to which a person has suffered from racial discimination, it may be necessary simply to take the susceptibility to this discrimination (and perhaps some other gross criterion such as present income) as the basis for allocation. The use of such an administrative basis would result in a certain degree of both over and underinclusiveness, but in most cases this degree would probably not be an intolerable one from the perspective of fairness and efficiency.

This reply to the charge of inconsistency ignores possible differences in the characteristic which is the justifying basis; it presupposes, as does the person making the charge of inconsistency, that race is the justifying basis for compensatory programs. This reply claims that even if race is held to be irrelevant when blacks are being mistreated and relevant when blacks are being helped, there is no inconsistency in this since different issues are involved, and a characteristic which is relevant to one issue is often irrelevant to another. Relevance involves a relation between a characteristic and an issue, "C is relevant to I," and because of this "C_1 is relevant to I_1" is not inconsistent with "C_1 is not relevant to I_2."

But for this reply to work it must be shown that there really are two issues here, that the issue of deciding whether to allocate a penalty or loss is a different issue from deciding whether to allocate a benefit. This seems to be what Mark Green is suggesting in his article "Reparations for Blacks" when he says, "It is a verbal gimmick to elide past prejudice with preferential treatment. A subsidy is obviously dissimilar to a penalty, a beneficiary different from a victim, although both fit under the discrimination rubic."[4] Green seems to hold that the crucial difference is between subsidies and penalties, between helping and harming, and that it is the fact that racial classifications are used in compensatory programs to do good that makes them permissible. Green's view seems to be that it is one thing to use race as a basis for doing harm but quite another to use it as a basis for providing help.

But is there a sufficient difference between deciding to allocate a subsidy and deciding to allocate a penalty or loss to enable us to say that different issues are being decided and that race can be relevant to the former and irrelevant to the latter? The best reason I have been able to discover for thinking that there is a sufficient difference derives from the fact that the allocation of losses and penalties is a much more dangerous enterprise than the allocation of help and benefits. Deciding to impose a penalty or loss involves making a person worse off, whereas deciding not to provide a benefit usually involves merely leaving a person as he is. Since the former decision involves weightier consequences in most cases, we may be inclined to allow that it is a different decision than the latter and to allow that different considerations can be relevant to the two issues. This will be to claim that because of this difference there are and should be tighter moral and legal restriction on grounds that can serve as a basis for distributing penalties and losses, and that even though it is impermissible to use race as the basis for imposing losses and penalties, it is permissible to use race as the basis for distributing benefits.

One problem with putting so much weight on the distinction between distributing benefits and distributing penalties and losses is that in many cases a single distribution does both. If the item which is being allocated is a scarce and important benefit (like a good job), giving it to one person will often be tantamount to denying it to another person with an equally good claim to it, and denying it to this person will often be a considerable loss to him. Here the allocative decision concerns both providing a benefit and causing a loss, and hence one cannot merely say that race is a permissible basis for the decision because it is a decision about whom to help. If in a situation like this we decide to help Jones because he is black, this may be tantamount to causing Smith to suffer a loss because he is nonblack. Cases like this do exist,[5] and in these cases the "different-issues" approach provides no help.

Leaving this problem aside, there is another difficulty with the "different-issues reply." Even if it is allowed that what is relevant to the distribution of a benefit is sometimes different from what is relevant to the distribution of penalties and losses, it still remains to be shown that race is the justifying basis for programs which provide special help to blacks. If this cannot be shown then one must fall back on the claim that race is only the administrative basis for such programs.

So the question that we must ask is whether race or ancestry as such can serve as a justifying basis for a program which distributes benefits rather than many burdens. And I am inclined to think that it cannot. The mere fact that many people in this country are of African ancestry does not in itself provide any justification for a program of benefits to these people—no more than the mere fact that many people in California are of Oklahoman ancestry provides a justifying basis for a program of benefits to them. One's race or ancestry could serve as a justifying basis for special benefits only if having this race or ancestry was, in itself, a special merit which deserved reward or special lack which required compensation. But unless one is prepared to return to racist and aristocratic principles, one must deny that one's race or ancestry is in itself a matter of special merit or special lack. And hence one must deny that race or ancestry, in itself, can serve as a justifying basis for a program of special benefits.

It might be replied, however, that this overlooks important aspects of the context. In a context where the members of one race have over a long period been subject to discrimination and mistreatment it might be argued that race can be the justifying basis for a program of benefits. I think, however, that as soon as one begins to emphasize the wrongs done to blacks, the losses they have suffered, and the special needs they have now, it becomes clear that these things are the justifying basis for help to blacks and not race per se.

Suppose, however, that the person making this reply continues by asserting that in this period in America so many people think that being black is a special defect or lack that in effect it is a special defect or lack which requires compensation. But again one must insist that it is not race itself that justifies compensation; it is rather the effects of people's misconceptions about race that do this. Race or ancestry in itself constitutes no merit or defect; it is only in combination with people's misconceptions about it that it can aspire to this status. It is the adverse effects of these misconceptions, not race per se, that provide the justifying basis for special help programs. Race simply is not plausible as a justifying basis for a program, even for a program of benefits.

If I am right about this the "different-issues reply" turns out not to be helpful since it presupposes that race is the justifying basis for compensatory programs. Unless some other option emerges, the defender of compensatory programs will have to use the "different-characteristics reply" to the charge of inconsistency. This view allows that race can sometimes serve as the administrative basis for programs but makes its use contingent on considerations of fairness and efficiency. Whether race or ancestry can serve as a reasonable administrative basis (or a part of such a basis) for a program designed to provide special benefits to victims of slavery and discrimination will depend on whether among the possible alternatives it is the classification which is most workable and involves the combination of over- and underinclusiveness which is least unfair.

NOTES

1. There are two senses of "discrimination." One of these is morally neutral and applies to the simple discernment of differences. The other implies moral disapproval and applies to differentiations which involve bias, prejudice, and the use of irrelevant characteristics. My concern here is with "discrimination" in the latter sense.
2. This is the position that I took in my article "Discrimination and Morally Relevant Characteristics," *Analysis* 32 (1972): 113–14. Also see J. L. Cowan's reply, "Inverse Discrimination," *Analysis* 33 (1972): 10–12.
3. The distinction between over- and underinclusive classifications is derived from Tussman and tenBroek, "The Equal Protection of the Laws," *California Law Review* 37 (1949): 341.
4. "Reparations for Blacks," *Commonweal* 90 (June 1969): 359. In saying that both subsidies and penalties "fit under the discrimination rubric," Green seems to overlook the connection between discrimination and the use of an irrelevant characteristic. He seems, that is, to slip into using the morally neutral sense when it is the other sense of "discrimination" that is in question.
5. See, for example, Bob Kuttner, "White Males and Jews Need Not Apply," *The Village Voice*, August 31, 1972.

How Can Comparable Worth Be Achieved?

SEAN DEFORREST

Perhaps the biggest issue in the equal rights movement in the 1980s is the concept of comparable worth. This highly controversial and complex topic is having a major impact on women's groups, the justice system, business, local government, and even presidential candidates. Solving this issue is no simple matter and the decisions made in the near future will have a lasting effect on American society. Let's examine the history of comparable worth, the questions it raises, and the solutions being proposed. A good way to start is to define comparable worth: A concept requiring equal pay for employees whose work is of comparable value even if their jobs are totally different from each other. Thus the comparable worth doctrine goes far beyond the simple notion of equal pay for equal work. To understand how the comparable worth issue evolved, let's look at the history of the equal pay concept.

The concept of equal pay for equal work has its roots in the 1963 Equal Pay Act, which determined equal work on the basis of four factors: skill level, effort, responsibility, and working conditions. It also permitted four exceptions: seniority systems, merit systems, quality or quantity measures, and differentials based on any factor other than sex. It is this last exception that is most controversial and most used by businesses as defendants in equal pay lawsuits.

The passage of the Civil Rights Act of 1964 and its Title VII provisions brought much broader implications to discrimination on the basis of race, color, religion, sex, or national origin. To clarify the relationship between the Equal Pay Act and the Civil Rights Act, Congress passed the Bennett Amendment to Title VII of the Civil Rights Act, which allowed differences in wages as outlined by the four exceptions in the original Equal Pay Act.

The law was narrowly interpreted from that point on, confining sex discrimination claims to situations involving equal work alone. However, comparable worth advocates argued that the Bennett Amendment allowed discrimination claims based on dissimilar jobs of comparable worth. The comparable worth champions were not to get a major break until the highly controversial 1981 Supreme Court decision in *County of Washington vs. Gunther*. The judges ruled in favor of the plaintiffs—female jail matrons—who claimed they were being discriminated against because they received only 70 percent of the pay received by typical male jail guards. By ruling in favor of the plaintiffs, the Court set a precedent for claims of wage discrimination in cases that involve dissimilar jobs.

The door had been opened for comparable worth advocates—the question was how far they could go. The Court in the *Gunther* case had left some important questions unanswered. It had not endorsed the comparable worth concept, nor had it set the standard and order of proof. In addition, the Court left itself wide open for attack by critics when it based its majority opinion on the fact that the female matrons received only 70 percent of the male guards' wage. As one critic stated, "None of the justices seem to ask themselves why, in a situation where the jobs were acknowledged to be dissimilar, there should be any 'right' relationship at all between their compensation levels."

THE ISSUE OF DISCRIMINATION

The best place to begin examining the comparable worth question is the issue of whether women are currently being discriminated against in terms of pay. No one doubts that women earn, on average, only 60 percent of men's income. Few question the data indicating that this disparity has been increasing over the past 20 years. The debate begins with the question of what causes the disparity. Let's summarize the various aspects of the problem.

First, critics of comparable worth point out that women make up a much larger portion of the part-time labor force than men do and that this trend is increasing. As job sharing becomes more respected and encompasses higher-level jobs, women are likely to exercise this option even more. In the past ten years, part-time employment of women has grown twice as fast as full-time employment of women. Part-time jobs pay less than full-time employment, of course—hence the earnings discrepancy.

Second, critics argue that women typically leave the paid labor force in order to bear and raise children, and that during this time their "stock of human capital" deteriorates. Shorter careers mean less long-run productivity—which, in turn, means less value. Because we operate in an open market, this is reflected in lower earnings. June O'Neill of the Urban Institute adds credibility to this claim by stating that women, on average, spend only 50–60 percent of their available years in the job market. The balance of the years off the job are spent primarily on raising families.

A third argument holds that women earn less because of their occupational choices—that until they begin choosing nontraditional jobs, the wage disparity will continue. Indeed, some maintain that at least some of the responsibility here must be borne by women themselves—that they must set their sights on higher-level jobs and acquire the skills needed to land them. For women who move into nontraditional jobs, the earnings differential will disappear.

The fourth argument used by opponents of comparable worth is that wages are set by the law of supply and demand and that tampering with the way the market sets wages violates the theoretical underpinnings of our economic system. To alter this would imply that jobs have some intrinsic value separate from their market value.

Most advocates of comparable worth agree that there are nondiscriminatory factors that contribute to wage disparity, but they argue nevertheless that discrimination exists. A recent study found that after taking into account factors that tend to cause productivity differences between men and women (such as education and experience), the portion of the sex differential attributable to pure discrimination was estimated at between 29 and 43 percent of male earnings.

Many other studies substantiate this claim. One of the most impressive was conducted by Lee Sigelman, H. Brinton Milward, and Jon M. Shepard of the University of Kentucky. Their research design involved salaries for 424 full-time executive, administrative, and managerial personnel at a large university. Contending that women either had positional disadvantages compared with men or were paid less for equal work, they began their research by conducting an extensive job audit to determine the responsibilities for various positions. They used more than 13 criteria, including complexity of position, range of policy discretion, and assets controlled.

The researchers obtained three variables—gender, earnings, and degree of responsibility—for the 424 employees and performed a regression analysis of the data. The findings showed a significant relationship between gender and salary ($r = -.251$). This correlation coefficient indicates that the male employees earned more than the females earned. In this study the difference averaged $5,343 per year.

If the positional theory is correct, adjusting for the responsibility level should have eliminated the $5,343 difference. But even after controlling the responsibility factor, an earnings gap of $2,000, or 37 percent of the original $5,343 difference, was still unexplained. This is even more significant when one considers that two factors, gender and responsibility, explained the majority of the variance in salary levels ($R = .768$, $R^2 = .587$). The researchers' conclusion was that both positional disadvantage (in terms of job responsibility) and wage discrimination explained the wage disparities between men and women at the university.

Mary Anne Devanna, research coordinator of the Columbia Business School for Research in Career Development, recently conducted another significant study that traced the careers of 45 men and 45 women who earned M.B.A.'s at Columbia University. Although the women started at the same levels of pay as the men, they were earning significantly less after ten years. "Although the number of women in managerial positions has clearly been increasing," said Devanna, "their salaries [compared with those of] male managers have not improved."

What these and other studies point out is that discrimination is a two-edged sword. Earnings disparity is caused by both wage discrimination *and* job segregation, and the problems are closely related. To say, as some critics do, that *the* solution is for women to be more assertive in managing their careers is naïve at best. The unavoidable conclusion is that although factors such as part-time work and leaving the marketplace to raise children explain part of the earnings gap, a significant portion is still directly attributable to wage discrimination. The question now is how society plans to alleviate this problem.

SOLUTIONS TO WAGE DISPARITY

Before examining the possible solutions to the wage disparity problem, it is important to stress that pay equity, *not* the method used to achieve pay equity, is the main issue. Comparable worth is a method that is currently receiving a great deal of publicity, but it is just one of several. The goal is to achieve pay equity and a number of methods currently available may fit the bill.

Comparable Worth—The Pros

The concept of comparable worth is directly tied to current job evaluation systems—after all, job evaluation is designed to measure the relative value of jobs. Proponents of comparable worth argue that current systems are outdated and not relevant to today's jobs. What is needed, they say, is a widespread upgrading of current systems. The first step must be the reevaluation of job content, either through questionnaires or through evaluation by industrial engineers. Next, new job evaluation systems might assign "worth points" to such factors as knowledge and skills, mental demands, accountability, and working conditions (education and training are also important in establishing comparable worth). These "worth points" could then be totaled to determine the value of each person's job.

The program could be implemented through one of four sources: employers themselves, through voluntary action; the federal government; local government in tandem with business; or labor unions. The volunteer route would require a good deal of concerted action by businesses. As one example of a successful volunteer program, AT&T is considering a new job evaluation system and is currently working with its unions to reach an agreement on the system.

Some professionals consider the federal government, through EEOC guidelines, to be the best source because they lack faith in voluntary action and believe that labor unions are weak in handling traditional women's jobs. Others point to the past problems with EEOC guidelines—difficulty with enforcement, administrative waste—and suggest voluntary action by local governments and businesses in tandem as the best source of a comparable worth program. Few experts believe that labor unions could be the key to developing new job evaluation standards.

Experts cite many benefits of implementing job evaluation programs based on comparable worth. First, such policies promise a higher living standard and greater financial independence for women and their families. This is especially important in light of the growing number of single female parents, working widows, and wives whose spouses are unemployed. Second, by increasing salaries for previously under-valued jobs, local governments and businesses would attract higher quality people of both sexes. Finally, in implementing these policies businesses would achieve such long-term benefits as higher productivity and more deeply committed employees.

Comparable Worth—The Cons

One of the strongest arguments against comparable worth policy is the potential cost involved. Human nature being what it is, jobs will tend to be evaluated upward. "You have to equalize up," says Jeanne Atkins, a staff attorney for the Women's Equity Action League. "That is fairly well settled in employment-discrimination law." The estimates of the cost can be staggering. Hay Associates, the consulting firm, estimates that eliminating wage disparities could total more than $320 billion and increase inflation by 10 percent. For example, the *Gunther* decision alone may result in $400 million in damages. Another recent example was the Iowa Legislature's decision to pay out $30 million to equalize salaries. The costs on a national level would certainly be extensive.

A reduction in our competitiveness in foreign markets could be another hidden cost. Increasing wages would increase costs to businesses—which could ultimately mean lost sales and revenues. We are already feeling the pain of decreased productivity, and comparable worth policy could compound the problem.

A second major problem with comparable worth policy is its implementation. The EEOC recently commissioned the National Academy to report on whether a feasible and reasonable objective measurement of a job's worth can be done. The National Academy concluded its study by saying it would need more time. Today, there is no practical program for implementing comparable worth policy. There is no general agreement about how such factors as training, education, and responsibility would be measured and weighed. Even if such a program were in existence, who would be responsible for selecting and applying the job-worth criteria?

A third concern about comparable worth involves its social ramifications. Many express concern that a comparable-worth approach to wage determination would create severe legal entanglements; they believe that because of the subjective nature of the topic, the courts could become inundated with discrimination suits.

A fourth argument is that comparable worth will have an adverse effect on certain segments of society. These critics argue about the increasing competition between the sexes, changing American social structure, decreasing male self-esteem, and decreasing morale and productivity in the workplace. Critics in this category seem to want to use comparable worth as a scapegoat for all of society's problems.

Finally, the most philosophical argument holds that, taken in its extreme, comparable worth policy could disrupt the balance of supply and demand. Experts argue that the consequences of tampering with supply and demand through enforcement of a comparable worth policy would create an oversupply of some jobs and a shortage of others. If so, this could be a serious argument against comparable worth programs.

Part V

CONTEMPORARY BUSINESS ISSUES

Modern business is undergoing dramatic changes. Smaller companies find it harder to compete as large corporations take bigger and bigger pieces of the economic pie. Today the 1,000 largest U.S. firms account for 72 percent of the sales, 86 percent of the employees, and 85 percent of the profits of all U.S. industrial corporations. Fewer than 150 corporations hold the same share of manufacturing assets as the 1,000 largest corporations in 1941. But size is only one of the ways in which business has changed. Other changes include alterations in corporate organizational structure, expansion into multinational markets, consumer unrest over advertising, and fears about pollution and the loss of natural resources. While these changes have been taking place, business has become more aware of itself not only as an economic institution but as an active participant in the surrounding community.

From an ethical standpoint the transformation of business is significant. Changes in the goals and structure of the corporation have caused changes in the expectations of employees and consumers. For example, the shift away from one-man domination of the corporation has prompted greater participation by employees in corporate decisions. Professional managers, many of whom do not even own stock in the companies they manage, now control most of the largest and most influential corporations in the world. Technological changes, too, have played their role, generating a wider array of products and vastly more efficient means, such as television, for advertising them. With these advances have come moral doubts about the content of advertisements and the psychological impact of advertising on society.

Society has also changed its views about economic growth. It was once routinely assumed that economic growth should be pursued at every turn: greater production, higher incomes, and larger gross national products. Now critics complain that clean air, abundant wildlife, and adequate energy sources will vanish if we persist unreflectively in our search for greater economic prosperity. We seem to be driven to the point of asking whether an ever-increasing standard of living is possible without endangering the ecological systems that support technology and human life. And more and more people are also asking whether the unabated quest for economic prosperity doesn't erode human values such as freedom and creativity.

THE ENVIRONMENT

Attention has been drawn in recent years to the fact that we live on a planet which, despite its apparent abundance, possesses finite natural resources. Never-ending economic growth involves either a never-ending consumption of these resources or the discovery of substitutes. Is it wise then, to persist in our goal of technological and economic expansion when our stocks of natural resources are continually dwindling? Critics argue that we live on a spaceship—the earth—which carries limited supplies. Considering our rapidly expanding population and economic output, we may soon approach the limits of those supplies, and human needs may outstrip the technological know-how required to develop substitutes. To avoid this disaster such critics propose a "no-growth" economy in which we actively work to replace lost resources.

In sharp contrast with the "no-growth" school, Wilfred Beckerman, a noted Oxford economist, argues that economic growth is both necessary and valuable. It enhances human life rather than discouraging it, and the quality of human life, perhaps even the existence of human life, depends on maintaining both economic and technological growth. Only a fraction of the world's population has achieved a decent standard of living, and economic growth, according to Beckerman, remains indispensable for the millions of humans around the globe trapped in poverty. One cannot argue that growth is undesirable until the minimal necessities of life are available for everyone. Moreover, Beckerman points out, people have actively interfered with nature for centuries, and although there have been periodic panics over the exhaustion of natural resources, the resources have not been exhausted. Rather, people continue to find more resources and to invent satisfactory substitutes. The problems connected with our use of resources, Beckerman concludes, cannot be solved by turning to a policy of no growth. Instead, in some of his writings he recommends strict international government control of the ecological side effects of business.

In his article "The Scarcity Society," William Ophuls discusses the dilemma of economic growth from an ethical point of view. In contrast with

Beckerman, Ophuls claims that for human life to continue, a program of ecological and economic equilibrium must be instituted to produce an economy in which population, resources, and environment are in balance. The solution recommended by both Beckerman and no-growth proponents is to control and regulate the economy in order to prevent environmental abuses. But this measure leads immediately, Ophuls says, to the loss of important personal human liberties. Given that people operate in accordance with their own personal ends (Ophuls calls this the "tragedy of the commons"), how is humanity to protect both the environment and vital natural resources without generating stifling and oppressive systems of social control?

Ophuls's solution to the problem is an ethical one: improve the ethical nature of man; restore the "civic virtue of a corrupt people." People, acting as individuals, must restore human dignity by developing the moral resources of self-restraint and human respect. We must impose our own laws and controls upon ourselves — individually.

In "Ethics and Ecology," the philosopher William Blackstone counters the economic optimism of thinkers such as Beckerman by arguing that, whatever the future holds, we must recognize that people have a *right* to reasonably clean air and water. Rights, Blackstone asserts, flow from the capacities that make us uniquely human, and these capacities require a livable environment for their proper development.

ADVERTISING

Advertising is big business. It accounts for one fifth of the total selling costs of American industry, lagging behind both sales promotion and direct salesmanship in its total cost.[1] In 1982 U.S. ad agencies grossed $6.51 billion, and their customers paid $44.2 billion for space and time in the mass media. Increasingly, however, critics are raising the question: "Is society getting what it pays for?"

Until the latter part of the nineteenth century, many of the commonest articles of consumption, such as soap and clothing, were made at home. Products were in short supply, and religious leaders habitually preached against the vanity of materialism. But following 1875 most consumer industries were fully mechanized, an event which resulted in an explosion of items for daily use and led to an obvious task: someone had to persuade the public that all the new consumer products were worth having. A significant portion of that burden fell to the growing industry of advertising. Once complete, the transformation that advertising helped create ushered in a dramatic new age.

A standard criticism of advertising is that it deceives. At least two major theories of advertising can be appealed to in making this criticism, the first relying on a conception of advertising as "persuasion," the second as "information." If, as John Kenneth Galbraith argues in "The Dependence Effect," the principal function of advertising is to establish the consumer's desire for a product (and hence his willingness to pay), advertising may be equated with persuasion. Just as Tom Sawyer encouraged his friends to help him whitewash his famous fence, so modern advertisers encourage consumers to buy their toothpaste, chewing gum, and deodorants. In both cases, clever salesmanship makes an item more attractive than it would be otherwise; but in both cases there is no guarantee that the listeners are better off with their new desires than they were without them.

A second theory of advertising sees it not as persuasion, but as information. How, its defenders ask, can you persuade people without telling them something? Furthermore, since a market economy relies on information to help consumers maximize their welfare in the process of choice, advertising's service to society is to provide consumers with two essential kinds of information about products: their characteristics (including quality) and their price. Yet insofar as advertising is seen as information, one can easily doubt the information value of many television and magazine advertisements. Advertisements frequently rely on mere association; for example, an advertisement for whiskey reads: "Increase the value of your holdings. Old Charter Bourbon Whiskey—The Final Step Up." This, and many advertisements like it, seem to provide little or no hard information about price or quality. Furthermore, the source of an advertisement is said to be "tainted," since the persons responsible for generating it have a vested interest in persuading consumers; they have a vested interest, in short, in making profits, not in being objective.

Yet another view, sometimes called the competitive efficiency view, defends the social importance of advertising. Taking off where the information theory began, it affirms the information value of advertising while granting that advertisements frequently contain little specific information about price or quality and, what is more, often "puff" or exaggerate the worth of products. But puffery, notes the theory, is an accepted part of salesmanship, and it would be a mistake to view the public as a collection of gullible fools. No one really believes an advertisement that suggests drinking Old Charter Bourbon will increase one's stock-market holdings. Specific product information, furthermore, is only one kind of information important for market efficiency: another is information about the existence or availability of the product, and this kind of information advertising supplies in abundance. Competition in the marketplace is efficient only when consumers are able to compare rival products; and this is possible only if they know what products are available.

In his article "Advertising and Behavior Control," Robert Arrington defends the information value of advertising and denies that in most instances it controls behavior or threatens autonomy. Advertising does not so much *create* desires, he argues, as *redirect* them. Hence, if we are to accept this account, our desires for Grecian Formula 16, Mazda Rx-7s, and Pongo Peach lipstick depend ultimately upon our prior hopes for youth, power, adventure, or ravishing beauty, not upon desires that Madison Avenue creates.

Whatever one thinks about the information value of advertising, the issue of children's advertising poses special problems. How, if at all, should advertisers shift their approach in light of the fact that children lack the judgment and experience required to evaluate information? Also, are there limits to the amount of puffery or violence that should appear in children's advertising? These questions, along with the more standard ones about advertising, are raised in the case study "Toy Wars."

CORPORATE GOVERNANCE

In the case study "A. H. Robins: The Dalkon Shield," we read about a well-publicized incident involving corporate governance, or the lack of it. For years, A. H. Robins Company manufactured and sold an IUD known as the Dalkon Shield. But despite claims by the company that its product was the best on the market, thousands of suits were brought against A. H. Robins for illness and death caused, according to the suits, by the Dalkon Shield. In 1985, in response to the suits, A. H. Robins declared bankruptcy. What brings about problems like those at Robins? What motives distinguish, and what systems separate, good from bad management? In this last section of the book, we take up the pressing issues of corporate governance.

In a provocative article, "Who Rules the Corporation," corporate critics Ralph Nader, Joel Seligman, and Mark Green assert that the legal image of the corporation, in which the board of directors controls the corporation from the vantage point of final power, is a myth. Managers rule the corporation, not directors, and what is more, the chief executive officer chooses the board members, not vice versa. The problem is that upper management's privileged position insulates it from moral criticism and allows serious breaches of morality and legality. In effect, business executives are unaccountable, and the only solution is a restructuring of the system of corporate governance that reestablishes their accountability. Thus restructuring, it is argued, will involve, among other things, the placing of professional full-time directors — persons who represent more than the narrow interests of stockholders — on corporate boards.

In a far more optimistic appraisal of the current state of corporate governance, the respected business executive Irving Shapiro (formerly board chairman of E. I. du Pont de Nemours & Company) argues that the present system of corporate governance is sound and its methods morally defensible. Changes are needed, but they should be gradual, not sudden, and of a kind that extends the successful reforms of the past decades, for example, the placing of more "outside directors" on the board (outside directors are persons who are not employed by the corporation they direct). A fundamental mistake would be made by adopting the "Noah's Ark" approach to board composition, in which board members would represent the many interest groups affected by the corporation: employees, suppliers, local communities, and shareholders. The mistake would lie in creating a board that lacked the managerial expertise and cohesiveness necessary to govern corporate affairs effectively.

NOTE

1. Roger Draper, "The Truth About Advertising," *New York Review of Books*, XXX-III, no. 7 (1986), p. 14.

The Environment

Case Study—Three Mile Island

It began with a brief but terrible bump in the night and quickly grew into the worst commercial nuclear accident in U.S. history. At the Three Mile Island power plant near Harrisburg, Pennsylvania, a balky valve malfunctioned, setting off an intricate chain of mechanical and human failures. In the control room of the plant's Unit II, warning lights flashed and an electronic alarm rang. Craig Faust, 32, and Ed Frederick, 29, working the night shift, studied the alarms and meters as the plant veered toward a state of emergency. They kept their heads, pushed and pulled as many as 50 buttons and levers in fifteen seconds and the reactor shut down. "What we saw we understood and we controlled," Frederick said. But it wasn't enough.

Within minutes, there was a serious leak of radioactive steam—and several more in the days following—spreading over an area up to 20 miles from the plant. Many experts agreed that the radiation posed no immediate threat to health, but others warned of cancer, genetic damage and other long-term effects from the low-level emissions.

"Time bomb": Pennsylvania Governor Richard Thornburgh considered a mass evacuation of parts of four surrounding counties. Instead, he advised people to stay inside their homes, then urged pregnant women and preschool children to move beyond a 5-mile radius of the plant. In Middletown, Goldsboro, Harrisburg, and other surrounding towns, few panicked. But schools closed, families packed up, and gasoline stations did a brisk business as an estimated 50,000 to 60,000 people headed away, for the weekend at least. "I just get the feeling we're all sitting on a time bomb," said

Louise Hardison of Londonderry Township. "It's rotten—the whole thing is rotten."

The episode came precariously close to turning into Everyman's nuclear nightmare—an out-of-control reactor spewing radioactivity into the countryside. At the weekend, there was still a distant possibility that the chain of events could take a nightmarish turn. Unless engineers were able to cool the crippled reactor, said Joseph M. Hendrie, the chairman of the Nuclear Regulatory Commission, it might still be necessary to evacuate thousands of people living 10 to 20 miles downwind of the plant. "They are way out in an unknown land with a reactor whose instruments and controls were never designed to cope with this situation," said MIT professor Henry Kendall, an outspoken nuclear critic. "They are like children playing in the woods."

There was no danger that the plant would explode like a nuclear bomb, but there were other possibilities nearly as apocalyptic. The problem was to cool the reactor. But damage suffered by its radioactive core in the first moments of the accident interfered with the cooling process, and the high heat spread damage to up to half the 36,816 nuclear fuel rods. A gas bubble inside the reactor vessel also threatened to block the circulation of water around the rods. To make matters worse, highly flammable hydrogen gas was accumulating inside the huge containment structure that holds the reactor, posing the threat of a conventional explosion that could scatter dangerous radioactive gas and debris widely through the area.

The greatest risk of all was a catastrophic "meltdown" of the sort fictionalized in a . . . film called "The China Syndrome." In theory, the experts said, the core could melt its way through the thick steel walls of the reactor vessel, penetrate the floor of the containment structure, contaminate the soil or hit a water pocket and send up gushers of radioactive steam and contaminants. If that happened, there might be thousands of deaths later on. "There is some risk of meltdown," Dr. Roger Mattson of the NRC told members of a Senate subcommittee on nuclear regulation last week.

Officials of the Metropolitan Edison Co., operators of the plant, consistently down-played the seriousness of the situation, and their accounts often disagreed with those of staff members from the NRC who were rushed to the scene. Radioactive steam apparently vented automatically—and uncontrollably. Government officials were not alerted in advance, raising complaints that the monitoring by Met-Ed and government agencies was so haphazard that the cumulative radiation absorbed by people in the vicinity might never be known. Beyond that, the General Accounting Office reported that Pennsylvania—like most states with nuclear facilities—did not have a federally approved plan for dealing with such on-site emergencies. And the GAO said there was no single Federal Agency that could direct the mass evacuation that might be prompted by a major disaster.

"Decisions": Industry officials insisted that the accident, as bad as it was, showed that safety systems did indeed prevent any immediate injuries or deaths. "We didn't injure anybody, we didn't seriously contaminate anybody and we certainly didn't kill anybody," said John Herbein, a Met-Ed vice president. . . .

* * *

Under the circumstances, the public fallout from the accident was bound to have a lengthy half-life of its own. "Every dose of radiation is an overdose," said Nobel Prize–winning biochemist George Wald, professor emeritus at Harvard. Protestors duly went on the march from New England to southern California. . . . And in Washington, the NRC itself came under attack. "Three Mile Island has had a very short operating period but a very long and troubled history," said Richard Pollock, head of Critical Mass, a Ralph Naderite group. "The NRC let this plant go forward despite the red flags which were waving. They look—but they do not see."

Cash: In the beginning it looked like Three Mile Island would generate nothing more menacing than megawatts. Completed in 1974 on a forested little island in the Susquehanna River, it replaced a small farm and a few cabins used by fishermen. Most local residents welcomed it because Federal economizing had closed nearby Olmstead Air Force Base, punching a hole in the local economy. With their high pay and overtime, men hired at the new plant could earn between $25,000 and $35,000 a year. In sleepy Middletown, workers coming off their shift began to fill Mat's Wining Wench tavern with good company and clinking cash. When people asked the watering hole's owner whether the new plant made him nervous, he said: "What happens, happens."

There appeared to be nothing to be nervous about: the plant seemed a marvel of advanced technology. Unit I and Unit II each had a reactor with a core of 36,816 fuel rods sheathed in zirconium and containing pellets of uranium oxide. The reactor produced heat by nuclear fission. Giant pumps pushed water heated by the reactor to two towering steam generators. Within the generators, the heat from each reactor's pressurized water loop was "exchanged" through tiny tubes to a second independent water loop that produced steam. This steam drove turbines that turned generators that sent 880,000 kilowatts of electricity humming out over high-tension wires to the 346,000 residents of Berks, York and Lebanon counties.

"Incidents": The plant was fitted out with multiple fail-safe protective systems. The core of the reactor was sealed in a 41-foot-high vessel with walls of steel 8 7/16ths inches thick. This awesome tube stood within a containment dome 190 feet high and 140 feet across. The dome, with its massive walls of concrete 4 feet thick over a sheathing of carbonized steel,

would hold in the fiercest radiation. In an emergency in the reactor core, the industry's scientific experts predicted, several cooling systems could flood the core, in effect turning the containment into a nuclear hot-water bottle that could be drained slowly and safely if the plant suffered what nuclear engineers often call nuclear "incidents."

No one expected any trouble at Three Mile Island. But when Unit II plugged into the northeastern power grid for full commercial operations on December 30, 1978, it promptly developed a number of worrisome bugs. In mid-January, it had to be shut down for almost two weeks after two safety valves ruptured during a test of the turbine. On February 1 a throttle valve developed a leak. The next day, a heater pump blew a seal. On February 6 a pump on a feedwater line tripped off. All the difficulties were promptly repaired, though the reason the feedwater pump had stuttered remained something of a mystery.

Alarms: Similar trouble apparently returned to haunt the plant last week. Early Wednesday, at about 4 A.M., Unit II was generating at 97 percent capacity, with the third shift manning the controls and machinery. "Somebody was screwing around with some of the equipment in the feed-water system," said Edson Case, deputy director of nuclear-reactor regulation for the NRC. "Whatever he was doing resulted in tripping the feedwater pumps off the line." Ordinarily, when the feedwater pumps go off, the turbine shuts down and the reactor cuts back on power. This time the turbine performed normally but the reactor did not. Heat and pressure in the reactor's primary water loop began to rise above normal operating levels (582 degrees Fahrenheit and 2,155 pounds per square inch pressure)—and alarms in the control room bean to flash and beep.

When the pressure hit 2,350 psi, about 200 pounds above normal, the reactor automatically "scrammed"—its boron control rods dropped down into the core to "poison" and finally shut down the fission process. There was never any danger of a nuclear explosion. "A reactor is not like a bottled-up bomb," says Mark Mills of the Atomic Industrial Forum, an industry group. "It won't explode. It can't run away like a fire."

Officials at Three Mile Island denied that the malfunction could have melted the core enough to produce the China syndrome—so named because the fiercely hot molten core eats its way into the floor of the containment building and straight through the earth below. It may stop about 50 feet down, cool into a glassy blob and emit intense radiation in all directions—or hit the water table and throw back a deadly radioactive geyser.

Valve: It didn't happen last week, but the Three Mile Island syndrome was unsettling enough in itself. As utility and NRC officials pieced things together, the scrammed reactor kept producing residual heat from the decay of fission products in its core. Heat and pressure in the primary water loop then mounted until a relief valve in a pressurizer opened, allowing the excess water to flow safely into a quench tank. But, instead of shutting off again, the valve stuck open. Water surged through the stuck relief valve, filled the quench tank and flooded out onto the floor of the reactor containment building. Water pressure in the primary loop then fell dangerously low. The main cooling pumps were shut off. An emergency cooling system kicked in, injecting still more water into the loop. It, too, flooded through the valve and out of the quench tank.

"Now things get conjectural," Case said. He speculated that while the emergency core-cooling system was on, a technician may have watched the water pressure build up — then turned off the system manually, thinking the crisis had passed. When the system was turned off, the water pressure in the loop fell again. "Whether he was right is not clear; whether he should have turned it back on again later is not clear," Case said. "But in any event, it was turned off for a long enough period of time that the pressure went back down again. At that point — and we're guessing — the water level got low enough that the core became uncovered, at least momentarily."

A hot and uncovered core is the nuclear engineer's nightmare. The best guess last week was that the heat grew severe enough to burst the protective zirconium cladding of some of the fuel rods. Radioactive elements — xenon and krypton gases — could then have contaminated water in the primary loop. This "hot" hot water then flowed out the relief valve through the broken quench tank and into the containment area. In very short order, there were 6 feet of radioactive water on the containment floor, clouds of deadly steam billowing to the roof and a "shine" of gamma radiation passing directly through the walls.

Sump: Plant operators said that the containment system had functioned properly. "There is no way the water could escape through the walls," said Frederick, because the walls were secure. But escape it did — the only question was how. Ordinarily, safety systems shut off all pipes into the containment building when the emergency core-cooling system is on. NRC investigators speculated last week that when the emergency core-cooling system was turned off, a basement sump pump was activated, pumping thousands of gallons of radioactive water out of the containment building into tanks in an auxiliary building never meant to contain high-intensity radiation. Utility officials conceded that the pump had indeed gone into operation. At least one of the tanks overflowed onto the floor of the auxiliary building — and radioactivity shot through a vent stack. . . .

The results were disturbing. The monitors detected between 20 and 30 millirems of radiation per hour in the atmosphere over the island and 5 to 7 millirems (or about one-eighth of the dose in a chest X ray) in the air 2 to 3 miles away. Radioactivity traveled 20 miles on winds that shifted from southeast to northwest. Maggie Reilly, chief of the environmental radiation unit of Pennsylvania's DER, said the most radiation anyone in the plant's vicinity had received was 100 millirems at the time of the accident. That added up to half the annual exposure for an average U.S. citizen—in a single flash—but it was still one-tenth of the level the U.S. Environmental Protection Agency considers immediately dangerous. Later, it turned out that four plant employees received mild overdoses of gamma radiation.

Met-Ed officials, trying earnestly to calm the growing crisis, only created more confusion and anxiety. "We aren't at the China syndrome level," plant spokesman William Gross said, but a few hours later, Met-Ed official Don Curry said: "We concede that it's not just a little thing." The same day, Sen. Gary Hart of Colorado, head of the Senate nuclear regulation subcommittee, arrived for an inspection. Hart told reporters that three key questions would need further investigation: Had Met-Ed recognized the emergency quickly enough? Did Unit II have inherent design flaws? Were the plant's systems adequate to handle a large overflow of radioactive water? Gov. Richard Thornburgh was more soothing: "There is no reason to disrupt your daily routine," he told Pennsylvanians late that afternoon, "nor any reason to feel that the public health has been affected by events on Three Mile Island."

But that reassurance faded on the next day, when the reactor failed to cool down as quickly as expected and new puffs of radiation escaped from the hot plant. One meter picked up 1,200 millirems per hour in a steam plume above the plant site; ground levels shot up to 25 millirems within a 3-mile radius. For a moment, Governor Thornburgh considered evacuating parts of four counties around the plant. After consulting the NRC and Met-Ed, he decided instead to advise residents to stay indoors and close their windows. He received a phone call from President Carter. "He was concerned that there be no panic, that there be no going off half-cocked," Thornburgh said. He later urged the evacuation of all pre-school toddlers and pregnant women within 5 miles of the plant. "There is no reason to panic," he said. But the alarm was palpable . . . and a small exodus was soon under way.

"A big balloon": Back at the plant, the immediate task was to cool down a very hot reactor. Dozens of engineers and more than 50 workers, clad in raincoats over white protective suits and equipped with scuba-like breathing gear or gas masks, desperately tried to shrink the bubble of gas trapped in the top of the reactor vessel. "You have to be very careful about the method you use to bring the reactor to a cold shutdown position," said Harold R. Denton, nuclear-reactor regulation director for the NRC—who arrived at the plant as President Carter's personal man on the scene. Reducing vessel pressure to cool the reactor would also allow the bubble to expand. "It's like a big balloon," said one worried Met-Ed official. If the bubble grew too large, it could block the flow of coolant or drive water levels down

far enough to expose the damaged core—raising the risk of a meltdown. None of the available solutions looked very attractive and all took time. "If there were a clear choice, it wouldn't take us this long to decide," said the NRC's Case. The first option was to continue slowly to cool the reactor, venting small amounts of the gas bubble through a pressurizer valve with the cooling water. The risk was that the process was so slow that oxygen and hydrogen might build up and explode. Another idea was to "purge" the reactor vessel with oxygen in the hope that it would combine with the hydrogen in the bubble to form water. But safety experts estimated that tactic could take up to 30 days. A third option was to turn on the emergency core-cooling system and attempt to blow the bubble out through the coolant pipes, but enough water might be lost to raise the risk of a meltdown.

Given the manifest dangers, NRC chairman Joseph M. Hendrie said it was possible that all residents in a wedge-shaped area 10 to 20 miles downwind of the plant might be evacuated before any attempt was made to do something about the bubble. "It may turn out to be a prudent, precautionary measure," said Hendrie. "We wouldn't necessarily at all wait for a demonstrated disaster."

. . . The ripples of the accident also promised to spread a long way. In New England, the Clamshell Alliance organized vigils at the Seabrook, Maine Yankee and Millstone nuclear power plants. The Clamshellers also planned to leaflet California Gov. Jerry Brown when he visited the New Hampshire legislature this week to argue for a balanced Federal budget. The complaint: that Brown has not been hard enough on the Diablo Canyon nuclear plant being constructed in his state. In Austin, Texas, where voters have narrowly approved referendums on the proposed South Texas Nuclear Project five times in the past, a sixth vote next week hung in the balance after the accident at Three Mile Island. "It hurt—it hurt bad," complained John Rogers of the Committee for Economic Energy, a pro-nuclear group.

The accident did nothing to ease the Carter Administration's rough passage through the energy crunch. Energy Secretary James Schlesinger, a nuclear advocate, said sunnily that the accident "underscores how safe nuclear [energy] has been in the past." That reassured no one, and it seemed likely Congress would look doubly hard at Administration plans for funding a revamped breeder-reactor program and for speeding up the regulatory process for licensing a nuclear plant. It can now take up to a dozen years to license and build. Sen. Edward Kennedy, chairman of the House-Senate Joint Economic Committee's subcommittee on energy, shot off a tart letter to Schlesinger attacking the license speedup. "It's more important to build these plants safely than to build them quickly," he said. Carter himself told a group of editors that the incident "will make all of us reassess our present safety regulations . . . and will probably lead inexorably toward even more stringent safety-design mechanisms and standards."

Whether the shock of the accident would jolt citizens and elected officials into broader action remained to be seen. The Government Accounting Office released the final draft of a report to Congress calling for the expansion of emergency planning zones around nuclear plants to a radius of 10 miles. So far only ten states—Pennsylvania not among them—have federally approved peacetime nuclear-emergency plans. The lapse alarmed critics. Robert D. Pollard, a former staffer of the NRC, charged that problems similar to those that touched off the accident at Three Mile Island had turned up at Rancho Seco in California, Oconee Units I, II and III in South Carolina, Davis-Besse Unit I in Ohio, Crystal River Unit III in Florida and Arkansas Nuclear One-I and One-II. "If anyone had been paying attention, Three Mile Island wouldn't have happened," he said.

Now that it has, the nation is in an exceptionally difficult energy bind. Every form of energy production involves risks. Coal, the chief alternative to nuclear power, has already claimed thousands of lives in mining accidents, and air pollution is a serious health menace. There isn't enough available oil and natural gas to carry the load, and solar energy for electricity is still years away.

Both Schlesinger and Carter were counting on more nuclear plants to reduce America's dependence on imported oil. They will try to keep on that course, undoubtedly coupled with tighter safety regulations. But anti-nuclear forces, backed now by a more worried populace, will be more potent than ever. Meltdowns and millirems are now part of America's vocabulary—and it remains to be seen whether the industry can recover from the nightmare that almost was.

The Case for Economic Growth

WILFRED BECKERMAN

For some years now it has been very unfashionable to be in favor of continued long-run economic growth. Unless one joins in the chorus of scorn for the pursuit of continued economic growth, one is in danger of being treated either as a coarse Philistine, who is prepared to sacrifice all the things that make life really worth living for vulgar materialist goods, or as a short-sighted, complacent, Micawber who is unable to appreciate that the world is living on the edge of a precipice. For it is widely believed that if growth is not

Wilfred Beckerman, "The Case for Economic Growth," *Public Utilities Fortnightly*, September 26, 1974. Abridged and reprinted by permission of the publisher and the author.

now brought to a halt in a deliberate orderly manner, either there will be a catastrophic collapse of output when we suddenly run out of key raw materials, or we shall all be asphyxiated by increased pollution. In other words, growth is either undesirable or impossible, or both. Of course, I suppose this is better than being undesirable and inevitable, but the antigrowth cohorts do not seem to derive much comfort from the fact. . . .

Hence it is not entirely surprising that the antigrowth movement has gathered so much support over the past few years even though it is 99 percent nonsense. Not 100 percent nonsense. There does happen to be a one percent grain of truth in it.

This is that, in the absence of special government policies (policies that governments are unlikely to adopt if not pushed hard by communal action from citizens), pollution will be excessive. This is because—as economists have known for many decades—pollution constitutes what is known in the jargon as an "externality." That is to say, the costs of pollution are not always borne fully—if at all—by the polluter. The owner of a steel mill that belches smoke over the neighborhood, for example, does not usually have to bear the costs of the extra laundry, or of the ill-health that may result. Hence, although he is, in a sense, "using up" some of the environment (the clean air) to produce his steel, he is getting this particular factor of production free of charge. Naturally, he has no incentive to economize in its use in the same way as he has for other factors of production that carry a cost, such as labor or capital. In all such cases of "externalities," or "spillover effects" as they are sometimes called, the normal price mechanism does not operate to achieve the socially desirable pattern of output or of exploitation of the environment. This defect of the price mechanism needs to be corrected by governmental action in order to eliminate excessive pollution.

But, it should be noted that the "externality" argument, summarized above, only implies that society should cut out "excessive" pollution; not *all* pollution. Pollution should only be cut to the point where the benefits from reducing it further no longer offset the costs to society (labor or capital costs) of doing so.

Mankind has always polluted his environment, in the same way that he has always used up some of the raw materials that he has found in it. When primitive man cooked his meals over open fires, or hunted animals, or fashioned weapons out of rocks and stones, he was exploiting the environment. But to listen to some of the extreme environmentalists, one would imagine that there was something immoral about this (even though God's first injunction to Adam was to subdue the earth and every living thing that exists in it). If all pollution has to be eliminated, we would have to spend the whole of our national product in converting every river in the country into beautiful clear-blue swimming pools for fish. I live in a town with a 100,000 population but without even a decent swimming pool for the humans, I am not prepared to subscribe to this doctrine.

Anyway, most of the pollution that the environmentalists make such a fuss about is not the pollution that affects the vast mass of the population. Most people in industrialized countries spend their lives in working conditions where the noise and stench cause them far more loss of welfare than the glamorous fashionable pollutants, such as PCB's or mercury, that the antigrowth lobby makes such a fuss about. Furthermore, such progress as has been made over the decades to improve the working conditions of the mass of the population in industrialized countries has been won largely by the action of working-class trade unions, without any help from the middle classes that now parade so ostentatiously their exquisite sensibilities and concern with the "quality of life."

The extreme environmentalists have also got their facts about pollution wrong. In the Western world, the most important forms of pollution are being reduced, or are being increasingly subjected to legislative action that will shortly reduce them. In my recently published book (*In Defense of Economic Growth*)[1] I give the facts about the dramatic decline of air pollution in British cities over the past decade or more, as well as the improvement in the quality of the rivers. I also survey the widespread introduction of antipollution policies in most of the advanced countries of the world during the past few years, which will enable substantial cuts to be made in pollution. By comparison with the reductions already achieved in some cases, or envisaged in the near future, the maximum pollution reductions built into the computerized calculations of the Club of Rome[2] can be seen to be absurdly pessimistic.

The same applies to the Club of Rome's assumption that adequate pollution abatement would be so expensive that economic growth would have to come to a halt. For example, the dramatic cleaning up of the air in London cost a negligible amount per head of the population of that city. And, taking a much broader look at the estimates, I show in my book that reductions in pollution many times greater than those that the Club of Rome purports to be the upper limits over the next century can, and no doubt will, be achieved over the next decade in the advanced countries of the world at a cost of only about one percent to 2 percent of annual national product.

When confronted with the facts about the main pollutants, the antigrowth lobby tends to fall back on the "risk and uncertainty" argument. This takes the form, "Ah yes, but what about all these new pollutants, or what about undiscovered pollutants? Who knows, maybe we shall only learn in a 100 years' time, when it will be too late, that they are deadly." But life is full of risk and uncertainty. Every day I run the risk of being run over by an automobile or hit on the head by a golf ball. But rational conduct requires that I balance the probabilities of this happening against the costs of insuring against it. It would only be logical to avoid even the minutest chance of some catastrophe in the future if it were costless to do so. But the cost of stopping economic growth would be astronomic. This cost does not merely comprise the loss of any hope of improved standards of living for the vast mass of the world's population; it includes also the political and social costs that would need to be incurred. For only a totalitarian regime could persist on the basis of an antigrowth policy that denied people their normal and legitimate aspirations for a better standard of living.

But leaving aside this political issue, another technical issue which has been much in the public eye lately has been the argument that growth will br brought to a sudden, and hence catastrophic, halt soon on account of the impending exhaustion of raw material supplies. This is the "finite resources" argument; i.e., that since the resources of the world are finite, we could not go on using them up indefinitely.

Now resources are either finite or they are not. If they are, then even zero growth will not save us in the longer run. Perhaps keeping Gross National Product at the present level instead of allowing it to rise by, say, 4 percent per annum would enable the world's resources to be spread out for 500 years instead of only 200 years. But the day would still come when we would run out of resources. (The Club of Rome's own computer almost gave the game away and it was obliged to cut off the printout at the point where it becomes clear that, even with zero growth, the world eventually begins to run out of resources!) So why aim only at zero growth? Why not cut output? If resources are, indeed, finite, then there must be some optimum rate at which they should be spread out over time which will be related to the relative importance society attaches to the consumption levels of different generations. The "eco-doomsters" fail to explain the criteria that determine the optimum rate and why they happen to churn out the answer that the optimum growth rate is zero.

And if resources are not, after all, finite, then the whole of the "finite resources" argument collapses anyway. And, in reality, resources are not finite in any meaningful sense. In the first place, what is now regarded as a resource may not have been so in the past decades or centuries before the appropriate techniques for its exploitation or utilization had been developed. This applies, for example, to numerous materials now in use but never heard of a century ago, or to the minerals on the sea bed (e.g., "manganese nodules"), or even the sea water itself from which unlimited quantities of certain basic minerals can eventually be extracted.

In the second place, existing known reserves of many raw materials will never appear enough to last more than, say, twenty or fifty years at current rates of consumption, for the simple reason that it is rarely economically worthwhile to prospect for more supplies than seem to be salable, at prospective prices, given the costs of exploitation and so on. This has always been the case in the past, yet despite dramatic increases in consumption, supplies have more or less kept pace with demand. The "finite resource" argument fails to allow for the numerous ways that the economy and society react to changes in relative prices of a product, resulting from changes in the balance between supply and demand.

For example, a major United States study in 1929 concluded that known tin resources were only adequate to last the world ten years. Forty years later, the Club of Rome is worried because there is only enough to last us another fifteen years. At this rate, we shall have to wait another century before we have enough to last us another thirty years. Meanwhile, I suppose we shall just have to go on using up that ten years' supply that we had back in 1929.

And it is no good replying that demand is growing faster now than ever before, or that the whole scale of consumption of raw material is incomparably greater than before. First, this proposition has also been true at almost any time over the past few thousand years, and yet economic growth continued. Hence, the truth of such propositions tells us nothing about whether the balance between supply and demand is likely to change one way or the other. And it is this that matters. In other words, it may well be that demand is growing much faster than ever before, or that the whole scale of consumption is incomparably higher, but the same applies to supply. For example, copper consumption rose about fortyfold during the nineteenth century and demand for copper was accelerating, around the turn of the century, for an annual average growth rate of about 3.3 percent per annum (over the whole century) to about 6.4 percent per annum during the period 1890 to 1910. Annual copper consumption had been only about 16,000 tons at the beginning of the century, and was about 700,000 tons at the end of it; i.e., incomparably greater. But known reserves at the end of the century were greater than at the beginning.

And the same applies to the postwar period. In 1946 world copper reserves amounted to only about 100 million tons. Since then the annual rate of copper consumption has trebled and we have used up 93 million tons. So there should be hardly any left. In fact, we now have about 300 million tons!

Of course, it may well be that we shall run out of some individual materials; and petroleum looks like one of the most likely candidates for exhaustion of supplies around the end of this century — if the price did not rise (or stay up at its recent level). But there are two points to be noted about this. First, insofar as the price does stay up at its recent level (i.e., in the $10 per barrel region), substantial economies in oil use will be made over the next few years, and there will also be a considerable development of substitutes for conventional sources, such as shale oil, oil from tar sands, and new ways of using coal reserves which are, of course, very many times greater than oil reserves (in terms of common energy units).

Secondly, even if the world did gradually run out of some resources, it would not be a catastrophe. The point of my apparently well-known story about "Beckermonium" (the product named after my grandfather who failed to discover it in the nineteenth century) is that we manage perfectly well without it. In fact, if one thinks about it, we manage without infinitely more products than we manage with! In other words, it is absurd to imagine that if, say, nickel or petroleum had never been discovered, modern civilization would never have existed, and that the eventual disappearance of these or other products must, therefore, plunge us back into the Dark Ages.

The so-called "oil crisis," incidentally, also demonstrates the moral hypocrisy of the antigrowth lobby. For leaving aside their mistaken interpretation of the technical reasons for the recent sharp rise in the oil price (i.e., it was not because the world suddenly ran out of oil), it is striking that the antigrowth lobby has seized upon the rise in the price of oil as a fresh argument for abandoing economic growth and for rethinking our basic values and so on. After all, over the past two or three years the economies of many of the poorer countries of the world, such as India, have been hit badly by the sharp rise in the price of wheat. Of course, this only means a greater threat of starvation for a few more million people in backward countries a long way away. That does not, apparently, provoke the men of spiritual and moral sensibility to righteous indignation about the values of the growth-oriented society as much as does a rise in the price of gasoline for our automobiles!

The same muddled thinking is behind the view that mankind has some moral duty to preserve the world's environment or supplies of materials. For this view contrasts strangely with the antigrowth lobby's attack on materialism. After all, copper, oil, and so on are just material objects, and it is difficult to see what moral duty we have to preserve indefinitely the copper species from extinction.

Nor do I believe that we have any overriding moral duty to preserve any particular animal species from extinction. After all, thousands of animal species have become extinct over the ages, without any intervention by mankind. Nobody really loses any sleep over the fact that one cannot now see a live dinosaur. How many of the people who make a fuss about the danger that the tiger species may disappear even bother to go to a zoo to look at one? And what about the web-footed Beckermanipus, which has been extinct for about a million years. . . .

In fact, I am not even sure that the extinction of the human race would matter. The bulk of humanity lead lives full of suffering, sorrow, cruelty, poverty, frustration, and loneliness. One should not assume that because nearly everybody has a natural animal instinct to cling to life they can be said, in any meaningful sense, to be better off alive than if they had never been born. Religious motivations apart, it is arguable that since, by and large (and present company excepted, of course), the human race stinks, the sooner it is extinct the better. . . .

Whilst economic growth alone may never provide a simple means of solving any of these problems, and it may well be that, by its very nature, human society will always create insoluble problems of one kind or another, the absence of economic growth will only make our present problems a lot worse.

NOTES

1. Jonathan Cape, London. The U.S.A. edition, under the title 'Two Cheers for the Affluent Society,' was published by the St. Martins Press in the fall of 1974.
2. The Club of Rome is an informal international organization of educators, scientists, economists, and others which investigates what it conceives to be the overriding problems of mankind. Its study, "The Limits to Growth," has become the bible of no-growth advocates (Potomac Associates, 1707 L Street, N.W., Washington, D.C., $2.75). The study assembled data on known reserves of resources and asked a computer what would happen if demand continued to grow exponentially. Of course, the computer replied everything would break down. The theory of "Beckermonium" lampoons this. Since the author's grandfather failed to discover "Beckermonium" by the mid-1800s, the world has had no supplies of it at all. Consequently, if the club's equations are followed, the world should have come to a halt many years ago. "Beckermonium" 's foundation is that the things man has not yet discovered are far more numerous and of greater importance than what has been discovered. (Editor's of *Public Utilities Fortnightly* Note.)

The Scarcity Society

WILLIAM OPHULS

. . . For the past three centuries, we have been living in an age of abnormal abundance. The bonanza of the New World and other founts of virgin resources, the dazzling achievements of science and technology, the availability of "free" ecological resources such as air and water to absorb the waste products of industrial activities, and other lesser factors allowed our ancestors to dream of endless material growth. Infinite abundance, men reasoned, would result in the elevation of the common man to economic nobility. And with poverty abolished, inequality, injustice, and fear—all those flowers of evil alleged to have their roots in scarcity—would wither away. Apart from William Blake and a few other disgruntled romantics, or the occasional pessimist like Thomas Malthus, the Enlightenment ideology of progress was shared by all the West. The words of John Locke and Adam Smith, the two men who gave bourgeois political economy its fundamental direction, are shot through with the assumption that there is always going to be more—more land in the colonies, more wealth to be dug from the ground, and so on. Virtually all the philosophies, values, and institutions typical of modern capitalist society—the legitimacy of self-interest, the primacy of the individual and his inalienable rights, economic laissez-faire, and democracy as we know it—are the luxuriant fruit of an era of apparently endless abundance. They cannot continue to exist in their current form once we return to the more normal condition of scarcity.

Worse, the historic responses to scarcity have been conflict—wars fought to control resources, and oppression—great inequality of wealth, and the political measures needed to maintain it. The link between scarcity and oppression is well understood by spokesmen for underprivileged groups and nations, who react violently to any suggested restraint in growth of output.

Our awakening from the pleasant dream of infinite progress and the abolition of scarcity will be extremely painful. Institutionally, scarcity demands that we sooner or later achieve a full-fledged "steady-state" or "spaceman" economy. Thereafter, we shall have to live off the annual income the earth receives from the sun, and this means a forced end to our kind of abnormal affluence and an abrupt return to frugality. This will require the strictest sort of economic and technological husbandry, as well as the strictest sort of political control.

The necessity for political control should be obvious from the use of the spaceship metaphor: political ships embarked on dangerous voyages need philosopher-king captains. However, another metaphor—the tragedy of the commons—comes even closer to depicting the essence of the ecopolitical dilemma. The tragedy of the commons has to do with the uncontrolled self-seeking in a limited environment that eventually results in competitive overexploitation of a common resource, whether it is a commonly owned field on which any villager may graze his sheep, or the earth's atmosphere into which producers dump their effluents.

Francis Carney's powerful analysis of the Los Angeles smog problem indicates how deeply all our daily acts enmesh us in the tragic logic of the commons:

> Every person who lives in this basin knows that for twenty-five years he has been living through a disaster. We have all watched it happen, have participated in it with full knowledge. . . . The smog is the result of ten million individual pursuits of private gratification. But there is absolutely nothing that any individual can do to stop its spread. . . . An individual act of renunciation is now nearly impossible, and, in any case, would be meaningless unless everyone else did the same thing. But he has no way of getting everyone else to do it.

If this inexorable process is not controlled by prudent and, above all, timely political restraints on the behavior that causes it, then we must resign ourselves to ecological self-destruction. And the new political structures that seem required to cope with the tragedy of the commons (as well as the imperatives of technology) are going to violate our most cherished ideals, for they will be neither democratic nor libertarian. At worst, the new era could be an anti-Utopia in which we are conditioned to behave according to the exigencies of ecological scarcity.

Ecological scarcity is a new concept, embracing more than the shortage of any particular resource. It has to do primarily with pollution limits, complex trade-offs between present and future needs, and a variety of other physical constraints, rather than with a simple Malthusian overpopulation. The case for the coming of ecological scarcity was most forcefully argued in the Club of Rome study *The Limits to Growth*. That study says, in essence, that man lives on a finite planet containing limited resources and that we appear to be approaching some of these major limits with great speed. To use ecological jargon, we are about to overtax the "carrying capacity" of the planet.

Critical reaction to this jeremiad was predictably reassuring. Those wise in the ways of computers were largely content to assert that the Club of Rome people had fed the machines false or slanted information. "Garbage in, garbage out," they soothed. Other critics sought solace in less empirical directions, but everyone who recoiled from the book's apocalyptic vision took his stand on grounds of social or technological optimism. Justified or not, the optimism is worth examining to see where it leads us politically.

The social optimists, to put their case briefly, believe that various "negative feedback mechanisms" allegedly built into society will (if left alone) automatically check the trends toward ever more population, consumption, and pollution, and that this feedback will function smoothly and gradually so as to bring us up against the limits to growth, if any, with scarcely a bump. The market-price system is the feedback mechanism usually relied upon. Shortages of one resource—oil, for example—simply make it economical to substitute another abundant supply (coal or shale oil). A few of these critics of the limits-to-growth thesis believe that this process can go on indefinitely.

Technological optimism is founded on the belief that it makes little difference whether exponential growth is pushing us up against limits, for technology is simultaneously expanding the limits. To use the metaphor popularized during the debate, ecologists see us as fish in a pond where all life is rapidly being suffocated by a water lily that doubles in size every day (covering the whole pond in thirty days). The technological optimists do not deny that the lily grows very quickly, but they believe that the pond itself can be made to grow even faster. Technology made a liar out of Malthus, say the optimists, and the same fate awaits the neo-Malthusians. In sum, the optimists assert that we can never run out of resources, for economics and technology, like modern genii, will always keep finding new ones for us to exploit or will enable us to use the present supply with ever-greater efficiency.

The point most overlooked in this debate, however, is that politically it matters little who is right: the neo-Malthusians *or* either type of optimist. If the "doomsdayers" are right, then of course we crash into the ceiling of physical limits and relapse into a Hobbesian universe of the war of all against all, followed, as anarchy always has been, by dictatorship of one form or another. If, on the other hand, the optimists are right in supposing that we can adjust to ecological scarcity with economics and technology, this effort will have, as we say, "side effects." For the collision with physical limits can be forestalled only by moving toward some kind of steady-state economy—characterized by the most scrupulous husbanding of resources, by extreme vigilance against the ever-present possibility of disaster should breakdown occur, and, therefore, by right controls on human behavior. However we get there, "Spaceship Earth" will be an all-powerful Leviathan—perhaps benign, perhaps not.

The scarcity problem thus poses a classic dilemma. It may be possible to avoid crashing into the physical limits, but only by adopting radical and unpalatable measures that, paradoxically, are little different in their ultimate political and social implications from the future predicted by the doomsdayers.

Why this is so becomes clear enough when one realizes that the optimistic critics of the doomsdayers, whom I have artificially grouped into "social" and "technological" tendencies, finally have to rest their different cases on a theory of politics, that is, on assumptions about the adaptability of leaders, their constituencies, and the institutions that hold them together. Looked at closely, these assumptions also appear unrealistic.

Even on a technical level, for example, the market-price mechanism does not coexist easily with environmental imperatives. In a market system a bird in the hand is always worth two in the bush.* This means that resources critically needed in the future will be discounted—that is, assessed at a fraction of their future value—by today's economic decision-makers. Thus decisions that are economically "rational," like mine-the-soil farming and forestry, may be ecologically catastrophic. Moreover, charging industries—and, therefore, consumers—for pollution and other environmental harms that are caused by mining and manufacturing (the technical solution favored by most economists to bring market prices into line with ecological realities) is not politically palatable. It clearly requires political decisions that do not accord with current values or the present distribution of political

---

* Of course, noneconomic factors may temporarily override market forces, as the current Arab oil boycott illustrates.

power; and the same goes for other obvious and necessary measures, like energy conservation. No consumer wants to pay more for the same product simply because it is produced in a cleaner way; no developer wants to be confronted with an environmental impact statement that lets the world know his gain is the community's loss; no trucker is likely to agree with any energy-conservation program that cuts his income.

We all have a vested interest in continuing to abuse the environment as we have in the past. And even if we should find the political will to take these kinds of steps before we collide with the physical limits, then we will have adopted the essential features of a spaceman economy on a piecemeal basis—and will have simply exchanged one horn of the dilemma for the other.

Technological solutions are more roundabout, but the outcome—greater social control in a planned society—is equally certain. Even assuming that necessity always proves to be the mother of invention, the management burden thrown on our leaders and institutions by continued technological expansion of that famous fishpond will be enormous. Prevailing rates of growth require us to double our capital stock, our capacity to control pollution, our agricultural productivity, and so forth every fifteen to thirty years. Since we already start from a very high absolute level, the increment of required new construction and new invention will be staggering. For example, to accommodate world population growth, we must, in roughly the next thirty years, build houses, hospitals, ports, factories, bridges, and every other kind of facility in numbers that almost equal all the construction work done by the human race up to now.

The task in every area of our lives is essentially similar, so that the management problem extends across the board, item by item. Moreover, the complexity of the overall problem grows faster than any of the sectors that comprise it, requiring the work of innovation, construction, and environmental management to be orchestrated into a reasonably integrated, harmonious whole. Since delays, planning failures, and general incapacity to deal effectively with even our current level of problems are all too obvious today, the technological response further assumes that our ability to cope with large-scale complexity will improve substantially in the next few decades. Technology, in short, cannot be implemented in a political and social vacuum. The factor in least supply governs, and technological solutions cannot run ahead of our ability to plan, construct, fund, and man them.

Planning will be especially difficult. For one thing, time may be our scarcest resource. Problems now develop so rapidly that they must be foreseen well in advance. Otherwise, our "solutions" will be too little and too late. The automobile is a critical example. By the time we recognized the dangers, it was too late for anything but a mishmash of stopgap measures that may have provoked worse symptoms than they alleviated and that will not even enable us to meet health standards without painful additional measures like rationing. But at this point we are almost helpless to do better, for we have ignored the problem until it is too big to handle by any means that are politically, economically, and technically feasible. The energy crisis offers another example of the time factor. Even with an immediate laboratory demonstration of feasibility, nuclear fusion cannot possibly provide any substantial amount of power until well into the next century.

Another planning difficulty: the growing vulnerability of a highly technological society to accident and error. The main cause for concern is, of course, some of the especially dangerous technologies we have begun to employ. One accident involving a breeder reactor would be one too many: the most minuscule dose of plutonium is deadly, and any we release now will be around to poison us for a quarter of a million years. Thus, while we know that counting on perfection in any human enterprise is folly, we seem headed for a society in which nothing less than perfect planning and control will do.

At the very least, it should be clear that ecological scarcity makes "muddling through" in a basically laissez-faire socioeconomic system no longer tolerable or even possible. In a crowded world where only the most exquisite care will prevent the collapse of the technological society on which we all depend, the grip of planning and social control will of necessity become more and more complete. Accidents, much less the random behavior of individuals, cannot be permitted; the expert pilots will run the ship in accordance with technological imperatives. Industrial man's Faustian bargain with technology therefore appears to lead inexorably to total domination by technique in a setting of clockwork institutions. C. S. Lewis once said that "what we call Man's power over Nature turns out to be a power exercised by some men over other men with Nature as its instrument," and it appears that the greater our technological power over nature, the more absolute the political power that must be yielded up to some men by others.

These developments will be especially painful for Americans because, from the beginning, we adopted the doctrines of Locke and Smith in their most libertarian form. Given the cornucopia of the frontier, an unpolluted environment, and a rapidly developing technology, American politics could afford to be a more or less amicable squabble over the division of the spoils, with the government stepping in only when the free-for-all pursuit of wealth got out of hand. In the new era of scarcity, laissez-faire and the inalienable right of the individual to get as much as he can are prescriptions for disaster. It follows that the political system inherited from our forefathers is moribund. We have come to the final act of the tragedy of the commons.

The answer to the tragedy is political. Historically, the use of the commons was closely regulated to prevent overgrazing, and we need similar controls—"mutual coercion, mutually agreed upon by the majority of the people affected," in the words of the biologist Garrett Hardin—to prevent the individual acts that are destroying the commons today. Ecological scarcity imposes certain political measures on us if we wish to survive. Whatever these measures may turn out to be — if we act soon, we may have a significant range of responses — it is evident that our political future will inevitably be much less libertarian and much more authoritarian, much less individualistic and much more communalistic than our present. The likely result of the reemergence of scarcity appears to be the resurrection in modern form of the preindustrial polity, in which the few govern the many and in which government is no longer of or by the people. Such forms of government may or may not be benevolent. At worst, they will be totalitarian, in every evil sense of that word we know now, and some ways undreamed of. At best, government seems likely to rest on engineered consent, as we are manipulated by Platonic guardians in one or another version of Brave New World. The alternative will be the destruction, perhaps consciously, of "Spaceship Earth."

There is, however, a way out of this depressing scenario. To use the language of ancient philosophers, it is the restoration of the civic virtue of a corrupt people. By their standards, by the standards of many of the men who founded our nation (and whose moral capital we have just about squandered), we are indeed a corrupt people. We understand liberty as a license for self-indulgence, so that we exploit our rights to the full while scanting our duties. We understand democracy as a political means of gratifying our desires rather than as a system of government that gives us the precious freedom to impose laws on ourselves — instead of having some remote sovereign impose them on us without our participation or consent. Moreover, the desires we express through our political system are primarily for material gain; the pursuit of happiness has been degraded into a mass quest for what wise men have always said would injure our souls. We have yet to learn the truth of Burke's political syllogism, which expresses the essential wisdom of political philosophy: man is a passionate being, and there must therefore be checks on will and appetite; if these checks are not self-imposed, they must be applied externally as fetters by a sovereign power. The way out of our difficulties, then, is through the abandonment of our political corruption.

The crisis of ecological scarcity poses basic value questions about man's place in nature and the meaning of human life. It is possible that we may learn from this challenge what Lao-tzu taught two-and-a-half millennia ago:

> Nature sustains itself through three previous principles, which one does well to embrace and follow.
>
> These are gentleness, frugality, and humility.

A very good life — in fact, an affluent life by historic standards — can be lived without the profligate use of resources that characterizes our civilization. A sophisticated and ecologically sound technology, using solar

power and other renewable resources, could bring us a life of simple suffi-
ciency that would yet allow the full expression of the human potential.
Having chosen such a life, rather than having had it forced on us, we might
find it had its own richness.

Such a choice may be impossible, however. The root of our problem
lies deep. The real shortage with which we are afflicted is that of moral
resources. Assuming that we wish to survive in dignity and not as ciphers in
some ant-heap society, we are obliged to reassume our full moral responsibility. The earth is not just a banquet at which we are free to gorge. The
ideal in Buddhism of compassion for all sentient beings, the concern for the
harmony of man and nature so evident among American Indians, and the
almost forgotten ideal of stewardship in Christianity point us in the direction
of a true ethics of human survival—and it is toward such an ideal that the
best among the young are groping. We must realize that there is no real
scarcity in nature. It is our numbers and, above all, our wants that have
outrun nature's bounty. We become rich precisely in proprotion to the
degree in which we eliminate violence, greed, and pride from our lives. As
several thousands of years of history show, this is not something easily
learned by humanity, and we seem no readier to choose the simple, virtuous
life now than we have been in the past. Nevertheless, if we wish to avoid
either a crash into the ecological ceiling or a tyrannical Leviathan, we must
choose it. There is no other way to defeat the gathering forces of scarcity.

Ethics and Ecology

WILLIAM T. BLACKSTONE

THE RIGHT TO A LIVABLE ENVIRONMENT
AS A HUMAN RIGHT

. . . Let us first ask whether the right to a livable environment can properly
be considered to be a human right. For the purposes of this paper, however,
I want to avoid raising the more general question of whether there are any
human rights at all. Some philosophers do deny that any human rights
exist.[1] In two recent papers I have argued that human rights do exist (even

Reprinted from *Philosophy and Environmental Crisis*, ed. William T. Blackstone, ©
1974 the University of Georgia Press. Reprinted by permission of the University of Georgia
Press.

though such rights may properly be overridden on occasion by other morally relevant reasons) and that they are universal and inalienable (although the actual exercise of such rights on a given occasion is alienable).[2] My argument for the existence of universal human rights rests, in the final analysis, on a theory of what it means to be human, which specifies the capacities for rationality and freedom as essential, and on the fact that there are no relevant grounds for excluding any human from the opportunity to develop and fulfill his capacities (rationality and freedom) as a human. This is not to deny that there are criteria which justify according human rights in quite different ways or with quite different modes of treatment for different persons, depending upon the nature and degree of such capacities and the existing historical and environmental circumstances.

If the right to a livable environment were seen as a basic and inalienable human right, this could be a valuable tool (both inside and outside of legalistic frameworks) for solving some of our environmental problems, both on a national and on an international basis. Are there any philosophical and conceptual difficulties in treating this right as an inalienable human right? Traditionally we have not looked upon the right to a decent environment as a human right or as an inalienable right. Rather, inalienable human or natural rights have been conceived in somewhat different terms; equality, liberty, happiness, life, and property. However, might it not be possible to view the right to a livable environment as being entailed by, or as constitutive of, these basic human or natural rights recognized in our political tradition? If human rights, in other words, are those rights which each human possesses in virtue of the fact that he is human and in virtue of the fact that those rights are essential in permitting him to live a human life (that is, in permitting him to fulfill his capacities as a rational and free being), then might not the right to a decent environment be properly categorized as such a human right? Might it not be conceived as a right which has emerged as a result of changing environmental conditions and the impact of those conditions on the very possibility of the realization of other rights such as liberty and equality?[3] Let us explore how this might be the case.

Given man's great and increasing ability to manipulate the environment, and the devastating effect this is having, it is plain that new social institutions and new regulative agencies and procedures must be initiated on both national and international levels to make sure that the manipulation is in the public interest. It will be necessary, in other words, to restrict or stop some practices and the freedom to engage in those practices. Some look upon such additional state planning, whether national or international, as unnecessary further intrusion on man's freedom. Freedom is, of course, one of our basic values, and few would deny that excessive state control of human action is to be avoided. But such restrictions on individual freedom now appear to be necessary in the interest of overall human welfare and the rights and freedoms of *all* men. Even John Locke with his stress on freedom as an inalienable right recognized that this right must be construed so that it is consistent with the equal right to freedom of others. The whole point of the state is to restrict unlicensed freedom and to provide the conditions for equality of rights for all. Thus it seems to be perfectly consistent with Locke's view and, in general, with the views of the founding fathers of this country to restrict certain rights or freedoms when it can be shown that such restriction is necessary to insure the equal rights of others. If this is so, it has very important implications for the rights to freedom and to property. These rights, perhaps properly seen as inalienable (though this is a controversial philosophical question), are not properly seen as unlimited or unrestricted. When values which we hold dear conflict (for example, individual or group freedom and the freedom of all, individual or group rights and the rights of all, and individual or group welfare and the welfare of the general public) something has to give; some priority must be established. In the case of the abuse and waste of environmental resources, less individual freedom and fewer individual rights for the sake of greater public welfare and equality of rights seem justified. What in the past had been properly regarded as freedoms and rights (given what seemed to be unlimited natural resources and no serious pollution problems) can no longer be so construed, at least not without additional restrictions. We must recognize both the need for such restrictions and the fact that none of our rights can be realized without a livable environment. Both public welfare and equality of rights now require that natural resources not be used simply according to the whim and caprice of individuals or simply for personal profit. This is not to say that all property rights must be denied and that the state must own all productive property, as the Marxist argues. It is to insist that those rights be qualified or restricted in the light of new ecological data and in the interest of the freedom, rights, and welfare of all.

The answer then to the question, Is the right to a livable environment a human right? is yes. Each person has this right qua being human and because a livable environment is essential for one to fulfill his human capacities. And given the danger to our environment today and hence the danger to the very possibility of human existence, access to a livable environment must be conceived as a right which imposes upon everyone a correlative moral obligation to respect.[4] . . .

ECOLOGY AND ECONOMIC RIGHTS

We suggested above that it is necessary to qualify or restrict economic or property rights in the light of new ecological data and in the interest of the freedom, rights, and welfare of all. In part, this suggested restriction is predicated on the assumption that we cannot expect private business to provide solutions to the multiple pollution problems for which they themselves are responsible. Some companies have taken measures to limit the polluting effect of their operations, and this is an important move. But we are deluding ourselves if we think that private business can function as its own pollution police. This is so for several reasons: the primary objective of private business is economic profit. Stockholders do not ask of a company, "Have you polluted the environment and lowered the quality of the environment for the general public and for future generations?" Rather they ask, "How high is the annual dividend and how much higher is it than the year before?" One can hardly expect organizations whose basic norm is economic profit to be concerned in any great depth with the long-range effects of their operations upon society and future generations or concerned with the hidden cost of their operations in terms of environmental quality to society as a whole. Second, within a free enterprise system companies compete to produce what the public wants at the lowest possible cost. Such competition would preclude the spending of adequate funds to prevent environmental pollution, since this would add tremendously to the cost of the product—unless all other companies would also conform to such antipollution policies. But in a free enterprise economy such policies are not likely to be self-imposed by businessmen. Third, the basic response of the free enterprise system to our economic problems is that we must have greater economic growth or an increase in gross national product. But such growth many ecologists look upon with great alarm, for it can have devastating long-range effects upon our environment. Many of the products of uncontrolled growth are based on artificial needs and actually detract from, rather than contribute to, the quality of our lives. A stationary economy, some economists and ecologists suggest, may well be best for the quality of man's environment and of his life in the long run. Higher GNP does not automatically result in an increase in social well-being, and it should not be used as a measuring rod for assessing economic welfare. This becomes clear when one realizes that the GNP

> aggregates the dollar value of all goods and services produced—the cigarettes as well as the medical treatment of lung cancer, the petroleum from offshore wells as well as the detergents required to clean up after oil spills, the electrical energy produced and the medical and cleaning bills resulting from the air-pollution that is caused by fuel used for generating the electricity. The GNP allows no deduction for negative production, such as lives lost from unsafe cars or environmental destruction perpetrated by telephone, electric and gas utilities, lumber companies, and speculative builders.[5]

To many persons, of course, this kind of talk is not only blasphemy but subversive. This is especially true when it is extended in the direction of additional controls over corporate capitalism. (Some ecologists and economists go further and challenge whether corporate capitalism can accommodate a stationary state and still retain its major features.[6]) The fact of the matter is that the ecological attitude forces one to reconsider a host of values which have been held dear in the past, and it forces one to reconsider the appropriateness of the social and economic systems which embodied and implemented those values. Given the crisis of our environment, there must be certain fundamental changes in attitudes toward nature, man's use of nature, and man himself. Such changes in attitudes undoubtedly will have far-reaching implications for the institutions of private property and private enterprise and the values embodied in these institutions. Given that crisis we can no longer look upon water and air as free commodities to be exploited at will. Nor can the private ownership of land be seen as a lease to use that land in any way which conforms merely to the personal desires of the owner. In other words, the environmental crisis is forcing us to challenge what had in the past been taken to be certain basic rights of man or at least to restrict those rights. And it is forcing us to challenge institutions which embodied those rights.

Much has been said . . . about the conflict between these kinds of rights, and the possible conflict between them is itself a topic for an extensive paper. Depending upon how property rights are formulated, the substantive content of those rights, it seems plain to me, can directly conflict with what we characterize as human rights. In fact our moral and legal history demonstrate exactly that kind of conflict. There was a time in the recent past when property rights embodied the right to hold human beings in slavery. This has now been rejected, almost universally. Under nearly any interpretation of the substantive content of human rights, slavery is incompatible with those rights.

The analogous question about rights which is now being raised by the data uncovered by the ecologist and by the gradual advancement of the ecological attitude is whether the notion of property rights should be even further restricted to preclude the destruction and pollution of our environmental resources upon which the welfare and the very lives of all of us and of future generations depend. Should our social and legal system embrace property rights or other rights which permit the kind of environmental exploitation which operates to the detriment of the majority of mankind? I do not think so. The fact that a certain right exists in a social or legal system does not mean that it ought to exist. I would not go so far as to suggest that all rights are merely rule-utilitarian devices to be adopted or discarded whenever it can be shown that the best consequences thereby follow.[7] But if a right or set of rights systematically violates the public welfare, this is prima facie evidence that it ought not to exist. And this certainly seems to be the case with the exercise of certain property rights today.

In response to this problem, there is today at least talk of "a new economy of resources," one in which new considerations and values play an important role along with property rights and the interplay of market forces.

Economist Nathaniel Wollman argues that "the economic past of 'optimizing' resource use consists of bringing into an appropriate relationship the ordering of preferences for various experiences and the costs of acquiring those experiences. Preferences reflect physiological-psychological responses to experience or anticipated experience, individually or collectively revealed, and are accepted as data by the economist. A broad range of noneconomic investigations is called for to supply the necessary information."[8]

Note that Wollman says that noneconomic investigations are called for. In other words the price system does not adequately account for a number of value factors which should be included in an assessment. "It does not account for benefits or costs that are enjoyed or suffered by people who were not parties to the transaction."[9] In a system which emphasizes simply the interplay of market forces as a criterion, these factors (such as sights, smells and other aesthetic factors, justice, and human rights—factors which are important to the well-being of humans) are not even considered. Since they have no direct monetary value, the market places no value whatsoever on them. Can we assume, then, that purely economic or market evaluations provide us with data which will permit us to maximize welfare, if the very process of evaluation and the normative criteria employed exclude a host of values and considerations upon which human welfare depend? The answer to this question is plain. We cannot make this assumption. We cannot rely merely upon the interplay of market forces or upon the sovereignty of the consumer. The concept of human welfare and consequently the notion of maximizing that welfare requires a much broader perspective than the norms offered by the traditional economic perspective. A great many things have value and use which have no economic value and use. Consequently we must broaden our evaluational perspective to include the entire range of values which are essential not only to the welfare of man but also to the welfare of other living things and to the environment which sustains all of life. And this must include a reassessment of rights.

ETHICS AND TECHNOLOGY

I have been discussing the relationship of ecology to ethics and to a theory of rights. Up to this point I have not specifically discussed the relation of technology to ethics, although it is plain that technology and its development is responsible for most of our pollution problems. This topic deserves separate treatment, but I do want to briefly relate it to the thesis of this work.

It is well known that new technology sometimes complicates our ethical lives and our ethical decisions. Whether the invention is the wheel or a contraceptive pill, new technology always opens up new possibilities for human relationships and for society, for good and ill. The pill, for example, is revolutionizing sexual morality, for its use can preclude many of the bad consequences normally attendant upon premarital intercourse. *Some* of the strongest arguments against premarital sex have been shot down by this bit of technology (though certainly not all of them). The fact that the use of the pill can prevent unwanted pregnancy does not make premarital sexual intercourse morally right, nor does it make it wrong. The pill is morally neutral, but its existence does change in part the moral base of the decision to engage in premarital sex. In the same way, technology at least in principle can be neutral—neither necessarily good nor bad in its impact on other aspects of the environment. Unfortunately, much of it is bad—very bad. But technology can be meshed with an ecological attitude to the benefit of man and his environment.

I am not suggesting that the answer to technology which has bad environmental effects is necessarily more technology. We tend too readily to assume that new technological developments will always solve man's problems. But this is simply not the case. One technological innovation often seems to breed a half-dozen additional ones which themselves create more environmental problems. We certainly do not solve pollution problems, for example, by changing from power plants fueled by coal to power plants fueled by nuclear energy, if radioactive waste from the latter is worse than pollution from the former. Perhaps part of the answer to pollution problems is less technology. There is surely no real hope of returning to nature (whatever that means) or of stopping *all* technological and scientific development, as some advocate. Even if it could be done, this would be too extreme a move. The answer is not to stop technology, but to guide it toward proper ends, and to set up standards of antipollution to which all technological devices must conform. Technology has been and can be used to destroy and pollute an environment, but it can also be used to save and beautify it. What is called for is purposeful environmental engineering, and this engineering calls for a mass of information about our environment, about the needs of persons, and about basic norms and values which are acceptable to civilized men. It also calls for priorities on goals and for compromise where there are competing and conflicting values and objectives. Human rights and their fulfillment should constitute at least some of those basic norms, and technology can be used to implement those rights and the public welfare.

NOTES

1. See Kai Nielsen's "Scepticism and Human Rights," *Monist*, 52, no. 4 (1968):571–94.
2. See my "Equality and Human Rights," *Monist*, 52, no. 4 (1968):616–39 and my "Human Rights and Human Dignity," in Laszlo and Gotesky, eds., *Human Dignity*.

3. Almost forty years ago Aldo Leopold stated that "there is as yet no ethic dealing with man's relationship to land and to the nonhuman animals and plants which grow upon it. Land, like Odysseus' slave girls, is still property. The land relation is still strictly economic entailing privileges but not obligations." (See Leopold's "The Conservation Ethic," *Journal of Forestry*, 32, no. 6 [October 1933]:634–43.) Although some important changes have occurred since he wrote this, no systematic ethic or legal structure has been developed to socialize or institutionalize the obligations to use land properly.

4. The right to a livable environment might itself entail other rights, for example, the right to population control. Population control is obviously essential for quality human existence. This issue is complex and deserves a separate essay, but I believe that the moral framework explicated above provides the grounds for treating population control both as beneficial and as moral.

5. See Melville J. Ulmer, "More Than Marxist," *New Republic*, 26 December 1970, p. 14.

6. See Murdock and Connell, "All about Ecology," *Center Magazine*, 3, no. 1 (January–February 1970), p. 63.

7. Some rights, I would argue, are inalienable, and are not based merely on a contract (implicit or explicit) or merely upon the norm of maximizing good consequences. (See David Braybrooke's *Three Tests for Democracy: Personal Rights, Human Welfare, Collective Preference* [New York: Random House, 1968], which holds such a rule-utilitarian theory of rights, and my "Human Rights and Human Dignity," for a rebuttal.)

8. Nathaniel Wollman, "The New Economics of Resources," *Daedalus* 96, pt. 2, (Fall 1967):1100.

9. Ibid.

Advertising

Case Study—Toy Wars

MANUEL G. VELASQUEZ

Early in 1986, Tom Daner, president of the advertising company of Daner Associates, was contacted by the sales manager of Crako Industries, Mike Teal.[1] Crako Industries is a family-owned company that manufactures children's toys and had long been a favorite and important client of Daner Associates. The sales manager of Crako Industries explained that the company had just developed a new toy helicopter. The toy was modeled on the military helicopters that had been used in Vietnam and that had appeared in the "Rambo" movies. Mike Teal explained that the toy was developed in response to the craze for military toys that had been sweeping the nation in the wake of the Rambo movies. The family-owned toy company had initially resisted moving into military toys, since members of the family objected to the violence associated with such toys. But as segments of the toy market were increasingly taken over by military toys, the family came to feel that entry into the military toy market was crucial for their business. Consequently, they approved development of a line of military toys, hoping that they were not entering the market too late. Mike Teal now wanted Daner Associates to develop a television advertising campaign for the toy.

The toy helicopter Crako designers had developed was about one and one-half feet long, battery-operated, and made of plastic and steel. Mounted to the sides were detachable replicas of machine guns and a detachable stretcher modeled on the stretchers used to lift wounded soldiers from a battlefield. Mike Teal of Crako explained that they were trying to develop a

Copyright © 1986 by Manuel G. Velasquez. Reprinted by permission of the author.

toy that had to be perceived as "more macho" than the top-selling "G. I. Joe" line of toys. If the company was to compete successfully in today's toy market, according to the sales manager, it would have to adopt an advertising approach that was even "meaner and tougher" than what other companies were doing. Consequently, he continued, the advertising clips developed by Daner Associates would have to be "mean and macho." Television advertisements for the toy, he suggested, might show the helicopter swooping over buildings and blowing them up. The more violence and mayhem the ads suggested, the better. Crako Industries was relying heavily on sales from the new toy, and some Crako managers felt that the company's future might depend on the success of this toy.

Tom Daner was unwilling to have his company develop television advertisements that would increase what he already felt was too much violence in television aimed at children. In particular, he recalled a television ad for a tricycle with a replica machine gun mounted on the handlebars. The commercial showed the tricycle being pedaled through the woods by a small boy as he chased several other boys fleeing before him over a dirt path. At one point the camera closed in over the shoulder of the boy, focused through the gun sight, and showed the gun sight apparently trying to aim at the backs of the boys as they fled before the tricycle's machine gun. Ads of that sort had disturbed Tom Daner and had led him to think that advertisers should find other ways of promoting these toys. He suggested, therefore, that instead of promoting the Crako helicopter through violence, it should be presented in some other manner. When Teal asked what he had in mind, Tom was forced to reply that he didn't know. But at any rate, Tom pointed out, the three television networks would not accept a violent commercial aimed at children. All three networks adhered to an advertising code that prohibited violent, intense, or unrealistic advertisements aimed at children.

This seemed no real obstacle to Teal, however. Although the networks might turn down children's ads when they were too violent, local television stations were not as squeamish. Local television stations around the country regularly accepted ads aimed at children that the networks had rejected as too violent. The local stations inserted the ads as spots on their non-network programming, thereby circumventing the Advertising Codes of the three national networks. Daner Associates would simply have to place the ads they developed for the Crako helicopter through local television stations around the country. Mike Teal was firm: if Daner Associates would not or could not develop a "mean and tough" ad campaign, the toy company would move their account to an advertiser who would. Reluctantly, Tom Daner agreed to develop the advertising campaign. Crako Industries accounted for $1 million of Daner's total revenues.

Like Crako Industries, Daner Associates is also a family-owned business. Started by his father almost fifty years ago, the advertising firm that Tom Daner now ran had grown dramatically under his leadership. In 1975 the business had grossed $3 million; ten years later it had revenues of $25 million and provided a full line of advertising services. The company was divided into three departments (Creative, Media, and Account Executive), each of which had about 12 employees. Tom Daner credited much of the company's success to the many new people he had hired, especially a group with M. B. A.s who had developed new marketing strategies based on more thorough market and consumer analyses. Most decisions, however, were made by a five-person executive committee consisting of Tom Daner, the Senior Account Manager, and the three department heads. As owner-president, Tom's views tended to color most decisions, producing what one of the members called a "benevolent dictatorship." Tom himself was an enthusiastic, congenial, intelligent, and widely read person. During college he had considered becoming a missionary priest but had changed his mind and was now married and the father of three daughters. His personal heros included Thomas Merton, Albert Schweitzer, and Tom Dooley.

When Tom Daner presented the Crako deal to his Executive Committee, he found they did not share his misgivings. The other Committee members felt that Daner Associates should give Crako exactly the kind of ad Crako wanted: one with a heavy content of violence. Moreover, the writers and artists in the Creative Department were enthused with the prospect of letting their imaginations loose on the project, several feeling that they could easily produce an attention-grabbing ad by "out-violencing" current television programming. The Creative Department, in fact, quickly produced a copy-script that called for videos showing the helicopter "flying out of the sky with machine guns blazing" at a jungle village below. This kind of ad, they felt, was exactly what they were being asked to produce by their client, Crako Industries.

But after viewing the copy, Tom Daner refused to use it. They should produce an ad, he insisted, that would meet their client's needs but that would also meet the guidelines of the national networks. The ad should not glorify violence and war but should somehow support cooperation and family values. Disappointed and somewhat frustrated, the Creative Department went back to work. A few days later they presented a second proposal: an ad that would show the toy helicopter flying through the family room of a home as a little boy plays with it; then the scene shifts to show the boy on a rock rising from the floor of the family room; the helicopter swoops down and picks up the boy as though rescuing him from the rock where he had been stranded. Although the Creative Department was mildly pleased with their attempt, they felt it was too "tame." Tom liked it, however, and a version of the ad was filmed.

A few weeks later Tom Daner met with Mike Teal and his team and showed them the film. The viewing was not a success. Teal turned down the ad. Referring to the network regulations, which other toy advertisements were breaking as frequently as motorists broke the 55 mile per hour speed law, he said, "That commercial is going only 55 miles an hour when I want one that goes 75." If the next version was not "tougher and meaner," Crako Industries would be forced to look elsewhere.

Disappointed, Tom Daner returned to the people in his Creative Department and told them to go ahead with designing the kind of ad they had originally wanted: "I don't have any idea what else to do." In a short time the Creative Department had an ad proposal on his desk that called for scenes showing the helicopter blowing up villages. Shortly afterwards a small set was constructed depicting a jungle village sitting next to a bridge stretching over a river. The ad was filmed using the jungle set as a background.

When Tom saw the result he was not happy. He decided to meet with his Creative Department and air his feelings. "The issue here," he said, "is basically the issue of violence. Do we really want to present toys as instruments for beating up people? This ad is going to promote aggression and violence. It will glorify dominance and do it with kids who are terrifically impressionable. Do we really want to do this?" The members of the Creative Department, however, responded that they were merely giving their client what the client wanted. That client, moreover, was an important account. The client wanted an aggressive "macho" ad, and that was what they were providing. The ad might violate the regulations of the television networks, but there were ways to get around the networks. Moreover, they said, every other advertising firm in the business was breaking the limits against violence set by the networks. Tom made one last try: why not market the toy as an adventure and fantasy toy? Film the ad again, he suggested, using the same jungle backdrop. But instead of showing the helicopter shooting at a burning village, show it flying in to rescue people from the burning village. Create an ad that shows excitement, adventure, and fantasy, but no aggression. "I was trying," he said later, "to figure out a new way of approaching this kind of advertising. We have to follow the market or we can go out of business trying to moralize to the market. But why not try a new approach? Why not promote toys as instruments that expand the child's imagination in a way that is positive and that promotes cooperative values instead of violence and aggression?"

A new film version of the ad was made, now showing the helicopter flying over the jungle set. Quick shots and heightened background music give the impression of excitement and danger. The helicopter flies dramatically through the jungle and over a river and bridge to rescue a boy from a flaming village. As lights flash and shoot haphazardly through the scene the helicopter rises and escapes into the sky. The final ad was clearly exciting and intense. And it promoted saving of life instead of violence against life.

It was clear when the final version was shot, however, that it would not clear the network censors. Network guidelines require that sets in children's ads must depict things that are within the reach of most children so that they do not create unrealistic expectations. Clearly the elaborate jungle set (which cost $25,000 to construct) was not within the reach of most children, and consequently most children would not be able to recreate the scene of the ad by buying the toy. Moreover, network regulations stipulate that in children's ads scenes must be filmed with normal lighting that does not create undue intensity. Again clearly the helicopter ad, which created excitement by using quick changes of light and fast cuts, did not fall within these guidelines.

After reviewing the film Tom Daner reflected on some last-minute instructions Crako's sales manager had given him when he had been shown the first version of the ad: The television ad should show things being blown up by the guns of the little helicopter and perhaps even some blood on the fuselage of the toy; the ad had to be violent. Now Tom had to make a decision. Should he risk the account by submitting only the rescue mission ad? Or should he let Teal also see the ad that showed the helicopter shooting up the village, knowing that he would probably prefer that version if he saw it? And was the rescue mission ad really that much different from the ad that showed the shooting of the village? Did it matter that the rescue mission ad still violated some of the network regulations? What if he offered Teal only the rescue mission ad and Teal accepted the "rescue approach" but demanded he make it more violent; should he give in? And should Tom risk launching an ad campaign that was based on this new untested approach? What if the ad failed to sell the Crako toy? Was it right to experiment with a client's product, especially a product that was so important to the future of the client's business? Tom was unsure what he should do. He wanted to show Teal only the rescue mission commercial, but he felt he first had to resolve these questions in his own mind.

NOTE

1. Although the events described in this case are real, all names of the individuals and the companies involved are fictitious; in addition, several details have been altered to disguise the identity of participants.

The Dependence Effect

JOHN KENNETH GALBRAITH

The theory of consumer demand, as it is now widely accepted, is based on two broad propositions, neither of them quite explicit but both extremely important for the present value system of economists. The first is that the urgency of wants does not diminish appreciably as more of them are satisfied or, to put the matter more precisely, to the extent that this happens it is not demonstrable and not a matter of any interest to economists or for economic policy. When man has satisfied his physical needs, then psychologically grounded desires take over. These can never be satisfied or, in any case, no progress can be proved. The concept of satiation has very little standing in economics. It is neither useful nor scientific to speculate on the comparative cravings of the stomach and the mind.

The second proposition is that wants originate in the personality of the consumer or, in any case, that they are given data for the economist. The latter's task is merely to seek their satisfaction. He has no need to inquire how these wants are formed. His function is sufficiently fulfilled by maximizing the goods that supply the wants.

The notion that wants do not become less urgent the more amply the individual is supplied is broadly repugnant to common sense. It is something to be believed only by those who wish to believe. Yet the conventional wisdom must be tackled on its own terrain. Intertemporal comparisons of an individual's state of mind do rest on doubtful grounds. Who can say for sure that the deprivation which afflicts him with hunger is more painful than the deprivation which afflicts him with envy of his neighbour's new car? In the time that has passed since he was poor his soul may have become subject to a new and deeper searing. And where a society is concerned, comparisons between marginal satisfactions when it is poor and those when it is affluent will involve not only the same individual at different times but different individuals at different times. The scholar who wishes to believe that with increasing affluence there is no reduction in the urgency of desires and goods is not without points for debate. However plausible the case against him, it cannot be proved. In the defence of the conventional wisdom this amounts almost to invulnerability.

However, there is a flaw in the case. If the individual's wants are to be urgent they must be original with himself. They cannot be urgent if they must be contrived for him. And above all they must not be contrived by the process of production by which they are satisfied. For this means that the whole case for the urgency of production, based on the urgency of wants, falls to the ground. One cannot defend production as satisfying wants if that production creates the wants.

Were it so that man on arising each morning was assailed by demons which instilled in him a passion sometimes for silk shirts, sometimes for kitchenware, sometimes for chamber-pots, and sometimes for orange squash, there would be every reason to applaud the effort to find the goods, however odd, that quenched this flame. But should it be that his passion was the result of his first having cultivated the demons, and should it also be that his passion was the result of his first having cultivated the demons, and should it also be that his effort to allay it stirred the demons to ever greater and greater effort, there would be question as to how rational was his solution. Unless restrained by conventional attitudes, he might wonder if the solution lay with more goods or fewer demons.

So it is that if production creates the wants it seeks to satisfy, or if the wants emerge *pari passu* with the production, then the urgency of the wants can no longer be used to defend the urgency of the production. Production only fills a void that it has itself created.

The even more direct link between production and wants is provided by the institutions of modern advertising and salesmanship. These cannot be reconciled with the notion of independently determined desires, for their central function is to create desires—to bring into being wants that previously did not exist.[1] This is accomplished by the producer of the goods or at his behest. A broad empirical relationship exists between what is spent on production of consumers' goods and what is spent in synthesizing the desires for that production. A new consumer product must be introduced with a suitable advertising campaign to arouse an interest in it. The path for an expansion of output must be paved by a suitable expansion in the advertising budget. Outlays for the manufacturing of a product are not more important in the strategy of modern business enterprise than outlays for the manufacturing of demand for the product. None of this is novel. All would be regarded as elementary by the most retarded student in the nation's most primitive school of business administration. The cost of this want formation is formidable. In 1956 total advertising expenditure—though, as noted, not all of it may be assigned to the synthesis of wants—amounted to about ten thousand million dollars. For some years it had been increasing at a rate in excess of a thousand million dollars a year. Obviously, such outlays must be integrated with the theory of consumer demand. They are too big to be ignored.

But such integration means recognizing that wants are dependent on production. It accords to the producer the function both of making the goods and of making the desires for them. It recognizes that production, not only passively through emulation, but actively through advertising and related activities, creates the wants it seeks to satisfy.

The businessman and the lay reader will be puzzled over the emphasis which I give to a seemingly obvious point. The point is indeed obvious. But it is one which, to a singular degree, economists have resisted. They have sensed, as the layman does not, the damage to established ideas which lurks in these relationships. As a result, incredibly, they have closed their eyes (and ears) to the most obtrusive of all economic phenomena, namely modern want creation.

This is not to say that the evidence affirming the dependence of wants on advertising has been entirely ignored. It is one reason why advertising has so long been regarded with such uneasiness by economists. Here is something which cannot be accommodated easily to existing theory. More pervious scholars have speculated on the urgency of desires which are so obviously the fruit of such expensively contrived campaigns for popular attention. Is a new breakfast cereal or detergent so much wanted if so much must be spent to compel in the consumer the sense of want? But there has been little tendency to go on to examine the implications of this for the theory of consumer demand and even less for the importance of production and productive efficiency. These have remained sacrosanct. More often the uneasiness has been manifested in a general disapproval of advertising and advertising men, leading to the occasional suggestion that they shouldn't exist. Such suggestions have usually been ill received.

And so the notion of independently determined wants still survives. In the face of all the forces of modern salesmanship it still rules, almost undefiled, in the textbooks. And it still remains the economist's mission — and on few matters is the pedagogy so firm — to seek unquestioningly the means for filling these wants. This being so, production remains of prime urgency. We have here, perhaps, the ultimate triumph of the conventional wisdom in its resistance to the evidence of the eyes. To equal it one must imagine a humanitarian who was long ago persuaded of the grievous shortage of hospital facilities in the town. He continues to importune the passers-by for money for more beds and refuses to notice that the town doctor is deftly knocking over pedestrians with his car to keep up the occupancy.

And in unravelling the complex we should always be careful not to overlook the obvious. The fact that wants can be synthesized by advertising, catalysed by salesmanship, and shaped by the discreet manipulations of the persuaders shows that they are not very urgent. A man who is hungry need never be told of his need for food. If he is inspired by his appetite, he is immune to the influence of Messrs. Batten, Barton, Durstine and Osborn. The latter are effective only with those who are so far removed from physical want that they do not already know what they want. In this state alone men are open to persuasion.

The general conclusion of these pages is of such importance for this essay that it had perhaps best be put with some formality. As a society becomes increasingly affluent, wants are increasingly created by the process by which they are satisfied. This may operate passively. Increases in consumption, the counterpart of increases in production, act by suggestion or emulation to create wants. Or producers may proceed actively to create wants through advertising and salesmanship. Wants thus come to depend on output. In technical terms it can no longer be assumed that welfare is greater at an all-around higher level of production than at a lower one. It may be the same. The higher level of production has, merely, a higher level of want creation necessitating a higher level of want satisfaction. There will be frequent occasion to refer to the way wants depend on the process by which they are satisfied. It will be convenient to call it the Dependence Effect.

The final problem of the productive society is what it produces. This manifests itself in an implacable tendency to provide an opulent supply of some things and a niggardly yield of others. This disparity carries to the point where it is a cause of social discomfort and social unhealth. The line which divides our area of wealth from our area of poverty is roughly that which divides privately produced and marketed goods and services from publicly rendered services. Our wealth in the first is not only in startling contrast with the meagreness of the latter, but our wealth in privately produced goods is, to a marked degree, the cause of crisis in the supply of public services. For we have failed to see the importance, indeed the urgent need, of maintaining a balance between the two.

This disparity between our flow of private and public goods and services is no matter of subjective judgment. On the contrary, it is the source of the most extensive comment which only stops short of the direct contrast being made here. In the years following World War II, the papers of any major city—those of New York were an excellent example—told daily of the shortages and shortcomings in the elementary municipal and metropolitan services. The schools were old and overcrowded. The police force was under strength and underpaid. The parks and playgrounds were insufficient. Streets and empty lots were filthy, and the sanitation staff was underequipped and in need of men. Access to the city by those who work there was uncertain and painful and becoming more so. Internal transportation was overcrowded, unhealthful, and dirty. So was the air. Parking on the streets had to be prohibited, and there was no space elsewhere. These deficiencies were not in new and novel services but in old and established ones. Cities have long swept their streets, helped their people move around, educated them, kept order, and provided horse rails for vehicles which sought to pause. That their residents should have a non-toxic supply of air suggests no revolutionary dalliance with socialism.

The contrast was and remains evident not alone to those who read. The family which takes its mauve and cerise, air-conditioned, power-steered, and power-braked car out for a tour passes through cities that are badly paved, made hideous by litter, blighted buildings, billboards, and posts for wires that should long since have been put underground. They pass on into a countryside that has been rendered largely invisible by commercial art. (The goods which the latter advertise have an absolute priority in our value system. Such aesthetic considerations as a view of the countryside accordingly come second. On such matters we are consistent.) They picnic on exquisitely packaged food from a portable icebox by a polluted stream and go on to spend the night at a park which is a menace to public health and morals. Just before dozing off an an air-mattress, beneath a nylon tent, amid the stench of decaying refuse, they may reflect vaguely on the curious unevenness of their blessings. Is this, indeed, the American genius?

The case for social balance has, so far, been put negatively. Failure to keep public services in minimal relation to private production and use of goods is a cause of social disorder or impairs economic performance. The matter may now be put affirmatively. By failing to exploit the opportunity to expand public production we are missing opportunities for enjoyment which otherwise we might have had. Presumably a community can be as well rewarded by buying better schools or better parks as by buying bigger cars. By concentrating on the latter rather than the former it is failing to maximize its satisfactions. As with schools in the community, so with public services over the country at large. It is scarcely sensible that we sould satisfy our wants in private goods with reckless abundance, while in the case of public goods, on the evidence of the eye, we practice extreme self-denial. So, far from systematically exploiting the opportunities to derive use and pleasure from these services, we do not supply what would keep us out of trouble.

The conventional wisdom holds that the community, large or small, makes a decision as to how much it will devote to its public services. This decision is arrived at by democratic process. Subject to the imperfections and uncertainties of democracy, people decide how much of their private income and goods they will surrender in order to have public services of which they are in greater need. Thus there is a balance, however rough, in the enjoyments to be had from private goods and services and those rendered by public authority.

It will be obvious, however, that this view depends on the notion of independently determined consumer wants. In such a world one could with some reason defend the doctrine that the consumer, as a voter, makes an independent choice between public and private goods. But given the dependence effect—given that consumer wants are created by the process by which they are satisfied—the consumer makes no such choice. He is subject to the forces of advertising and emulation by which production creates its own demand. Advertising operates exclusively, and emulation mainly, on behalf of privately produced goods and services.[2] Since management and emulative effects operate on behalf of private production, public services will have an inherent tendency to lag behind. Car demand which is expensively synthesized will inevitably have a much larger claim on income than parks or public health or even roads where no such influence operates. The engines of mass communication, in their highest state of development, assail the eyes and ears of the community on behalf of more beer but not of more schools. Even in the conventional wisdom it will scarcely be contended that this leads to an equal choice between the two.

The competition is especially unequal for new products and services. Every corner of the public psyche is canvassed by some of the nation's most talented citizens to see if the desire for some merchantable product can be cultivated. No similar process operates on behalf of the nonmerchantable services of the state. Indeed, while we take the cultivation of new private wants for granted we would be measurably shocked to see it applied to public services. The scientist or engineer or advertising man who devotes himself to developing a new carburetor, cleanser, or depilatory for which the public recognizes no need and will feel none until an advertising campaign arouses it, is one of the valued members of our society. A politician or a public servant who dreams up a new public service is a wastrel. Few public offences are more reprehensible.

So much for the influences which operate on the decision between public and private production. The calm decision between public and private consumption pictured by the conventional wisdom is, in fact, a remarkable example of the error which arises from viewing social behaviour out of context. The inherent tendency will always be for public services to fall behind private production. We have here the first of the causes of social imbalance.

NOTES

1. Advertising is not a simple phenomenon. It is also important in competitive strategy and what creation is, ordinarily, a complementary result of efforts to shift the demand curve of the individual firm at the expense of others or (less importantly, I think) to change its shape by increasing the degree of product differentiation. Some of the failure of economists to identify advertising with want creation may be attributed to the undue attention that its use in purely competitive strategy has attracted. It should be noted, however, that the competitive manipulation of consumer desire is only possible, at least on any appreciable scale, when such need is not strongly felt.
2. Emulation does operate between communities. A new school or a new highway in one community does exert pressure on others to remain abreast. However, as compared with the pervasive effects of emulation in extending the demand for privately produced consumers' goods there will be agreement, I think, that this intercommunity effect is probably small.

Advertising and Behavior Control

ROBERT L. ARRINGTON

Consider the following advertisements:

1. "A woman in *Distinction Foundations* is so beautiful that all other women want to kill her."
2. Pongo Peach color from Revlon comes "from east of the sun . . . west of the moon, where each tomorrow dawns." It is "succulent on your lips" and "sizzling on your finger tips (And on your toes, goodness knows)." Let it be your "adventure in paradise."
3. "Musk by English Leather—The Civilized Way to Roar."
4. "Increase the value of your holdings. Old Charter Bourbon Whiskey—The Final Step Up."
5. Last Call Smirnoff Style: "They'd never really miss us, and it's kind of late already, and its quite a long way, and I could build a fire, and you're looking very beautiful, and we could have another martini, and its awfully nice just being home . . . you think?"
6. A Christmas Prayer. "Let us pray that the blessings of peace be ours—the peace to build and grow, to live in harmony and sympathy with others, and to plan for the future with confidence." New York Life Insurance Company.

These are instances of what is called puffery—the practice by a seller of making exaggerated, highly fanciful, or suggestive claims about a product or service. Puffery, within ill-defined limits, is legal. It is considered a legitimate, necessary, and very successful tool of the advertising industry. Puffery is not just bragging; it is bragging carefully designed to achieve a very definite effect. Using the techniques of so-called motivational research, advertising firms first identify our often hidden needs (for security, conformity, oral stimulation) and our desires (for power, sexual dominance and dalliance, adventure) and then they design ads which respond to these needs and desires. By associating a product, for which we may have little or no direct need or desire, with symbols reflecting the fulfillment of these other, often subterranean interests, the advertisement can quickly generate large numbers of consumers eager to purchase the product advertised. What woman in the sexual race of life could resist a foundation which would turn other women envious to the point of homicide? Who can turn down an adventure in paradise, east of the sun where tomorrow dawns? Who doesn't

Robert L. Arrington, "Advertising and Behavior Control," *Journal of Business Ethics*, Vol. 1, No. 1, February 1982, pp. 3–12. Copyright © 1982 by D. Reidel Publishing Company. Reprinted by permission.

want to be civilized and thoroughly libidinous at the same time? Be at the pinnacle of success—drink Old Charter. Or stay at home and dally a bit—with Smirnoff. And let us pray for a secure and predictable future, provided for by New York Life, God willing. It doesn't take very much motivational research to see the point of these sales pitches. Others are perhaps a little less obvious. The need to feel secure in one's home at night can be used to sell window air conditioners, which drown out small noises and provide a friendly, dependable companion. The fact that baking a cake is symbolic of giving bith to a baby used to prompt advertisements for cake mixes which glamorized the "creative" housewife. And other strategies, for example involving cigar symbolism, are a bit too crude to mention, but are nevertheless very effective.

Don't such uses of puffery amount to manipulation, exploitation, or downright control? In his very popular book *The Hidden Persuaders*, Vance Packard points out that a number of people in the advertising world have frankly admitted as much:

> As early as 1941 Dr. Dichter (an influential advertising consultant) was exhorting ad agencies to recognize themselves for what they actually were—"one of the most advanced laboratories in psychology." He said the successful ad agency "manipulates human motivations and desires and develops a need for goods with which the public has at one time been unfamiliar—perhaps even undesirous of purchasing." The following year *Advertising Agency* carried an ad man's statement that psychology not only holds a promise for understanding people but "ultimately for controlling their behavior."[1]

Such statements lead Packard to remark: "With all this interest in manipulating the customer's subconscious, the old slogan 'let the buyer beware' began taking on a new and more profound meaning."[2]

B. F. Skinner, the high priest of behaviorism, has expressed a similar assessment of advertising and related marketing techniques. Why, he asks, do we buy a certain kind of car?

> Perhaps our favorite TV program is sponsored by the manufacturer of that car. Perhaps we have seen pictures of many beautiful or prestigeful persons driving it—in pleasant or glamorous places. Perhaps the car has been designed with respect to our motivational patterns: the device on the hood is a phallic symbol; or the horsepower has been stepped up to please our competitive spirit in enabling us to pass other cars swiftly (or, as the advertisements say, 'safely'). The concept of freedom that has emerged as part of the cultural practice of our group makes little or no provision for recognizing or dealing with these kinds of control.[3]

In purchasing a car we may think we are free, Skinner is claiming, when in fact our act is completely controlled by factors in our environment and in our history of reinforcement. Advertising is one such factor.

A look at some other advertising techniques may reinforce the suspicion that Madison Avenue controls us like so many puppets. T.V. watchers surely have noticed that some of the more repugnant ads are shown over and over again, *ad nauseam*. My favorite, or most hated, is the one about A-1 Steak Sauce which goes something like this: Now, ladies and gentlemen, what *is* hamburger? It has succeeded in destroying my taste for hamburger, but it has surely drilled the name of A-1 Sauce into my head. And that is the point of it. Its very repetitiousness has generated what ad theorists call *information*. In this case it is indirect information, information derived not from the content of what is said but from the fact that it is said so often and so vividly that it sticks in one's mind—i.e., the information yield has increased. And not only do I always remember A-1 Sauce when I go to the grocers, I tend to assume that any product advertised so often has to be good—and so I usually buy a bottle of the stuff.

Still another technique: On a recent show of the television program "Hard Choices" it was demonstrated how subliminal suggestion can be used to control customers. In a New Orleans department store, messages to the effect that shoplifting is wrong, illegal, and subject to punishment were blended into the Muzak background music and masked so as not to be consciously audible. The store reported a dramatic drop in shoplifting. The program host conjectured whether a logical extension of this technique would be to broadcast subliminal advertising messages to the effect that the store's $15.99 sweater special is the "bargain of a lifetime." Actually, this application of subliminal suggestion to advertising has already taken place. Years ago in New Jersey a cinema was reported to have flashed subthreshold ice cream ads onto the screen during regular showings of the film—and, yes, the concession stand did a landslide business.

Puffery, indirect information transfer, subliminal advertising—are these techniques of manipulation and control whose success shows that many of us have forfeited our autonomy and become a community, or herd, of packaged souls?[4] The business world and the advertising industry certainly reject this interpretation of their efforts. *Business Week*, for example, dismissed the charge that the science of behavior, as utilized by advertising, is engaged in human engineering and manipulation. It editorialized to the effect that "it is hard to find anything very sinister about a science whose principle conclusion is that you get along with people by giving them what they want."[5] The theme is familiar: businesses just give the consumer what he/she wants; if they didn't they wouldn't stay in business very long. Proof that the consumer wants the products advertised is given by the fact that he buys them, and indeed often returns to buy them again and again.

The techniques of advertising we are discussing have had their more intellectual defenders as well. For example, Theodore Levitt, Professor of Business Administration at the Harvard Business School, has defended the practice of puffery and the use of techniques depending on motivational research.[6] What would be the consequences, he asks us, of deleting all exaggerated claims and fanciful associations from advertisements? We would be left with literal descriptions of the empirical characteristics of products and their functions. Cosmetics would be presented as facial and bodily lotions and powders which produce certain odor and color changes; they would no longer offer hope or adventure. In addition to the fact that these products would not then sell as well, they would not, according to Levitt, please us as much either. For it is hope and adventure we want when we buy them. We want automobiles not just for transportation, but for the feelings of power and status they give us. Quoting T. S. Eliot to the effect that "Human kind cannot bear very much reality," Levitt argues that advertising is an effort to "transcend nature in the raw," to "augment what nature has so crudely fashioned." He maintains that "everybody everywhere wants to modify, transform, embellish, enrich and reconstruct the world around him." Commerce takes the same liberty with reality as the artist and the priest—in all three instances the purpose is "to influence the audience by creating illusions, symbols, and implications that promise more than pure functionality." For example, "to amplify the temple in men's eyes, (men of cloth) have, very realistically, systematically sanctioned the embellishment of the houses of the gods with the same kind of luxurious design and expensive decoration that Detroit puts into a Cadillac." A poem, a temple, a Cadillac—they all elevate our spirits, offering imaginative promises and symbolic interpretations of our mundane activities. Seen in this light, Levitt claims, "Embellishment and distortion are among advertising's legitimate and socially desirable purposes." To reject these techniques of advertising would be "to deny man's honest needs and values."

Phillip Nelson, a Professor of Economics at SUNY-Binghamton, has developed an interesting defense of indirect information advertising.[7] He argues that even when the message (the direct information) is not credible, the fact that the brand is advertised, and advertised frequently, is valuable indirect information for the consumer. The reason for this is that the brands advertised most are more likely to be better buys—losers won't be advertised a lot, for it simply wouldn't pay to do so. Thus even if the advertising claims made for a widely advertised product are empty, the consumer reaps the benefit of the indirect information which shows the product to be a good buy. Nelson goes so far as to say that advertising, seen as information and especially as indirect information, does not require an intelligent human response. If the indirect information has been received and has had its impact, the consumer will purchase the better buy even if his explicit reason for doing so is silly, e.g., he naively believes an endorsement of the product by a celebrity. Even though his behavior is overtly irrational, by acting on the indirect information he is nevertheless doing what he ought to do, i.e., getting his money's worth. " 'Irrationality' is rational," Nelson writes, "if it is cost-free."

I don't know of any attempt to defend the use of subliminal suggestion in advertising, but I can imagine one form such an attempt might take. Advertising information, even if perceived below the level of conscious awareness, must appeal to some desire on the part of the audience if it is to trigger a purchasing response. Just as the admonition not to shoplift speaks directly to the superego, the sexual virtues of TR-7's, Pongo Peach, and Betty Crocker cake mix present themselves directly to the id, bypassing the pesky reality principle of the ego. With a little help from our advertising friends, we may remove a few of the discontents of civilization and perhaps even enter into the paradise of polymorphous perversity.

The defense of advertising which suggests that advertising simply is information which allows us to purchase what we want, has in turn been challenged. Does business, largely through its advertising efforts, really make available to the consumer what he/she desires and demands? John Kenneth Galbraith has denied that the matter is as straightforward as this.[8] In his opinion the desires to which business is supposed to respond, far from being original to the consumer, are often themselves created by business. The producers make both the product and the desire for it, and the "central function" of advertising is "to create desires." Galbraith coins the term "The Dependence Effect" to designate the way wants depend on the same process by which they are satisfied.

David Braybrooke has argued in similar and related ways.[9] Even though the consumer is, in a sense, the final authority concerning what he wants, he may come to see, according to Braybrooke, that he was mistaken in wanting what he did. The statement "I want x," he tells us, is not incorrigible but is "ripe for revision." If the consumer had more objective information than he is provided by product puffing, if his values had not been mixed up by motivational research strategies (e.g., the confusion of sexual and automotive values), and if he had an expanded set of choices instead of the limited set offered by profit-hungry corporations, then he might want something quite different from what he presently wants. This shows, Braybrooke thinks, the extent to which the consumer's wants are a function of advertising and not necessarily representative of his real or true wants.

The central issue which emerges between the above critics and defenders of advertising is this: do the advertising techniques we have discussed involve a violation of human autonomy and a manipulation and control of consumer behavior, *or* do they simply provide an efficient and cost-effective means of giving the consumer information on the basis of which he or she makes a free choice? Is advertising information, or creation of desire?

To answer this question we need a better conceptual grasp of what is involved in the notion of autonomy. This is a complex, multifaceted concept, and we need to approach it through the more determinate notions of (a) autonomous desire, (b) rational desire and choice, (c) free choice, and (d) control or manipulation. In what follows I shall offer some tentative and very incomplete analyses of these concepts and apply the results to the case of advertising.

(a) AUTONOMOUS DESIRE

Imagine that I am watching T.V. and see an ad for Grecian Formula 16. The thought occurs to me that if I purchase some and apply it to my beard, I will soon look younger—in fact I might even be myself again. Suddenly I want to be myself! I want to be young again! So I rush out and buy a bottle. This is our question: was the desire to be younger manufactured by the commercial, or was it 'original to me' and truly mine? Was it autonomous or not?

F. A. von Hayek has argued plausibly that we should not equate non-autonomous desires, desires which are not original to me or truly mine, with those which are culturally induced.[10] If we did equate the two, he points out, then the desires for music, art, and knowledge could not properly be attributed to a person as original to him, for these are surely induced culturally. The only desires a person would really have as his own in this case would be the purely physical ones for food, shelter, sex, etc. But if we reject the equation of the nonautonomous and the culturally induced, as von Hayek would have us do, then the mere fact that my desire to be young again is caused by the T.V. commercial—surely an instrument of popular culture transmission—does not in and of itself show that this is not my own, autonomous desire. Moreover, even if I never before felt the need to look young, it doesn't follow that this new desire is any less mine. I haven't always liked 1969 Aloxe Corton Burgundy or the music of Satie, but when the desires for these things first hit me, they were truly mine.

This shows that there is something wrong in setting up the issue over advertising and behavior control as a question whether our desires are truly ours *or* are created in us by advertisements. Induced and autonomous desires do not separate into two mutually excusive classes. To obtain a better understanding of autonomous and nonautonomous desires, let us consider some cases of a desire which a person does not *acknowledge* to be his own even though he *feels* it. The kleptomaniac has a desire to steal which in many instances he repudiates, seeking by treatment to rid himself of it. And if I were suddenly overtaken by a desire to attend an REO concert, I would immediately disown this desire, claiming possession or momentary madness. These are examples of desires which one might have but with which one would not identify. They are experienced as foreign to one's character or personality. Often a person will have what Harry Frankfurt calls a second-order desire, that is to say, a desire *not* to have another desire.[11] In such cases, the first-order desire is thought of as being nonautonomous, imposed on one. When on the contrary a person has a second-order desire to maintain and fulfill a first-order desire, then the first-order desire is truly his own, autonomous, original to him. So there is in fact a distinction between desires which are the agent's own and those which are not, but this is not the same as the distinction between desires which are innate to the agent and those which are externally induced.

If we apply the autonomous/nonautonomous distinction derived from Frankfurt to the desires brought about by advertising, does this show that advertising is responsible for creating desires which are not truly the agent's own? Not necessarily, and indeed not often. There may be some desires I feel which I have picked up from advertising and which I disown—for instance, my desire for A-1 Steak Sauce. If I act on these desires it can be said that I have been led by advertising to act in a way foreign to my nature. In these cases my autonomy has been violated. But most of the desires induced by advertising I fully accept, and hence most of these desires are autonomous. The most vivid demonstration of this is that I often return to purchase the same product over and over again, without regret or remorse. And when I don't, it is more likely that the desire has just faded than that I have repudiated it. Hence, while advertising may violate my autonomy by leading me to act on desires which are not truly mine, this seems to be the exceptional case.

Note that this conclusion applies equally well to the case of subliminal advertising. This may generate subconscious desires which lead to purchases, and the act of purchasing these goods may be inconsistent with other conscious desires I have, in which case I might repudiate my behavior and by implication the subconscious cause of it. But my subconscious desires may not be inconsistent in this way with my conscious ones; my id may be cooperative and benign rather than hostile and malign. Here again, then, advertising may or may not produce desires which are 'not truly mine'.

What are we to say in response to Braybrooke's argument that insofar as we might choose differently if advertisers gave us better information and more options, it follows that the desires we have are to be attributed more to advertising than to our own real inclinations? This claim seems empty. It amounts to saying that if the world we lived in, and we ourselves, were different, then we would want different things. This is surely true, but it is equally true of our desire for shelter as of our desire for Grecian Formula 16. If we lived in a tropical paradise, we would not need or desire shelter. If we were immortal, we would not desire youth. What is true of all desires can hardly be used as a basis for criticizing some desires by claiming that they are nonautonomous.

(b) RATIONAL DESIRE AND CHOICE

Braybrooke might be interpreted as claiming that the desires induced by advertising are often irrational ones in the sense that they are not expressed by an agent who is in full possession of the facts about the products advertised or about the alternative products which might be offered him. Following this line of thought, a possible criticism of advertising is that it leads us to act on irrational desires or to make irrational choices. It might be said that our autonomy has been violated by the fact that we are prevented from following our rational wills or that we have been denied the 'positive freedom' to develop our true, rational selves. It might be claimed that the desires induced in us by advertising are false desires in that they do not reflect our essential, i.e., rational essence.

The problem faced by this line of criticism is that of determining what is to count as rational desire or rational choice. If we require that the desire or choice be the product of an awareness of *all* the facts about the product, then surely every one of us is always moved by irrational desires and makes nothing but irrational choices. How could we know all the facts about a product? If it be required only that we possess all of the *available* knowledge about the product advertised, then we still have to face the problem that not all available knowledge is *relevant* to a rational choice. If I am purchasing a car, certain engineering features will be, and others won't be, relevant, *given what I want in a car*. My prior desires determine the relevance of information. Normally a rational desire or choice is thought to be one based upon relevant information, and information is relevant if it shows how other, prior desires may be satisfied. It can plausibly be claimed that it is such prior desires that advertising agencies acknowledge, and that the agencies often provide the type of information that is relevant in light of these desires. To the extent that this is true, advertising does not inhibit our rational wills or our autonomy as rational creatures.

It may be urged that much of the puffery engaged in by advertising does not provide relevant information at all but rather makes claims which are not factually true. If someone buys Pongo Peach in anticipation of an adventure in paradise, or Old Charter in expectation of increasing the value of his holdings, then he/she is expecting purely imaginary benefits. In no literal sense will the one product provide adventure and the other increased capital. A purchasing decision based on anticipation of imaginary benefits is not, it might be said, a rational decision, and a desire for imaginary benefits is not a rational desire.

In rejoinder it needs to be pointed out that we often wish to purchase subjective effects which in being subjective are nevertheless real enough. The feeling of adventure or of enhanced social prestige and value are examples of subjective effects promised by advertising. Surely many (most?) advertisements directly promise subjective effects which their patrons actually desire (and obtain when they purchase the product), and thus the ads provide relevant information for rational choice. Moreover, advertisements often provide accurate indirect information on the basis of which a person who wants a certain subjective effect rationally chooses a product. The mechanism involved here is as follows.

To the extent that a consumer takes an advertised product to offer a subjective effect and the product does not, it is unlikely that it will be purchased again. If this happens in a number of cases, the product will be taken off the market. So here the market regulates itself, providing the mechanism whereby misleading advertisements are withdrawn and misled customers are no longer misled. At the same time, a successful bit of puffery, being one which leads to large and repeated sales, produces satisfied customers and more advertising of the product. The indirect information provided by such large-scale advertising efforts provides a measure of verification to the consumer who is looking for certain kinds of subjective effect. For example, if I want to fell well dressed and in fashion, and I consider buying an Izod Alligator shirt which is advertised in all of the magazines and newspapers, then the fact that other people buy it and that this leads to repeated advertisements shows me that the desired subjective effect is real enough and that I indeed will be well dressed and in fashion if I purchase the shirt. The indirect information may lead to a rational decision to purchase a product because the information testifies to the subjective effect that the product brings about.

Some philosophers will be unhappy with the conclusion of this section, largely because they have a concept of true, rational, or ideal desire which is not the same as the one used here. A Marxist, for instance, may urge that any desire felt by alienated man in a capitalistic society is foreign to his true nature. Or an existentialist may claim that the desires of inauthentic men are themselves inauthentic. Such concepts are based upon general theories of human nature which are unsubstantiated and perhaps incapble of substantiation. Moreover, each of these theories is committed to a concept of an ideal desire which is normatively debatable and which is distinct from the ordinary concept of a rational desire as one based upon relevant information. But it is in the terms of the ordinary concept that we express our concern that advertising may limit our autonomy in the sense of leading us to act on irrational desires, and if we operate with this concept we are driven again to the conclusion that advertising may lead, but probably most often does not lead, to an infringement of autonomy.

(c) FREE CHOICE

It might be said that some desires are so strong or so covert that a person cannot resist them, and that when he acts on such desires he is not acting freely or voluntarily but is rather the victim of irresistible impulse or an unconscious drive. Perhaps those who condemn advertising feel that it produces this kind of desire in us and consequently reduces our autonomy.

This raises a very difficult issue. How do we distinguish between an impulse we *do* not resist and one we *could* not resist, between freely giving in to a desire and succumbing to one? I have argued elsewhere that the way to get at this issue is in terms of the notion of acting for a reason.[12] A person acts or chooses freely if he does so for a reason, that is, if he can adduce considerations which justify in his mind the act in question. Many of our actions are in fact free because this condition frequently holds. Often, however, a person will act from habit, or whim, or impulse, and on these occasions he does not have a reason in mind. Nevertheless he often acts voluntarily in these instances, i.e., he could have acted otherwise. And this is because if there *had been* a reason for acting otherwise of which he was aware, he would in fact have done so. Thus acting from habit or impulse is not necessarily to act in an involuntary manner. If, however, a person is aware of a good reason to do x and still follws his impuse to do y, then he can be said to be impelled by irresistible impulse and hence to act involuntarily. Many kleptomaniacs can be said to act involuntarily, for in spite of their knowledge that they likely will be caught and their awareness that the goods they steal have little utilitarian value to them, they nevertheless steal. Here their 'out of character' desires have the upper hand, and we have a case of compulsive behavior.

Applying these notions of voluntary and compulsive behavior to the case of behavior prompted by advertising, can we say that consumers influenced by advertising act compulsively? The unexciting answer is: sometimes they do, sometimes not. I may have an overwhelming, T.V. induced urge to own a Mazda Rx-7 and all the while realize that I can't afford one without severely reducing my family's caloric intake to a dangerous level. If, aware of this good reason not to purchase the car, I nevertheless do so, this shows that I have been the victim of T.V. compulsion. But if I have the urge, as I assure you I do, and don't act on it, or if in some other possible world I could afford an Rx-7, then I have not been the subject of undue influence by Mazda advertising. Some Mazda Rx-7 purchasers act compulsively; others do not. The Mazda advertising effort *in general* cannot be condemned, then, for impairing its customers' autonomy in the sense of limiting free or voluntary choice. Of course the question remains what should be done about the fact that advertising may and does *occasionally* limit free choice.

In the case of subliminal advertising we may find an individual whose subconscious desires are activated by advertising into doing something his calculating, reasoning ego does not approve. This would be a case of compulsion. But most of us have a benevolent subconsciousness which does not overwhelm our ego and its reasons for action. And therefore most of us can respond to subliminal advertising without thereby risking our autonomy. To be sure, if some advertising firm developed a subliminal technique which drove all of us to purchase Lear jets, thereby reducing our caloric intake to the zero point, then we would have a case of advertising which could properly be censured for infringing our right to autonomy. We should acknowledge that this is possible, but at the same time we should recognize that it is not an inherent result of subliminal advertising.

(d) CONTROL OR MANIPULATION

Briefly let us consider the matter of control and manipulation. Under what conditions do these activities occur? In a recent paper on "Forms and Limits of Control" I suggested the following criteria:[13]

A person C controls the behavior of another person P *if*

1. C intends P to act in a certain way A;
2. C's intention is causally effective in bringing about A; and
3. C intends to ensure that all of the necessary conditions of A are satisfied.

These criteria may be elaborated as follows. To control another person it is not enough that one's actions produce certain behavior on the part of that person; additionally one must intend that this happen. Hence control is the intentional production of behavior. Moreover, it is not enough just to have the intention; the intention must give rise to the conditions which bring about the intended effect. Finally, the controller must intend to establish by his actions any otherwise unsatisfied necessary conditions for the production of the intended effect. The controller is not just influencing the outcome, not just having input; he is as it were guaranteeing that the sufficient conditions for the intended effect are satisfied.

Let us apply these criteria of control to the case of advertising and see what happens. Conditions (1) and (3) are crucial. Does the Mazda manufacturing company or its advertising agency intend that I buy an Rx-7? Do they intend that a certain number of people buy the car? *Prima facie* it seems more appropriate to say that they *hope* a certain number of people will buy it, and hoping and intending are not the same. But the difficult term here is 'intend'. Some philosophers have argued that to intend A it is necessary only to desire that A happen and to believe that it will. If this is correct, and if marketing analysis gives the Mazda agency a reasonable belief that a certain segment of the population will buy its product, then, assuming on its part the desire that this happen, we have the conditions necessary for saying that the agency intends that a certain segment purchase the car. If I am a member of this segment of the population, would it then follow that the agency intends that I purchase an Rx-7? Or is control referentially opaque? Obviously we have some questions here which need further exploration.

Let us turn to the third condition of control, the requirement that the controller intend to activate or bring about any otherwise unsatisfied necessary conditions for the production of the intended effect. It is in terms of this condition that we are able to distinguish brainwashing from liberal education. The brainwasher arranges all of the necessary conditions for belief. On the other hand, teachers (at least those of liberal persuasion) seek only to influence their students—to provide them with information and enlightenment which they may absorb *if they wish*. We do not normally think of teachers as controlling their students, for the students' performances depend as well on their own interests and inclinations.

Now the advertiser—does he control, or merely influence, his audience? Does he intend to ensure that all of the necessary conditions for purchasing behavior are met, or does he offer information and symbols which are intended to have an effect only *if* the potential purchaser has certain desires? Undeniably advertising induces some desires, and it does this intentionally, but more often than not it intends to induce a desire for a particular object, *given* that the purchaser already has other desires. Given a desire for youth, or power, or adventure, or ravishing beauty, we are led to desire Grecian Formula 16, Mazda Rx-7s, Pongo Peach, and Distinctive Foundations. In this light, the advertiser is influencing us by appealing to independent desires we already have. He is not creating those basic desires. Hence it seems appropriate to deny that he intends to produce all of the necessary conditions for our purchases, and appropriate to deny that he controls us.

Let me summarize my argument. The critics of advertising see it as having a pernicious effect on the autonomy of consumers, as controlling their lives and manufacturing their very souls. The defense claims that advertising only offers information and in effect allows industry to provide consumers with what they want. After developing some of the philosophical dimensions of this dispute, I have come down tentatively in favor of the advertisers. Advertising may, but certainly does not always or even frequently, control behavior, produce compulsive behavior, or create wants which are not rational or are not truly those of the consumer. Admittedly it may in individual cases do all of these things, but it is innocent of the charge of intrinsically or necessarily doing them or even, I think, of often doing so. This limited potentiality, to be sure, leads to the question whether advertising should be abolished or severely curtailed or regulated because of its potential to harm a few poor souls in the above ways. This is a very difficult question, and I do not pretend to have the answer. I only hope that the above discussion, in showing some of the kinds of harm that can be done by advertising and by indicating the likely limits of this harm, will put us in a better position to grapple with the question.

NOTES

1. Vance Packard, *The Hidden Persuaders* (Pocket Books, New York, 1958), pp. 20–21.
2. *Ibid.*, p. 21.
3. B. F. Skinner, "Some Issues Concerning the Control of Human Behavior: A Symposium," in Karlins and Andrews (eds.), *Man Controlled* (The Free Press, New York, 1972).

4. I would like to emphasize that in what follows I am discussing these techniques of advertising from the standpoint of the issue of control and not from that of deception.

5. Quoted by Packard, *op. cit.*, p. 220.

6. Theodore Levitt, "The Morality (?) of Advertising," *Harvard Business Review* 48 (1970), 84–92.

7. Phillip Nelson, "Advertising and Ethics," in Richard T. De George and Joseph A. Pichler (eds.), *Ethics, Free Enterprise, and Public Policy* (Oxford University Press, New York, 1978), pp. 187–98.

8. John Kenneth Galbraith, *The Affluent Society*; reprinted in Tom L. Beauchamp and Norman E. Bowie (eds.), *Ethical Theory and Business* (Prentice-Hall, Englewood Cliffs, 1979), pp. 496–501.

9. David Braybrooke, "Skepticism of Wants, and Certain Subversive Effects of Corporations on American Values," in Sidney Hook (ed.), *Human Values and Economic Policy* (New York University Press, New York, 1967); reprinted in Beauchamp and Bowie (eds.), *op. cit.*, pp. 502–8.

10. F. A. von Hayek, "The *Non Sequitur* of the 'Dependence Effect,' " *Southern Economic Journal* (1961); reprinted in Beauchamp and Bowie (eds.), *op. cit.*, pp. 508–12.

11. Harry Frankfurt, "Freedom of the Will and the Concept of a Person," *Journal of Philosophy* **LXVIII** (1971), 5–20.

12. Robert L. Arrington, "Practical Reason, Responsibility and the Psychopath," *Journal for the Theory of Social Behavior* 9 (1979), 71–89.

13. Robert L. Arrington, "Forms and Limits of Control," delivered at the annual meeting of the Southern Society for Philosophy and Psychology, Birmingham, Alabama, 1980.

Corporate Governance

Case Study—A. H. Robins:
The Dalkon Shield

A. R. GINI AND T. SULLIVAN

On August 21, 1985, A. R. Robins of Richmond, Virginia—the seventeenth largest pharmaceutical house in America and corporately rated as number 392 in the Fortune 500—filed for reorganization under Chapter 11 of the 1978 Federal Bankruptcy Code. On the surface, Robins seemed to be a thriving company. Its popular products, including Robitussin cough syrup, Chap Stick lip balm, and Sergeant's flea and tick collars for cats and dogs, generated record sales in 1985 of $706 million with a net income in excess of $75 million. Robins' petition for protection under Chapter 11 stems directly from the "blitz of litigation" over a product it has not produced since 1974, the Dalkon Shield intrauterine birth control device. At the time it filed for bankruptcy Robins had been deluged with more than 12,000 personal injury lawsuits charging that the Dalkon Shield was responsible for countless serious illnesses and at least 20 deaths among the women who used it.

In many ways this bankruptcy petition mimes and mirrors (Johns-) Manville's unprecedented request for reorganization in 1982. Manville, the nation's, if not the world's, largest producer of asbestos, claimed that it was succumbing to a "blitz of toxic torts" and therefore could not carry on with business as usual. In August 1982 Manville was facing 16,500 suits on behalf of people who claimed to have contracted cancer and other diseases caused by asbestos and the asbestos-related products that the company produced.

Like Manville, A. H. Robins is defending and explaining its actions by claiming that it simply cannot go on and fulfill its immediate and potential obligations to its stockholders, customers, employees, and litigants (claimants) unless it takes dramatic financial action. In filing for Chapter 11 Robins has won at least temporary respite from its legal woes. Although the company will continue operating during the reorganization, all suits now pending are frozen and no new suits can be filed. While the company develops a plan to handle its liabilities, it is up to the bankruptcy courts to deal with all present claims as well as to establish guidelines for the handling of any future claims.[1] Whatever the final results, the Dalkon Shield case may well turn out to be the worst product liability nightmare that a U.S. drugmaker or major corporation has ever suffered.[2]

✻ ✻ ✻

The A. H. Robins Company is essentially a family owned and operated organization. The original company was founded by Albert Hartley Robins, a registered pharmacist, in 1866 in Richmond, Virginia. His grandson, E. Claiborne Robins, built and directed the company into a multinational conglomerate which was able to obtain Fortune 500 status by the middle of the twentieth century. While E. Claiborne Robins remains Chairman of the Board, E. Claiborne Junior is now the firm's president and CEO. Both the family and the company are much liked and respected in their home state. Generations of employees have repeatedly claimed that E. Claiborne Senior was at his worst a "benevolent despot" and at his best a kind and gentle man sincerely interested in quality control as well as his employees' well being. By all reports E. Claiborne Junior seems to be following in his father's footsteps. Moreover, the family's kindness has not been limited to its employees. In 1969 E. Claiborne Senior personally donated over $50 million to the University of Richmond. Since then the Robins family has given at least $50 million more to the university, and additional millions to other universities and to diverse other causes. In December 1983 *Town and Country* magazine listed Claiborne Senior among the top five of "The Most Generous Americans."

Both the family and the company take pride in having "always gone by the book" and always giving their customers a good product at a fair price. In its 120 years of operation the company had done business without having a single product-liability lawsuit filed against it. Critics now claim that Robins has been involved in a directly ordered, prolonged institutional cover-up of the short- and long-term effects of the use of the Dalkon Shield. Moreover, many critics claim that, more than just stonewalling the possible side effects of the Shield, Robins is guilty of marketing a product they knew to be relatively untested, undependable, and therefore potentially dangerous. Robins is accused of having deceived doctors, lied to women, perjured itself to federal judges, and falsified documentation to the FDA. According to Morton Mintz, Robins' most outspoken critic, thousands, probably tens of thousands, of women who trusted the doctors who trusted A. H. Robins paid a ghastly price for the use of the Dalkon Shield: chronic pelvic infections, impairment or loss of childbearing capacity, children with multiple birth defects, unwanted abortions, recurring health problems, and chronic pain.

IUDs are among the most ancient forms of contraception, known for more than two thousand years. Exactly how an IUD prevents conception is not known. It may interfere with the fertilization of the eggs, but most experts believe that when inserted into the uterus it prevents pregnancy by making it difficult for a fertilized egg to attach itself to the wall of the uterus. Over the centuries the materials used in the fabrication of IUDs include ebony, glass, gold, ivory, pewter, wood, wool, diamond-studded platinum, copper, and plastic.[3] The Dalkon Shield was developed by Dr. Hugh J. Davis, a former professor of obstetrics and gynecology at the Johns Hopkins University, and Irwin Lerner, an electrical engineer. In 1970 they sold their rights to the Shield to Robins, who agreed to pay royalties on future sales and $750,000 in cash. Between 1971 and 1974 Robins sold 4.5 million Dalkon Shields around the world, including 2.85 million in the United States.

By the late 1960s large numbers of women had become concerned about the safety of the Pill. These women formed an ever-growing potential market for an alternative means of birth control. Many of these women switched to "barrier" methods of birth control, particularly the diaphragm, which, when used with spermicidal creams or jellies, can be highly effective, though inconvenient. Others turned to IUDs, which, although convenient, previously had been considered unsafe—causing pelvic infections, irregular bleeding, uterine cramps, and accidental expulsion. Robins leapt at an opportunity to develop a new market with their product. The company's task was to convince physicians that the Shield was as effective as oral contraceptives in preventing pregnancies and that it was safer, better designed, and afforded greater resistance to inadvertent expulsion from the uterus than other IUDs.[4]

In January 1971 Robins began to sell the Dalkon Shield, promoting it as the "modern, superior," "second generation" and—most importantly—"safe" intrauterine device for birth control. The Shield itself is a nickel-sized plastic device that literally looks like a badge or a shield with spikes around the edges and a thread-sized "nylon tail string," which allowed both the wearer and the physician a means to guarantee that the device had not been expelled. The Shield was relatively inexpensive. The device itself sold for between $3.00 and $4.50 (its production costs were an incredibly low figure of $.25 a Shield). The only other cost associated with the Shield was the doctor's office fee for insertion and a recommended yearly pelvic examination. Dr. Hugh Davis claimed that the Dalkon Shield was the safest and most effective IUD because it is "the only IUD which is truly anatomically engineered for optimum uterine placement, fit, tolerance, and retention."[5] Davis was able to persuade a large number of physicians of the effectiveness of the Shield in an article he published in the "Current Investigation" section of the *American Journal of Obstetrics and Gynecology* in February 1970. The article described a study conducted at the Johns Hopkins Family Planning Clinic involving 640 women who had worn the Shield for one year. His analysis was based on 3,549 women-months of experience. Davis cited five pregnancies, ten expulsions, nine removals for medical reasons, and three removals for personal reasons. His startling results: tolerance rate (non-expulsion), 96 percent; pregnancy rate, 1.1 percent. The A. H. Robins Company reprinted no fewer than 199,000 copies of the Davis article for distribution to physicians.[6]

While various executives strongly recommended that other studies be commissioned to validate Davis's results, in January 1971 Robins began to market and sell the Shield on the basis of Davis's limited analysis. Robins' decision to produce and sell the Shield based on Davis's statistics may not coincide with the highest standards of scientific research, but it did not violate any FDA statutes and was therefore perfectly legal. At the time Robins produced the Shield, FDA had no regulatory policies in force regarding IUDs of any kind. While FDA had the authority to regulate the production, testing, and sales of all new prescriptions, it could only *recommend* testing on new medical devices. It could not monitor, investigate, or police a device unless charges of lack of effectiveness, injury, or abuse were formally leveled against the device or the producer.

In December 1970 Robins commissioned a major long-term study to reinforce Davis's results. The study concentrated on ten clinics, seven in the United States and one each in Canada, Nova Scotia, and British Columbia. Between December 1970 and December 1974 (six months after Robins suspended domestic sales) 2,391 women were fitted with the Shield. The first results came out in November 1972, with only about half of the women enrolled in the study. The statistics showed a sixteen month pregnancy rate of 1.6 percent. The Robins home office was more than pleased and immediately communicated this information to its sales staff. Thirteen months later, with all the women now participating in the program, less happy figures began to show up. The pregnancy rate after six months was 2.1 percent; after twelve months, 3.2 percent; after eighteen months, 3.5 percent; and after twenty-three months, 4.1 percent. In a final report published as a confidential internal document in August 1975 the final figures and results were even more devastating. The pregnancy rate after six months was 2.6 percent; after twelve months, 4.2 percent; after eighteen months, 4.9 percent; and after twenty-four months, 5.7 percent. Two of the scientists involved in this project submitted a minority report claiming that the Shield was even less effective than these already damaging figures indicated. They claimed that the pregnancy rate during the first year was much higher: after six months, 3.3 percent; and after twelve months, 5.5 percent. This twelve-month pregnancy rate is exactly five times *higher than* the rate Robins advertised and promoted—1.1 percent—to catapult the Shield to leadership in the IUD business.[7] This minority report was never disclosed to the medical community by Robins. Nor did Robins communicate these results to its own sales force. It did report some of these findings to FDA in July 1974, but only after the company had suspended domestic sales earlier that June.

Soon after the Shield entered the marketplace, independent research results began to appear in both national and foreign journals of medicine. In 1970 and 1971 Dr. Mary O. Gabrielson, working out of clinics in San Francisco and Oakland, did an eighteen-month study on 937 women with results that Robins would not want to advertise. The rate of medical removals was 26.4 percent; the pregnancy rate, 5.1 percent. In 1973 the *British Medical Journal* published a study showing a 4.7 percent pregnancy rate in Shield users.[8] Again because there was no law requiring disclosure of this new research information, Robins did not rush to inform the general public, the medical community, or the FDA.

At the same time that the Robins Company was receiving research results pointing to poor statistical effectiveness of the Shield, they also began to receive more and more "single physician experience" reports warning and complaining about some of the medical consequences from using the Shield. These physician's reports plus the statistics generated from controlled clinical reports began to portray the Shield as neither effective nor safe.

The primary cause of concern for Shield users proved to be a much higher incidence of uterine/pelvic bacterial infections. PID (pelvic inflammatory disease) is a highly virulent and very painful, difficult to cure, life threatening infection, which more often than not impairs or destroys a woman's ability to bear children. Of those women who conceived with the Shield in place (approximately 110,000 in the United States), an estimated 60 percent of them miscarried after suffering severe bacterial infections (PID). In 1974 FDA reported that over 245 women in their fourth to sixth month of pregnancy suffered the relatively rare bacterially-induced miscarriage called septic spontaneous abortions. For fifteen women, these septic abortions were fatal.[9] Moreover, hundreds of women throughout the world who had conceived while wearing the Shield gave birth prematurely to children with grave congenital defects, including blindness, cerebral palsy, and mental retardation.[10]

Scientists now believe that the systemic cause for these virulent forms of bacterial infection is the nylon tail of the Shield itself. The Dalkon Shield tail string runs between the vagina, where bacteria are always present, and the uterus, which is germ free. It then passes through the cervix, where cervical mucus is the body's natural defense against bacterial invasion of the uterus. Robins claimed that cervical mucus would stop all germs from entering and infecting the uterus. To the naked eye, the Dalkon Shield tail string is an impervious monofilament, meaning that bacteria on it could not get into it. Actually, however, it is a cylindrical sheath encasing 200 to 450 round monofilaments separated by spaces. While the string was knotted at both ends, neither end was actually sealed. Therefore, any bacteria that got into the spaces between the filaments would be insulated from the body's natural antibacterial action while being drawn into the uterus by "wicking," a phenomenon similar to that by which a string draws the melting wax of a candle to the flame. Scientists believe that the longer the Shield and its string/tail is in place, the greater the chances for its deterioration and infiltration, thereby inducing infection in the uterus. Scientists now also contend that the "syndrome of spontaneous septic abortions" that occurred to women who had the Shield in place in the early second trimester of their pregnancy was caused by the tail string. That is, radical and sudden infection occurred when the uterus expanded to the point where it tended to pull the tail string into itself thereby bringing on instant, often lethal, contamination.[11]

In the summer of 1983 the Centers for Disease Control in Atlanta and the FDA recommended that all women still using the Shield should contact their physicians and have it immediately removed. The Agencies found that women using the Shield had a fivefold increase in risk for contracting PID as compared to women using other types of IUDs. No change in contraceptive practice was recommended for women using any other type of IUD.[12] In April 1985 two studies funded by the National Institute of Health announced yet another dire warning. These studies showed that childless IUD wearers who have had PID run a higher risk of infertility if their devices were Shields than if they were other makes.[13]

Throughout all of this, A. H. Robins officials appeared to be unaware of, or at best indifferent to, the issues, facts, and effects of their product. The company assumed the position of complete denial of any intentional wrongdoing or any malicious intent to evade full public disclosure of pertinent medical information about the safety and effectiveness of the Shield. On numerous separate occasions both in public forums and under oath, E. Claiborne Robins, Senior, has claimed near ignorance of Robins' sixteen-year involvement with the Dalkon Shield. At a series of depositions taken in 1984 Robins Senior swore that he was unable to recall ever having discussed the Shield with his son, the company's chief executive officer and president. When asked, "You certainly knew, when you started marketing this device, that PID was a life-threatening disease, did you not?" Robins testified: "I don't know that. I never thought of it as life-threatening." Did he know it could destroy fertility? "Maybe I should, but I don't know that. I have heard that, but I am not sure where." Carl Lunsford, senior vice-president for research and development, swore he could recall no "expression of concern" by any company official about PID, and he didn't remember having "personally wondered" about the toll it was taking. He had not tried to find out how many users had died. He had not "personally reviewed" *any* studies on the Shield's safety or effectiveness. When asked if he had "any curiosity" regarding the millions of dollars the company had been paying out in punitive damages to settle lawsuits, his answer was, "No."[14] The case of William Forrest, vice-president and general counsel of A. H. Robins, further strains belief. He has been described by E. Claiborne Junior as one of the company's "two most instrumental" persons in the Dalkon Shield situation. He was in effect in charge of all Shield matters and related legal issues for over a decade. In a trial proceeding, Forrest testified that his wife had worn a Shield until it was surgically removed. She had also had a hysterectomy. Although IUD removals and hysterectomies were frequently connected and simultaneous events for many infected Shield wearers, Forrest steadfastly denied any connection in his wife's case and gave vague and widely differing dates for the two events. He and his wife, he explained, did not discuss such matters in detail. Indeed, Forrest gave a series of confusing accounts of his wife's hysterectomy and its possible relationship to the Shield she had worn.

> Q: Did her doctor advise her that her hysterectomy was in any way related to the Dalkon Shield?
>
> A: Not that I know of, no, sir.
>
> Q: Did you ever ask her that?
>
> A: I don't recall. I may have asked her that. I don't recall the doctor telling her that. . . .
>
> Q: . . . Are you telling the ladies and gentlemen of the jury that you and your wife have never had a discussion concerning whether or not the Dalkon Shield played a part in her hysterectomy?
>
> A: Well, certainly, as I indicated to you, we had very general discussions. Now, if I asked her whether that played a part, I don't recall specifically if I did. If I did, to my knowledge, there was no indication that it did.[15]

The company's response to all claims of faulty product design and limited testing procedures has been counter assertions or counter claims regarding the faulty or improper use of the product by the user or the physician. The company has steadfastly maintained that there were no special dangers inherent in the device. In a report to FDA they stated: "Robins believes that serious scientific questions exist about whether the Dalkon Shield poses a significantly different risk of infection than other IUDs." Their continuous theme has been that doctors, not the device, have caused any infections associated with the Shield. The company was committed to the notion that pregnancy and removal rates could be kept extremely low by proper placement of the Shield. They also contended that user abuse played a part in the Shield's supposed malfunctioning. They defined user abuse as poor personal hygiene habits, sexual promiscuity or excessive sexual activity, or physical tampering with the device itself.

According to three different independent investigative reports,[16] the company's public face of calm denial and counterargument masked an internal conspiring to conceal information from the public, the court system, and the FDA. These reports (books) claim documented evidence of the multilevel cover-up. They claim that Robins quashed all documentation debating and contesting Dr. Hugh Davis's celebrated pregnancy rate of only 1.1 percent, and that Robins knew of the real significance and traumatic effect of the wicking process of the tail string but did nothing about it. Not only did the company know that the nylon cord used on the tail could degenerate and cause infection, but as early as the summer of 1972 the company was warned in writing by one of its chief consultants, Dr. Thad Earl, that pregnant women should have the Shield immediately removed to avoid "abortion and septic infection." These reports also contend that on at least three separate occasions executives and officials of Robins lost or destroyed company files and records specifically requested by the Federal Appellate Courts and the FDA.

By May 1974 Robins could no longer avoid the evidence presented to it by FDA implicating the Shield in numerous cases of spontaneous septic abortions and in the death of at least four women as a result. These findings were disclosed in a letter sent by the company to 120,000 doctors. In June 1974 Robins suspended the U.S. distribution and sale of the Shield. In January 1975 Robins called back and completely removed the Shield from the market. The company termed the action a "market withdrawal," not a recall, because it was undertaken voluntarily and not at the direct order of FDA. In September 1980 Robins again wrote the medical community suggesting as a purely precautionary measure that doctors remove the Shield from their patients. In Octover 1984 Robins initiated a $4 million television, newspaper, and magazine advertising campaign warning and recommending that all women still wearing the device have it removed at Robins's expense. In April 1985 Robins publicly set aside $615 million to settle legal claims from women who had used the Shield. This reserve is the largest provision of its kind to date in a product liability case. In May 1985 a jury in Wichita, Kansas, awarded nearly $9 million to a woman who had charged that the use of the Shield caused her to undergo a hysterectomy. The award was the largest ever made in the history of litigation involving the Shield. Officials of the Robins Company felt that adverse decisions of this magnitude could mean that their $615 million fund would prove to be inadequate. On August 21, 1985, Robins filed for Chapter 11 protection, citing litigation relating to the Shield as the main cause for its actions. Company spokesmen said that it hoped that the Federal Bankruptcy Court in Richmond would set up a payment schedule that would enable it to survive while insuring that victims "would be treated fairly." E. Claiborne Robins, Jr., called it "essential that we move to protect the company's economic viability against those who would destroy it for the benefit of a few."[17] The intriguing financial irony in all of this is that when Robins filed for Chapter 11 it had already spent, at a conservative estimate, $500 million in settlements, litigation losses, and legal fees for a product it had only manufactured for three years and from which it had only realized $500,000 in real profits![18]

*   *   *

The central issues in this case revolve around the answers to four critical questions:

1. Is A. H. Robins telling the truth about its knowledge of the health factors involved in the use of the Dalkon Shield? Is it true that they had no awareness of the connection between PID and spontaneous septic abortions and the nylon tail of the Shield? Or is it the case, as many of their critics contend, that they have conspired for over sixteen years to both deny and cover up any knowledge of the short- and long-term effects of wearing the Shield?

2. Even if Robins is not guilty of conspiring to misinform its customers, why didn't simple "prudence" lead the company to go public immediately when "single physician experience" and the results of their own and outside testing procedures indicated from the beginning that there were serious drawbacks, limitations, and dangers inherent in the product? Moreover, after suspending production in 1974 because of FDA findings, why did Robins wait until 1984 to recommend that all women still wearing the Shield have it removed?

3. Is the 1978 Federal Bankruptcy Code a proper and valid means of seeking relief from immediate and possible future liability?

4. Is it simply the case, as Morton Mintz—Dalkon critic and corporate watchdog—has stated, that Robins knowingly and willfully placed greed before human welfare because the corporate structure itself is oriented toward profit and away from liability?

Robins claims that it produced a well-conceived, well-researched, and perfectly acceptable product well within the standards of the industry. They contend that any and all ill effects arising from the use of the Shield are the results of unexpected and unforeseeable technical or material breakdowns. At no time did they conspire to defraud the public. They maintain that family honor and the general reputation of the company simply would not allow for such behavior. Officials of the company further claim that just because their actions are unusual and unorthodox, it does not mean that they are acting in an immoral or illegal fashion. They insist that filing for bankruptcy was unavoidable and in the best interest of its stockholders and creditors. Moreover, they feel that in the long run their decision will better benefit those who have suffered from medical complications arising from the use of the Shield. Robins perceives the filing for Chapter 11 as the only orderly way possible for the company to treat everyone fairly.

In all candor it must be remembered that Robins's actions are not without danger. To the extent that Robins is using Chapter 11 as a shelter against the rush of product-liability litigation, the company is nevertheless taking a gamble. Robins must now operate under the eye of a federal bankruptcy judge, and as Lawrence King, Professor of Law at NYU, has said in regard to the Manville case, "Once you file, there is always a risk of liquidation."[19] For example, as part of their reorganization arrangement with the court, Robins agreed to a class action procedure in which they would begin a 91 nation advertisement campaign to announce to all former users their right to file a claim for compensation for any health problems that may have been caused by the Shield. All potential claimants are given a case number and sent a questionnaire to determine if they qualify for a financial settlement. As of June 1986 more than 300,000 claims have been filed against Robins![20] Numbers such as these may completely overwhelm the bankruptcy court's ability to reorganize and reestablish the company on a sound financial basis.

There are several lessons lurking in this case. The first of them has to do with the dangers held by the combination of a legalistic society and a highly technological one—or, perhaps more clearly, in a society based upon notions of individual freedom suddenly caught up in rapid innovation. Generally speaking, we hold, in America, that that which is not specifically prohibited is permitted. The danger comes when technology continually creates inventions for which there are no categories and hence no rules. FDA clearly is charged with safeguarding health and monitoring the pharmaceutical industry, among others. The Dalkon Shield is clearly a contraceptive capable of creating physical good or ill, and yet because it is a device, neither a food nor drug, and because neither FDA nor A. H. Robins would act at the outset on anything other than the exact literal definition of the rules, no real consideration was given to the medical consequences of the Shield. FDA felt it lacked the authority and A. H. Robins felt no moral imperative that was not specifically imposed upon them. We have left all interpretations of intention, all exercise of reasonableness, to the court systems—expert and de facto agents. The second lesson can be found in that the Dalkon Shield itself may have been a genuinely safe, useful product, even a breakthrough, as the first effective IUD. The danger was ancillary to the device—the "wicking" action of the tail string—and had Robins followed the usual FDA approval guidelines for drugs, this flaw might have been discovered, and perhaps eliminated. It was in adhering only to the letter of the regulations and in using this exclusion of devices to rush into production and quicker profits that the company began a course which may end in its own demise.

Given all of this conflicting data, perhaps there is only one thing we can say with certainty in regard to Robins's production of the Dalkon Shield: "In the pharmaceutical world, products that fail can cripple companies as well as people."[21]

NOTES

1. A. R. Gini, "Manville: The Ethics of Economic Efficiency?" *Journal of Business Ethics*, 3 (1984), p. 66.
2. *Time*, September 2, 1985, p. 32.
3. Morton Mintz, *At Any Cost* (New York: Pantheon Books, 1985), p. 25.
4. Ibid., p. 29.
5. Ibid., p. 82.
6. Ibid., pp. 29–31.
7. Ibid., pp. 86–88.
8. Ibid., pp. 81, 82.
9. *FDA Consumer*, May 1981, p. 32.
10. Morton Mintz, "At Any Cost," *The Progressive*, November 1985, p. 21.
11. *At Any Cost*, pp. 131–48 and 149–72.
12. *FDA Consumer*, July–August 1983, p. 2.
13. *Wall Street Journal*, April 11, 1985, p. 1.
14. Mintz, "At Any Cost," *The Progressive*, p. 24.
15. Mintz, *At Any Cost*, p. 111.
16. Mintz, *At Any Cost* (New York: Pantheon Books, 1985). Sheldon Engelmayer and Robert Wagman, *Lord's Justice* (New York: Anchor Press/Doubleday, 1985). Susan Perry and Jim Dawson, *Nightmare: Women and the Dalkon Shield* (New York: Macmillan Publishing, 1985).
17. *New York Times*, August 22, 1985, pp. 1, 6.
18. *Time*, November 26, 1984, p. 86.
19. Gini, "Manville: The Ethics of Economic Efficiency?" p. 68.
20. *Wall Street Journal*, June 26, 1986, p. 10.
21. *U.S. News and World Report*, September 2, 1985, p. 12.

Who Rules the Corporation?

RALPH NADER, MARK GREEN, AND JOEL SELIGMAN

All modern state corporation statutes describe a common image of corporate governance, an image pyramidal in form. At the base of the pyramid are the shareholders or owners of the corporation. Their ownership gives them the right to elect representatives to direct the corporation and to approve fundamental corporate actions such as mergers or bylaw amendments. The intermediate level is held by the board of directors, who are required by a provision common to nearly every state corporation law "to manage the

Excerpted from *Taming the Giant Corporation*, by Ralph Nader, Mark Green, and Joel Siligman, reprinted by permission of W. W. Norton & Company, Inc. Copyright © 1976 by Ralph Nader.

business and affairs of the corporation." On behalf of the shareholders, the directors are expected to select and dismiss corporate officers; to approve important financial decisions; to distribute profits; and to see that accurate periodic reports are forwarded to the shareholders. Finally, at the apex of the pyramid are the corporate officers. In the eyes of the law, the officers are the employees of the shareholder owners. Their authority is limited to those responsibilities which the directors delegate to them.

In reality, this legal image is virtually a myth. In nearly every large American business corporation, there exists a management autocracy. One man—variously titled the President, or the Chairman of the Board, or the Chief Executive Officer—or a small coterie of men rule the corporation. Far from being chosen by the directors to run the corporation, this chief executive or executive clique chooses the board of directors and, with the acquiescence of the board, controls the corporation.

The common theme of many instances of mismanagement is a failure to restrain the power of these senior executives. A corporate chief executive's decisions to expand, merge, or even violate the law can often be made without accountability to outside scrutiny. There is, for example, the detailed disclosures of the recent bribery cases. Not only do these reports suggest how widespread corporate foreign and domestic criminality has become; they also provide a unique study in the pathology of American corporate management.

At Gulf Corporation, three successive chief executive officers were able to pay out over $12.6 million in foreign and domestic bribes over a 15-year period without the knowledge of "outside" or nonemployee directors on the board. At Northrop, chairman Thomas V. Jones and vice president James Allen were able to create and fund the Economic and Development Corporation, a separate Swiss company, and pay $750,000 to Dr. Hubert Weisbrod, a Swiss attorney, to stimulate West German jet sales without the knowledge of the board or, apparently, other senior executives. At 3M, chairman Bert Cross and finances vice president Irwin Hansen ordered the company insurance department to pay out $509,000 for imaginary insurance and the bookkeeper to fraudulently record the payments as a "necessary and proper" business expense for tax purposes. Ashland Oil Corporation's chief executive officer, Orwin E. Atkins, involved at least eight executives in illegally generating and distributing $801,165 in domestic political contributions, also without question. . . .

The legal basis for such a consolidation of power in the hands of the corporation's chief executive is the proxy election. Annually the shareholders of each publicly held corporation are given the opportunity of either attending a meeting to nominate and elect directors or returning proxy cards to management or its challengers signing over their right to vote. Few shareholders personally attend meetings. Sylvan Silver, a Reuters correspondent who covers over 100 Wilmington annual meetings each year, described representative 1974 meetings in an interview: At Cities Service Company, the 77th largest industrial corporation with some 135,000 shareholders, 25 shareholders actually attended the meeting; El Paso Natural Gas with 125,000 shareholders had 50 shareholders; at Coca Cola, the 69th largest corporation with 70,000 shareholders, 25 shareholders attended the annual meeting; at Bristol Meyers with 60,000 shareholders a like 25 shareholders appeared. Even "Campaign GM," the most publicized shareholder challenge of the past two decades, attracted no more than 3,000 of General Motors' 1,400,000 shareholders, or roughly two-tenths of one percent.

Thus, corporate directors are almost invariably chosen by written proxies. Yet management so totally dominates the proxy machinery that corporate elections have come to resemble the Soviet Union's euphemistic "Communist ballot"—that is, a ballot which lists only one slate of candidates. Although federal and state laws require the annual performance of an elaborate series of rituals pretending there is "corporate democracy," in 1973, 99.7 percent of the directorial elections in our largest corporations were uncontested. . . .

THE BEST DEMOCRACY MONEY CAN BUY

The key to management's hegemony is money. Effectively, only incumbent management can nominate directors—because it has a nearly unlimited power to use corporte funds to win board elections while opponents must prepare separate proxies and campaign literature entirely at their own expense.

There is first management's power to print and post written communications to shareholders. In a typical proxy contest, management will "follow up" its initial proxy solicitation with a bombardment of five to ten subsequent mailings. As attorneys Edward Aranow and Herb Einhorn explain in their treatise, *Proxy Contests for Corporate Control:*

> Perhaps the most important aspect of the follow-up letter is its role in the all-important efforts of a soliciting group to secure the *latest-dated* proxy from a stockholder. It is characteristic of every proxy contest that a large number of stockholders will sign and return proxies to one faction and then change their minds and want to have their stock used for the opposing faction.

The techniques of the Northern States Power Company in 1973 are illustrative. At that time, Northern States Power Company voluntarily employed cumulative voting, which meant that only 7.2 percent of outstanding shares was necessary to elect one director to Northern's 14-person board. Troubled by Northern's record on environmental and consumer issues, a broadly based coalition of public interest groups called the Citizens' Advocate for Public Utility Responsibility (CAPUR) nominated Ms. Alpha Snaby, a former Minnesota state legislator, to run for director. These groups then successfully solicited the votes of over 14 percent of all shareholders, or more than twice the votes necessary to elect her to the board.

Northern States then bought back the election. By soliciting proxies a second, and then a third time, the Power Company was able to persuade (or confuse) the shareholders of 71 percent of the 2.8 million shares cast for Ms. Snaby to change their votes.

Larger, more experienced corporations are usually less heavy-handed. Typically, they will begin a proxy campaign with a series of "build-up" letters preliminary to the first proxy solicitation. In Campaign GM, General Motors elevated this strategy to a new plateau by encasing the Project on Corporate Responsibility's single 100-word proxy solicitation within a 21-page booklet specifically rebutting each of the Project's charges. The Project, of course, could never afford to respond to GM's campaign. The postage costs of soliciting GM's 1,400,000 shareholders alone would have exceeded $100,000. The cost of printing a document comparable to GM's 21-page booklet, mailing it out, accompanied by a proxy statement, a proxy card, and a stamped return envelope to each shareholder might have run as high as $500,000.

Nor is it likely that the Project or any other outside shareholder could match GM's ability to hire "professional" proxy solicitors such as Georgeson & Company, which can deploy up to 100 solicitors throughout the country to personally contact shareholders, give them a campaign speech, and urge them to return their proxies. By daily tabulation of returned proxies, professional solicitors are able to identify on a day-by-day basis the largest blocks of stock outstanding which have yet to return a favorable vote. . . .

THE STATE OF THE BOARD

But does not the board of directors with its sweeping statutory mandate "to manage the business and affairs of every corporation" provide an internal check on the power of corporate executives? No. Long ago the grandiloquent words of the statutes ceased to have any operative meaning. "Directors," William O. Douglas complained in 1934, "do not direct." "[T]here is one thing all boards have in common, regardless of their legal position," Peter Drucker has written. *"They do not function."* In Robert Townsend's tart analysis, "[M]ost big companies have turned their boards of directors into nonboards. . . . In the years that I've spent on various boards I've never heard a single suggestion from a director (made as a director *at* a board meeting) that produced any result at all."

Recently these views are corroborated by Professor Myles Mace of the Harvard Business School, the nation's leading authority on the performance of boards of directors. In *Directors—Myth and Reality*, Mace summarized the results of hundreds of interviews with corporate officers and directors.

Directors do not establish the basic objectives, corporate strategies or broad policies of large and medium-size corporations, Mace found. Management creates the policies. The board has a right of veto but rarely exercises it. As one executive said, "Nine hundred and ninety-nine times out of a thousand, the board goes along with management. . . ." Or another, "I can't think of a single time when the board has failed to support a proposed policy of management or failed to endorse the recommendation of management."

The board does not select the president or other chief executive officers. "What is perhaps the most common definition of a function of the board of directors—namely, to select the president—was found to be the greatest myth," reported Mace. "The board of directors in most companies, except in a crisis, does not select the president. The president usually chooses the man who succeeds him to that position, and the board complies with the legal amenities in endorsing and voting his election." A corporate president agreed: "The former company president tapped me to be president, and I assure you that I will select my successor when the time comes." Even seeming exceptions such as RCA's 1975 ouster of Robert Sarnoff frequently turn out to be at the instigation of senior operating executives rather than an aroused board.

The board's role as disciplinarian of the corporation is more apparent than real. As the business-supported Conference Board conceded, "One of the most glaring deficiencies attributed to the corporate board . . . is its failure to monitor and evaluate the performance of the chief executive in a concrete way." To cite a specific example, decisions on executive compensation are made by the president—with perfunctory board approval in most situations. In the vast majority of corporations, Professor Mace found, the compensation committee, and the board which approves the recommendations of the compensation committee, "are not decision-making bodies." . . .

Exceptions to this pattern become news events. In reporting on General Motors' 1971 annual shareholders' meeting, the *Wall Street Journal* noted that "The meeting's dramatic highlight was an impassioned and unprecedented speech by the Rev. Leon Sullivan, GM's recently appointed Negro director, supporting the Episcopal Church's efforts to get the company out of South Africa. It was the first time that a GM director had ever spoken against management at an annual meeting." Now Reverend Sullivan is an unusual outside director, being General Motor's first black director and only "public interest" director. But what makes Leon Sullivan most extraordinary is that he was the first director in *any* major American corporation to come out publicly against his own corporation when its operations tended to support apartheid. . . .

REVAMPING THE BOARD

The modern corporation is akin to a political state in which all powers are held by a single clique. The senior executives of a large firm are essentially not accountable to any other officials within the firm. These are precisely the circumstances that, in a democratic political state, require a separation of powers into different branches of authority. As James Madison explained in the *Federalist* No. 47:

> The accumulation of all powers, legislative, executive, and judiciary, in the same hands, whether of one, a few or many, and whether hereditary, self-appointed, or elective, may justly be pronounced the very definition of tyranny. Were the federal constitution, therefore, really chargeable with this accumulation of power, or with a mixture of powers, having a dangerous tendency to such an accumulation, no further arguments would be necessary to inspire a universal reprobation of the system.

A similar concern over the unaccountability of business executives historically led to the elevation of a board of directors to review and check the actions of operating management. As a practical matter, if corporate governance is to be reformed, it must begin by returning the board to this historical role. The board should serve as an internal auditor of the corporations, responsible for constraining executive management from violations of law and breach of trust. Like a rival branch of government, the board's function must be defined as separate from operating management. Rather than pretending directors can "manage" the corporation, the board's role as disciplinarian should be clearly described. Specifically, the board of directors should:

- establish and monitor procedures that assure that operating executives are informed of and obey applicable federal, state, and local laws;
- approve or veto all important executive management business proposals such as corporate bylaws, mergers, or dividend decisions;
- hire and dismiss the chief executive officer and be able to disapprove the hiring and firing of the principal executives of the corporation; and
- report to the public and the shareholders how well the corporation has obeyed the law and protected the shareholders' investment.

It is not enough, however, to specify what the board should do. State corporations statutes have long provided that "the business and affairs of a corporation shall be managed by a board of directors," yet it has been over a century since the boards of the largest corporations have actually performed this role. To reform the corporation, a federal chartering law must also specify the manner in which the board performs its primary duties.

First, to insure that the corporation obeys federal and state laws, the board should designate executives responsible for compliance with these laws and require periodic signed reports describing the effectiveness of compliance procedures. Mechanisms to administer spot checks on compliance with the principal statutes should be created. Similar mechanisms can insure that corporate "whistle blowers' and nonemployee sources may communicate to the board—in private and without fear of retaliation—knowledge of violations of law.

Second, the board should actively review important executive business proposals to determine their full compliance with law, to preclude conflicts of interest, and to assure that executive decisions are rational and informed of all foreseeable risks and costs. But even though the board's responsibility here is limited to approval or veto of executive initiatives, it should proceed in as well-informed a manner as practicable. To demonstrate rational business judgment, the directorate should require management "to prove its case." It should review the studies upon which management relied to make a decision, require management to justify its decision in terms of costs or rebutting dissenting views, and, when necesssary, request that outside experts provide an independent business analysis.

Only with respect to two types of business decisions should the board exceed this limited review role. The determination of salary, expense, and benefit schedules inherently possesses such obvious conflicts of interest for executives that only the board should make these decisions. And since the relocation of principal manufacturing facilities tends to have a greater effect on local communities than any other type of business decision, the board should require management to prepare a "community impact statement." This public report would be similar to the environmental impact statements presently required by the National Environmental Policy Act. It would require the corporation to state the purpose of a relocation decision; to compare feasible alternative means; to quantify the costs to the local community; and to consider methods to mitigate these costs. Although it would not prevent a corporation from making a profit-maximizing decision, it would require the corporation to minimize the costs of relocation decisions to local communities.

To accomplish this restructuring of the board requires the institutionalization of a new profession: the full-time "professional" director. Corporate scholars frequently identify William O. Douglas' 1940 proposal for "salaried, professional experts [who] would bring a new responsibility and authority to directorates and a new safety to stockholders" as the origin of the professional director idea. More recently, corporations including Westinghouse and Texas Instruments have established slots on their boards to be filled by full-time directors. Individuals such as Harvard Business School's Myles Mace and former Federal Reserve Board chairman William McChesney Martin consider their own thoroughgoing approach to boardroom responsibilities to be that of a "professional" director.

To succeed, professional directors must put in the substantial time necessary to get the job done. One cannot monitor the performance of Chrysler's or Gulf's management at a once-a-month meeting; those firms' activities are too sweeping and complicated for such ritual oversight. The obvious minimum here is an adequate salary to attract competent persons to work as full-time directors and to maintain the independence of the board from executive management.

The board must also be sufficiently staffed. A few board members alone cannot oversee the activities of thousands of executives. To be able to appraise operating management, the board needs a trim group of attorneys, economists, and labor and consumer advisors who can analyze complex business proposals, investigate complaints, spot-check accountability, and frame pertinent inquiries.

The board also needs timely access to relevant corporate data. To insure this, the board should be empowered to nominate the corporate financial auditor, select the corporation's counsel, compel the forwarding and preservation of corporate records, require all corporate executives or representatives to answer fully all board questions respecting corporate operations, and dismiss any executive or representative who fails to do so.

This proposed redesign for corporate democracy attempts to make executive management accountable to the law and shareholders without diminishing its operating efficiency. Like a judiciary within the corporation, the board has ultimate powers to judge and sanction. Like a legislature, it oversees executive activity. Yet executive management substantially retains its powers to initiate and administer business operations. The chief executive officer retains control over the organization of the executive hierarchy and the allocation of the corporate budget. The directors are given ultimate control over a narrow jurisdiction: Does the corporation obey the law, avoid exploiting consumers or communities, and protect the shareholders' investment? The executive contingent retains general authority for all corporate operations.

No doubt there will be objections that this structure is too expensive or that it will disturb the "harmony" of executive management. But it is unclear that there would be any increased cost in adopting an effective board. The true cost to the corporation could only be determined by comparing the expense of a fully paid and staffed board with the savings resulting from the elimination of conflicts of interest and corporate waste. In addition, if this should result in a slightly increased corporate expense, the appropriateness must be assessed within a broader social context: should federal and state governments or the corporations themselves bear the primary expense of keeping corporations honest? In our view, this cost should be placed on the corporations as far as reasonably possible.

It is true that an effective board will reduce the "harmony" of executive management in the sense that the power of the chief executive or senior executives will be subject to knowledgeable review. But a board which monitors rather than rubber-stamps management is exactly what is necessary to diminish the unfettered authority of the corporate chief executive or ruling clique. The autocratic power these individuals presently possess has proven unacceptably dangerous: it has led to recurring violations of law, conflicts of interest, productive inefficiency, and pervasive harm to consumers, workers, and the community environment. Under normal circumstances there should be a healthy friction between operating executives and the board to assure that the wisest possible use is made of corporate resources. When corporate executives are breaking the law, there should be no "harmony" whatsoever.

ELECTION OF THE BOARD

Restructuring the board is hardly likely to succeed if boards remain as homogeneously white, male, and narrowly oriented as they are today. Dissatisfaction with current selection of directors is so intense that analysts of corporate governance, including Harvard Law School's Abram Chayes, Yale political scientist Robert Dahl, and University of Southern California Law School Professor Christopher Stone, have each separately urged that the starting point of corporate reform should be to change the way in which the board is elected.

Professor Chayes, echoing John Locke's principle that no authority is legitimate except that granted "the consent of the governed," argues that employees and other groups substantially affected by corporate operations should have a say in its governance:

> Shareholder democracy, so-called, is misconceived because the shareholders are not the governed of the corporations whose consent must be sought. . . . Their interests are protected if financial information is made available, fraud and overreaching are prevented, and a market is maintained in which their shares may be sold. A priori, there is no reason for them to have any voice, direct or representational, in [corporate decision making]. They are no more affected than nonshareholding neighbors by these decisions. . . .

> A more spacious conception of "membership," and one closer to the facts of corporate life, would include all those having a relation of sufficient intimacy with the corporation or subject to its powers in a sufficiently specialized way. Their rightful share in decisions and the exercise of corporate power would be exercised through an institutional arrangement appropriately designed to represent the interests of a constituency of members having a significant common relation to the corporation and its power.

Professor Dahl holds a similar view: "[W]hy should people who own shares be given the privileges of citizenship in the government of the firm when citizenship is denied to other people who also make vital contributions to the firm?" he asks rhetorically. "The people I have in mind are, of course, employees and customers, without whom the firm could not exist, and the general public, without whose support for (or acquiescence in) the myriad protections and services of the state the firm would instantly disappear. . . ." Yet Dahl finds proposals for interest group representation less desirable than those for worker self-management. He also suggests consideration of codetermination statutes such as those enacted by West Germany and ten other European and South American countries under which shareholders and employees separately elect designated portions of the board.

From a different perspective, Professor Stone has recommended that a federal agency appoint "general public directors" to serve on the boards of all the largest industrial and financial firms. In certain extreme cases such as where a corporation repeatedly violates the law, Stone recommends that the federal courts appoint "special public directors" to prevent further delinquency.

There are substantial problems with each of those proposals. It seems impossible to design a general "interest group" formula which will assure that all affected constituencies of large industrial corporations will be represented and that all constituencies will be given appropriate weight. Even if such a formula could be designed, however, there is the danger that consumer or community or minority or franchisee representatives would become only special pleaders for their constituents and otherwise lack the loyalty or interest to direct generally. This defect has emerged in West Germany under codetermination. Labor representatives apparently are indifferent to most problems of corporate management that do not directly affect labor. They seem as deferential to operating executive management as present American directors are. Alternatively, federally appointed public directors might be frozen out of critical decision-making by a majority of "privately" elected directors, or the appointing agency itself might be biased.

Nonetheless, the essence of the Chayes-Dahl-Stone argument is well taken. The boards of directors of most major corporations are, as CBS's Dan Rather criticized the original Nixon cabinet, too much like "twelve grey-haired guys named George." The quiescence of the board has resulted in important public and, for that matter, shareholder concerns being ignored.

An important answer is structural. The homogeneity of the board can only be ended by giving to each director, in addition to a general duty to see that the corporation is profitably administered, a separate oversight responsibility, a separate expertise, and a separate constituency so each important public concern would be guaranteed at least one informed representative on the board. There might be nine corporate directors, each of whom is elected to a board position with one of the following oversight responsibilities:

1. Employee welfare
2. Consumer protection
3. Environmental protection and community relations

4. Shareholder rights
5. Compliance with law
6. Finances
7. Purchasing and marketing
8. Management efficiency
9. Planning and research

By requiring each director to balance responsibility for representing a particular social concern against responsibility for the overall health of the enterprise, the problem of isolated "public" directors would be avoided. No individual director is likely to be "frozen out" of collegial decision-making because all directors would be of the same character. Each director would spend the greater part of his or her time developing expertise in a different area; each director would have a motivation to insist that a different aspect of a business decision be considered. Yet each would simultaneously be responsible for participating in all board decisions, as directors now are. So the specialized area of each director would supplement but not supplant the director's general duties. . . .

To maintain the independence of the board from the operating management it reviews also requires that each federally chartered corporation shall be directed by a purely "outside" board. No executive, attorney, representative, or agent of a corporation should be allowed to serve simultaneously as a director of that same corporation. Directorial and executive loyalty should be furthered by an absolute prohibition of interlocks. No director, executive, general counsel, or company agent should be allowed to serve more than one corporation subject to the Federal Corporate Chartering Act.

Several objections may be raised. First, how can we be sure that completely outside boards will be competent? Corporate campaign rules should be redesigned to emphasize qualifications. This will allow shareholder voters to make rational decisions based on information clearly presented to them. It is also a fair assumption that shareholders, given an actual choice and role in corporate governance, will want to elect the men and women most likely to safeguard their investments.

A second objection is that once all interlocks are proscribed and a full-time outside board required, there will not be enough qualified directors to staff all major firms. This complaint springs from that corporate mentality which, accustomed to 60-year-old white male bankers and businessmen as directors, makes the norm a virtue. In fact, if we loosen the reins on our imagination, America has a large, rich, and diverse pool of possible directorial talent from academics and public administrators and community leaders to corporate and public interest lawyers.

But directors should be limited to four two-year terms so that boards do not become stale. And no director should be allowed to serve on more than one board at any one time. Although simultaneous service on two or three boards might allow key directors to "pollinize" directorates by comparing their different experiences, this would reduce their loyalty to any one board, jeopardize their ability to fully perform their new directorial responsibilities, and undermine the goal of opening up major boardrooms to as varied a new membership as is reasonable.

The shareholder electoral process should be made more democratic as well. Any shareholder or allied shareholder group which owns .1 percent of the common voting stock in the corporation or comprises 100 or more individuals and does not include a present executive of the corporation, nor act for a present executive, may nominate up to three persons to serve as directors. This will exclude executive management from the nomination process. It also increases the likelihood of a diverse board by preventing any one or two sources from proposing all nominees. To prevent frivolous use of the nominating power, this proposal establishes a minimum shareownership condition.

Six weeks prior to the shareholders' meeting to elect directors, each shareholder should receive a ballot and a written statement on which each candidate for the board sets forth his or her qualifications to hold office and purposes for seeking office. All campaign costs would be borne by the corporation. These strict campaign and funding rules will assure that all nominees will have an equal opportunity to be judged by the shareholders. By preventing directorates from being bought, these provisions will require board elections to be conducted solely on the merit of the candidates. . . .

Finally, additional provisions will require cumulative voting and forbid "staggered" board elections. Thus any shareholder faction capable of jointly voting approximately 10 percent of the total number of shares cast may elect a director.

A NEW ROLE FOR SHAREHOLDERS

The difficulty with this proposal is the one that troubled Juvenal two millennia ago: *Quis custodiet ipsos custodes,* or Who shall watch the watchmen? Without a full-time body to discipline the board, it would be so easy for the board of directors and executive management to become friends. Active vigilance could become routinized into an uncritical partnership. The same board theoretically elected to protect shareholder equity and internalize law might instead become management's lobbyist.

Relying on shareholders to discipline directors may strike many as a dubious approach. Historically, the record of shareholder participation in corporate governance has been an abysmal one. The monumental indifference of most shareholders is worse than that of sheep; sheep at least have some sense of what manner of ram they follow. But taken together, the earlier proposals—an outside, full-time board, nominated by rival shareholder groups and voted on by beneficial owners—will increase involvement by shareholders. And cumulative voting insures that an aroused minority of shareholders—even one as small as 9 or 10 percent of all shareholders—shall have the opportunity to elect at least one member of the board.

But that alone is hardly sufficient. At a corporation the size of General Motors, an aggregation of 10 percent of all voting stock might require the allied action of over 200,000 individuals—which probably could occur no more than once in a generation. To keep directors responsive to law and legitimate public concerns requires surer and more immediate mechanisms. In a word, it requires arming the victims of corporate abuses with the powers to swiftly respond to them. For only those employees, consumers, racial or sex minorities, and local communities harmed by corporate depredations can be depended upon to speedily complain. By allowing any victim to become a shareholder and by permitting any shareholder to have an effective voice, there will be the greatest likelihood of continuing scrutiny of the corporation's directorate. . . .

Shareholders are not the only ones with an incentive to review decisions of corporate management; nor, as Professors Chayes and Dahl argue, are shareholders the only persons who should be accorded corporate voting rights. The increasing use by American corporations of technologies and materials that pose direct and serious threats to the health of communities surrounding their plants requires the creation of a new form of corporate voting right. When a federally chartered corporation engages, for example, in production or distribution of nuclear fuels or the emission of toxic air, water, or solid waste pollutants, citizens whose health is endangered should not be left, at best, with receiving money damages after a time-consuming trial to compensate them for damaged property, impaired health, or even death.

Instead, upon finding of a public health hazard by three members of the board of directors or 3 percent of the shareholders, a corporate referendum should be held in the political jurisdiction affected by the health hazard. The referendum would be drafted by the unit triggering it—either the three board members or a designate of the shareholders. The affected citizens by majority vote will then decide whether the hazardous practice shall be allowed to continue. This form of direct democracy has obvious parallels to the initiative and referendum procedures familiar to many states—except that the election will be paid for by a business corporation and will not necessarily occur at a regular election. . . .

This type of election procedure is necessary to give enduring meaning to the democratic concept of "consent of the governed." To be sure, this proposal goes beyond the traditional assumption that the only affected or relevant constituents of the corporation are the shareholders. But no longer can we accept the Faustian bargain that the continued toleration of corporate destruction of local health and property is the cost to the public of doing business. In an equitable system of governance, the perpetrators should answer to their victims.

Power and Accountability: The Changing Role of the Corporate Board of Directors

IRVING S. SHAPIRO

The proper direction of business corporations in a free society is a topic of intense and often heated discussion. Under the flag of corporate governance there has been a running debate about the performance of business organizations, together with a flood of proposals for changes in the way corporate organizations are controlled.

It has been variously suggested that corporate charters be dispensed by the Federal Government as distinct from those of the states (to tighten the grip on corporate actions); that only ousiders unconnected to an enterprise be allowed to sit on its board of directors or that, as a minimum, most of the directors should qualify as "independent"; that seats be apportioned to constituent groups (employees, women, consumers and minorities, along with stockholders); that boards be equipped with private staffs, beyond the management's control (to smoke out facts that hired executives might prefer to hide or decorate); and that new disclosure requirements be added to existing ones (to provide additional tools for outside oversight of behavior and performance).

Such proposals have come from the Senate Judiciary Committee's antitrust arm; from regulatory agency spokesmen, most notably the current head of the Securities and Exchange Commission, Harold Williams, and a predecessor there, William Cary; from the professoriat in schools of law and business; from the bench and bar; and from such observers of the American scene as Ralph Nader and Mark Green.[1]

Excerpted from a paper presented in the Fairless Lecture Series, Carnegie-Mellon University, October, 24, 1979. Reprinted by permission.

Suggestions for change have sometimes been offered in sympathy and sometimes in anger. They have ranged from general pleas for corporations to behave better, to meticulously detailed reorganization charts. The span in itself suggests part of the problem: "Corporate Governance" (like Social Responsibility before it) is not a subject with a single meaning, but is a shorthand label for an array of social and political as well as economic concerns. One is obliged to look for a way to keep discussion within a reasonable perimeter.

There appears to be one common thread. All of the analyses, premises, and prescriptions seem to derive in one way or another from the question of accountability: Are corporations suitably controlled, and to whom or what are they responsible? This is the central public issue, and the focal point of this paper.

One school of opinion holds that corporations cannot be adequately called to account because there are systemic economic and political failings. In this view, nothing short of a major overhaul will serve. What is envisioned, at least by many in this camp, are new kinds of corporate organizations constructed along the lines of democratic political institutions. The guiding ideology would be communitarian, with the needs and rights of the community emphasized in preference to profit-seeking goals now pursued by corporate leaders (presumably with Darwinian abandon, with natural selection weeding out the weak, and with society left to pick up the external costs).

BOARDS CHANGING FOR BETTER

Other critics take a more temperate view. They regard the present system as sound and its methods of governance as morally defensible. They concede, though, that changes are needed to reflect new conditions. Whether the changes are to be brought about by gentle persuasion, or require the use of a two-by-four to get the mule's attention, is part of the debate.

This paper sides with the gradualists. My position, based on a career in industry and personal observation of corporate boards at work, is that significant improvements have been made in recent years in corporate governance, and that more changes are coming in an orderly way; that with these amendments, corporations are accountable and better monitored than ever before; and that pat formulas or proposals for massive "restructuring" should be suspect. The formula approach often is based on ignorance of what it takes to run a large enterprise, on false premises as to the corporate role in society, or on a philosophy that misreads the American tradition and leaves no room for large enterprises that are both free and efficient.

The draconian proposals would almost certainly yield the worst of all possibilities, a double-negative trade-off. They would sacrifice the most valuable qualities of the enterprise system to gain the least attractive features of the governmental system. Privately owned enterprises are geared to a primary economic task, that of joining human talents and natural resources in the production and distribution of goods and services. That task is essential, and two centuries of national experience suggest these conclusions: The United States has been uncommonly successful at meeting economic needs through reliance on private initiative; and the competitive marketplace is a better course-correction device than governmental fiat. The enterprise system would have had to have failed miserably before the case could be made for replacing it with governmental dictum.

Why should the public have any interest in the internal affairs of corporations? Who cares who decides? Part of the answer comes from recent news stories noting such special problems as illegal corporate contributions to political campaigns, and tracking the decline and fall of once-stout companies such as Penn Central. Revelations of that kind raise questions about the probity and competence of the people minding the largest stores. There is more to it than this, though. There have always been cases of corporate failures. Small companies have gone under too, at a rate far higher than their larger brethren.[2] Instances of corruption have occurred in institutions of all sizes, whether they be commercial enterprises or some other kind.

Corporate behavior and performance are points of attention, and the issue attaches to size, precisely because people do not see the large private corporation as entirely private. People care about what goes on in the corporate interior because they see themselves as affected parties whether they work in such companies or not.

There is no great mystery as to the source of this challenge to the private character of governance. Three trends account for it. First is the growth of very large corporations. They have come to employ a large portion of the work force, and have become key factors in the nation's technology, wealth and security. They have generated admiration for their prowess, but also fear of their imputed power.

The second contributing trend is the decline of owner-management. Over time, corporate shares have been dispersed. The owners have hired managers, entrusted them with the power to make decisions, and drifted away from involvement in corporate affairs except to meet statutory requirements (as, for example, to approve a stock split or elect a slate of directors).

That raises obvious practical questions. If the owners are on the sidelines, what is to stop the managers from remaining in power indefinitely, using an inside position to control the selection of their own bosses, the directors? Who is looking over management's shoulder to monitor performance?

The third element here is the rise in social expectations regarding corporations. It is no longer considered enough for a company to make products and provide commercial services. The larger it is, the more it is expected to assume various obligations that once were met by individuals or communities, or were not met at all.

With public expectations ratcheting upward, corporations are under pressure to behave more like governments and embrace a universe of problems. That would mean, of necessity, that private institutions would focus less on problems of their own choice.

If corporations succumbed to that pressure, and in effect declared the public's work to be their own, the next step would be to turn them into institutions accountable to the public in the same way that units of government are accountable.

But the corporation does not parallel the government. The assets in corporate hands are more limited and the constituents have options. There are levels of appeal. While the only accountability in government lies within government itself—the celebrated system of checks and balances among the executive, legislative, and judicial branches—the corporation is in a different situation: It has external and plural accountability, codified in the law and reinforced by social pressure. It must "answer" in one way or another to all levels of government, to competitors in the marketplace who would be happy to have the chance to increase their own market share, to employees who can strike or quit, and to consumers who can keep their wallets in their pockets. The checks are formidable even if one excludes for purposes of argument the corporation's initial point of accountability, its stockholders (many of whom do in fact vote their shares, and do not just use their feet).

The case for major reforms in corporate governance rests heavily on the argument that past governmental regulation of large enterprises has been impotent or ineffectual. This is an altogether remarkable assertion, given the fact that the nation has come through a period in which large corporations have been subjected to an unprecedented flood of new legislation and rule making. Regulation now reaches into every corporate nook and cranny—including what some people suppose (erroneously) to be the sanctuary of the boardroom.

Market competition, so lightly dismissed by some critics as fiction or artifact, is in fact a vigorous force in the affairs of almost all corporations. Size lends no immunity to its relentless pressures. The claim that the largest corporations somehow have set themselves above the play of market forces or, more likely, make those forces play for themselves, is widely believed. Public opinion surveys show that. What is lacking is any evidence that this is so. Here too, the evidence goes the other way. Objective studies of concentrated industries (the auto industry, for instance) show that corporate size does not mean declining competitiveness, nor does it give assurance that the products will sell.

Everyday experience confirms this. Consider the hard times of the Chrysler Corporation today, the disappearance of many once-large companies from the American scene, and the constant rollover in the membership list of the "100 Largest," a churning process that has been going on for years and shows no signs of abating.[3]

If indeed the two most prominent overseers of corporate behavior, government and competition, have failed to provide appropriate checks and balances, and if that is to be cited as evidence that corporations lack accountability, the burden of proof should rest with those who so state.

The basics apply to Sears, Roebuck as much as to Sam's appliance shop. Wherever you buy the new toaster, it should work when it is plugged in. Whoever services the washing machine, the repairman should arrive at the appointed time, with tools and parts.

Special expectations are added for the largest firms, however. One is that they apply their resources to tasks that invite economies of scale, providing goods and services that would not otherwise be available, or that could be delivered by smaller units only at considerable loss of efficiency. Another is that, like the elephant, they watch where they put their feet and not stamp on smaller creatures through clumsiness or otherwise.

A second set of requirements can be added, related not to the markets selected by corporations individually, but to the larger economic tasks that must be accomplished in the name of the national interest and security. In concert with others in society, including big government, big corporations are expected to husband scarce resources and develop new ones, and to foster strong and diverse programs of research and development, to the end that practical technological improvements will emerge and the nation will be competitive in the international setting.

Beyond this there are softer but nonetheless important obligations: To operate with respect for the environment and with careful attention to the health and safety of people; to honor and give room to the personal qualities employees bring to their jobs, including their need to make an identifiable mark and to realize as much of their potential as possible; to lend assistance in filling community needs in which corporations have some stake; and to help offset community problems which in some measure corporations have helped to create.

This is not an impossible job, only a difficult one. Admitting that the assignment probably is not going to be carried out perfectly by any organization, the task is unlikely to be done even half well unless some boundary conditions are met. Large corporations cannot fulfill their duties unless they remain both profitable and flexible. They must be able to attract and hold those volunteer owners; which is to say, there must be the promise of present or future gain. Companies must have the wherewithal to reinvest significant amounts to revitalize their own capital plants, year after year in unending fashion. Otherwise, it is inevitable that they will go into decline versus competitors elsewhere, as will the nation.

Flexibility is no less important. The fields of endeavor engaging large business units today are dynamic in nature. Without an in-and-out flow of products and services, without the mobility to adapt to shifts in opportunities and public preferences, corporations would face the fate of the buggy-whip makers.

Profitability and flexibility are easy words to say, but in practice they make for hard decisions. A company that would close a plant with no more than a passing thought for those left unemployed would and should be charged with irresponsibility; but a firm that vowed never to close any of its plants would be equally irresponsible, for it might be consigning itself to a pattern of stagnation that could ultimately cost the jobs of the people in all of its plants.

The central requirement is not that large corporations take the pledge and bind themselves to stated actions covering all circumstances, but that they do a thoughtful and informed job of balancing competing (and ever changing) claims on corporate resources, mediating among the conflicting (also changing) desires of various constituencies, and not giving in to any one-dimensional perspective however sincerely felt. It is this that describes responsible corporate governance.

Certainly, corporations do not have the public mandate or the resources to be what Professor George Lodge of the Harvard Business School would have them be, which is nationally chartered community-oriented collectives.[4] Such a mission for corporations would be tolerable to society only if corporations were turned into minigovernments—but that takes us back to the inefficiency problem noted earlier. The one task governments have proven they almost always do badly is to run production and distribution organizations. The only models there are to follow are not attractive. Would anyone seriously argue that the public would be ahead if General Motors were run along the lines of Amtrak, or Du Pont were managed in the manner of the U.S. Postal System?

Once the roles are defined, the key to success in running a large corporation is to lay out a suitable division of labor between the board and the management, make that division crystal clear on both sides, and staff the offices with the right people. Perhaps the best way to make that split is to follow the pattern used in the U.S. Constitution, which stipulates the powers of the Federal Government and specifies that everything not covered there is reserved to the states or the people thereof. The board of directors should lay claim to five basic jobs, and leave the rest to the paid managers.

The duties the board should not delegate are these:

1. The determination of the broad policies and the general direction the efforts of the enterprise should take.
2. The establishment of performance standards—ethical as well as commercial—against which the management will be judged, and the communication of these standards to the management in unambiguous terms.

3. The selection of company officers, and attention to the question of succession.
4. The review of top management's performance in following the overall strategy and meeting the board's standards as well as legal requirements.
5. The communication of the organization's goals and standards to those who have a significant stake in its activities (insiders and outsiders both) and of the steps being taken to keep the organization responsive to the needs of those people.

The establishment of corporate strategy and performance standards denotes a philosophy of active stewardship, rather than passive trusteeship. It is the mission of directors to see that corporate resources are put to creative use, and in the bargain subjected to calculated risks rather than simply being tucked into the countinghouse for safekeeping.

That in turn implies certain prerequisites for board members of large corporations which go beyond those required of a school board member, a trustee of a charitable organization, or a director of a small, local business firm. In any such assignments one would look for personal integrity, interest and intelligence, but beyond these there is a dividing line that marks capability and training.

The stakes are likely to be high in the large corporation, and the factors confronting the board and management usually are complex. The elements weighing heavily in decisions are not those with which people become familiar in the ordinary course of day-to-day life, as might be the case with a school board.

Ordinarily the management of a corporation attends to such matters as product introductions, capital expansions, and supply problems. This in no way reduces the need for directors with extensive business background, though. With few exceptions, corporate boards involve themselves in strategic decisions and those involving large capital commitments. Directors thus need at least as much breadth and perspective as the management, if not as much detailed knowledge.

If the directors are to help provide informed and principled oversight of corporate affairs, a good number of them must provide windows to the outside world. That is at least part of the rationale for outside directors, and especially for directors who can bring unique perspective to the group. There is an equally strong case, though, for directors with an intimate knowledge of the company's business, and insiders may be the best qualified to deliver that. What is important is not that a ratio be established, but that the group contain a full range of the competences needed to set courses of action that will largely determine the long-range success of the enterprise.

BOARDS NEED WINDOWS

The directors also have to be able and willing to invest considerable time in their work. In this day and age, with major resources on the line and tens of thousands of employees affected by each large corporation, there should be no seat in the boardroom for people willing only to show up once a month to pour holy water over decisions already made. Corporate boards need windows, not window dressing!

There are two other qualities that may be self-evident from what has been said, but are mentioned for emphasis. Directors must be interested in the job and committed to the overall purpose of the organization. However much they may differ on details of accomplishment, they must be willing to work at the task of working with others on the board. They ought to be able to speak freely in a climate that encourages open discussion, but to recognize the difference between attacking an idea and attacking the person who presents it. No less must they see the difference between compromising tactics to reach consensus and compromising principles.

Structures and procedures, which so often are pushed to the fore in discussions of corporate governance, actually belong last. They are not unimportant, but they are subordinate.

Structure follows purpose, or should, and that is a useful principle for testing some of the proposals for future changes in corporate boards. Today, two-thirds to three-quarters of the directors of most large corporations are outsiders, and it is being proposed that this trend be pushed still further, with the only insider being the chief executive officer, and with a further stipulation that he not be board chairman. This idea has surfaced from Harold Williams, and variations on it have come from other sources.

The idea bumps into immediate difficulties. High-quality candidates for boards are not in large supply as it is. Conflicts of interest would prohibit selection of many individuals close enough to an industry to be familiar with its problems. The disqualification of insiders would reduce the selection pool to a still smaller number, and the net result could well be corporate boards whose members were less competent and effective than those now sitting.

Experience would also suggest that such a board would be the most easily manipulated of all. That should be no trick at all for a skillful CEO, for he would be the only person in the room with a close, personal knowledge of the business.

The objective is unassailable: Corporate boards need directors with independence of judgment; but in today's business world, independence is not enough. In coping with such problems as those confronting the electronics corporations beset by heavy foreign competition, or those encountered by international banks which have loans outstanding in countries with shaky governments, boards made up almost entirely of outsiders would not just have trouble evaluating nuances of the management's performance; they might not even be able to read the radar and tell whether the helmsman was steering straight for the rocks.

If inadequately prepared individuals are placed on corporate boards, no amount of sincerity on their part can offset the shortcoming. It is pure illusion to suppose that complex business issues and organizational problems can be overseen by people with little or no experience in dealing with such problems. However intelligent such people might be, the effect of their governance would be to expose the people most affected by the organization—employees, owners, customers, suppliers—to leadership that would be (using the word precisely) incompetent.

It is sometimes suggested that the members of corporate boards ought to come from the constituencies—an employee-director, a consumer-director, an environmentalist-director, etc. This Noah's Ark proposal, which is probably not to be taken seriously, is an extension of the false parallel between corporations and elected governments. The flaw in the idea is all but self-evident: People representing specific interest groups would by definition be committed to the goals of their groups rather than any others; but it is the responsibility of directors (not simply by tradition but as a matter of law as well) to serve the organization as a whole. The two goals are incompatible.

If there were such boards they would move at glacial speed. The internal political maneuvering would be Byzantine, and it is difficult to see how the directors could avoid an obvious challenge of accountability. Stockholder suits would pop up like dandelions in the spring.

One may also question how many people of ability would stand for election under this arrangement. Quotas are an anathema in a free society, and their indulgence here would insult the constituencies themselves—a woman on the board not because she is competent but only because she is female; a black for black's sake; and so on ad nauseam.

A certain amount of constituency pleading is not all bad, as long as it is part of a corporate commitment. There is something to be said for what Harold Williams labels "tension," referring to the divergence in perspective of those concerned primarily with internal matters and those looking more at the broader questions. However, as has been suggested by James Shepley, the president of Time, Inc., "tension" can lead to paralysis, and is likely to do so if boards are packed with groups known to be unsympathetic to the management's problems and business realities.

As Shepley commented, "The chief executive would be out of his mind who would take a risk-laden business proposition to a group of directors who, whatever their other merits, do not really understand the fine points of the business at hand, and whose official purpose is to create 'tension.' "[5]

Students of corporate affairs have an abundance of suggestions for organizing the work of boards, with detailed structures in mind for committees on audit, finance, and other areas; plus prescriptions for membership. The danger here is not that boards will pick the wrong formula—many organization charts could be made to work—but that boards will put too much emphasis on the wrong details.

The idea of utilizing a committee system in which sub-groups have designated duties is far more important than the particulars of their arrangement. When such committees exist, and they are given known and specific oversight duties, it is a signal to the outside world (and to the management) that performance is being monitored in a no-nonsense fashion.

It is this argument that has produced the rule changes covering companies listed on the New York Stock Exchange, calling for audit committees chaired by outside directors, and including no one currently active in management. Most large firms have moved in that direction, and the move makes sense, for an independently minded audit committee is a potent instrument of corporate oversight. Even a rule of that kind, though, has the potential of backfiring.

Suppose some of the directors best qualified to perform the audit function are not outsiders? Are the analytical skills and knowledge of career employees therefore to be bypassed? Are the corporate constituencies well served by such an exclusionary rule, keeping in mind that all directors, insiders or outsiders, are bound by the same legal codes and corporate books are still subject to independent, outside audit? It is scarcely a case of the corporate purse being placed in the hands of the unwatched.

Repeatedly, the question of structure turns on the basics: If corporations have people with competence and commitment on their boards, structure and process fall into line easily; if people with the needed qualities are missing or the performance standards are unclear, corporations are in trouble no matter whose guidebook they follow. Equally, the question drives to alternatives: The present system is surely not perfect, but what is better?

By the analysis presented here the old fundamentals are still sound, no alternative for radical change has been defended with successful argument, and the best course appears to be to stay within the historical and philosophical traditions of American enterprise, working out the remaining problems one by one.

NOTES

1. U.S. Senate, Committee on the Judiciary Subcommittee on Antitrust, Monopoly and Business Rights; Address by Harold M. Williams, *Corporate Accountability*, Fifth Annual Securities Regulation Institute, San Diego, California (January 18, 1978); W. Cary, *A Proposed Federal Corporate Minimum Standards Act*, 29 Bus. Law. 1101 (1974) and W. Cary, *Federalism and Corporate Law: Reflections Upon Delaware*, 83 Yale L. J. 663 (1974); D. E. Schwartz, *A Case for Federal Chartering of Corporations*, 31 Bus. Law. 1125 (1976); M. A. Eisenberg, *Legal Modes of Management Structure in the Modern Corporation; Officers, Directors and Accountants*, 63 Calif. L. Rev. 375 (1975); A. J. Goldberg, *Debate on Outside Directors*, New York Times, October 29, 1972 (§3, p. 1); Ralph Nader and Mark Green, *Constitutionalizing the Corporation: The Case for Federal Chartering of Giant Corporations* (1976).

2. See "Sixty Years of Corporate Ups, Downs and Outs," *Forbes*, September 15, 1977, p. 127 et seq.
3. See Dr. Betty Bock's Statement before Hearings on S. 600, Small and Independent Business Protection Act of 1979, April 25, 1979.
4. G. Lodge, *The New American Ideology* (1975).
5. Shepley, *The CEO Goes to Washington*, Remarks to Fortune Corporation Communications Seminar, March 28, 1979.

Biographical Information

KENNETH D. ALPERN

Kenneth Alpern is a member of the Philosophy Department at DePaul University. He works in ethical theory and the history of ethics as well as in applied ethics. Presently he is writing on moral and legal problems raised by technological innovations in human reproduction.

ROBERT L. ARRINGTON

Robert Arrington is Professor of Philosophy and Associate Dean of the College of Arts and Sciences at Georgia State University. He received his undergraduate degree from Vanderbilt University and did his graduate work at Tulane University. He was an Honorary Woodrow Wilson Fellow, and he held an ACLS Fellowship in 1974–75. His areas of specialization include ethics and the philosophy of Wittgenstein. He currently is at work on a book on moral epistemology.

GORDON H. BARLAND

Gordon H. Barland, Ph.D., is the president of Barland & Associates, a Salt Lake City-based firm specializing in forensic polygraph, teaching, and research in the areas of deception detection. A widely published author, he holds a Ph.D. in psychophysiology from the University of Utah, and conducts polygraph examinations for a large number of clients, including the U.S. Army.

WILFRED BECKERMAN

Born in England and educated at Cambridge, Wilfred Beckerman has served on numerous economic institutions, organizations, and committees, including the Royal Commission on Environmental Pollution and the Board of Trade. He is presently the governor and executive committee member of the National Institute for Economic and Social Research. A prominent contributor to economic journals and author of numerous books, his latest publication is *Poverty and Social Security in Britain since 1962*.

WILLIAM T. BLACKSTONE

William Blackstone received his B.A. from Elan College and his M.A. and Ph.D. from Duke University. He was a professor of philosophy and religion at the University of Georgia, where he was also chairman of the Division of Social Sciences. A member of the American Philosophical Association and numerous other philosophical societies, William Blackstone authored *Philosophy and the Human Conditions, Religious Knowledge and Religion,* and many other books and articles on ethical and environmental issues.

ANDREW CARNEGIE

Andrew Carnegie was born in Scotland in 1835 and emigrated to the United States with his family in 1848. He worked in a cotton factory and as a telegraph operator and introduced sleeping cars for the Pennsylvania Railroad. Foreseeing the future demand for iron and steel, he left the railroad and founded the Keystone Bridge Company, and began to amass his fortune. The Carnegie companies were incorporated into USS in 1901, when Carnegie retired and devoted himself to philanthropy, for which he is deservedly famous today.

ALBERT CARR

Albert Carr was born in 1902 and educated at the University of Chicago, Columbia University, and the London School of Economics. He was active in business and politics, serving as economic advisor to President Truman. He wrote numerous books and articles, among them *Truman, Stalin, and Peace*, and *Business as a Game*. In addition, he authored several film and television plays. He died of a heart attack in 1971.

THOMAS L. CARSON

Thomas Carson is Associate Professor of Philosophy at Loyola University of Chicago. He has published widely in the areas of moral philosophy and applied ethics. His most important publications are *The Status of Morality* (Reidel, 1984), "Bribery, Extortion and The Foreign Corrupt Practices Act," *Philosophy and Public Affairs*, (1985), "Relativism and Nihilism," *Philosophia*, (1985), "Strict Compliance and Rawls's Critique of Utilitarianism," *Theoria*, (1983), and "Hare's Defense of Utilitarianism," *Philosophical Studies*, (1986).

JOANNE B. CHIULLA

After receiving her Ph.D. in Philosophy from Temple University in 1984, Professor Chiula spent two years as a Post-Doctoral Fellow in Business and Ethics at the Harvard Business School. In 1986 she was a Visiting Scholar in Social Responsibility at the Wharton School of the University of Pennsylvania. Dr. Chiula now teaches in the Management Department and the Department of Legal Studies at Wharton.

SEAN DEFORREST

Sean DeForrest is executive vice-president of American Lock & Supply, Inc., in Anaheim, California. He holds a B.A. in finance and an M.A. in management from California State University at Fullerton. He is listed in *Who's Who* in California and is a member of the Door Hardware Institute and the Phi Kappa Phi Honor Society.

THOMAS J. DONALDSON

Thomas Donaldson is the Henry J. Wirtenberger Professor of Ethics at Loyola University of Chicago. Books he has authored or edited include *Corporations and Morality*, (1982); *Issues in Moral Philosophy*, (1986); and *Case Studies in Business Ethics*, (1984). He is a founding member and past president of the Society for Business Ethics and a member of the editorial boards for the *Journal of Business Ethics* and the *Employee Responsibilities and Rights Journal*. He is general editor of the book series *Soundings*, which publishes books dealing with ethics, economics, and business, for Notre Dame University Press.

FRIEDRICH ENGELS

Friedrich Engels (1820–1895) was the intellectual companion of colleague Karl Marx and is generally considered the author of orthodox Marxism as a system of historical materialism and dialectic. Engels published numerous texts, edited his colleague's manuscripts (most notably *Das Kapital*), and published what is perhaps his best known work, *Dialectics of Nature*, in 1925.

DAVID EWING

David Walkley Ewing attended Amherst College and received an LL.B. from Harvard in 1949. Until recently he was the managing editor of the *Harvard Business Review* and a consultant on editorial problems to business and industrial firms. His works include *Long Range Planning for Management*, *Effective Marketing Action*, *The Managerial Mind*, and *Writing for Results*.

PETER A. FRENCH

Peter French is Lennox Distinguished Professor and Chairman of the Department of Philosophy at Trinity University. He received a B.V. from Gettysburg College, an M.A. from the University of Southern California, and a Ph.D. from the University of Miami. He is the editor of *Midwestern Studies in Philosophy* and has taught at the University of Delaware, the University of Minnesota, and Dalhousie University. His published works include *The Scope of Morality* and *Ethics in Government*.

MILTON FRIEDMAN

Milton Friedman, U.S. laissez-faire economist and professor at the University of Chicago, is one of the leading modern exponents of liberalism in the nineteenth-century European sense. He is the author of *Capitalism and Freedom* and *A Monetary History of the United States*. He was awarded the Nobel Prize for Economics in 1976.

JOHN KENNETH GALBRAITH

John Kenneth Galbraith, perhaps best known for having served as a key advisor to John F. Kennedy, was educated at the University of Toronto and the University of California at Berkeley. He taught at Harvard and Princeton until 1942, when he was called to serve in a variety of government positions. He later returned to Harvard but remained active in public affairs. A prolific writer, he is the author of *American Capitalism: The Concept of Countervailing Power* and *The Liberal Hour*.

A. R. GINI

A. R. Gini is Associate Professor of Philosophy at Loyola University of Chicago. His published works include articles and case studies on a variety of problems in American philosophy, philosophical anthropology, and business ethics. He is presently working on a text entitled *Work: The Process and the Product*.

KENNETH E. GOODPASTOR

Kenneth Goodpastor received his A.B. from the University of Notre Dame and his M.A. and Ph.D. from the University of Michigan. He has published widely on moral philosophy and applied ethics, including *Perspectives on Morality: Essays of William K. Frankena, Ethics and Problems of the 21st Century*, and *Regulation, Values, and the Public Interest*. In 1980 Kenneth Goodpastor joined the faculty of Harvard University, Graduate School of Business Administration, where he currently teaches a course entitled "Ethical Aspects of Corporate Policy."

MARK GREEN

Mark Green is currently the Director of the Corporate Accountability Research Group. He is a well-known and respected critic of the American Business System and U.S. government policy, and has often co-authored articles and shared projects with Ralph Nader.

BARRY R. GROSS

Barry Gross is a professor of philosophy at York College, City University of New York, and a visiting scholar of law at Columbia University. He received his B.A. from New York University, his M.A. from the University of Colorado, and his Ph.D. from the University of Toronto. He has previously taught at Northern Illinois University and DePaul University, and is a member of the Mind Association and the American Philosophical Association. He is the editor of *Reverse Discrimination* as well as the author of *Discrimination in Reverse: Is Turn About Fair Play?* and numerous articles.

JAMES M. GUSTAFSON

James Gustafson is a professor of theological ethics at the University of Chicago and a member of the American Theological Society. He received a B.S. from Northwestern University, a B.D. from the Chicago Theological Seminary and the University of Chicago, and his

Ph.D. from Yale University. He has written numerous books on ethics and religion, including *Theology and Christian Ethics*. His latest book is *Ethics From a Theocentric Perspective* (Chicago: University of Chicago Press, 1981).

FRIEDRICH A. HAYEK

Friedrich Hayek, an Austrian-born economist noted for his conservative views and criticisms of the Keynesian welfare state, shared the Nobel Prize for Economics with Gunnar Myrdal in 1974. Hayek received a doctorate from the University of Vienna and later held positions at the University of London and the London School of Economics and Political Science. He taught at the University of Chicago and accepted a lifetime chair at Freidburg. He is the author of *The Road to Serfdom* and *Law, Legislation, and Liberty*.

MICHAEL HOOKER

Michael Hooker, a Woodrow Wilson Fellow and President of Bennington College, received a B.A. from the University of North Carolina and an M.A. and Ph.D. from the University of Massachusetts. He was a professor at both Harvard and Johns Hopkins, and is currently a member of the American Philosophical Association and the Leibniz Society. He has published widely on cartesian issues and edited several texts on Descartes and Leibniz.

ELMER W. JOHNSON

Elmer Johnson, formerly senior partner of the Kirkland and Ellis law firm of Chicago, is Vice President, Group Executive, and General Counsel of General Motors Corporation. As Group Executive, he headed up the Public Affairs Staffs until April 1, 1985, when he was given charge of the Operating Staffs. He also serves as a member of the Administration Committee at General Motors.

IMMANUEL KANT

Immanuel Kant was born in 1724 in East Prussia, where he took his master's degree at Konigsberg in 1755 and began teaching in the university as a *Privatdozent*, teaching a wide variety of subjects including mathematics, physics, and geography, in addition to philosophy. Kant's publications during this period, primarily concerning the natural sciences, won him considerable acclaim in Germany, but he is best known today for his three critiques—the *Critique of Pure Reason*, the *Critique of Practical Reason*, and the *Critique of Judgment*—written and published after he obtained his professorship. Kant died in 1804.

ARTHUR L. KELLY

Arthur Kelly is a graduate of Yale University with an M.B.A. from the University of Chicago. He was formerly a management consultant with A. T. Kearney, Inc., and later served as president and chief executive officer of LaSalle Steel Company. Currently Mr. Kelly is president of KEL industries, a Chicago holding and investment company, and serves on a number of boards of directors.

STEVEN KELMAN

Steven Kelman received his B.A. and Ph.D. from Harvard and did postgraduate studies at the University of Stockholm as a Fulbright scholar. He is associate professor of public policy, John F. Kennedy School of Government, Harvard University. Dr. Kelman has written on assignment for the *New Yorker*, and has contributed to numerous periodicals. He is the author of *Regulating America, Regulating Sweden: A Comparative Study of Occupational Safety and Health Policy* and *What Price Incentives?*

A. CARL KOTCHIAN

Carl Kotchian is the former president of Lockheed Corporation. He currently serves as a consultant to Lockheed.

JOHN LADD

John Ladd, a professor of philosophy at Brown University, received an A.B., A.M., and Ph.D. from Harvard University and an M.A. from the University of Virginia. A member of numerous societies and associations, including The American Philosophical Association and The New York Academy of Sciences, he authored *The Structure of a Moral Code* and *Ethical Issues Relating to Life and Death*.

JOHN LOCKE

John Locke was born in 1632, and educated in classics, Near-Eastern languages, scholastic philosophy, and later in medicine. Active and influential in the political affairs of his time, Locke was forced to flee England and his position at Oxford after his close friend the Earl of Shaftesbury was tried for treason in 1681. After events turned to his advantage he returned to England from exile in Holland and subsequently published his two most famous works, the *Essay Concerning Human Understanding* and *Two Treaties of Government*. Following years of bad health, England's famous empiricist and political philosopher died in 1704.

GEORGE CABOT LODGE

George C. Lodge, a graduate of Harvard, is Professor of Business Administration at the Harvard School of Business Administration. He has served as a political reporter and columnist for the *Boston Herald*, Director of Information of the U.S. Department of Labor, and Assistant Secretary of labor for International Affairs. He has authored numerous books and articles, including *Spearheads in Democracy* and *The New American Ideology*.

DAVID T. LYKKEN

David Lykken holds a professorship of psychiatry and psychology at the University of Minnesota, where he received his Ph.D. in clinical psychology and neuropsychiatry. He is widely regarded as one of today's foremost experts on the use of polygraphs.

KARL MARX

Karl Marx, the famous German political philosopher and revolutionary socialist, was born in 1818. His radical Hegelianism and militant atheism precluded an academic career in Prussia, and he subsequently lived the life of an exile in Paris and London. Financially supported by Friedrich Engels, he devoted himself to research and the development of his theory of socialism, and to agitation for social reforms. The *Communist Manifesto* was written in collaboration with Engels in 1847. His greatest work, *Das Kapital*, remained unfinished at the time of his death in 1883 and was carried to completion by Engels from posthumous papers.

JOHN B. MATTHEWS

John Matthews has had a long successful career teaching business policy at Harvard Business School, where he is the Joseph C. Wilson Professor of Business Administration.

THOMAS F. MCMAHON, C. S. V.

Fr. Thomas McMahon is professor of Socio-Legal Studies at Loyola University of Chicago and director of the Loyola Center for Values in Business. He received his S.T.D. from the University of St. Thomas Aquinas in Rome and an M.B.A. from George Washington University. In addition to numerous articles on business ethics, he published the first book-length research report on the teaching of socio-ethical issues. He received the 1980 Consumer Educator Award on the Better Business Bureau of Greater Chicago. He is currently engaged in an empirical study of the vocation of business managers.

RALPH NADER

A lawyer and famous consumer advocate, Ralph Nader received as A.B. from Princeton and an LL.B. from Harvard. He received national attention in 1965 when he published *Unsafe at Any Speed*, critical of General Motors, and was subsequently investigated by General Motors, who violated his rights of privacy according to a congressional decision. He is the author of *Taming the Giant Corporation* and *Who's Poisoning America*, among many other publications.

JAMES W. NICKEL

James Nickel is Director for the Center for the Study of Value and Social Policy and a professor of philosophy at the University of Colorado, Boulder. He has previously taught at Wichita State University and the University of California at Berkeley. He was educated at Tabor College and the University of Kansas. He is a National Endowment for the Humanities Younger Humanist Fellow and a visiting scholar at Columbia School of Law. He has published widely on political issues and moral problems.

WILLIAM OPHULS

William Ophuls, formerly a foreign service officer and a lecturer in political science at Yale, is writing two books on the ecological crisis.

MARK PASTIN

Mark Pastin, a professor of philosophy and director of the Center for Ethics at Arizona State University, received his B.A. from the University of Pittsburgh and his A.M. and Ph.D. from Harvard University. He is a National Endowment for the Humanities Research Fellow and a visiting professor of philosophy at the University of Michigan, Ann Arbor, and at the University of Maryland. He has published widely in journals on ethics and epistemology.

JOHN RAWLS

John Rawls is Professor of Philosophy at Harvard University and is among the leading moral and political theorists of this century. His book A *Theory of Justice* is a contemporary classic; it has prompted wide-ranging comment and discussion, not only by philosophers, but by economists, sociologists, political and legal theorists, and others. He is the author of articles too numerous to mention.

MICHAEL J. SANDEL

Professor Michael Sandel teaches political philosophy at Harvard University. He is the author of numerous articles and books including *Liberalism and the Limits of Philosophy*.

JOEL SELIGMAN

Joel Seligman is a professor in the Department of Law at Northeastern University.

IRVING S. SHAPIRO

Irving Shapiro is chairman of the finance committee and former chairman of the board with E. I. du Pont Nemours & Co.

ADAM SMITH

Adam Smith, first known as a moral philosopher, is now famous as a political economist. He was born in 1723 in Scotland and was later elected Professor of Logic at the University of Glasgow. He published *Theory of Moral Sentiments* in 1759 to great acclaim. He resigned his professorship at Glasgow, and after ten years of work published *The Wealth of Nations*, for which his fame has endured. In 1778 he was appointed a commissioner of customs for Scotland. He died in 1790.

WALTER T. STACE

Walter Terence Stace, born in London in 1886, was a prominent English philosopher whose Utilitarian theories sought to reconcile naturalism and religious experience. Major works include *The Philosophy of Hegel*, *The Concept of Morals*, and *Mysticism and Philosophy*.

WILLIAM GRAHAM SUMNER

William Sumner was born in 1840 and died in 1910. He was a famous sociologist and economist and an outspoken advocate of Darwinism. In *Folkways*, published in 1907, he declared the origination of customs and morals in the instinctive responses to sensual stimuli. His work is the basis of *The Science of Society*, volume 4.

KERMIT VANDIVIER

Kermit Vandivier was formerly a data analyst and technical writer at the B. F. Goodrich plant in Troy, Ohio, where he blew the whistle in 1967. Mr. Vandivier is now a journalist for the Troy Daily News.

ROBERT M. VEATCH

Robert Veatch is Professor of Medical Ethics at the Kennedy Institute of Ethics as well as holding appointments in the Philosophy Department and in the Medical School at Georgetown University. He is a frequent author and lecturer on numerous topics in health care ethics. Among his books are *Death, Dying, and the Biological Revolution, Case Studies in Medical Ethics,* and *A Theory of Medical Ethics.*

MANUEL G. VELASQUEZ

Manuel Velasquez is associate professor of philosophy at the University of Santa Clara. He received his B.A. from Gonzaga University and his M.A. and Ph.D. from the University of California at Berkeley. He is a member of the American Philosophical Association and the American Catholic Philosophy Association. He is the author of *Business Ethics,* and co-editor with Cynthia Rostankowski of *Ethical Theory.*

RICHARD WASSERSTROM

Richard Wasserstrom is Professor of Philosophy at the University of California, Santa Cruz, and a practicing attorney in the civil rights. He received a Ph.D. in philosophy from the University of Michigan, an LL.B. from Stanford University, and an LL.D. from Amherst College. He is the author of *Philosophy and Social Issues: Five Studies, The Judicial Decision, Today's Moral Problems,* and numerous articles in ethics and social and legal philosophy.

JAMES A. WATERS

James Waters received his B.A. and B.S. in chemical engineering from the University of Notre Dame, and his M.B.A. and Ph.D. in organizational behavior from Case Western Reserve University. He has worked extensively in the chemical, plastic, and petroleum industries in a variety of managerial positions. He is visiting professor of organizational behavior at McGill University.

MAX WAYS

Max Ways began as a reporter for the *Baltimore Sun* and the *Philadelphia Record* and eventually made his way to the board of editors of *Fortune,* a position from which he recently retired. He has served in various editorial capacities for *Fortune* and continues to write for the magazine.

PATRICIA H. WERHANE

Patricia Werhane is Professor of Philosophy and Associate Dean of the College of Arts and Sciences at Loyola University of Chicago. She is the author and/or editor of several articles and books in aesthetics, ethics, and business ethics including *Persons, Rights, and Corporations* (1983), *Philosophical Issues in Rights* (1984), and *Profit and Responsibility* (1985). She is a founding member and former president of the Society for Business Ethics. She serves on the editorial board of the *Journal of Business Ethics* and is co-editor of the *Employee Responsibilities and Rights Journal.*

RICHARD E. WOKUTCH

Richard Wokutch is an associate professor of management at Virginia Polytechnic Institute and State University. He received a Ph.D. in business administration from the University of Pittsburgh, and has held positions at the University of Delaware and the Science Center in Berlin, West Germany. He has published widely in journals of business and ethics.